A NEW HISTORY OF KOREA

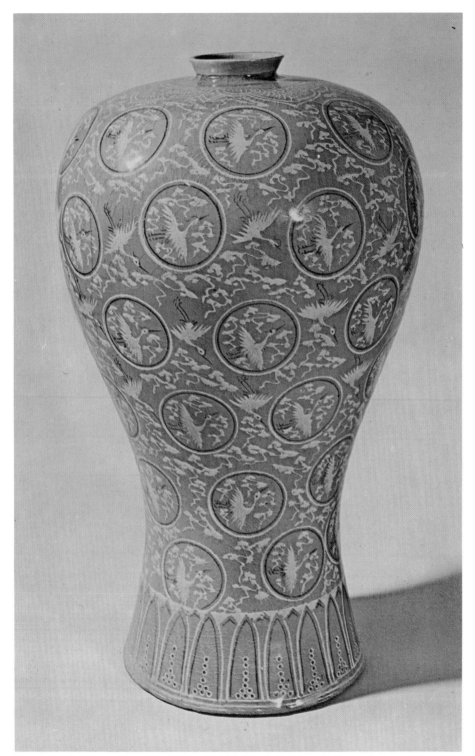

The "Thousand Crane Vase," in the widely admired *maebyŏng* or baluster shape.
One of the finest examples of incised slip-filled celadon ware. Koryŏ, mid-12th century.
Seoul, Kansong Museum of Fine Arts.

A NEW HISTORY
OF KOREA

Ki-baik Lee

Translated by Edward W. Wagner
with
Edward J. Shultz

Published for the
HARVARD-YENCHING INSTITUTE
by
HARVARD UNIVERSITY PRESS
Cambridge, Massachusetts
London, England

Originally published in Korea under the title of 韓國史新論.

This translation is published simultaneously
in the Republic of Korea
by Ilchokak, Seoul.
Printed in the United States of America.
10 9 8

Library of Congress Cataloging-in-Publication Data

Yi, Ki-baek.
 A new history of Korea.

 Translation of: Han'guksa sillon.
 Bibliography: p.
 Includes index.
 1. Korea — History. I. Title.
DS907.16.Y5313   1984   951.9   83-246
ISBN   0-674-61575-1 (cloth)
ISBN   0-674-61576-X (paper)

To the people of Korea

That the record of those enduring qualities of strength, and fortitude, and cultural creativity that so distinguish their long, proud history may become more widely known.

PREFACE TO THE TRANSLATION

As the author indicates in his preface to the 1967 revised edition, already at that time an English translation of *Han'guksa Sillon* (*A New History of Korea*) seemed to be a most worthwhile undertaking. A promise was made, in fact, to translate the new edition as soon as a busy schedule might permit. Even now it occasions considerable embarrassment to recall that more than a decade passed before a first step was taken toward fulfilling this commitment.

Yet, in the context of the late 1960's, there was every incentive to go forward with the planned translation without delay. No new English language history of Korea had appeared since that by an American missionary, Homer B. Hulbert, in 1905 and another by a Canadian missionary, James Scarth Gale, a generation later in 1927. Between 1969 and 1972 no fewer than five survey histories were to appear, three of them translations, but this could not be foreseen in 1967 and turned out to be, after all, no great embarrassment of riches. Meanwhile, academic interest was entering a period of substantial growth, and in history as in most other fields of Korean studies the need for a good, basic text was acute.

At the same time, if a Korean text were to be translated, there were excellent reasons why it ought to be Professor Ki-baik Lee's *Han'guksa Sillon*. As the years have passed, moreover, these considerations have become all the more persuasive. Because it first appeared in 1961, underwent major revisions in 1967 and 1976, and has been further improved in the course of numerous reprintings, *Han'guksa Sillon* is the only survey history of Korea to keep abreast of the mounting volume of monographic work being produced by Korean scholarship today. This process of continuous revision has resulted in a refined narrative structure that smoothly carries forward the author's descriptive and interpretive purposes.

Han'guksa Sillon also is noteworthy for its treatment of cultural history, which it skillfully interweaves with the narration of political, social, and economic history. In other words, the author presents cultural developments not merely as isolated expressions of the creative spirit of the Korean people, but as an integral component of the overall Korean historical experience.

Again, *Han'guksa Sillon* offers not simply a narrative but an interpretation of Korean history. The author has elaborated a comprehensive overview of the developmental process through which Korean history has passed, focusing on changes over time in the composition of the leadership elite and in the locus of political power in Korean society. Although some aspects of this treatment remain controversial, the interpretation nonetheless is innovative and it gives the book an overall integrity and thrust that distinguish it from other survey histories.

Finally, in the near quarter century since it first appeared, *Han'guksa Sillon* has enjoyed unparalleled acceptance among both an academic readership and the educated public. It is widely used as a college text, and it is clearly the general history of choice outside the campus as well. Both the 1967 edition and that of 1976 have been translated into Japanese, and a Chinese translation currently is underway in Taipei. An English translation, then, is indeed long overdue.

Although begun in 1979, the present translation relates closely to the most recent printing of *Han'guksa Sillon*, that of January, 1984. This is because the many changes and improvements the author made in the text during the intervening years were incorporated into the translation as they occurred. For the translation proceeded in close consultation with the author from start to finish. At perhaps as many as sixty separate sessions he answered questions, solved problems, offered background explanations, discussed issues, and provided fresh insights. Without his invaluable assistance the translation hardly could have been completed at all and certainly would have suffered much in quality.

The translation is, essentially, a full rendering of the text proper, with only an occasional bit of detail eliminated. The short introductory chapter ("A New Understanding of Korean History") and concluding chapter ("The Ruling Elite and the Course of Korean History"), however, have been omitted from the present translation with the consent of the author. The detailed and useful Classified List of References appended to the book also has not been translated, since this bibliography is principally concerned with primary source materials and secondary studies written in the languages of East Asia. Readers who command these languages may consult any recent printing of *Han'guksa Sillon*. Nor have the selections of journal articles appended to each topical subsection of the text been rendered into English, since these, too, are preponderantly in Korean or Japanese. On the other hand, with the needs of a Western readership in mind, a Select Bibliography containing book-length, English-language works has been appended. The Dynastic Lineages of the original work, diagramming lines of descent within the royal houses of the various historical Korean states, have been reproduced with slight modifications, in particular the addition of reign dates. The Index-Glossary attempts, as its principal objective, to include all of the names and terms found in the translation, with Chinese characters or *han'gŭl* provided wherever appropriate. In most instances the maps have been enlarged to show the entirety of the Korean peninsula, or to provide a fuller setting for the reader less familiar with the geography of Korea and Northeast Asia. The plates feature some of the same illustrations that grace the original, but others have been especially selected for the English translation.

Han'guksa Sillon was written for a readership well acquainted with the course of Korean history, with the drama of its events, and with its dramatis personae. This has posed a problem for the translation, which attempts, at the same time, to meet the needs both of the serious student and of the informed general reader. A series of special footnotes was contemplated, but in the end it was decided to include explanatory phrasing in the text itself. No doubt some readers will wish that this effort had been taken a step or two further.

All readers surely will regret the fact that the author does not carry his narrative beyond the April, 1960, Student Revolution. Moreover, the coverage of the crowded years after Korea's liberation in August, 1945, is quite cursory in comparison with what has gone before. This shortcoming is particularly serious for the Western reader, whose prior knowledge of Korea and much of his interest often will be confined to the last thirty to forty years. Certain events of this period, however, make it difficult for the historian either to gain access to all the information he requires or to venture a balanced account of Korea's recent history. Fortunately, a large body of published material exists in English that will enable readers to educate themselves in this regard and form independent judgments.

Names and terms have been romanized in accordance with accepted norms in the English-speaking world, generally on the basis of the culture in which they originated. Those that are Korean are spelled in accordance with the prescriptions of the McCune-Reischauer system, happily now adopted as well by the Ministry of Education, Republic of Korea. For Japanese the Hepburn system is employed and for Chinese the Wade-Giles. Problems remain, principally the question of how to treat place names in those areas of northeastern China that once were ruled or contested by Korean peoples. In these cases the attempt has been to make the romanization accord with the contemporary historical situation.

The task of translation is never easy and often enough is thankless. A conscientious effort to produce an accurate and readable English translation of an academic text such as this will inevitably owe much to the skilled and generous assistance of a great many people. The primary obligation to the author, Professor Ki-baik Lee, already has been recorded. Also of great value has been the careful attention given the manuscript, in full or in part, by a number of colleagues in the field: Edward J. Baker, Jonathan W. Best, Gari K. Ledyard, and Karl Moskowitz most notably, but also Yong-ho Choe, Michael C. Kalton, Hugh H. W. Kang, Yŏn-ung Kwŏn, Mark Peterson, Michael Robinson, and Chae-ryong Sim. Less direct assistance came from several other specialists whose published works in their respective fields guided the translation through some of its most unfamiliar byways. Peter H. Lee for literature (to whom acknowledgement also is due for permission to use a translation of his) and Sang-woon Jeon for science and technology must be mentioned first, but important contributions of this sort also came, however unwittingly, from Martina Deuchler, Chong-Sik Lee, Richard J. Pearson and, indeed, many others. Editorial assistance, and many useful substantive suggestions as well, were provided by M. Rebecca Bernen, Sherrill M. Davis, Milan Hejtmanek, Scott Kalb, Homer Williams, and Jeong-ro Yoon. Help in overcoming particular translation problems was sought in many places, but these and numerous other contributions, ranging from the ordinary to the inspirational, cannot well be acknowledged here. Those who collaborated in these respects will have been thanked directly.

Substantial financial support for the translation work was received from the U.S. Office of Education under its Fulbright program, from the Scholarship Foundation of the Korean Traders Association, and from the International Cultural Society of Korea. Certain costs related to the translation project also were borne by the Korea Institute, Harvard University. The obligation to each of these is recorded here with a renewed sense of gratitude.

Finally, appreciation must be expressed for the unstinting support given throughout the long and arduous translation and publication process by the Korean publisher, Ilchokak. The warmth of understanding of its president, Man Nyun Han, and the wholehearted devotion of his staff have been indispensable in giving life to this translation.

When all is said and done, of course, the translation must stand on its own merit. The debt owed to all those who have assisted in transforming *Han'guksa Sillon* into *A New History of Korea* can in some measure be requited only by the contribution it may make to a wider awareness of the nature of the Korean historical experience.

Seoul, Korea
Spring, 1984

AUTHOR'S PREFACES

Preface to the 1967 Revised Edition

My initial work titled *Kuksa Sillon* (*A New History of Our Nation*) appeared in the spring of 1961, nearly six years ago. During these years study of the history of Korea has greatly advanced. It is not merely that explications of particular historical events have been put forward, but repeated efforts have been made to achieve a fuller overall understanding of Korean history. In the light of these new research findings it has become necessary to revise the original text in a great many places. Furthermore, it seemed to me the time had come to venture, however tentatively, a restructuring of the standard periodization of Korea's history, something I had not been able to do in the 1961 publication.

Fortunately, an opportunity to address the shortcomings of the original work soon arose. This came about when I received an invitation from the Harvard-Yenching Institute to spend a year at Harvard University as a research scholar. Edward W. Wagner had proposed to undertake an English translation of *Kuksa Sillon* and, if this were to eventuate, I was anxious that the translation be based on a thoroughly revised manuscript. It was to producing this new manuscript that, upon taking up residence at Harvard, I immediately set my hand.

Even though a revision of an earlier work, it was no easy matter to bring the new version to completion. Chapters and sections within chapters all had to be redesigned, while many new studies had to be read and evaluated. My pace, as always, was deliberate and, as I bemoaned the all too swift passing of each day, I found much of my short year at Harvard consumed by this task.

Through such travail was born this new, revised edition bearing the title *Han'guksa Sillon* (*A New History of Korea*). To be sure, here and there the reader will find passages identical with those of the original book, but overall the contents are so markedly different as to constitute a new work. That is why the book has been renamed and the type reset.

Having read and pondered the completed manuscript, I find more than an occasional ground for dissatisfaction. In particular, the pages devoted to the recent history of Korea need to be increased still further. Setting aside a short, separate chapter for the eventful years since Liberation in 1945 is, I realize, only a short step in the right direction. Still, I have endeavored there as well to perceive Korean history as an integral and on-going developmental process.

With all its flaws and imperfections, if this book but serves as a single foundation stone upon which a genuine understanding of the history of Korea partially may rest, what greater fulfillment could an author ask?

Winter, 1966
Cambridge, Massachusetts

Preface to the 1976 Revised Edition

Han'guksa Sillon (*A New History of Korea*) originally was written in the conviction that its narrative might be so constructed as to channel the flow of Korean history into a coherent, directed current. If this bold design of mine has proved to be something of an engineering conceit, I neverthe-less have been greatly encouraged by the favorable response of my readers to the attempt.

Still, it has been my constant thought that at some point I must make a further effort to more neatly systematize those elements of Korean his-tory that earlier had fit but uneasily into the model I had fashioned. This was all the more required by the mountain of fresh studies produced in re-cent years by Korean historians. I resolved, therefore, to defer the gratifi-cations of pursuing my own research interests and, instead, to force myself to undertake yet another thorough revision. The fruit of these labors, the present edition of *Han'guksa Sillon,* has been reworked most importantly in the following respects:

First of all, the introductory chapter titled "A New Understanding of Korean History" has been rewritten and a concluding chapter, "The Rul-ing Elite and the Course of Korean History," has been added. The purpose in both these instances has been to put forward with greater clarity my views on the successive developmental stages through which Korean history has passed.

Secondly, in conformity with this same objective, chapters and sections have been rearranged and their contents reshaped accordingly. As before, the overriding consideration has been to design chapters that reflect a scheme of periodization based on changes in the nature of the ruling elite, with the principal events in each period grouped appropriately under sec-tion headings and recounted in an interrelated sequence of subsections. The flow of the narrative, in turn, has been modified to better reveal this underlying and integrating theme.

Third, the bibliographical references appended to each subsection have been made selective rather than comprehensive, and in the process older works have been replaced by more recent studies. Since truly extensive bibliographical compilations, suitably annotated, now are available in the Korean studies field, a survey history such as this surely is freed from any obligation to be bibliographically all-encompassing. Nevertheless, in the substantial appendix entitled Classified List of References, brief explanatory remarks have been supplied as guideposts to those who may wish to pursue a topic further.

By and large, these three areas of change constitute the substance of the present revision. At first glance this may appear to have been a simple undertaking, but for me it has not been easy to recast the book in this fashion. To begin with, considerable effort was expended merely in absorbing the findings of the many important studies that have appeared during the past decade. Moreover, the impact of this new scholarship on the direction the revision should take had to be dealt with as each issue in turn arose, thus occasioning frequent delays in the progress of the work. No doubt I would have fallen even further behind schedule were it not for the considerable assistance rendered by the editorial staff of the publisher, Ilchokak.

As I now apply the final, finishing touches to this endeavor, I feel as if a heavy burden has slipped from my shoulders. My only wish, as it was on the occasion of the earlier edition, is that this work may serve as a single foundation stone upon which a genuine understanding of the history of Korea partially may rest.

Finally, it should be observed that this book stands upon the research achievements that have nurtured it, those many fine studies by my fellow historians who devote their energies to seeking new insights into the nature of the Korean historical experience. To all these colleagues I wish to express my appreciation.

Summer, 1976
Looking Out on Inwang Mountain

CONTENTS

Chapter 3. Aristocratic Societies Under Monarchical Rule

Chapter 4. The Fashioning of an Authoritarian Monarchy

Chapter 5. The Age of Powerful Gentry Families

Chapter 6. The Hereditary Aristocratic Order of Koryŏ

Chapter 7. Rule by the Military

Chapter 8. Emergence of the Literati

Chapter 9. The Creation of a *Yangban* Society

Chapter 10. The Rise of the Neo-Confucian Literati

Chapter 11. The Emergence of Landed Farmers and Wholesale Merchants

Chapter 12. Instability in the *Yangban* Status System and the Outbreak of Popular Uprisings

Chapter 13. Growth of the Forces of Enlightenment

Chapter 14. Nationalist Stirrings and Imperialist Aggression

Chapter 15. Development of the Nationalist Movement

Chapter 16. The Beginnings of Democracy

MAPS, CHARTS, AND TABLES

Chapter 1

The Communal Societies of Prehistoric Times

1. The Paleolithic Age

The Paleolithic Period in Korea

It is not at present possible to estimate at what precise period people began to live on the historical stage that we call Korea. Until just a few years ago, Paleolithic remains had been reported only at Tonggwanjin near Chongsŏng in North Hamgyŏng province. At this site, together with fossils of mammoths and other mammals, a few stone and bone artifacts believed to have been fashioned by man were discovered. However, it is possible that these artifacts belong instead among the many Neolithic remains scattered about in this vicinity and, accordingly, some scholars are reluctant to link them definitely with the fossil remains from the same site and assign them to the Paleolithic period. In recent years, however, Paleolithic remains have been reported from a number of excavations, and so it has become possible to suggest at least an outline of the Paleolithic period in Korea.

At present the best known Paleolithic sites in the Korean Peninsula are those at Kulp'o-ri (in Unggi county in North Hamgyŏng province), at Sangwŏn (in Chunghwa county in South P'yŏngan), at Sŏkchang-ni (in Kongju in South Ch'ungch'ŏng), and at the Chŏmmal Cave, P'ojŏn-ni (in Chech'ŏn county in North Ch'ungch'ŏng province) [see map p. 4]. In addition several other Paleolithic sites now are in process of investigation. On the basis of the reports from these many sites it may be presumed that Paleolithic man lived in virtually every part of the peninsula.

The time frame for the Paleolithic period is not yet clear. However, extrapolating from the fact that two cultural layers from the Late Paleolithic at the Sŏkchang-ni site have been dated respectively to approximately 30,000 and 20,000 years ago, it may be surmised in general that Paleolithic man began to inhabit the Korean peninsula some 40,000 to 50,000 years before the present. Over a span of many millennia, then, these people slowly made advances in their culture and mode of life. It is not known, however, whether the Korean people of today are the ethnic descendants of these Paleolithic inhabitants of their land.

Culture and Mode of Life of Paleolithic Man in Korea

Paleolithic man in Korea both lived in caves and built habitations on level ground. Examples of the former are found at Kŏmŭnmoru Cave in Sangwŏn and Chŏmmal Cave at P'ojŏn-ni, while the latter type is illustrated by a dwelling site at Sŏkchang-ni. The Sŏkchang-ni dwelling site dates from the late Paleolithic period and is marked by a hearth and other remains found within an area that appears to have been partially enclosed by a wall. The existence of a hearth suggests that fire was used both for warmth and for the cooking of food.

These Paleolithic people lived by gathering fruit, berries, and edible roots and also by hunting and fishing. The implements needed for hunting and preparing food were fashioned by chipping stone. At first a lump of rock was struck until a number of pieces had been broken off, leaving a usable tool of sorts with sharp edges or points, but later the pieces that had thus been broken off were given additional edge or sharpness by chipping or flaking and were themselves used. Stone implements made in this way were of a number of varieties conforming to their intended purpose—handaxes, choppers, and points used in hunting and butchering; side-scrapers and end-scrapers used in preparing food; and gravers used as tools for working stone and wood.

Since a concerted group effort would have been required for hunting, it is likely that some fixed form of communal life obtained among Paleo-lithic man, but there is no way to know what precise form this took. Additionally it is speculated that later Paleolithic man relied on the power of magic to secure success in hunting and to ward off personal calamity.

2. Neolithic Man in Korea

The Appearance of Neolithic Man

It is thought that Neolithic man, characterized by the making of polished stone tools and the use of pottery, appeared in Korea about 4000 B.C. Korea's earliest Neolithic inhabitants likely were of the same ethnic stock as those who lived at that time in Siberia, and they are known to have used round-bottomed plain pottery. But no more than a handful of sites in-habited by these Neolithic people are known, chiefly Kulp'o-ri at Unggi in North Hamgyŏng and Tongsam-dong on Yŏngdo island off Pusan, and accordingly at present we possess only sketchy knowledge about Korea's Early Neolithic period.

From sometime around 3000 B.C. the active presence of Neolithic man is in evidence throughout the Korean Peninsula. It was at this time that people appeared who used pottery with the geometric designs (often called "comb pattern pottery") characteristic of the Neolithic period. Geometric-design pottery is gray in color with a V-shaped pointed bottom, and it is distinguished by designs on the outer surface of parallel lines that resemble markings made by a comb. The fact that such pottery has been found widely in places like Ch'ŏngho-ri in Taedong county in South P'yŏngan and Amsa-dong in the Kangdong ward of Seoul suggests something of the geographical range of activity of the people who made it. Pottery with identical geometric designs has been discovered in the Maritime Territory of Siberia, in the basins of the Amur and Sungari Rivers in Manchuria, and in regions of Mongolia, thus providing insight into the geographic extent of the area in which its makers lived and the course of their eastward and southward migration.

Then, about 1800 B.C., a third pottery culture characterized by painted designs spread into the Korean peninsula from Manchuria and experienced further development as its impact slowly became more pervasive.Geometric-design pottery now underwent changes in both shape and design, and such new forms as thunderbolt design pottery appeared. Remains of this new culture have been found at such places as Nongp'o-dong (in Ch'ŏngjin, North Hamgyŏng), at Chit'am-ni (in Pongsan, Hwanghae), and at Kyo-dong (in Ch'unch'ŏn, Kangwŏn province) [see map p. 4].

Neolithic culture in Korea thus experienced three major stages of development as these three successive waves of migration spilled down into the peninsula. Unlike that of Korea's Paleolithic people, the ethnic stock of the Neolithic people is seen as continuing unbroken to form one element of the later Korean race. It is believed, then, that in the course of a long historical process these Neolithic peoples merged with one another and, combining with the new ethnic groups of Korea's Bronze Age, eventually came to constitute what we now think of as the Korean people.

Mode of Life of Neolithic Man in Korea

Neolithic dwelling sites in Korea are found mainly at water's edge, along the seashore and the banks of rivers. As time went on, however, Neolithic man also ventured into inland areas.

The food of these Neolithic people largely was supplied by the marine life in the waters beside which they lived. The stone sinkers so frequently found at these Neolithic sites attest to the use of nets for catching fish. They also fished with hook and line, of course, and gathered varieties of shellfish. Food was procured by hunting as well, and bones of such animals as deer, roe deer, and wild boar have been found, while arrowheads and spear points appear among the stone artifacts discovered at Neolithic sites. And the presence of acorns, for example, provides proof of the gathering activities of these Neolithic people. Thus at first having relied for their food on hunting, fishing, and gathering, these people subsequently began to practice agriculture. This is known from the discovery among later remains of stone hoes used in turning over the soil and of stone sickles for harvesting,

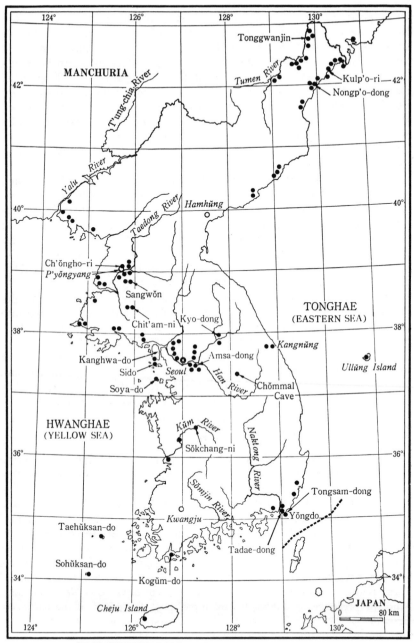

MANCHURIA

Tonggwanjin

Tumen River

Kulp'o-ri
Nongp'o-dong

T'ung-chia River

Yalu River

Taedong River

Hamhŭng

Ch'ŏngho-ri
P'yŏngyang

Sangwŏn

Chit'am-ni   Kyo-dong

TONGHAE
(EASTERN SEA)

Kangnŭng

Ullŭng Island

Kanghwa-do

Sido

Soya-do

Seoul

Amsa-dong

Han River

Chŏmmal
Cave

HWANGHAE
(YELLOW SEA)

Kŭm River

Sŏkchang-ni

Naktong River

Sŏmjin River

Tongsam-dong

Kwangju

Yŏngdo

Taehŭksan-do

Sohŭksan-do

Tadae-dong

Kogŭm-do

Cheju Island

JAPAN

0   80 km

**GEOMETRIC DESIGN POTTERY SITES IN KOREA
(NEOLITHIC AGE, ca. 3000–800 B.C.)**

together with kernels of grain thought to be millet. Grain and acorns were ground by millstones to make meal for food preparation.

Neolithic man in Korea lived mainly in pit dwellings. These usually were dug in circular or in rough square form, posts then being set up to support a straw thatch covering to keep out the wind and rain. In size a diameter of about six meters and a depth of sixty centimeters were typical. In general the hearth is found in the center of the floor of the dwelling, and this must have been used for cooking. Storage pits are located next to the hearth or near the entrance, indicating that various implements and supplies of grain were kept close at hand. The location of the various finds suggests that the space within the dwelling was divided into living quarters and areas in which cooking and other household activities were performed. It is not yet clear, however, in what way the pit dwellings of that time were grouped together to form small communities. It is evident, though, that Neolithic man in Korea at times lived in natural or man-made caves.

Clothing at first consisted of animal skins, prepared by scraping away the flesh with stone knives and then sewing them together by the use of bone needles. Later cloth came to be woven on primitive looms from animal fur or such fibers as hemp, and the clothing made in this way was adorned with shells and decorative bits of stone.

3. Society and Culture in the Neolithic Period

Communal Clan-Centered Society

There is almost no direct evidence suggesting what form society took in the Neolithic period when Korea was inhabited, most notably, by the people who made geometric-design pottery. Judging from the fact that a number of their dwellings are found clustered at a single site, it may be conjectured that already some form of settled communal life was being practiced. But since no investigation of such a settlement as an integral unit has yet been carried out, there is no way at present that this evidence of the clustering of dwellings can be used to suggest the pattern of social organization. However, myths, legends, and traditional patterns of behavior described in records from later periods reflect certain features of the social structure of that age. When this information is assessed in the light of studies of primitive societies in the modern world, it is possible to make out in rough outline the nature of the society of this early time.

The basic unit of the society of this time was the clan. This is indicated, for example, by the "six villages" of the Pak Hyŏkkŏse legend. These consanguineous social groupings, each bound together by its distinct blood line, are thought to have been totemistic, differentiated one from the other by the object in the natural world with which a particular clan closely identified itself. For example, it would appear that Hyŏkkŏse's Pak clan took the horse as its totem and the Kim clan of Alchi and Aryŏng the chicken.

These clan entities formed distinct communities and decided important matters at clan assemblages. It is widely supposed that the later *Hwabaek* (Council of Nobles) institution of Silla represents a continuation of this ancient tradition. To be sure, the clan was headed by a chieftain, but he was chosen by his clansmen and, if he was thought to have erred, he always was subject to removal from his position. This is inferred from the nature of the kingship among the Puyŏ people in the early period of their history. And as may be surmised from the *ture* form of communal labor arrangements found in Korean villages in later times, the primary productive activities of hunting, fishing, and agriculture likely were performed in common in the Neolithic period. The conduct of religious ceremonies too on a communal basis is suggested by the later customs known to us as *yŏnggo* (a shamanistic ceremony performed to invoke a god or spirit), *tongmaeng* (an ancestor worship ritual perhaps originating in a cult honoring the founder-king of Koguryŏ), and *much'ŏn* (a "dance to Heaven," a form of heaven worship). Moreover, the interment of the dead in communal tribal graves may be presumed from the practice among the Okchŏ people of burying an entire family in a single large coffin.

The clan community was an economically independent and self-sufficient entity. Economic activities, whether gathering or hunting and fishing, were not permitted within the territories claimed by other clans. Should a violation of this prohibition occur then compensation had to be given, as may be inferred from the practice of the Eastern Ye people (of Korea's northeastern coastal plain) known as *ch'aekhwa* ("responsibility for damages"). Nevertheless, some economic exchange among different clan communities did take place, as can be seen in the example of a particular kind of stone being brought from a considerable distance for use in fashioning certain implements.

It will be evident from the above that these consanguineous clan communities were societies possessing a markedly closed character. Nevertheless exogamous marriage was practiced, with partners invariably sought not within the community but from other clans. That this was so is presumed from the Eastern Ye custom prohibiting marriage within the "same surname" or clan grouping. It also has been asserted that descent was determined by the mother's lineage during some part of the Neolithic period. The Koguryŏ institution of a "son-in-law chamber" (*sŏok*)—the custom of the groom going to the bride's home following marriage and living with her in the son-in-law chamber upon first receiving the formal consent of her parents, he then being permitted to bring his wife back to his clan only after their children had reached a certain age—has been thought to have been a survival of such an earlier practice. Recently, however, doubts have been expressed that a matrilineal descent system existed in Korea in Neolithic times.

This describes the general structural features of the clan community as they now can be surmised, but the clan was not the only form that social organization took in the Neolithic period. Larger social configurations, or tribes, came into being with the merging either of related clan units that had split off from one another as population increased, or of clans linked by marriage ties. These tribes tended to find their unity in territorial as well as simply blood ties, but the principles governing the structure of their societies were substantially the same as those of the clan. That is, matters of concern to the tribe as a whole were decided at assemblies of the clan chieftains, and the leader of the tribe was chosen by these same clan representatives. The raising of Pak Hyŏkkŏse to kingship by an assembly of the clan leaders of Silla's "six villages" and the similar elevation of Suro by the "nine chieftains" of Kaya are thought to be embellished accounts of such a practice of selecting a tribal leader.

Shamanistic Beliefs

Neolithic man in Korea held animistic beliefs, being convinced that every object in the natural world was possessed of a soul. Man, too, of course had a soul and it was believed that this soul was immortal. Accordingly, in burying the body of one who had died, a variety of special attentions were shown. Stones were placed around the corpse in an effort to protect it from evil spirits, articles that the deceased had used during his lifetime were buried with him, and the corpse was laid with its head toward the east, in the direction of the sunrise.

The souls of natural objects such as mountains, rivers, and trees were thought of in the same way as those of men, and certain of these were accorded status as divinities. Foremost among these was the sun, and its worship is perhaps best evidenced by the numerous instances that can be found of myths of human birth from eggs. For example, Yuhwa is said to have conceived after the rays of the sun shone on her body and to have produced an egg from which the founder of Koguryŏ, Chumong, was born. Again, Pak Hyŏkkŏse's birth is described as being from an egg, and it is related that the name he was given, Pak (or *palk*, "brightness," a concept expressed in the Chinese character transcription of another native word used to designate him), is owed to the fact that light radiated from his body. Both these legends indicate that exalted personages were thought to be children of the sun.

While good spirits like the sun were believed to bring good fortune to human beings, it also was believed that evil spirits such as those who dwelled in darkness brought misfortune upon man. Accordingly, it was necessary that there be adepts in magic, intermediaries with the ability to drive off evil spirits and invoke the gods so as to bring about a happy outcome. It is supposed that these tribal magicians performed ceremonies designed to forestall calamity by means of chants and dancing, for a tradition of such practices can be found in the routines of the *ch'ŏn'gun* ("Heaven prince") of the Samhan period. Primitive religious practices of this same form are found throughout the world, and in the area of Northeast Asia they are known by the general term of shamanism.

Primitive Art Forms

Geometric-design ("comb pattern") pottery may be said to be the representative art form of the Neolithic period. The outer surface of this pottery, which was made in the shape of a somewhat rounded V, was decorated by drawing series of parallel slanted lines, the direction of different groupings of lines being varied to create geometric patterns such as the common fishbone design. These designs, rather than being conceived of as simply decorative, seem to have had a religious significance. In most primitive art parallel slanted lines are thought to symbolize water, and so it may well be that the decorations on the geometric design pottery also were intended to represent water, the major source of early Korean Neolithic man's food. But with the advent of agriculture straight line designs gave way to curved, and maze-like jagged broken-line designs suggesting thunderbolts also began to appear. This design is thought to symbolize lightning as the heavenly force that brought forth all creation.

The only sculptured object that has yet been found is the head of a small clay figurine of some animal, uncovered at the Amsa-dong site. It is not clear what animal it represents, but it was done in a strikingly graphic manner. A mask made from a shell, with holes put in it for the eyes and mouth, has been found at Tongsam-dong, and bits of stone that probably were used for ornamentation also have been discovered. All of these objects, it may be supposed, were made to serve religious purposes, such as ceremonies to pray for a bountiful supply of food or to drive away evil spirits.

That music and dance were a vital adjunct of the lives of Korean Neolithic man may be surmised in the light of such later ceremonial observances as those referred to above, called *yŏnggo* (a shamanistic ceremony for invoking a spirit), *tongmaeng* (an ancestor worship ritual), and *much'ŏn* (a dance perfomed to worship Heaven). These performances also surely had a religious significance.

Thus the art forms of the Neolithic period were closely bound to religious practices. And the art objects produced by Korean Neolithic man are rather characterized by abstraction than by realism, for their purpose was to give expression to some symbolic meaning.

Chapter 2

Walled-Town States and Confederated Kingdoms

1. The Use of Bronze and the Formation of Walled-Town States

The Use of Bronze Implements

Whatever the impact caused by successive waves of Neolithic peoples and cultures entering the Korean peninsula, the life of the Korean Neolithic population changed relatively little over an extended period of time. This tranquility was broken, however, by the advent of the use of bronze.

The first use of bronze implements in Korea is generally put at around the ninth or eighth centuries B.C. There are some, however, who date this occurrence earlier and others who assign it to a somewhat later date. The Bronze Age in Korea is thought to have lasted generally until about the fourth century B.C., but of course this time span varied to some extent in different areas of the peninsula.

The bronze culture of these centuries constituted a unitary and independent development, and its domain extended from the Sungari and Liao river basins in Manchuria down into the Korean peninsula. Two typical bronze implements in use at this time, the mandolin-shaped dagger and the multi-knobbed coarse-lined mirror, by and large have not been unearthed outside this region. The narrow-bottomed, two-handled, brownish red undecorated pottery used in this period also is found only in this area. Occasionally a black or other pottery piece resembling contemporary Chinese specimens also has come to light in this region, but the undecorated pottery is predominant. Moreover, it is a well-known fact that discoveries of dolmen burial sites have been overwhelmingly concentrated in this same area. It may be asserted, then, that this region of southern Manchuria and the Korean peninsula was the arena in which Korean Bronze Age man played out his historical role.

The relationship between these Bronze Age people and Korea's Neolithic inhabitants is unclear. Nevertheless, however close together geometric-design and designless pottery in some instances have been found, the two types are manifestly to be distinguished one from the other. This suggests that the peoples who produced the two likely led different modes of life and that there would have been ethnic differences as well. At the same time, the fact that these two types of pottery sometimes are found at the same sites indicates that there was a transition period when the two cultures were in contact. Similarly, the repetition of motifs found on the geometric-design pottery in the decoration of the mandolin-shaped bronze daggers and multi-knobbed coarse-lined bronze mirrors bespeaks cultural continuity between the two peoples. Yet geometric-design pottery no longer is found once the Bronze Age was well under way, and this can be taken to signify that the Bronze Age people had become the arbiters of the new societies then developing in Korea.

The Life of Bronze Age Man

Remains of Korean Bronze Age man, whose characteristic artifacts are mandolin-shaped bronze daggers and designless pottery, are chiefly found on higher ground that overlooks flatlands along river courses. This fact suggests that, unlike the Neolithic people who used geometric design pottery, Bronze Age man was a slope dweller.

The juxtaposition of these finds with the surrounding terrain indicates that the food supply of Bronze Age man in Korea was greatly dependent on agriculture. Although farming implements made of bronze have not themselves been found, the existence of such woodworking tools of bronze manufacture as axes and knives tells us that a variety of wooden agricultural implements must have been produced. The fact that rice cultivation began to be practiced from this time is known from the use of crescent-shaped stone knives and grooved stones shaped like an axe head that served as hoes. The former was a hand-held tool used at harvest time to cut the rice stalks, while the latter was an implement for turning over the soil preparatory to planting. Both these tools were used in rice culture in China and it is thought, accordingly, that rice agriculture itself had been transmitted from China by this early date. These Bronze Age people of course also hunted and fished, but the fact that they cultivated rice implies a considerable degree of sophistication in their agriculture.

Some weapons also were made of bronze, most notably spear points and arrowheads. The existence of these bronze weapons suggests that conquest by warfare was a hallmark of this period, and it is by this means, presumably, that the Bronze Age people were easily able to gain ascendancy over the Neolithic inhabitants who had only stone weapons.

The Bronze Age people too lived mainly in pit dwellings. Circular construction now gradually fell into disuse as rectangular design came to dominate. A typical depth was around fifty centimeters, but the existence of thirty centimeter depths indicates that surface level dwellings were not far in the future. The hearth generally was located to one side, and in the case of larger dwellings two hearths sometimes are found. On the whole, pottery vessels were stored in the inner recesses of the dwelling where the females

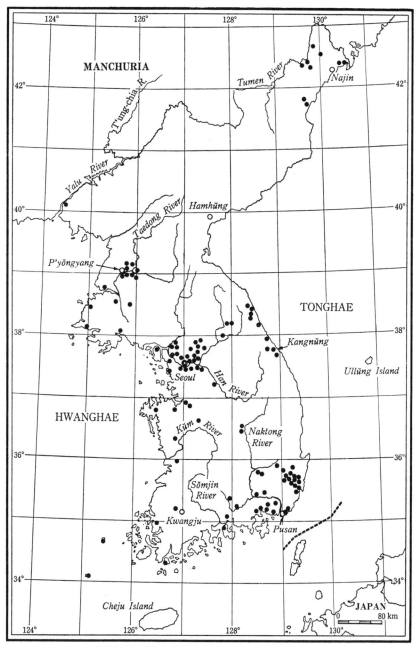

MANCHURIA

Tung-chia R.

Tumen River

○ *Najin*

Yalu River

Taedong River

Hamhŭng ○

P'yŏngyang

TONGHAE

Kangnŭng

Seoul

○ *Ullŭng Island*

Han River

HWANGHAE

Kŭm River

Naktong River

Sŏmjin River

Kwangju ○

Pusan

34°

Cheju Island

JAPAN

0   80 km

DESIGNLESS POTTERY SITES IN KOREA
(BRONZE AGE, ca. 800–300 B.C.)

performed their functions, while implements for outdoor use were left near the entrance, the living space occupied by the male members of the household. Dwelling sites of course were grouped into settlements, but their precise arrangement has not yet been made clear. However, the fact that clusters of dwelling sites have been found in a single location suggests that settlements were gradually growing in size. The dwelling sites of this period increasingly show evidence of damage by fire, and this is likely to reflect both the more frequent occurrence of blazes that would accompany heightened use of fire and also deliberate destruction by burning that would result from warfare and conquest.

Dolmen and stone cist tombs are the predominant forms of burial that survive from the Bronze Age. The existence of these dolmen, together with numerous menhir or large upright stones, has caused the culture of this age to be called megalithic. Dolmen in Korea, which are found in great numbers in every part of the country, are of two basic forms of construction—the table style and the *paduk* (Japanese *gō*) board style. The table style (also called the northern style) was constructed by placing several upright stones in a rough square and covering them with a flat capstone, and its distribution has been found to be preponderantly north of the Han River. The *paduk* board style (also known as the southern style), on the other hand, employed a large boulder as a capstone placed atop several smaller rocks, and it is found most widespread in the area south of the Han River. There also are dolmen tombs without supporting stones, where the capstone has been placed directly atop the burial chamber, and these are found in both northern and southern halves of the peninsula. The burial objects taken from dolmen tombs include some made of bronze, but the frequent appearance of polished stone daggers is especially noteworthy. In stone cist burial a box-shaped coffin was made in a shallow pit by laying out flat stones, and this form of burial sometimes occurs in conjunction with dolmen tombs. Additionally, a stone mound tomb built over a stone cist has been discovered, but to date at only one site.

The Formation of Walled-Town States

Stone and wooden implements were much used in the Bronze Age as well, and in fact bronze implements were precious articles, difficult to obtain. Such objects as mandolin-shaped bronze daggers and multi-knobbed coarse-lined bronze mirrors were the possessions of only a privileged few whose authority thus was symbolized by their ownership.

This consideration holds true for dolmen burial as well. Dolmen were individual tombs for interment of a single corpse, and dolmen tombs with capstones as long as nine meters and weighing up to seventy tons were constructed. In some cases, moreover, these huge slabs had to be brought from sites many miles distant. Clearly, then, the individual buried in such a tomb had the power to command the labor services of a very large number of people. Moreover, the authority of such a figure appears not to have been limited to his lifetime but to have passed to subsequent generations. This conjecture is based on the consideration that dolmen are found in clusters of at least three or four or indeed in groups of thirty or forty, and in rare cases of over one hundred, and they were built in orderly array along a straight line—all of which suggests that their construction was undertaken at different times. Accordingly, we may be certain that the individuals buried in dolmen tombs were not simply leading members of a communal social structure but rather were those who wielded authority in a stratified society.

Who, then, were these individuals who owned the bronze symbols of authority and who enjoyed enough power to be buried in dolmen tombs? Most likely they were the successors to the tribal chieftains of the Neolithic period, those who carried on that tradition of leadership. But the leaders of Bronze Age societies surely obtained a more plentiful product from agriculture and also seized greater spoils in war, and in this way they would have been able to command greater economic wealth.

The territories ruled by Bronze Age chieftains could not have been so very extensive. Probably they controlled no more than the agricultural population that farmed the narrow plains beyond the earthen fortifications they built on hillside plateaus. These petty states in the past frequently were termed tribal states, but it is appropriate to call them instead walled-town states. This is because, even though they retained a tribal character, they must have possessed a political structure built around a territorial unit that subsumed populations other than the tribe alone. These walled-town states were the earliest form of state structure to exist in Korea, and accordingly the origins of state formation in Korea are to be sought therein.

2. The Formation and Development of Old Chosŏn

The Evolution of the Society of Old Chosŏn

Societies with articulated political structures now began to develop everywhere around the walled-town states that had been formed with the advent of the use of bronze implements. In the northern regions Puyŏ arose in the Sungari river basin, Yemaek along the middle reaches of the Yalu, Old Chosŏn in the basins of the Liao and Taedong Rivers, Imdun in the Hamhŭng plain on the northeast seacoast, and Chinbŏn in the region of Hwanghae province, while south of the Han River the state of Chin emerged. By about the fourth century B.C. these states had developed to the point where their existence was known even in China. Among them the most advanced was Old Chosŏn, which had established itself in the basins of the Liao and Taedong Rivers, the region where bronze artifacts are most plentifully found.

As a walled-town state Old Chosŏn appears originally to have occupied the Taedong river basin at P'yŏngyang. At this time it must have been but a small political entity dominating the plains in the vicinity of P'yŏngyang. Its early leaders seem to have borne the title *tan'gun wanggŏm*, and it is thought likely that they combined political and religious functions in a single personage. The fact that the *tan'gun wanggŏm* is said to have descended from Hwanin, who is taken to signify a sun god, would appear to represent an attempt to enhance symbolically the dignity and authority of his role as political leader.

This walled-town state of Old Chosŏn proceeded to combine with the other walled-town states scattered throughout the region between the Taedong and Liao rivers to form a single large confederation, the head of which came to be designated as its king. Old Chosŏn at this stage might appropriately be called a confederated kingdom, for this suggests that—although it bore the same name as before—it had undergone great societal development. It is difficult to be certain just when this transformation in the social fabric of Old Chosŏn occurred, but it clearly must have been before the fourth century B.C. This is revealed by a record noting that, when the North China state of Yen began to use the term "king" (*wang*) upon the decline of the Chou kingdom around this time, Old Chosŏn also took the same title for its ruler. And this Chinese term for king is more properly descriptive of the ruler of a confederated kingdom than of the leader of a small walled-town state. It is also recorded that Old Chosŏn planned an attack on Yen about this time, and this would not have been possible unless it had reached the more advanced stage of development of a confederated kingdom. Yen and Old Chosŏn were then confronting each other across their Liao River boundary, and in the light of Yen assertions that Old Chosŏn was arrogant and cruel, it can be surmised that Old Chosŏn boasted formidable strength as an independent power in Northeast Asia.

The Use of Iron

Two new metal cultures of differing provenance were transmitted to Korea in the fourth century B.C. as a consequence of the expansive thrusts of the Chinese and Hsiung-nu peoples. One was the iron culture of China and the other was a bronze culture of Scytho-Siberian origin. The two cultures intermingled in Manchuria and came to the Taedong river basin by way of the middle Yalu and the upper reaches of the Ch'ŏngch'ŏn River. The Taedong river region thus became a reservoir of the new metal cultures, and from there they soon came to spread in all directions. Moreover, these cultural waves went on to cross the sea and penetrate even into Japan, where they gave rise to the Yayoi culture.

The use of iron implements wrought a variety of changes in the then prevailing mode of life. First of all, agriculture underwent striking development. This is known not merely from the existence of hoeing implements made of iron but from the discovery of such sophisticated iron farming tools as plowshares and sickles. The plowshares suggest the possibility that already at this time draft animals were being used to till the soil. Nevertheless, it seems probable that for the most part fields still were made ready for planting by human labor, with the use of such tools as wooden hand-plows and iron hoes. It is more likely, therefore, that even the iron plowshares were pulled by men rather than by animals. Still, the use of iron sickles meant that rice could be harvested not by cutting down the stalks one at a time but rather in clusters. In this way food production increased markedly in comparison with that of the Bronze Age. The increased output, however, was not shared equally by the whole society but doubtless tended to be monopolized instead by a ruling class. Accordingly, the gap between the rich and the poor must have been further widened.

Other frequently found artifacts from the Iron Age include such iron weapons as daggers and spear points as well as bronze daggers, spear points, and spears. A type of short and finely wrought bronze dagger (known as the *sehyŏng tonggŏm*) and the bronze spear are particularly notable for their unique design, which is not found in the artifacts of neighboring peoples. Such horse trappings as iron bits and bronze bells, as well as axle caps and other components of horse-drawn vehicles, also have been unearthed, and it seems clear that these objects of metal manufacture must have been possessed only by a small elite stratum. It is not difficult to imagine how this ruling elite, armed with sharp weapons made of metal and mounted on horseback or riding on horse-drawn vehicles, must have imposed its authority. It also is evident that objects like the multi-knobbed fine-patterned bronze mirrors would have served as symbols of their authority.

People of this new metal age continued to live in pit dwellings, but the use of *ondol* devices (an arrangement of flues under the floor) for heating begins to be in evidence, and wooden houses built on ground level also were in use at this time. Bronze belt buckles in the shape of animals are a noteworthy example of clothing ornamentation from this period. The prevailing forms of burial were earthen tombs measuring three meters long and one meter wide, into which the corpse appears to have been directly entered, and jar-coffin interments utilizing two large urns laid mouth to mouth (with the length of the one for the lower part of the corpse sometimes extended by a third jar) to contain the body. And a new pottery form, a hard, higher fired Chinese-style gray stoneware, now appeared. In all probability the ground level wooden houses, the animal-shape belt buckles, and the earthen tombs were appurtenances of the life style of the ruling elite.

That this new metal culture was deeply influenced by Chinese culture is demonstrated above all by the discovery of Chinese coins, such as the "crescent knife coin" (*ming-tao-ch'ien*), at many Korean sites. But it would be a mistake to assume from this evidence that the transmission of its iron culture to the Taedong river basin was accompanied by extension of Chinese political domination over that portion of the Korean peninsula and to attempt, as some have done, to reinterpret the Kija Chosŏn legend in this light. Such a theory is refuted by a number of considerations—in particular by the fact that the cultural mainstream of this period is represented by unique artifacts like the short and finely wrought bronze dagger, the bronze spear, and the multi-knobbed fine-patterned bronze mirror, as well as by the existence of a number of elements of north Asian steppe culture origin, like the Scytho-Siberian style animal-shape belt buckles. Furthermore, the fact that numerous molds for casting bronze and iron have been found in the region of Old Chosŏn suggests that this new metal culture was not colonial but indigenous.

Wiman Chosŏn

Under the pressure of the powerful Chinese state of Yen, which invaded the Liaotung Peninsula at the end of the fourth century B.C., Old Chosŏn entered a period of gradual decline. Commanded by one Ch'in K'ai, the Yen invasion forces advanced rapidly, until this strategic region had been taken and attached as a commandery to the Yen domain. Liao-tung Commandery subsequently came under the control of the new Ch'in empire, but during the intervening years it had witnessed the comings and goings of numerous Chinese officials, military men, and merchants. Then, not long after Ch'in had unified China, it fell around 206 B.C. to Liu Pang, the founder of the Han dynasty. Han enfeoffed Lu Wan as king of Yen in the former Yen domain, but he then turned against Han and sought haven among the Hsiung-nu to the north. During this period of continuous political upheaval, increasing numbers of people took refuge in areas further to the east. Among these refugees was a man known as Wiman, who is reported to have taken with him a band of over a thousand followers. At first entrusted by King Chun of Old Chosŏn with defense of his northwestern border, Wiman strengthened his power base among the refugee population and presently drove King Chun from his throne and himself assumed the kingship (sometime between 194 and 180 B.C.). At this point King Chun is said to have fled southward to the state of Chin, where he called himself the "Han king."

Beginning with the Yen invasion of around 300 B.C., there thus had occurred a continuous penetration of Chinese political, military, and economic power into the region of the kingdom of Old Chosŏn. Ultimately, then, this transformation in the area's power structure led to the establishment of a new kingdom by Wiman, whose state of course bore the hallmark of the stronger Chinese civilization. But the formerly prevailing view that Wiman Chosŏn represented a colonial regime ruled by a migrant Chinese population has been challenged by many contemporary scholars. It is pointed out first of all that ethnically Wiman is likely to have been not a man of

Yen but Old Chosŏn, an assertion based on the fact that he is said to have worn his hair in a different kind of topknot and to have been dressed in Chosŏn style when he led his followers into Old Chosŏn, and that he continued to use "Chosŏn" in the name of his kingdom. Secondly it is argued that many men of Old Chosŏn, most notably the official (*Igyesang*) Sam, occupied high positions under Wiman's rule. These considerations strongly suggest that, however much Wiman Chosŏn may have relied on migrant Chinese with their more sophisticated knowledge of iron culture, it could not simply have been a Chinese colonial regime. On the contrary, Wiman Chosŏn surely took the form of a confederated kingdom grounded on the former Old Chosŏn power structure. In this way, then, the society of Old Chosŏn came to take on new form and entered a stage of rapid advance.

With its superior military and economic strength, Wiman Chosŏn was able to subjugate its neighboring states to the north, east and south. Chinbŏn, lying between Chabiryŏng Pass and the Han River, and Imdun in the southern Hamgyŏng area were forced to submit, thus giving Wiman Chosŏn control of a territory stretching over some several hundred miles [see map p. 18]. Having so grown in strength and domain, Wiman Chosŏn now barred Chin (located south of the Han River) and other smaller states near its borders from direct contact with the Han Chinese, seeking thus to profit as an intermediary in the area's trade with China. This action was not well received by Han China, which also was concerned about the threat posed by the possibility of ties between Wiman Chosŏn and the Hsiung-nu, then expanding into Manchuria from their heartland in Mongolia. At this point, taking advantage of the defection of Namnyŏ, the ruler of Ye, Han sought to bring pressure to bear on Wiman Chosŏn by establishing the Ts'ang-hai Commandery in Ye territory (in the area of the mid-Yalu and the T'ung-chia river basin). But in fact this was accomplished only on paper, as after a few years Han abandoned its aggressive designs in the area, most likely because of the resistance of the Ye people.

Political negotiations having failed to heal the long standing breach in relations between Wiman Chosŏn and Han, a major crisis ensued when a Chinese envoy named She Ho, who earlier had been rewarded after killing a Chosŏn commander and fleeing back to China, was himself killed in retaliation by Chosŏn soldiers. This became the pretext for Emperor Wu of Han, already engaged in aggressive military campaigns along the whole periphery of his empire, to finally launch an armed assault against Wiman Chosŏn (109 B.C.). Wiman Chosŏn fought hard against the invaders for a year, but resistance was weakened by the defections and collaborationist activities of a peace faction, culminating in the assassination of King Ugŏ (Wiman's grandson). Led by the high official Sŏnggi the struggle went on for a time but could not be maintained, and with the fall of its capital Wanggŏm-sŏng (at modern P'yŏngyang) in 108 B.C., Wiman Chosŏn perished.

Wiman Chosŏn's ability to mount such stiff resistance presumably was

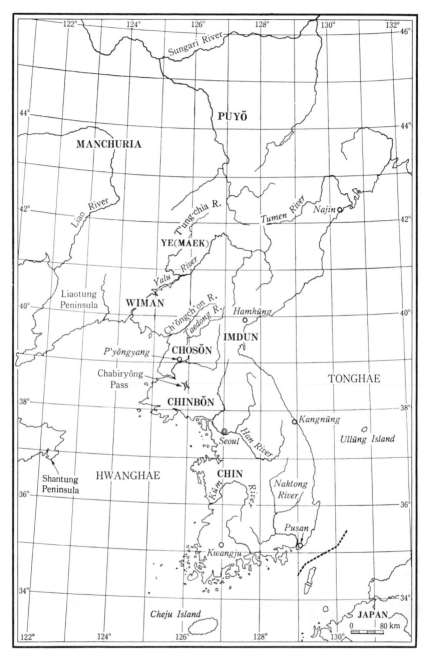

KOREA AT THE TIME OF WIMAN CHOSŎN
(2ⁿᵈ CENTURY B.C.)

owing to its attainment of a level of metal culture rivaling that of the Han Chinese invaders. Dissension within the ruling class, however, opened the way for the downfall of this ambitious kingdom.

The Han Chinese Commanderies

In 108 B.C. Han China established the three commanderies of Lo-lang, Chen-fan, and Lin-t'un within the former domain of Wiman Chosŏn, which had been subjugated in that same year, and in the next year completed the formation of the so-called Four Chinese Commanderies by creating Hsüan-t'u in the former territory of the Ye. The locations of these Chinese administrative units are not precisely known, but one widely accepted view places them as follows: Lo-lang (Korean: Nangnang) in the Taedong river basin area of Old Chosŏn; Chen-fan (Korean: Chinbŏn) in the former Chinbŏn region from the Chabi Pass south to the Han River; Lin-t'un (Korean: Imdun) in the old Imdun area of southern Hamgyŏng province; and Hsüan-t'u (Korean: Hyŏndo) in the Ye territory spanning the middle reaches of the Yalu and the T'ung-chia river basin. According to this theory the territorial extent of the Four Chinese Commanderies was limited to the area north of the Han River, thus leading to the interesting conclusion that they were designed to administer four distinct and integral socio-political entities.

Whatever the case, it is clear that Han China was forced by the opposition of the local populations to make major adjustments in the boundaries of each of these four administrative units. Only twenty-five years after they had been established, Han China abolished both Chen-fan and Lin-t'un, attaching the areas under their jurisdiction to Lo-lang and Hsüan-t'u respectively (82 B.C.). But at the same time some of the more remote districts presumably had to be abandoned. Less than a decade later, in 75 B.C., Han moved Hsüan-t'u Commandery far to the west, out of the former Ye territory to a region centering on modern Hsing-ching in east-central Manchuria. This likely was occasioned by clashes with the growing power of the emerging Koguryŏ state. In consequence, jurisdiction over areas that originally had come under Lin-t'un Commandery now was transferred from Hsüan-t'u to Lo-lang.

Nor could Lo-lang itself enjoy uninterrupted tranquility in the administration of its territory. At the beginning of the Later Han dynasty a revolt occurred led by Wang T'iao, a powerful member of the Lo-lang gentry. This was suppressed in 30 A.D. by Wang Tsun, the newly arrived governor of Lo-lang, but it had significant repercussions. It was around this time that the Korean Han societies in the region of the Chin state south of the Han River began to display new vigor, and from this point on many people of Old Chosŏn who had come under the rule of Lo-lang sought refuge there. The growing strength of these societies eventually evoked a response from the Kung-sun rulers of the Liao-tung region (where they had created an independent domain at the end of the Later Han dynasty), who established a new commandery, Tai-fang (Korean: Taebang), in the area south of Lo-lang formerly administered by the Chen-fan Commandery (ca. 204 A.D.). In 313, however, Lo-lang fell to Koguryŏ pressure and at about the same time Tai-fang disappeared as Paekche expanded its frontiers northward.

Lo-lang was the core area in which Chinese colonial policy in Korea was carried out. As its administrative center the Chinese built what was in essence a Chinese city where the governor, the officials under him, merchants, and many other Chinese colonists came to live. Their way of life in general can be surmised from the investigation of remains unearthed at T'osŏng-ni, across the Taedong River to the southwest of P'yŏngyang where the administrative center for Lo-lang is thought to have been located. The richness of the life style of these Chinese officials, merchants, and others who enjoyed the status of colonial overlords in Lo-lang's capital is plainly evident in the variety of burial objects that have been found in the wooden and brickwork tombs in which these Chinese were interred. Although some of these objects were made locally in Lo-lang, for the most part they were brought in from China. Accordingly, the culture of Lo-lang was a Chinese culture, and from the standpoint of those who produced and used these burial objects, this culture had no connection whatever with the people of Old Chosŏn who now were under Chinese rule.

Despite the sumptuousness of Lo-lang's colonial administrative center, China's colonial policy does not seem to have been marked by severe political repression. Living among themselves apart from the native Old Chosŏn populace, it may be conjectured that the Chinese were content to exercise a certain degree of control while permitting substantial political freedom to the people they governed. On the other hand, it would appear that the impact of the Chinese administration on the economic life of the native population was substantial. Records of the mobilization of 1,500 people from Lo-lang to cut timber in the area of the Han states to the south, or of the acts of thievery committed at night by Chinese merchants constitute fragmentary evidence to be sure, but they offer a hint, at least, that such was the case. Moreover, since salt and iron were government monopolies in China, Lo-lang officials must have shown great interest in the extraction of these local resources, and iron from the Pyŏnhan state, it is known, was supplied to both Lo-lang and Tai-fang. To obtain such vital products from areas outside Chinese control, it was standard practice for the Chinese to effect tributary relationships with native leaders by granting them titular office and rank, official seals, and ceremonial attire.

The impact of the Chinese commanderies must have been particularly pronounced in the area under direct Chinese dominion, where the Chinese way of life and institutional arrangements gradually but inexorably penetrated the fabric of the Old Chosŏn society. This influence is perhaps typified by the fact that Old Chosŏn's original body of law, consisting of only eight prohibitory articles, was expanded to over sixty provisions as a result of the Chinese presence. We are told that the continuous nighttime thievery of Chinese merchants in Lo-lang was prompted by the realization that the people of Old Chosŏn were not in the habit of keeping their goods in secure custody, and that this experience weakened the faith of the native inhabitants in their traditional values, thus necessitating the proliferation of provisions in the code of laws. It may be conjectured, then, that close contact with the Chinese, with their highly developed sense of private property, set in motion a disintegrative process in Old Chosŏn society. For example, the fact that a segment of the native population is said to have come to use Chinese type eating and drinking utensils may be taken to signify the emergence of a new China-oriented elite class possessed of wealth and power. Within the area under Chinese control, however, there could be no expectation of independent political development by the Old Chosŏn people.

The impact of the Chinese commanderies also was felt in neighboring states. In these areas the cultural influence was by far the most important, for the fruits of the highly advanced Chinese culture were much coveted. This is apparent from the fact that for the most part the leaders of the Han states in the southern half of the peninsula willingly accepted the grants of office and rank, official seals, and ceremonial attire that constituted formal tokens of their submission to Lo-lang's authority. The ability to absorb Chinese culture while maintaining their political independence, it should be noted, allowed these native societies to weather the crises that at times confronted them and achieve impressive new development.

3. The Formation of Confederated Kingdoms

Puyŏ

Puyŏ (Chinese: Fu-yü) emerged in the region of the Sungari river basin in Manchuria [see map p. 18]. Its heartland is generally thought to have been in the area of Nung-an, a location marked by an unusually broad expanse of flatlands.

The first clear reference to Puyŏ concerns events of about the fourth century B.C., and from the beginning of the first century A.D. the name appears frequently in the historical records. By this time Puyŏ had grown in power to the point where it was regarded, along with the Hsiung-nu and Koguryŏ, as a potential menace to Wang Mang's short-lived (8–23 A.D.) Hsin dynasty in China. Accordingly, it may be assumed that by this time at the latest Puyŏ had succeeded in forming a confederated kingdom. Further evidence of this is the record that not long thereafter, in 49 A.D., the Puyŏ ruler was using the Chinese appellation for "king" (*wang*).

In fact, there appears to have been good reason for China to welcome the rise of Puyŏ on the Manchurian scene. This was because Puyŏ lay between the Hsien-pei on China's northern frontier and Koguryŏ to China's northeast, and so by making common cause with Puyŏ, China would be able to check the expansion of these two powerful peoples. At the same time, Puyŏ's relationship with Koguryŏ to its south, as well as with the nomadic peoples to its north, long had been one of hostility, and for this reason the rulers of Puyŏ, too, were anxious for friendly ties with China. The Chinese thus became convinced of the peaceful inclinations of the Puyŏ people, and the mutuality of interests between the two nations presently found concrete expression in a series of events.

The first recorded instance of Puyŏ envoys being sent to China was in 49 A.D., and from this point on embassies were sent almost every year. To be sure, clashes between Puyŏ and the Chinese commanderies in Manchuria are reported to have occurred on several occasions, but on the whole the relationship remained close and, moreover, China received embassies from Puyŏ with the utmost cordiality. At the end of the Later Han, when the Kung-sun house was in control of Liao-tung and reigned over China's easternmost regions, it formed marriage ties with Puyŏ. Again, when Kuan-ch'iu Chien, a general of the North China kingdom of Wei, invaded Koguyrŏ in 244 A.D., Puyŏ demonstrated its commitment to the support of Chinese interests by supplying provisions to the Wei army. Forty years later, in 285 A.D., the Puyŏ king, Ŭiryŏ, committed suicide when his country was invaded by the Hsien-pei ruler Mu-jung Hui. Since the king's sons and brothers had fled to Okchŏ in northeast Korea, the continued existence of the Puyŏ state was now in jeopardy. But the ruler of the Chinese state of Chin offered his support to Ŭira, a member of the Puyŏ royal house, putting him on the empty throne and thus making possible the restoration of the Puyŏ kingdom. Subsequently, however, Puyŏ suffered repeated invasions from the south by Koguryŏ.

Throughout the course of its history Puyŏ had reached accommodation with a succession of Chinese states as a means of defending itself against the incursions of Koguryŏ and the nomadic peoples to its north, and with Chinese support Puyŏ had sought first to expand and then to preserve its sovereign power. But when the Chinese Chin kingdom was driven south by the nomadic tribes to its north, in 316, Puyŏ found itself isolated and exposed. Thus, in the invasion by the Hsien-pei ruler Mu-jung Huang in 346, the Puyŏ king, Hyŏn, and over 50,000 of his people were taken prisoner. A generation later, upon the extinction of the Hsien-pei state of Earlier Yen in 370, Puyŏ passed under the protection of Koguryŏ. Subsequently, with the rise of the Wu-chi (Malgal) people in northeastern Manchuria, the Puyŏ royal house was driven from its ancient territory and surrendered itself to Koguryŏ. The last vestiges of Puyŏ's existence now had been extinguished.

The Rise of Koguryŏ

Legend has it that Koguyrŏ was founded in 37 B.C. by Chumong and a band of his followers from Puyŏ, in a region thought to be centered on the middle Yalu and T'ung-chia river basin. Already by about the fourth century B.C., however, a precursor to Koguryŏ had consolidated its strength in this area. This was the people known as the Yemaek, and it would appear that this political entity was ruled by the Ye "lord" Namnyŏ, who in an account of events of the second century B.C. is said to have held dominion over a population of 280,000. Thus the leadership elite of Koguryŏ was not native to the area it came to rule, but the state that evolved there must have represented a coalescence of this new force with the indigenous society.

When the Ye leader Namnyŏ sought Han dynasty support in his resistance against domination by Wiman Chosŏn, Han responded by establishing the Ts'ang-hai Commandery in the mid-Yalu region of Manchuria (128 B.C.), but this turned out to be a mere exercise in map drawing. Subsequently the Hsüan-t'u Commandery was established in this area, in 107 B.C., but some thirty years later it had to be pulled back deeper into Manchuria (75 B.C.). Since this removal westward of the Hsüan-t'u Commandery must have been occasioned by the resistance of powerful native forces in this region, it is to be inferred that already at this time Koguryŏ was in the process of taking form as a confederated kingdom.

Thus Koguryŏ came into being and proceeded to develop in a context of conflict with the Chinese. Accordingly Koguryŏ was in need of strong military forces, and in the course of its early armed struggles the military character of Koguryŏ's ruling elite was continuously reinforced. It would appear that even in times of peace this warrior aristocracy did not engage in any kind of productive activities but devoted itself entirely to training for combat. For the warriors of Koguryŏ, in fact, warfare was the most productive activity they might pursue, as is indicated by their consuming interest in such spoils of war as land, populations, and domestic animals. Only through warfare could they compensate for the inadequacy of the resources within their boundaries. It is no wonder, then, that unlike the Puyŏ the Koguryŏ people gave the impression to the Chinese of being vigorous, warlike, and fond of attacking their neighbors.

By the beginning of the first century A.D. the Koguryŏ state already had developed to the point of adopting the Chinese title of "king" (*wang*) for its ruler, and it now sought to break out of its territorial confines in all directions. The areas toward which Koguryŏ directed its expansion were the basins of the Liao River to the southwest and the Taedong River to the south, and in addition the Sungari river basin to the northwest and the plains along the northeast coast of the Korean peninsula. Since these regions at that time were all either directly administered by China or within its sphere of influence, open warfare between Koguryŏ and China was inevitable. The most violent of these clashes was with Wang Mang's Hsin dynasty. Wang Mang had enlisted Koguryŏ forces in a campaign against the Hsiung-nu, but before battle was joined the Koguryŏ contingents had a change of heart, with the result that a clash broke out between the Chinese and Koguryŏ armies (12 A.D.). And Wang Mang had to console himself with whatever satisfaction he might derive from the peculiarly Sino-centric concept of subjecting Koguryŏ to terminological degradation, labeling it Ha("low")guryŏ instead of Ko("high")guryŏ.

Koguryŏ's conflict with China became more intense in the reign of King T'aejo (53–146?), who pursued a vigorous expansion of his kingdom's territory. Subjugating the Okchŏ to his southeast, T'aejo secured a base to his rear which could give meaningful support to Koguryŏ's warfare against China. The northeast littoral of Korea, then the homeland of the Okchŏ and the neighboring Eastern Ye people, earlier had been occupied by the Imdun people before becoming a Chinese colony with the establishment of the Lin-t'un (Imdun) Commandery. But now this whole area was brought under the dominion of Koguryŏ. Koguryŏ, however, permitted the chieftains of the native communities to retain their authority and levied tribute through them. We are told, for example, that the Okchŏ people carried "Yemaek cloth," fish, salt, and other local products on their backs to Koguryŏ, over a distance of perhaps 200 to 300 miles. King T'aejo also mounted repeated attacks against the Chinese Liao-tung and Hsüan-t'u Commanderies as he pursued his plans to advance westward. Under T'aejo's successors Koguryŏ incursions into the Liao-tung region continued as before. In particular, when the Kung-sun house sought to extend its sway from its base in Liao-tunɔ in the late second century, Koguryŏ fought against this new Chinese thrust with fierce tenacity.

The State of Chin and the Three Han (Samhan) States

It would appear that a culturally homogeneous political entity also took form south of the Han river basin in Korea, in conjunction with the phenomenon of dolmen tomb burial. This assumption is based on the consideration that *paduk*-style dolmen, which in terms of burial objects are best typified by the polished stone dagger, are widely distributed in the region south of the Han. These artifacts likely represent the earliest manifestation of the emerging state of Chin.

The first recorded mention of the state of Chin refers to an event of the second century B.C., when Wiman Chosŏn occupied the Taedong river basin. At this time Chin sent a communication to Han China seeking to open direct contact between the two. This suggests a strong desire on the part of Chin to enjoy the benefits of Chinese metal culture. But due to the obstruction of Wiman Chosŏn, which dominated international trade in the region at that time, Chin's hopes were frustrated. This was the period, however, when refugees from the territory of Old Chosŏn, with its more advanced knowledge of metalworking, were streaming into the Chin domain and finding their places in the Chin society. Outstanding examples of this movement are the last king of Old Chosŏn, Chun, fleeing south to escape

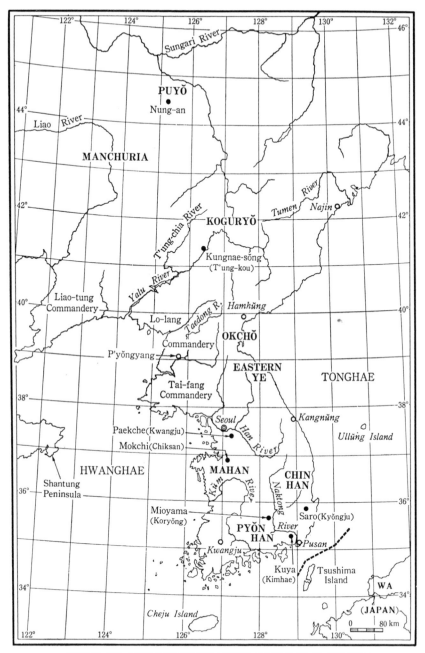

KOREA IN THE CONFEDERATED KINGDOMS PERIOD
(ca. 1ˢᵗ—3ʳᵈ CENTURIES A.D.)

Wiman, and the migration to Chin just before the downfall of Wiman Chosŏn of a high official, referred to as the *Yŏkkyegyŏng*, at the head of over two thousand households. The absorption of these refugees into its population enabled Chin to take advantage of a more developed iron culture and, in consequence, Chin society underwent rapid change.

The wide dissemination of iron culture played an important role in the development of the societies in the region south of the Han River. In conjunction with this it should be observed that rice agriculture began to be practiced more widely around this time, as is witnessed by the discovery of carbonized grains of rice in the Kimhae shell mound. As the flow of the migration continued, and indeed increased, the newcomers' knowledge of the arts of governing and of metal culture combined with the strengths of the indigenous Chin society to produce a steady growth in its power. This process eventually led to the restructuring of the Chin territory into three new political entities, known collectively as the Samhan: Mahan, Chinhan, and Pyŏnhan. It has long been assumed that Mahan was located in the region of modern Kyŏnggi, Ch'ungch'ŏng, and Chŏlla provinces, Chinhan to the east of the Naktong River in Kyŏngsang province, and Pyŏnhan in Kyŏngsang province to the west of the Naktong [see map p. 25]. One modern view, however, places Chinhan in the Han river basin.

4. Society and Polity in the Confederated Kingdoms

Village Communities and their Farming Populations

Agriculture gradually increased in importance from the onset of the Bronze Age. In addition to the expected growing of a variety of grains in dry fields, rice culture was also practiced in paddies. Rice became particularly prevalent in the Samhan states, and it is believed that reservoirs for rice irrigation already were being constructed at this time. That agriculture was the principal food source in this period is plainly indicated by the fact that the kings of Puyŏ were held responsible for disastrous harvests and were either removed from the throne or killed in consequence. And the fact that the most important ceremonial observances were one held to pray for a bounteous crop after seed was sown in the fifth month and a thanksgiving festival celebrated after the harvest was completed in the tenth month provides further evidence of the importance of agriculture.

There were, of course, a variety of other economic activities besides agriculture. In Puyŏ, for example, the raising of livestock was practiced on a large scale, to the point where the names of domestic animals like the ox, horse, pig, and dog are found attached to designations for official posts. In the south as well, in the Samhan region, domestic animals were raised, and bones of horses and cattle have turned up in the Kimhae shell mound. A variety of long-tailed chicken, too, is said to have been found in the Samhan area. At the same time, hunting also was a major activity, particularly in states like Koguryŏ situated in mountainous terrain. The unearthing from the Kimhae shell mound of bones of wild boar and deer, as well as the discovery of a scene incised on a rock at Pan'gudae in Ulchu county of North Kyŏngsang province depicting such wild animals, testify to the great importance attached to hunting. The Pan'gudae rock drawing also contains whales and other marine life, thus providing evidence that coastal peoples engaged in fishing too. This would have been regarded as a particularly vital source of food by societies like Okchŏ and Eastern Ye which inhabited the narrow eastern coastal plains.

Nevertheless, the principal productive activity in this period was agriculture. The basic unit for carrying on the work of farming was the village community. Most of the farming population in these village communities possessed freeman, or commoner, social status, being what the Chinese called "low households" (*hsia-hu*). Above this preponderant component of free peasants were the village headmen (*homin*) and below them there were slaves in some number. Private ownership of land by the individual peasant likely already had developed, but it is believed that the free peasants, the primary work force in the village community, also tilled communal fields. That the village possessed such a communal character is speculative, but there are sites on which large buildings stood that may have served as community gathering places, while the written record includes references to institutions that are thought to represent assemblies of youth and communal labor practices in the Samhan states. There was, of course, a portion of the farming population that could not take part in village communal arrangements, presumably peasants who had been reduced to hiring out their labor. But these were the exceptions and for the most part peasants performed their labor as free men within the communal structure of the farming community. Heavily burdened with taxes in kind and with obligations to provide labor service to the state, this free Korean peasantry was regarded by the Chinese as being exploited in the manner of agricultural slaves. Moreover, the freeman peasant was not permitted to bear arms and fight in time of war but rather was limited to service in transporting provisions. In sum, the societies of the walled-town states and confederated kingdoms period stood on a foundation of village communities inhabited by such a peasant farming population as this.

The Structural Pattern of the Walled-Town State

The farming population that lived in the village community was governed by the ruling elite of the walled-town state. Those who made up this ruling class originally must have been members of the same clans, and enjoying the same status, as the peasants, but by now they had developed into a ruling elite living in walled towns apart from the village communities. To be sure, a kingly authority had emerged at the apex of society in the walled-town state, but at this time power in reality was exercised by this ruling elite.

As presumptive evidence of the existence of such a ruling elite in the walled-town state, the practice in Wiman Chosŏn of attaching a geographical name to official titles designating a "chief minister" (*sang*) or a "high minister" (*kyŏng*) may be cited (two specific instances of this are the officials mentioned above known as the *Igyesang* and *Yŏkkyegyŏng*). When Wiman first fled to Old Chosŏn it is recorded that King Chun gave him a territory of "100 *li*" and charged him with defense of the western border. It may well be that this territory conformed in general to the boundaries of one of the walled-town states that earlier had come together to constitute the confederated kingdom of Old Chosŏn, and that the position of Wiman and his followers thus was akin to that of its former ruling elite. The "four outlying provinces" (*sach'ulto*) in Puyŏ that were administered by "governors" (*ka*) likely represent a development in the direction of a local government structure under centralized control, but this presumably was an outgrowth from an original walled-town state pattern.

In early Koguryŏ the small states that it either subjugated or brought into confederation evince with comparative clarity the form of walled-town states. The Piryu and Kalsa "countries" that surrendered to Koguryŏ are examples of walled-town states, as are the various "*na*" entities—Kwanna, Chona, Hwanna, Chuna, and Yŏnna. The Chinese used a different character for the names of the *na* states, recording them (in modern Korean pronunciation) as Sono (or Yŏnno), Chŏllo, Sunno, and Kwanno. Originally small independent entities, with their surrender to the confederated kingdom of Koguryŏ they were transformed into something like provincial administrative units and their ruling elites are thought to have been those known as *sangga*.

The many small "countries" of the Samhan area, numbering seventy-eight in all in the Chinese records, surely also were walled-town states. In Korean sources these appear with names like Sabŏl, Chomun, Aptok, Isŏ, and Korhwa, and the ruling elites of the larger entities were called *sinji* and those of the smaller *ŭpch'a*. Among these walled-town states were Paekche in the region of modern Kwangju just south of the Han River and Saro at modern Kyŏngju. The later Paekche kingdom developed out of the former, which was founded by immigrant people from regions to the north; its founder-king is said to have been Onjo. The later Silla kingdom emerged from the walled-town state of Saro, founded we are told by Pak Hyŏkkŏse, and the historical record also contains some information concerning Saro's structure and development.

Situated on the Kyŏngju plain, Saro appears to have been formed by the descendants of six clan groupings—the Kŭmnyang, Saryang, Ponp'i, Moryang, Hanji, and Sŭppi. Tradition has it that Pak Hyŏkkŏse was elevated to the position of first ruler of Saro, and since he was a member of the Kŭmnyang clan it would seem that Saro's leaders at first were chosen from that lineage group. Aryŏng, Hyŏkkŏse's queen, came from the Saryang clan, and so this presumably was Saro's second most powerful lineage. Subsequently leadership of Saro was seized by T'arhae, a man from the coastal region east of Saro who possessed the attributes of both a skilled metalworker and also of a shaman. Apparently by this time Saro already had broken out of the confines of the Kyŏngju plain and had developed a federative relationship with other walled-town states in its region. The terms used to designate Saro's rulers during this period were first *kŏsŏgan* and then *ch'ach'aung* before *isagŭm* was adopted. These titles are to be interpreted as having meant "chief," "shaman," and "successor prince" respectively and are not to be taken as representing kings of a centralized aristocratic state such as Saro, in the form of Silla, was to become.

There is no way to know to what extent the Saro model was followed by the many other walled-town states, but it is likely that there was substantial similarity. The results of studies of dolmen and other old tombs in the Taegu area tell us that a walled-town state in which power was shared among a number of elite lineages existed in that region as well. Accordingly, we may be justified in making the same general assumptions about the formative process and structure of the other walled-town states.

The Development of Kingly Authority

The Korean confederated kingdoms all represent the joining together of a number of walled-town states, but the formative process did not adhere to a uniform chronology, since some developed earlier or more rapidly than others. The case of the Samhan, as seen in the "Account of the Eastern Barbarians" (*Tung-i chuan*) in the Chinese source *San-kuo chih,* was perhaps a model of normal development. With the so-called "Chin-king" of the Mokchi state [see map p. 25] as their titular leader (he is said to have been elevated to his position by the common consent of the Mahan people), the numerous walled-town states of the Samhan had entered into a confederated relationship in the third century A.D.—although to be sure the twelve states of the Pyŏnhan region at some point removed themselves from this association. On the other hand, since the Chinese commanderies formed diplomatic ties with each of the walled-town states on an individual basis, a divisive policy designed to disrupt the process of union among them, political development in these states was hindered in varying degrees. Walled-town states like Okchŏ and Eastern Ye, which had come under the direct dominion of Koguryŏ, are instances of still more retarded development. Indeed, these states never were able to reach the stage of entering into a federative relationship.

In contrast, the political restructuring of both Puyŏ and Koguryŏ went forward at an unusually rapid pace. In both these states it appears that at first kings were chosen by some sort of elective process. This is indicated by the fact that in Puyŏ the kings were held accountable for poor harvests and accordingly were either replaced or killed, and that in later Koguryŏ the position of chief minister, called *taedaero,* was an elective one. If this assumption is correct, then the kingship in these two states may have alternated among two or more royal houses. A concrete suggestion of this is the record of the kingship in Koguryŏ passing from the Sono (or Yŏnno) lineage to the Kyeru. This same phenomenon appears later in the history of Silla, at the time when it still had not evolved beyond the stage of a confederated kingdom. Moreover, a distinctive feature of succession to the throne in this period was that it often followed the principle of younger brother succeeding older brother, and this too suggests that the institution of kingship still was in an early stage of development.

Subsequently, however, the right to the throne came to inhere in a single royal house and succession became hereditary, passing from father to son. These developments occurred in conjunction with the energetic wars of conquest launched by these emerging kingdoms. The territories thus newly acquired were ruled as subject domains and tribute was levied upon their populations, and this resulted in the further enhancement of kingly power. The chronology of this process of change is suggested by the instances of the Puyŏ king Ŭiryŏ (?–285) succeeding his father on the throne at the age of six and of father to son succession to the throne being established in Koguryŏ from the reign of King Sansang (196–227). At about the same time a system of regional government under centralized control appears to have been put in practice. One suggestion of this is seen in the Puyŏ institution of the "four outlying provinces" (*sach'ulto*), and another is the fact that Koguryŏ's system of the five "enclaves" (*pu*), with names indicating the directions of north, east, south, west, and center, was created in the reign of King Kogukch'ŏn (179–196).

Yet these new institutional arrangements still contained features of the former federative patterns. This is indicated by the fact that, like the king himself, the so-called *taega* of Koguryŏ had retinues of household retainers known as *saja, choŭi,* and *sŏnin,* while the *taega* officials of Puyŏ (known, for example, as *maga, uga, chŏga,* and *kuga,* that is, the horse, ox, pig, and dog "governors") also appear to have been served by *saja* household retainers. Accordingly, it is not amiss to suggest that actual political authority lay less with the king than in the hands of the *taega,* who are believed to have been senior members of the royal clan or of the various lineages from which the queens were drawn. The *taega* not only possessed political power but economic wealth as well. There seems to be no question that the *taega* elite had the first claim on the tax levies collected from the peasants through their village headmen. They wore silk clothing and also furs that were the envy of the Chinese, and their crown-like headgear and fez-like caps were extravagantly decorated with gold and silver ornaments. Not only this, but they dined off the finest Chinese-style tableware (called *chodu*). Moreover, they were powerful enough figures to command in extreme cases that as many as one hundred servants or attendants be killed and buried with them. It is also clear that they owned considerable numbers of slaves. It was natural, then, that the society in which they lived should develop attitudes of reverential respect toward them. The fact that visitors performed the ritual of bowing from a kneeling position with the arms extended and hands flat on the ground, and spoke in quiet tones, testifies to this.

Thus in late Puyŏ and early Koguryŏ the *taega* may be said to have constituted the elite stratum of their societies but, unlike the *sinji* and *ŭpch'a* of the Samhan, they cannot be considered to have been the actual rulers of walled-town states. Instead, they were well along in the process of development as an aristocratic political force in a centralized state. Accordingly, in Puyŏ and Koguryŏ, the structure of the confederated kingdom was undergoing marked change, and in the process the kingly authority was being strengthened. One illustration of this is found in the circumstance of the growing political importance of the *taesa* officials (for the most part originally the stewards of the royal household) in Puyŏ. Accordingly it may be said that the transformation of these two northern confederated kingdoms into centralized aristocratic states with the kingly authority paramount already was well underway.

5. Culture in the Confederated Kingdoms Period

Law

The chief characteristics of law in this period were its simplicity and its severity. The societies of this age were content with the minimum degree of legal regulation necessary to maintain the norms of social order. Whatever prohibitions were needed to maintain social order were considered good, and any violation of such prohibitions was deemed to be evil and so to be punished; there was little concern for adjusting severity of punishment to differing degrees of transgression. Since it was believed the gods had ordained that good be upheld and evil punished, law possessed a religious significance as well, and criminal judgments were passed and executions carried out in conjunction with the performance of religious ceremonies.

In Old Chosŏn a law code consisting of eight articles was observed, but the stipulations of only three of these are known with certainty:

1. He who kills another shall immediately be put to death.
2. He who causes bodily injury to another shall pay compensation in grain.
3. He who steals another's possessions shall be made the slave of his victim; however, exemption from such penalty may be obtained by payment of 500,000 "coppers."

We also are told that the wives of Old Chosŏn were faithful and did not engage in loose sexual conduct. On the basis of this bit of evidence from the historical record, it seems reasonable to assume that another of the eight articles in Old Chosŏn's law code may have been a provision prohibiting female adultery.

The following record exists concerning four legal provisions said to have been observed in Puyŏ:

1. He who kills another is put to death and the members of his family enslaved.
2. Those who commit robbery must compensate their victims twelve times over.
3. Women who commit adultery are put to death.
4. Jealousy on the part of a wife is considered particularly heinous and is punishable by death, with the corpse being left to rot in the mountains south of the capital; however, should the family of such a woman wish to claim the body, it may be done upon suitable payment in cattle or horses.

Thus despite some minor variations in the provisions of the laws of Old Chosŏn and Puyŏ as we know them, on the whole they exhibit common features. The laws of Koguryŏ, the Samhan, Okchŏ, and Eastern Ye, although only scant knowledge of their content has come down to us, also seem likely to have contained much the same provisions. In short, it may be supposed that in this period the five crimes of murder, bodily injury, thievery, female adultery, and jealousy on the part of a wife were commonly held to be the most serious offenses.

These legal provisions constitute important evidence for an understanding of the social values of this age. First of all, the penalties for murder and for causing bodily injury indicate a high regard for individual human life and working capacity, and the penalties for thievery show considerable respect for private property. Especially in Old Chosŏn concern over the crime of thievery was so great, we are told, that even though the perpetrator were to redeem his freedom by paying an indemnity, the shamefulness of the act in the eyes of society would make it impossible for him to find a marriage partner. Next, the penalties for female adultery and jealousy are thought to have served the purpose of safeguarding a patriarchal family system. The importance attached in Puyŏ to legal stipulations relating to the family system is particularly striking, and it is likely that the cruel punishment of the crime of jealousy reflects a widespread practice of polygamy within Puyŏ's upper class. Nor is there any reason to suppose that such a penalty for jealousy was limited to Puyŏ alone, for there is the clear example of the punishment of the Lady of Kwanna, the famed long-haired beauty of Koguryŏ, who was put to death for the crime of jealousy.

Religion

It is believed that in the earlier stages of the historical process in Korea religious and political functions were combined as one, and that the two became distinct as more formidable political power developed. This is because ruling political elites were now content with secular power alone and entrusted religious ceremonies to masters of ritual. In the Samhan these masters of ritual were called "Heaven prince" (*ch'ŏn'gun*), and they are said to have had authority over separate settlements known as *sodo*. It is recorded that a tall wooden pole was erected in the *sodo* on which were hung bells and a drum, and that these were used in religious ceremonies. This immediately calls to mind the staging of a *kut* ceremony by a modern Korean female shaman. Now, if someone who had committed a crime entered within the precincts of the *sodo* he could not be apprehended there, and although there are a number of varying theories concerning the *sodo*, it seems most likely that it was a sacred place. Thus a change had come about in the primitive beliefs in animism or shamanism. The duties of the religious leader, no longer simply those of the practitioner of magic who believed that he could move the gods by the power of his own invocations, rather had become those of the master of ritual who supplicated the gods for their favor. Nor was there any further need for these duties to be undertaken by the political powerholders themselves. At this point, then, the functions of religious and political leadership can be considered to have become distinct.

The harvest thanksgiving festival was the most lavish religious observance. The *yŏnggo* ("spirit-invoking drums") of Puyŏ, *tongmaeng* ("Chumong founder-worship") of Koguryŏ, *much'ŏn* ("dance to Heaven") of the Eastern Ye, and the celebration held in the Samhan in the tenth lunar month all represent such harvest festivals. They were performed in the tenth lunar month, at the conclusion of the harvest—with the exception of Puyŏ's *yŏnggo* which was held in the twelfth month, probably as a survival of a tradition of the primitive hunting society out of which Puyŏ evolved. No less important than the harvest festival was the ceremony performed in the spring to pray for a bounteous year. We are told that in the Samhan this was observed in the fifth month, after seed had been sown. And it is related that on the occasion of these major religious festivals the entire populace thronged together, giving themselves over to eating, drinking, singing, and dancing for several days on end.

The fact that high and low alike, without class distinctions, could celebrate these religious festivals together, indicates that in the sphere of religion the traditions of the earlier egalitarian lineage-centered communities still had some force. But even here changes in the direction of role differentiation and social stratification are evident. One example of this is the establishment by a king of Koguryŏ of a shrine to its dynastic founder, at which the king himself performed rites. At the same time, a lineage elder of the earlier Sono (or Yŏnno) royal house also was permitted to establish such a shrine to its first king, and this record of the sharing of an important royal prerogative constitutes evidence too of inherent limitations on the development of kingly authority in Koguryŏ.

Belief in the immortality of the soul and the lavish burial rites that were its corollary also were common features of the religious life of this period. We are told that in Puyŏ it was customary to delay burial for five months, and since it was regarded as a mark of honor to delay as long as possible, in the summer ice was used to prevent decomposition of the corpse. Indeed, the proprieties were deemed best served when the chief officiant performed the burial ceremony only when finally compelled to do so by others. Numerous burial objects were placed in the tomb and in some cases sacrificial burial was practiced, with as many as one hundred attendants being buried with their master. Burial was lavish in Koguryŏ too, many burial objects being interred with the deceased, and graves were covered with slabs of stone piled one atop the other in pyramidal shape. Similar concern for the afterlife of the deceased in the Samhan is revealed by the record that both cattle and horses were involved in some way in the funeral ceremony, and it was there too that the wings of large birds were buried with the deceased to supply the means for the soul to fly from the body. This provides an interesting confirmation of the belief the people of this area held in the immortality of the soul. It is clear, of course, that the practice of such lavish burials is indicative of belief in ancestor worship, which in turn was based on the conviction that the living soul of an ancestor exerts a continuous influence on the well-being of descendants of a later generation. Thus, as the pattern evolved of family headship and the throne passing from father to son, the performance of rituals for ancestors too came to be an important right, as well as obligation, for the lineal successor.

Finally, it is known that divination was practiced in this period. In Puyŏ, in time of war, an ox was killed in a ceremony dedicated to Heaven, and if the cleft in the hoof were found to have widened it was thought to portend disaster, and if not then the omen was considered propitious. This form of divination appears to be similar to the tortoise shell ("oracle bone") divination practiced in the Chinese Shang (Yin) dynasty. Divination too at first was a duty incumbent upon the king, but it is supposed that with the expansion of his political authority it gradually fell under the specialized province of the shaman.

Fine Arts

As bronze implements came into use and agriculture developed apace, activity in the realm of fine arts also increased. Yet viewed overall, the traditions of the Neolithic Age remained strong and the art of the confederated kingdoms period continued to evidence a close link with religion.

A conscious effort to achieve beauty of expression can be perceived in the design and decoration of many bronze artifacts. A truly impressive variety of such creations in bronze has been discovered: dagger hilts decorated with carvings of birds or horses or flanked by a pair of bells; belt buckles in the shape of horses or tigers; ceremonial implements with two, or five, or sometimes eight bells dangling from them; shaman ritual tree-poles adorned with a pair of birds; shoulder armor incised with deer and other animal designs; shield-shaped ceremonial objects and dagger handles with carvings of animals or farming scenes; and bronze mirrors decorated with minutely incised geometric patterns, like the so-called multi-knobbed fine-patterned mirrors. On the whole, this decorative work is characterized by the realism of the carvings of animals and by the geometric patterns of the incised linear designs. Among the bronze artifacts are numerous ceremonial implements made for religious purposes, and it seems likely that these were used in the performance of various rituals by the "Heaven prince" and other shaman. And since even the decorations on articles intended for the secular use of political leaders probably had a magical significance, these designs too may be said to have been religious in character.

Except for a single figurine of a woman, no clay figures from this period have yet been discovered. In a related form of sculpture, however, several small human figures made of bone have been found. Although small and artless in their execution, these deserve notice as carvings of religious images.

The works of art from this period that recently have drawn the most attention from academic circles are drawings incised on rocks. The one at Yangjŏn-dong in Koryŏng county consists of a number of concentric circles in a rather geometric design, crosses, and human masks. That at Ch'ŏnjŏn-ni in Ulchu county presents a variety of geometric designs—circles, triangles, and diamond shapes—set off by sketches of animals. And also in Ulchu county, at Pan'gudae, an incised rock drawing has been found that depicts hunting scenes on land and by boat on the sea, with pictures of whales, tortoises, and other marine life, of wild animals like the deer, tiger, bear, boar, and rabbit, and of humans as well. The concentric circles in these drawings probably symbolized the sun and contain a suggestion of praying for abundance, as was done in other agricultural societies where sun worship was practiced. The other geometric designs also may be interpreted as expressing religious meaning of an analogous sort. The animals generally are drawn in pairs, and this clearly symbolizes the procreative process and at the same time conveys the notion of prayer for bounty in nature. And the hunting and fishing scenes likely were drawn as a supplication for success in these essential activities. These drawings incised on chiseled rock surfaces suggest the vitality of the mode of life of the people of that age.

For celebrations like the spring festival to pray for abundance and the fall harvest thanksgiving, song and dance were essential. In the Samhan, we are told, a score or more of people would stamp the ground in concert with alternating high and minced step, moving their hands and feet the while in time to a beat. No doubt singing and dancing of this sort was performed at all of the great celebrations known to date from this period—the "spirit-invoking drums" of Puyŏ, the "Chumong founder-worship" of Koguryŏ, the "dance to Heaven" of the Eastern Ye, and others. These performances were not simply entertainments but were religious ceremonies, traditions doubtless handed down from the earlier clan-centered societies.

Chapter 3

Aristocratic Societies Under Monarchical Rule

1. The Development of the Three Kingdoms

The Growth of Koguryŏ and the Rise of Paekche

The right to the throne in Koguryŏ was permanently secured by the Ko house of the Kyeru lineage in the time of King T'aejo (53–146?), and from the reign of Kogukch'ŏn (179–196) the processes of strengthening the kingly authority and of centralizing the nation's political structure went ahead still more rapidly. In the first place, the five tribal enclaves that represented survivals from the earlier traditional society were restructured into five "provinces" (*pu*), with names that connoted the directions of north, south, east, west, and center. This signifies the strengthening of the centralized governmental structure. Secondly, succession to the throne on the whole no longer went from brother to brother but changed to a father to son pattern, and this represents a further enhancement of the power of the kingship. Thirdly, it became established practice for queens to be taken from the Myŏngnim house of the Yŏnna (Chŏllo) lineage. The creation of this special tie between the royal house and a single aristocratic lineage may be seen as an attempt to place restraint on other potential power centers opposed to the growth of monarchical authority. Such changes as these constitute the setting in which Koguryŏ pressed ahead with its advance toward the basins of the Liao River to the west and the Taedong River to the south. And eventually, under King Mich'ŏn in 313, Koguryŏ succeeded in seizing the territory of the Lo-lang Commandery and occupying the Taedong river region. At the same time, however, Koguryŏ came into sharp confrontation with Paekche, which had pushed northward to gain hold over the former domain of the Tai-fang Commandery in modern Hwanghae province.

It has been noted earlier that Paekche originally developed out of one of the walled-town states (also known as Paekche) that comprised the Mahan area, over which the "Chin-king" had ruled. It is not certain just when this original Paekche emerged as a confederated kingdom incorporating the various walled-town states in the Han river basin. But by the year 246, when the Lo-lang and Tai-fang commanderies (then under the dominion of

Wei, one of the Chinese Three Kingdoms) launched a large-scale attack against the Han river region, a new force already was gaining in strength in this area, for the purpose of the Wei army's attack was to disrupt and prevent the consolidation of this new power. In the ensuing warfare the governor of Tai-fang, Kung Tsun, was killed in battle, and this provides testimony to the strength of this newly emerging power. This surprisingly strong entity surely was not Mahan but rather the newly confederated kingdom of Paekche led, no doubt, by King Koi (traditional reign dates 234–286), who is known to have been active in other arenas around this time.

King Koi is thought to have been the same historical figure as Kui, the man Paekche later was to honor as its founder-king with commemorative ceremonies performed four times yearly. In the twenty-seventh year of Koi's reign, 260, we are told that six ministers (*chwap'yŏng*) were appointed to conduct the affairs of state along appropriate functional lines, sixteen grades of official rank were created, and colors for official dress were prescribed in accordance with rank. It is further recorded that in 262 King Koi decreed that officials who accepted bribes or those guilty of extortionate practices would be required to pay three-fold compensation and in addition would be barred from office for life. And the king displayed his majesty by receiving his subjects bedecked in stunning finery. All this conjures up a vivid image of a powerful political leader.

The structuring of Paekche into a centralized, aristocratic state appears to have been completed in the reign of King Kŭn Ch'ogo (346–375). A formidable warrior king, in 369 he destroyed Mahan, which by this time seems to have moved its capital southward to the modern Iksan area, and took possession of the whole of its territory. Then, in 371, Paekche struck northward into the Koguryŏ domain as far as P'yŏngyang, killing the Koguryŏ king, Kogugwŏn, in the course of the campaign. Paekche thus came to hold sway over a sizeable portion of the Korean Peninsula, including all the modern provinces of Kyŏnggi, Ch'ungch'ŏng, and Chŏlla, as well as parts of Hwanghae and Kangwŏn. Furthermore, King Kŭn Ch'ogo solidified his international position by making overtures to the Eastern Chin state in the Yangtze river region and to the Wa people in Japan.

It is not surprising that from the time of this warrior king the power of the throne in Paekche came to be increasingly authoritarian. Father to son succession to the kingship is thought to have begun from King Kŭn Ch'ogo. It was also from his reign that the so-called "age of Chin family queens" began, as Kŭn Ch'ogo's immediate successors continued to choose their consorts from this single aristocratic house. Kŭn Ch'ogo's command to the scholar Kohŭng to compile the *Sŏgi*, a history of Paekche, clearly reflects the king's desire to exult in his expanded royal authority and his well ordered state. Kŭn Ch'ogo was succeeded by Kŭn Kusu (375–384), whose death was immediately followed by King Ch'imnyu's adoption of Buddhism (in 384) and the implanting of the new value system of that faith.

Koguryŏ in Full Flourish

The invasions of the Earlier Yen (founded by the Mu-jung tribe of the Hsien-pei) and of Paekche, both in the time of King Kogugwŏn, dealt a severe blow to Koguryŏ. To surmount its difficulties it was necessary for Koguryŏ to reshape the pattern of its institutions. This task was undertaken by King Sosurim (371–384), who adopted Buddhism and established a National Confucian Academy (the *T'aehak*) in 372 and in the next year promulgated a code of administrative law. If Buddhism would serve to give the nation spiritual unity, then the National Confucian Academy was essential to the creation of a new bureaucratic structure, and an administrative code would systematize the state structure itself. Unfortunately we do not know the contents of the statutory code enacted at this time, but there is no question that it signifies Koguryŏ's initial completion of a centralized aristocratic state structure.

These internal arrangements laid the groundwork for the external expansion that presently would ensue. It was King Kwanggaet'o (391–413) who pursued most vigorously the task of adding new domains to Koguryŏ by conquest. The great military campaigns of this king, whose name literally means "broad expander of domain," are recorded in detail on the huge stone stele still standing at his tomb in Kungnae-sŏng (at modern T'ung-kou, on the Manchurian side of the mid-Yalu river), then the capital of Koguryŏ. According to this inscription, in the course of his reign of just twenty-odd years, King Kwanggaet'o conquered a total of sixty-four fortress domains and 1,400 villages. Leading his cavalry forth across all of Koguryŏ's land boundaries, he won a succession of notable victories: in the west he occupied Liao-tung, long the focal point of a fierce struggle between Koguryŏ and both Chinese and non-Chinese states; he subdued the Su-shen people, a Tungusic tribe to Koguryŏ's northeast, thus making himself the master of Manchuria; to the south he attacked Paekche, extending Koguryŏ's frontier into the region between the Imjin and Han rivers; and far to the southeast, in the Naktong river basin, he crushed a Wa Japanese force attacking Silla. Kwanggaet'o instituted his own era name, *Yŏngnak* ("Eternal Rejoicing"), thus arrogating to Koguryŏ a status of equality with China. After his death he was honored with a long eulogistic title that, with abundant good reason, proclaimed his awesome kingly achievements.

Kwanggaet'o was succeeded by King Changsu ("the long-lived;" 413–491), who during his seventy-nine years on the throne continued his father's enterprises and brought Koguryŏ to its flourishing height. He held China in check by employing a diplomatic strategy of maintaining ties with both the Northern and Southern Dynasties, thus enabling him to manipulate these two contending forces to Koguryŏ's advantage. And in 427 he transferred the Koguryŏ capital to P'yŏngyang, creating a new epicenter for the nation. This move from a region of narrow mountain

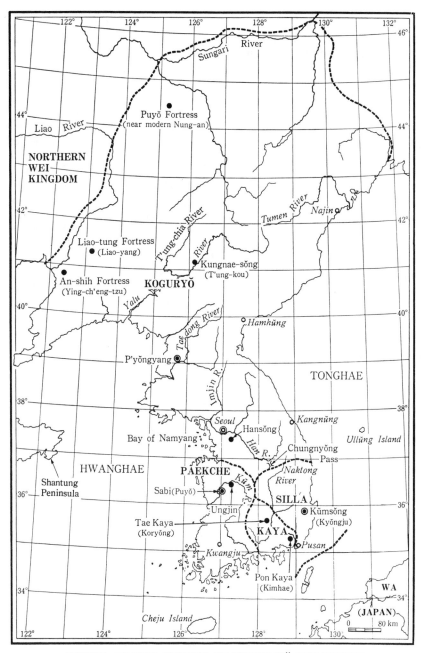

**KOREA AT THE HEIGHT OF KOGURYŎ EXPANSION
IN THE 5th CENTURY**

valleys to a broad riverine plain indicates that the capital could no longer remain primarily a military encampment but had to be developed into a metropolitan center for the nation's political, economic, and social life. And indeed this period saw the perfecting of Koguryŏ's political, economic, and other institutional arrangements.

The shift of Koguryŏ's capital far southward to P'yŏngyang of course posed a serious threat to Paekche and Silla. The alliance that these two now forged (in 433), as well as Paekche's embassy to the Chinese Northern Wei kingdom in 472 to appeal for military support against Koguryŏ's southward aggression, were developments dictated by the acute peril Paekche, in particular, faced. But in vain, for in 475 Koguryŏ seized the Paekche capital at Hansŏng (modern Kwangju just south of Seoul), captured King Kaero, and beheaded him. Paekche moved its capital south to Ungjin (modern Kongju), barely managing to preserve its national existence. The Koguryŏ dominion thus had come to extend southward to a line drawn from the area of Chungnyŏng Pass (linking modern North Kyŏngsang and North Ch'ungch'ŏng provinces) to the Bay of Namyang [see map p. 39]. Koguryŏ had fashioned a great empire with well functioning institutional machinery, embracing a vast territory stretching far into Manchuria and the Korean Peninsula, and so now came to contend for supremacy on the field of battle with China.

The Rise of Silla and Kaya

As already narrated, Silla evolved out of Saro, one of the twelve walled-town states in the Chinhan area of southeastern Korea. This state of Saro took the lead in forming a confederated structure with the other walled-town states in the region, and it is thought that the appearance of the first ruler from the Sŏk clan, King T'arhae (traditional dates 57–80 A.D.), marks the beginning of this gradual process. By the time of King Naemul (356–402), then, a rather large confederated kingdom had taken shape, controlling the region east of the Naktong River in modern North Kyŏngsang province. Through both conquest and federation, Saro now had reached the stage where it rapidly would transform itself into the kingdom of Silla. Naemul, the central figure in this unfolding historical drama, adopted a title befitting his new position as the ruler of a kingdom. Instead of *isagŭm* ("successor prince"), the term used by his predecessors, Naemul took the title *maripkan,* a term based on a word meaning "ridge" or "elevation." From this point on, the kingship no longer alternated among three royal houses but was monopolized on a hereditary basis by Naemul's Kim clan. In the course of his reign Naemul sought help from Koguryŏ in thwarting the designs of Paekche, which was making use of both Kaya and Japanese Wa forces to harass the fledgling Silla kingdom. This effort was successful, but it led to a slowing of the pace of Silla's development.

The lower reaches of the Naktong River, where Kaya emerged, originally were the territory of the twelve "states" of Pyŏnhan. These had not come under the dominion of the "Chin-king" but through confederation had formed an independent entity. Among the original twelve states, Kuya at modern Kimhae honored Suro as its first king and developed into the Pon ("original") Kaya kingdom, while in the region of Koryŏng the Mio-yama state accepted Ijinasi as its first ruler and evolved into Tae ("great") Kaya [see maps pp. 25 and 39]. Pon Kaya and Tae Kaya then joined with the other walled-town states in the lower Naktong region to form the Kaya federation.

With its Naktong River location, Kaya (and in particular Pon Kaya at the mouth of the river) engaged in vigorous maritime activities, maintaining contacts far up the western coast of the peninsula with the Chinese commanderies of Lo-lang and Tai-fang, northward along the east coast with the Ye people, and southward with the Wa in Japan. But Kaya was caught between Silla and Paekche, and the struggle between those two kingdoms rendered it impossible for Kaya to achieve full political and societal development. Moreover, when Paekche brought in Wa troops to attack Silla by way of Kaya, Silla and Kaya came into sharp conflict and this eventually led to the dispatch of a force by Koguryŏ's King Kwang-gaet'o in support of Silla (400 A.D.). Thereafter Kaya came under persistent harassment from Silla, until first Pon Kaya, in 532, and then Tae Kaya, in 562, succumbed to Silla's growing might. The other petty states in the lower Naktong region suffered the same fate, thus bringing about the downfall of the Kaya federation.

The Flourishing of Silla and the Resurgence of Paekche

Silla had taken the step of fixing the right to the kingship in the house of Kim in the time of King Naemul, and before long, with the reign of Nulchi (417–458), the pattern of father to son succession to the throne was established. Shortly thereafter the six clan communities were reorganized into administrative "districts" (*pu*), bringing a step closer to fruition the design for centralization of governmental authority. It is not clear just when this restructuring was carried out, but it appears to have been under King Chabi (458–479) or King Soji (479–500), that is, sometime in the latter half of the fifth century. The establishment of post stations throughout the country and the opening of markets in the capital where the products of different locales might be traded were among the consequences, no doubt, of such a centralizing thrust in Silla's governance of its domain. Meanwhile, to counter the pressure being exerted on its frontiers by Koguryŏ, Silla had concluded an alliance with Paekche, in 433. It was under King Chabi, most likely, that Silla was able to fully free itself from Koguryŏ's interference in its internal affairs, and in the process Silla's ties with Paekche became further strengthened. The fact that Silla forged marriage ties with King Tongsŏng of Paekche after the transfer of the Paekche

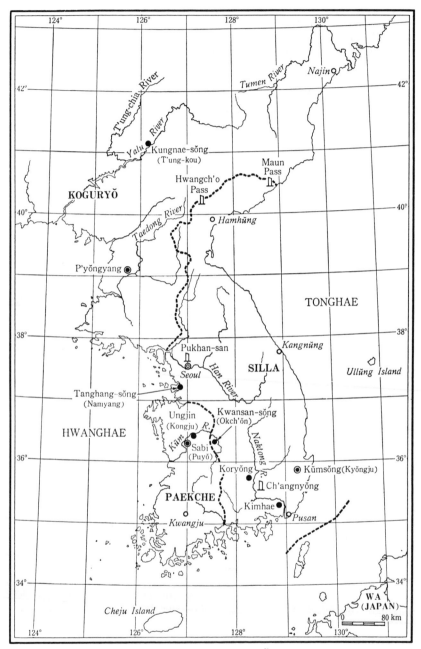

SILLA UNDER KING CHINHŬNG (540–576)
(⌂: sites of four monument stones)

capital to Ungjin in 475 is recounted in a well known tale, and in the ensuing years the two countries carried out joint military operations on several occasions.

Having experienced these domestic and external developments, Silla finally completed the structuring of a centralized aristocratic state in the reign of King Pŏphŭng (514–540). Under his predecessor, King Chijŭng (500–514), Silla had achieved important advances in its agricultural technology, as plowing by oxen was introduced and, from about this same time, irrigation works were carried out extensively. The resulting increase in agricultural production must have been one factor in promoting change in Silla society. In the political sphere, then, the nation's name was declared to be "Silla" and the Chinese term *wang* ("king") was adopted in place of the native title of *maripkan*. These Sinifications were not merely terminological changes but reflected Silla's readiness to accept China's advanced political institutions. Another significant political development of this period was the emergence of the Pak clan as the source of queens for Silla's kings.

The foundation thus having been readied, an administrative structure fully characteristic of a centralized aristocratic state was created in Silla in the reign of King Pŏphŭng. The clearest indication of this development is the promulgation of a code of administrative law in 520. Although its provisions are not known with certainty, it is believed to have included such basic regulations as those delineating the seventeen-grade office rank structure, prescribing proper attire for the officialdom, and instituting the *kolp'um* ("bone-rank") system. The adoption of an independent era name, *Kŏnwŏn* ("Initiated Beginning"), in 536 also is deserving of note, for it is evidence of the firm establishment of royal authority within Silla and of Silla's confident view of itself as a nation of equal standing in its international community even with China. The official adoption of Buddhism as the state religion, sometime between 527 and 535, is another memorable event of King Pŏphŭng's reign. This provided an ideological underpinning for national unity and solidarity in the newly centralized Silla state.

At this point it became possible for Silla too to go on the offensive in its relations with its neighbors. To be sure, this expansionist process had been at work over a considerable period of time. King Chijŭng had subjugated Usan (the Eastern Sea island of Ullŭng) in 512, and then in 532 King Pŏphŭng had conquered Pon Kaya (the modern Kimhae region), thus creating a springboard for advance northwestward in the Naktong river basin. But it was King Chinhŭng (540–576) who pushed ahead most vigorously with Silla's territorial expansion. In 551 Silla attacked the Koguryŏ domain in the Han river basin region, in concert with King Sŏng, the architect of Paekche's recent resurgence. The ten counties in the upper reaches of the Han thus fell to Silla, and before long Silla drove Paekche forces out of the lower Han region, thus securing for itself the whole of the Han river basin. The enraged King Sŏng then launched a frontal assault on

Silla in 554 but was himself killed in battle at Kwansan Fortress (modern Okch'ŏn). The Silla-Paekche alliance, which had endured for 120 years, at last was sundered. Silla's occupation of the Han river basin not only brought with it additional human and material resources but was important as well for providing a gateway through which Silla might communicate with China across the Yellow Sea. In 562, moreover, King Chinhŭng destroyed Tae Kaya (the modern Koryŏng area), thus completing Silla's acquisition of the fertile Naktong river basin. In the northeast, too, Chinhŭng advanced Silla's frontiers into the Hamhŭng plain. The four monument stones erected at Ch'angnyŏng, Pukhan-san, Hwangch'o Pass, and Maun Pass [see map p. 42] to mark the monarch's personal tour of inspection of his new frontiers offer eloquent testimony to Chinhŭng's achievements as a conqueror king.

Paekche, it will be recalled, had been forced to move its capital southward to Ungjin (modern Kongju) in 475 and for a time faced a threat to its very existence. Through the efforts of King Tongsŏng (479–501) and King Muryŏng (501–523), however, Paekche's fortunes somewhat revived. It was around this time that twenty-two districts (*tamno*) were created in the regions outside the capital and a prince or other member of the royal family enfeoffed in each in an effort to strengthen national unity. But if a foundation for renewed national development were to be laid, it was essential for Paekche to escape the confines of the mountain-ringed Ungjin and administer its domain from a new capital more favorably located. With this objective in mind King Sŏng (523–554) moved his capital to Sabi, on the broad plain at modern Puyŏ, and at the same time he renamed his kingdom "Southern Puyŏ." It is believed likely that the system of twenty-two separate central government offices and a territorial administrative structure consisting of five capital districts (*pu*) and five provinces (*pang*) came into being in conjunction with the removal of the capital to Puyŏ. Furthermore, King Sŏng entrusted Kyŏmik and other monks with the task of fostering the spread of Buddhism, thus to make firm the nation's spiritual foundation. At the same time he further strengthened Paekche's ties with the Southern Dynasties of China.

Having restructured his kingdom and built up its strength, King Sŏng now turned his efforts toward recovery of Paekche's former territory in the Han river basin. To this end he made a pact with King Chinhŭng of Silla and, taking advantage of internal dissension in Koguryŏ, struck northward. With the occupation of the lower reaches of the Han, he had for the moment attained his objective, but when Silla unexpectedly seized this fruit of his long and arduous endeavors, King Sŏng saw his dreams end in failure. Enraged, the Paekche king tried to strike back at Silla but was himself killed in battle, as we have seen. Thereafter Paekche looked upon Silla as its mortal enemy and, making common cause with its former foe, Koguryŏ, launched one attack after another against Silla.

2. The Foreign Relations of the Three Kingdoms

The Unfolding of Relations with Foreign States

In the relations of the Three Kingdoms with their neighbors in Northeast Asia, the relationship with China was pivotal. The general characteristics of the policies adopted by the Three Kingdoms toward China may be summarized as follows. First, as they vigorously pursued their expansionist policies of conquest, the Three Kingdoms at times made bold to launch military assaults against China itself, and naturally they in turn had to face Chinese attacks. This was the case particularly with Koguryŏ, whose frontiers bordered on China. And indeed such conflict was the dominant theme of relations with China in the Three Kingdoms period. Secondly, in the process of mapping out their own strategies for the unification of the peninsula, all of the Three Kingdoms took appropriate advantage of the conflict at this time in China between the Northern and Southern Dynasties and, moreover, attempted in their diplomacy to make use of the nomadic peoples of the northern regions and of the Wa (Japanese) to the south. Nevertheless, thirdly, none of the Three Kingdoms showed any hesitation in adopting whatever elements of Chinese culture might be needful for its own development. The relations between the Korean states and China during the Three Kingdoms period, then, proceeded to unfold within the framework of these general characteristics.

It already has been explained that Koguryŏ, at an early stage in its national existence, directed repeated attacks against the Chinese dominions in the Liao and Taedong river basins, and in the reign of King Tongch'ŏn (227–248), with an assault against Hsi An-p'ing at the mouth of the Yalu, Koguryŏ sought to cut the land route linking China proper with its Lo-lang colony. The Chinese state of Wei soon retaliated with an invasion of Koguryŏ led by Kuan-ch'iu Chien in 244, resulting in the capture of the Koguryŏ capital of Hwando-sŏng (also called Kungnae-sŏng, at modern T'ung-kou on the Manchurian side of the mid-Yalu). When Wei again sent an invasion force, led by Wang Ch'i, against Koguryŏ in the very next year (245), King Tongch'ŏn could only save himself by seeking refuge in the distant northeast coastal region. The fall of the Wei kingdom in 265 was followed by a brief reunification under the Chin dynasty (266–316), but this was a fragile unity and China was increasingly beset by attacks from the nomadic peoples on its northern frontier. Seizing upon this opportunity, Koguryŏ renewed its pressure against Liao-tung and at the same time drove out the Chinese from their Lo-lang colony (313), thus gaining control over the former domain of Old Chosŏn in the Taedong river basin.

But in China the kingdom of Chin now was driven south into the Yangtze

river region, while sixteen ephemeral kingdoms, all but three founded by
five different non-Chinese peoples, rose and fell in China's northern regions. When one of these, the Hsien-pei Earlier Yen state (founded by the
Mu-jung tribe), advanced further into Manchuria, Koguryŏ was again
compelled to engage in a bloody struggle for control of the Liao river
region. The consequences for Koguryŏ were disastrous, as an invasion
force in 342 under the king of the Earlier Yen, Mu-jung Huang, stormed
into the Koguryŏ capital, burned the royal palace to the ground, dug up
the corpse of the previous king (Mich'ŏn), and seized the queen mother
and fifty thousand other Koguryŏ captives. A generation later in 371, the
Paekche army of King Kŭn Ch'ogo dealt the Koguryŏ of King Kogugwŏn
an equally harsh blow by thrusting north all the way to P'yŏngyang and
killing the Koguryŏ monarch in the battle for the city. To overcome the
nation's deepening crisis, a number of new institutional arrangements
were put into effect under King Sosurim (371–384), as already has been
recounted. This laid the groundwork for Koguryŏ's brilliant expansion
under King Kwanggaet'o (391–413), who finally succeeded in occupying
the whole of the Liao-tung area, subjugated the Su-shen forest dwellers
on Koguryŏ's northeastern frontier, and in the end created a vast kingdom extending over two-thirds of the Korean Peninsula and much of
Manchuria as well.

With its greatly expanded frontiers, Koguryŏ now adopted a policy of
friendly relations with the more distant Chinese states and military confrontation with those closer to its borders. Thus the bitter struggle with the
nearby Northern Dynasties of China continued, while Koguryŏ at the same
time sought diplomatic contact across the sea with China's Southern
Dynasties. Koguryŏ also formed ties with the nomadic peoples on China's
northern frontier as a further means to hold China at bay. Paekche, for its
part, attempted to restrain Koguryŏ by establishing relations not only
with the Southern Dynasties but with the Northern Dynasties as well. Not
only this, but Paekche also called on forces from the petty states of
Wa in Kyūshū, Japan, founded by a people who had migrated from the
Paekche area, to mount attacks against Silla. This caused Silla to turn to
Koguryŏ for support, with the result that a Koguryŏ army sent by King
Kwanggaet'o drove the Wa back beyond Silla's borders. The ensuing pressure from Koguryŏ itself, however, led Silla to seek its salvation rather in
an alliance with Paekche (in 434, under Silla King Nulchi).

However intense the conflict of the Three Kingdoms with China may
have been, it did not diminish the ardor of the Korean states for the introduction of Chinese culture. The most notable illustrations of this are the
adoption of Chinese legal and other institutions, of the Buddhist and Confucianist ideologies, and of the Chinese written language. Nevertheless,
despite the forging of peaceful diplomatic ties and the close cultural contact, the history of the warfare between Korea's Three Kingdoms and
China constitutes the principal theme of the relationship. And it is the

struggle between Koguryŏ and the Sui and T'ang dynasties that marks the climax of this violent conflict.

Koguryŏ's Struggle with Sui and T'ang

In the latter half of the sixth century a major change occurred in the balance of power among the Three Kingdoms. With its occupation of the Han river basin Silla had advanced into the central regions of the peninsula, but this conquest had earned it the enmity of both Koguryŏ and Paekche, against whose combined forces Silla now stood alone. The new Koguryŏ-Paekche alliance moved quickly to attack Silla, in particular its communication link with China through Tanghang-sŏng (modern Namyang to the west of Suwŏn). It was in the course of one such campaign against Silla that the famed Koguryŏ commander, Ondal, was killed in battle.

New tensions began to appear in the latter half of the sixth century not only in the Korean Peninsula but on the continent as well. In China the Sui dynasty succeeded in once again unifying the empire (589) after the prolonged division of the period of the Northern and Southern Dynasties, while a new power rising in the steppe region of north-central Asia, the T'u-chüeh (Turks), posed an immediate threat to the victorious Sui. With its kingdom extending over the northern half of the Korean peninsula and far into Manchuria, Koguryŏ now sought to form ties with the T'u-chüeh to confront Sui, and at the same time its Paekche ally was in contact with the Japanese across the sea. Thus to oppose the north-south alignment of forces represented by the T'u-chüeh, Koguryŏ, Paekche, and Japan, Sui and Silla joined hands to form an east-west axis. The confrontation between these two power blocs foreboded the great storm that soon would break over Northeast Asia, and it was the showdown between Koguryŏ and Sui that represented the first decisive test of strength.

Koguryŏ was the first to open hostilities, with a bold assault across the Liao River against Liao-hsi, in 598. The Sui emperor, Wen Ti, launched a retaliatory attack on Koguryŏ but met with reverses and turned back in mid-course. Yang Ti, the next Sui emperor, proceeded in 612 to mount an invasion of unprecedented magnitude, marshalling a huge force said to number over a million men. And when his armies failed to take Liao-tung Fortress (modern Liao-yang), the anchor of Koguryŏ's first line of defense, he had a nearly a third of his forces, some 300,000 strong, break off the battle there and strike directly at the Koguryŏ capital of P'yŏngyang. But the Sui army was lured into a trap by the famed Koguryŏ commander Ŭlchi Mundŏk, and suffered a calamitous defeat at the Salsu (Ch'ŏngch'ŏn) River. It is said that only 2,700 of the 300,000 Sui soldiers who had crossed the Yalu survived to find their way back, and the Sui emperor now lifted the siege of Liao-tung Fortress and withdrew his forces to China proper. Yang Ti continued to send his armies against Koguryŏ but again without success, and before long his war-weakened empire crumbled.

When the T'ang dynasty succeeded the fallen Sui, Koguryŏ anticipated further attacks from China and so strengthened its defenses by constructing a wall a thousand *li* in length across its northwestern frontier. At about the same time, internal schism developed within the Koguryŏ aristocracy and, after a wholesale slaughter of the king (Yŏngnyu) and others who opposed him, Yŏn Kaesomun emerged as a military strong man wielding absolute political power (642). Yŏn Kaesomun now took a still more forceful posture in foreign relations, setting Koguryŏ on a collision course with both T'ang and Silla. Rejecting the request of the Silla envoy Kim Ch'un-ch'u for assistance in repelling attacks from Paekche, he demanded instead that Silla yield up the Han river basin. And he also spurned T'ang representations that Koguryŏ call a halt to its military operations against Silla. Before long, in 645, Koguryŏ's defiant stance occasioned the launching of a large-scale T'ang invasion of Koguryŏ.

Crossing the Liao River, the Emperor T'ai Tsung reduced the Liao-tung Fortress (at modern Liao-yang) and a number of others, but he suffered a massive defeat at An-shih Fortress (modern Ying-ch'eng-tzu) and was compelled to turn back. Although a minor link in Koguryŏ's chain of defensive strongholds, An-shih Fortress withstood a siege of more than sixty days, during which period the T'ang army threw all its strength into as many as six or seven assaults in a single day. But the stubborn defenders, commanded by one Yang Man-ch'un, hurled back each fresh attack and in the end the fortress could not be breached. Subsequently Emperor T'ai Tsung made several further attempts to invade Koguryŏ, but these attacks too all were repulsed.

Koguryŏ's victories over the Sui and T'ang invasion armies occupy a special place in the annals of the resistance of the Korean people to foreign aggression. The conquest of Koguryŏ was to be but one stage in the grand imperial design of both Sui and T'ang to achieve hegemony over all of East Asia. Accordingly, had Koguryŏ been beaten, Paekche and Silla as well likely would have fallen under Chinese dominion. But Koguryŏ held firm, serving as a breakwater against which the repeated Chinese invasions foundered, and the peoples of the Korean peninsula thus were saved from the grave peril of foreign conquest. It is for this reason that Koguryŏ's triumphs hold such importance in the pages of Korean history.

3. Political and Social Structure of the Three Kingdoms

Emergence of a Central Aristocracy

After long processes of development and considerable travail, all of the Three Kingdoms created centralized aristocratic states. Power in each of the three societies was concentrated in those who lived in the kingdom's capital, and among these it was the aristocratic families (in particular the lineages of the kings and their queens), whose special privileges derived from rigidly hierarchic social status systems, that appear to have occupied a position of primacy in the political and economic spheres, and in the cultural arena as well. The period of the Three Kingdoms, then, was the age in which this extremely limited number of aristocratic lineages consolidated their dominant positions over their respective societies.

Little of a definite nature is known about the Koguryŏ social status system, but there appears to have been a distinct stratum of the aristocracy from which the chief minister, the *taedaero*, was drawn and which itself was empowered to choose appointees to that highest office. Doubtless this upper aristocracy was centered on the royal houses and on the lineages from which the Koguryŏ monarchs took their queens. This can be surmised from the fact that, in addition to the royal Ko house of the Kyeru lineage, the most honorable title of esteem, *koch'uga*, could be worn only by those of the former royal house of the Sono lineage and of the Myŏngnim house of the Yŏnna (Chŏllo) lineage that furnished the royal consorts. Beneath this uppermost layer of the aristocracy were several other social strata, and it appears that marriage could not be contracted freely between different status groups.

In Paekche, we are told, there were eight renowned families—the Sa, Yŏn, Hyŏp, Hae, Chin, Kuk, Mok, and Paek. The principal government offices appear to have been monopolized by the royal Puyŏ house and by the Chin and Hae families of the Paekche queens, while the chief administrative positions in important regions outside the capital (such as the twenty-two *tamno* districts) were entrusted exclusively to members of the royal house. It may be assumed, therefore, that the families of the kings and their queens occupied the predominant position in Paekche society as well. It is believed, moreover, that only a distinct and limited group of aristocratic families could participate in Paekche institutional arrangements like the *chŏngsa-am* council, a body whose function is understood to have been to elect a chief minister to head the officialdom. The "colored vestments" system of Paekche that ranked the officialdom into sixteen grades arranged in three tiers, like the similar Silla institution, probably bore a close relationship to the social status structure.

The "bone-rank" (*kolp'um*) institution of Silla provides the clearest illustration of the actual structure of aristocratic society in the period of the Three Kingdoms. This was a system that conferred or withheld a variety of special privileges, ranging from political preferment to aspects of everyday life, in accordance with the degree of respect due a person's bone-rank—that is, hereditary bloodline. There were two levels of so-called bone-rank itself, "hallowed-bone" (*sŏnggol*) and "true-bone" (*chin'gol*), and in addition six grades of "head-rank" existed, "head-rank six" down through "head-rank one." The hallowed-bone status was held by those in the royal house of Kim who possessed the qualification to become king, but subsequently, just prior to the Silla unification, this higher bone-rank ceased to exist. Those of true-bone rank also were members of the Kim royal house but originally lacked qualification for the kingship; after the disappearance of the hallowed-bone rank, however, the throne was occupied by those who held true-bone status. True-bone rank also included the Pak lineage that had been a royal house early in Silla and from which royal consorts later came, as well as the "new Kim lineage" descended from the royal house of the Pon Kaya state. The reason for distinguishing between those of hallowed-bone and true-bone rank within the same Silla royal house of Kim is not entirely clear, but apparently it was done on the basis of maternal lineage. Head-ranks six, five, and four comprised the general aristocracy, with six (also called *tŭngnan*, puzzlingly explained as meaning "obtained with difficulty") being next below true-bone status. Head-ranks three, two, and one, if they ever formally existed, must have designated the "ordinary people" (*p'yŏngin*) or "common people" (*paeksŏng*)—that is, the non-privileged general populace.

As already indicated, the various bone-ranks accorded their holders differential access to the enjoyment of political and social privilege. The most important aspect of this, the allocation of official rank and government position, is illustrated in the accompanying chart. For example, holders of true-bone rank could advance to the highest official rank (that of *ibŏlch'an* or *kakkan*), but holders of head-rank six were restricted to no higher than the sixth office rank (*ach'an*), holders of head-rank five to the tenth office rank (*taenama*), and holders of head-rank four to the twelfth office rank (*taesa*). These limitations naturally were reflected in appointment to official position. As one instance, the post of *yŏng*, the head of a ministry or department, could only be held by those of the fifth office rank (*taeach'an*), or higher, and accordingly these ministerial level posts were occupied by those of the true-bone rank alone. Similarly, the post of *kyŏng* or vice-minister was filled by those who held the sixth (*ach'an*) through the eleventh (*nama*) office ranks and thus could be occupied by holders of either head-rank six or five, but this was the highest post to which such men might be appointed. Lower posts in the ministries, those of *taesa, saji,* and *sa*, could be held by men of head-rank four as well as by those of the higher head- and bone-ranks. And on the military side, the general officers who exercised the highest command functions in Silla's army held office ranks ranging from first (*ibŏlch'an*) through ninth (*kŭppŏlch'an*), but it nevertheless was stipulated that only those of the true-bone rank could receive such vital appointments.

Thus an individual's political preferment was inextricably bound to the status he held in the bone-rank system. Not only this, but bone-rank also determined the scale of the residence in which a Silla citizen might live. For example, a true-bone house could not exceed 24 "feet" in length or width, a head-rank six house 21 feet, a head-rank five house 18 feet, a head-rank four or commoner's house 15 feet. Moreover, sumptuary regulations based on bone-rank governed the color of official attire, vehicles

Relationship of Bone-Rank Gradations in Silla to Office Rank and Post

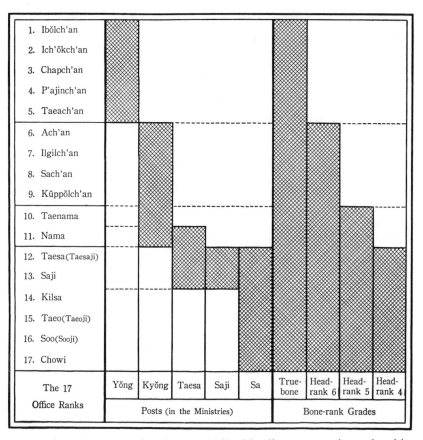

The 17 Office Ranks	Yŏng	Kyŏng	Taesa	Saji	Sa	True-bone	Head-rank 6	Head-rank 5	Head-rank 4
1. Ibŏlch'an									
2. Ich'ŏkch'an									
3. Chapch'an									
4. P'ajinch'an									
5. Taeach'an									
6. Ach'an									
7. Ilgilch'an									
8. Sach'an									
9. Kŭppŏlch'an									
10. Taenama									
11. Nama									
12. Taesa(Taesaji)									
13. Saji									
14. Kilsa									
15. Taeo(Taeoji)									
16. Soo(Sooji)									
17. Chowi									
	Posts (in the Ministries)					Bone-rank Grades			

and horse trappings, and various utensils. Needless to say, in such a hierarchic society as that of Silla, predominant power was wielded by those who enjoyed the highest hereditary social status, namely those of true-bone rank. And since the core element within the true-bone rank was comprised of the royal house and that of the queens, it may be asserted that Silla society was dominated by these two lineage groups. The fact that the honorific title of *kalmun wang*, Silla's counterpart of *koch'uga* in Koguryŏ, was bestowed only on members of the royal and consort families also can be seen as a reflection of this fundamental characteristic of Silla society.

Political Structure

The Three Kingdoms alike evolved from early pluralistic political systems to monolithic bureaucratic structures centered upon the kingship.

Office Rank Systems of the Three Kingdoms

Koguryŏ's 12 Office Ranks

1. *taedaero*	2. *t'aedaehyŏng*	3. *ulchŏl*	4. *t'aedaesaja*
5. *choŭidudaehyŏng*	6. *taesaja*	7. *taehyŏng*	8. *suwisaja*
9. *sosaja*	10. *sohyŏng*	11. *chehyŏng*	12. *sŏnin*

Paekche's 16 Office Ranks

1. *chwap'yŏng*
2. *talsol*   3. *ŭnsol*   4. *tŏksol*   5. *hansol*   6. *nasol* ⎫ (purple robes)
7. *changdŏk*   8. *sidŏk*   9. *kodŏk*   10. *kyedŏk*   11. *taedŏk* (scarlet robes)
12. *mundok*   13. *mudok*   14. *chwagun*   15. *chinmu*   16. *kŭgu* (blue robes)

Silla's 17 Office Ranks

1. *ibŏlch'an*   2. *ich'ŏkch'an*   3. *chapch'an*   4. *p'ajinch'an* ⎫ (purple robes)
                  5. *taeach'an*
6. *ach'an*   7. *ilgilch'an*   8. *sach'an*   9. *kŭppŏlch'an* (scarlet robes)
10. *taenama*   11. *nama*   (blue robes)
12. *taesa(ji)*   13. *saji*   14. *kilsa*   15. *taeo(ji)*
                   16. *soo(ji)*   17. *chowi*   (yellow robes)

The aristocratic officials of Koguryŏ, for example, were classified into twelve grades, the topmost of which was the *taedaero*, a term that also designated the chief minister. Especially noteworthy in the Koguryŏ structure is the existence of the several *hyŏng* ("elder brother") ranks—*t'aedaehyŏng, choŭidudaehyŏng, taehyŏng, sohyŏng,* and *chehyŏng.* The term *hyŏng* in this context connotes an elder, and it is thought that, in the process of Koguryŏ's transformation into a centralized aristocratic state, those who in former days had been tribal or clan chieftains were given the *hyŏng* rank appropriate to their earlier positions and in this way were integrated into the new socio-political structure. It also should be observed that a number of the office ranks of Koguryŏ have appended to them the term *saja*—*t'aedaesaja, taesaja, suwisaja,* and *sosaja.* Unlike the *hyŏng* with their background as tribal or clan leaders, it appears that the holders of *saja* ranks emerged from among those who had been the actual administrators of the powerful royal and aristocratic houses that they served. In such ways, then, was the pluralistic political structure of Koguryŏ's past converted into a unitary office rank system.

The three tier Paekche office rank system had *chwap'yŏng* and the various *sol* ranks at the top, the several *tŏk* ranks in the middle stratum, and a bottom layer consisting of *mundok* and under. The three strata were distinguished further by the color of official attire worn by those in each tier—purple for the top tier, scarlet for the middle, and blue for the bottom. As in the case of Silla, the Paekche system likely reflects a correlation between official rank and social status. At any rate, it seems clear that such a monolithic office rank structure as that of Paekche must have been instituted in consonance with the creation of a centralized aristocratic state. In looking at the office rank system of Silla, terms like *ch'an* (which also appears as *kan*) and *chi* (-*ji*) that suggest the tribal leaders of an earlier age are immediately apparent and, as in Koguryŏ and Paekche, these signify the creation of a unitary structure that integrated diverse elements from Silla's past.

With regard to government structure in the Three Kingdoms period, there are virtually no records in the case of Koguryŏ. In Paekche, however, we know that while its capital was still at Hansŏng (Paekche's capital was moved from Hansŏng at modern Kwangju to Ungjin at modern Kongju in 475) there were six *chwap'yŏng*, or ministers, who headed the administrative departments entrusted with royal secretariat duties, fiscal administration, the conduct of rites and ceremonies, palace and capital security, penal matters, and provincial military forces. In the course of Paekche's last century and a quarter, when the capital was at Sabi (modern Puyŏ), a relatively complex government structure was elaborated, consisting of twenty-two departments—twelve within the palace itself and ten to administer the affairs of the government proper. In Silla a number of central government departments were created over a period of time, and responsibilities (such as military affairs, surveillance of official conduct, the handling of royal secretariat and fiscal matters) were assigned to them along functional lines.

The most significant feature of the political process in each of the Three Kingdoms is the role played by conciliar bodies in political decision making. The fact that the chief minister in Koguryŏ was elected by a council of the high aristocracy, and that those who held the fifth office rank (*chouidudaehyŏng*) and above assembled in conclave to discuss and decide important government matters, are indications of the existence of such a council composed of high aristocratic officials. Similarly, the *chŏngsa-am* institution, which is thought to have chosen the chief minister of Paekche through a balloting procedure, suggests something of the nature of conciliar government in that state. However, it is the *Hwabaek* institution, Silla's Council of Nobles, that provides the clearest illustration of this phenomenon. The *Hwabaek* was a council headed by the single aristocrat who held "extraordinary rank one," *sangdaedŭng,* and was composed of those of "extraordinary rank two," *taedŭng,* all of whom are thought to have been of true-bone lineage. Its function was to render decisions on the most important matters of state, such as succession to the throne and the declaration of war; the original decision to formally adopt Buddhism also was made by the *Hwabaek* council. The principle of unanimity governed *Hwabaek* decisions, and deliberations on particularly vital matters, we are told, were convened at sites bearing special religious significance—at Mt. Ch'ŏngsong on the eastern edge of the capital at Kyŏngju, Mt. Uji on the south, the P'ijŏn field on the west, and Mt. Kŭmgang on the north. The existence and function of these conciliar institutions, as corporate assemblies of the high aristocracy, imparted a distinctive character to the political processes of the Three Kingdoms.

In each of the Three Kingdoms the authority of the central government extended over the countryside, which gradually came to be divided into administrative districts. Fortresses were built in the regions where formerly tribal communities had claimed territorial rights, and these were made the centers of local administration. Subsequently the local administrative units were called by the Chinese term *kun,* or districts, and in Koguryŏ the governor of such a district bore the title *ch'ŏryŏgŭnji* (or *tosa*), in Paekche *kunjang,* and in Silla *kunt'aesu,* but in fact the general term *sŏngju* ("castle lord," or "master of the keep") was applied to all these district governors. Eventually numbers of districts were combined to form larger, provincial-type administrative units, which in Koguryŏ consisted of five *pu* (north, east, south, west, and inner), in Paekche five *pang* (center, north, east, south, and west), and in Silla several *chu* (such as upper, lower, and new). The governors of these were called *yoksal* (a transliteration of a native word), *pangnyŏng* ("provincial governor"), and *kunju* ("military commandant"), respectively, in Koguryŏ, Paekche, and Silla. And in the capitals of the Three Kingdoms, where the ruling aristocracies resided, special administrative divisions were created, five *pu* ("districts") in both Koguryŏ and Paekche, and six in Silla. The residents of the capital in each case enjoyed a position superior to that of people who lived in the provincial areas, as will be seen below.

Military Organization

With the development of the Three Kingdoms into centralized aristocratic states, military units came to be organized on a national level and, as political institutions had been, were put under the authority of the king. In this structural sense, then, the king had become the commander-in-chief of his nation's military forces and, in fact, the monarchs of the Three Kingdoms frequently led their soldiers in person and fought alongside them in battle. Little concrete information is available on the organization of the units in the new military structure, but it is known that in Silla six divisions called *chŏng* ("garrisons") were established, one in each of the *chu* provincial administrations. The six *chŏng* were commanded by generals of true-bone status, were composed of men who lived in the capital, and so had the character of elite units drawn from elite lineages. These soldiers, accordingly, looked upon their military service as an honor and privilege, rather than as a burdensome duty. In addition to this garrison army nucleus in Silla, there also were units called *sŏdang* ("oath bannermen"), the ranks of which are believed to have been filled by men who, something like retainers, pledged their individual services and loyalty to their commanders.

Apparently to supplement the elite units that constituted the core of the military forces of the Three Kingdoms, companies of quite young men (often in their midteens) were organized, like the *hwarang* ("flower of youth") bands of Silla. The special character of the *hwarang* derives from its adaptation of a traditional communal institution dating back to Silla's formative period. As had been the case with the communal assemblies of youth in the earlier clan-centered society, the *hwarang* bands cultivated an ethos that served the needs of the state. This is indicated by the fact, or so the evidence suggests, that the *hwarang* warrior youth honored the "five secular injunctions" laid down in the early 600's by the famed Buddhist monk Wŏn'gwang. (These were: (1) to serve the king with loyalty, (2) to serve one's parents with filiality, (3) to practice fidelity in friendship, (4) to never retreat in battle, and (5) to refrain from wanton killing.) There was also a religious character to the activities of the *hwarang,* as they made pilgrimages to sacred mountain and river sites in Silla and prayed for their nation's tranquility and prosperity by performing ceremonial singing and dancing. But the most important function of the *hwarang,* after all, was military. In time of peace the *hwarang* cultivated the military arts, and in time of war they joined in the fighting at the front lines. The many tales of valor and prowess in battle told of such *hwarang* heroes as Sadaham, Kim Yu-sin, and Kwanch'ang are among the most famous episodes in all of Korean history.

Each of the Three Kingdoms also organized military forces on the district or local level, and in fact the units of local administration served at the same time as the basic units of local military organization. In each of the fortresses that served as the centers of district administration, military units of fixed strength were garrisoned, and it is thought that the *kyŏngdang* institution of Koguryŏ was instituted as a means to reinforce these local units. Like the *hwarang,* the *kyŏngdang* carried on an earlier tradition of communal bodies of unmarried males, and the youthful members of the *kyŏngdang* devoted themselves to cultivating moral values and practicing the military arts. The *sŏngju,* the "castle lord," of course was the commander of a district's military contingents, and the provincial governors who exercised jurisdiction over a number of fortified district centers also doubled as military commanders. Accordingly, one cannot escape the feeling that each of the Three Kingdoms had given itself the structure of a single, monolithic military organization.

Village Headmen and the Farming Population

With the emergence of centralized aristocratic states centered on monarchical power, the concepts evolved that all of the nation's land belonged to the king and that all of the people were his subjects. This was a new phenomenon, one that cannot be found in earlier ages. Nevertheless, this does not mean that private ownership of land disappeared, or that the people of the nation all alike came under the direct dominion of the king. To commanders for their victories in battle, or to the aristocratic holders of government office, large grants of land and numerous prisoners of war were given as befitting their distinguished service and exalted station, and in consequence the private land and slave holdings of the aristocracy increased continuously. The kings themselves were no exception, as can be seen from the fact that the *Naegwan* department in the Paekche government structure, which was a ministry of royal household affairs, occupied itself principally with matters relating to cereal grains and handcrafted products. At times prisoners of war or criminals were forcibly resettled in villages known in Silla, for example, as *hyang* or *pugok,* where they formed communities of low caste laborers. In fact, the social compulsion to relegate large segments of the populace to unfree status constitutes a special characteristic of the aristocratic states of the Three Kingdoms period.

Nevertheless, the independent peasants whose status was that of freemen, and who cultivated their own plots of land throughout the country, comprised the preponderant class in these societies. Their lives and livelihood, of course, were subject to direct control by the state, which levied grain and tribute taxes (in the form of local products) upon them and commandeered their labor services. On a per capita or perhaps a household basis, the free peasantry was required to pay both a cloth and a grain tax, and they were mobilized for prescribed periods of time to man local defenses or as corvee laborers to construct fortifications, irrigation works, or the like. Indeed, one is almost tempted to suggest that the interest of the state in controlling the peasantry was more for their labor power than for the product of the land they worked.

Since the peasants who lived in the villages of the Three Kingdoms still did some farming on a cooperative basis, for example the growing of hemp, it is clear that the earlier communal traditions persisted. Nevertheless, on the whole they were self-reliant farmers who each worked his own land independently and, in consequence, considerable social differentiation developed among them. Some peasants, for example, lost their land and thus fell into a new class of tenant farmers. This phenomenon can be seen in the biography of Ŭlbul, the later King Mich'ŏn of Koguryŏ, which records his experience as a tenant farmer in the household of Ŭmmo, a rich landowner of Susil village. Tenant farmers were poor peasants who eked out a livelihood by working others' land, and it seems likely that the so-called *yuin* ("wanderers") of Koguryŏ belonged to this class of agricultural laborers. Because of their landless plight, the taxes levied on the *yuin* were lighter than those collected from the peasants who possessed their own holdings. Koguryŏ's "relief loan law" (*chindaepŏp*) that enabled peasants to borrow grain from state storehouses during the spring famine season, to be repaid after the autumn harvest, must have been enacted in part, at least, in response to the appearance of such a landless class in that state's agricultural society.

The villages, where the peasants led their lives, were the basic units in the provincial administrative structure. Central government control over the villages apparently was exercised through village chiefs or headmen, and in the case of Silla at least it is possible to perceive, however imperfectly, how the system actually worked. The village chiefs of Silla were natives of their particular local areas, and their position in society was determined by status gradations different from those available to residents of the capital. They held the rank of either "true village headman" (*chin-ch'onju*) or "secondary village headman" (*ch'a-ch'onju*), and they enjoyed social status privileges that corresponded to those of head-ranks five and four. Village headmen, however, received office rank in local government grades that were not a part of the structure of office ranks held by residents of the capital, the office rank level to which they were permitted to rise being predetermined in accordance with their social standing as "true village headmen" or "secondary village headmen." This circumstance meant, of course, that they were denied access to other government office. Aspects of their daily lives, too, were subject to restrictive regulations related to their standing as village headmen.

4. The Aristocratic Culture of the Three Kingdoms

Historiography and Confucianism

The Chinese writing system, introduced to Korea in much earlier times along with continental iron culture, came into considerably more widespread use during the Three Kingdoms period. The use of this foreign written language without modification, however, entailed a number of disadvantages, so that it was natural for Koreans to devise ways of adapting Chinese characters to suit their own needs. Specifically, a method was developed of representing a Korean word either with a Chinese character having its sound or with one sharing its meaning. There was a fixed set of rules for this method of transcription, which later influenced the creation of the Japanese writing system known as *Man'yō-gana*. Originally limited to recording native proper nouns, Korean transcription practice subsequently was expanded into a full-fledged writing system. As can be seen in the Oath Inscription of 612 (see below), Chinese characters at first simply were arranged in Korean word order. Later, however, certain characters came to be used to put a sentence partially into Korean syntax and so to clarify its meaning. This writing system is known as *idu*. A more sophisticated system, called *hyangch'al,* then was developed. In general, as used in the writing of *hyangga, hyangch'al* expressed Korean nouns with Chinese characters having the same meaning, while verb stems and inflections, and other grammatical elements, were written by arbitrary use of Chinese characters having the desired pronunciation. On the other hand, there also was a system used in reading Chinese texts whereby Korean grammatical elements, written in fixed patterns with Chinese characters, were inserted appropriately in the text. This is called *kugyŏl* and the record that Sŏl Ch'ong read nine

Chinese classics in the native Silla language is taken to mean that he used the *kugyŏl* system of textual explication.

With the development of ways of writing, a variety of state supported compilation activities were undertaken, chief among which were national histories. We are told that a work in one hundred volumes entitled *Yugi* (*Extant Records*) was produced in early Koguryŏ and that this was re-worked into a five-volume *Sinjip* (*New Compilation*) in the year 600 by Yi Mun-jin. In Paekche a history called *Sŏgi* (*Documentary Records*) was compiled by Kohŭng in the reign of Kŭn Ch'ogo (346–375), and the *Kuksa* (*National History*) was done in Silla by Kŏch'ilbu in 545. None of these histories has survived, but it is thought that in large part their contents were incorporated by Kim Pu-sik into his twelfth century *Samguk sagi* (*History of the Three Kingdoms*). The fact that each of the Three Kingdoms compiled its own history around the time it promulgated a code of laws, elaborated an institutional infrastructure, and began a period of outward expansion likely reflects a common desire to put their sovereign dignity on display both at home and abroad. Accordingly, the compilation of these national histories may be regarded as monuments to the creation of the Koguryŏ, Paekche, and Silla centralized aristocratic states.

All of the Three Kingdoms laid great stress on inculcating the Confucian ethos as a means of maintaining their aristocratic social orders. Already in 372 Koguryŏ had established a National Confucian Academy (*T'aehak*) at which Confucianism was taught. Subsequently, at the *kyŏngdang* in each locality, the unmarried youth of Koguryŏ were assembled for intensive instruction in the reading of Chinese texts as well as for archery practice. And it is recorded that, at a relatively early date, the people of Koguryŏ were reading the Five Classics of Confucianism, Ssu-ma Ch'ien's *Historical Records* (*Shih chi*) and the *History of the Han Dynasty* (*Han shu*), the *Yü-p'ien* Chinese character dictionary, and an anthology of Chinese literature called the *Wen hsüan* (*Literary Selections*). In Paekche, since the title of "savant" (*paksa*, the modern term for an academic "doctor") was given to teachers of the Chinese Classics, Confucian educational institutions also must have existed, and it is recorded that works from the corpus of Chinese classics, philosophies, and histories were being read. Confucianism came later to Silla than to its neighboring kingdoms, but there too Confucian moral values were widely propagated among the people. The precept of fidelity, so valued by the members of the *hwarang* bands, was of particular importance in welding Silla society together and, through the inculcation of loyalty, this cohesive force was directed upward to fasten upon the authority of the throne. Thus Confucianism contributed importantly to the creation of a social ethos that would foster national unity among the Silla people. It is in such a context that the values expressed in the monk Wŏn'gwang's "five secular injunctions" and in the Oath Inscription of 612 (a text incised on a stone tablet in which two Silla youth swore to strictly observe the code of loyalty and to complete the reading of certain

Chinese canonical works) are to be understood. Nor is there reason to think that either Koguryŏ or Paekche differed from Silla in respect to the contribution Confucian precepts made to the solidarity of their societies.

The Acceptance of Buddhism

The widely used date for the initial acceptance of Buddhism is the year 372, when the monk Sundo came to Koguryŏ from the Earlier Ch'in state then in control of northeastern China and transmitted images of the Buddha and Buddhist sutras. Twelve years later the monk Malananda brought Buddhism to Paekche from the Eastern Chin state in the Yangtze river valley. In both these instances it would appear that a receptive attitude toward the adoption of Chinese culture already had developed and that the new doctrine was conveyed through officially sanctioned missions from states in China with which the recipients had friendly relations. Accordingly, Buddhism was welcomed by the royal houses of Koguryŏ and Paekche without giving rise to any significant discord. In Silla, too, Buddhism was first disseminated not very much later, certainly by the mid-fifth century, by the monk Ado (also known as Mukhoja) who entered Silla from Koguryŏ. Nevertheless, this missionary effort was an individual initiative limited to an outlying area of Silla and it ended in failure when it met with local hostility. Buddhism was brought to the Silla royal house perhaps a century later, with the arrival of the monk-envoy Wŏnp'yo from the southern Chinese state of Liang (502–557). Subsequently King Pŏphŭng (514–540) made every effort to secure the acceptance of Buddhism but for a long time was thwarted by the opposition of the Silla aristocracy, which led to the storied martyrdom of the high court noble Ich'adon in 527. This incident, however, served as the catalyst that eventually brought about the official recognition of Buddhism near the end of Pŏphŭng's reign, most likely in 535.

In all of the Three Kingdoms the principal initiative for the acceptance of Buddhism was taken by the royal houses. This is seen with particular clarity in the case of Silla. Only when Buddhism had been transmitted to the royal house of Silla, a century after it first had been propagated among the populace, was the way finally opened for official recognition of this alien religion. Moreover it was the king and those who served his person who turned aside the opposition of the aristocracy and forcibly carried through the official sanction of Buddhism. The fact that Buddhism came to be so strongly supported and promoted by the royal house probably was because it was seen to be well-suited as a spiritual prop with which to undergird the new governing structure centered on the authority of the throne. The concept of a single body of believers all alike devoted spiritually to observing the way of the Buddha, taken together with the notion of the whole of the nation's people serving the king as one, surely played a major role as a force for unity and cohesion in these early Korean states. At the same time, however, it should not be forgotten that without the acquiescence of the powerful aristocracy the official acceptance of Buddhism likely would not have come about. It is plausible that, in societies like these marked by such strict social stratification, the Buddhist teaching of reincarnation, of a rebirth based on *karma*, was welcomed as a doctrine giving recognition to the privileged position of the aristocracy. It may be argued, then, that Buddhism came to be accepted as a system of thought peculiarly suited to the needs of a centralized aristocratic state headed by a king.

In consequence of this, the aspect of Buddhism as a doctrine for the protection of the state was a powerful attraction of that faith in the Three Kingdoms period. Buddhism of course also was a vehicle for seeking the well-being of the individual, for example through prayers for recovery from illness or for having children, but its practice as a faith assuring the well-being of the state is still more strongly in evidence. It is not surprising, therefore, that such sutras as the *Inwang kyŏng* (*Sutra of the Benevolent Kings*) were held in particular esteem. In keeping with the doctrines of this sutra, ceremonies called "Assemblies for Sutra Recitation by One Hundred Monks" (*paekchwa kanghoe*, also known as Inwang Assemblies) were held to pray for the well-being of the state. Another ceremony, called the *p'algwanhoe* ("Festival of the Eight Vows"), also was significant as a vehicle for prayers for the state. Among the numerous Buddhist temples in the Three Kingdoms, Paekche's Wanghŭng-sa ("Temple of the King Ascendant") and Silla's Hwangnyong-sa ("Temple of the Illustrious Dragon"), both dedicated to dissemination of the doctrines of state protection, were built on the grandest scale. Particularly noteworthy is the fact that it was an article of faith among the people of Silla that the nine-story pagoda of the Hwangnyong-sa symbolized Silla's destiny to conquer nine other East Asian nations (including China and Japan) and receive their tribute in fealty. And the conviction that the Maitreya Buddha, the Buddha of the Future, had experienced several reincarnations on Silla soil in the form of famed *hwarang* warriors is another reflection of the belief in Buddhism as the protector of the state. Moreover, there is no question that the exhortations of monks to fight bravely in battle, to safeguard not only the state and its ruler but the way of the Buddha as well, gave courage to the soldiers called upon to wage their nation's wars.

A look at the Buddhist sects that flourished during the Three Kingdoms period will also serve to illustrate the close nexus that existed between state and religion. The most important sect was the Vinaya, and the monks Kyŏmik of Paekche and Chajang of Silla were major figures in this school. Chajang, in fact, occupied the position of Chief Abbot of State, and so exercised supervision over the entire Buddhist establishment in Silla. The emphasis on the Vinaya doctrines, which set forth the "disciplines" or rules governing monastic life, also had a political significance, in that the unity of belief and discipline fostered by the religion could be made to serve the purposes of the state as well. To this end Silla established a hierarchy of abbot administrators at the district, province, and national levels who applied the rules of the Vinaya order to control the temples and monks of the whole country. A Buddhism analogous to the later tantric doctrines also flourished at this time, and the widespread belief that the power of the Buddha could effect miraculous cures, drive off invading armies, and even slay malevolent dragons explains much about the appeal of Buddhism to the people of that age. In the later years of Koguryŏ and Paekche, however, a change was taking place in the Buddhist faith as practiced in those kingdoms, one evidence of which was the growing popularity of the Nirvana school. The Nirvana doctrine, which holds that the imperishable Buddha nature exists within all living creatures, was espoused most notably by the Koguryŏ monk Podŏk to counter the appeal of the Taoist belief in immortality.

Since Buddhism received such extensive support from the state, it is not surprising that at times monks performed the function of political advisers. Two well-known examples of this are the Silla monks Wŏn'gwang, to whom the king turned for advice on how to rule, and the aforementioned Chajang whose proposal as Chief Abbot of State led to the construction of the nine-story pagoda at Hwangnyong-sa. Buddhist monks, moreover, played the pioneering role in bringing new elements of Chinese culture into Korea, since they made up the majority of those who traveled to China for study during the Three Kingdoms period (a phenomenon known then as "study in the West"). The monks also provided ethical guidance to the people. Wŏn'gwang's formulation of the "five secular injunctions" and the undertaking of moral instruction to *hwarang* youth by monks who lived with them in their bands illustrate aspects of this function.

Poetry, Song, and Music

It is not certain what form poetry took in Koguryŏ and Paekche, but the *hyangga* ("native songs") exist for Silla, and the gentle rhythms that run through these simple poetic songs are regarded as admirable expressions of Korean literary sensibility. A full appreciation of the *hyangga*, however, requires an awareness of its religious character. For *hyangga* were written principally by *hwarang* or by Buddhist monks and often were vehicles for entreating divine intervention in human affairs. The *hyangga*, then, represents a transformation of shamanist incantations into Buddhistic supplications. The monk Yungch'ŏn's "Song of the Comet," the singing of which is said to have made a comet disappear and to have caused Japanese invaders to retreat as well, is a rare *hyangga* from the Three Kingdoms period, and it aptly illustrates the religious nature of Korea's earliest poetic form.

With its close relationship to poetry, the music of this age also was replete with religious overtones. There is no lack of evidence attesting to this religious function of music—the fact that the *hwarang* bands often gave themselves over to dance and song; the historical reference to Silla King Chinhŭng who, when he sent Kŏch'ilbu to attack the Han river region, himself proceeded to Nangsŏng (modern Ch'ungju) where he summoned Urŭk and his disciple Imun to perform music; the anecdote about the pestle pounding refrain composed by Master Paekkyŏl, who seems to have believed in the miraculous power of onomatopoetic sound. In such a context as this, it is understandable that music flourished in all of the Three Kingdoms.

Some thirty or forty varieties of musical instruments, including wind, string, and percussion, are known to have been in use during this age. Of particular renown is the "black crane zither" (*hyŏnhakkŭm*) that Wang San-ak of Koguryŏ created by modifying the seven-stringed zither of the Chinese state of Chin. Wang San-ak is said to have composed more than one hundred melodies for his instrument, which later found its way into Silla and there produced such virtuoso performers as Okpogo. Detailed records on the music of Paekche have not survived, but in light of the fact that Paekche instruments, instrument makers, and master performers found their way into Japan, it seems clear that music in Paekche was no less developed than in Koguryŏ and Silla. The distinctive zither of the Kaya area, the *kayagŭm,* also is famous. The *kayagŭm* was brought to Silla by Urŭk, who then taught the art of playing it to Kyego and many other Silla disciples. A repertoire of one hundred eighty-five melodies, we are told, existed for the *kayagŭm* alone.

Fine Arts

The art of the Three Kingdoms period is characterized by its simple, forthright esthetic appeal. To be sure, the childlike sense of the grotesque that is a hallmark of earlier Korean art occasionally still is found, for example in tiny clay figures, but on the whole this now has disappeared. At the same time, rather than being the product of a mature craftsmanship, this was an art of realism possessed of a robust beauty. It is only natural that the artistic creations of the Three Kingdoms period, an age when a new social order was being shaped by an aristocratic elite as yet unspoiled and unsophisticated, should be fundamentally both forthright and robust in their beauty of expression. Gradually then, the concomitant flourishing of Buddhism both enriched the intellectual content of Three Kingdoms art and markedly advanced artistic techniques, and in consequence works began to appear in which a more refined sense of beauty can be discerned.

No specimens of free-standing Koguryŏ architecture remain, and we can only surmise the form it took indirectly, through the ancient tombs that remain in such abundance in the vicinity of P'yŏngyang and of the earlier Koguryŏ capital at Kungnae-sŏng (T'ung-kou) inside Manchuria. These tombs fall into two types, those built with stone and those of earthen construction. The former are pyramidal in shape and were made by placing slabs of stone one atop the other. An outstanding example is the Tomb of the General (*Changgun Ch'ong*), which is typical in the feeling these tombs give that the powerful figures interred therein possessed an unyielding strength. The earthen tombs, on the other hand, consist of mounds of earth piled atop a burial chamber formed by stone slabs. The Tomb of the Twin Pillars (*Ssangyŏng Ch'ong*) is one of the major earthen tombs, and the octagonal twin columns at the entrance to the burial chamber, as well as the painted representations of columns and their capitals in the four corners of the chamber, and of ridge and ceiling beams painted on the ceiling, give us some notion of Koguryŏ architectural style. That no Koguryŏ structures related to Buddhism have survived no doubt is because both pagodas and other temple buildings in that kingdom were made of wood.

Turning to Paekche, there are records of the construction of magnificent palace buildings and pavilions, as well as of huge temples like the Wanghŭng-sa, but stone pagodas represent the only surviving evidence of Paekche architecture. The best known of these are the pagoda on the site of the Chŏng-nim-sa temple at Puyŏ and that of the Mirŭk-sa temple at Iksan. The latter is an immense structure that retains the more fluid style of a wooden pagoda, while the Chŏngnim-sa example expresses the greatest possible beauty within so simplified a form. In the case of Silla, too, we read of the construction of temples of massive proportions, but today we can see only the sites on which they stood. Even the famed nine-story wooden pagoda of the Hwangnyong-sa temple, which is said to have been built by the Paekche master craftsman Abiji, was destroyed by fire during the thirteenth century Mongol invasions. Nevertheless, the majestic stone-brick pagoda of the Punhwang-sa temple and the graceful curved lines of the stone Ch'ŏm-sŏngdae observatory, both in Kyŏngju, provide insight into architectural modes of Old Silla. It should be noted, finally, that temples in the Three Kingdoms period at first were designed with a single pagoda and three main shrine halls but later changed to the familiar pattern of one of each of these structures.

Sculpture from the Three Kingdoms consists almost entirely of Buddhist images. The outstanding Koguryŏ examples are the gilt bronze standing Tathagata Buddha (dated uncertainly at 539 A.D) and the gilt bronze half-seated Maitreya in meditation pose, to both of which their sculptors gave benignly musing smiles. In Paekche statues like the stone Buddha carved in the face of a cliff at Sŏsan, and the renowned gilt bronze meditating half-seated Maitreya with its low and unadorned four-peaked diadem, exhibit characteristic Paekche artistry in the elegance of their facial contours and indulgence of their smiles. Silla also can boast of a masterfully executed gilt bronze sculpture of a meditating half-seated Maitreya Bodhisattva, wearing a tall jeweled crown topped by a sculpted pagoda. More linearly rendered than its Paekche counterpart, this Silla statue is admired for the sense of spiritual strength that it conveys. Here it should be noted that all of the Three Kingdoms produced numerous statues of Sakyamuni (the historic Buddha) and also of the meditating half-seated Maitreya figure, and this constitutes a salient feature of the Buddhist sculpture of this period. Little is known of the artists who created the imposing array of Three Kingdoms sculpture, but the Silla monk Yangji is credited with not only many Buddha figures but with guardian demons and decorated roof, wall, and flooring tiles as well. These latter expressions of the sculptor's art in the Three Kingdoms period are highly regarded for the beauty of their designs.

The best known paintings of the Three Kingdoms period, of course, are the murals of the old tombs of Koguryŏ. Painted on the four walls of the burial chamber of earthen tombs and on the corbeled vaulted ceilings, and treating a variety of themes, these murals provide precious, indeed exuberant material for the study of the way of life and thought of the Koguryŏ people. These Koguryŏ tombs customarily are named after the theme of the paintings that adorn their walls—for example the Tomb of the Four Spirits, the Tomb of the Wrestlers, the Tomb of the Dancers, and the Tomb of the Hunters. Perhaps the most famous of the murals are found at Uhyŏn-ni in South P'yŏngan province in the great Tomb of the Four Spirits—the azure dragon of the East, the white tiger of the West, the vermilion phoenix of the South, and the tortoise and snake of the North. The spirited lines and bold colors of the Koguryŏ murals make these paintings so pulsate with animation that the viewer feels as if, for example, a mounted Koguryŏ warrior is riding by in full gallop before his very eyes. Mural paintings are found in old Paekche tombs as well, the result of Koguryŏ influence, and the best known are those in the brickwork tomb at Songsan-ni, Kongju, and in the stone-chambered tomb at Nŭngsan-ni, Puyŏ. The Paekche murals, however, convey a sense of much greater refinement than those of Koguryŏ. Artists of both countries, like Tamjing of Koguryŏ and Prince Ajwa of Paekche, went to Japan, where their artistry was so acclaimed that such outstanding works as the murals at the Hōryūji temple and the portrait of Shōtoku Taishi, both in Nara, traditionally were attributed to them. Silla too produced famous artists, judging from the appearance in the records of the names of master painters like Solgŏ, but none of their works survive. Silla tombs have no murals for the simple reason that Silla tomb architecture did not employ a separately constructed, walled burial chamber. Quite recently, however, a painting of a "heavenly horse," done on a rectangular section of bark that served as a mudguard, came to light at a tomb then named after this find (the Tomb of the Heavenly Horse), and this specimen suggests that Silla painting, too, was characterized by a robustness of spirit and a high level of artistry.

The old tombs of Koguryŏ and Paekche, constructed with a horizontal entrance way leading inward from the surface of the burial mound, were relatively easy to pilfer, and for this reason virtually no burial objects remain. But with the recent discovery of the fully intact tomb of King Mu-ryŏng (501–523) at Songsan-ni, Kongju, it has been possible to gain an appreciation of the superb artistry of Paekche craftsmen, as evidenced for example in the ornamentation of the gold crowns found there. It is Silla, however, that has left us by far the most tomb artifacts, a happy result of the fact that the Silla style of tomb construction, utilizing a vertical shaft for interment beneath an earth-covered mound of stones, made grave robbing almost impossible. Among the multitude of burial objects so far excavated, the most bedazzling are those fashioned of pure gold—gold crowns and shoes, girdles and earrings, finger rings and bracelets, and there is wondrous jewelry made of gemstones and molten glass as well. Gold crowns have been unearthed from quite a number of tombs, including the Tomb of the Golden Crown, the Tomb of the Lucky Phoenix, the Tomb of the Golden Bell, and the Tomb of the Heavenly Horse, and they are especially prized for the unique Silla style of their form and adornment. Nevertheless, the historical significance of these artistic creations lies less in their remarkable esthetic qualities than in the fact that they are symbols of the power and authority of the Silla kings and queens in whose tombs they are found.

Chapter 4

The Fashioning of an Authoritarian Monarchy

1. The Silla Unification and the Founding of the Parhae Kingdom

Silla Unifies the Korean Peninsula

While Koguryŏ was occupied by its bloody wars with Sui and T'ang, Paekche hastened to take the offensive against Silla. The campaigns of King Ŭija (641-660), admired in his own time as a paragon of courage and fidelity, were particularly effective. Early in his reign, in 642, his forces captured Taeya-sŏng (modern Hapch'ŏn) and some forty other strongpoints in the fortified zone marking the contested Silla-Paekche border. Thus imperiled, Silla was forced to pull its line of defense back to the Naktong River. It was at this juncture that Kim Ch'un-ch'u, the later King Muyŏl of Silla, undertook the hazardous diplomatic mission of asking military assistance from Silla's other enemy, Koguryŏ. But Yŏn Kaesomun, who at that time held power in Koguryŏ, demanded the return of the Han river region as the price for his help, and so Kim Ch'un-ch'u's efforts came to naught. Silla then sent Kim to China to seek an alliance with T'ang. T'ang acceded to Silla's request and settled upon the strategy of first overcoming Paekche and then striking against Koguryŏ in a pincers movement from both the north and south.

In the year 660, then, the Chinese Emperor Kao Tsung sent an invasion fleet against Paekche under the command of Su Ting-fang, while Silla forces led by Kim Yu-sin marched to attack Paekche in concert. The T'ang troops effected a landing on the south bank at the mouth of the Paek River (the present Kŭm River), by which time the Silla army already had crossed the pass at T'anhyŏn, east of Taejŏn. Having ignored the advice given him some time earlier by a high official named Sŏngch'ung and now repeated by another loyal official, Hŭngsu, the Paekche king belatedly sent Kyebaek to block the Silla advance. But this suicide detachment, badly outnumbered, was defeated at Hwangsan (modern Yŏnsan), whereupon the Silla and T'ang armies plunged ahead toward the Paekche capital at Sabi. Before long Sabi fell, and with the surrender of King Ŭija, who had taken refuge at Ungjin (modern Kongju), the kingdom of Paekche perished.

Despite the submission of the king, a member of the royal family named Poksin and the monk Toch'im raised a force at Churyu-sŏng (modern Hansan) to resist the invaders of their land. For a time their efforts met with marked success, as over two hundred strongpoints were retaken. Then, upon the return of the Paekche Prince P'ung from Japan, the restoration forces made him their king and, laying siege to Sabi, Ungjin, and other occupied strongholds, not only harassed the T'ang garrisons but on a number of occasions inflicted defeat on the T'ang and Silla armies sent against them. One is tempted to observe that, had its rulers earlier been worthy of receiving such support from the people they governed, Paekche might not so easily have fallen. Yet the restoration movement also developed leadership problems, as Poksin killed the monk Toch'im and was in turn killed by P'ung. Seizing the opportunity presented them by this internal conflict, the combined Silla-T'ang armies attacked and seized the main restorationist stronghold at Hansan. At this point, remnant units of the restoration forces surrendered one after another, and when their final redoubt at Imjon-sŏng (modern Taehŭng) fell, the three-year struggle to restore the Paekche kingdom came to an end.

Having finally destroyed Paekche, T'ang and its Silla ally redirected their efforts to the conquest of Koguryŏ. This of course had been the original intention. Already in 661, the Chinese commander Su Ting-fang had sailed his fleet to the Taedong River to make a frontal attack on P'yŏngyang. To be sure, the Chinese force was defeated by Yŏn Kaesomun and had to withdraw, but Koguryŏ's power to resist by now had been seriously weakened. The attrition resulting from long years of continuous warfare and the disaffection engendered by Yŏn Kaesomun's dictatorial rule both were factors at work in this process of enfeeblement. After Yŏn Kaesomun's death, a power struggle broke out among his sons and younger brother, and this internal conflict thrust Koguryŏ headlong toward its doom. For when the eldest son (Namsaeng) was driven out by the second son (Namgŏn), he fled to the old capital at Kungnae-sŏng and surrendered to T'ang, while the younger brother, Yŏn Chŏngt'o, went over to Silla. Loath to let slip such an opportunity, T'ang mounted a fresh invasion under Li Chi in 667 and Silla launched a coordinated offensive. This time the T'ang army received every possible assistance from the defector Namsaeng, and although Koguryŏ continued to hold out for another year, the end finally came in 668. Pledging his loyalty to Ansŭng, an illegitimate son of the last Koguryŏ king, a former middle-rank official named Kŏmmojam carried on a resistance movement for two years, until he was assassinated at the instigation of the man he served. Ansŭng then fled to the protection of Silla and was given the title of "King of Koguryŏ" (later changed to King Podŏk).

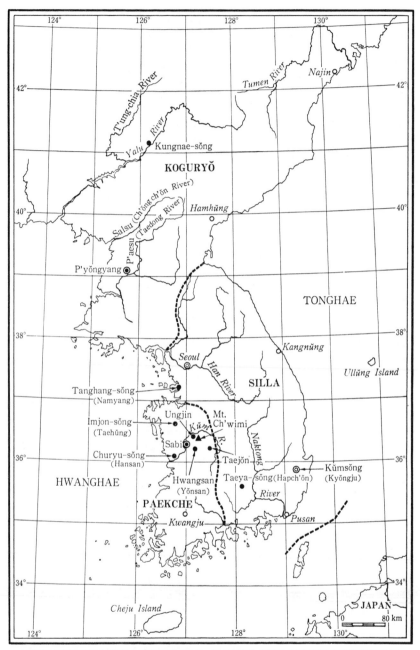

THE UNIFICATION STRUGGLE AMONG THE THREE KINGDOMS
(7ᵗʰ CENTURY)

Silla's Expulsion of T'ang

The intention of the Chinese in sending armies to conquer Paekche and Koguryŏ was to bring the entire Korean Peninsula under T'ang imperial control. With this in mind, T'ang now established five commanderies in the regions that had been the five provinces (*pang*) of the former Paekche kingdom and began to administer the area directly. Shortly thereafter, T'ang created the Great Commandery of Kyerim as the mechanism through which the Silla domain would be ruled and appointed Silla King Munmu as its governor-general. With the same objective of appearing inoffensive in the eyes of the Korean inhabitants by disguising the reality of the alien dominion it sought to impose, T'ang named Puyŏ Yung, a son of King Ŭija, governor of the Ungjin Commandery in the former Paekche area. T'ang then put pressure on Puyŏ Yung and a reluctant King Munmu to meet at Mt. Ch'wiri (the present Mt. Ch'wimi on the north bank of the Kŭm River near Kongju) and enter into a pact of friendship. These actions were aimed not only at winning over the people of Paekche but also at thwarting Silla's designs on the former Paekche territory. Subsequently, after the fall of Koguryŏ, T'ang created nine additional commanderies to govern that kingdom's former domains, while at the same time establishing the Protectorate-General to Pacify the East (An-tung Tu-hu-fu) at P'yŏngyang and giving it jurisdiction over not only the Koguryŏ area but over Silla and former Paekche lands as well. The effect of this was that, contrary to its expectations, Silla was receiving no different treatment from T'ang than were the conquered kingdoms of Koguryŏ and Paekche.

But Silla was unwilling to accept such an outcome. Accordingly, almost from the moment of Koguryŏ's collapse Silla launched a fresh campaign, this time in an effort to win control over the former Koguryŏ domain. Silla rendered assistance to the restorationist forces of Kŏmmojam in their effort to drive out the Chinese and formally invested Ansŭng as king of Koguryŏ. Moreover, Silla sent armies into the Paekche region and in numerous battles defeated the Paekche units of Puyŏ Yung and the T'ang occupation forces. Finally, in 671, Silla captured Sabi fortress and there established the province of Soburi, thus seizing control over the whole of the former Paekche kingdom. T'ang countered by declaring Kim In-mun (King Munmu's younger brother and long resident in China) to be the king of Silla, though without obtaining his consent, and mounting an attack against its erstwhile Korean ally. But the Silla army met the T'ang forces in a series of battles in the region of the Han river basin and succeeded in driving them back, in 676. In the end, T'ang removed its Protectorate-General to Pacify the East from P'yŏngyang to Liao-tung-ch'eng (modern Liao-yang just south of Mukden in Manchuria), in effect recognizing Silla's claim to hegemony in the Korean Peninsula. Thus Silla now had come

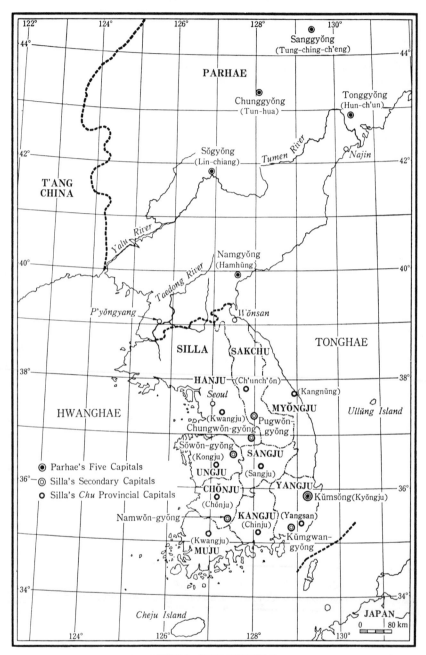

SILLA AND PARHAE
(ADMINISTRATIVE DIVISIONS)

to occupy all of the territory south of a line roughly extending from the Taedong River across to the Bay of Wŏnsan.

The fact that Silla repulsed the T'ang aggression by force of arms and preserved the independence of the Korean peninsula is of great historical significance. The T'ang ambition to destroy Paekche and Koguryŏ and conquer Silla as well, thus bringing the whole of Manchuria and the Korean peninsula under its dominion, posed no less grave a crisis for the Korean people than the establishment of the Four Han Chinese Commanderies nearly seven hundred years earlier. Clearly, Korean society and culture would not have been able to develop unhindered under T'ang political domination. Fortunately, however, Silla was fully able to resist T'ang aggression and maintain its national independence. This constituted the foundation on which the development of the society and culture of Unified Silla rested and what is more it laid the groundwork for the independent historical development of the Korean people.

To be sure, Silla did not succeed in unifying the whole of the territory occupied by the Three Kingdoms. The wide area of Manchuria over which Koguryŏ had held sway remained outside Silla control, and there refugee emigres from Koguryŏ now established the kingdom of Parhae. Strictly speaking, moreover, Silla's unification did not include the entire Korean Peninsula, since the more northerly areas came under Parhae control. This fact, nevertheless, does not diminish the importance of the Silla unification, the significance of which above all lies in the creation of an environment wherein the process of the formation of the Korean people might take an independent course. To be sure, Unified Silla and Parhae confronted each other hostilely much like southern and northern halves of a partitioned nation, but in the end it was the territory and people of Unified Silla, and the society and culture fashioned there, that formed the mainstream of subsequent Korean history. In this sense the historical significance of the Silla unification scarcely can be overemphasized.

The Founding of Parhae

It already has been related that after the fall of Koguryŏ one part of its former domain came under the rule of Silla; the rest of Koguryŏ's vast territory, however, was not destined to be governed by a single unified state. The Liao-tung region came under T'ang control and was placed under the jurisdiction of its Protectorate-General to Pacify the East. Thinking to placate the people of that area, formerly subjects of Koguryŏ, T'ang enfeoffed the last Koguryŏ king, Pojang, as "King of Ch'ao-hsien (Chosŏn)" and appointed him governor of Liao-tung, but he plotted insurrection and so was soon recalled and banished. Subsequently his son Tŏngmu also was appointed governor of Liao-tung and his immediate descendants, who succeeded him in that position, gradually were able to secure virtual autonomy for the region they governed, to the point where historians sometimes refer to it as "Lesser Koguryŏ."

Meanwhile, in the broad plain bisected by the Sungari River in south central Manchuria, where the ancient Puyŏ kingdom had flourished and which also had been under the dominion of Koguryŏ, the new state of Parhae (Chinese: P'o-hai) was established. The founder of Parhae was a former Koguryŏ general, Tae Cho-yŏng (later called King Ko). Upon the fall of Koguryŏ he had been taken prisoner and forced to settle at Ying-chou (modern Ch'ao-yang in southwest Manchuria) but, seizing upon the occasion of an insurrection by Khitan people, he led a band of followers eastward to Tung-mou-shan (near modern Tun-hua in Chi-lin province), where he proclaimed himself king of the independent state of Chin (in 698; the name Parhae dates from 713). He ruled not only over people of Koguryŏ ethnic stock but also over a large Malgal population then living in eastern Manchuria. The Malgal were a semi-nomadic Tungusic people scattered in many tribes over a wide expanse of Manchuria, southern Siberia, and northeast Korea; having been subject to the Koguryŏ domain in Manchuria, it was natural that they would now come under the rule of Parhae. Despite the presence of these numerous Malgal tribesmen in the population of the Parhae kingdom, the ruling class was comprised of Koguryŏ people who clearly regarded their state as representing a revival of Koguryŏ. This is evident in the text of an official communication conveyed by a Parhae envoy to Japan, in which Parhae called itself the "state of Ko[gu]ryŏ."

The international position in which the new state of Parhae found itself was extremely delicate. Having been subjected to strong Chinese pressure from the time of its founding, for some decades Parhae remained hostile toward T'ang. Indeed, in 732 King Mu (719-737) even sent a force by sea to attack the port of Teng-chou on the Shantung Peninsula. At the same time, Parhae also found itself in confrontation with Silla, with the result that in 721 Silla even undertook to build a defensive wall along its northern frontier. The pressure exerted by Parhae, in fact, appears to have been the major reason why Silla was forced to be content with a northern boundary limited to the Taedong River–Bay of Wŏnsan line. It was natural, therefore, that Silla and T'ang should join hands in 733 to strike at Parhae in concert from two sides. To overcome this twofold danger, Parhae established formal diplomatic ties with the T'u-chüeh people to China's north and crossed the sea to the south to make similar contact with Japan.

In this perilous international setting, King Mu nevertheless succeeded in expanding his domain to encompass the whole of northeastern Manchuria, thus clearly demonstrating Parhae's status as a fully independent kingdom. In the ensuing reign of King Mun (737-794), moreover, Parhae took advantage of the An Lu-shan rebellion in T'ang to extend its sway as far as the Lesser Koguryŏ area, thus bringing the Liaotung Peninsula under its dominion. Later, however, accord with the Chinese was reached and Parhae proceeded to assimilate T'ang institutions and culture. In both territorial extent and cultural achievement Parhae reached its zenith in the time of King Sŏn (818-830), when it occupied a vast area reaching to the Russian Maritime Territory to the east, K'ai-yüan in south-central Manchuria to the west, the South Hamgyŏng region in the Korean Peninsula to the south, and the Amur River to the north.

The Change of Direction in Korea's Foreign Policy

The relationship of Koguryŏ, Paekche, and Silla with China during the Three Kingdoms period was mainly one of conflict. To be sure, contact with China took other forms as well, such as diplomatic alliances and cultural borrowing, but seen in larger perspective this was predominantly a history of armed conflict. Not long after the Silla unification, however, both Silla and Parhae came to establish peaceful diplomatic relations with T'ang. This represents, then, a major change in the character of Korea's relationship with China.

The relationship of Silla and Parhae with China can be considered under two broad headings. The first of these is economic exchange. Carried on within the framework of T'ang's tributary system, much of Korea's export trade at first comprised raw materials, but gradually a marked increase in handcrafted articles occurred. From beginning to end, however, the demand for imported goods remained the stronger impetus for Korean trade with China, as many kinds of luxury fabrics and handcrafted goods were eagerly sought for consumption by the members of the aristocracy. In the end this led to a decree handed down by Silla's King Hŭngdŏk in 834 minutely regulating such ostentatious displays of wealth.

Cultural borrowing was the other major facet of the relationship with T'ang China. Both Silla and Parhae imported large numbers of books and art works from T'ang. Moreover, Korean monks and students—at the outset mostly monks—traveled to T'ang to study Buddhism or Confucian scholarship and, after their return, contributed to cultural development in their homelands. Viewed overall, the importation of T'ang civilization was a major factor in the blooming of the native cultures of Silla and Parhae.

Economic and cultural interchange also took place with Japan, and Parhae in particular, in consequence of its confrontation with Silla, communicated frequently with that island nation across the sea to its south. Silla, moreover, even had contacts with Arab merchants, and thus a trickle of that distant culture found its way into Korea.

2. The Government and Society of Unified Silla

An Authoritarian Throne and the Aristocracy

At the same time that Silla was unifying the peninsula and thus gaining dominion over a much increased territory and population, internally new political and social developments were taking shape. The Silla people themselves thought of these developments as marking the end of the early period and the beginning of the middle period of their history. It is now necessary to inquire into the nature of these changes in the Silla polity and society.

A growing authoritarianism in the power exercised by the throne was the most important change accompanying the Silla unification. During the early history of Silla, in the Three Kingdoms period, the throne had been occupied by rulers of "hallowed-bone" lineage, but this highest lineage rank came to an end with the two seventh century queens, Sŏndŏk (632-647) and Chindŏk (647-654). The next monarch was T'aejong, King Muyŏl, a man of the "true-bone" lineage. He came to the throne after suppressing the rebellion of Pidam, as *sangdaedŭng* the head of the Council of Nobles, and prevailing over another *sangdaedŭng*, Alch'ŏn, in a contest for the kingship. In short, he took the throne after overcoming the power of the aristocracy represented by the *sangdaedŭng Hwabaek* leaders. King Muyŏl's mother was from the Kim royal house, the daughter of a king, and moreover his queen was the younger sister of Kim Yu-sin, whose Kaya royal lineage was called the "new house of Kim." Thereafter it became established practice for Silla queens to be chosen from a narrow segment of the Kim royal house itself, thus breaking away from the tradition requiring that both the king's mother and his queen come from the former royal house of Pak. The significance of this is the evidence it provides of the growth of the authority of the king at the expense of his rivals for power, the aristocratic families. The fact that Muyŏl was followed on the throne by his direct lineal descendants and that the records no longer mention the honorific title of *kalmun wang*, hitherto often bestowed upon younger brothers of the king in recognition of their specially privileged position, are further indications of the heightened authority of the kingship.

It was King Sinmun (681-692) who firmly established the authority of the throne. To accomplish this he carried out a determined purge of those leading figures upon whom aristocratic power centered. The same year he came to the throne, in 681, he took advantage of an abortive coup led by the father of his first queen, Kim Hŭm-dol, to search out all those implicated and have them killed. He proceeded to sentence to death the *sangdaedŭng* Kun'gwan as well, on the charge that he had possessed knowledge of the planned insurrection but had failed to report it. King Sinmun's purge was an act of extraordinary boldness, and it appears to have brought the process of strengthening the authority of the throne to its decisive stage. The king now accelerated the restructuring of those political and military institutions upon which the exercise of royal power depended. Then in the reign of his second son, Sŏngdŏk (702-737), the paramount authority of the throne in Silla finally was secured, and with this accomplished the kingdom at last was able to enjoy unaccustomed domestic tranquility.

To say that the authority of the throne had become paramount is not to suggest that the bone-rank system, the linchpin of the Silla social and political order, was itself shaken. Those of true-bone lineage continued to constitute the dominant status group, the major difference being that now the ruling house of Kim had come to wield almost exclusive political power. Another difference was that, with regard to the royal house itself, it now functioned importantly as a mainstay of the authority of the throne instead of as a force inhibiting exercise of kingly power.

As the power of the true-bone aristocracy became weakened overall, the role of the aristocracy holding head-rank six in the stratified Silla order was correspondingly enhanced. Here too can be seen one aspect of the social change taking place in this age. As before, the restraints on the upward mobility of those of head-rank six prevented them from serving in the topmost positions of *sangdaedŭng* or *chungsi* (see below) and even from being appointed as chief officers (*yŏng*) in the ministries of the central government. However, these less privileged members of the aristocracy set themselves against the true-bone nobles, clinging so determinedly to their status prerogatives, and so aligned their interests with those of the throne. Despite the obstacles created by the social status system, therefore, the throne and head-rank six found common cause and, accordingly, men of head-rank six now began to come to the fore in Silla society. In particular because of their deeper learning and insight, their advice on governmental matters was sought by the king, and in this way they performed an important political role in the later years of Unified Silla.

The Structuring of the Governmental Apparatus

In consonance with the greatly strengthened power of the throne, changes now occurred in the workings of the organs of the central government. Specifically, it had become possible for Unified Silla to make more extensive use of the detailed stipulations of administrative law in conducting the affairs of government. King Munmu's testamentary injunction to appropriately revise Silla's legal codes apparently reflects just such an aim. Yet the administrative structure of Unified Silla, in form at least, adhered in general to that of the Three Kingdoms period. For example, the various ministries—of military affairs, disbursements, rites, tax collections, official surveillance, and justice—remained in existence as before. Moreover, the position of *sangdaedŭng,* the occupant of which in effect represented the aristocracy as the head of the *Hwabaek,* continued to exist as it had since first being established by King Pŏphŭng in 531. Nevertheless, a significant change is evident in the comparative importance that came to be attached to the Chancellery Office (*Chipsabu*), created in 651 at the end of the Three Kingdoms period, as the highest administrative organ of the Silla government. Rather than representing the interests of the aristocracy, the *Chipsabu* was a kind of executive council responsive to the dictates of the king. In consequence, the chief officer of the *Chipsabu*, who served in essence as a prime minister, stood in an antithetical position to that of the *sangdaedŭng*. And the fact that the head of the *Chipsabu*, called the *chungsi*, was regarded as politically more important than the *sangdaedŭng* is an indication that the political structure of Unified Silla had become more authoritarian.

Unified Silla came into being through a process of territorial expansion, and in order to administer the enlarged national domain it was necessary to create an expanded system of provincial and local government. The basic units of local administration in the Unified Silla period were the *chu*, or province, the *kun*, or prefecture, and the *hyŏn*, or county. Nine *chu* (*-ju*) were established soon after unification, in 685. Three were in the former Silla-Kaya territory (Sangju, Yangju, and Kangju); three were in the area of the Paekche kingdom (Ungju, Chŏnju, and Muju); and three again were in regions formerly ruled by Koguryŏ (Hanju, Sakchu, and Myŏngju), and this nine-fold division appears to have been consciously modeled after the nine *chou* (*chu*) pattern of the ancient Chinese state of Hsia [see map p. 70]. From the first the *chu*, or provinces, were governed by an official called a *ch'onggwan*, a title with lighter military overtones than the term hitherto used (*kunju*, or military commandant), and in the late ninth century the title was changed again, to *todok*, or governor. These titular changes probably reflect a gradual evolution in the character of the duties of this office, from those more military in nature to those more purely administrative. The provinces were divided into prefectures (*kun*), headed by *t'aesu*, or prefects, and the *kun* in turn had jurisdiction over a number of counties, or *hyŏn*, headed by magistrates (*yŏng*). The *hyŏn* were further subdivided into villages (*ch'on*) and certain special settlements (for those of unfree status) known as *hyang, so,* and *pugok*.

Unified Silla also carried out a policy of forcibly resettling the aristocracies of the states it had conquered in urbanized centers called *sogyŏng* (secondary capitals). In 685, the same year the nine *chu* system was inaugurated, five of these secondary capitals were designated—Chungwŏn-gyŏng (at modern Ch'ungju), Pugwŏn-gyŏng (at Wŏnju), Kŭmgwan-gyŏng (at Kimhae), Sŏwŏn-gyŏng (at Ch'ŏngju), and Namwŏn-gyŏng (at Namwŏn). Shortly after the unification Silla considered moving its capital from Kyŏngju westward to Taegu, but in the end was unable to do so. This provides an indication of how tenaciously the Silla aristocracy clung to its base of power in Kyŏngju, despite its location off in one corner of the peninsula. The secondary capital system represented both a conciliatory gesture to the peoples Silla had conquered and a means by which to exercise control over them, but at the same time it seems to have served as a counterbalance to the unfavorable geographical location of the capital. Such a consideration may explain why some members of the capital aristocracy also were resettled in the secondary capitals, with the result that these came to play a special role in the social and cultural life of Unified Silla.

By fashioning this system of provincial and local administration, Silla at the same time created a mechanism for governing its newly occupied territories. Prisoners of war were enslaved and the inhabitants of rebellious districts were reduced to unfree status and transported to the special *hyang, so,* and *pugok* settlements. On the other hand, some of those in the conquered areas were magnanimously accorded a "bone-rank" status and office rank based on the social station they formerly had occupied in their own societies. On the whole, however, the newly subjugated peoples were routinely absorbed into the regular administrative divisions—the provinces, prefectures, counties, and villages. To be sure, the governors, prefects, and county magistrates were always appointed from among the capital aristocracy, but the village headmen and the functionaries on the staffs of the provincial, prefectural, and county governments came from influential local families. It was necessary, therefore, for the central government to devise a means to prevent these local elites from growing too strong. To serve this end, it is thought, Silla developed the institution that modern historians call *sangsuri,* a kind of hostage system whereby representatives of these powerful local families were required to undertake low level military or court duties in the capital on a rotation basis.

Changes in the Economic Life of the Aristocracy

Even before unification the Silla aristocracy had received grants of "tax villages" (*sigŭp*), other agricultural land to be held in perpetuity, horse farms, and grain, thus accumulating immense wealth. For example, Kim Yu-sin was rewarded with hereditary rights to a village of five hundred households, five hundred *kyŏl* of farm land, and six horse farms. Among one hundred seventy-four horse farms in Silla in 669, twenty-two were allocated to the palace and ten to various government offices, while the rest all were distributed to Kim Yu-sin, Kim In-mun, and other members of the aristocracy. All these were awards bestowed in recognition of specific instances of meritorious service to the state. On the other hand, government officials were paid for their services by allocation of "stipend villages" (*nogŭp*). The recipients of this form of salary payment not only took the grain tax from the lands within their grants for their own use but also, it is thought, were able to command the labor services of the peasants who worked these lands.

Not long after the unification, however, the "stipend village" method of salary payment was abolished, in 689, and in its place (already in 687) officials were allocated "office-land" (*chikchŏn*), from which they were permitted to receive only the grain tax. This change reflects an attempt to limit so far as possible the direct control of the aristocracy over the peasant population and, as such, it was a development that went hand in hand with the growth of the power of the throne. Nevertheless, the "stipend village" system subsequently was revived while the "office-land" and "annual grain grants" (*sejo*) methods of paying official salaries were discontinued. This represents a renewed effort on the part of the aristocracy to break loose from the restraints placed on it by the dominant authority of the throne, and it indicates that, to this extent at least, aristocratic power had reasserted itself. It occasions little surprise, then, to encounter in the official *New History of T'ang (Hsin T'ang shu)* the following account of the wealth of the elite of Unified Silla:

> Emoluments flow unceasingly into the houses of the highest officials, who possess as many as 3,000 slaves, with corresponding numbers of weapons, cattle, horses, and pigs.

The lives of the aristocracy were centered on the capital at Kyŏngju (then called by a name that means "city of gold"). Remains still found today in Kyŏngju, such as those of the Imhae-jŏn ("Pavilion on the Sea," a banquet hall built out into the water of the man-made Anapchi lake) and the P'osŏkchŏng (a slightly winding channel of finely sculpted stone around which wine cups were circulated as revelers competed in matching poetic wits), bear mute witness to the extravagant lives and pleasures of the Silla aristocracy. There is a late ninth century record informing us that, at its flourishing height, Kyŏngju had a population of 178,936 households divided among 1,360 residential quarters in 55 wards, with 35 mansions of the immensely wealthy and separate residences for use in the four seasons. Within the walls of Kyŏngju there was said to be not a single thatched roof house but instead unbroken lines of tiled homes with enclosed courtyards, while the never-ending sounds of music and song filled the streets night and day. This too offers testimony to the wealth and luxury enjoyed by the aristocratic ruling class.

Reorganization of the Military System

The dominant power of the throne in Unified Silla is clearly evident also in the nature of its military organization. Among the important military units in Silla before the unification were the *yukchŏng*, or "six garrisons." These are thought to have been organized along lines that reflected earlier tribal traditions, and with the Silla unification they went out of existence. Instead, in conformity with the changes elsewhere in Silla society, a new pattern of military organization was instituted, characterized by nine "oath bannermen" divisions (*sŏdang*) and ten garrison units again called *chŏng*.

The nine *sŏdang*, as finally constituted in the reign of King Sinmun (681-692), formed a national army that was stationed in the capital. Believed to have come into existence as a volunteer army, the *sŏdang* units gradually were expanded until, after the unification, nine divisions had been organized. The tunics of each of these had collars of a distinctive color—green, purple, white, scarlet, yellow, black, cobalt, red, and blue. A special characteristic of the *sŏdang* was that they drew their recruits not only from the native Silla population but also from the former inhabitants of Koguryŏ and Paekche, and from Malgal tribesmen as well. The *sŏdang* divisions appear to have operated under the direct authority of the king, to whom each unit took an oath of loyalty. Thus the emergence of the nine *sŏdang* as the core units of Silla's army, replacing the "six garrisons" which had been under the command of the aristocracy, may be said to have been another consequence of the deliberate efforts made to strengthen the authority of the throne.

Complementing the nine *sŏdang* divisions in Kyŏngju were the "ten garrisons" (*sip chŏng*), units stationed outside the capital. The two most important of these were positioned at modern Ich'ŏn and Yŏju, garrisoning Hanju province, the largest province and also strategically the key frontier area for the defense of the kingdom. The remaining eight garrisons were at modern Sangju, Ch'ŏngyang, Namwŏn, Talsŏng, Haman, Naju, Hongch'ŏn, and Ch'ŏngsong, one in each of the other eight provinces. Distributed uniformly as they were throughout the whole of the Silla domain, it is not difficult to imagine that these units not only were entrusted with the defense of the country but were charged with internal security duties as well. Once again this bespeaks the centralized character of governmental authority in Unified Silla.

There were many other military units as well, although of lesser importance. They too were a part of the carefully designed military structure that, along with the administrative system of the nine provinces and the five secondary capitals, constituted major links in the institutional arrangements through which Unified Silla governed.

The Life of the People

The years of warfare that marked the Silla unification were accompanied by increasing impoverishment of the lives of the common people. More and more of them could not repay their debts and were reduced to slavery. Social class divisions thus gradually had widened. Slavery was prevalent, particularly in the capital where the aristocracy was so firmly ensconced. Large numbers of artisans and laborers with slave status were attached to the various palace and government agencies that supplied the requirements of the royal household at one extreme and produced weapons and ships at the other. If, as the *New History of T'ang* relates, the houses of the highest officials possessed as many as three thousand slaves, then it may be surmised that the number owned by the aristocracy in its entirety comprised a substantial portion of the total Silla population.

The ordinary farming population lived in village or hamlet (*ch'on*) units, the smallest division within the local administrative structure. A hamlet normally consisted of ten or so consanguineous households that had naturally developed into such a small cluster of peasant dwellings. These hamlets were brought under government control in groups consisting of several hamlets administered by a village headman, and to serve the state's purposes a census register was prepared for each hamlet. In 1933 a portion of one such Silla census register, believed to date from 755 and covering four hamlets in the vicinity of Ch'ŏngju, was discovered in the Shōsōin imperial repository in Nara, Japan. The contents of this document indicate that Silla census registers were compiled anew every three years and, in addition to giving household and population statistics, recorded the numbers of cattle and horses, of mulberry, nut-bearing pine, and walnut trees, and the area of different types of land, while indicating as well changes from the previous census in both human and livestock populations.

In this census document, the population was registered in six categories based on age: able-bodied adult men and women, adolescents, pre-adolescents, small children, the aging, and the aged. These age groupings were established as the basis for exacting labor service from the population, and in turn households were classified in accordance with the number of able-bodied adults (those subject to corvee) they contained. There were nine such grades of households, and since an arbitrary "census household" unit representing a fixed number of able-bodied adults was employed to record subtotals of those subject to corvee duty, it was a simple matter to calculate the size of the labor pool available to the state in a particular hamlet.

Agricultural lands recorded in this document include several categories of paddy and dry fields, as well as "hemp fields," which were cultivated by the people of the hamlets. A special allocation of paddy land is recorded for the village headman and allotments for the villagers as well are separately described. These latter are believed to correspond to the so-called *chŏngjŏn* parcels of "able-bodied land" which other sources tell us were first apportioned in 722. It appears most likely that the product of one designated category of paddy land and of the "hemp fields" went to the state, the yield from what is thought to have been a kind of "office-land" (*chikchŏn*) to the support of government officials, and the harvest from certain paddy lands, the terms for which include "village headman" or "commoner households" respectively, to those local inhabitants. From the fact that not only land but also three particularly valued kinds of trees are recorded, it may be assumed that these were subject to taxation as well. This again indicates that the capital aristocracy made every effort to extract as much as possible from the peasant population.

On essentially the same level as the village in Silla's local administrative structure were other units called *hyang, so,* and *pugok*. In contrast to the free commoner population of the villages, these were inhabited by unfree people whose status was essentially one of slavery. Either conquered peoples or those guilty of crimes against the state, they were transported to these special settlements to labor at such tasks as farming, stock raising, or other manual work. The existence of numerous such communities of unfree laborers located in every region of the country is one distinguishing feature of Silla society.

3. The Flourishing of Silla Culture

The Growth of Buddhism

Buddhism was the dominant system of thought in Unified Silla. As the religion was revered and professed alike by all the people, from the king on high to the populace at large, Buddhism played a vital role in Silla society. It was natural, therefore, that many eminent monks would make the journey to T'ang China or even to far away India to study the way of the Buddha. After Wŏn'gwang, who traveled to Sui China in the late sixth century, such famed monks as Chajang, Ŭisang, and Wŏnch'ŭk studied Buddhism in China. Wŏnch'ŭk is particularly noteworthy for the major contributions he made to the development of Buddhism in China through the sutra translations and other writings he produced during his long sojourn in the T'ang empire. On the other hand, Hyech'o went on to India and described his pilgrimage to Buddhist holy places in a well-known account entitled *Record of a Journey to the Five Indian Kingdoms (Wang och'ŏnch'ukkuk chŏn)*.

The many monks who returned to Silla after studying in China brought back with them the doctrines of the various Buddhist sects that had proliferated under the T'ang dynasty. Five major doctrinal sects that became established in this way in Silla were the Nirvana school, the Vinaya, the Buddha-Nature, the Avatamsaka and the Dharmalaksana. Among these it was the Avatamsaka (Hwaŏm; Chinese Hua-yen) that was accorded the most devout belief by aristocratic society when Silla was in full flourish. The Hwaŏm doctrine was implanted in Silla by Ŭisang, who had been a leading disciple of the great Chinese master Chih-yen. He is credited with founding Pusŏk-sa after his return to Silla and making it the religious center from which the new sect was widely disseminated, and many disciples emerged under his tutelage. Hwaŏm preached the doctrine of all encompassing harmony, that the one contains the multitude and yet the multitude is as one, a concept that sought to embrace the myriad of sentient beings within the single Buddha mind. Such a doctrine was well suited to a state with a centralized power structure under an authoritarian monarchy, and this likely is the reason why the Hwaŏm teaching was welcomed by the ruling elite of Unified Silla's aristocratic society.

Wŏnhyo (617-686), on the other hand, condemned the sense of confrontation that characterized the attitude of the various sects toward one another. Unlike most eminent monks of that day Wŏnhyo did not make the journey to China, and yet the profundity of his Buddhist learning won respect even in T'ang. He is said to have principally espoused the thought of the Buddha-Nature school, but his learning in the Buddhist canon was unusually broad. His mastery of the Avatamsaka sutra was so profound that at times he is identified with the Hwaŏm school, and in addition to the texts of these two schools he wrote commentaries to the Wisdom (Prajna), Lotus, Nirvana, Amitabha, and Diamond sutras, to the *Treatise on the Awakening of Faith of the Greater Vehicle,* and many others. He thus took no single sutra or treatise as the sole source book for his faith. Instead, he created a unique synthesis of Buddhist thought that argued the necessity of viewing Buddhist doctrine from a higher level of abstraction, so as to achieve a harmonious integration of the points of contradiction and dispute among the many sects. His work entitled *Treatise on the Harmonization of Disputes among the Ten Schools (Simmun hwajaeng non)* expounds this conception of his, and this explains why in a later age he was given the posthumous title of National Mentor Hwajŏng ("harmonious quiescence"). Wŏnhyo's thought can be viewed as an effort to reconcile conflicts in the religious domain paralleling those inherent in the authoritarian structure of Unified Silla society.

The great popularity of Pure Land Buddhism, principally among the common people, is another striking feature of the history of Buddhism in the Unified Silla period. The Pure Land creed was a Buddhism for the masses, a faith which even the unlettered could understand and profess. No grasp of the abstruse doctrines of the Buddhist sutras was required, for it was enough only to invoke the name of the Buddha by chanting "*Nammu Amit'a Pul,*" thus professing one's belief in the Amitabha Buddha. If one but performed this extremely simple devotion, which formed the core of the Pure Land teachings, then one could be reborn in the "Pure Land," in the Western Paradise where Amitabha dwelled. Pure Land became the Buddhism for the masses precisely because it held out such a hope to those whose day to day lives were filled with suffering. Pure Land Buddhism found no comfort in earthly existence, which it termed a "sea of torment," but instead preached the desirability of rebirth into the paradise of the next world. As the Pure Land faith swept over Silla society, thousands of people turned their backs on the world of their daily lives and entered the novitiate in mountain temples. Tales even spread of those who, while still alive, had flown heavenward and been reborn in the Western Paradise. The popularity of the Pure Land faith brought significant change to Silla Buddhism, and it may be said to reflect a tendency among the common people toward alienation from the world, a feeling of despair that arose out of the gross inequities in Silla society under authoritarian rule. It was also Wŏnhyo who was responsible for the widespread propagation of Pure Land Buddhism. Great as were his attainments in Buddhist scholarship, he is even more worthy of admiration for his role as an itinerant monk, which he undertook following the storied occasion when he broke his vows by fathering a son (the famous Sŏl Ch'ong) by a Silla princess. Traveling in penance to hamlets in every part of the country, Wŏnhyo preached the Pure Land creed that all men might be reborn in paradise. His own understanding of the Pure Land faith is well expressed in his work *The Way of Bringing Troubled Minds to Rest* (*Yusim allak to*), in which he writes:

The deeper meaning of the Pure Land is that it always has been for everyman, not for the Bodhisattva.

One source tells us that, in consequence of his efforts, eight or nine of every ten Silla people embraced Buddhism, a record that vividly testifies to Wŏnhyo's role as the great evangelist of popular Buddhism.

The Rise of Confucianism

A new phenomenon in Silla of the middle period, following the unification, was the appearance of Confucianism to rival Buddhism as a distinct system of thought. The establishment of a National Confucian College (*Kukhak*) in 682 was one result of this development. Not long thereafter, in 717, portraits of Confucius, the "ten philosophers," and the seventy-two Confucian worthies were brought from T'ang and installed in the National Confucian College. And around 750 this state institution was renamed the *T'aehakkam* (National Confucian University) and two faculty ranks were created for those appointed to teach there. The curriculum was divided into three courses of study, with the subjects taught in each designated as follows:

(1) *Analects, Classic of Filial Piety, Book of Rites, Classic of Changes*
(2) *Analects, Classic of Filial Piety, Tso chuan* (the *Tradition of Tso* interpretation of the *Spring and Autumn Annals*), *Classic of Songs*
(3) *Analects, Classic of Filial Piety, Book of History, Literary Selections*

Thus the *Analects* and *Classic of Filial Piety* were required subjects in each course of study, while other classical Chinese texts, including works on rites, history, and literature, filled out the curriculum. Entrance into the National Confucian University was permitted only to those members of the aristocracy who held the twelfth office rank (*taesa*) or below, including those without office rank, and it is conjectured that in practice this meant mainly those who possessed head-rank six.

With the foundation thus laid by the establishment of a national educational institution, a kind of state examination system for the selection of government officials was inaugurated in 788. The candidates who took this examination, called the *toksŏ samp'umkwa* ("examination in the reading of texts in three gradations"), were graded on three levels of proficiency in reading Chinese texts and then given appointments. The examination was based on the texts studied at the state university, but there also is a record stating that those who demonstrated still broader learning—being well versed in the Five Classics, Three Histories (Ssu-ma Ch'ien's *Historical Records, History of the [Earlier] Han, History of the Later Han*), and the works of Chou China's Hundred Schools—were extraordinarily appointed to higher level positions. The establishment of this state examination system apparently reflected a desire to emphasize Confucian learning, rather than merely bone-rank lineage, as the basis for selecting government officials.

The essential implications of this Confucianism in which the Silla state was displaying such lively interest were in conflict with the values of the traditional bone-rank order, with its core of true-bone aristocrats, and with the Buddhist doctrine that buttressed it. It was primarily those of head-rank six background who championed Confucian thought. These men argued the paramount importance of a set of moral standards applicable to the world of human affairs, and they criticized the ambivalent view of man and his mundane existence fostered by the Buddhist emphasis on life in the hereafter. Two such Confucian figures of the Unified Silla period were Kangsu and Sŏl Ch'ong. A man of head-rank six from the Imna (a Kaya state) area, Kangsu is remembered for his signal service in authoring Silla's diplomatic correspondence with T'ang, but he also attacked Buddhism as an "otherworldly" teaching and took the view that moral worth is a more important criterion for advancement than social background. The son of the monk Wŏnhyo, Sŏl Ch'ong also was of head-rank six lineage, and he is best known for developing the *kugyŏl* system of explicating Chinese texts by inserting native Korean grammatical elements. But he also presented a letter of admonition to the throne known as the *P'ung wang sŏ* ("Parable for the King"), in which he urged that monarchs should renounce pleasure seeking and strictly observe moral standards. It may be said, therefore, that under Silla's authoritarian political structure Confucianism stood in opposition to traditional true-bone privilege and, indeed, developed in partnership with the power of the throne.

Scholarship and Technology

In the field of historical studies Kim Tae-mun, a scholar who flourished in the earlier years of the eighth century, stands out above all others. The author of a number of works on Silla history and geography—*Tales of Silla (Kyerim chapchŏn)*, *Biographies of Eminent Monks (Kosŭng chŏn)*, *Chronicles of the Hwarang (Hwarang segi)*, *Book of Music (Ak pon)*, and *Record of Hansan (Hansan ki)*, his deep concern for the native Silla tradition stands out in an age obsessed with T'ang Chinese culture. Unfortunately, however, none of his works survive, and we can only find traces of them in the much later *History of the Three Kingdoms* and *Memorabilia of the Three Kingdoms*. A man of true-bone lineage, Kim Tae-mun appears to have sought to counter the impact of Chinese Confucian learning by reawakening awareness of Silla's traditional culture.

It was a deeply held conviction of this age that good government depended on maintaining a harmonious balance between the forces of *yin* and *yang*, thus enabling natural phenomena to bring blessings upon mankind. Consequently, out of a background of primitive astrological practices, astronomy and calendrical science now developed. One result of this was the construction of the Ch'ŏmsŏngdae observatory at the end of the Three Kingdoms period (sometime between 632-647), where it is assumed that basic astronomical observations were conducted by the use of a sundial and other simple instruments. Kim Am was a later eighth century astronomer-astrologer of considerable renown. Having studied the occult arts of *yin-yang* doctrine in China, he produced his own treatise entitled *The Principles of Transformation of Substances* (*Tun'gap ipsŏng pŏp*), and after returning to Silla he was appointed "savant of celestial phenomena." There is another record that Kim Am, while serving as Commander of the P'aegang Garrison (the modern P'yŏngsan area), taught his troops a "six column battle formation," from which account it may be assumed that he was also well versed in military science.

Mathematical knowledge also greatly advanced and was given practical application in a number of areas. The ground plan of the Sŏkkuram stone grotto temple to the Buddha at Kyŏngju and the projection of its domed ceiling, as well as the balanced proportions of the Pagoda of Many Treasures (Tabo-t'ap) and Pagoda That Casts No Shadow (Muyŏng-t'ap) at Kyŏngju's Pulguk-sa temple, and of other similar Silla monuments, all reflect the application of precise mathematical concepts. Knowledge of scientific principles also is evident elsewhere in Silla architecture, for example in the extreme care taken to provide for enough circulation of air to prevent damage from excessive moisture.

Finally, the art of woodblock printing was developed in order to reproduce a variety of texts, especially Buddhist sutras and classical Confucian writings. The copy of the Dharani sutra found not long ago within the Pagoda That Casts No Shadow, which therefore must date from before the erection of the pagoda in 751, is the world's oldest extant example of woodblock printing.

The Hyangga

It already has been noted that the *hyangga* is a poetic genre the themes of which relate to Buddhism or to religious practices in general. A form already written in Silla of the Three Kingdoms period, after the unification it continued to develop with the appearance of many poems such as Siro's "Ode to Knight Tamara" (*Mo Tamara-rang ka*), Master Wŏlmyŏng's "Dedication" (*Tosol ka*) and "Requiem for a Deceased Sister" (*Che mangmae ka*), and Master Ch'ungdam's "Ode to Knight Kilbo" (*Ch'an Kilbo-rang ka*) and "Ode on Benevolent Rule" (*Anmin ka*). And at the end of the ninth century Queen Chinsŏng commanded the monk Taegu and the high courtier Wihong to compile an anthology of *hyangga*; the work they produced bore the title *Samdae mok* (*Collection of Hyangga from the Three Periods of Silla History*), but it has not survived.

> Here now I sing the flower strewing song—
> Oh offering of flowers, do you
> As my pious heart commands:
> Attend and bring the Maitreya Bodhisattva
> From the distant Tusita Heaven.

This is a modern rendering of the concise and difficult text of the original *hyangga* "Dedication" (*Tosol ka*), which poignantly expresses the ardent devotion with which a prayer is offered, in the form of a gift of flowers, for the compassion of the Maitreya Bodhisattva. Silla's *hyangga* poets composed their songs with the object at times of entreating Heaven to bring tranquility to the state, at times to extol the virtue of the Buddha, at times out of longing for a deceased loved one, and at other times simply as prayers. The *hyangga*, in sum, represents a beautiful literary expression of the religious feelings of the Silla people.

Fine Arts

The artistic creations of Unified Silla were the products of fully matured techniques. Having outgrown the rusticity of the Three Kingdoms period, art now revealed a highly developed esthetic sense. Although the art of Unified Silla employed the technique of realistic representation, the purpose was not thus to portray objects just as they appear in real life but rather to seek to give expression to a concept of idealized beauty. Moreover, in the works produced at this time, an effort to create a world of unflawed harmony is made evident. The special characteristic of the art of the Unified Silla period, then, is its attempt to create a beauty of idealized harmony through the application of refined artistic craftsmanship.

The art of the Unified Silla period may be said to be represented at its finest by the Pulguk-sa temple in Kyŏngju and the nearby Sŏkkuram grotto. Both are said to have been built in 751 by the chief minister (*chung-si*) of the time, Kim Tae-sŏng. A large temple with original floor space exceeding 2,000 *kan* (unit for the space enclosed by four pillars) in the combined area of its buildings, its wooden structures dating from Silla were destroyed by fire during the late sixteenth century Japanese invasions and what we see today is a modern restoration. The beautiful "cloud bridge stairway" leading up to the entrance gate (called the Mauve Mist Gate), consisting of a lower flight known as the Bridge of White Clouds and an upper flight named the Bridge of Azure Clouds; the novel shape of the stone supports for the two front pillars of the Floating Shadow Pavilion to the right, or west, of the Mauve Mist Gate; the balanced proportions of the two pagodas, the Pagoda of Many Treasures and the Pagoda That Casts No Shadow, that form a complementary pair to the left and right of the Taeung-jŏn (Hall of Sakyamuni, the temple proper)—all these display this same mature beauty of harmony. The stone pagoda, in particular, is widely admired as a unique expression of Silla artistry—in contrast, the emphasis in China was on brick pagodas and in Japan on those of wooden construction. Of all the many remaining stone pagodas, the Pagoda That Casts No Shadow and the Pagoda of Many Treasures, together with the Lion Pagoda at the Hwaŏm-sa temple, are regarded as the crowning glories among such monuments built in the Unified Silla period.

The Sŏkkuram was modeled after the stone cave temples of China, but in China these were cut into the face of natural rock cliffs, whereas the Sŏkkuram is a man-made stone grotto designed as a setting for the worship of a principal statue of Buddha. The Sŏkkuram has a rectangular antechamber and a circular interior chamber with a domed ceiling formed by carefully cut blocks of stone. This domed ceiling evidences not only great technical skill but also a solidity reflecting sophisticated knowledge of the mechanics of stress. Yet it is its sculpture that makes the Sŏkkuram unique. Most prominently the large stone statue of the Sakyamuni Buddha in the center of the interior chamber, the eleven-headed Goddess of Mercy and the various Bodhisattvas and Arhat (disciples of Buddha) carved in relief in a semicircle on the surrounding wall, the two *Inwang* ("benevolent kings") on the walls of the antechamber, and the Four Deva Kings standing guard along the passageway—each of these adds its own distinctive note to the symphony of beauty presented by the Sŏkkuram as an integral whole. To be sure, in their roundness of face and ampleness of body there is evidence of influence from T'ang Buddhist sculpture, but the Sŏkkuram examples suggest a deeper sense of spiritual beauty. Other famous Silla sculptures include the four-sided stone Buddha at the Kulbul-sa temple as well as the Amitabha Buddha and Maitreya Bodhisattva at Kamsan-sa, and it is worth noting that the many representations of the Amitabha Buddha (he who presides over the Western Paradise) are a particular feature of this age.

In considering art forms accompanying Buddhism the castings of bronze temple bells cannot be overlooked. The oldest extant bell from Silla is that dated 725 at the Sangwŏn-sa temple on Mt. Odae, but the best known is Pongdŏk-sa's so-called Emille Bell (now in the national museum in Kyŏngju), cast in 771 to posthumously honor King Sŏngdŏk. This bell measures seven feet six inches (2.27 meters) in diameter and is eleven feet (3.3 meters) high, making it the largest surviving Korean bell. It also is the most exquisitely wrought, in the shape of the bell itself and in the beauty of its decoration with flying angel-Buddha and lotus flower motifs. We are told that the bell at Hwangnyong-sa was an enormous one, weighing 500,000 *kŭn* (well over 300 tons in terms of the modern *kŭn* unit), but it has not survived. The bells of Silla have a unique shape, a blending of the forms in which the striker and clapper bells were cast in ancient China; this, together with their exquisitely executed raised designs, give them a beauty unequalled by the temple bells of China or Japan. Unified Silla has left us not only these bells but many superb examples of stone lanterns, stone stupas, stone water basins, support stones for iron pennant poles, end tiles for roofing, paving tiles, and other objects associated with Buddhist architecture.

Tomb mounds are the treasure house of Silla works of art unrelated to Buddhism. It has been noted above that the vertical shaft interment practice of pre-unification Silla, in tombs with layers of stone covered over by mounds of earth, made pillaging difficult, so that gold crowns and a variety of other magnificent burial objects have been preserved. After the unification, however, the prevalent style of tomb architecture took on a different form, characterized by a horizontal shaft or passageway leading to a stone burial chamber. In constructing these tombs, the much smaller earthen mound covering the burial chamber itself was faced with upright supporting slabs of stone, on which were carved representations of the twelve zodiacal animal deities. The concept was that these animal figures (rat, bull, tiger, etc.), all bearing weapons, would guard the soul of the deceased. The idea of the twelve zodiacal animals itself was borrowed from China, but their use in tomb architecture is a unique Silla development that has no counterpart in China. The rendering of these animals, which the merest inadvertence might have turned into comic figures, is done with a dexterous skill that provides yet another proof of the consummate artistry of the Silla people. The best examples of the twelve zodiacal animal deities are found at the tomb of Kim Yu-sin and at Kwaerŭng (thought to be the tomb of King Wŏnsŏng), and the latter in particular, with its additional stone statues of a civil and a military official and of two lions, represents the fully developed form of this type of Unified Silla tomb.

In regard to the art of calligraphy, finally, its stylistic development and attainments can be judged from Kim In-mun's inscription on the capstone of the stele for King Muyŏl's tomb, from the Hwaŏm sutra passages carved on stone at the Hwaŏm-sa temple, and from the many surviving stele found at Silla's Buddhist temples. The most renowned Silla calligrapher was Kim Saeng, whose work is said to have been of such surpassing artistry as to be mistakenly attributed to the brush of fourth century China's famed Wang Hsi-chih. No actual specimen of Kim Saeng's calligraphy remains today, but the text of the stele for the late Silla monk Nanggong Taesa (832-916), which modeled its characters on then extant specimens of the work of Kim Saeng, gives us a glimpse of the style of this great master.

4. The Society and Culture of Parhae

Government and Society

Parhae, it has been noted, was a kingdom founded by people of Koguryŏ stock and, accordingly, it was they who monopolized political power in Parhae. For example, the envoys dispatched from Parhae to foreign states for the most part had the surname Ko, that of the Koguryŏ royal house, or other surnames of Chinese type, and it is thought that these important figures were of Koguryŏ lineage.

The majority of those over whom this elite class ruled were Malgal people. Some of them succeeded in moving upward into the ruling elite, in particular, it would seem, followers of Kŏlsabiu who supported Tae Cho-yŏng in founding his new kingdom. On the whole these Malgal figures held the title of *suryŏng*, or "chief," and they occupied an important, if peripheral, place in Parhae's elite structure. Although very few in number, some members of Parhae embassies bore Malgal surnames, and it is likely that these belonged to this same small Malgal elite class. Nevertheless, the bulk of the Malgal constituted a subject people, some of whom at times were reduced to forced labor or slave status and so became an unfree class serving masters who belonged to the ruling class of Koguryŏ origins. Even though the upper stratum of Parhae society absorbed the high culture of T'ang and designed a sophisticated system of government, this could not conceal the inherent fragility of a social structure so sharply divided along ethnic lines.

The basic administrative organs of the Parhae central government consisted of three chancelleries—the *Chŏngdangsŏng* (directed the actual administration of state affairs), *Sŏnjosŏng* (served as a secretariat through which royal edicts were promulgated and possessed some rights of policy review), and *Chungdaesŏng* (an organ with policy initiation and report functions)—and six ministries (the *Ch'ungbu* for personnel administration, the *Inbu* for finance, the *Ŭibu* for rites, the *Chibu* for military affairs, the *Yebu* for punishments, and the *Sinbu* for public works). It is clear, then, that in form this was modeled after the T'ang system. In Parhae, however, the chief minister of the *Chŏngdangsŏng* (whose title was *taenaesang* or "great minister of the court") occupied a superior position to that of the "chief minister of the left" or "chief minister of the right" who headed the other two chancelleries. Thus in its actual functioning the Parhae central administrative structure did not entirely conform to that of T'ang, and it also was distinctive in the heavy Confucianist overtones of its office nomenclature. This Parhae structure was different from that of Unified Silla, which was content to leave the earlier, traditional administrative arrangements essentially intact, merely creating an overall supervisory organ, the *Chipsabu*. In short, in devising a carefully structured administrative system embellished by weighty Confucianist terminology, Parhae appears to have sought to make manifest the authority and prestige of its governmental mechanisms.

Parhae also set up a systematic structure for provincial and local administration. The capital of Parhae, called Sanggyŏng or "High Capital," was located at modern Tung-ching-ch'eng in Hei-lung-chiang province,

Manchuria, and there were four secondary capitals—the "Central Capital" at modern Tun-hua in Chi-lin province, Manchuria, "Eastern Capital" at Hun-ch'un in Chi-lin, "Southern Capital" at Hamhŭng in South Ham-gyŏng province, Korea, and "Western Capital" at Lin-chiang in Chi-lin [see map p. 70]. In addition, fifteen major towns, called *pu*, were established throughout the country, and five major roadways were laid to link Parhae with its neighboring states. No such meticulous concern was shown, however, for the condition of the Malgal people who lived under this orderly administrative structure.

Cultural Aspects

Once peaceful diplomatic relations with T'ang had been established, Parhae acted vigorously to introduce Chinese culture. A large number of students were sent to T'ang to study and, as was the case with Silla, many of them passed the T'ang civil service examinations. As a result of such cultural interaction, Parhae modeled not only its government structure after that of T'ang but other institutional features as well. For example, the Parhae capital of Sanggyŏng was laid out on the pattern of the T'ang capital at Chang-an. The entire city was surrounded by a rectangular outer wall, while an inner wall was constructed in the north central area of the capital around the palace and government buildings. A broad thoroughfare linked the south gate of the inner citadel with the south gate of the outer wall, thus bisecting the city and creating residential quarters on either side.

Nevertheless, many elements of Koguryŏ derivation also are found in Parhae culture. It appears, for example, that Parhae's establishing of five capitals was based on Koguryŏ's provincial administrative structure consisting of five *pu*. Other features of Parhae culture that likely reflect Koguryŏ models include the *ondol* installation (Korean system of heating by means of flues laid under the floor) discovered at the site of the Parhae palace in the inner citadel of the capital at Sanggyŏng, and the stone burial chamber structure of Parhae tombs with a horizontal entrance shaft. Moreover, the style of Buddhist statuary found at Parhae temple sites, as well as the lotus blossom and woven cloth motifs with which Parhae roofing end tiles were decorated, also have a distinct Koguryŏ flavor. It is unfortunate that the few remains we have from Parhae do not permit a full elucidation of the organic relationship of Parhae culture with that of Koguryŏ. But the fact that many among the small number of Parhae artifacts can be linked with Koguryŏ models provides an ample basis for informed conjecture as to the principal roots of Parhae culture.

Parhae's Place in History

The cultural level of the Parhae kingdom was so advanced that an official

Chinese history described it as the "flourishing land in the East." But since the population was composed of two disparate elements, the ruling elite of Koguryŏ descent and a subject class of native Malgal people, the Parhae state possessed an inherent structural weakness. This instability in its social fabric was the main reason why Parhae succumbed so easily to attack by the Khitan in 926.

Moreover, once Parhae fell, there was no way for its culture to be transmitted to later historical ages. This is because the custodians of Parhae culture, the ruling elite of Koguryŏ ethnic stock, now took refuge in the new Korean state of Koryŏ, leaving behind the indigenous Malgal people who, having shared little in the Parhae cultural efflorescence, were incapable of perpetuating it. The Malgal in turn, after nearly two centuries of subjection to Khitan rule, founded their own state (the Jurchen Chin dynasty), drove out the Khitan, and emerged as masters of all Manchuria and of the northern half of China as well. Memories of the greatness of Parhae no doubt contributed to the ultimate realization on the part of the Malgal people of their own capacity to develop into such a powerful East Asian state.

With the fall of Parhae, then, Manchuria ceased to serve as a stage for the unfolding drama of Korean history. Parhae was to be the last state through which the Korean people dominated Manchuria either politically or culturally. It is here that the place of Parhae in the history of the Korean people is to be found. After the downfall of Parhae, its ruling class of Koguryŏ descent came over to Koryŏ and contributed to that state's reunification of the Korean people. But they were unable to play a major role, either politically or culturally, in the mainstream of the ensuing age of Korean history. This explains why, even though Parhae and Silla constituted in essence northern and southern halves of a single partitioned nation, the view that regards Silla as the legitimate standard bearer of Korean history has long prevailed in the historiography of Korea.

Chapter 5

The Age of Powerful Gentry Families

1. Contradictions within the Bone-Rank Status System

Schism within the True-Bone Aristocracy

Although Silla civilization reached its zenith during the reign of King Kyŏngdŏk (742–765), beneath the surface signs of renewed conflict within Unified Silla society had appeared. For a movement had arisen among the true-bone aristocracy to break the authoritarian power of the throne. To thwart these efforts King Kyŏngdŏk instituted a program of political reform built around a policy of increased Sinicization, but this had no appreciable effect. Under the next king, Hyegong (765–780), then, a large scale rebellion broke out.

The political turbulence began in 768 with a plot against the throne led by Kim Tae-gong. This incident grew into a conflict of unprecedented dimensions, a power struggle described as involving ninety-six nobles (surely a much exaggerated number) who held Unified Silla's highest office rank (*kakkan*), and it continued for three years. A few years later (in 774) a highborn member of the aristocracy, Kim Yang-sang, succeeded in seizing power, reducing the king to little more than a figurehead. Kim Ŭn-gŏ and others made several attempts to restore the authority of the throne but failed, and in the end King Hyegong was killed by Kim Yang-sang and his supporters. Claiming to be a tenth generation descendant of the late fourth century King Naemul, Kim Yang-sang himself took the throne (King Sŏndŏk, 780–785). He was followed by Kim Kyŏng-sin (King Wŏnsŏng, 785–798), said to have been a twelfth generation descendant of King Naemul, and subsequent Silla rulers all came from King Wŏnsŏng's line of descent. Thus the line of King Muyŏl, the architect of Silla's unification, came to an end, and with it the middle period of Silla history. What is usually called the "late period" (*hadae*) of Unified Silla's existence designates this last century and a half during which King Wŏnsŏng's descendants occupied the throne.

This change from a flourishing middle period to a late period of decline in the history of Silla was brought about by the aristocracy's resistance to the trend toward the authoritarian rule of the throne. In consequence, the politics of Silla's late period is marked by the decisive role played by ephemeral coalitions of aristocratic forces. Instead of the chief minister (*chungsi*) of the Chancellery Office (*Chipsabu*), the *sangdaedŭng*, the head of the Council of Nobles (*Hwabaek*), again stood in the spotlight. But a reaction against these developments soon set in, and it came to a head in the rebellion of Kim Hŏn-ch'ang in 822. Kim Hŏn-ch'ang was the son of Kim Chu-wŏn, a descendant of King Muyŏl whose rightful claim to the throne upon the death of King Sŏndŏk in 785 had been usurped by King Wŏnsŏng with the backing of the aristocracy. Driven by this old grievance, Kim Hŏn-ch'ang mounted a large-scale insurrection from a base at Ungju (modern Kongju), going so far as to proclaim the founding of a new state (Changan) and the adoption of an era name for his rule. For a time a wide area in the modern Ch'ungch'ŏng, Chŏlla, and Kyŏngsang provinces rallied to his cause, but a coalition of forces among the Kyŏngju aristocracy brought about his defeat. His son, Kim Pŏm-mun, subsequently carried on the struggle, attempting to establish a capital at Hansan (near Seoul), but he too failed.

Members of the aristocracy had joined forces to break the authoritarian power of the throne, but now they found themselves torn by internecine strife. It was the increase in the individual wealth of the nobles, who had succeeded in abolishing the "office-land" and "annual grain grants" methods of remuneration and restoring the former "stipend village" system, that destroyed the solidarity of the corporate aristocracy. With the aim of seizing political power, ambitious nobles used their vast economic resources to create personal military forces, arming their slaves and recruiting the landless peasants who roamed the Silla countryside. At this point it was no longer blood lineage but political leverage and armed might that became decisive in determining succession to the throne. This is well illustrated by the succession struggle that broke out upon the death of King Hŭngdŏk in 836.

At first King Hŭngdŏk's cousin, Kim Kyun-jŏng, was put foward as king, but he was slain by the partisans of a nephew, Kim Che-ryung, who became King Hŭigang (in 836). After ruling for scarcely a year, amidst worsening turmoil created by other contenders for the throne, he took his own life and was succeeded by a second cousin, King Minae (in 838). Whereupon Kim U-jing, a son of Kim Kyun-jŏng, obtained the support of forces under the command of the Commissioner of the Ch'ŏnghae Garrison, Chang Po-go, attacked Kyŏngju, removed King Minae from the throne, and took it for himself (King Sinmu, 839). Under these circumstances, whoever might emerge victorious in the struggle for the kingship could no longer represent the aristocracy as a whole but only his own partisans who had raised him to the throne. Accordingly, each new king became the target of revenge of the factions he had defeated. Twenty kings occupied the throne during the approximately one hundred fifty years of the later period of Silla, and a goodly number of them fell victim to the almost unceasing political turmoil. This fact alone is graphic evidence of the parlous state into which the Silla social order had fallen.

The Role Played by the Head-Rank Six Aristocracy

Because of the limitations imposed by their social status, men of head-rank six were not afforded opportunity to hold positions of real political power. Rather than seeking advancement in official rank and position, therefore, their standing in Silla society led many of these lesser nobles into avenues of political participation congenial to their learning and informed judgment. There are numerous examples of the distinctive services rendered by such men of head-rank six background—Kangsu and Sŏl Ch'ong were Confucian scholars who enjoyed the full confidence and favor of the king; Yŏsam won renown for his skillful explication of a dream that troubled the later King Wŏnsŏng; Nokchin's sage counsel dispelled the anxieties of the *sangdaedŭng* Ch'unggong over appointments of officials; and Ch'oe Ch'i-wŏn submitted a detailed proposal to Queen Chinsŏng for dealing with the major issues of his day.

These men all were aware of the fact that the examination system in T'ang China provided opportunity for advancement in public office in accordance with an individual's demonstrated abilities. Accordingly, criticism began to be heard from such men concerning the inequities of Silla's bone-rank system. In his trenchant proposal referred to above, Ch'oe Ch'i-wŏn no doubt included a recommendation that men of talent be appointed to office on the basis of an examination system like that of T'ang. But such a major departure from Silla practices would have been unacceptable, and it is recorded that when his advice went unheeded he abandoned his official career and spent the rest of his days in unsettled retirement away from the capital. Ch'oe Ch'i-wŏn was not alone, for other scholars of head-rank six background took the same critical stance toward the bone-rank status system, in extreme cases even working actively against the interests of their Silla homeland. Ch'oe Sŭng-u holding office under Later Paekche and Ch'oe In-yŏn (Ch'oe Ŏn-wi) serving the Koryŏ state illustrate the seriousness of this disaffection. Thus mounting opposition to the Silla true-bone aristocracy was clearly evident among the lesser nobles of head-rank six.

2. The Rise of Powerful Local Gentry

The Growth of Maritime Trade

Around the middle of the ninth century the intense political strife among the true-bone aristocracy that had arisen out of the struggle for the throne began to show signs of abating. A spirit of reconciliation seems now to have prevailed among the previously warring factions, apparently owing to the need to deal with the threat to aristocratic hegemony posed by regional power centers that had begun to show their strength. At this juncture, then, Silla history entered a new phase, as power shifted away from the capital at Kyŏngju toward key centers in outlying areas.

The leaders of these regional power centers, who found the avenues of political participation at the central government level blocked by the bone-rank system, turned their attention to opportunities open to them beyond Silla's shores. Thus they came to look upon maritime trade as a major outlet for their energies. Silla's foreign trade hitherto had been carried on under the guise of official tribute missions, but at this point private trading activities began to flourish. This signified, of course, the emergence of new forces economically and militarily powerful enough to enable them to carry on such trade. Trade flourished not only with T'ang China but with Japan as well, and in consequence the Japanese even posted additional Silla language interpreters on Tsushima Island.

These trading activities led to the appearance of special Korean settlements in areas of the Shantung Peninsula and Kiangsu province, places Silla people frequently visited, and these were called Silla Quarters. So-called Silla Offices were established in these settlements with jurisdiction over the affairs of the residents, and the officials of these agencies were appointed from among the Koreans themselves. The residents also established their own Buddhist temples, where they prayed for the safe journey of their sailors and ships. These temples were called Silla Temples, and the best known among them is the Pŏphwa-wŏn established at Ch'ih-shan village in Wen-teng prefecture, Shantung, by Chang Po-go. The Japanese monk Jikaku (Ennin), who journeyed to T'ang in 840, tells us in his *Account of a Pilgrimage to T'ang in Search of the Law* (*Nyū Tō kyūhō junrei kōki*) that as many as two hundred fifty Silla people assembled at one time in the Pŏphwa-wŏn to listen to sermons on Buddhist texts.

Chang Po-go at the Ch'ŏnghae Garrison (on modern Wando island off the southwest coast of Chŏlla province) is the figure most prominent for the scale of his maritime activities, but other names are known to us as well—such as Wang Pong-gyu who operated out of Kangju (modern Chinju), and the man known as Chakchegŏn (the grandfather of the founder of the Koryŏ dynasty, Wang Kŏn) who was active in the Kaesŏng area. The individuals who dominated maritime trade in such flourishing ports as Namyang and Naju are not named in the records, but there must have been families in these regional centers as well whose wealth and power were derived from seaborne commerce.

The Emergence of Powerful Military Garrisons

Military garrisons in Silla originally were established at strategic locations to defend the country's land frontiers, the Northern Garrison (Puk-chin) at Samch'ŏk and the P'aegang-jin at modern P'yŏngsan being prime examples. But as the threat of piracy to Silla's maritime commerce intensified, a succession of garrisons also came to be established at important coastal points, such as the Ch'ŏnghae Garrison (on Wando island), Tangsŏng Garrison (at modern Namyang not far southwest of Seoul), and Hyŏlgu Garrison (on Kanghwa Island) [see map p. 102]. The most important of these was the Ch'ŏnghae Garrison.

The Ch'ŏnghae Garrison was established in 828 by Chang Po-go. He had journeyed to China as a young man and had pursued a successful military career in the service of T'ang. Outraged at the frequent incidents of his countrymen being captured by sea marauders and sold into slavery, Chang Po-go returned to Silla and appealed to King Hŭngdŏk (826–836) to formally establish a garrison on Wando, athwart the vital sea lanes in Korea's southern waters, where he already had created a strong military base. The king consented and appointed Chang to command the Ch'ŏnghae Garrison. With a force of 10,000 men, very much in the nature of his own private army, he patrolled Silla's coastal waters and put an end to the depredations of Chinese pirates. At the same time, he controlled a flourishing trade with China and Japan and became, in effect, the master of the Yellow Sea.

Chang Po-go not only ruled the sea lanes, but he intruded himself as well into the thick of the political strife in the capital. The military support he provided enabled Kim U-jing (King Sinmu), who came to him for help after losing out in an earlier struggle for the throne, to storm the capital and claim the kingship (839). A few years later, however, the protests of the capital aristocracy prevented King Munsŏng (839–857; Sinmu's son) from taking Chang Po-go's daughter as his second queen, and in the end this episode led to Chang's death at the hands of an assassin (846). Not long thereafter the Ch'ŏnghae Garrison itself was abolished (851).

For a time Chang Po-go and his Ch'ŏnghae Garrison command had represented a powerful force indeed. But he failed in his efforts to participate directly in the politics of the capital, nor was he able to create an independent political force that might contend for supremacy with the government in Kyŏngju. The capital aristocracy was torn by schism and its power had begun to crumble, but it still was strong enough to preserve the bone-rank system on which its dominance rested. Thus the islander Chang Po-go, guilty of heresy against the Silla social order, met his downfall, and the 10,000 troops under his command were removed to Pyŏkkol county (modern Kimje) where they no longer could pose the threat of insurrection. But other military garrisons had developed in much the same way as had that at Ch'ŏnghae, and before long these would serve as sources of military support for the ambitions of powerful gentry families in the Silla countryside.

The Rise of Castle Lords

Chang Po-go appears to have been the scion of a gentry family that had established itself on Wando. It would be only natural, then, for him to base his operations on his home island, form a personal armed force around other members of his lineage, and finally succeed in establishing a military garrison there. Certainly at this time there were many analogous cases of powerful families that for several generations had exercised de facto control over particular regions away from the capital. Typically these leading gentry houses built fortifications around the population centers from which they held sway, and so they were known as "castle lords" (*sŏngju*). They also are referred to in the historical records as "generals" (*changgun*), since they commanded their own private soldiery recruited from the local populace and based at their strongholds.

It appears that some castle lords arose from among those originally of capital aristocracy background who had been forced in one way or another to remove to areas of the Silla countryside. Coming from both the true-bone aristocracy and those of head-rank six, these erstwhile Kyŏngju nobles no doubt sought in this way to create new power bases for themselves in the particular locality where they and their close kinsmen had taken refuge. On the other hand many castle lords represented indigenous local elites, families that had furnished village headmen over a long period of time. In the original Silla local administrative structure the task of these petty officials was to govern the rural population, but by now the stronger village headmen had brought the others in their immediate environs under their control, thus creating an expanded power base. Castle lords of both types of background came to occupy a position on the local scene that, in effect, usurped that of the prefecture and county magistrates dispatched from the capital.

The castle lords exercised economic jurisdiction in the villages over which their power extended. They both levied taxes on the peasant population and exacted corvee labor service from them. This shift in the locus of economic control over the countryside signified a growing erosion of the economic foundation of the central government. This constituted a grave problem upon which the very survival of Silla hinged.

3. The Later Three Kingdoms

Peasant Uprisings

The growing strength of the castle lords weakened the hold of the central government of Silla over the countryside, and this made it impossible to collect taxes from the peasants. Moreover, the financial needs of the capital aristocracy in the late years of Silla grew ever more pressing as it sought increasingly to indulge its taste for a life-style of opulence and pleasure, while at the same time the resources available to the government in Kyŏngju were in the process of shrinking. In an attempt to overcome its fiscal crisis, the government in 889 resorted to forced collections of taxes from the provincial and county areas. But this resulted in a dual burden being imposed upon the peasant population, for they now had to suffer not only the exactions of the castle lords under whom they lived but the levies of the central government as well.

Even in Unified Silla's most flourishing period the tax and corvee burdens on the peasant population had led numbers of them to abandon their land and roam the countryside. Some of these landless wanderers remained a population of drifters, enduring lives of bare subsistence as best they could, and some joined together in brigand bands and lived by plundering. Still others, however, sought to start life anew under the protection of local gentry families. Whatever the case, all these developments had a destabilizing impact on the old social order centered on the capital. The government's decision to use force to collect taxes from the countryside, then, represented a last gasp effort to preserve the aristocratic order. But its effect was to drive the peasantry into seething rebellion.

The first flames of peasant revolt flared in the Sangju area in 889. This uprising was on a sizeable scale, and it is said that the government forces sent to suppress it were loath to do battle with the powerful peasant insurgents arrayed against them. An unending succession of rebellions now erupted in every corner of the country. Yanggil at Wŏnju, Kihwŏn at Chuksan, Kyŏnhwŏn at Chŏnju, and Yanggil's lieutenant Kungye were the most prominent among the many leaders of rebel armies [see map p. 102]. Moreover, a large force of brigands that called itself the Red Trousered Banditti (*Chŏkkojŏk*) seized control of the region southwest of the capital. And countless other peasant insurgent bands, called "grass brigands" (*ch'ojŏk*) in the records, rose spontaneously across the land.

Later Paekche and T'aebong

The early rebel leaders had been no more than commanders of rebel forces in a particular limited locale. Before long, however, two leaders emerged at the head of forces strong enough to create new state entities in the areas they controlled and challenge Silla for the mantle of legitimacy. These were Kyŏnhwŏn and Kungye who, claiming that the states they founded were restorations of Paekche and Koguryŏ respectively, set in motion a three-cornered contest for mastery of the Korean peninsula. The nearly half century span consumed by this struggle is known as the Later Three Kingdoms period.

Kyŏnhwŏn was from poor peasant stock in the Sangju area. Starting out as an ordinary soldier, Kyŏnhwŏn was advanced from the ranks in reward for valor in defending Silla's southwestern coastal region. As rebellion flared throughout the country, he led a band of followers to seize Kwangju and then proceeded to establish his base of operations at Chŏnju, where in 892 he proclaimed the founding of the state of Later Paekche with the avowed objective of avenging the last Paekche king, Ŭija. Despite his peasant background and his early career as a foot soldier, once he sat on a throne of his own making he proved to be an intractable and despotic ruler. His eventual attempt to disinherit his eldest son and pass on the kingship of Later Paekche to his fourth son, Kŭmgang, of whom he was particularly fond, was a manifestation of this willful trait of character, one that ultimately became his undoing. He harbored the bitterest enmity toward Silla, as can be seen in his claim to represent a revival of Paekche and in his pillaging of Kyŏngju in 927, when he killed King Kyŏngae, abducted Kyŏngae's younger brother and highest officials, and seized large quantities of treasure, arms, and the capital's skilled craftsmen. Had Kungye and Wang Kŏn not stood in his way, he surely would have had little difficulty in toppling Silla.

Kungye was a Silla prince who most likely was driven out of the capital as one victim of the political power struggle. He at first became a monk, but as Silla became caught up in turmoil he threw in his lot first with Kihwŏn (in 891) but later became a lieutenant of Yanggil. Given command of a contingent of Yanggil's forces, he succeeded in capturing wide areas of Kangwŏn, Kyŏnggi, and Hwanghae provinces and in assembling a large army under his personal control. At this point he overthrew Yanggil and in 901 proclaimed the founding of the state of Later Koguryŏ as the successor to the former Koguryŏ kingdom. Kungye first made Songak (modern Kaesŏng) his capital, but subsequently he renamed his state Majin and built a new capital at Ch'ŏrwŏn, where he once more gave his state a new name, T'aebong. Kungye then set about creating an administrative structure replete with a chancellery to oversee government affairs, a number of ministries and other offices, and an office rank system in nine grades. In formal aspect, then, Kungye now sat at the helm of an impressive state apparatus.

Having been forced to give up his position in Silla society as a son of the king, Kungye from the beginning harbored strong enmity toward his homeland. He required his subjects to refer to Silla as the "nation of the damned," and he is said to have killed all those from Silla who entered his territory. Like Kyŏnhwŏn in Later Paekche, Kungye ruled over his domain with untempered despotism. As the rationale for his despotic rule he made use of the mystique of Buddhism, claiming himself to be the Maitreya Buddha and designating his eldest and second sons both Bodhisattvas. As is usual with such tyrants, Kungye was inordinately suspicious of the motives of those around him, and many who served him fell victim to his claim to possess the supernatural power to read others' minds. Forced to maintain himself in power by acts of terror, Kungye in the end was driven from his throne by his own generals and was killed as he fled by the people he had ruled.

The Founding of Koryŏ

It was Wang Kŏn who was put forward to succeed Kungye as king of the northern region. Wang Kŏn had emerged from a gentry family in the Songak (Kaesŏng) area. With the military power of the garrisons Silla had established at border locations like P'aegang and Hyŏlgu as a backdrop, he had striven for preeminence in the world of his time. His connections with the maritime activities centered around the Hyŏlgu Garrison on Kanghwa Island seem to have been particularly close. At first Wang Kŏn had taken part in a number of campaigns as a subordinate commander of Kungye, but he had won particular recognition for his seaborne operations against the southwest coastal region. Occupying Kŭmsŏng (Naju), Chindo, and other coastal points, he had blocked Later Paekche's communications with China and Japan, and at the same time he had inhibited its ability to attack northward. Such a strategy as this must have derived from Wang Kŏn's long familiarity with maritime activities. Because of these achievements he had been appointed *sijung* (chief minister), and so now Wang Kŏn was put forward by the generals who ousted Kungye and rose to the kingship (918).

Wang Kŏn renamed his state Koryŏ, adopted the era name *Ch'ŏnsu* ("Heaven's Mandate"), and moved the capital to Songak (Kaesŏng). No differently than Kungye, Wang Kŏn considered himself to be the successor to the mantle of Koguryŏ. His purpose in moving the capital to his own home area, however, was to give expression to the fact that he had founded a new state. The move to Kaesŏng not merely secured his military and political base but also clearly demonstrated his standing as a local gentry figure. The fact that he belonged to this local elite class, unlike Kungye and Kyŏnhwŏn, meant that he had a local power base that would support him, a firm base that would not be shaken by a single political crisis. Moreover, as a leading local gentry figure, he would be able to form strong ties with other local gentry. It was these fundamental conditions that made it possible for Wang Kŏn to unite the Later Three Kingdoms.

In foreign relations Wang Kŏn, unlike Kungye, employed a policy of friendship with Silla. He established close ties with Silla first in order to destroy his rival Kyŏnhwŏn, but at the same time he sought by this means to secure his position as the successor to Silla's traditions and authority. Upon hearing that Kyŏnhwŏn had invaded the Silla capital and killed King Kyŏngae, Wang Kŏn personally led his forces into battle against the Later Paekche ruler. When he visited the Silla capital, it is said, he won the admiration of the Silla people, who felt toward him as if they were welcoming their parents. Nevertheless, Wang Kŏn did not neglect to develop a military strategy toward Silla. Fifty *li* north of the Silla capital he established the Irŏ-jin (Sin'gwang-jin) garrison as a permanent encampment for Koryŏ troops.

4. Unification by Koryŏ

Unification of the Later Three Kingdoms

Koryŏ had exchanged hostages for a time with Later Paekche in an effort at effecting a truce. On the whole, however, the two countries found themselves in an unceasing state of hostilities. Their battlefield was the region just west of the Naktong River, from Koch'ang (Andong) past Sangju to Kangju (Chinju) [see map p. 102]. In the struggle for possession of what remained of Silla, the battleground had become Silla's outer perimeter. Silla already had completely lost control over its hinterland and now was helpless. The local gentry leaders in their fortified towns looked to their own interests as they made overtures to either Wang Kŏn's Koryŏ or Kyŏnhwŏn's Later Paekche.

Neither Koryŏ nor Later Paekche was remiss in developing relations with China. Later Paekche had ties principally with southern China, whereas Koryŏ maintained relations with northern China through the Shantung Peninsula. It was not only a period of internal disorder in Korea but the time of the chaotic Five Dynasties in China; nevertheless, contacts between the Chinese and Korean states were frequent. These contacts had trade as one objective, but they also gave the appearance of a type of diplomatic war. However, the solution to the problem of the Later Three Kingdoms lay within the borders of Korea. In an age of disorder like that of the Five Dynasties, the outcome could not be influenced by China.

With the victory of the Koryŏ forces at Koch'ang in 930 the existing stalemate was broken, and the tide of battle turned to favor Koryŏ. Later Paekche now was forced to retreat from Silla's outer domain, whereupon Koryŏ intensified its frontal pressure against Later Paekche. Sending an army into the South Ch'ungch'ŏng area, Koryŏ crushed Later Paekche's forces at Unju (Hongsŏng) in 934. At this point, the fighting developed entirely to Koryŏ's advantage.

Later Paekche had lost the advantage not only in battle but also faced internal disarray. Kyŏnhwŏn had designated his fourth son, Kŭmgang, to succeed him, whereupon the eldest son, Sin'gŏm, confined his father in the Kŭmsan-sa temple in Kimje and took the throne of Later Paekche for himself. Kyŏnhwŏn managed to escape to Koryŏ and, entrusting himself to his old enemy Wang Kŏn, plotted revenge against his son. Meanwhile, the last ruler of Silla, Kyŏngsun, had come to reign over a kingdom in name only, a domain limited to the narrow confines of the Kyŏngju region. At this juncture, late in the year 935, he took his fate into his own hands by tendering formal surrender to Koryŏ. Thus it was that Wang Kŏn succeeded in securing the position as successor to the Silla tradition and mantle of authority. In the following year Koryŏ troops, with Kyŏnhwŏn in the

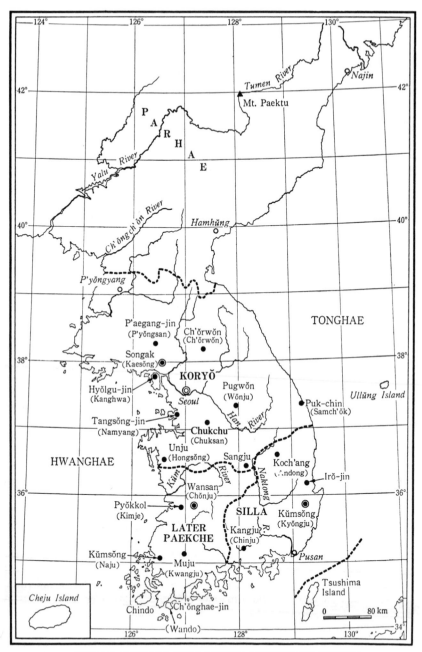

**KOREA IN THE LATER THREE KINGDOMS PERIOD
(LATE 9ᵗʰ—EARLY 10ᵗʰ CENTURIES)**

lead, brought about the collapse of Later Paekche as well. At last Wang Kŏn had succeeded in uniting the Later Three Kingdoms.

When Parhae perished at the hands of the Khitan around this same time, much of its ruling class, who were of Koguryŏ descent, fled to Koryŏ. Wang Kŏn warmly welcomed them and generously gave them land. Along with bestowing the name Wang Kye ("Successor of the Royal Wang") on the Parhae crown prince, Tae Kwang-hyŏn, Wang Kŏn entered his name in the royal household register, thus clearly conveying the idea that they belonged to the same lineage, and also had rituals performed in honor of his progenitor. Thus Koryŏ achieved a true national unification that embraced not only the Later Three Kingdoms but even survivors of Koguryŏ lineage from the Parhae kingdom.

Strategy of Alliance with Local Gentry

King T'aejo (Wang Kŏn's posthumous title) had succeeded in bringing order out of the chaos of the Later Three Kingdoms and establishing a new unified dynasty. Regarding himself as the successor to Koguryŏ, he pursued a policy of expansion to the north, extending his borders to the Ch'ŏngch'ŏn River, and at the same time he broke the chains of the bone-rank order which had shackled Silla's society. On the other hand, however, he still intended to wear the mantle of authority that traditionally had been Silla's. Accordingly he took to wife a woman from the Silla royal house, and he treated the Silla nobility, King Kyŏngsun (Kim Pu) foremost among them, with extreme generosity. Because of this, many individuals of Silla lineage entered into the Koryŏ bureaucracy. This was in marked contrast to the cool treatment Later Paekche people received. Thus Koryŏ became the full-fledged successor to Silla. Wang Kŏn was no longer merely a nameless upstart castle lord from a border region, but a personage who had inherited long historical traditions.

Unification by T'aejo, however, signified only the extinction of the competing regimes. The castle lords continued to maintain the quasi-independent status of their regional strongholds, in no way differently than in the chaotic Later Three Kingdoms period. Accordingly, officials to govern the local areas could not be dispatched from the central government. There were also the men to whom T'aejo owed his throne, the military commanders of local gentry background who had shared his victories and defeats on the battlefield. With the prisoners and other spoils of war they had seized and in command of their own armed retinues, they constituted a prideful and powerful force. The continued viability of T'aejo's rule much depended on their consent and cooperation. He established marriage ties with more than twenty local gentry families throughout the country, such as the Chŏngju Yu clan, the P'yŏngsan Yu and Pak clans, and the Kwangju Wang clan, and in some cases he firmed the alliance by bestowing the royal surname, thus establishing fictive family ties.

In spite of this policy, the existence of these political forces of local gentry background was the cause of considerable anxiety on the part of Wang Kŏn. That he wrote and promulgated a volume of "Political Precautions" and eight compilations of "Bureaucratic Precepts" may be seen as resulting from this concern. For even though today we cannot know the content of these documents, it is clear that they set forth the norms that were to govern the conduct of those who served his Koryŏ state. T'aejo died, however, without being able to establish stable royal power, leaving behind for his successors the testament known as the *Ten Injunctions* (*Sip hunyo*), precepts in the realm of government and values to be honored by later kings.

King T'aejo's fears were well founded, for two years after his death the Wang Kyu rebellion occurred. Wang Kyu was a royal in-law, having given two daughters to T'aejo as his fifteenth and sixteenth queens, one of whom bore a son, the Prince of Kwangju. Wang Kyu sent another daughter into the palace as a secondary queen for Hyejong, Wang Kŏn's eldest son and successor, and at the same time sought to bring the Prince of Kwangju to the throne by falsely informing Hyejong that two younger brothers were disloyal and, ultimately, by attempting to kill Hyejong. His position thus threatened, Hyejong survived uneasily for a time, always protected by an armed bodyguard, but before long he died. Wang Kyu finally was eliminated early in the reign of Chŏngjong, Hyejong's successor, by the military power of the P'yŏngyang garrison commander, Wang Sing-nyŏm, but this incident well conveys the unstable nature of the royal authority at this time.

Royal Authority and the Local Gentry

Having crushed Wang Kyu's treason plot, King Chŏngjong thought to strengthen the frail royal authority by moving the seat of government to the "Western Capital," P'yŏngyang. In this design the geomantic theories that T'aejo had emphasized in his *Ten Injunctions* certainly were at work. But it would seem as well that Chŏngjong had a strong desire to escape from the too close embrace of those who had been rewarded for merit in founding Koryŏ, who were expanding their power around Kaesŏng. Chŏngjong died, however, after a reign of only four years, and he had not been able to move the capital.

Improved prospects for stable royal authority in Koryŏ had to await the reforms of King Kwangjong. His initial move in this direction was the enactment of a Slave Review Act. During the chaotic period of the Later Three Kingdoms, military commanders and local gentry had forced prisoners and refugees into slavery. This increase in slaves signified an increase in their masters' economic and military strength, and to check this growth it was necessary to decrease the number of slaves. To this end, the Slave Review Act determined those who originally had been commoners and restored them to free status.

Besides this, Kwangjong adopted the proposal of the Chinese scholar Shuang Chi and established a civil service examination system in 958. The purpose was to employ in the bureaucracy new civilian officials, men of learning, in place of the old military officials from the ranks of those who had participated in the founding of Koryŏ. New people now were to be appointed on the basis of new criteria. Thus the enactment of the civil service examination system constituted a fundamental effort at establishing a new bureaucratic structure that would serve to strengthen royal authority. To give a heightened degree of hierarchy to this newly established bureau-cratic structure, he instituted gradations in court robes in 960, distinguishing officials of different rank levels by the purple, red, scarlet, or green color of the attire prescribed for each. Beyond these reforms, a series of actions such as styling himself "Emperor," calling Kaesŏng the "Imperial Capital," assigning more dignified characters to P'yŏngyang as the "Western Capital," and adopting independent era names constitutes another dimension of Kwangjong's efforts to strengthen the royal authority.

The greatest discontent with these reforms was felt by those high mili-tary and civil officials who had been rewarded for their services in founding Koryŏ, and by their heirs. As a result a merciless purge occurred. Even being a military commander who had fought side by side with his father, Wang Kŏn, brought no immunity, as Kwangjong liquidated all who would not submit to the authority of the throne. Thus he was able to assert royal authority over at least the aristocrats in the center of the kingdom at Kaesŏng. The next step, then, was the enactment of the Stipend Land Law (*chŏnsikwa*), instituted initially by the next king, Kyŏngjong, in 976, a measure designed to create an economic underpinning for a central government bureaucracy newly remodeled on the foundation laid by Kwangjong's reforms.

5. Culture of the Gentry Period

Growth of Confucianism

During the height of royal authoritarian rule in Silla, Confucianism gradu-ally won wider acceptance as a doctrine providing a unique moral basis for effective government. However, Confucianism had not been able to develop to the point where it could put forward strong reform measures to achieve its political ideals. But during the later years of Silla, when the bone-rank system was in decline, Confucianism emerged as an ideology of political reform.

Originally Confucianism had developed with its base in the National Confucian College. In Silla's later years, however, the number of Confucian students going to study Confucianism firsthand in T'ang China increased dramatically. Ch'oe Ch'i-wŏn is an outstanding representative of this group, as are Ch'oe Sŭng-u and Ch'oe In-yŏn (Ch'oe Ŏn-wi), and together they are known as the Three Ch'oe. Ch'oe Ch'i-wŏn in particular was renowned in China as well for his literary ability, and he is remembered for a number of works, such as *Chungsan igwe chip* and *Kyewŏn p'ilgyŏng*, both collections of essays, and *Chewang yŏndaeryŏk*, a historical chronology.

These men urged that the government appoint men distinguished by learning in preference to those qualified merely by bone-rank lineage. They hoped in this way to create a different kind of centralized aristocratic state, one with men of talent who possessed a Confucian training as its core element. We cannot be certain, since Ch'oe Ch'i-wŏn's policy proposals unfortunately have not been preserved, but it may be assumed that his memorials too were filled with ideas of this sort. But such ideas were unacceptable in a Silla that stubbornly adhered to the bone-rank order right up to the moment of its collapse. In consequence, a chorus of voices was raised among the Confucianists in criticism of Silla's antiquated bone-rank system. One such protest was that of Wang Kŏ-in, arrested in Queen Chinsŏng's reign on charges of having criticized the government by use of language with hidden meanings. Ch'oe Ch'i-wŏn too, when his proposals were not accepted, gave up his position and spent the rest of his days in self-imposed exile from the capital. In the end, however, it was Confucian scholars of Ch'oe Ch'i-wŏn's persuasion who performed the function of providing the political ideology of the new Koryŏ dynasty.

Popularity of Sŏn (Zen) Buddhism

The new trend in Buddhism in the late Silla period was the popularity of Sŏn. The Sŏn, or Contemplative School, took a position in contrast to that of the Kyo, or Textual School, which differentiated its sects on the basis of the particular sutra each relied upon. In brief, Sŏn argued that faith need not be grounded in the written word and put its emphasis instead on getting away from the complexities of doctrine by cultivating the spiritual essence of the human mind. Thus the advocacy of the path of sudden enlightenment by the Sŏn sect went hand in hand with the position it took against scripture reading. The method of this path of sudden enlightenment is *sŏn*, or meditation. Through *sŏn*, through meditation, it is possible to comprehend the Buddha nature that inherently exists in the minds of all of us. In this respect it may be said that Sŏn contains an individualistic aspect.

Sŏn is said to have first entered Korea in the seventh century during Queen Sŏndŏk's reign (632–647), but it was only vaguely understood at that time. Then under King Hŏndŏk at the beginning of the ninth century, starting with the founding of the Mt. Kaji sect at Porim-sa by the monk Toŭi, the Sŏn faith gradually started to spread more widely, leading to the establishment of the so-called Nine Mountain Sects of Sŏn.

The great popularity of Sŏn is explained by the warm reception it received from the gentry families in the countryside. Most of the nine sects of the Sŏn school had close ties with the local gentry. For example, the Mt. Sagul sect received patronage from Wang Sun-sik, a gentry figure in Myŏngju (Kangnŭng), and the Mt. Sumi sect at Kaesŏng had close ties with Wang Kŏn. In fact, many of the founders of the Nine Mountain Sects were from local gentry families. Some of these, of course, traced their ancestry to the capital aristocracy, but their families had long been settled in the countryside and become local gentry. Thus naturally the Nine Mountain Sects all took root in outlying areas near the strongholds of the powerful local gentry who supported them.

Sŏn in short developed as the religion of the local gentry. The individualistic element in Sŏn provided an ideological basis for the assertion of their independence by the local gentry, who stood in opposition to the centralized ruling structure in the capital. To be sure, the Silla royal house sought to make use of Sŏn Buddhism in its efforts to restore the crumbling central power structure, but to play such a role was not in keeping with the fundamental character of the Sŏn religion of this era.

Geomantic Theories

Another way of thought that became widespread with the rise of the local gentry was geomancy. It was the monk Tosŏn who greatly enhanced the appeal of geomancy, for he combined with it the Buddhist idea of achieving merit through good works, as well as the Taoistic *yin-yang* and Five Elements theories. According to Tosŏn, the natural features of a land area and their configuration deeply affect a country's or an individual's fate. In the lie of the land there is decay or prosperity, the favorable and unfavorable, and by selecting a flourishing or propitious site for a building or for constructing a tomb, the country or an individual would be able to enjoy good fortune. On the other hand, since a decadent or inauspicious site brings misfortune, one must forestall calamity by constructing temples to remedy topographical defects, just as one might apply a poultice to the human body. Tosŏn likened the Korean peninsula to a branching tree with its roots at Mt. Paektu, and at other times he saw it in the shape of a ship. He is said to have wandered all over Korea divining the auspiciousness and inauspiciousness of the topographical features.

From the standpoint of this sort of geomantic theory, the gentry of each locality regarded their own home ground as auspicious, and they appear to have sought to legitimize their standing as gentry on this basis. The case of the Wang family in Kaesŏng may be said to be a prime example of this, for Wang Kŏn's unification of the Later Three Kingdoms was believed to be the result of Kaesŏng's virtuous topography. Specifically, we are told that Wang Kŏn's ancestors believed implicitly the geomantic forecast that if they planted pine trees on Mt. Songak, thus making the mountain green, and then moved their house to a site near the southern slope, a hero who would unite Korea's ancient Samhan would emerge from among their descendants. They proceeded to carry this out and Wang Kŏn's unification was the result. Wang Kŏn himself was a sincere if ingenuous believer in such geomantic theories, so much so that he asserted in the fifth of his *Ten Injunctions*:

> I carried out the great undertaking of reunifying the country by availing myself of the latent virtue of the mountains and streams of the Samhan.

Although all the local gentry must have considered their home areas to be topographically auspicious, there appear to have been degrees of auspiciousness based on the actual power of the particular gentry family. The term "great flower manifestation," signifying a place where trees flowered with large blooms, bespoke the most auspicious location. On the other hand, the strongholds of opponents were designated as adverse sites. The best example of this is Wang Kŏn in his *Ten Injunctions* labeling the area of Later Paekche, which had resisted him to the end, a "perverse and rebellious land."

Art

The later period of Silla is commonly acknowledged to be a time of decline in the arts. It must not be overlooked, however, that several new trends appeared in association with the thought and society of this age. First to be noted is the popularity of prayer pagodas among the nobility. With the frequent changes in power surrounding the succession struggles, true-bone aristocrats competed with each other in constructing prayer pagodas to pray for their good fortune. Examples can be seen in the three-tiered stone pagoda at Ch'angnim-sa in Kyŏngju for King Munsŏng, the three-tiered stone pagoda at the Piro-am hermitage at Tonghwa-sa on Mt. P'algong, Taegu, for King Minae, and the three-tiered double pagoda at Porim-sa in Changhŭng for King Hŏnan. Such prayer pagodas were built not only for kings, but also for aristocrats in the capital and for gentry in the local areas.

In Buddhist sculpture, the great popularity of images of the Vairocana Buddha, the supreme Buddha deity, was a special characteristic of this age. Many of these images, unlike those of earlier periods, were cast in iron, the Vairocana sitting cross-legged at Porim-sa in Changhŭng or at To-p'ian-sa in Ch'ŏrwŏn being typical examples. Huge stone carvings like the standing Bodhisattva (the so-called Ŭnjin Maitreya), done at Nonsan's Kwanch'ok-sa in the reign of Kwangjong (mid-10th century), and others carved on the face of rock cliffs also are characteristic of this age.

Memorial stupas and monument stones also began to be in vogue in this period. Stupas were made as tombs in which to preserve the remains of noted monks. Since the Sŏn school as a matter of principle did not rely on texts but transmitted the awakening experience from the mind of a teacher to that of a learner, it looked upon the function of the master-disciple relationship as being of fundamental importance. One suspects it was for this reason that, after a master died, his cremated remains were extraordinarily venerated, as a symbol of the sect or school that he had taught. Thus memorial stupas to honor Sŏn masters came to be built in considerable numbers, the oldest known being that for Monk Yŏmgŏ erected in 790. It was common for the stupa to have an eight-sided pedestal, and some of the best are the Master Ch'ŏlgam stupa for Toyun, the founder of the Mt. Saja sect, one of the Nine Mountain Sects of Sŏn, at Ssangbong-sa in Hwa-sun, and the stupa at Kongju's Kap-sa. Accompanying the stupa usually is a monument stone recording the Sŏn master's achievements, and among these an outstanding example is one to Master Wŏllang from the Wŏl-gwang-sa temple, formerly in Ch'ungju and now at Kyŏngbok Palace in Seoul. These stupas and monuments, with their out-thrusting capstone elements and the vigorously carved swirl-design motifs that remind one of whirlpools, well reflect the tumultuous society of the age.

The writings inscribed on these monuments are important both as materials for the study of calligraphic styles and as historical sources that transmit the story of the development of Sŏn. Most widely known of all these are the "four mountain inscriptions" done by the hand of Ch'oe Ch'i-wŏn.

Chapter 6

The Hereditary Aristocratic Order of Koryŏ

1. Beginnings of Koryŏ's Aristocratic Order

Toward Aristocratic Government

The reforms of Kwangjong (949–975) dealt a serious blow to high officials of local gentry origin. To serve him, Kwangjong principally appointed scholars without distinguished lineage background who had passed the state examination and Chinese who had no power base in Koryŏ. However, the influence of these officials evaporated with Kwangjong's death, as Confucian scholars of Silla's head-rank six lineages came to assume leading political roles. Ch'oe Sŭng-no was a major such figure.

Ch'oe Sŭng-no had as his goal the creation of an aristocratic society with a centralized power structure. Unlike the local gentry, he was a scholar who had no base in the countryside but rather had been a Koryŏ government official at the time of Silla's surrender. Therefore his concern was with advancing in the central bureaucracy, and this orientation naturally caused his political views to favor centralization of power. He opposed, however, the growth of royal absolutism, and he abhorred the absolute monarch who would ignore the opinions of the aristocracy. He wanted to construct an aristocratic society in which the political process would operate with the aristocracy at its center. These views of Ch'oe Sŭng-no clearly appear in the twenty-eight point policy memorial he submitted not long before his death in 989 to King Sŏngjong.

Sŏngjong (981–997), in dealing with the political situation after the failure of Kwangjong's reforms, relied on the views of Confucian scholars such as Ch'oe Sŭng-no. Under Sŏngjong, for the first time, officials were dispatched from the capital to head the provincial administrative units, and he instituted a reform of the local government structure that marked the inauguration of Koryŏ's county functionary system, thus effecting a downgrading of the position of the local gentry. Still, wishing to absorb into the capital aristocracy as many of the local gentry as possible, he spared no effort to educate their youth. Always attentive to the opinions of aristocratic officials well-versed in the Chinese classics, he sought to reflect these ideas in his political decisions. In this way the foundation for Koryŏ's aristocratic order was laid.

Establishment of the Aristocratic Order

The aristocrats of Silla's head-rank six lineages contributed much to the reordering of Koryŏ's social and political structure, in the process solidifying their own position. At the same time, increasing numbers of men from gentry families in the area around Kaesŏng also appeared on the central political stage as civil officials. Thus unlike Silla, where the true-bone members of the royal lineage had been at the center of the political process, Koryŏ relied on aristocrats from many different clans to govern. These aristocratic clans called Kyŏngju (the former Silla capital), or the areas from which their forbears had originated as local gentry, their *pon'gwan* (clan seat), and the *pon'gwan* came to serve as a symbol of aristocratic power and privilege. Thus Koryŏ society attached great importance to lineage background, and indeed aristocratic families were listed on separate census registers from those that recorded the commoner population.

These aristocratic lineages used marriage as a strategy to expand the power of their families. The more influential in society the family with which one formed marriage ties, the greater the honor to one's own house and the more quickly one might enhance its standing and bring it into greater political prominence. Accordingly, the highest aspiration was to marry with Koryŏ's most aristocratic family, the royal clan. This brought with it not only the greatest distinction, but it also provided a shortcut to grasping political power. Thus were born the exalted lineages that monopolized power as marriage kinsmen of the royal family.

Such clans were the Ansan Kim and the Inju (Inch'ŏn) Yi families. The Ansan Kim clan monopolized power in this way under four kings, for over fifty years, from the time Kim Ŭn-bu presented three daughters as queens to Hyŏnjong (1009–1031) down into Munjong's reign (1046–1083). Then the Inju Yi clan, which had maintained marriage ties with the Ansan Kim, came to take over its monopoly of political power with the marriage of three daughters of Yi Cha-yŏn to King Munjong. The dominance of the Inju Yi clan continued for over eighty years, until early in the reign of Injong (1122–1146), six kings later. The magnitude of its power can be judged from the fact that Yi Cha-gyŏm (a grandson of Yi Cha-yŏn) even dreamed of a new dynasty of the Inju Yi clan, with himself as its first ruler. Besides these families, Yun Kwan's P'ap'yŏng Yun clan, Ch'oe Ch'ung's Haeju Ch'oe clan, and Kim Pu-sik's Kyŏngju Kim clan were all famous lineages of this day. Thus in Koryŏ there emerged a society centering on new hereditary aristocratic houses, and it was these that controlled the workings of the political process.

The heartland of this aristocracy was of course the capital at Kaesŏng. Kaesŏng after all was the heart of the whole nation, where all those who shaped its destiny congregated. The aristocrats who held positions in the central government all were denizens of Kaesŏng who resided permanently in the capital, returning to their former places of origin in the countryside only if found guilty of official misconduct and so compelled to do so. The palace was built at the foot of Mt. Songak on the Full Moon Terrace (Manwŏl-tae), a site that geomantic lore regarded as highly propitious, and around it were streets filled with great government buildings, monasteries and temples, and the houses of the inhabitants, forming a city divided into neighborhoods, blocks, and wards. Although the thatched houses of the ordinary populace clustered together like anthills or beehives, the palaces, government structures, and temple buildings displayed an appearance of proud splendor. A wall built by over 30,000 laborers and completed in 1029 surrounded the city at its outer limits.

Remodeling of the Social Structure

In Koryŏ men of a new social class, not those of Silla true-bone origin, had emerged as masters of its destiny, and in this circumstance a restructuring of the social status system was inevitable. The governing elite in the earlier Koryŏ period comprised those of gentry origin from the districts around the capital and aristocrats of Silla head-rank six background, and the new social structure took form around this dominant force.

The Koryŏ social structure was characterized above all by a close connection between it and the political system. A number of "orders" (*pan* or -*ban*) were created whose names indicated fixed political functions, and as a basic principle the population segments in each grouping were assigned the right and obligation to perform their particular function on a hereditary basis. For example, those in the civil official order (*munban*) filled civil offices, those in the military officer order (*muban*) filled military offices, those in the court functionary order (*namban*) filled various palace service offices, and those in the soldiering order (*kunban*) filled the ranks of the military units. To be sure, the clerical and petty functionary force in the local and central bureaucracies, the artisans, and the like were not designated terminologically as "orders," but in reality they too were hereditarily fixed in their occupations. The peasant population, called *paekchŏng*, was not eligible to hold government office, and below the *paekchŏng* were *ch'ŏnmin* (lowborn) who were slaves.

Social status in these several gradations was inherited within kinship boundaries defined by a unit of fixed size. Although it is not clear today how inclusive a unit this was, it appears to have been in the nature of what might be termed a family or lineage rather than a clan as a whole. A number of measures were adopted to ensure the inheritance of social status. The state established a "protected appointment" system whereby one son of a man who reached the fifth rank or above in either the civil or military order could receive a government appointment. Soldiers and local functionaries also passed on their occupations to their descendants. The economic underpinning of this hereditary status system, then, was provided by state allocation of so-called *yŏngŏpchŏn*, support land held in perpetuity.

Although social status in the Koryŏ system was hereditary in principle, in fact changes in status took place continually. The phenomenon of upward movement from a lower into a higher status occurred with particular frequency. Especially noteworthy were instances of movement of local clerks into the civil official order and of soldiers into the military officer order. Since most of the aristocrats in the civil official order originally had emerged from local gentry background, there were many cases of civil officials and local clerks sharing the same lineage. That local clerks could easily advance into the civil official order is due to this fact. The local clerks, however, did not enjoy the privilege of a protected appointment, and so their only recourse was to enter the officialdom via the civil service examination. Thus the Koryŏ civil service examination performed an important function in bringing about social change.

There were many instances as well of soldiers advancing into the military officer order because of meritorious service, and these constitute examples of major upward movement. Furthermore, since the ranks of the soldiery were replenished by recruits not only from the free peasantry (*paekchŏng*) but from among the slave population as well, there were also cases of members of these classes advancing through the soldiering order into the military officer order. Thus it is a particular characteristic of the Koryŏ period that this sort of constant change took place within the framework of a status system based on the principle of hereditary social classes.

2. The Aristocratic Ruling Structure

Political Structure

The new Koryŏ political structure began to take shape in 983 under Sŏngjong and was completed in 1076 under Munjong. The administrative structure of Koryŏ was so built around the Three Chancelleries (*Samsŏng*) that it may be called the "threefold chancellery system." The names given these (*Chungsŏsŏng*, *Munhasŏng*, and *Sangsŏsŏng*) appear to have had little relation to the functions each performed, and the first two, in reality, merged into a single organ called the Chancellery for State Affairs (*Chungsŏmunhasŏng*), or the Directorate of Chancellors (*Chaebu*). The officials of the Directorate of Chancellors consisted of directors holding rank two or above who made policy decisions, and undersecretaries of rank three or below who were entrusted with the functions of proposing policy and acting as policy critics, that is as censors. In contrast, the third chancellery (*Sangsŏsŏng*, or Secretariat for State Affairs) was responsible for carrying out policy through the Six Boards subordinated to it that handled actual government administration. These were Personnel, Military Affairs, Taxation, Punishments, Rites, and Public Works. Personnel managed personnel matters for civil offices; Military Affairs handled personnel matters for military offices, other military affairs, and postal stations; Taxation administered the census and tax collections; Punishments dealt with statute law and litigation; Rites was responsible for the conduct of ceremonies, foreign relations, government schools, and the state examinations; and Public Works had charge of the state's woodlands and fishing ponds, the output of artisans at government workshops, and general construction activities.

Another major organ of Koryŏ's central government, ranking in importance with the Three Chancelleries, was the Royal Secretariat (*Chungch'uwŏn*, later called the *Ch'umirwŏn*). Sometimes referred to as the Directorate of Advisers (*Ch'ubu*), the Royal Secretariat was established in Sŏngjong's reign and its duties were not only the transmission of royal commands but also the handling of urgent military matters.

The Directorate of Chancellors and Directorate of Advisers (Royal Secretariat) in turn were known by the single terms Two Directorates (*Yangbu*) or Privy Council (*Chaech'u*), and the joint sessions of their highest officers, at which matters of grave national import were decided, were called "Convenings of the Privy Council," or *Todang*. The existence of such a conciliar organ for considering overall state policy well reveals one important characteristic of Koryŏ aristocratic government.

Outside the Two Directorates was the Censorate (*Ŏsadae*, later *Sahŏnbu*), with the important duties of evaluating administrative performance and censuring the wrongdoing of officials. The Censorate and the undersecretaries in the Directorate of Chancellors together were known as the Surveillance Chancellery (*Taesŏng*), and by virtue of its mandate to scrutinize appointments of officials and propose changes in statutes (called *sŏgyŏng*), this key organ exerted a significant restraint on autocratic exercise of royal power.

As for the countryside, the establishment of twelve provinces (*mok*) in 983 marked the beginning of the dispatch of officials from the capital to administer local government. After a number of further changes, the restructuring of local government reached a definitive stage in the ninth year of Hyŏnjong, 1018. At this point the whole country was divided into a capital region (*kyŏnggi*), large circuits (*to*), and border regions (*kye*), and within these were established three capitals, five regional military commands (*tohobu*), and eight provinces (*mok*), with further subdivisions into districts (*kun*), counties (*hyŏn*), and garrisons (*chin*). The number of circuits, the primary administrative division for the country as a whole, was increased or reduced at various times, but in the end the number was set at five (Yanggwang, Kyŏngsang, Chŏlla, Kyoju, and Sŏhae). Along with these, two border districts, the Northern (or Western) Border Region (Pukkye, or Sŏgye) and the Eastern Border Region (Tonggye) were established along Koryŏ's northern boundary and the northeast littoral, and these were special military zones [see map p. 115]. Accordingly, the

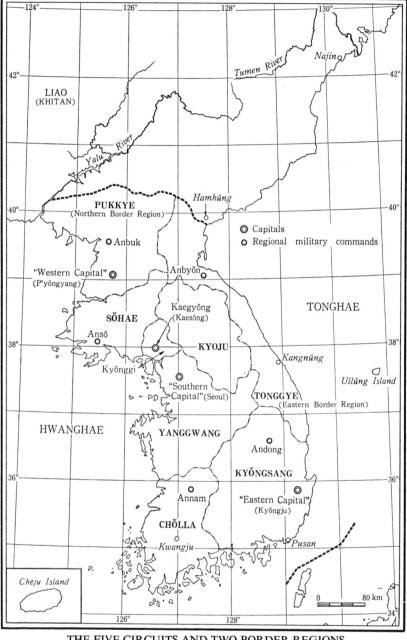

- ◎ Capitals
- ○ Regional military commands

LIAO
(KHITAN)

Tumen River

Najin

Yalu River

PUKKYE
(Northern Border Region)

Hamhŭng

○ Anbuk

"Western Capital" ◎
(P'yŏngyang)

Anbyŏn ○

Kaegyŏng
(Kaesŏng)

SŎHAE

TONGHAE

Ansŏ ○

KYOJU

Kangnŭng ○

Kyŏnggi

Ullŭng Island

◎
"Southern
Capital"(Seoul)

TONGGYE
(Eastern Border Region)

HWANGHAE

YANGGWANG

○
Andong

KYŎNGSANG

○
Annam

◎
"Eastern Capital"
(Kyŏngju)

CHŎLLA

Kwangju

Pusan

Cheju Island

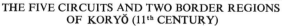

0   80 km

THE FIVE CIRCUITS AND TWO BORDER REGIONS
OF KORYŎ (11ᵗʰ CENTURY)

military commanders (*pyŏngmasa*) appointed to head the border regions were charged with different duties than the superintendents (*anch'alsa*) of the circuits. The border regions and circuits also differed in that districts and counties were established in the latter, whereas the border regions were subdivided principally into garrisons.

The location of the three capitals was closely related to geomantic theories. At first they were situated at Kaesŏng (the main capital), at P'yŏngyang (the western capital), and at Kyŏngju (the eastern capital); subsequently a "southern capital" at Seoul replaced Kyŏngju as one of the three capitals. The five regional military commands were located at Andong, Annam, Ansŏ, Anbuk, and Anbyŏn [see map p. 115]. As the names themselves suggest, the principle was to situate these at the four compass points (the vulnerable northern frontier, however, required two), and entrust them with the pivotal role in the military defense of the realm.

Central government officials were dispatched to head all of the above provincial and local administrative units. These officials could not be appointed to head their own home districts and their terms of office were fixed. This is because the central government feared the growth of regional power centers. Under these officials dispatched from the capital, however, were local headmen (*hojang*) and other petty functionaries, and it was these who were charged with performing administrative tasks involving direct contact with the population at large. Originally of local gentry background, these petty functionaries constituted the elite stratum of local society, and since they were more knowledgeable about conditions in their own home areas than the centrally appointed officials, who were transferred after short terms in office, the influence they exerted was tremendous. In order to check their power, central government officials who had come from a particular locality were sent as inspector-general (*sasimgwan*) to their home districts, and in addition a kind of hostage (*kiin*) system was developed that required young male members of local influential families to be assigned to duties in the capital. Finally, the district, county, and garrison administrative units were made up of villages (*ch'on*) headed by village chiefs, and these played an intermediate role in governing the village people.

Military Organization

Koryŏ had emerged in a setting of military conflict, had had to use military might to destroy its powerful Later Paekche foe, and had already experienced numerous military clashes with the Khitan in the north. Understandably, then, Koryŏ devoted considerable attention to problems of military organization. T'aejo Wang Kŏn himself had marched at the head of a powerful army which drew on the military strength of the Kaesŏng region, and this was the core force in the unification of the Later Three Kingdoms. This army, which had been under T'aejo's personal command, became the nucleus of the Two Guards and Six Divisions into which the forces of the central government were organized. The term Six Divisions refers to the Division of the Left and Right (*Chwauwi*), Divine Tiger Division (*Sinhowi*), Elite Striking Division (*Hŭngwiwi*), Internal Security Division (*Kŭmowi*), Thousand Bull Division (*Ch'ŏnuwi*), and Capital Guards Division (*Kammunwi*), and it is thought that the formation of these took place under King Sŏngjong around 995. The first three of these Six Divisions constituted the core of the nation's combat forces, and they were charged not only with defense of the capital but with guarding the frontiers as well. The Internal Security Division, on the other hand, exercised police powers in the capital, the Thousand Bull Division was used for state ceremonies, and the Capital Guards Division stood guard at the palace and city gates and government buildings. The Two Guards units, the Soaring Falcon Guards and Dragon-Tiger Guards, were formed later and, as the king's personal bodyguards, ranked above the Six Divisions.

Each of the Two Guards and Six Divisions had a general (*sangjanggun*) and lieutenant general (*taejanggun*) as its commander and deputy commander. These generals and lieutenant generals, who held the highest positions among military officers, had their own joint deliberative organ called the Council of Generals (*Chungbang*), a counterpart to the Privy Council (*Todang*) of the civil officials. In a Koryŏ dominated by civil officials, however, the power of the *Chungbang* was in no way commensurate with that of the Privy Council. The Two Guards and Six Divisions were composed of regiments of 1,000 soldiers each. The regiments were classified into infantry, cavalry, prison guards, army ceremonial, naval ceremonial, and gate guard regiments, there being a total of forty-five regiments in all. The commanding officer of a regiment was a commander and all the commanders also met in a joint deliberative body called the Council of Commanders (*Changgunbang*).

The rank and file of the Two Guards and Six Divisions were professional military men from families belonging to the soldiering order, whose social status and military service obligation were hereditary, and they were separately recorded in a military census roster as military householders. The state granted them "soldier's land" (*kuninjŏn*) and assigned two "supporting households" to cultivate it, thus providing for the soldier's livelihood and equipment expenses. When the number of soldiers fell below strength a recruitment was held, and those selected to fill the ranks were enrolled as military householders and given an allocation of soldier's land. The military recruitment system normally sought out young and vigorous men from among the *paekchŏng* peasantry. However, *ch'ŏnmin* (lowborn) also might be selected, and this is one reason for the decline in the social status of the soldiers.

Although at first the private forces of the gentry in the countryside were brought together into the so-called Resplendent Army (*Kwanggun*) and were placed under the control of the central government (in 947), later these were reorganized into provincial garrison forces. The provincial forces stationed in the border regions differed from those in the circuits. In the border regions, since these were military zones along the frontier, regular army forces were stationed in each garrison (*chin*) administrative unit. These forces, which might well be called frontier garrisons, were built around an assault group supported by flanking forces of the left and right. This then was a force at the ready, on permanent station, one that could do battle the moment an incident broke out. On the other hand, the provincial armies in the circuits were composed of units that undertook police (*posŭnggun*), local militia (*chŏngyonggun*), and labor battalion (*ilp'umgun*) functions.

Civil Service Examinations and Protected Appointments

The civil service examinations that served as a basis for appointment to office were of three basic types: the *chesul ŏp* or Composition Examination course, the *myŏnggyŏng ŏp* or Classics Examination course and the *chap ŏp* or Miscellaneous Examination course. The *chesul* selected candidates on the basis of their ability to compose in set Chinese literary forms such as *shih* poetry, rhyme prose (*fu*), sacrificial ode (*sung*), and the problem-essay (*ts'e*), while the *myŏnggyŏng* examined knowledge of such Confucian canonical works as the *Book of History*, *Classic of Changes*, *Classic of Songs*, and *Spring and Autumn Annals*. Both these were conducted for the purpose of selecting civil officials, but the literary composition examination was regarded as especially important. This can be seen in the fact that during the Koryŏ dynasty over 6,000 men passed the composition examination while scarcely 450 passed the classics examination. Clearly the aristocratic class of this era esteemed literary accomplishment more than knowledge of the Confucian classics.

In contrast, the so-called miscellaneous examinations were held to select specialists to serve in capacities demanding technical knowledge, principally in statute law, accounting, medicine, divination, and geomancy. The standing of these examinations, therefore, was lower than that of the literary composition and classics examinations. Moreover, since state examinations for the selection of military officials first came into being in King Kongyang's reign at the very end of the dynasty, it is not really incorrect to say that there was no military examination in the Koryŏ period.

In Koryŏ, if a man were but freeborn (a *yangin*), he was qualified to sit for the examinations, while *ch'ŏnmin* (lowborn) and the children of monks were ineligible. In reality, however, it was virtually impossible for the general peasant population, despite their freeborn status, to take the examinations. The official in charge of an examination was called a *chigonggŏ*, and it was considered a great honor to be named to this duty. The examination officer and the successful candidates formed a master-disciple relationship, behaving toward each other much as would father and son. This relationship was for life and indeed social groupings based on it came into existence. Such groups constituted a support force for the advancement of their members in the government.

Under the bone-rank system in Silla the criterion for official appointment was social class, and thus no great need was felt for an examination system by which to select officials. In Koryŏ, however, the members of the many hereditary aristocratic houses, all of whom possessed privileged social status, all were entitled to participate in political life. Not only this, but a way was opened for those of local functionary background also to advance into the central bureaucracy and to enter the ranks of the aristocracy. In other words, to a degree that stands out in sharp contrast with the Silla period, it was possible for large numbers of men to become government officials in Koryŏ. This made necessary a new method of selecting personnel, namely the state civil service examination. These examinations, so very attractive to the petty functionaries in the countryside, also provided an avenue for members of all the hereditary aristocratic families to participate in government. It was thus a system of bureaucratic recruitment that secured advantage to both these segments of the ruling class.

Nevertheless, the civil service examination system in Koryŏ was not the only mechanism used for selecting officials. This is because the aristocratic society of Koryŏ had not yet achieved the broader social base that characterized the *yangban* aristocratic society of the subsequent Yi dynasty. The hereditary aristocratic families of Koryŏ additionally wanted to have a recruitment system that would preserve their position of special privilege. The protected appointment system (*ŭmsŏ*) accomplished this. This was a provision enabling one son of an official of the fifth rank or above to receive an official appointment; that is, if a man but became a middle-rank official, then one of his sons automatically could enter the officialdom. This tells us that, after all, the bureaucratic system of Koryŏ was undergirded by strong aristocratic institutions. Implicit here too is the fact that Koryŏ's was an aristocratic society that respected hereditary privilege. As in the case of the Inju Yi clan, the protected appointment system also came to be abused by houses that, once having seized power, used it as an instrument for the aggrandizement of their own special position.

Educational Institutions

In T'aejo's reign schools already existed in Kaesŏng and P'yŏngyang, but it was with the establishment of the National University (*Kukchagam*) in 992 under Sŏngjong that the foundation was laid for Koryŏ's educational system. In this respect like a modern university, Koryŏ's *Kukchagam* contained a number of colleges within it, namely the so-called Six Colleges of the Capital—University College (*Kukchahak*), High College (*T'aehak*), Four Portals College (*Samunhak*), Law College (*Yurhak*), Calligraphy College (*Sŏhak*), and Accounting College (*Sanhak*), institutions created during Injong's reign (1122–1146). Although all were separate colleges, it was not a case of each offering a distinctive curriculum. University College, High College, and Four Portals College all were places to study, principally, the sources of the Chinese tradition, such as the Five Classics, the *Classic of Filial Piety*, and the *Analects*. Their difference lay in the different entrance requirements for their students: University College admitted the sons of military or civilian officials of the third rank or higher, High College the sons of fourth and fifth rank officials, and Four Portals the sons of officials of ranks six and seven. Finally, sons of eighth and ninth rank officials, as well as of commoners, were admitted to the Law College, the College of Calligraphy, or the College of Accounting to study one of these technical specialties. The stipulation of such entrance qualifications offers still another insight into the status consciousness of Koryŏ's aristocratic society.

Local educational facilities had not yet been organized by Sŏngjong's reign (981–987). In his zeal for spreading education to the countryside, however, Sŏngjong at first brought youth from the local areas to study in the capital, and when his program failed, he sent scholars of the Classics, of medicine, and of other subjects to the countryside to teach. Under Injong, then, along with the establishment of the Six Colleges of the Capital, schools were set up in rural areas to educate local youth. Insomuch as one objective of the civil service examination system was to absorb men of local gentry background into the central bureaucratic structure and transform them into members of the capital aristocracy, it was natural for the government to display this enthusiasm for local education.

3. Aristocratic Society and the Economic Structure

The Land System

The so-called Stipend Land Law (*chŏnsikwa*) occupied a central position in the Koryŏ land system. The Stipend Land Law evolved from the *yŏkpunjŏn* system of 940, which had allocated grants of land as rewards for merit following the reunification. Although the term *chŏnsikwa* was first used in 976, at that time it still retained the character of land grants to a privileged few. Finally in 998, the first year of King Mokchong, a comprehensive system was instituted, allocating land in eighteen stipend grades based on the office rank structure created three years earlier under Sŏngjong. The land allocated to an official in accordance with the provisions of the Stipend Land Law thus constituted his salary. Consequently, when an official died the allocated land was to be returned to the state. Furthermore, the collection of land rents was managed by the state and direct collection by officials was not permitted. The Stipend Land Law also provided for "soldier's land" (*kuninjŏn*) to be given to those peasant families enrolled in the soldiering order.

Besides such stipend land, so-called privileged merit land (*kongŭm-*

jŏn) also was an important form of remuneration for higher officials. This generally was given in graded amounts to those of the fifth rank or above as grants in perpetuity (*yŏngŏpchŏn*), and it thus could be bequeathed to one's descendants. Accordingly, it might also be disposed of at will. *Kongŭmjŏn* was cultivated by tenant farmers and the grantee collected the rent on his own authority. Thus this land in effect was privately owned, and it may be said to have provided firmer support for aristocratic class status than did office holding itself. Like enabling sons of fifth and higher rank officials automatically to obtain appointments, the purpose of *kongŭmjŏn* was to help perpetuate the privileged position of the high aristocracy.

Allocations of land to local government functionaries (*hyangni*) and to soldiers also were significant. The former were given "local service land" (*oeyŏkchŏn*) to compensate them for the duties they undertook. And just as their services were a hereditary responsibility, so was this land inheritable and thus may be termed land granted in perpetuity. Since they were able to collect the rents themselves, moreover, this land too was tantamount to private land. "Soldier's land" (*kuninjŏn*) was land given in compensation for military service. Although the regulations governing allocation of soldier's land were incorporated into the Stipend Land Law, it was different in character from stipend land. It was inheritable, since the military service obligation was hereditary, and "support households" were attached to each soldier to cultivate his land. However, if a soldier had no son or grandson to carry on his obligations when he retired from active service, he was made to return his soldier's land and was given instead a modest pension land allocation (*kubunjŏn*) for his support. Such pension land also was given to families of officials and deceased soldiers, including war widows, who had no means of livelihood.

In addition there was "royal estate land" (*naejangjŏn*) that belonged to the palace; although in effect privately held by the royal household, this land had the peculiarity of being managed through special administrative districts. Finally, "public agency land" (*konghaejŏn*) was allotted to cover the expenses of government offices, and there were lands owned by the monasteries or temples.

Economic Underpinning of the Aristocratic Class

The Koryŏ land system reflected the underlying premise that all land in the country was the king's land. This was an extremely idealistic concept, however, and it did not mean that all land was owned by the state. To be sure, there was "public land" (*kongjŏn*) that the state directly managed. The rents from this land were transported to Kaesŏng by ship and were used for public expenditures, the foremost of which was official salaries. Although the income from stipend land went to individual officials, since the state collected the rents for them and since the land reverted to the state when officials died, it too may be included in the category of "public land." In other words, this "public" land had the character of providing economic benefits to that key segment of the "public" consisting of the aristocracy as a whole.

In contrast to this, there was "private land" (*sajŏn*) that served the private interests of the individual aristocrat. This is demonstrated most graphically by the "privileged merit land" (*kongŭmjŏn*). Nominally such land was allocated by the state in the same manner as the various kinds of stipendiary land, but in reality the recipient could bequeath it or freely dispose of it, and he could also collect the rents directly. Therefore it was the same as privately owned land, and this is one reason why it also was called *yŏngŏpchŏn* ("land held in perpetuity"). "Local service land" (*oeyŏkchŏn*) and "soldier's land" (*kuninjŏn*) were also *yŏngŏpchŏn*, but these were received as payment for service to the state and so, although they could be passed on to one's descendants, they could not be disposed of otherwise. Monastery and temple lands were not called *yŏngŏpchŏn* but were no different in character. All these varieties of "private land," despite the existence of minor hindrances, in effect were the same as privately owned land.

As the power of the aristocracy grew, "stipend land" like "merit land" came to be inherited, and it turned into private land from which rents were collected directly by the aristocrats. And by such stratagems as reclaiming wasteland, by receiving special grants from the king, or by seizing the land of others by force, the aristocracy increased its holdings of private land still further. The rents from private land, in contrast to the 25% rate on public land, amounted to half the harvest, in accordance with the prevalent crop sharing system. This is why the aristocrats were particularly interested in accumulating private land. Built on a foundation of private landholding, the fortunes of the aristocracy steadily grew fatter.

The aristocracy used its wealth to reap still greater profits. They built granaries to store their share of the harvest, then profited by lending grain at high interest. Such granaries were operated not only by individual aristocrats, but by the state and the monasteries as well. There were also so-called endowments (*po*) that profited from the interest on grain loans. These were of many varieties, in accordance with the purpose they served. Some were established to provide support for Confucian students or for monks to study, while others provided for relief of the poor or were established to cover the expenses of the *p'algwanhoe* festivals.

Both grain and cloth were used in these profit-making activities. Because commerce in general had not developed significantly, there was not a great need for currency. Coins were minted in Sŏngjong's reign, in 996, and under Sukchong in 1102 the copper coins known as *Haedong t'ongbo* ("circulating treasure of Korea") were made, but these did not come into widespread use. However, silver vases (*hwalgu*) made about this same time in the shape of the Korean peninsula and containing one *kŭn* (600 grams as a modern weight) of silver were much used among the aristocracy for large-scale transactions or as bribes.

Life of the People

Koryŏ was built on an agricultural economy, and those who directly tilled the land, the peasantry, formed the foundation of the society. The freeborn farmers who made up the majority of the peasantry were commonly called *paekchŏng*, a name reflecting the fact that they lacked any fixed role in the service of the state. Accordingly, they were not eligible to receive a land allowance from the state. They cultivated land commonly known as "people's land" (*minjŏn*), a sub-category of public land, and this meant that they paid one fourth of the harvest as rent to the state. They also tilled the private lands of the aristocracy, and since the rent in this case was one half the yield, their obligation was that much greater. Not only did the peasantry pay these rents, but a tribute tax paid in cloth usually was imposed upon them as well. In some cases this was levied on special products of an area, such as fruit or hempen cloth. Furthermore, adult males from the age of 16 to 60 were liable for corvee labor duty, and they were mobilized for all sorts of construction projects. They had to provide their own food while performing labor service, and for that reason there were instances of poor people working from morning to night without sustenance.

Treated even worse than the freeborn peasantry were those living in such special administrative districts as *hyang*, *pugok*, *so*, *yŏk*, *chin*, and *kwan*. In contrast to the *hyang* and *pugok*, which were restricted residence areas for lowborn people assigned to farm labor, the *so* generally were concentrations of laborers who mined and worked with gold, silver, copper, or iron, or who made silk, paper, or pottery. Although the *yŏk* (post station) and *chin* (ferry) were transportation facilities established at important land and sea routes, and the *kwan* (hostelry) were inns for overnight travelers, all those who served in these establishments possessed a lower social status than commoners. It should be noted that the existence of these special aggregations of people was a legacy inherited from Silla, and that gradually their distinctive character disappeared as they were merged with the freeborn population.

At the very bottom of the society was the slave class. There were government slaves belonging to the state and private slaves belonging to individuals. The task of government slaves was to perform various duties in the palace and government offices, but they were also allocated to civilian and military officials as their personal attendants. Private slaves belonged to members of the royal household, the aristocracy, and to temples, and they worked at such household chores as cooking and gathering firewood. They of course inherited their slave status and could be bought or sold. Besides these household slaves, there were out-resident slaves who cultivated their master's lands in the countryside. However, these out-resident slaves possessed their own personal property and only paid rents to their masters, so that actually their situation was much like that of the tenant farmers. The tendency was for the number of these out-resident slaves to gradually increase, but at the same time a new feature of Koryŏ society appeared as some of them accumulated property and were able to rise in class status to become commoners. On the other hand, there were outcasts, those such as butchers and wicker workers (*hwach'ŏk* or *yangsuch'ŏk*, the *paekchŏng* of the Yi dynasty) or entertainers (*chaein*, the *kwangdae* of the Yi dynasty) whose occupations were despised, with the consequence that they were treated socially as slaves.

The freeborn peasantry and the others directly involved in the production of wealth generally led lives of poverty. Their hardship forced many to abscond, and this had repercussions on the economic foundations of the country. It was necessary, therefore, for the government to develop a social policy to deal with this situation, to include at least minimal relief programs. Among the relief mechanisms Koryŏ employed were these: a special endowment, called *Chewibo*, that used certain commodities as capital and applied the interest to poor relief; the East and West Infirmaries that cared for the indigent sick; the *Hyemin'guk* that functioned as a public dispensary; and a network of storehouses, such as "righteous granaries" (*ŭich'ang*) that stored grain in normal times for public relief in years of poor harvests, and Ever Normal Storehouses (*sangp'yŏngch'ang*) that served to smooth out fluctuations in commodity prices. There are also many examples of Buddhist establishments functioning as relief agencies, and at such monasteries as Kaeguk-sa in Kaesŏng and Pot'ong-wŏn at the Imjin ferry, bands of itinerant beggars were fed in mess halls. But this was a social policy of temporary expedients; it did not constitute a solidly based program of poverty relief.

4. Foreign Relations

Struggle with the Khitan

Contact with the Khitan started from T'aejo's reign. Not many years after the Khitan overthrew Parhae in 926 and so came to share a common border with Koryŏ, they sent an embassy to present fifty camels to the Koryŏ king (942). T'aejo, however, regarded the Khitan as uncivilized and immoral, and he banished the envoys to an island, letting the camels starve to death under the Manbugyo, a bridge in Kaesŏng. At the same time, T'aejo welcomed refugees from Parhae, worked to restore P'yŏngyang, the former Koguryŏ capital, and in other ways too sought to realize his dream of recovering the ancient territories of the Koguryŏ kingdom. In consequence, already in T'aejo's time Koryŏ's boundary line had expanded northward to the Ch'ŏngch'ŏn River.

Later kings continued this northern expansion policy. Chŏngjong (945–949) planned to move the capital to P'yŏngyang and so undertook construction there on a large scale; it also was he who formed the Resplendent Army (*Kwanggun*) to prepare against invasion by the Khitan. From the time of Kwangjong (949–975), then, Koryŏ began to actively push toward the Yalu, establishing numerous garrison forts across the Ch'ŏngch'ŏn River.

It was inevitable that in carrying out this policy of northern expansion Koryŏ would come into conflict with the Khitan. Although Sung China was the original target of their attacks, the Khitan could not rid themselves of misgivings about Koryŏ's intentions. The kingdom of Ting-an (Korean: Chŏngan) had arisen along the middle reaches of the Yalu, founded by Parhae remnants, and, using Jurchen (a proto-Manchu people of eastern Manchuria) envoys to communicate with Sung China via the sea route, Ting-an had taken a hostile stance toward the Khitan. This gave further provocation to the Khitan, and before long the situation erupted in a Khitan invasion of Koryŏ.

In 991 the Khitan built a fort at Naewŏn-sŏng on the lower Yalu River and so severed communications between the Jurchen and Sung China, and in 993 they sent an invasion force across the Yalu under Hsiao Sun-ning. This time, however, through the diplomatic maneuvers of Sŏ Hŭi, Koryŏ was able to overcome the crisis. Sŏ Hŭi not only managed to persuade Hsiao's forces to make a voluntary withdrawal, but he also obtained Khitan consent to incorporate the area up to the Yalu into Koryŏ territory. This came about because the Khitan were unable to bring their full strength to bear on Koryŏ, since they were engaged at this time in a struggle with Sung China. Consequently, the Khitan were forced to be satisfied with a Koryŏ promise to enter into friendly relations once the Jurchen lands south of the Yalu had come into Koryŏ's possession, thus opening a land link between them. Nor could the Khitan deny Sŏ Hŭi's assertion that Koryŏ was the successor to Koguryŏ and thus might lay claim to the Manchurian territories formerly under Koguryŏ dominion. The success of Sŏ Hŭi's dazzling diplomatic maneuver doubtless owed much to his correct assessment of the international situation and of Koryŏ's position therein. After the Khitan army withdrew, Koryŏ set about building a number of fortresses in the area southeast of the Yalu, and the so-called Six Garrison Settlements East of the River that became an issue later on were constructed as part of this process. This term refers to garrison forts at modern Ŭiju, Yŏngch'ŏn, Sŏnch'ŏn, Ch'ŏlsan, Kusŏng, and Kwaksan [see map p. 127].

Not long after this, the Khitan expressed their unhappiness with Koryŏ's control over the area southeast of the Yalu and demanded that Koryŏ turn over the Six Garrison Settlements. In fact, the Khitan had become alarmed by the growing strength of the forces Koryŏ was stationing in this border area. But of course Koryŏ rejected this demand. At this point the Khitan took advantage of a period of political turbulence in Koryŏ to launch a second invasion under the personal command of the Khitan emperor, Sheng Tsung. This was the time when Kang Cho, the powerful military commander of the northwest frontier region, had deposed King Mokchong, eliminated the rival Kim Ch'i-yang faction, and enthroned Hyŏnjong (1009–1031). But Kang Cho underestimated the enemy's strength and was defeated, captured, and killed. He had refused to the end to vow allegiance to the Khitan emperor and so died a hero's death. Now the Khitan army occupied Kaesŏng, while King Hyŏnjong fled south, all the way to Naju. Fearing that their supply lines might be cut, however, the Khitan withdrew without gaining any particular advantage, stipulating the sole condition that the Koryŏ king pay homage in person at the Khitan court. This of course was not a commitment Koryŏ willingly would honor, and accordingly such a royal journey never was undertaken.

Subsequently the Khitan launched several small-scale attacks, to press demands for Hyŏnjong's appearance at their court and surrender of the region of the Six Garrison Settlements, before mounting their third great invasion in 1018. Led by Hsiao P'ai-ya, this time the Khitan army was harassed at every turn and then, retreating, was all but annihilated by a massive Koryŏ attack at Kuju (Kusŏng) executed by Kang Kam-ch'an. The Koryŏ victory was so overwhelming that scarcely a few thousand of the 100,000 man invasion force survived. The Khitan invasions of Koryŏ thus ended in failure. Koryŏ had resolutely resisted foreign aggression and had driven the invaders back. The result was that the two nations worked out a settlement and peaceful relations were maintained between them thereafter.

Campaigns against the Jurchen and Relations with Chin

About the time peace was worked out with the Khitan, Koryŏ began to be troubled by the Jurchen. The long wall stretching from the mouth of the Yalu a thousand *li* eastward to the sea at Toryŏnp'o (modern Yŏnp'o), laboriously built over a twelve year period from 1033 to 1044, was intended for defense not only against the Khitan but also against the Jurchen.

The Jurchen had been under Parhae rule, but after Parhae perished they had looked upon Koryŏ and the Khitan as suzerain powers. They had not yet achieved a level of societal development that would enable them to create their own state entity. Therefore, because of its advanced culture, they looked upon Koryŏ in particular as their "parent country" and as the source of the trappings of civilization they so desired to acquire. It was Koryŏ, then, that supplied their needs for grain, cloth, iron agricultural implements, and iron weapons, for which they exchanged horses and furs. There were many Jurchen who remained in their original places of abode and yet put their trust in Koryŏ, while still others migrated into the Koryŏ domain. To these Koryŏ gave land and dwellings, thus furnishing them with the means to maintain their livelihood.

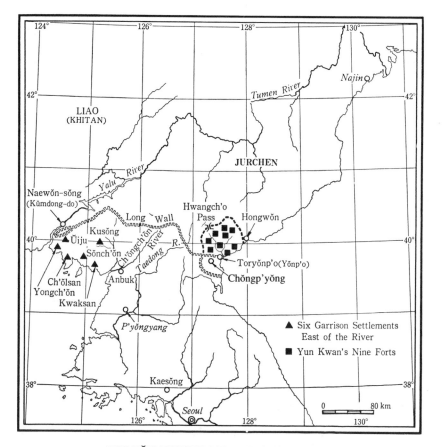

KORYŎ'S NORTHERN FRONTIER REGION
(LATE 10ᵗʰ TO EARLY 12ᵗʰ CENTURIES)

The situation changed, however, when a new urge toward unification of all the Jurchen crystallized under the leadership of Ukkonae, the chieftain of the Wan-yen tribe in northern Manchuria. As the power of the Wanyen tribe extended even to the Jurchen who had submitted to Koryŏ, the relationship between the two became increasingly stormy. On several occasions there were military clashes, but the Koryŏ standing army, the Six Divisions, had deteriorated and moreover consisted mostly of infantry, so that the usual outcome was defeat by the mounted Jurchen. It was for this reason that King Sukchong created a new military organization called the Extraordinary Military Corps (*Pyŏlmuban*). It appears to have taken its name from the fact that it was a special military organization existing apart from the Six Divisions, the regular army, and it was made up of a cavalry corps (*Sin'gigun*), an infantry (*Sinbogun*), and a so-called *Hangmagun*

("Subdue Demons Corps"). The cavalry and infantry corps were formed around members of aristocratic families and the freeborn peasantry (*paek-chŏng*), respectively, while Buddhist monks were enlisted into the *Hang-magun*. They trained year-round, preparing for a massive assault against the Jurchen.

Such an assault was carried out by Yun Kwan in 1107. Crossing the pass at modern Chŏngp'yŏng, he occupied the Hamhŭng plain as far north as Hongwŏn, a region hitherto inhabited by Jurchen tribesmen. In the occupied area he constructed the so-called Nine Forts [see map p. 127] and garrisoned them for defense. However, unceasing Jurchen attacks alternating with diplomatic appeals, as well as jealousy in the Koryŏ court of Yun Kwan's success, led ultimately to the return of the region of the Nine Forts to the Jurchen.

Later Ukkonae's younger brother A-ku-ta united the Jurchen and succeeded in founding a state, called Chin, in 1115. Chin not only overran the Khitan Liao dynasty in 1125 but also captured the Sung capital at Kai-feng and took prisoner the Sung emperor and his father, who had reigned before him (1127). In the course of these events Chin put increased pressure on Koryŏ as well, and finally demanded that Koryŏ enter into a suzerain-subject relationship. There were many in Koryŏ who were outraged at this, calling it an insolent demand. Nevertheless, Yi Cha-gyŏm, in power at the time, judged that peaceful relations with the continent would contribute to maintaining his own political dominance, and so he assented to Chin's demands. As a result there was no military invasion of Koryŏ by the Chin dynasty.

Relations with Sung China

From the beginning Koryŏ admired the advanced civilization of Sung China and so sought to satisfy its material and cultural wants by maintaining a harmonious relationship with Sung. Thus, through the visits of official embassies and the travels of private merchants, Koryŏ exported such raw materials as gold, silver, copper, ginseng, and pine nuts, and hand-crafted items favored by the Sung people such as paper, brushes, ink, and fans, in return importing silk, books, porcelain, medicines, spices, and musical instruments. These imports had a significant impact on Koryŏ's culture. For example, Sung woodblock editions contributed to the development of Koryŏ woodblock printing and Sung porcelain to the development of Koryŏ celadon ware. Thus the relationship between the two countries rested on a peaceful foundation of cultural and economic exchange, and this was precisely in conformity with the desires of the Koryŏ aristocracy.

As the military pressures exerted by the Khitan (Liao) and Chin mounted, however, Koryŏ-Sung relations required a delicate readjustment. This is because Sung hoped to attack the Khitan and Chin from both sides, in alliance with Koryŏ. Koryŏ, however, was unwilling to provoke the Khitan or Chin by any action not strictly necessary, and so Koryŏ did not accede to the Sung demands. After the two Sung emperors were taken prisoner by Chin and Sung retreated south of the Yangtze River, Sung asked Koryŏ to intercede to secure the release of the two emperors, but Koryŏ refused again to help. Koryŏ had understood the thrust of events on the continent and so was determined to remain aloof from the confrontation between Chin and Sung.

In this situation, Koryŏ and Sung even suspended for a time their exchange of envoys. In general, however, the trade relationship carried on through the travels of merchants, and the exchange of envoys as well, continued as before. Moreover, even Arab ships that so busily plied their trade with Sung entered Yesŏng harbor, the port for Kaesŏng, bringing mercury, spices, and medicines. Thus Yesŏng harbor came to flourish at that time as an international commercial port.

5. Aristocratic Culture

Confucianism and Private Academies

In a state committed to the principle of rule by civil officials in accordance with Confucian political ideals, it was natural that Confucianism prospered. Confucian political ideology rejects the Buddhist doctrine of reward for good works and takes as its ideal a centralized state governed by an elite whose rule is sanctioned by a morality grounded not in religious belief, but in a rational view of the universe and man's place within it. This political vision gradually received wide support among the Koryŏ aristocracy. The result was that Confucianism, which had had little appeal in comparison with Buddhism in the Silla era just past, would develop to the point where it someday would be able to suppress Buddhism as an institutionalized religion.

Now in Koryŏ society the importance attached to aristocratic pedigree in turn acted to modify certain features of Confucian doctrine. One consequence of this can be seen in the new phenomenon of the rise of private academies as the principal agencies for the education of aristocratic youth. In Munjong's reign (1046–1083) the great Confucian scholar Ch'oe Ch'ung, known as the Confucius of Korea, established a school (the "Nine Course Academy") at which lectures were given in nine specialized areas of study; this was known as Master Ch'oe's Assembly and it marked the beginning of the private academies. Master Ch'oe's Assembly was the precursor of a dozen such private academies that sprang up around that time, and these were known as the Twelve Assemblies (*Sibi to*). Just as Ch'oe Ch'ung had held the top government post of chancellor, most of the men who founded the Twelve Assemblies were former high officials and many were eminent scholars of the day who had officiated at the state examinations. These circumstances, together with the emphasis placed on lineage background, created a tendency among the sons of aristocratic families to consider it a greater honor to attend one of these twelve private academies than the government's National University (*Kukchagam*). Consequently, it seems, the notion of a new lineage orientation, one's academic line of descent, came to exert a hold on the Koryŏ aristocratic mind.

The flourishing of private academies of course brought on the decline of the state schools. Concerned over this, a succession of kings attempted to breathe new life into the state system. First Yejong (1103–1122), in imitation of Ch'oe Ch'ung's Nine Course Academy, established lectures in seven specialized fields: *Classic of Changes, Book of History, Classic of Songs, Rituals of Chou, Book of Rites, Spring and Autumn Annals,* and a new field of military studies, appointing to lectureships outstanding scholars in each field. He also set up a type of scholarship foundation called the Fund for Nurturing Worthies (*Yanghyŏn'go*) and established academic institutes on the palace grounds, the Ch'ŏngyŏn Pavilion and the Pomun Pavilion, recruiting scholars and collecting books for study of the classics and history. Injong (1122–1146), Yejong's successor, continued this effort by establishing the Six Colleges of the Capital and local schools as well, thus completing the creation of Koryŏ's government school system. From these institutions a succession of eminent scholars like Kim In-jon, Kim Pu-sik, Yun Ŏn-i, and Chŏng Chi-sang emerged.

The development of Confucianism brought with it a mode of thought that favored a rational approach to the problems of human society. Confucianism was looked upon as the orthodox doctrine by which to order family relationships and to govern the state, and both the monarch and the aristocracy came to regard it as vital to the moral cultivation of political leaders. Kim Pu-sik's *History of the Three Kingdoms* (*Samguk sagi*) indeed was compiled from this perspective. The oldest Korean history extant, the *Samguk sagi* is an orthodox Confucianist history, compiled in annalistic form. However, just as Korean values imposed constraints on the operation of the Koryŏ state examination system, so were there limitations to the Koryŏ aristocracy's conversion to Confucian rationalism. Koryŏ Confucians by no means completely rejected Buddhism; instead, regarding it as the doctrine for achieving spiritual tranquility and otherworldly salvation, they felt that it could exist side by side with Confucianism. Accordingly, many men were versed in both, and in this respect they differed from the Confucian scholars of late Koryŏ and the Yi dynasty.

The Buddhist Tripitaka and the Ch'ŏnt'ae Sect

Koryŏ Buddhism achieved a systematization with the woodblock printing of the Tripitaka, the Buddhist canon, as rendered in Chinese translations. The carving of the Tripitaka commenced in the early years of Hyŏnjong's reign (1009–1031) and was not completed until 1087. The printing of the Tripitaka originally was undertaken as a kind of prayer to bring a halt to the Khitan invasions. However, beyond that objective, the printing of the Tripitaka must be seen as motivated also by the intention to systematize the doctrines of the Buddhist scriptures. The woodblocks for this printing, which were stored at Taegu's Puin-sa temple, were destroyed in the thirteenth century Mongol invasions, and the so-called *Koryŏ Tripitaka* that remains today at Haein-sa temple represents a new edition begun on Kanghwa Island, where the court had taken refuge from the Mongol scourge, and completed in 1251. The *Koryŏ Tripitaka*, despite being done under wartime conditions, is regarded as the finest among some twenty versions of the Tripitaka originating in East Asia, in terms of its accuracy, the beauty of the calligraphic style, and the exquisite carving of the woodblocks. Meanwhile the monk Ŭich'ŏn (1055–1101) established the Directorate for Buddhist Scriptures and published treatises and commentaries found in Sung, Liao, and Japan, as well as in Koryŏ. This was the *Supplement to the Tripitaka* (*Sok changgyŏng*), and although not all of it is extant, its contents can be surmised from the listings of publications in Ŭich'ŏn's other work, the *New Catalogue of Buddhist Sectarian Writings* (*Sinp'yŏn chejong kyojang ch'ongnok*).

The Tripitaka in short was a complete collection of Buddhist scriptures, and its publication in effect systematized the doctrines of the Kyo or Textual School. Even Ŭich'ŏn, who favored the unity of the Textual and Contemplative (Sŏn, i.e., Zen) Schools, failed to include Sŏn-related works in his *Supplement to the Tripitaka*. In spite of this preference of the Koryŏ aristocracy for the Textual School, in a Koryŏ that had developed on a foundation of local gentry support, Sŏn too prospered as before. Thus the Buddhist world of Koryŏ found itself divided into two streams of sectarian belief existing side by side, and disunity and conflict arose from their respective prejudices. The Ch'ŏnt'ae sect took root in Koryŏ as an attempt to reform the Buddhist establishment by resolving these conflicts.

Ch'ŏnt'ae had first been advocated in Kwangjong's reign (949–975) by such figures as Ch'egwan (?–970), author of *Essentials of the Four Stages of Teaching in T'ient'ai* (*Ch'ŏnt'ae sa kyoŭi*). But these Koryŏ monks were active mainly in China rather than in their homeland, and accordingly a Ch'ŏnt'ae sect did not come into existence in Koryŏ at this early period. It was Ŭich'ŏn (also known as Taegak Kuksa), then, who established Ch'ŏnt'ae as an independent sect, and it quickly came to be a major force in the world of Koryŏ Buddhism. Ŭich'ŏn, the fourth son of King Munjong, from an early age had deeply immersed himself in the study of Buddhist scriptures and commentaries, and he also was broadly learned in Confucianism and Taoism. After returning from Sung China in 1086, where he had studied Hwaŏm (Hua-yen) and Ch'ŏnt'ae (T'ien-t'ai), he sought to reform the Koryŏ Buddhist world in which the Textual School (especially the Hwaŏm sect) and Sŏn stood in conflict. Urging the unity of the Textual and Contemplative (Sŏn) Schools, Ŭich'ŏn propagated the Ch'ŏnt'ae doctrine as a faith adherents of both schools might embrace. Although heavily doctrinal, Ch'ŏnt'ae asserted that concentrating one's spiritual energy by ridding the mind of random thoughts, thus to observe the nature of things with correct insight, was the means by which a clear perception of ultimate truth might be achieved. With the acceptance of this teaching, Koryŏ Buddhism entered upon a new phase of development. For in the course of founding the Ch'ŏnt'ae sect Ŭich'ŏn gathered about him outstanding talents from the Nine Mountain Sects of Sŏn and this, together with such other actions as his exclusion of Sŏn literature from his compilation of the *Supplement to the Tripitaka*, aroused the Sŏn sect and gave it a renewed sense of self-awareness and cohesiveness, thus giving rise to the Chogye sect. In this way the Koryŏ Buddhist scene came to take on a new complexion.

Buddhism and Aristocratic Society

Buddhism's impact on everyday life was of greater significance for Koryŏ society than its development as a system of religious belief. The Koryŏ aristocracy continued to regard Buddhism not merely as an otherworldly religion but as a faith that would influence the fortunes of the state and of individuals in the contemporary world. Underlying this attitude was the belief in salvation through good works, a doctrine that promised well-being through the accumulated effect of pious acts. This belief fully explains why Koryŏ constructed so many temples and monasteries and dutifully observed the various Buddhist ceremonies.

T'aejo himself had built many temples, beginning with ten in Kaesŏng, including Pŏbwang-sa ("Temple of the Buddha King"), Wangnyun-sa ("Temple of the Royal Destiny"), and Hŭngguk-sa ("Temple of the Flourishing Kingdom"), and in the first of his *Ten Injunctions* he said:

> The success of the great enterprise of founding our dynasty is entirely owing to the protective powers of the many Buddhas. We therefore must build temples for both Sŏn and Kyo (Textual) Schools and appoint abbots to them, that they may perform the proper ceremonies and themselves cultivate the way.

It can be perceived, therefore, that the founding of temples had not simply a religious meaning. The Hŭngwang-sa temple, extending over 2,800 *kan* (as a modern measure of area about 9,270 square meters) of floor space and completed after twelve years of construction in 1067, is perhaps the most notable example of a temple built with the objective of ensuring dynastic well-being. The proliferation of temples in Koryŏ—there were as many as seventy in Kaesŏng alone—itself conveys a clear picture of Koryŏ as a thoroughly Buddhist state.

Koryŏ also observed a variety of state Buddhist festivals. The largest were the *yŏndŭnghoe* on the fifteenth of the first month and the *p'algwanhoe* on the fifteenth of the eleventh month. Both these festivals combined Buddhist rites with indigenous practices, and in celebrating them the king and his subjects entreated the various Buddhas and the spirits of heaven and earth to bring tranquility to the nation and to the royal house by presenting performances of music, dance, and various entertainments. Besides these there were other annual ceremonies, such as the "prayer for happiness celebration" held on the king's birthday, the "memorial convocation" on the anniversary of the late king's death, the assembly of monks to celebrate Buddha's birthday (eighth day of the fourth month), a ceremony to commemorate the king's oath to seek to attain Bodhisattva-hood (fifteenth day of the sixth month), the "festival for the dead" (prayer offerings for the deliverance of the souls of the deceased, held on the fifteenth day of the seventh month), and a convocation marking the end of the year. There were also "Inwang meetings" to pray for peace in the nation and maigre (vegetarian) feasts for monks, held for the same purpose as the Inwang meetings and in conjunction with them. These fed as many as 100,000 monks at one time, while even larger feasts called "open assemblies" (*much'a taehoe*) were not limited to monks but offered food to all who appeared. As the occasion required other observances took place, such as the freeing of domestic animals and burning of fishing nets in accordance with the Buddhist injunction against killing, and convocations of monks to explicate and recite scriptures. It already has been remarked that the publication of the Tripitaka was undertaken early in the eleventh century with the objective of repelling enemy invasions, and such pious acts as copying sutras with infinite care in gold and silver on dark blue paper in fact were motivated by the desire to supplicate Buddha for the realization of individual wishes. "Scripture processions" of monks reading sutras, or simply displaying them while walking about the streets praying for the fortune of the nation and the blessing of the people, were familiar scenes at that time.

This respect for Buddhism led to the establishment of an examination for its clergy, on the model of the state civil service examination. The "monk examination" was divided into two sections, one for monks of the Textual School and the other for Sŏn monks, and those who passed were given cleric ranks. These graded titles started with Monk Designate (*taesŏn*), while the highest rank for a Textual School monk was Patriarch (*sŭngt'ong*) and for a Sŏn monk, Great Sŏn Mentor (*taesŏnsa*). Higher still than these were the titles Royal Preceptor (*wangsa*) and National Preceptor (*kuksa*), which were considered the greatest honors that monks could achieve. Monks received land allotments from the state and were exempt from corvee labor duties, considerations that contributed to an increase in the number of monks. Many royal princes also entered the clergy, and the fact that members of the royal house and the aristocracy often became monks doubtless had much to do with the wealth possessed by the monasteries.

Monasteries expanded their landholdings through donations from the royal house and aristocracy, through commendation by the peasants, and by outright seizure. Because this land enjoyed the special privilege of tax exemption, the Buddhist establishment grew ever more powerful economically. Using income from their land, monasteries produced still more wealth by setting up Buddhist endowments, relief granaries, and similar agencies for loaning grain at high interest. And they also increased their riches through commerce, wine-making, and raising livestock.

In order to protect their growing wealth the monasteries felt it necessary to use armed might, and so they trained monks as soldiers. The number of armed monks appears to have gradually increased, and they even were used as a military force for national purposes. An outstanding example of this is the Subdue Demons Corps of warrior-monks that was mobilized against the Jurchen invasions. But the phenomenon of monks bearing arms also was related to the power struggles among the aristocracy, and so their influence extended to the political arena as well.

Esteem for Writing in Chinese

In the beginning of the Koryŏ period the Silla *hyangga* tradition still retained some vitality. Only the works of the monk Kyunyŏ (917–973) remain to us, and indeed the eleven poems of his "Ten Vows of Samantabhadra" constitute a major portion of the surviving *hyangga* corpus. These pieces, however, excel more in their refined craftmanship than in artistic inspiration, and in feeling they are less poems than formal hymns. After Kyunyŏ some *hyangga* continued to be written for a time, but before long this form disappeared.

It was literature written in Chinese that now came to flourish. The Koryŏ aristocracy was rather different in character from its counterparts in the Three Kingdoms and Unified Silla periods. Civil officials who delighted in Confucian doctrine and Chinese literature, they took pride in their ability to memorize phrases from the Chinese classics and recite Chinese poetry. A practice known as the Monthly Composition Exercise required civil officials to compose poems each month on themes set by the king, while students still in school sharpened their literary skills by writing poems within stipulated time limits—contests that were called Notched Candle Poetics. In this way learning in Chinese literature, poetry in particular, developed apace, gradually becoming an essential ingredient in the education of aristocratic youth. Originally Chinese poems simply were recited, but later they came to be sung, or chanted, just as *hyangga* had been. Thus much Chinese poetry was used as lyrics, sung either to Chinese or to native tunes.

Fine Arts

Celadon ware, the product of the Koryŏ aristocracy's life of luxury, surely best exemplifies Koryŏ artistic achievement. Koryŏ celadon ware developed under the influence of Sung celadon but is deemed to be superior to the Sung exemplar, and the Chinese as well traditionally have praised it as the world's finest ceramic art. The excellence of Koryŏ celadon first of all is seen in its beautiful color. Although some were done in yellow-green or a yellowish-brown color, the jade-green pieces are particularly lovely. Secondly, the widely varied shapes in which Koryŏ celadon ware was made—whether flasks, jars, cups, wine pitchers, plates, water droppers (for use in mixing ink), brush holders, incense burners, teapots, flower vases, or flower pots—had their exquisite forms enhanced by the perfect harmony of the designs executed upon them. Particularly charming and attractive are the incense burners, water pitchers and water droppers fashioned after the shapes of such plants or animals as chrysanthemums, lotus flowers, pomegranates, bamboo shoots, melons, parrots, mandarin ducks, the phoenix, rabbits, monkeys, turtles, dragons, lions, and fish. A third outstanding feature is the beauty of the decorations on the Koryŏ celadon ware. At first designs either were incised or carved in relief, but later inlay was used, a distinctive technique found only in Koryŏ celadon ware. Clouds and cranes, waterfowl and willows, peonies, chrysanthemums, pomegranates, gourds, grapes, lotus flowers, arabesque scrolls, and stylized floral clusters are among the many design motifs employed. Koryŏ celadon ware thus displays a refined beauty in which shape, color, and design are harmoniously combined. These celadon pieces were made, however, more for ostentatious display than for actual use, so that theirs is less a robust beauty than a delicate, exquisite loveliness. Indeed it may be said that this celadon ware embodied the yearning of the Koryŏ aristocracy for Taoistic nothingness and Buddhistic quiescence. For in its flawless harmony, it seems, they found expression of their weary longing for the spiritual realm that lies beyond the world of mundane existence.

The many objects fashioned of bronze found in aristocratic homes—most notably incense burners with silver inlay, *kundika* (ritual ewers), candelabra, and mirrors represent not only another beautiful art form but enable us to perceive the richness of the Koryŏ aristocracy's way of life. Nevertheless, the celadon wares are to be considered the crowning glories of Koryŏ fine arts. They are the products of an aristocratic taste that appreciated sheer elegance, yes, but also grace and charm. But there is no lack of other artistic creations that express the refined tastes of the Koryŏ aristocracy. The stone memorial stupas so admired for their elaborate and delicate workmanship are but one example. Outstanding specimens of these are the Silsang-t'ap erected about 1017 for the National Preceptor Hongbŏp, at Ch'ungju's Chŏngt'o-sa temple (now moved to Kyŏngbok Palace), and the Hyŏnmyo-t'ap built about 1085 for National Preceptor Chigwang, at Pŏpch'ŏn-sa in Wŏnju (now also in the Kyŏngbok Palace grounds).

In contrast, the larger the size of Koryŏ structures and sculptures, the more clumsy their workmanship. Although the pagodas of early Koryŏ followed the Silla style, one senses a retrogression. In time, however, a distinctive Koryŏ development took place, leading to pagodas with a softened look rather than the sharp, straight-line beauty of the Silla pagoda. An excellent example of this is the seven-tiered pagoda at Hyŏnhwa-sa in Kaep'ung built in the early eleventh century. Octagonal shaped pagodas influenced by Sung styles also were in vogue and are well represented by the nine-tiered pagoda at Wŏlchŏng-sa on Mt. Odae, again a graceful product of aristocratic taste. There also were masterpieces of Buddhist statuary like the clay Amitabha at Pusŏk-sa in Yŏngju, but in general the sculpture of this age was not outstanding.

The art of painting also flourished markedly. The people of Koryŏ seem not to have held Chinese works in particularly high regard, yet few Koryŏ painters have left their names to us. Still, there is Yi Yŏng of Injong's reign (1122–1146), renowned as a master painter, and his "Yesŏng River Scene" (*Yesŏng-gang to*) is said to have won praise from the Sung Emperor Hui Tsung. Yi Yŏng's son, Yi Kwang-p'il, also was famed, his artistry exalted in his own time as a glory of Koryŏ. No works of these two survive, however. For their calligraphic art Yu Sin (d. 1104), the monk T'anyŏn (1070–1159), and Ch'oe U (d. 1249) were best known, and together with Kim Saeng of Silla they are called the "Four Worthies of Divine Calligraphy." On the whole the aristocracy of this earlier Koryŏ period preferred the clean and simple lines of Ou-yang Hsün's calligraphy.

6. Disturbances in the Aristocratic Order

The Treason of Yi Cha-gyŏm

The hereditary aristocracy of Koryŏ had created a number of institutional arrangements, the examination system and the Stipend Land Law among them, designed to restrain the arbitrary exercise of royal authority and so to maintain the privileged position enjoyed by the ruling elite as a whole. But when powerful families took advantage of the protected appointment system to monopolize government posts and expand their private land-holdings (by securing royal grants, opening up new land, and by simple seizure of the land of poor peasants), the balance of power among the great hereditary houses was broken. Under these circumstances it was only natural that conflict should break out among the aristocratic ruling elite themselves, eruptions that often assumed the character of armed insurrection. Several such disturbances occurred in rapid succession in the reigns of Injong (1122–1146) and Ŭijong (1146–1170), the very period that may be said to have marked the zenith of aristocratic culture.

The first to thus shatter Koryŏ's domestic tranquility was Yi Cha-gyŏm, the man who brought the Inju (Inch'ŏn) Yi house to the pinnacle of its power. Yi Cha-gyŏm had given a daughter as queen to Yejong and he contrived to put Injong, the son of that union, on the throne in 1122. Then to Injong as well he gave two daughters, assuring by this reduplicated in-law connection his own monopoly of power. His kinsmen and partisans all rose rapidly, while those who stood in his way were driven from office. One of his supporters was the military hero Ch'ŏk Chun-gyŏng who had served with distinction in the campaigns against the Jurchen; he stood ready to back Yi Cha-gyŏm with armed force. Thus secure in their hold on political power, Yi Cha-gyŏm and his faction enlarged their personal holdings of land and property by seizing those of others, thereby achieving as well a dominant economic position in Koryŏ society.

Now grown arrogant, Yi Cha-gyŏm placed credence in a prophecy that the "eighteen child" (an anagram on the character for his surname) would become king, and he came to cherish the ambition of deposing In-jong and himself assuming the throne. To forestall such a plot, Injong laid plans with officials close to him to oust Yi from power. The king's design was foiled, however, by the prompt military counteraction of Ch'ŏk Chun-gyŏng, and Injong was held in confinement while those around him were put to death (1126). After this triumph Yi Cha-gyŏm flaunted his power still more audaciously, even attempting to murder the king. But at this point, in 1127, he himself was driven out by the opportunistic Ch'ŏk Chun-gyŏng, was sent into banishment, and is heard of no more. The power of the Inju Yi that had seemed so awesome thus abruptly collapsed.

Revolt of Myoch'ŏng

The Yi Cha-gyŏm incident had demonstrated the weakened state of royal authority and the power potential of the aristocracy. Accordingly, no sooner had this grave menace been overcome than Injong contemplated a series of political reform measures that would restore the authority of the throne, a program that he delineated in a fifteen point decree handed down in 1127. But this was a time of tribulation in foreign relations as well, when the Jurchen established the Chin dynasty (1115) and were exerting repeated pressures on Koryŏ. It was at this point that several men of P'yŏngyang—the monk Myoch'ŏng, Paek Su-han, and Chŏng Chi-sang most notably, sought to take advantage of the troubled situation at home and abroad to seize the reins of power.

Myoch'ŏng urged Injong to abandon Kaesŏng, where his palace had been burned to the ground by Yi Cha-gyŏm, and move his capital to P'yŏngyang. To this end he utilized the theories of the geomancer's art. Arguing that the virtue of the Kaesŏng topography was depleted while that of P'yŏng-yang was full of vigor, he asserted that moving the capital to P'yŏngyang would make possible the reinvigoration of the dynasty. Once rewarded for his merit in bringing about dynastic revival, Myoch'ŏng then would be in a position to take power into his own hands. The immediate consequence of Myoch'ŏng's repeated urgings was the king's decision to construct the Taehwa ("Great Flowering") Palace near P'yŏngyang, completed in

1129. Myoch'ŏng and his supporters now went further, to propose that the king not only declare himself emperor and adopt his own reign name, thus asserting Koryŏ's equality with Sung and with Chin, but also launch an attack against the Jurchen Chin. Their argument was that, if only the capital were transferred to P'yŏngyang, the virtue of its topography would assure the easy success of these enterprises.

The position taken by Myoch'ŏng and those around him, who might be designated the P'yŏngyang, geomancy-credulous, xenophobic faction, came under attack from the Kaesŏng, Confucianist, China-oriented faction best represented by Kim Pu-sik, and the superstitious behavior of the former provided the grist for the latter's harshest denunciation. At first Myoch'ŏng succeeded in swaying Injong, deeply disturbed as he was by Yi Cha-gyŏm's insurrection. But when mounting opposition in Kaesŏng made it evident that he would not be able to sway the king as he desired, Myoch'ŏng determined to resolve the issue by military force. Raising an army in P'yŏngyang, Myoch'ŏng called his short-lived state Taewi ("Great Accomplishment"), adopted the reign name *Ch'ŏn'gae* ("Heavenly Commencement"), and labeled his army the "Heaven-Sent Force of Loyalty and Righteousness" (1135). But early the next year P'yŏngyang fell to government forces commanded by Kim Pu-sik, and Myoch'ŏng's revolt was suppressed.

Chapter 7

Rule by the Military

1. The Military Seize Power

The Military Officers Revolt

Aristocratic rule in Koryŏ was grounded in the principle of civil supremacy, and this led to an inferior position in the society for military officials. They ranked below the civil officials politically, and economically too they were relegated to a lower status. Even military positions to which military men in principle ought to have been appointed were being given to civil officials. The renowned Kang Kam-ch'an (948–1031) made his name as a military commander against the Khitan, but he did not emerge from a military official background. This was true of Yun Kwan (?–1111) as well, and of Kim Pu-sik (1075–1151). In sum, the military officer was the target of discrimination, and of exploitation too, at the hands of the civil officials. It was for this reason that as early as 1014 a coup d'etat was attempted, with initial success, by disguntled military officers such as Ch'oe Chil and Kim Hun, both of whom had distinguished themselves against the Khitan.

Mistreatment of the military reached new heights under King Ŭijong (1146–1170), a monarch who reflected the tranquility of that day in his fondness for peaceful arts. Ŭijong built a number of pavilions with names like "Tranquility," "Joyful Pleasure," and "Beauty Attained," and around them he dug lily ponds and sculpted hillsides for the enjoyment of himself and his court. So absorbed was he in pursuing the life of the esthete that he scarcely found time to set foot in the palace. The civil officials who followed him about of course shared in his pleasures, but the lot of the military men detailed to guard the king and his retinue was wretched. Not only ordinary soldiers but even redoubtable commanders were required to serve as mere military escorts. Military men suffered indignities as well at the hands of civil officials. In one storied incident Kim Ton-jung, the son of Kim Pu-sik, used a candle to set fire to the beard of Chŏng Chung-bu, a military officer, while the outrageous behavior of Han Noe in striking Lieutenant General Yi So-ŭng in the face was the proximate spark that ignited the military revolt in 1170. That the military officers would rise in revolt was a foregone conclusion; the only question had been what fresh provocation would set it in motion.

Another cause of the military revolt is to be found in the deteriorating economic position of the professional soldier. It already has been noted that, as those who bore the burden of military service, the professional soldiery were to have their livelihood assured through government grants of land. This was what the law stipulated, yes, but in reality few such allocations of land had been made. On the contrary, even what land they had been given was taken from them and reassigned for use in paying official stipends. Mobilized not only for wartime service but frequently for corvee duty in time of peace as well, the professional soldiery were looked upon as little more than menial laborers. For some time, then, their plight had been worsening, and many of them already had simply taken to flight to escape their burdens. Their discontent now had almost reached the point of exploding.

The military revolt broke out in the twenty-fourth year of Ŭijong's reign, 1170. Commanders Chŏng Chung-bu, Yi Ŭi-bang, Yi Ko and others assigned to escort the king on a royal progress to the Pohyŏn-wŏn temple, outside of Kaesŏng, instigated the uprising with the cry: "Death to all who but wear the civil official headdress!" With officers and soldiers united in common cause, the revolt met with quick success. The military proceeded to remove Ŭijong and place his younger brother Myŏngjong (1170–1197) on the throne. In the course of the revolt, it scarcely need be added, the offending Kim Ton-jung, Han Noe, and countless other civil officials were massacred. Three years later, when Kim Po-dang's attempt to restore Ŭijong to the throne ended in failure, his dying utterance of "The civil bureaucrats all joined in plotting with me!" set off another purge of civil officials who had escaped death earlier. Subsequently the efforts of Cho Wi-ch'ong and others to oust the military junta in Kaesŏng by armed force all were thwarted. Thus it was that political power passed from the civil officials into the hands of the military.

Power Struggle Within the Military

After their seizure of power the military officials managed state affairs through the central mechanism of the *Chungbang*, the supreme military council, and they sought to effect a military monopoly of government positions, from the most prestigious on high to the meanest office on the bottom rung of the bureaucratic ladder. Then, like their civil official predecessors, they utilized their positions to expand their private landholdings and take control of the country's economic resources as well. This newly acquired political stature and economic wealth soon led to the arming of family retainers and household slaves, with the aim of developing personal military forces. It now had become an age when nothing mattered but raw power. This was in marked contrast to the earlier Koryŏ period dominated by civil officials, who had attached primary importance to exalted lineage background. Thus success in grasping political power came to be determined not by marriage connections with the royal house but by how much force-in-being one could muster. In consequence, the locus of power shifted again and again from one military strong man to another.

At first political power was shared among Chŏng Chung-bu, Yi Ŭi-bang, and Yi Ko, the three leading figures in the military revolt, and they made decisions jointly using the instrument of the *Chungbang* council. But presently Yi Ŭi-bang killed Yi Ko and sought to consolidate his power by marrying his daughter to the crown prince, whereupon he in turn was assassinated by the Chŏng Chung-bu faction. Chŏng then ruled alone, increasingly dictatorial, until he was killed by the young commander Kyŏng Tae-sŭng in 1179. The assassination of Chŏng Chung-bu created an atmosphere of marked unease in the ranks of the military men, who looked upon Kyŏng (a man of aristocratic background) as the enemy of them all. Aware of the danger in their hostility, Kyŏng Tae-sŭng sought to protect himself by creating a force of some one hundred picked men, calling it his *Tobang* ("residence reinforcements"). But before long, in such an atmosphere of tension, Kyŏng took ill and died. After his death power was seized by Yi Ŭi-min, a rival who now returned from self-exile in the countryside where he had gone to stay out of harm's way. Originally of slave status, Yi Ŭi-min ruled with extreme tyranny, until he was killed in 1196 by the brothers Ch'oe Ch'ung-hŏn and Ch'oe Ch'ung-su. Thus for some twenty-five years a kaleidoscopic succession of military men had burst upon the scene, held power fitfully, and disappeared again. But the advent of Ch'oe Ch'ung-hŏn marked the end of these decades of disorder.

Ch'oe Ch'ung-hŏn Seizes Power

The revolt of the military greatly altered the course of Koryŏ history, for it resulted in the establishment of military rule. This shift of political power into military hands produced upheaval in Koryŏ society. The struggle for power among the military men themselves and uprisings by the slave population were among the principal manifestations of these years of disorder. It was Ch'oe Ch'ung-hŏn (1149–1219) who now brought the situation under control. He had risen in the military, won recognition in the fighting against the rebel Cho Wi-ch'ong, and now emerged into prominence. After ousting Yi Ŭi-min he proceeded to rid himself as well of all who disobeyed his orders, even though they might be among his own supporters. His younger brother, Ch'oe Ch'ung-su, and his nephew, Pak Chin-jae, were among the victims of this consolidation of power. Thus having suppressed one after another those who opposed him, in the end he succeeded in establishing a personal dictatorship.

He also rendered powerless the authority of the throne. Within the short span of sixteen years he deposed two kings, Myŏngjong and Hŭijong, and set four on the throne—Sinjong (1197–1204), Hŭijong (1204–1211), Kangjong (1211–1213), and Kojong (1213–1259). The monarchy lay completely under his control. This fact is borne out by the *History of Koryŏ* (*Koryŏ sa*) in its evaluation of King Sinjong:

> Sinjong was put upon the throne by Ch'oe Ch'ung-hŏn, and all matters of life and death, decisions to accept or to reject, were in Ch'oe's hands. Sinjong stood above his subjects holding only empty authority. Alas, he was nothing but a puppet.

Yet the fact that he preserved the Wang house and the monarchy, while in reality managing the affairs of government himself, surely was due to the impossibility of purging Koryŏ society of its strong attachment to the tradition of a hereditary aristocracy. Unlike Yi Ŭi-bang and Ch'oe Ch'ung-su, however, he had no thought to try to enhance his own authority by intermarriage with the royal house, as the civil officials had done in the past. He strove to the end to rely on his own resources.

Ch'oe Ch'ung-hŏn also used his strength to break the power of the Buddhist monasteries and temples, which constituted the sole remaining reservoir of military might with ties to the king and the civil officials. There were occasions, indeed, when several thousand armed monks stormed Kaesŏng in an attempt to overthrow military rule. But Ch'oe Ch'ung-hŏn forced the Buddhist clergy, in particular the illegitimate princes who had become monks, to leave the capital. And he crushed the armed monks by military force.

Ch'oe Ch'ung-hŏn also put down uprisings by peasants and by slaves that threatened his regime's stability. While subduing these insurgencies by military means, he also employed conciliatory tactics. To some of the leaders he gave office and rank, and he freed the lowborn inhabitants of the forced labor areas known as *pugok, hyang,* and *so,* merging these administrative units into the regular county (*hyŏn*) system. One way or another, then, these uprisings of the lowborn and peasants were pacified. The foundation for a Ch'oe regime that Ch'oe Ch'ung-hŏn put in place by the efforts of his lifetime was made still stronger by his son Ch'oe U (also known as Ch'oe I), who completed the structuring of military rule.

2. Peasant and Slave Uprisings

Outbreak of Popular Uprisings

The trend toward peasants abandoning the land for a life of wandering already had appeared at the beginning of the twelfth century, in the reign of Yejong (1105–1122). That the phenomenon was particularly severe in the area around Kaesŏng and in Sŏhae (Hwanghae) province appears to have been due to the severity of the tribute exactions and corvee mobilizations enforced there for the benefit of the central aristocracy. These rootless people from time to time formed gangs of brigands and caused disturbances in local areas. Thus already in a state of unrest, the peasants now were further agitated by the social upheaval brought about by the military revolt, after which the sudden rise to high station by those in the lower classes became a common occurrence. It is not surprising, then, that large-scale popular insurrections now came to break out in many parts of the country.

The first such popular uprising to occur under the rule of the military broke out in 1172 in the Western Border Region (P'yŏngan province), in areas such as Ch'angsŏng, Sŏngch'ŏn, and Ch'ŏlsan. Since this was a military zone, the inhabitants in effect all were soldiers, and they too were much inspirited by the military officers revolt. They became enraged, however, at the highhanded actions of the local officials, and so rose in revolt. Following that, the remnants of Cho Wi-ch'ong's defeated forces, supported by the peasantry, entrenched themselves on Mt. Myohyang and continued to cause disturbances for many years.

Popular uprisings in the southern areas spread apace with the outbreak in 1176 of the revolt of Mangi and Mangsoi in the Myŏnghak forced labor district attached to Kongju. The rebels subjugated the Kongju garrison and occupied the Ch'ŏngju and Asan region on their march north toward Kaesŏng, but in the end, after holding out for more than a year, they were subdued. A few years later, in 1182, a rising of soldiers and government slaves occurred in Chŏnju. The soldiery of Chŏnju rebelled against the cruelty of the local officials under whose harsh supervision they were compelled to labor on shipbuilding, and, together with the government slaves who rushed to join them, they held the city for some forty days. Meanwhile, lesser outbreaks occurred one after another in many parts of the country.

These early popular uprisings on the whole came about spontaneously. They resulted from resistance on the part of soldiers, peasants, and slaves against the oppression of local officials and their minions. The objective of the rebels was simply to free themselves from such unjust treatment. It is likely that they also sought freedom from the lowly status Koryŏ society assigned them, but this was not a dominant theme. The situation had not developed to the point where they would join forces with others of lowly social status in an effort to achieve the liberation of them all.

Popular Uprisings Spread

Popular uprisings entered a new phase with the insurrections of Kim Sami and Hyosim in 1193, for the two rebel bands were able to combine forces and form a common front, and the rebellion also came to develop sustained momentum. To begin with, Kim Sami rose in Ch'ŏngdo and Hyosim separately at a nearby location in North Kyŏngsang (thought to have been at modern Ulsan), but later they merged into a single force whose numbers were reckoned in the tens of thousands. The commander of the government troops sent against them met with failure and killed himself, and it was not until the next year that government forces emerged victorious in a battle at Miryang. Its strength thus was broken, but one easily can imagine the scale of this insurrection from the fact that more than 7,000 rebels died in the Miryang battle alone.

Again, the peasant rebels who rose in 1199 at Myŏngju (Kangnŭng) occupied Samch'ŏk and Ulchin on their way to joining forces with a rebel band at Kyŏngju. In 1200 the rebellious slaves of Chinju united with low-born peasants in revolt at Hapch'ŏn in a common insurgency. Moreover, rebels who rose at Kyŏngju in 1202, with the battle cry of reviving Silla, made common cause with other rebel bands at Ch'ŏngdo, Ulchin, and elsewhere in the province. In the Kyŏngsang area, then, such close cooperation among rebel forces had given them strength to continue their struggle for some ten years. By this time, it is clear, the rebellions that arose in Koryŏ were large-scale efforts aimed at restructuring the social order and, beyond that, at the seizure of political power.

These uprisings occurred not only in the countryside but in Kaesŏng as well. One such was the revolt plotted by Manjŏk in 1198, just two years after Ch'oe Ch'ung-hŏn seized power. Its principal significance lies in the fact that it involved the entire slave population in the capital and frankly aimed both at emancipation and at the seizure of power. Although the plot came to light before the rising actually got under way, it is famous for the stirring words uttered by Manjŏk to the government and private slaves he had assembled at Kaesŏng's North Mountain:

> Since the events of 1170 and 1173 many high officials have arisen from among the slave class. Are generals and ministers born to these glories? No! For when the time is right anyone at all can hold these offices. Why then should we only work ourselves to the bone and suffer under the whip? . . . If each one kills his master and burns the record of his slave status, thus bringing slavery to an end in our country, then each of us will be able to become a minister or general.

In the end all of these popular uprisings were suppressed, but they remain of great significance. This is because they demonstrate that the very foundation of the Koryŏ social order had been shaken. The masses who directly shouldered the burdens of economic production had given expression to their demand for improvement in their status. They had taken a course of action, moreover, that would assure a political response to their demands, which included liberation for the slave class, above all, but also a thorough revamping of the hereditary status system. Their movement could not but have an impact on government policy, and the widespread establishment of the *kammu* system (the posting of magistrates to smaller counties hitherto lacking such officials dispatched from the capital) and the abolition of the special forced labor districts were its more immediate results. The military officers revolt not only had brought a new elite to power at the top, but had given rise as well to great change in the bottom layers of Koryŏ society.

3. The Military Rule of the Ch'oe

Creation of Private Armed Retinues

The authority of the Ch'oe house as military rulers rested on the strength of its own private soldiery. In the decades following the military officers revolt, the powerful military figures had created personal guard units by arming their household retainers and slaves. The household retainers (*mun'gaek*), like their counterparts in the European feudal order, served their powerful lords with utmost fidelity, but in the Koryŏ case, with the backing of their masters as patrons, they might even enter the bureaucracy. Private armed retinues, with these retainers as officers and the household slaves as soldiers, first were institutionalized in Kyŏng Tae-sŭng's *Tobang* private guards unit, and this was the model for Ch'oe Ch'ung-hŏn's like-named personal armed force. Ch'oe organized his private soldiery into six "watches," having each in turn stand guard at his residence, and later the force was expanded to thirty-six "watch" units. Thus the number of men in the Ch'oe armed retinue was immeasurably greater than the one hundred or so in Kyŏng Tae-sŭng's private guards. The result was that the regular army deteriorated, its function gone, as its most able men joined the armed retinue of the Ch'oe house. In addition to this basic force, Ch'oe U formed a cavalry unit called the Elite Horse (*Mabyŏlch'o*). Although a part of the Ch'oe private armed force, the Elite Horse appears in particular to have performed ceremonial duties.

The *Sambyŏlch'o* (Three Elite Patrols) provided further military backing for the Ch'oe regime. It originated with Ch'oe U's establishment of a Night Patrol (*Yabyŏlch'o*) to put a stop to the marauding of vicious gangs of young toughs that constituted one element among the military. As its numbers grew, the Night Patrol was divided into units of the left and right, and when later a unit called the *Sinŭigun* ("Army of Transcendent Righteousness") was formed from fighters who had escaped after being captured in the wars with the Mongols, the three together came to be known as the *Sambyŏlch'o*, the Three Elite Patrols. In contrast to the principal duty of the Ch'oe private guards unit, which was to assure the personal safety of its master, the *Sambyŏlch'o* took on the public functions performed by police and by combat forces. The fact that separate units had to be organized to take over these functions is clear evidence that the Six Divisions of the regular army, to which these duties originally had been entrusted, no longer existed in anything but name. To replace them, it was now the Ch'oe house rather than the appropriate state mechanism that created the *Sambyŏlch'o*. Therefore, although the *Sambyŏlch'o* were maintained at public expense and were entrusted with public functions, in reality they were tantamount to another private Ch'oe armed force. The fact that the *Sambyŏlch'o* were disbanded upon the collapse of military rule would seem to prove this point.

The economic underpinning that made possible the growth of these private armed retinues was the personal landholdings of the military officer group. Private landholding already had begun to expand during the heyday of aristocratic rule, and the process became still more pronounced with the seizure of the lands of civil officials by military men following the military officers revolt. The military men dispatched their household retainers and slaves to take by force the lands they coveted, and they themselves directly collected the grain taxes. In the case of the Ch'oe, the whole of the Chinju region in effect was appropriated as their own private preserve, from which they took all of the revenues. Thus the Ch'oe, who epitomize the wealth and power enjoyed by Koryŏ's military rulers, were able to accumulate huge stores of grain, so much that they supplied from their own holdings the salaries for officials that the empty government granaries were unable to provide. This vast wealth constituted the economic foundation for the private armed might developed by the house of Ch'oe.

Control Mechanisms of the Ch'oe Regime

The mechanism through which the military exercised control immediately following the military officers revolt was the Council of Generals (*Chungbang*). This joint deliberative body of all generals and lieutenant generals unquestionably was an instrument that would respond appropriately to the wishes of the military rulers. However, during the transition period from severe strife and struggle among the military to authoritarian rule by the Ch'oe house, the Council of Generals, after all an instrument of joint rule by the military, came to be pushed into the background. In its place, new control mechanisms better suited to the Ch'oe dictatorship were set in place one by one.

Ch'oe Ch'ung-hŏn obtained the title of Marquis of Chin'gang (Chinju) from the king and proceeded to establish an administrative authority that he called the *Hŭngnyŏngbu* ("Office of Flourishing Tranquility"). This title of enfeoffment and creation of a governing authority gave formal legitimacy to the military rule of the Ch'oe. But it appears to have been another body, the Directorate of Decree Enactment (*Kyojŏng Togam*), that served as the highest organ of the Ch'oe "shogunate." Until the collapse of military rule the position of chief of this office continued to be occupied by whatever military man actually held the reins of power. After Ch'oe Ch'ung-hŏn who first established it, his descendants U (I), Hang, and Ŭi of course, and also Kim Chun, Im Yŏn, Im Yu-mu, and others who seized power in the final days of military rule, all in turn headed the Directorate of Decree Enactment. The issuance of orders by the Ch'oe to collect taxes or to investigate wrongdoing by officials was done in their capacity as directors of this office. In the formal sense an appointment to this position was received from the king, but in reality the military men who held it succeeded automatically to this highest office in the military regime.

Unlike the military strong men who preceded them, however, the Ch'oe were not content to act as overlords of a purely military regime. As the supreme arbiters of power in Koryŏ, the Ch'oe established a Personnel Authority (*Chŏngbang*) in their own residence to handle official appointments. It was Ch'oe U who created this office, and although authority in such matters of course had rested with the Ch'oe even earlier, it was at this point that institutionalization occurred, and this provides evidence that the rule of the military had achieved a certain stability. Men of civil attainments were attached to this office—the title "secretary for personnel administration" (*chŏngsaek sŭngsŏn*) appears to have been given to just such men—and herein is found the distinctive feature of the Personnel Authority among the instruments of military rule. It was this development that paved the way for the gradual reappearance of civil officials in positions of power, and this helps to explain why the Personnel Authority alone continued to exist even after the downfall of its creators.

In connection with the role of civil officials, the existence of the Household Secretariat (*Sŏbang*) also must be noted. This too was established by Ch'oe U and was formed from men of letters among his household retainers. It is said to have been divided into three "watches" that stood duty in turn, and it is a likely supposition that the so-called secretaries for personnel administration were selected for appointment from among the members of this Household Secretariat. The Ch'oe thus surrounded themselves not only with a retinue composed of military men from the *Tobang* guards and Three Elite Patrols but with a civilian staff as well. In this way they sought to make it clear that they were not merely military men concerned with military power alone, but rather that they were prepared to exercise full authority in both the civil and military spheres. In short, the Ch'oe had made themselves the dominant figures in both the civil official and the military official orders—they were, in fact, *yangban* (officials of the "two orders") who controlled all of the affairs of government in thirteenth century Koryŏ.

4. The Struggle with the Mongols

The Military Regime's Resistance Against the Mongols

The Mongols arose as a nomadic herding people in the steppe region of north central Asia. The wealth produced by the agricultural peoples to their south naturally aroused their acquisitive instincts, and so it was that the empires of Chin and Sung, and Koryŏ too, became prime targets of Mongol invasion. After defeating Chin there was a further reason for the Mongols to extend the swath of their conquests to Koryŏ—the objective of securing a base for the subjugation of the Southern Sung and Japan.

The first contact between Koryŏ and the Mongols resulted from their joint effort to destroy a motley army of Khitan who had fled from Manchuria across the Yalu to escape the Mongols. When Chin came under sustained Mongol attack, the Khitan had taken the opportunity to assert their independence, but following the fall of the Chin capital in 1215, Mongol pressure drove the Khitan into Koryŏ territory. After creating considerable turmoil in Koryŏ's northern regions for more than two years, the Khitan made a defensive stand at Kangdong Fortress, east of Pyŏngyang, but soon were compelled to surrender by the combined Mongol-Koryŏ siege forces (1219). After this incident the Mongols regarded themselves as Koryŏ's benefactors and came to collect annual tribute. Their demands were too heavy, however, and on several occasions Koryŏ refused to accede to them. This was the immediate cause for the beginning of a rift between the two. Subsequently, in 1225, the Mongol envoy Chu-ku-yü was killed enroute back from Koryŏ, and the Mongols eventually used the incident as a pretext for launching their first invasion of Koryŏ, in 1231.

The Mongol army led by Sartaq ran into stubborn resistance from Pak Sŏ at Kuju (Kusŏng) but, abandoning his siege there, Sartaq drove toward the capital at Kaesŏng. When Koryŏ now sued for peace, the Mongols left military governors (*daruhaci*) behind in the northwest region of Korea and withdrew their troops. But Ch'oe U resolved to resist the Mongols and so moved the capital to Kanghwa Island the next year (1232), an action calculated to exploit the one Mongol weakness, their fear of the sea. At the same time that the ruling class entered Kanghwa, the populace in general was made to take refuge in the mountain fortresses or on islands off the coast. Koryŏ's decision to resist the Mongols provoked further invasions. To be sure, the Mongol force again withdrew upon the death of their commander, Sartaq, at the hands of the monk Kim Yun-hu in the battle at Ch'ŏin-sŏng (Yongin), later in 1232, but thereafter Mongol assaults continued as before. In the end, over a thirty year period, the Mongols launched a total of six invasions of Koryŏ.

To one standing on a hill on the mainland opposite, the shoreline of Kanghwa Island lies visible just across the water. Nevertheless, the Mongols could only glare across this narrow strip of sea and call to the Koryŏ defenders to come out onto the mainland. The Koryŏ response was that they would come out, if the Mongols first withdrew their forces. To which the Mongols in turn rejoined that they would withdraw, if first the Koreans came back across to the mainland. It was a pointless exchange of verbal taunts, for the real question was the strength of will on the part of the Ch'oe house to continue to resist. So long as their determination to resist could not be broken, it would be well-nigh impossible for the Mongols to capture Kanghwa.

Meanwhile, secure in their haven on Kanghwa, the members of the ruling class were able to continue their extravagant lives of luxury no differently than they had in Kaesŏng. It was just as if they had moved intact to Kanghwa all the facilities of the capital—the palaces, mansions, temples, polo fields, everything. The merriment on the occasion of the great annual festivals, such as the *p'algwanhoe* and *yŏndŭnghoe*, also was the same. This was because the amount of the grain tax revenues as well, sent by ship along safe coastal routes, was little different than before.

The Struggle of the People

The resistance of the military regime to the Mongols at first was carried on with the support of the peasantry and the lowborn classes. At the time of the first Mongol invasion, the brigand bands on Mt. Kwanak gave themselves up and joined in the battle against the Mongol enemy. The resistance of the army of slaves at Ch'ungju, led by Chi Kwang-su, is particularly famous. They fought bravely to the end to defend the town, even though the aristocratic officials all had fled.

While moving the capital to Kanghwa the military regime had instructed the peasantry to take refuge in mountain fortresses and on islands off the coast. These areas thus became the base points for the struggle against the Mongols. Unable to overcome the stout resistance of these redoubts, the Mongols adopted the tactic of laying waste by fire to the ripened grain fields. Food supplies then ran short, and because of this the peasantry suffered much hardship. Moreover, when a mountain fortress fell to the Mongols, the strength of its defenders exhausted, they were cruelly slaughtered by their conquerors. The most severe suffering and destruction resulted from the invasion led by Jalairtai in 1254. On this occasion it is said that the number of captives the Mongols took back with them reached more than 200,000, while the corpses of the dead were too many to be counted and the entire region through which the Mongols passed was reduced to ashes. The population thus declined and whole villages fell into ruin. It was also during this time that many irreplaceable cultural treasures were lost, outstanding among them the nine-story wooden pagoda at Hwangnyong-sa in Kyŏngju and the woodblocks for the Tripitaka produced two hundred years earlier and stored at the Puin-sa monastery in Taegu.

As the villages became devastated, the life of the peasants inevitably became one of hardship. But the government on Kanghwa, instead of pressing ahead with positive measures to safeguard the peasantry, by constant harsh exactions only made its condition more miserable. Such exploitation by the aristocratic elite not only bred hostility toward their rulers in the hearts of the peasants, but also dampened their desire to fight against the Mongols. This alienation of the people could not but pose a grave threat to the government on Kanghwa.

Collapse of the Military Regime and Peace with the Mongols

The Ch'oe had carried on resistance against the Mongols with the backing of the peasantry, but now that their support had weakened, a grave crisis overtook the military regime. Whether or not this crisis could be overcome would determine whether or not the regime would survive. Its trust in the power of the Buddha led the government to undertake another woodblock carving of the Tripitaka, and the result was the so-called *Koryŏ Tripitaka*, famed for its exquisite artistry, that remains to this day at Haein-sa near Taegu. The government also offered up anxious prayers to the deities of heaven and earth. It was in such an atmosphere that sentiment for peace with the Mongols arose among the king and the civil officials in particular.

It was observed above that once the Ch'oe had begun to make use of men of letters, the voices of the civil officeholders, who for some time had been completely ignored, more and more demanded to be heard. At the outset they had held opposing views with regard to moving the capital to Kanghwa, and even after the move they took every opportunity to urge peace. This policy of the civil officials to make peace with the Mongols was directly related to the question of the further expansion of their role in the governing process. That is, their aim was to attempt to curb the power of the military men by reaching an accommodation with the Mongols. In order to achieve this objective peace was necessary, but to bring about peace would necessitate the downfall of those who advocated continued resistance, the military rulers. Accordingly, the civil officials, in collusion with a segment of the military officials, had initiated a move toward overthrowing the Ch'oe house, a move toward peace.

The last of the Ch'oe dictators, Ch'oe Ŭi, was assassinated by the civil official Yu Kyŏng and the military official Kim Chun in 1258. Authority thus reverted for the moment to the king and a decision to make peace with the Mongols was reached. In the next year, then, the crown prince (later King Wŏnjong) went to the Mongols and conveyed Koryŏ's desire for peace, and to clearly signal this intent to cease resisting, Kanghwa's walled fortifications were torn down.

The military men, however, still were not happy about peace with the Mongols. Although Kim Chun went along with the current of opinion around him, taking no active steps to thwart those working for peace, he nevertheless was not enthusiastic about the peace policy. Then, when Im Yŏn killed Kim Chun and seized power from him, the opposition to making peace came out into the open. In the end, Im Yŏn went so far as to depose the king, Wŏnjong, who had put the pro-Mongol policy into effect. These events suggest that an inseparable linkage had formed between the pursuit of a policy of resistance to the Mongols and the perpetuation of military rule. However, rapprochement already had reached the point where Koryŏ was subject to strong Mongol interference, and at the same time national solidarity had so disintegrated that the populace no longer could be rallied behind a policy of resistance. Mongol pressure soon restored Wŏnjong to the throne, and at his request Mongol troops were brought in. Under these circumstances, with the assassination by royal command of Im Yu-mu (Im Yŏn's son who took power after his father's death), the flickering pulse of military rule that had been sustained since the downfall of the Ch'oe house now was utterly extinguished. This was the same year (1270) in which Koryŏ returned the capital to Kaesŏng and completely abandoned the struggle against the Mongols.

Anti-Mongol Struggle of the Sambyŏlch'o

As already noted, the Three Elite patrols (*Sambyŏlch'o*) had constituted the military underpinning of military rule. They were also in the forefront of the struggle against the Mongols, bedeviling the enemy forces with their sudden forays and harrying tactics. The Three Elite Patrols, then, were the mainstay of military rule, the core force in the resistance against the Mongols. Accordingly, when the military regime was toppled and peace terms worked out with the Mongols, they were bitterly resentful. When the return to Kaesŏng was announced, therefore, the Three Elite Patrols immediately rose in revolt. Under the leadership of Pae Chung-son, they first blocked all transit between Kanghwa and the mainland. A royal kinsman, Wang On, the Marquis of Sŭnghwa, was put forward as king, a government was established, and officials were appointed, thus creating an anti-Mongol regime in opposition to the government at Kaesŏng.

Kanghwa Island, to be sure, was the base from which the struggle with the Mongols had been waged for more than forty years. But the situation was different now that Wŏnjong's government at Kaesŏng was working hand in hand with the Mongols. It was necessary for the Three Elite Patrols to secure a permanent base of operations out of reach of the Kaesŏng government. The rebels went south, therefore, to the island of Chindo, off the southwest tip of the peninsula. There they not only built a palace complex on a large scale and readied the other appurtenances of a capital city, but they brought the nearby islands and the adjacent coastal region under their control, thus creating a distinct maritime kingdom.

Chindo, however, fell to a combined Koryŏ-Mongol assault in mid-1271, the central figures in the revolt being nearly all lost. Led by Kim T'ong-jŏng, the survivors fled to Cheju Island to continue their resistance, but Cheju too was subjugated, in 1273, bringing to a close almost four years of insurrection. The bitter end struggle of the Three Elite Patrols provides a clear indication of how strong was the spirit of resistance to the Mongols among the military men of Koryŏ.

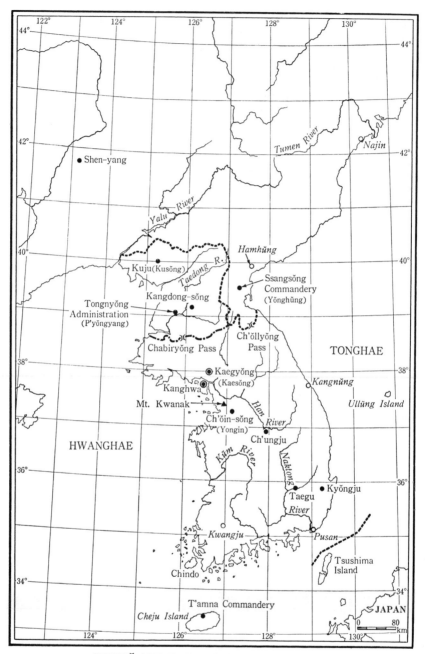

KORYŎ AND THE MONGOLS (13th CENTURY)

5. The Culture of the Age of the Military

Prose Tales and Narrative Poems

When the military seized power, men of letters had no recourse but to abandon thought of government careers, and some of them buried themselves in mountain villages where they passed their days in the enjoyment of poetry and wine. Such figures were O Se-jae, Im Ch'un, Yi Il-lo (1152–1220), and their companions, who likened themselves to third century China's Seven Sages of the Bamboo Grove. There were others too, men who sought to again enter government service in the way now opening to them, as retainers of the house of Ch'oe. Yi Kyu-bo (1168–1241) and Ch'oe Cha (1188–1260) are two outstanding figures of this sort. But there were limits to the political advancement of these men as well, and in this respect they shared common ground with those who eschewed government service entirely.

These two groups thus came to form a unitary literary community, and the genre that developed as their common mode of expression was the prose tale. Examples are Im Ch'un's "Fortunes of Master Coin" (*Kongbang chŏn*), Yi Kyu-bo's "Story of Mr. John Barleycorn" (*Kuk sŏnsaeng chŏn*), and "Story of Madame Bamboo" (*Chuk puin chŏn*) by Yi Kok (1298–1351), all tales that personified everyday objects. Yi Il-lo's *Collection to Dispel Leisure* (*P'ahan chip*), Yi Kyu-bo's *Notes on Poems and Other Trifles* (*Paegun sosŏl*), and Ch'oe Cha's *Collection to Relieve Idleness* (*Pohan chip*) represent another variety—potpourris of anecdotal material, poems and stories, and casual commentary designed to entertain. The precursor of literature of this genre may be sought in a collection of stories called *Tales of the Bizarre* (*Sui chŏn*) by Pak Il-lyang (?–1096), but writings of this kind were immensely popular in the period of military rule and later influenced such works as *Scribblings of Old Man Oak* (*Yŏgong p'aesŏl*) by Yi Che-hyŏn (1287–1367).

Koryŏ's enhanced consciousness of national identity, aroused by the trauma of reaching accommodation with a succession of bellicose neighbors, naturally found its reflection in the literature of the period. One manifestation of this awareness of nationhood, in narrative poetic form, is Yi Kyu-bo's "Saga of King Tongmyŏng" (*Tongmyŏng wang p'yŏn*), the semi-legendary founder of Koguryŏ. His purpose in writing this, Yi Kyu-bo avers, was "simply to let the world know that our country always has been a land of hero-sages." Koryŏ, in other words, was a nation that might take immense pride in being a cultured people possessed of a long history and tradition.

Establishment of the Chogye Buddhist Sect

After the seizure of power by the military a new development occurred in Koryŏ Buddhism. This was the establishment of the Chogye sect within the Sŏn (Zen) School. The monk Ŭich'ŏn, to be sure, had advocated the unity of the Sŏn contemplative and Kyo textual schools, but he had put his emphasis on the latter. When he founded the *Ch'ŏnt'ae* (*Chinese: T'ien-t'ai*) sect in Koryŏ, he not only brought into it many of the promising young monks of the Nine Mountain Sects of Sŏn, but he also failed to include a single Sŏn text in his *New Catalogue of Buddhist Sectarian Writings*. But sometime during the period of military rule, or thereabouts, the Nine Mountain Sects of Sŏn took the new name of the Chogye sect, and before long circumstances combined to bring about its flourishing development.

The monk responsible for the growing acceptance of the teachings of the Chogye sect was Chinul (1158–1210), also known as the National Preceptor Pojo, who converted the present Songgwang-sa monastery in South Chŏlla into a base for the propagation of his new approach to Sŏn. Chinul made "sudden-enlightenment [followed by] gradual-cultivation" his basic precept. "Sudden-enlightenment" connotes the awakening to the fact that the human mind is none other than the Buddha-mind, while "grad-ual-cultivation" means that even after the awakening is achieved there must be unremitting cultivation of the mind. This path of sudden-enlighten-ment and gradual-cultivation requires "twofold training in quiescence and knowing" (*chŏnghye ssangsu*), which are the dual aspects of true mind. Although priority is given in this process to meditation, invoking of the name of Buddha and reading sutras are considered important as well. In other words, unlike Ŭich'ŏn, Chinul advocated a harmonization of the Sŏn and Kyo schools that would give primacy to Sŏn. The Korean Chogye sect that embraced this precept of Chinul is a distinctive feature of Koryŏ Buddhism. After Chinul the development of the Chogye sect was continued by such outstanding successors as the National Preceptor Chin'gak (Hyesim, 1178–1234).

The flourishing of the Chogye sect following the period of military rule signifies the indigenous development of Koryŏ Buddhism. Korean Chogye Buddhism represented a challenge to the established authority of the doctrines of the Textual School, which preached that one might gain profit in this world by accumulating merit in accordance with the teachings of the sutras. It was also a repudiation of the secular Buddhism that had catered to the royal family and the aristocratic civil officials. The Chogye sect, then, with substantial support from the military rulers, proceeded to develop in mountain monasteries throughout Korea as a unique stream of Buddhist faith and practice. Furthermore with its emphasis on cultivation of the mind-nature, Chogye Buddhism played a key role in preparing the ground for the acceptance of Neo-Confucianism in the years soon to come.

Chapter 8

Emergence of the Literati

1. The Pro-Yüan Policy and the Powerful Families

Surrender to the Mongols

The first ordeal Koryŏ suffered following the conclusion of peace with Yüan (the Mongols had proclaimed the Yüan Dynasty in 1271) was its forced participation in the Mongol expeditions against Japan. For some time, through the intermediacy of Koryŏ, Yüan had sought to secure Japan's formal acknowledgment of its suzerainty. It would appear that the Mongol rulers were primarily motivated by strategic considerations—a plan to make use of Koryŏ and Japan, both of which had close maritime connections with Sung China, in pressing its attack against the stubborn Southern Sung dynasty. At any rate, Yüan demands forced Koryŏ to set forth with Mongol armies on two occasions, 1274 and 1281, to subjugate Japan, but both campaigns ended in failure. One reason for the failure, of course, was the natural unfamiliarity of the Mongols with summer weather conditions in the seas between Korea and Japan. At the same time, however, other factors were the stout resistance of the Kamakura Shogunate, which held power in Japan at that time, and the resistance of Koryŏ as well, not at all pleased to take part in the attempted invasion. Koryŏ was responsible for the construction of warships and the provision of supplies for both invasions, and this constituted a fearsome burden for the Koryŏ peasantry already exhausted from the thirty year struggle against the Mongols.

However agonizing an experience for Koryŏ, the campaigns against Japan were but a momentary tempest. More important were the deleterious changes in the fabric of Koryŏ itself, brought about by the relationship with Yüan. In order to strengthen the royal authority within Koryŏ, Wŏnjong sought permission for his son, the later King Ch'ungnyŏl, to wed a Yüan princess. Having adopted a policy of reconciliation, the Yüan emperor acceded to this request. King Ch'ungnyŏl thus was given a daughter of the Yüan emperor Shih Tsu (Kublai Khan) as his queen, and thereafter a succession of Koryŏ kings had princesses of the Yüan imperial house as their primary consorts, while sons born to these queens would normally succeed to the throne. Thus Koryŏ became a "son-in-law nation" to Yüan, in a sense an appanage under the Mongol imperial house. Subsequently it became the practice for Koryŏ crown princes to reside in Peking as hostages until called to the kingship. Even after their accession they would visit Peking frequently, leaving the throne in Kaesŏng empty. During the Mongol period the Koryŏ kings came to take Mongol names, wear their hair in Mongol style, wear Mongol dress, and use the Mongol language. The royal houses of the two nations had become a single family.

The Koryŏ king now was no longer the independent ruler of his kingdom but rather, as a son-in-law of the Yüan imperial house, occupied a fixed position within the Yüan empire. He was able to utilize this position to enhance his authority within the country to a certain extent, but this small benefit was gained only at the immense sacrifice of the degradation of the Koryŏ royal house. The characters "progenitor" (*cho*) and "ancestor" (*chong*) no longer could be used in creating a posthumous "temple name" for the king. Instead, the character for "king" (*wang*) itself was used, with the character "loyal" (*ch'ung*) added as a prefix to give expression to the spirit of loyalty with which the Koryŏ kings were to serve the Mongol Yüan. All other terms relating to the king and his actions similarly were downgraded, such as the royal first person pronoun, the mode of addressing the king, the term designating the crown prince, and the name for a royal decree. Moreover, there were several instances when Yüan determined the succession, deposing a king and raising another to the throne in his place. There also were times when members of Koryŏ's aristocratic ruling class, in collusion with the Mongols, schemed to drive a king from the throne. The consequence of this situation was to weaken the institution of the kingship itself within the Koryŏ polity.

Nor could the organs of government in Koryŏ remain as before. The Three Chancelleries were merged to form a single Council of State and the Royal Secretariat was given a new name (*Milchiksa*) that suggested diminished importance. The Six Boards, too, had not only their names changed but underwent a restructuring. Personnel and Rites were combined into an Office of Proprieties, the Board of Taxation became the Office of Census Registration, the Board of Military Affairs the Office of Military Rosters, the Board of Punishments the Office of Legal Administration, while the Board of Public Works was abolished. This revamping of offices and their names had the same depreciatory purpose as the downgrading of terminology related to the king.

Development of the Relationship with Yüan

Despite these many changes the Koryŏ royal house maintained to the end its position as sovereign ruler of an independent nation. This was a legacy of the struggle against the Mongols waged by the military regime. Yüan regarded it as fortunate indeed to have secured the peaceful submission of a nation that had persisted in a stubborn resistance against them for some thirty years. Thus while Yüan placed Korea under onerous restraint, it also worked hard to soothe Koryŏ feelings. The Koryŏ relationship with Yüan proceeded to develop in this setting of simultaneous repression and conciliation.

The Mongols had established the Eastern Expedition Field Headquarters (*Chŏngdong Haengsŏng*) in Korea in 1280 in order to prosecute the second campaign against Japan, and they continued it in operation even after abandoning any thought of subjugating Japan. The Koryŏ king, then, was automatically appointed to head this instrumentality with the title of Minister of the Left, and its subordinate officials were appointed by the king in this capacity. Accordingly, the Eastern Expedition Field Headquarters was simply a channel for official liaison between Koryŏ and Yüan. Nevertheless, at times Yüan attempted to interfere in internal Koryŏ politics through the Eastern Expedition Field Headquarters, and one such occasion arose when the Mongol K'uo-li-chi-ssu took up his post as a high official of the Headquarters. Due to Koryŏ opposition, however, his attempt to dictate policy failed. Moreover, a move initiated by Koryŏ renegades to abolish the Koryŏ kingdom and attach it directly to Yüan as one of its provinces also ended in failure, due to the stubborn opposition of the Koryŏ officialdom.

Sizeable portions of Koryŏ territory, nevertheless, were placed under direct Yüan dominion. The Ssangsŏng Commandery in Hamgyŏng province, the Tongnyŏng Administration in P'yŏngan province, and the T'amna Commandery on Cheju Island were offices established by Yüan to administer such areas [see map p. 152]. The Ssangsŏng Commandery was located at modern Yŏnghŭng and to it was attached the territory north of the Ch'ŏllyŏng Pass; the Tongnyŏng Administration was at P'yŏngyang and administered the area north of the Chabiryŏng Pass; and the T'amna Commandery was set up on Cheju to direct the vast livestock raising operation established there by the Mongols. Upon request from Koryŏ the latter two territories reverted before long to Koryŏ control, but the Ssangsŏng Commandery continued in existence until King Kongmin recovered it by force of arms in 1356, and this sowed the seeds of the vexing problems surrounding the Ming establishment of its Ch'ŏllyŏng Commandery.

Yüan's economic levies on Koryŏ sorely afflicted a nation laid waste by prolonged warfare. Under a variety of pretexts Yüan demanded Koryŏ gold, silver, cloth, grain, ginseng, and falcons. Worse, they even demanded young women and eunuchs. The demand for falcons in particular led to many abuses, as the numerous falconries, backed by Mongol power, enjoyed a variety of special privileges. All these impositions, in the final analysis, came to rest on the backs of the peasants, who thus had to bear the double burden of exactions by Yüan and by their own government. This led to many peasants abandoning their land and wandering about the countryside, whereupon the Koryŏ ruling class, with its huge agricultural estates, rounded up the wanderers and put them to work as farm laborers. Gradually, then, the Mongols came to regard this wealthy, propertied ruling class as a more reliable instrument for promoting Yüan interests than the powerless royal house.

Another political problem that arose between Koryŏ and Yüan concerned the so-called King of Shenyang, who had jurisdiction over Koryŏ people living in Manchuria. When King Ch'ungnyŏl was in the Yüan capital as crown prince he was invested as King of Shenyang, and subsequently, when King Ch'ungsŏn relinquished the throne and lived in the Yüan capital, he too received the same title. The reason for appointing Koryŏ royalty as kings of Shenyang was not only to make it easier to control the Koryŏ people living in that area, but it also was useful in maintaining Mongol control over Koryŏ itself. The result, not surprisingly, was to give rise to a confrontation between the King of Shenyang and the Koryŏ king. An example of this was the bitter struggle for the succession to the Koryŏ throne that erupted between Wang Ko, King Ch'ungsŏn's nephew and his successor as King of Shenyang, and Kings Ch'ungsuk and Ch'unghye. This clash between the two kings is noteworthy as one achievement of the Yüan divide and conquer policy.

The Powerful Families and Their Estates

As Yüan influence in Koryŏ grew ever more pronounced, new forces emerged in Koryŏ society under Yüan aegis. There were men like Cho In-gyu, who became a powerful figure as a Mongolian language interpreter, and there were those who, like Yun Su, rose to important station through the falconries established to fulfill the Yüan tribute demand. Then, too, some succeeded by dint of distinguished service in escorting the king on his journeys to Yüan, while others made their marks as members of the retinues of Yüan princesses who came to Koryŏ. There also were instances of men advancing themselves through valorous service in the Mongol campaigns against Japan, receiving as a reward appointments as "commander of ten thousand." To be sure, some families had remained powerful from early Koryŏ times while others had risen to prominence in the period of military rule, but the new forces spawned by the relationship with the Mongols, the emergence of the so-called high and mighty lineages, gave a new complexion to late Koryŏ society. This is because these powerful families, by their unrestrained personal aggrandizement, brazenly monopolized the benefits that the ruling class as a whole should have derived from the governing process.

Not only as ranking civil and military officials, but also in the new capacity of discussants, members of these powerful families came to participate in the deliberations of the Privy Council (*Top'yŏngŭisasa*, or *Todang*), the government's highest conciliar body. In consequence, the number of participants in this highest level decision-making process, originally but twelve officials altogether, now had risen to seventy or eighty. What is more, these same men possessed vast estates and hundreds of slaves, and so had acquired great economic power. The original Stipend Land Law having broken down, the government had adopted a salary land (*nokkwajŏn*) system in its place. This was done in 1271, the year after peace was made with the Mongols and the capital was returned to Kaesŏng. But the salary land system, which allocated land in the eight county districts in the province around the capital to current office holders, in reality was not a matter of great interest to the powerful families. The private landholdings that they had amassed by obtaining royal grants, by bringing new land under cultivation, and by outright seizure were the focus of their economic concerns. Private landholdings had been growing for a long time, but it was after the downfall of the military regime, when the heightened power of the dominant families secured for them such special privileges as tax and corvee exemption, that the term "agricultural estates" (*nongjang*) came into use. The great tracts of land that were under the direct control of the king also partook fully of this same character. Some of the holdings of the powerful families at the end of Koryŏ were vast estates that made mountains and rivers their boundaries, or that extended over whole counties, while the king's own estates, we are told, numbered as many as three hundred and sixty.

The powerful families that owned these estates were absentee landlords who lived in Kaesŏng, and their holdings were to be found in every corner of the country. Accordingly, the estate owners had to send household retainers or slaves to collect their rents. The estates were cultivated by both tenant farmers and slaves, some of whom had been acquired along with the land while others had been culled from among the vagrant agricultural population. Due to the prevalence of what has been called outright seizure, which seems to have been a kind of sharecropping forced upon the peasant by strong-arm methods, it also developed that a single tenant farmer had to pay rents to several owners. The tenant farmers, therefore, often preferred to become slaves, thus receiving the protection of an estate owner. The condition of this new slave element was like that of the out-resident slaves in general: they were permitted to have their own personal property and were, in essential respects, still tenant farmers.

The increase in private estates ate away at the government's own land resources, thus causing severe depletion of state revenues. In consequence, if a newly appointed official lacked a private estate inherited from an ancestor, he had to lead a life of virtual poverty no matter how high his bureaucratic position might be. Furthermore, the increase in the privately owned slave population caused a reduction in the numbers of those on whom the state might impose corvee duty. This in turn required that the government mobilize instead the slaves of its own officials. In short, the situation had reached the point where the government no longer could assure the collective well-being of the very interests for whose benefit it primarily existed.

2. Growth of the Power of the Literati

Emergence of the Literati (Sadaebu)

A new bureaucratic class appeared following the disintegration of aristo-cratic government during the period of military rule. These were the *sadaebu*, not only educated and knowledgeable men, but men who were adept too in the administration of the affairs of government. In short, they were scholar-bureaucrats, or literati, and after the collapse of military rule they came to perform an ever more important political role. Rather than by means of a protected appointment as scions of hereditary aristocratic families, these scholar-bureaucrats strove for political advancement via the examination system, on the basis of scholarly achievement. At the same time a new kind of military officer was emerging, one who had achieved a rise in status and entered the formal bureaucratic ranks by obtaining a sinecure appointment, either through distinguished military service or by purchase. The members of this rising military class generally were known as *hallyang*.

Literati also emerged from among the clerical force in the central govern-ment, but many more came from the ranks of the petty functionaries (*hyangni*) in the local administrations. The literati of this origin were small and middle-level landowners who possessed small-scale agricultural estates in their home localities, or they were independent farmers. With their own honest labor they had built up their holdings by opening up new land to cultivation or by purchase. These landowners lived on their land, operating their farms either with tenant and slave labor or by working the land them-selves, so that the term "agricultural estates" as applied to their holdings meant something quite different from the latifundia owned by the powerful families in the capital as absentee landlords. Understandably, then, these literati despised the powerful families who had acquired their huge estates by illegal means backed by political muscle. The literati, on the other hand, tended to be men of personal honesty and integrity.

These literati, the rural landowners who had emerged from among the class of local functionaries, might advance to serve at the national level, but when they retired they returned to enjoy life back in their country districts. Being banished from the capital on some charge or other held no terrors for these men, since it only meant being required to return to their rural homes. To the contrary, they themselves took every opportunity to go back to live on their small estates in the countryside, and indeed they did so in such numbers that the government actually levied a special tax on office rankholders who thus left Kaesŏng to take up residence outside the capital. In the end, the emergence of the literati from among independent rural landowners brought a profound change to the political scene in Koryŏ.

The Reforms of King Kongmin

So long as the powerful families were backed by the might of the Yüan dynasty, no effort to correct the abuses for which they were responsible could succeed. One such attempt that met with failure was the reform movement initiated in 1298, his first year on the throne, by King Ch'ungsŏn, with the support of the young scholar-officials of the Secretariat of Letters (*Sarimwŏn*). Consequently, it was clear that a reform effort could achieve some measure of success only if it were undertaken in a context of weakened Yüan capacity for intervening in Koryŏ's internal affairs. It was not until King Kongmin (1351–1374) came to the throne, at a time when Yüan was beginning to be driven northward by the rising Chinese dynasty of Ming, that such an opportunity presented itself. This explains why Kongmin's reforms had two facets: externally a policy directed against Yüan and internally an attempt to suppress the powerful families.

It was Kongmin, then, who abolished the Yüan liaison organ, the Eastern Expedition Field Headquarters, purged the pro-Yüan faction led by Ki Ch'ŏl (brother of the Korean queen of Yüan emperor Shun), restored the old government structure, and recovered Koryŏ's lost territory by sending an army to attack the Yüan commandery headquarters at Ssangsŏng, Hamgyŏng province. In his later years he even sent troops across the Yalu to attack the Yüan Tung-ning Commandery at Hsing-ching, Manchuria (modern Hsin-pin, about eighty miles east of Mukden). These aggressive acts of defiance of course provoked a reaction from both Yüan and its Korean adherents. Within Koryŏ Kim Yong led an attempt to assassinate the king at the Hŭngwang-sa temple, while for its part Yüan proclaimed that King Kongmin had been deposed. The king was able to frustrate these designs against him, however, and resolutely proceed with his policy. Upon the founding of the Ming dynasty, in 1368, King Kongmin immediately adopted a pro-Ming stance and initiated an exchange of envoys.

While employing an anti-Yüan pro-Ming foreign policy, internally Kongmin endeavored to undermine the dominant position of the powerful families through a variety of reforms. His first move was to abolish the Personnel Authority (*Chŏngbang*). This had been an instrument of the autocratic rule of the Ch'oe house in the period of military rule, and it had remained in existence even after the downfall of the military. In control of personnel matters, it had placed restraints on discretionary exercise of the royal authority and it also had impeded the rise of the new, young literati officials. Later in his reign Kongmin grew fond of Sin Ton (the monk P'yŏnjo), appointed him a National Preceptor, created for him the extraordinary post of Prime Minister Plenipotentiary, and had him carry out a sweeping reorganization of the government. This appointment of Sin Ton, an obscure monk, to such a powerful position itself signifies that political reform could only be carried out through the agency of someone who had no ties with the powerful families. Sin Ton first of all ousted Yi Kong-su and others of exalted lineage background, appointing in their stead men without such connections. Then, with the consent of the king, he established a special agency, the Directorate for Reclassification of Farmland and Farming Population, and with himself at its head set about returning lands and slaves seized by the powerful families to their original owners, and in many cases setting slaves free.

These actions naturally were well received by the populace as a whole, and Sin Ton was even hailed as a saint. But he so incurred the hostility of the powerful families that in the end they encompassed his downfall and death. Presently King Kongmin too was killed; a man more of artistic temperament than he was a political adept, he was unequal to the task of freeing Koryŏ from the grip of the powerful families, with their still formidable sources of strength.

3. The Founding of the Chosŏn (Yi) Dynasty

Yi Sŏng-gye Seizes Power

On two occasions during Kongmin's reign, in 1359 and 1361, Koryŏ was invaded from across the Yalu by the so-called Red Turbans, a powerful brigand force of Chinese. On one occasion they occupied Kaesŏng and the king was forced to flee all the way south to Andong in Kyŏngsang province. But these were very short-lived incursions, unlike the raids of Japanese marauders (*waegu*) that extended over a long period of time and affected the whole country. The raids of the seaborne Japanese marauders had begun as early as the reign of King Kojong (1213–1259), but they only became rampant after 1350. Although armed but lightly, the Japanese came at will by sea, landed at random along the whole of the Koryŏ coast, and devastated the farming villages. In consequence the peasants moved inland and let the rich farmlands of the coastal regions lie fallow. The Japanese even attacked Kanghwa Island, at the very threshold of the capital, thus throwing Kaesŏng itself into panic. Moreover, since they might appear anywhere at any time, maritime traffic became paralyzed, grain no longer could be transported by coastal shipping, and taxes in kind from the local areas could not be brought to the capital. Thus Kaesŏng, where the aristocratic ruling class was concentrated, faced imminent economic collapse.

In order to bring an end to the *waegu* attacks, Koryŏ on several occasions made diplomatic representations to Japan, but to no avail. The Japanese authorities themselves lacked the power to suppress them. But the campaigns of military commanders like Ch'oe Yŏng and Yi Sŏng-gye did succeed in sapping the strength of the attackers. Ch'oe Mu-sŏn, too, achieved outstanding success in destroying the Japanese ships by means of a variety of gunpowder weapons he produced at the government's cannon foundry. Moreover, Pak Wi led a direct assault on the marauders' lair on Tsushima Island in 1389. Thus the incidence of Japanese raids gradually diminished. At the same time, in consequence of their victories in battle against the Japanese, the influence of Koryŏ's military commanders, Ch'oe Yŏng and Yi Sŏng-gye in particular, mounted.

Sharp disagreement between Ch'oe Yŏng and Yi Sŏng-gye arose, however, over Koryŏ policy toward the continent. This was an issue of long standing, a dispute that had beset Koryŏ from a generation before. Kongmin had been succeeded by an eleven year-old boy born to a slave woman of the monk Sin Ton; known as King U (1375–1388), he owed his throne to the backing of the military hero and high official Yi In-im. Yi thus came to wield predominant power, and he abandoned Kongmin's pro-Ming policy for a pro-Yüan orientation. Yi Sŏng-gye, Chŏng Mong-ju, and others strongly opposed this change, attacking it unceasingly as a grievous error.

This most crucial foreign policy issue still had not been resolved when, early in 1388, Ming proclaimed its intention to establish a Ch'ŏllyŏng Commandery. Since Ch'ŏllyŏng is the pass at the southern end of the Hamgyŏng littoral, this would be tantamount to Ming annexing the whole of the northeastern territory that had been administered under the Yüan Ssangsŏng Commandery. It was at this juncture that the Yi In-im faction was driven out and power seized by Ch'oe Yŏng and Yi Sŏng-gye. Outraged upon receipt of this Ming proclamation, Ch'oe Yŏng determined to invade the Liao-tung region of Manchuria, and with the agreement of King U a troop mobilization was quickly carried out throughout the country. Within scarcely two months the expedition was launched on its way, with Ch'oe Yŏng as commander-in-chief and Cho Min-su and Yi Sŏng-gye as deputy commanders.

But events were given an unexpected turn by Yi Sŏng-gye, who had opposed the expedition from the start. Marching his army back from Wihwa Island in the mouth of the Yalu, he pointed it at King U and Ch'oe Yŏng. In a nearly bloodless coup Yi Sŏng-gye ousted the king and Ch'oe from power, seizing political control himself. He thus had grasped the historic moment for the overthrow of Koryŏ and the establishment of a new dynasty.

Reform of Private Landholding

Yi Sŏng-gye and his supporters, such men as Chŏng To-jŏn and Cho Chun, used their newly won power to depose King Ch'ang as well (U's son who had been raised to the throne at the urging of Cho Min-su), on the ground that he was a grandson of Sin Ton, and in his place put King Kongyang, a true member of the Wang royal house (1389). They then carried out a sweeping land reform, advocated all along by the newly risen literati class but hitherto impossible to put into effect. They were opposed, to be sure, by a moderate reform group led by Yi Saek, but this element was ousted from the ruling circle. The literati reform advocates, by and large adherents of Neo-Confucianism, not only opposed the Buddhist establishment on ideological grounds but also because, like the powerful families, it had amassed great estates and was eating away at the nation's economic fabric. In a word, then, the reform of private landholding signified the destruction of the old economic order and the establishment of a new one by the rising literati class.

The land reform began with the undertaking of a cadastral survey of landholding throughout the country. Then in 1390 all the existing registers of public and private land were set afire and destroyed. In the next year the basic statute governing the new land system, the Rank Land Law (*kwajŏnpŏp*), was promulgated. Its terms provided for stipend land, taken only from the Kyŏnggi region around the capital, to be allocated to members of the official class in accordance with the rank level each had attained. Needless to say, this resulted in the Yi Sŏng-gye faction receiving substantial allocations of land. The land in the rest of the country all was subsumed under the category of state land, with the result that the agricultural estates were in effect confiscated. Accordingly, the economic foundation of the powerful families was destroyed, and this in turn bespoke their downfall. And more: the land reform at the same time symbolized the downfall of the Koryŏ dynasty itself. On the other hand, the increase in state land brought about a corresponding increase in government revenues, and this secured the economic foundation of the new dynasty of Yi Korea.

Establishment of the Dynasty of Chosŏn

Yi Sŏng-gye had seized political and military power by his march back from the Yalu, and he had forced kings U and Ch'ang from the throne as false pretenders, enthroning King Kongyang in their place. By resolutely carrying out the land reform he had taken actual economic power as well into his own hands. The only requirement still to be met to effect the establishment of a new dynasty was the formality itself. There were, it ensued, some complications in the way of carrying out this formality. Powerful opponents such as Chŏng Mong-ju still stood in the way, but he was assassinated by Yi Sŏng-gye's fifth son Pang-wŏn (the later King T'aejong). Having struck down its last adversary, the Yi Sŏng-gye faction forced Kongyang to abdicate the throne and then seated their leader upon it. Thus did Yi Sŏng-gye found his royal house, and so perished the Koryŏ house of Wang.

Yi Sŏng-gye represented new forces that emerged toward the end of the Koryŏ dynasty. The prelude of the early Yi dynasty panegyric *Songs of Flying Dragons* eulogizes the virtue of the ancestors of the Yi founder, comparing the Yi house to a deep rooted tree and a spring of deep waters, in these words:

The tree that strikes deep root
Is firm amidst the winds.
Its flowers are good,
Its fruit abundant.

The stream whose source is deep
Gushes forth even in a drought.
It forms a river
And gains the sea.

(translated by Peter H. Lee)

In reality, however, the dynastic founder Yi Sŏng-gye was not the scion of a famous family with a long history. His ancestors had migrated in slow stages from their original home in Chŏnju, North Chŏlla province, finally settling down to live in Hamhŭng. In an area still heavily populated by Jurchen, the Yi gradually attained a position of influence as military commanders, emerging as a powerful gentry family of that region. Yi Cha-ch'un was the first member of the lineage to achieve prominence in Koryŏ when he obtained an appointment under the Yüan Ssangsŏng Commandery. Yi Cha-ch'un's cooperation was decisive in enabling King Kongmin to retake the Ssangsŏng Commandery, and he was rewarded with the post of Military Commander of the Northeast Region. Yi Sŏng-gye was the second son of this man.

Yi Sŏng-gye himself won advancement through his success in the numerous battles of his day. He played a major role in repulsing the attacks of the Red Turban bandits and Japanese marauders, as well as in the campaign against the Yüan Tung-ning Commandery in Manchuria. In consequence of these and other exploits, he had become one of the two most widely acclaimed military commanders of that age. Having ousted the other, Ch'oe Yŏng, in the aftermath of his march back from the Yalu, Yi Sŏng-gye seized power as the leader of the new literati class. Finally, put forward by Chŏng To-jŏn and others among the literati bureaucrats, he had succeeded in establishing a new dynasty.

Yi Sŏng-gye named his dynasty Chosŏn, after the most ancient Korean kingdom, and moved the capital to Hanyang (Seoul), both actions important manifestations of the founding of a new dynasty. Indeed, the founder took no small pains with the establishment of a new capital. Both in terms of its geomantic setting and in its scale he strove to ensure that Seoul would mirror the prestige of his new kingdom. From this time on Seoul has been the political, economic, and cultural center of Korea.

4. The Culture of the New Literati Class

The Dissemination of Neo-Confucianism

In the reign of King Ch'ungnyŏl (1274–1308), through the efforts of An

Yu and others, Confucian studies were greatly encouraged by such means as the rebuilding of the National Academy (*Kukhak*) and of the National Shrine to Confucius (*Munmyo*), as well as by the ample endowment of a foundation for the support of students. Hitherto focused on belles-lettres and on philological glosses, scholarly attention now turned toward substantive study of the Chinese classics and histories, and a Superintendency to Teach Classics and Histories was even created. King Ch'ungsŏn too, after the throne had reverted to his father in 1298, went to the Yüan capital with Paek I-jŏng and developed close relationships with Yüan scholars. He returned to Koryŏ ten years later to succeed to the kingship, but he spent nearly all of his five-year reign again in Yüan. After he was removed from the throne in 1313 he built the Hall of Ten Thousand Volumes in the Yüan capital and, accompanied by such Koryŏ figures as Yi Che-hyŏn, associated with Yüan scholars as before. These circumstances too gave great impetus to the development of Confucian studies in late Koryŏ.

The special characteristic of late Koryŏ Confucianism lies in its acceptance of Neo-Confucian doctrine. Neo-Confucianism is a philosophical Confucianism that explains the origins of man and the universe in metaphysical terms. At the same time, the political ethic that it expounds lays stress on the mutual relationship of ruler and subject, and it is an intolerant doctrine, quick to reject all other teachings. The new literati class of that time, unable to find fulfillment either in Buddhism or in the belletristic, philology-centered Confucianism, now made Neo-Confucianism their spiritual mainstay. The first to profess the new doctrine was An Yu (1243–1306). Subsequently Paek I-jŏng (fl. 1275–1325) also studied Neo-Confucianism in Yüan China, and he was followed by his disciple Yi Che-hyŏn (1287–1367). Other famed Neo-Confucianists at the end of Koryŏ were Yi Sung-in (1349–1392), Yi Saek (1328–1396), Chŏng Mong-ju (1337–1392), and Kil Chae (1353–1419), as well as men like Chŏng To-jŏn (1337?–1398) and Kwŏn Kŭn (1352–1409) who served on into the early years of Chosŏn.

This spread of Neo-Confucianism gave rise to a growing repudiation of Buddhism. In the beginning, rather than denouncing Buddhism itself, men like Yi Che-hyŏn and Yi Saek were content to attack the abuses of the temples and the misconduct of the monks. But Chŏng To-jŏn, for example, completely rejected Buddhism as destructive of mores and ruinous to the state. Those of this persuasion attacked not only Buddhism but such features of Koryŏ life as marriage within the lineage and unrestrained pleasure seeking as well. The discontinuance of Buddhistic funeral and memorial rites and the establishment of household shrines for ancestral tablets, as prescribed by the *Family Rites of Chu Hsi*, also are phenomena first seen at this time.

The Writing of Histories

Beginning with the compilation in Hyŏnjong's reign (1009–1031) of official *Annals* (*Sillok*) for the first seven kings of the dynasty, annals for all the Koryŏ rulers were prepared. Today, however, none of these survive, and we are left with the *History of the Three Kingdoms* (*Samguk sagi*), compiled by Kim Pu-sik at the command of King Injong in 1145, as the oldest extant history. The *Samguk sagi*, an official history in annals form with separate chronological tables, treatises, and biographies, was written on the basis of native sources like the early Koryŏ *Old History of the Three Kingdoms*, as well as with reference to the Chinese histories. Reflecting the background of the author and his times, it was compiled from an aristocratic point of view and a Confucianist historiographical perspective. We are told of a slightly later work by Kim Kwan-ŭi, entitled *Abridged Chronological History* (*P'yŏnnyŏn t'ongnok*), but this does not survive. There is also the *Lives of Eminent Korean Monks* (*Haedong kosŭng chŏn*) written by the monk Kakhun in 1215, again by royal command, and a portion of this remains. This work may be seen as a kind of orthodox history of Buddhism in Korea, written from the viewpoint of the Textual School that had flourished in congenial partnership with aristocratic power in Koryŏ.

Subsequently a more active interest in historical compilation developed, resulting in such works as Wŏn Pu's *Chronicle of Past and Present* (*Kogŭm nok*), Chŏng Ka-sin's *Reflections from the Mirror of This Age* (*Ch'ŏnch'u kŭmgyŏng nok*), Min Chi's *Annotated Events of the Present Dynasty* (*Ponjo p'yŏnnyŏn kangmok*), all done between 1274 and 1313, and Yi Che-hyŏn's somewhat later *Concise History* (*Saryak*). None of these has been handed down, however, and only Yi Che-hyŏn's personal judgments as the chronicler remain from his *Saryak*. All of these government sponsored histories, in the tradition of the *Samguk sagi*, employed the perspective of Confucian moralism to view history didactically as a mirror for government.

Of quite a different character are *Memorabilia of the Three Kingdoms* (*Samguk yusa*) by the monk Iryŏn (1206–1289) and *Songs of Emperors and Kings* (*Chewang un'gi*) by Yi Sŭng-hyu (1224–1300), both written during Ch'ungnyŏl's reign (1274–1308). The unique feature of both these is that they begin Korean history with Tan'gun. The suffering of the people of Koryŏ during the Mongol period, it would seem, strengthened their sense of identity as a distinct race and gave force to the concept of their descent from a common ancestor. A second characteristic is that these works present reminiscences of earlier ages in a manner clearly evidencing the deep respect the authors felt for the traditions and legacy of their past history. Thus many historical materials neglected by the author of the *Samguk sagi* came to be utilized in these two histories, making them still more valuable. The Sŏn monk Iryŏn's *Memorabilia of the Three Kingdoms* is a particularly rich source of information on ancient folkways and institutions; among general histories it stands in contrast to the *Samguk sagi* and, in terms of Buddhist histories, to the *Lives of Eminent Korean Monks*.

Kyŏnggi-*Style Poems and "Long Poems"*

The literary form in which the literati of this age expressed themselves was the so-called *kyŏnggi*-style poem. This newly developed poetic form used the Chinese language, but to exalt Korea's own land and its lore. It began with the "Song of the Confucian Academicians" (*Hallim pyŏlgok*) composed by the young Confucian officials of the Academy of Letters during the period of military rule, a poem that vividly depicts the exultant view of life held by the literati now emerging onto the political stage. The "Song of Kangwŏn Province" (*Kwandong pyŏlgok*) by An Ch'uk (1287–1348) and other works followed, in which the proud spirits of the literati bureaucrats are given piquant expression. At the same time poems about fishermen that depict the solitary pastimes of the literati living on their countryside estates also appeared.

If *kyŏnggi*-style poems and those on fishing were the upper-class genre of the literati, the "long poem" (*changga*), the authors of which are largely unknown, was the literary form of the common people. Such *changga* as "Green Mountain Song" (*Ch'ŏngsan pyŏlgok*), "A Song of the Western Capital" (*Sŏgyŏng pyŏlgok*), "Would You Now Leave Me?" (*Kasiri*), "A Song of Chŏngŭp County" (*Chŏngŭp sa*), and the "Tongdong Refrain" (*Tongdong*) are considered to rank with the *hyangga* of Silla in their literary quality. But because they are poems that developed out of the folk song tradition, they give full and frank expression to the feelings of the people. In extreme cases, such as the poem "The Turkish Bakery" (*Ssanghwajŏm*), the *changga* unblushingly depict scenes of licentiousness. On the other hand *changga* also reflect the life realities of the peasantry, as in this passage that begins the "Green Mountain Song," redolent with the sorrow of landless peasants as they are forced to abandon their farms for a life of wandering:

> Let us live, let us live,
> Let us live in a green mountain.
> Eating wild grapes and vine berries,
> Let us live in a green mountain.

These *changga*, nevertheless, came to be sung frequently on such occasions as palace banquets, and so they also underwent development as songs for the enjoyment of the upper classes.

Fine Arts

Discussion of wooden structures in Korea is not possible before the mid-Koryŏ period, for the earliest surviving building is the Hall of Paradise (Kŭngnak-chŏn) at the Pongjŏng-sa temple in Andong, thought to date from the thirteenth century. But the best example of Koryŏ architecture in wood is the Hall of Eternal Life (Muryangsu-jŏn) at Pusŏk-sa in Yŏngju, which appears to have been built at about the same time. Its tapered columns, shapely three-tiered roof supports, the buoyant lines of the dual roof-edge, and the ceiling-less open work of the hall within give an overall solemn dignity of appearance that is characteristic of Korean wooden buildings. Other noteworthy structures from the late Koryŏ are the Hall of the Founder (Chosa-dang) also at Pusŏk-sa, the Hall of Sakyamuni (Taeung-jŏn) at Sudŏk-sa in Tŏksan, and as an example of early Yi dynasty architecture, the South (Great) Gate (Namdaemun) in Seoul.

The distinctive feature of painting in the later Koryŏ period is that this art more and more came to be practiced by the non-professional, by the literati, to give expression to their sensibilities in what may be called a romantic style. This is evidenced by the frequency with which paintings of this age portrayed the literatus as recluse, the pleasures of alfresco fellowship, the "four gentlemen" (orchid, chrysanthemum, bamboo, and plum) and, in particular, representations of bamboo done in black writing brush ink. The concept of poem and painting as a unitary mode of expression, put forward by men of letters like Yi Kyu-bo and Yi Che-hyŏn, may be said to be another by-product of the new trend, which grew out of the elegant life-style of the newly risen literati class. But there is little opportunity to directly assess late Koryŏ literati painting today; perhaps no more than three or four works from this period are known, one of them, "Hunting on Mt. Heaven" (*Ch'ŏnsan suryŏp to*), rather uncertainly attributed to King Kongmin himself. Fortunately this is not the case with Buddhist painting, for such works as the monk Hyehŏ's "Portrait of the Willow Goddess of Mercy" (*Yangnyu Kwanŭm sang*), painted with refinement and splendor, have been handed down to today. Other renowned temple paintings are the depictions of the Deva guardian kings on a wall of Pusŏk-sa's Hall of the Founder and the water flower mural at the Sudŏk-sa temple; this last, although discovered less than fifty years ago, now is preserved only in a reproduction.

An unusual late Koryŏ stone pagoda is the one at the Kyŏngch'ŏn-sa temple in Kaep'ung (now moved to the Kyŏngbok Palace grounds in Seoul), which was built during the reign of King Ch'ungmok (1344–1348). A ten-story pagoda done in marble, the three-tiered pedestal and first three stories each protrude alternate square-shaped and triangular edges, eight in all, providing twenty surfaces on which to carve Buddhistic images; the top seven stories, then, are typically square. This pagoda exhibits a Yüan influence and in turn served as the model for the Wŏn'gak-sa pagoda (in Seoul's Pagoda Park), constructed in the time of the Yi king Sejo (mid-15th century). The stone memorial stupas of this late period took the unadorned form of stone bells, a marked change from the ornamental ones of earlier Koryŏ times. That for the monk Hyegŭn at Sillŭk-sa in Yŏju is a classic example, and stone stupas in this form also became precursors of Yi dynasty stupas. Finally worthy of note is the existence down to today of superb wood-crafted articles such as the masks for the Hahoe masked drama.

In calligraphy the spare style of the Sung Chinese master Ou-yang Hsün, so widely practiced in the earlier period, gave way to the markedly different, elegant style called *sung-hsüeh*, after a penname of the famed painter-calligrapher of the early Yüan period, Chao Meng-fu. A renowned calligrapher of this school in Korea is Yi Am (1297–1364). This calligraphic style went on to become the predominant mode of the Yi dynasty.

Science and Technology

The great concern from the early years of Koryŏ for the establishment of libraries led not only to the acquisition and preservation of books but to their duplication as well. Tens of thousands of rare books were kept as treasured possessions in Koryŏ, so that on occasion even the Sung government sent to Koryŏ to secure works unavailable in China. Printing thus flourished and a wide variety of books were published. At first most printing was done by the woodblock technique, of which the publication of the Tripitaka is an outstanding example.

Woodblock printing, of course, was an extremely convenient way to satisfy a widespread demand for one particular work. Once the blocks were carved the printing itself not only was a simple matter, but the blocks could be kept for a comparatively long time to make possible any number of subsequent editions. But when many kinds of works were needed in a limited number of copies, printing by movable type was more efficient, in spite of the drawback of having to cast and set type. In Koryŏ books were essential only to the small number of those in the educated upper-class, and so the normal run of an edition also was small. It was natural, then, for Koryŏ to direct its attention toward printing by movable type and to proceed to develop this art.

It is said that printing by movable type was invented in the eleventh century by Pi Sheng of the Northern Sung dynasty, but he used clay type, a method not widely imitated and which soon ceased to be used or remembered. In Koryŏ there is a record of the use of cast metal type in the year 1234 for the printing of the work *Prescribed Ritual Texts of the Past and Present (Sangjŏng kogŭm yemun)*. It is clear that the type used to print this book was metal movable type, and it likely was not many years earlier that Koryŏ began to print with such movable type. Thus Koryŏ's use of this printing method is the earliest in the history of the world. This early experimental period was followed, at the very end of the Koryŏ dynasty in 1392, by the establishment of a National Office for Book Publication charged with the casting of type and printing of books. Thus the foundation for the flourishing of movable type printing in the Yi dynasty was laid in the later Koryŏ period.

A major development at this time in material used for clothing in Korea also must be noted. Up to now hemp had been the principal material for people's clothing, with ramie and silk also used in the more elegant wear of the aristocracy. At this point the cultivation of the cotton plant began in Korea and cotton cloth emerged as a major material for clothing. Cotton seeds were brought back from Yüan China in 1363 by Mun Ik-chŏm (1329–1398), who had gone there as the secretary to a Koryŏ envoy. He gave the seeds for planting to his father-in-law, Chŏng Ch'ŏn-ik, who not only succeeded in growing them but also devised a cotton gin and built a spinning wheel as well. The wide recognition of the value of growing cotton and the spread of its cultivation throughout the country are stories that belong to the Yi dynasty, but this late Koryŏ development was responsible for a marked improvement in the clothing of the Korean people.

Important development also took place in this period in regard to medical knowledge. Although Koryŏ medicine was influenced by Sung China, on the other hand study and exploitation of Korea's own traditional folk remedies gave impetus to the development of an indigenous medical science. Compilation of the work *Emergency Remedies of Folk Medicine* (*Hyangyak kugŭp pang*) was an outgrowth of this emphasis; published in 1236, it is Korea's oldest extant medical treatise. A number of other such treatises were compiled at this time, including the thirteenth century work *Folk Remedies of Samhwaja* (*Samhwaja hyangyak pang*), widely used as a diagnostic guide, and these constituted a foundation for the preparation of the *Compilation of Native Korean Prescriptions* (*Hyangyak chipsŏng pang*) in the early Yi dynasty.

The manufacture of gunpowder for the first time in Korea is another development of this period. It already had been used in Sung and Yüan China, but the method of producing it was a closely guarded secret, not to be officially revealed to Koryŏ. When raids by Japanese marauders were at their destructive height, however, a man of minor official background named Ch'oe Mu-sŏn perceived the need for more powerful weapons and worked tirelessly to formulate gunpowder. Eventually learning its secret from a Yüan Chinese, Ch'oe persuaded the Koryŏ court to establish a Superintendency for Gunpowder Weapons (1377) where cannon of various kinds could be made and gunpowder employed in other weaponry as well. He also equipped the navy with newly built ships, which, with their cannon, achieved major successes in repulsing the Japanese marauders.

Chapter 9

The Creation of a *Yangban* Society

1. The Development of *Yangban* Society in Chosŏn

The Literati and the Kingship

Military strength was the principal factor that enabled Yi Sŏnggye to establish a new dynasty and become its first ruler (as King T'aejo, 1392–1398). At the same time, had the literati not given him their support, he surely could not have occupied the throne. In Chosŏn's early years the "Dynastic Foundation Merit Subjects" (*kaeguk kongsin*) of literati background, who had elevated him to the kingship, wielded political power from their base in the joint deliberative organ called the Privy Council (*Top'yŏngŭisasa*). Yi T'aejo's role was no more than to give sanction to the Council's decisions and to order them carried out. The literati powerholders, then, set about devising a corpus of administrative law infused with the ideals of Confucianist government, a code embodying the cardinal principles and practices by which the Yi dynasty political process would operate. Such efforts at comprehensive codification of Confucianist principles were the *Administrative Code of Chosŏn* (*Chosŏn kyŏngguk chŏn*), compiled by Chŏng To-jŏn, and the *Six Codes of Governance* (*Kyŏngje yukchŏn*), a compilation of administrative law that Chŏng prepared with Cho Chun following the march back from the Yalu in 1388.

This governance of the Dynastic Foundation Merit Subjects strikes one as being simply a repetition of Koryŏ aristocratic rule, and this is why the king from his perspective and the numerous other literati beneath the highest levels in the bureaucracy became disaffected. The result was the liquidation of Chŏng To-jŏn by T'aejo's fifth son, Yi Pang-wŏn (the later King T'aejong, 1400–1418). The ambitious T'aejong in the end took the throne for himself, having first ordered the assassination of T'aejo's designated heir, the youngest son Pang-sŏk, and then disposing of the rival claim of his next older brother, Pang-gan. Before actually taking the throne T'aejong already had seized political power, had abolished private armed retinues and instituted centralized military control, and had proceeded to change the Privy Council into a State Council (*Ŭijŏngbu*) with greatly diminished authority, since he entrusted overall conduct of government business to six ministries each authorized to approach the throne directly. T'aejong had the *Six Codes of Governance* revised and expanded to reflect these new structural arrangements, creating the *Basic Six Codes* (*Wŏn yukchŏn*) and the *Supplemental Six Codes* (*Sok yukchŏn*).

Sejong (1418–1450), T'aejong's successor, established the Hall of Worthies (*Chiphyŏnjŏn*), assigned outstanding scholars to it, and had them study the ancient statutes and institutions of China. He wanted to reorganize the political structure of Chosŏn on this model, and one result of the work of the Hall of Worthies was the six-volume *Orthodox Code* (*Chŏngjŏn*). In consequence of this process the political voice of the scholars in the Hall of Worthies came to be heard ever more loudly, and indeed the feeling grew that actual political control was now in their hands. Sejo's usurpation of the throne, it may be suggested, represented a reaction against this development. With the backing of disaffected elements among the literati, Sejo in 1455 deposed his nephew Tanjong (subsequently having him put to death) and mounted the throne himself. In the process he killed a great many of those who opposed him, beginning with the elder statesmen Hwangbo In and Kim Chong-sŏ and his own younger brother, the Prince of Anp'yŏng, who was close to them. Sejo then carried out a bloodbath in which Sŏng Sam-mun, Pak P'aeng-nyŏn, Ha Wi-ji, Yi Kae, Yu Ŭng-bu, and Yu Sŏng-wŏn, who came to be known in later days as the "six martyred ministers" (*sa yuksin*), and other scholars of the Hall of Worthies met their deaths. He too then set to work compiling, once again, a statutory code that would define the structure and functioning of Chosŏn's government, producing finally the *National Code* (*Kyŏngguk taejŏn*). With some minor revisions this version of the *National Code* actually was promulgated in the second year of Sŏngjong's reign (1471). Thus was set in place the administrative structure of the kingdom of Chosŏn, a dynasty that attached greater importance to a governing process directed by civil and military bureaucrats enforcing prescribed procedures than to one dominated by a joint deliberative organ situated at the highest level.

Yangban *Society*

The literati was the dominant social class that directed the Yi dynasty polity. It was the literati, after all, who constituted the *yangban*, the members of the "two orders" of officialdom who served in the bureaucracy as civil or military officials. This is why, subsequently, the term *yangban* came to be used broadly to designate the status group in Yi society privileged to occupy civil and military posts in the bureaucracy. And precisely because it was this *yangban* class that directed the government, economy, and culture of Yi dynasty society, it may fittingly be designated a *yangban* society.

Yi society's dominant *yangban* class was much more broadly based than the ruling classes of Koryŏ or earlier ages. For a far greater number of lineages gained recognition as *yangban* in Yi Korea than was the case with the true-bone aristocracy of Silla or with the small hereditary aristocracy of the Koryŏ period. The increased size of the *yangban* class in turn greatly increased the importance of an examination system for the recruitment of officials. In order to protect the common interests of the whole *yangban* class, then, the Yi dynasty found it wise to put primary emphasis on state examinations. Accordingly, government service via so-called protected appointments was strictly limited, in consequence making it difficult to advance solely on the basis of family background. Confucianist academic training was a necessary condition for qualifying for office via the examination system, and to provide this training a number of educational organs were available to the *yangban* class. Moreover, the *yangban* in actual practice were exempted from the usual service obligations to the state, whether corvee labor or military duty. They were to devote themselves exclusively to study, to the cultivation of self that Confucian doctrine holds must underlie the governing of others, and so the privilege that enabled them to become officials took the place of other service obligations to the state.

The *yangban* who thus alone enjoyed a variety of special privileges naturally could not be other than elitist. The door to advancement in the society that had been so widely opened to the class of local functionaries (*hyangni*) gradually became closed to them. *Yangban* married only among themselves and so of course *yangban* status became hereditary. They did not even live side by side with those who were not *yangban*. In Seoul the northern and southern quarters and in the countryside separate villages rather than the towns were where *yangban* residences were located. But within the *yangban* class itself there also were distinctions. First of all, the military order was less well regarded than the civil order. Further, a law banning those of illegitimate birth from important government office made it difficult and, during much of the dynasty, impossible for the sons of *yangban* by secondary wives, and their descendants, to sit for the examinations that would qualify them for civil office appointments. Sons and grandsons of *yangban* widows who remarried could not serve in government office at all. There was regional discrimination as well, and residents of the northern provinces of P'yŏngan and Hamgyŏng, with few exceptions, were unable to gain appointment to the higher offices. All of these limitations may be viewed as part of a self-selection process at work within *yangban* society. For the *yangban* feared that an increase in their numbers would erode their position of special privilege.

The sole profession of the *yangban* was the holding of public office. Yet they did not serve in the technical posts that alike were components of the bureaucracy. Positions as medical officers, translator-interpreters, technicians in the astronomy and meteorology office, accountants, statute law clerks, scribes, and government artists all were the hereditary preserve of the so-called middle people (*chungin*). Nor did the *yangban* perform the routine duties of petty clerks and local civil functionaries (*sŏri* and *ajŏn*) or of military cadre members (*kun'gyo*). These too, on their lower level, were the preserve of hereditary classes of functionaries. To be sure, in the broad sense that they too were assured of substantive positions within the administrative apparatus, these specialists, clerks, and military cadre also comprised segments of the ruling class, but they must be clearly distinguished from the *yangban*. The *yangban* also were not interested in working at agriculture, manufacture, or commerce, for these were but the occupations of farmers, artisans, and merchants. The *yangban* scholars might well dream of achieving an ideal polity through the moral cultivation of Chosŏn's people, but this did not mean in fact that they were prepared to do away with distinctions of social status.

2. Administrative Structure of the *Yangban* Bureaucratic State

The Political Framework

The highest organ of Yi government was the State Council (*Ŭijŏngbu*). A successor to the Privy Council of Koryŏ, the Yi State Council too was a deliberative organ, and its joint decisions were made by three High State Councillors. These three officials discussed important matters of state, conveyed their consensus to the king and, receiving his decision, transmitted it to the appropriate government agency. But in comparison with the Koryŏ Privy Council, the State Council of Chosŏn had far fewer officials, and since many important matters of government were referred for disposition directly to the Six Ministries (*Yukcho*), the State Council gradually declined in authority.

The Six Ministries, on the other hand, came to have the authority to memorialize the king directly on matters under their purview and then to put into execution his decisions. Although the respective areas of jurisdiction of Chosŏn's Six Ministries—those of Personnel, Taxation, Rites, Military Affairs, Punishments, and Public Works—were little different from those of Koryŏ's Six Boards, their political importance was far greater. The Yi dynasty's political structure, therefore, might aptly be termed a "ministries system," which in turn suggests that the political structure of Chosŏn was more bureaucracy centered than that of Koryŏ. Another agency that performed a vital role was the Royal Secretariat (*Sŭngjŏngwŏn*), the organ through which documents were transmitted to and from the king, and there were times when it ignored other agencies and exercised authority on its own.

An instrumentality designed to prevent abuses in the exercise of political and administrative authority was the so-called *Samsa*, a combined term for the Office of Special Advisers (*Hongmun'gwan*), Office of the Inspector-General (*Sahŏnbu*), and Office of the Censor-General (*Saganwŏn*). The Office of Special Advisers, a successor to the Hall of Worthies that Sejo had abolished, maintained a library, searched out administrative and legal precedents, authored major state documents, and so undertook the role of an advisory organ to the king. The Office of the Inspector-General was a surveillance organ, criticizing the political issues of the day, scrutinizing official conduct, and rectifying public mores. The Office of the Censor-General, on the other hand, was to examine critically and censure as necessary the conduct of the king himself, a function that imposed restraint on the arbitrary exercise of the power of the throne. Together, these two organs of remonstrance were entrusted with a unique authority, called *sŏgyŏng*, to look into the family background and career records of those nominated for middle- and lower-ranking positions, preliminary to giving or withholding approval of their appointments. Taken as a whole, the *Samsa* as advising and censoring bodies on the one hand, and the State Council and Six Ministries as responsible for policy and its execution on the other, were positioned so as to create a system of checks and balances, thus preventing power becoming over concentrated in one branch of government. The very existence of the *Samsa*, with its constant, keen scrutiny of the public and private conduct of the king and his high officials, provides a key to understanding the nature of Yi Korea's literati-centered *yangban* society.

As for provincial and local government, the country was divided into the eight provinces of Kyŏnggi, Ch'ungch'ŏng, Kyŏngsang, Chŏlla, Hwanghae, Kangwŏn, Hamgil (Hamgyŏng), and P'yŏngan, and within the provinces counties of several types (*pu, mok, kun, hyŏn*) were demarcated [see map p. 177]. A governor (*kwanch'alsa* or *kamsa*, also called *pangbaek*) was appointed to each province, with jurisdiction over the various county magistrates (*puyun, pusa, moksa, kunsu, hyŏllyŏng, hyŏn'gam*). The county magistrate was the so-called shepherd of the people, the official who governed them directly, and his principal duty was to collect taxes and mobilize corvee labor for the central government. Accordingly, local government as Yi Korea conceived it was little more than an additional administrative apparatus for the support of the *yangban* class.

Charged with broad administrative and judicial duties, the provincial and local officials were appointed for terms limited to one year for provincial governors and five years for county magistrates, and the latter were not permitted to serve in the counties in which they resided. This is because it was feared that a magistrate might act in collusion with local *yangban* who were their kinsmen against the interests of the *yangban* class as a whole. On the other hand, a so-called Local Agency (*Hyangch'ŏng*) was organized in each county by its *yangban* residents and through it they wielded considerable influence. This office, a successor to Koryŏ's similar institution (the *Yuhyangso*), was directed by an overseer (*chwasu*) and his

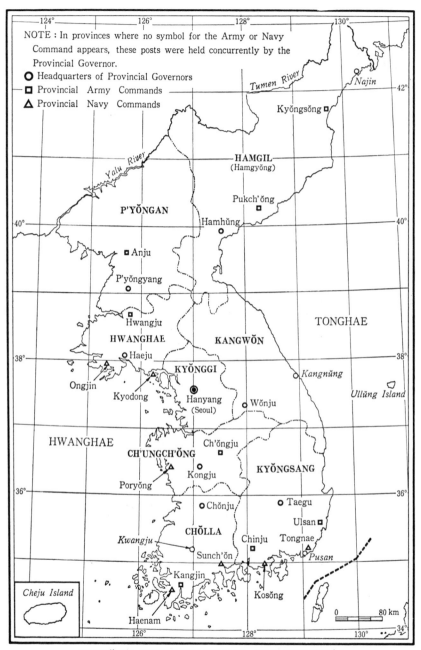

NOTE : In provinces where no symbol for the Army or Navy
Command appears, these posts were held concurrently by the
Provincial Governor.
○ Headquarters of Provincial Governors
□ Provincial Army Commands
△ Provincial Navy Commands

Tumen River
Najin
Kyŏngsŏng □

HAMGIL
(Hamgyŏng)
Pukch'ŏng □
Hamhŭng ○

Yalu River
P'YŎNGAN
□ Anju
P'yŏngyang ○

□
Hwangju
HWANGHAE   KANGWŎN   TONGHAE
○ Haeju
KYŎNGGI   ○ Kangnŭng
Ongjin   △
Kyodong   Ullŭng Island
Hanyang △ ○ Wŏnju
(Seoul)

HWANGHAE   Ch'ŏngju
CH'UNGCH'ŎNG   □
△   ○   KYŎNGSANG
Poryŏng   Kongju
○ Chŏnju   ○ Taegu
Ulsan □
CHŎLLA   Chinju   Tongnae
Kwangju   □
Sunch'ŏn △   Pusan △
△
Kangjin □   Kosŏng △
Cheju Island
Haenam   0   80 km

CHOSŎN'S EIGHT PROVINCES AND REGIONAL
MILITARY COMMANDS (15th CENTURY)

assistants (*pyŏlgam*), and it undertook responsibility for assisting the magistrate, rectifying public mores, and scrutinizing the conduct of the county's petty functionaries (*hyangni*). In consequence it served as a power base for the local *yangban* and exerted great influence on local adminis- tration. At the same time, there was a Capital Liaison Office (*Kyŏng- jaeso*) in Seoul for each county, headed by central government officials who had originated in that county, and these functionaries sought to ensure that the Local Agency served national rather than local interests.

In each provincial and local administrative unit duties were allocated among six "chambers" (*pang*)—personnel, taxation, rites, military af- fairs, punishments, and public works—on the model of the Six Ministries in the capital. The duties of these offices were discharged by a hereditary class of petty functionaries (*hyangni*, also known as local *ajŏn*) native to the area in which they served. For liaison purposes an *ajŏn* from each county was stationed in Seoul (and thus was known as a *kyŏngjŏri*) and at the headquarters of the provincial governor (known as a *yŏngjŏri*). Thus it was the *ajŏn*, or *hyangni*, that actually carried on the operations of the local government offices, and since they were an indigenous element, they could serve as a bridge between the magistrates who governed in the name of the king, and the Local Agency that represented *yangban* power in the locality. *Hyangni* had existed in Koryŏ as well, but they were a powerful group from among which men constantly rose to the ranks of the aristocracy in the capital; the vital difference in the *hyangni* of the Yi dynasty is that they were barred from rising to *yangban* status.

Military Organization

The military system had been in extreme disarray ever since the late Koryŏ period, and so Yi T'aejo exerted no little effort to set it in order. He established the Three Armies Headquarters (*Ŭihŭng Samgunbu*) to assume control over the military apparatus, but since members of the royal household, merit subjects, and others still retained personal armed retinues, he was unable to bring about centralization of military authority in the hands of the government. It was T'aejong who resolutely abolished these private armed forces and so accomplished this end. In 1400, when he himself was the real arbiter of national affairs under his brother, King Chŏngjong, T'aejong entirely did away with the private armed retinues, attaching their soldiers to the Three Armies Headquarters. This overall command was reorganized by Sejo in 1464 into the Five Military Com- mands Headquarters (*Owi Toch'ongbu*), which was given authority over the fivefold division of the forces that garrisoned the capital.

The restructuring of the various army units stationed in the capital in 1457 fixed the pattern of Yi Korea's military organization. The term "Five Commands" (*Owi*) refers to the divisions of the Center, East, West, South and North, and each of these had military jurisdiction over the corresponding region of the country. Each division consisted of five brigades (*pu*), each brigade of four regiments (*t'ong*), and under the regiments were battalions (*yŏ*), companies (*tae*), and platoons (*o*). The troops that formed the core of the Five Commands, such as armored soldiers, were professional military men selected through tests of their military skills. From among the commoner population, of course, there were troops drafted to serve as "conscript soldiers" (*chŏngbyŏng*) in the capital garrisons, but this system was not well enforced and moreover such troops did not comprise a significant portion of Yi Korea's standing army.

From an overall perspective, provincial armies in fact were a more important component of the Yi defense structure than were the Five Commands in the capital. Each province had its own Army Command and Navy Command with jurisdiction over the army and navy forces in its area, and under these were a number of garrisons (*chin*). In Hamgyŏng and Kyŏngsang provinces, though, as a defense against Jurchen (Yain) and Japanese incursions, there were two Army Commands and two Navy Commands, and Chŏlla province too, with its long coastline, had two Navy Commands [see map p. 177]. The military men attached to the garrisons in the provinces were called "garrison forces" (*chinsugun*) and they were of three kinds: the combat soldiers who defended the garrison fortifications, their support or labor battalions, and the sailors who manned the ships. The land garrison forces were by far the most important of these, with their core element of units made up of commoner peasants. Assigned to military service in accordance with a system of rotation, when they were stood down these peasant-soldiers returned to their farms.

The central government and provincial forces, which thus had existed under separate command structures, later came to be merged. That is, a garrison-command structure was created, centering on the fortified garrison points to which were assigned those same commoner peasants who formerly had been rotated up into the capital garrison or dispatched to defend the strongholds in the provinces. The two types of troops, then, had been combined into a single force of conscript soldiers, serving under a single command structure. In consequence the commoner peasant-soldier, the core of the national defense force, became simply a conscript who normally went about his farming but then would be called up in turn to active duty in Seoul or at the garrison forts. This did not mean, however, that all those in the category of commoner peasants became conscript soldiers, for some served as "sustainers" who provided economic support for the conscript soldiers on active duty. This arrangement was brought to final form by the Paired Provisioner System (*popŏp*), under which one of a team of two or three able-bodied men was to be supported while on active service by the others, the "provisioners" supplying the conscripted soldier with a fixed amount of cotton cloth and being so supported when they in turn were called up.

Finally, in order to quickly inform the capital of military crises that might occur in the provinces, there was a system of beacon fires, and in order to speedily convey more detailed information on such situations a network of post stations was maintained. The post station system also was used for the transmission of government documents in general, for government transport purposes, and for official travel.

Examinations and Education

The examination system put into effect in Koryŏ as a means of recruiting officials took on still more central importance in Yi Korea. Since Chosŏn restricted protected appointments to the sons of officials of the second rank and above, unless one passed through the examination system the path to higher office in effect was closed. For the *yangban*, then, the examinations truly were the gateway to success. While it is true that anyone of commoner, or free, status possessed the qualification to sit for the examinations, it still is not too much to say that the *yangban* monopolized the examinations leading to appointment to the civil offices so prized by Chosŏn's *yangban* society. This is because the opportunities for the kind of education needed to pass the examinations were made available almost exclusively to the *yangban*.

Qualifying examinations for appointment to civil offices were conducted at two levels, the licentiate or lower level (*saengjinkwa,* or *sokwa*) and the erudite or higher level (*munkwa,* or *taekwa*). The licentiate examinations were of two kinds: the Classics Licentiate Examination (*saengwŏnkwa*) that examined candidates on the Four Books and Five Classics of China, and the Literary Licentiate Examination (*chinsakwa*) that tested skill in composing such Chinese literary forms as *shih* poetry, rhyme prose (*fu*), documentary prose (*p'iao*), and the problem-essay (*ts'e*). From an early age *yangban* youth attended private elementary schools (*sŏdang*) where they learned the basic Chinese characters and practiced writing them. Then, from age seven, they advanced to one of the Four Schools (*sahak*) in Seoul or to the County School (*hyanggyo*) established in each county. The Confucian students of these schools, after several years of study, were thereby qualified to sit for the licentiate examinations, and if they passed a first stage examination held at the provincial level they proceeded to Seoul for a second stage examination, which determined those who would receive degrees. Depending on which examination they took, those who passed were called Classics Licentiates (*saengwŏn*) or Literary Licentiates (*chinsa*). These Licentiates might then enter the National Confucian Academy (*Sŏnggyun'gwan*) in Seoul, the country's highest educational organ, and the students who attended the National Confucian Academy could sit for the Erudite Examination (*munkwa*). Here too the successful candidates, typically thirty-three in number, had to survive preliminary and second examination stages. Finally a Palace Examination (*chŏnsi*) was held in the presence of the king, and those who had passed were individually ranked, in the categories of pass with distinction, high pass, and pass. The man who took the first place in the examination, the so-called *changwŏn*, was accorded specially favored treatment, being appointed to a middle level post of the junior sixth rank.

What has just been described, however, represents the processes of recruitment for civil offices as they were designed institutionally, and it was by no means the case that only this one track had to be followed. As the means of preparing for the examinations, for example, *yangban* society increasingly preferred their own privately established institutions to the government's Four Schools in Seoul or County Schools in the countryside. Moreover, although it originally was prescribed that so-called regular examinations be carried out every third year, in reality examinations also were held irregularly at other times. There was the Augmented Examination (*chŭnggwangsi*) held to celebrate such important events of national felici-tation as the accession of a new king, there were Special Examinations (*pyŏlsi*) given on more usual joyous occasions involving the royal family, and there were the Royal Visitation Examinations (*alsŏngsi*) administered from time to time by the king in person when he inspected the progress of students at the National Confucian Academy (*Sŏnggyun'gwan*). As these and other irregular examinations increased, the triennial examinations (*singnyŏnsi*) diminished in importance, and this but reflected changes in the nature of *yangban* literati society.

Military examinations had been held for the first time at the very end of the Koryŏ period, and these were continued in the Yi dynasty. The military examination tested skills in military arts such as archery, lance marksmanship, and low saddle maneuvering, as well as knowledge of the Classics and military texts. The military examination, in parallel with the civil, was carried out in three stages, and the twenty-eight men who passed each triennial examination were known as *sŏndal* (perhaps meaning those who had arrived at the threshold of appointment to office). Although the military examination was far less important than the civil, the fact that it was formally established as an integral part of Chosŏn's examination system meant that the way had been opened for the regular recruitment of military officials, and this in turn signified the formal com-pletion of the *yangban* bureaucratic structure. But the military examination too later changed complexion and became an avenue through which even lowborn (*ch'ŏnmin*) might advance.

There were four Miscellaneous Examinations (*chapkwa*) for the selection of technical specialists, in foreign languages, medicine, astronomy (includ-ing meteorology and geomancy), and law. Those who won degrees were employed in the Office of Translators, the Palace Medical Office, the Office for Observance of Natural Phenomena, and in the Ministry of Punishments, respectively, and it was these same agencies that undertook the schooling of the aspiring technical specialists. The literati of Yi Korea looked down on these specialized studies, calling them a "hodgepodge

of learning," and on the whole the youth of the *chungin* ("middle people")
class undertook these studies and sat for these examinations on a hereditary basis.

3. Social and Economic Structure of the *Yangban* Bureaucratic State

Patterns of Yangban *Landholding*

The land system of Yi Korea rested on the foundation of the reform carried out by Yi Sŏng-gye (T'aejo) at the end of Koryŏ. In accordance with
the Rank Land Law (*kwajŏnpŏp*) put into effect at that time, both incumbent
and former officials were to receive allocations of land in accordance with
the rank they held in the government's eighteen office ranks structure.
It was stipulated that such land would be allocated only from that available in the Kyŏnggi area, the province around the capital, the purpose
being to prevent the expansion out into the countryside of the economic
power of the *yangban* bureaucrats. Although in principle grants of rank
land were limited to the lifetime of the recipient, an official's widow, if she
did not remarry, was permitted to hold a portion of her husband's land
(this was called "fidelity land," *susinjŏn*), and similarly, if both parents were
deceased, "fostering land" (*hyuryangjŏn*) was retained for the upbringing
of the children. In consequence, there was a marked tendency, from the
beginning, for rank land to be held hereditarily.

These circumstances soon combined to create a shortage of land available for distribution to those newly eligible to receive rank land allocations.
The problem was exacerbated by the fact that grants of "merit land"
(*kongsinjŏn*), also generally limited to Kyŏnggi province, continued to
increase. Merit land in the Yi dynasty, being given only to so-called Merit
Subjects, differed from that of similar name (*kongŭmjŏn*) in the Koryŏ
system, but it too was permitted to be passed on to one's descendants. With
the founding of the new dynasty and the ensuing succession disputes
several rosters of Merit Subjects had been promulgated, and the accompanying grants of land to these officials had further depleted the stock of
land in Kyŏnggi. As a result, in 1466 Sejo revoked the Rank Land Law and
enacted an Office Land Law (*chikchŏnpŏp*) in its place. By its provisions
land was to be allocated only to incumbent officeholders, no longer to
former officials as well. But this new system too could not remain in effect
for long, and around 1556 it was itself abolished. At this point, then,
officials were paid only salaries and were no longer given land.

In addition to rank or office land and land granted to meritorious
officials, there was also "military land" (*kunjŏn*). Allocated to the *hallyang*
military junior officer class that still was a force in the countryside, this
category of land differed from the "soldiers' land" (*kuninjŏn*) of the Koryŏ

in that, like rank land, it too tended to be held on to hereditarily, on the ground that it was needed for the support of widows and orphaned children. There was *naesusajŏn*, too, tracts of land set aside to meet the needs of the palace, in the manner of Koryŏ's "royal estate land." The allocation of "public agency land" (*konghaejŏn*) to the many central government offices, on the other hand, soon was abandoned in favor of a system of meeting the expenses of government out of grain tax and local tribute receipts. Land continued to be assigned, however, for the support of local government agencies (*nŭmjŏn*), but the so-called local service land (*oeyŏkchŏn*) formerly given to the *hyangni*, the petty functionaries of local government, was abolished. Finally, allocations were made of "school land" (*hakchŏn*) to support the government's education organs, "temple land" (*sawŏnjŏn*) for Buddhist temples, and "garrison land" (*kuktunjŏn*) to provide stores for provincial and local military establishments.

In underlying concept, the land system of Yi Korea postulated that ownership of all the nation's land formally resided in the king. The term "public land" (*kongjŏn*), however, did not mean land owned by the state, but rather designated land from which the state directly collected a "rent" originally set at ten percent of the harvest. Similarly, "private land" (*sajŏn*) was distributed to individual rank or office holders, but what the government granted was the right to collect the rent and not ownership rights. Nevertheless, *yangban* recipients of such grants often were able to convey the right to collect the rent on a particular allotment of land to their heirs, and ultimately to convert this limited right to one of outright ownership. Despite the formal principle of state ownership, therefore, the extent of private ownership of land steadily increased.

In point of fact, private ownership of land had been widespread from the outset. Most land distributed under the Rank Land Law actually belonged to the category of "people's land" (*minjŏn*), which meant that private ownership rights to it were recognized by the state. These rights generally appear to have come into existence at the end of Koryŏ, in many cases as a direct consequence of the confiscation of the large estates that preceded the Rank Land Law reform. Typical owners of "people's land" possessed only enough to cultivate themselves, but many—especially the *yangban*—had far more, and many others had less. The *yangban*, of course, had their land cultivated either by slaves or by tenant farmers, while those very small owners whose land could not support them hired out their labor as tenants on land owned by others. In all these cases, a half and half crop sharing arrangement normally prevailed between owner and cultivator, with the owner paying the ten percent rent to the state from his share. Such a crop sharing system gradually spread as well to rank land, merit subject land, and other forms of land allocation. In consequence of these circumstances, from the beginning of the Yi dynasty both landowning by the *yangban* and their income from the land (which might be used to buy still more land) continuously increased, and once again the term "agricultural estates" (*nongjang*) came to be used to describe the large holdings of the more wealthy members of the ruling class.

The Life of the Peasants

It was the peasants, of course, who tilled the land. The peasants of this period had mastered a far better agricultural technology than their predecessors. They knew how to use a variety of fertilizers to improve the fertility of the land. In consequence they were able to cultivate the land year after year without having to let it lie fallow. Moreover, although direct sowing of seed remained predominant, the method of transplanting rice seedlings had become known. Reservoirs to combat the effects of drought also were constructed, numbering over six hundred in Kyŏngsang province alone. Efforts were exerted, too, to develop strains of seed better adapted to the Korean climate. These improvements in agricultural technology inevitably resulted in increased yields.

The position of the peasant in Yi Korean society also improved. It would appear that there was a significant number of independent peasants in this period, owner-operators who employed hired hands (*kogong*) to help them cultivate their small holdings. The typical peasant, of course, still was one who toiled as a tenant farmer on the various kinds of *yangban* owned land, but his social status was that of freeborn commoner (*yangin,* or *sangmin*). There also were "out-resident" (*oegŏ*) slaves who tilled their owner's land and who were classed as "lowborn" (*ch'ŏnmin*), but since these formed independent households and were themselves responsible for their livelihood, they did not differ particularly from the peasant tenant farmers.

At the same time, the peasants were fixed on the land and were unable to move as they wished. In order to prevent them from abandoning the land they worked, an "identification tag" (*hop'ae*) law was enacted. The *hop'ae*, on which was recorded the name, date of birth, class status, and county of residence of the registrant, was like a modern citizen's identification card, and it was required to be in one's personal possession at all times. Subsequent to the rebellions of Yi Ching-ok in 1453 and of Yi Si-ae in 1467, which drew support from peasants who had migrated to Hamgyŏng province, the *hop'ae* law was further strengthened. Moreover, by the provisions of a law (*oga chakt'ongpŏp*) that organized households into units of five, neighbors were made mutually responsible for ensuring that members of the unit did not abscond from their locality of residence. In consequence, the peasant household of Yi Korea in general was a self-sufficient unit living generation after generation in one place, providing its own needs for food, clothing, and shelter.

In return for having land to cultivate, the peasant farmer was required to pay a land tax. The Rank Land Law had set this at one-tenth the harvest, but under Sejong in 1444 the Tribute Tax Law (*kongpŏp*) was promulgated, and the tax rate was lowered to one-twentieth. The tax on "public land," which was collected by the government, went first to storehouse collection points and then was transported to Seoul by riverine and coastal shipping. The Tribute Tax Law also sought to correct a number of abuses that had arisen in the procedures prescribed for estimating the harvest potential of different plots of land, and so the new enactment stipulated that land be classified into six grades of fertility and that weather conditions in a particular year be judged on the basis of a nine-fold classification. The land grading system employed a flexible unit of area measurement (called the *kyŏl*), standardization being sought in terms of estimated yield rather than the size of a parcel of land. The scheme for calculating the effect of weather on the harvest, on the other hand, was linked directly to the tax assessment, with the tax burden being reduced in less productive years. In the light of all this it would appear that the peasant paid a land tax not merely modest to begin with, but one reasonably adjusted in his favor when conditions became difficult. But it would be a mistake to conclude, therefore, that the peasant's burden was light. For between the peasant and the state stood the landlord, with whom the peasant had to share the fruits of his labor on an equal basis. Since this form of crop sharing was by far the most prevalent arrangement, the peasant's actual burden was half or more of his harvest.

An additional burden on the peasant was the tribute tax. Known also as "local tribute" (*t'ogong*), since it was levied on products indigenous to a particular locale, it met a wide range of government needs. Included in such tribute articles were a variety of handcrafted items such as utensils, fabrics, paper, and woven mats, as well as refined metals, marine products, furs, fruits, and lumber. The tribute tax was a still more onerous charge on the peasant than the land tax, the more so since its cost, originally to be borne by the local magistracy, ultimately came to be shouldered by the peasants.

Finally, for the able-bodied commoner male, there was the obligation of military and corvee labor service. Military service was performed on a rotation basis, while corvee labor was required each year for a fixed period of time. Such labor included cultivating the land the king himself tilled in an annual symbolic ritual, construction work on palaces, royal tombs, and town walls, mining and other resource extracting. For each eight *kyŏl* units (or approximately sixteen acres of grade-one land) under cultivation one laborer was to be made available for corvee duty, and the work obligation was to extend over no more than six days in a single year. In reality, however, corvee drafts could be mustered whenever the government saw fit, and it was for this purpose, too, not merely to ensure stability in agricultural production, that the able-bodied peasant farmer was fixed in his locale of residence by the requirement to wear an identification tag (*hop'ae*) at all times.

Handcrafts and Artisanry

Household industry, principally the production of cotton cloth, was looked upon as a means of making the peasant family economically self-sufficient. The traditional arts of fabricating silk, hemp, and ramie cloth of course continued to be practiced, but now with the expansion of the cultivation of cotton the making of cotton cloth became wide spread. Cotton not only was used by the peasants for their own clothing, but it also was important to the government as material for military dress and as an item in Korea's foreign trade, so much so that it came to be permitted to substitute payment in cotton cloth for other forms of taxation. The making of farm implements was another occupation of the peasant villages, undertaken by blacksmiths who are thought, however, to have combined this work on a part-time basis with their normal farming activities.

Just as in the Koryŏ period, in the early Yi dynasty the work of craftsmen and artisans was performed preponderantly under government aegis. As a general rule, all workers with special skills were enrolled on separate rosters as "government artisans" and were attached to the various agencies in Seoul or to the provincial and local governments and the military garrison commands. Thus some 640 artisans were assigned to the Government Arsenal to make weapons, 590 to the Bureau of Royal Attire to make court robes, 380 to the Palace Kitchen Management to produce utensils for the royal table, 91 to the Paper Manufactory to meet the government's needs for paper. Altogether some 2,800 such skilled workers were employed in Seoul and more than 3,500 in the provinces. Though registered on the appropriate government rosters, these artisans did not devote themselves exclusively to supplying the government's requirements. Pressed into government service only for certain periods during the year, they normally worked for themselves on orders from private clients, paying the government a tax for the privilege. In many instances these artisans were government slaves and their social status was that of the lowborn, but in reality they formed independent households and managed their own household economies. Accordingly, they distinctly were not slave laborers and, moreover, the proportion of commoner artisans continuously increased.

Thus the output of artisans in early Chosŏn was mostly produced under state aegis, but at the same time, in the urban areas, there was a growing pattern of work undertaken on private initiatives. Originally the artisans who supplied the needs of private clients did so as they could when periodically furloughed from employment by the government, but later private artisans appeared who operated entirely on their own. While these private artisans produced luxury goods on order from *yangban* clients, in the main they made household necessities for the general populace and sold them in the markets. Prominent among such items were brassware utensils, horsehair hats, and leather shoes.

Commerce and Currency

From an early time there were shops in Seoul centering along the main thoroughfare of Chongno, but these were established by the government and leased to merchants for their premises. Somewhat later the so-called Six Licensed Stores (*yuguijŏn*), purveying silk, cotton cloth, thread, paper goods, ramie cloth, and fish products, came to typify this pattern of commercial activity. Granted the monopolistic privilege of dealing in designated articles, these stores operated in effect by government license, in exchange for which they paid a tax in the form of delivery on demand of items required by the government. But there were small shops as well, free of any tax obligations, and markets were opened too in a number of places.

In the local areas permanent markets called *changmun* ("market gate") began to develop from the early Yi dynasty. These were established by peasants who fled their land either because of famine or to avoid the burdens of military service or taxation. But such markets were deemed to constitute a threat to the Yi dynasty order and so they were suppressed. With the development of market towns centering around these thus forestalled, it was only the periodic markets that could flourish. Generally opened every five days, the periodic markets trafficked in such items as agricultural produce, handcrafted articles, marine products, and medicinal substances. The vendors were itinerant pack and back peddlers (*pobusang*), the former mostly dealing in luxury goods of finer craftsmanship and the latter, the back peddlers, selling mainly coarser necessities of life like products of the farm and sea. These peddlers even organized themselves into a guild, the *Pusangch'ŏng*, that was formally sanctioned by the government. The back and pack peddlers who worked the countryside had their counterpart in itinerant peddlers who traveled the coastal sea lanes, but theirs was not so flourishing a trade.

With commercial activities in Yi Korea conducted in this fashion, a money economy could not so easily develop. In 1401 currency was printed on paper made from the bark of the paper mulberry, in 1423 copper coins called "circulating treasure of the realm" (*Chosŏn t'ongbo*) were minted, and in 1464 iron currency in the shape of an arrowhead was introduced, but on the whole these were intended for government use in collecting taxes. Accordingly, whatever significance they have from the standpoint of administrative practice, they were not able to meet the needs of society. They did not, therefore, gain wide circulation, and as before the medium of exchange in important transactions was cloth. With the growth in the production of cotton cloth, however, the unit of exchange now shifted from hempen cloth to cotton.

The Situation of the Lowborn

In the Yi dynasty, too, the most significant component of the lowborn class was the slave population. There were two basic categories of slaves: public slaves owned by the government and private slaves belonging to individuals. Government slaves in turn were divided into those who owed labor service and those obligated to pay a tax in lieu of labor service, the former working at the behest of government agencies for a certain portion of the year and the latter required to pay a kind of head tax. This differentiation is applicable to privately owned slaves as well, since there were household slaves (*solgŏ nobi*) who performed miscellaneous duties in their master's house or tilled the land adjacent to it, and also out-resident slaves (*oegŏ nobi*) who paid a fixed fee to their owners. Slave status was strictly hereditary, in accordance with a law according a child the status of its mother, and like horses and cattle, slaves were bought and sold at officially set prices. Nevertheless, public slaves and out-resident slaves formed independent households and managed their livelihood on their own, for the most part engaging in tilling the land. Their economic position, therefore, was little different from that of the tenant farmers.

In addition to the slaves, outcasts (*paekchŏng*) who hereditarily worked at such occupations as butchering, tanning, and wickerwork, and who lived among themselves in separate hamlets, also possessed lowborn status. They were the ones, in short, who had been labeled with those other terms for outcast (*yangsuch'ŏk* and *hwach'ŏk*) in the Koryŏ period. In an effort to assimilate them to the general farming population King Sejong gave them land and had them taught how to work it, and this is how they came to be called *paekchŏng*, the term originally used to designate peasant farmers in general. This meant, then, that *paekchŏng* in point of law were accorded treatment as commoners, but in fact this did not in any way transform them into peasant farmers. To the contrary, they continued to pursue their hereditary occupations, treated as before as lowborn. Finally, there were traveling troupes of entertainers known as *kwangdae* and *sadang* who also were classed as lowborn.

In the Yi dynasty, too, there was a substantial population of the lowborn, but the economic position of slaves had improved, the *paekchŏng* for their part had been legally defined as commoners, and the forced labor settlements of lowborn, the *hyang, so,* and *pugok* of the Koryŏ period, had been completely abolished. The process was yet to extend over some hundreds of years, but it is a noteworthy development that the general tendency was for the lowborn to move up into commoner status, the status of free men.

4. Foreign Policy of Early Chosŏn

Relations with Ming China

Yi Korea used the term *sadae* ("serving the great") to describe its foreign policy toward Ming China, and every effort was made to maintain a friendly relationship. The pro-Ming policy espoused by Chosŏn's founder, Yi Sŏng-gye, in the course of his struggle with the old Koryŏ aristocracy, was necessary as well to confer legitimacy on the authority of the new regime and its ruler. This was all the more required in the light of the constitutional weakness, as it were, of the Yi kingship. With his unremarkable family background Yi Sŏng-gye was looked upon askance by the old aristocracy, who were not about to offer him their services ungrudgingly. He was in need of authoritative sanction for his regime, and he chose to make political use of Ming China to this end.

The Yi government dispatched three regular embassies to Ming each year. These were the embassy to offer felicitations on the occasion of the New Year (*hajŏngsa*), that to congratulate the Ming emperor on his birthday (*sŏngjŏlsa*), and one to honor the birthday of the imperial crown prince (*ch'ŏnch'usa*). Subsequently embassies also were sent on a regular basis to mark the passing of the winter solstice (*tongjisa*) and additionally whenever a ruler died, a succession to the throne occurred, or a queen formally was invested in either Chosŏn or Ming. The purpose of all these missions chiefly was political, but they served also as the medium for cultural borrowing and economic exchange. Articles exported in this way by Chosŏn included horses, ginseng, furs, ramie cloth, and straw mats with floral designs, while in return Korea obtained silk fabrics, medicines, books, and porcelain ware.

Thus the relationship with Ming China on the whole proceeded satisfactorily, but it was not without complications. One such problem was that known as "clarifying the royal lineage." When the *Ming Dynasty Administrative Code* (*Ta Ming hui-tien*) was promulgated in 1511, it again recorded a long held Ming misapprehension that Yi Sŏng-gye was the son of the notorious, and anti-Ming, Yi In-im. As it had done on several occasions beginning in the earliest years of the dynasty, the Yi government asked that this error be corrected. But this request again and again was ignored by Ming, until it became a heated issue. Ultimately, after nearly two centuries of protest, the matter was settled in 1584 by the insertion of a footnote in a new edition of this Ming compilation.

Settlement of the Northern Regions and the Problem of the Jurchen

Yi T'aejo, who had risen to power from his base in the northeast, took early steps to gain control over all of this region, and he succeeded in

THE SIX GARRISON FORTS AND FOUR YALU OUTPOSTS (ca. 1450)

incorporating the territory up to the Tumen River frontier into his kingdom. The native inhabitants of the area, however, a Jurchen people called Yain or "barbarians" by the Koreans, launched frequent raids against their new masters and for a time the Yi were compelled to draw back to Kyŏngsŏng [see map above]. It fell to Sejong, then, to again take positive measures to assert hegemony over this territory, and he set Kim Chong-sŏ to the task. In consequence six garrison forts were established in the northeast, at Chongsŏng, Onsŏng, Hoeryŏng, Kyŏngwŏn, Kyŏnghŭng, and Puryŏng, thus making permanent the Tumen River boundary. At the same time, expeditions were sent against the Yain in the Yalu region, with Ch'oe Yun-dŏk and Yi Ch'ŏn in command, and this led to the creation of four outposts along the upper Yalu, at Yŏyŏn, Chasŏng, Much'ang, and Uye. In this way that region too was incorporated into the domain of Chosŏn. Subsequently, for a time, the Four Yalu Outposts were abolished as county administrative units, but the Yalu River continued as before to mark Korea's northern boundary. The purpose of this opening up of the north lay not only in bringing new land under cultivation but in extending the frontier to the natural defense line formed by the two rivers, and to consolidate its control the government on several occasions sent colonists to settle the newly acquired territories. At this point, then, was fashioned the domain that Korea occupies today.

Originally the Yain maintained a half-agricultural, half-hunting economy, and they had to obtain from Chosŏn food, clothing, and other basic necessities, as well as tools of production such as agricultural implements. It was in quest of these that they invaded Korean territory, and the key element in Chosŏn's pacification policy was the opening of markets at Kyŏngsŏng and Kyŏngwŏn where Yain horses and furs might be bartered for cloth, farm implements, and grain. Their ritual submission and immigration also were encouraged, and to those who thus pledged their allegiance the government gave titular rank, food and clothing, and houses in which to live. Nevertheless their pillaging activities did not completely cease, and a major incident developed in 1583 when one tribal chief, Ni-t'ang-gae, led a Yain rebellion. Kyŏngwŏn and other garrison forts fell to him one after the other and his strength reached impressive proportions, but after a hard struggle he was subdued by government forces under Sin Ip.

Policy Toward the Japanese

The threat posed by Japanese marauders gradually had subsided by the end of Koryŏ but had not been eliminated completely, and in the early Yi incidents of pillaging continued to occur from time to time. Unable to produce enough food to provide for themselves on their mountainous, rocky islands, when Chosŏn refused to trade with them the Japanese on Tsushima had no recourse but to launch forays by ship against their neighbors, as they long had done in the past. When Sejong sent Yi Chong-mu to attack Tsushima in 1419 his purpose was to wipe out the bases from which these Japanese marauders mounted their attacks.

It was of course the Japanese who suffered the consequences of Chosŏn's hardened policy. The Sō house, the rulers of Tsushima, now sent repeated missions to Korea to express their contrition, and in response the Yi government took a conciliatory position, granting the Japanese limited trading privileges. Three ports were opened to them along the southeast coast of Korea, at Naeip'o (Ungch'ŏn), Pusanp'o (Tongnae), and Yŏmp'o (Ulsan), and trading and living quarters (*Waegwan*) were established in each to enable the Japanese to conduct their business. In consequence Japanese vessels fairly streamed into the three ports, carrying away with them large quantities of rice and cotton cloth. The Korean side then decided to work out a treaty that would limit the volume of goods given or allowed to be traded to the Japanese, and such an agreement was reached in 1443. According to its terms Tsushima might send no more than fifty trading ships each year and these would be permitted in port only upon presentation of credentials carrying the stamp of authorization of the lord of Tsushima. Moreover, the amount of rice and beans granted each year as a special allowance for the lord of Tsushima was set at only two hundred *sŏk* (enough to feed perhaps 100 people).

Sometime later, in 1510, the Japanese residing at the three ports rose in arms against the Korean garrison commander, with whom they had been at odds, and created a major disturbance. After this was put down, Japanese privileges at the three ports were abolished and trade relations were severed. But the entreaties of the lord of Tsushima led to a new treaty, in 1512, by which trade again was allowed but with the number of ships and the allowance of rice and beans stipulated in the 1443 treaty cut in half.

Items exported to Japan in this period were necessities such as rice and other grains, cotton, hemp and ramie cloth, and handcrafted articles like mother-of-pearl inlay, porcelain ware, and floral design mats. Cultural items also were involved in the trade, including the Buddhist Tripitaka, Confucian writings, histories, temple bells and Buddhist images, and these all made considerable impact on Japanese culture. In exchange the Japanese offered minerals not found in Korea, such as copper, tin, and sulphur, as well as luxury items for *yangban* consumption such as medicines and spices.

5. *Yangban* Bureaucratic Culture

The Creation of Han'gŭl

The creation of *han'gŭl*, an indigenous alphabet for the Korean people, is an achievement that must be writ large in the annals of early Yi dynasty culture. It was an awareness that his people must have a writing system designed to express the language of their everyday speech, and a concern that all his subjects be able to readily learn and use it, that impelled King Sejong to devise *han'gŭl*. Called at that time the "proper sounds to instruct the people" (*hunmin chŏngŭm*), the preface to its explication stated clearly the thinking behind its creation:

> The sounds of our language differ from those of China and are not easily conveyed in Chinese writing. In consequence, though one among our ignorant subjects may wish to express his mind, in many cases he after all is unable to do so. Thinking of these, my people, with compassion, We have newly devised a script of twenty-eight letters, only that it become possible for anyone to readily learn it and use it to advantage in his everyday life.

Moved by these considerations, Sejong brushed aside the opposition of a segment of the literati-officials around him and, enlisting the services of such scholars in the Hall of Worthies as Sŏng Sam-mun, Chŏng In-ji, and Sin Suk-chu, he created the *han'gŭl* alphabet, the proudest cultural achievement of the Korean people. The new alphabet was promulgated in his twenty-eighth year on the throne, in 1446.

Unfortunately, however, this masterful creation for the Korean people was not welcomed by the *yangban* ruling class of that day. This was because they had in mind to retain their monopoly on access to learning by continuing to use the difficult Chinese writing system. Sejong, however, with the intent of furthering the moral education of the populace as a whole, pushed firmly ahead with the development of the *han'gŭl* alphabet.

Soon after proclaiming the new alphabet, Sejong established the Office for Publication in Han'gŭl (also called the Office for Vulgate Publication) and had it author a number of major works. Chief among these are the *Songs of Flying Dragons* (*Yongbi ŏch'ŏn ka*), a eulogy of the virtues of the royal ancestors; the *Songs of the Moon's Reflection on a Thousand Rivers* (*Wŏrin ch'ŏn'gang chi kok*) and *Episodes from the Life of the Buddha* (*Sŏkpo sangjŏl*), the two hymns together being titled the *Wŏrin Sŏkpo*; and texts for study of Chinese characters such as *Dictionary of Proper Korean Pronunciations* (*Tongguk chŏngun*). King Sejo, a son of Sejong, went on to establish a Superintendency for Sutra Publication which put out numerous *han'gŭl* translations of Buddhist texts, a genre known as "vulgate elucidations" (*ŏnhae*). Agricultural manuals for peasant farmers to read and military texts whose contents were to be kept secret from those outside Korea's borders also were written in *han'gŭl*. At the same time, ladies of the palace and the wives and daughters of *yangban* families came to use *han'gŭl* extensively, for example in exchanging letters. Nevertheless, the many works of major importance compiled under government auspices continued on the whole to be written in Chinese, thus revealing the limitations that still existed on the wider use of *han'gŭl*.

A Pragmatic Scholarship

In the early Yi dynasty scholarship developed apace in many fields and the results were widely published. The state itself zealously bent its energies to the compilation and publication of a variety of scholarly works. In particular, in the period from the reign of Sejong (1418–1450) through that of Sŏngjong (1469–1494), the concerted efforts of the scholars in the Hall of Worthies and the Office of Special Advisers produced many government sponsored publications. These books, in the main, were written from a Confucian perspective and were designed for use in the actual governing and shaping of Korean society. Much of the scholarship of that age, therefore, was of a practical kind and was closely related to the realities of the new dynasty, which had cast itself as a Confucian state.

Histories deserve first mention among the works produced under the aegis of the government. The concept of history as a mirror, or exemplar, for government naturally heightened the interest of the state in the compilation of histories. The tradition of preparing a history of each reign began in 1413 with the completion of the *Annals of King T'aejo*. This process was continued thereafter to the end of the dynasty, giving us the basic record known collectively as the *Annals of the Dynasty of Chosŏn* (*Chosŏn wangjo sillok*). The *Annals* were drafted by historians in the Office for Annals Compilation (*Ch'unch'ugwan*), and to ensure their safe transmission to posterity copies were placed in special repositories (*Sago*) in four widely separated parts of the country—in Seoul, Sŏngju, Ch'ungju, and Chŏnju. The *Precious Mirror for Succeeding Reigns* (*Kukcho pogam*) was a work that drew examples from the *Annals* of words of guidance and acts of good government by earlier monarchs for the edification of later ages. From its initial appearance in 1458 it too continued to be compiled throughout the dynasty. Chosŏn also was determined to prepare an official history of the preceding dynasty, and after a prolonged effort that began in T'aejo's time, the much revised final version of the *History of Koryŏ* (*Koryŏ sa*) was completed in 1451. Being an official history, the *Koryŏ sa* cast its account of the Koryŏ period so as to make clear the legitimacy of the founding of the new Yi dynasty. At almost the same time, in 1452, the *Essentials of Koryŏ History* (*Koryŏ sa chŏryo*) was compiled in strict chronological format in contrast to the annals-treatises-biographies structure of the *Koryŏ sa*. In 1485 there also appeared Korea's first overall history, the *Comprehensive Mirror of the Eastern Kingdom* (*Tongguk t'onggam*), which treated in chronological fashion, for ease of reference, the whole of Korean history from Tan'gun through the end of Koryŏ. Since this was a time of enhanced ethnic consciousness among Koreans, when Tan'gun was honored as the progenitor of the Korean race by the establishment of a national shrine at P'yŏngyang and the performance there of ancestral rites, it was natural that a comprehensive history should begin with an account of the Tan'gun era.

Gazetteers, or geographies, must next be mentioned. The *Geographical Description of the Eight Provinces* (*P'alto chiri chi*) was the first to be compiled, in 1432, and eventually it was incorporated as a treatise into the *Annals of King Sejong*. It included those items of information deemed needful in the governing of the country, such as the administrative history of each local government jurisdiction, its topographical features, control checkpoints, fortifications, land area, population, native products, roads and post stations, garrisons, troop levies, beacon communication sites, mausolea and tombs, surnames found in the area, and historical personages. A fuller work, the *Augmented Survey of the Geography of Korea* (*Tongguk yŏji sŭngnam*) was compiled in 1481 under new guidelines. In this work treatment of aspects of cultural geography was much expanded, under such headings as pavilions, temples, shrines, historical remains, famed officials who had governed the particular district, other historical figures associated with the area, poetical creations inspired by the surrounding scenery, and other compositions taking the local schools and shrines, for example, as their themes. This, then, was a geographical treatise designed to reflect the interests and values of the literati class. A further enlarged version appeared in 1531 and it is this edition that has been preserved.

The *Exemplar for Efficient Government* (*Ch'ip'yŏng yoram*) was the first manual for administrators. Compiled in 1441, it was an attempt to provide guidance for officials in the form of selections from administrative achievements and failures in the past. A work that prescribed the mode of conduct of major state ceremonies was the *Five Rites of State* (*Kukcho orye ŭi*). Begun under Sejong and completed in 1474, it dealt with rites for royal succession, funerals, and marriages, as well as with ceremonies of welcome for foreign envoys and military reviews. There was also the *Conduct of the Three Bonds* (*Samgang haengsil*), prepared in 1432, which employed drawings and accompanying texts to portray models of the loyalty, filiality, and fidelity that ideally characterized proper relationships between ruler and official, father and son, and husband and wife. It hardly need be added that the purpose behind this work was to widely encourage those ethical values that form the basis of Confucian morality, thus to further sustain the *yangban* social order.

Science and Technology

Science and technology also developed in many areas in the early Yi dynasty and a number of inventions and publications appeared. Worthy of mention first of all is the agricultural manual called *Straight Talk on Farming* (*Nongsa chiksŏl*), compiled under Sejong in 1430. This manual was designed to meet the specific conditions of Korean agriculture, on the premise that the climate and soil of Korea are different from those of China and so make it problematical to apply unmodified the practices of Chinese agriculture. Sejong first had each provincial jurisdiction survey and report the methods used by the older, experienced farmers in its area and then put together this handbook on ways of storing seed, improving fertility, transplanting rice seedlings, and the like. During Sŏngjong's reign (1469-1494), the high ranking scholar-official Kang Hŭi-maeng made a comprehensive compilation (entitled *Kŭmyang chamnok*) of agricultural practices with which he was personally familiar or that were explained to him in his home district of Sihŭng, just south of Seoul, adding to this description his own observations. Although authored by a single individual in the light of the specific agricultural techniques of his own area, the contents of the book were of such value that it was appended to a new edition of *Straight Talk on Farming* published in 1492, an edition that reached a wide readership.

At the same time, the closely agriculture-related sciences of astronomy and meteorology also greatly advanced, especially in the time of Sejong.

A particularly fine example of the applied science of that day is the gauge to measure rainfall created in 1442, some two hundred years before such a device appeared in the West. The rain gauge made at this time was an iron instrument, a cylinder approximately 42.5 cm. deep and 17 cm. in diameter, and ceramic models of it were set up at each county seat to measure and record the volume of rainfall. Not only was attention given to rainfall but to the effect on agriculture of wind conditions as well: instruments called "wind streamers," a simple form of anemoscope, were installed to gauge the direction of the wind and to assist in estimating its velocity. Further, in 1434 an observatory was built on the grounds of Kyŏngbok Palace and an armillary sphere with which to make celestial observations was mounted therein. The genius of Chang Yŏng-sil and his assistants also created various types of astronomical clocks, sundials, and clepsydras (water clocks). Attendant upon the advances in astronomical knowledge were refinements in calendrical science, culminating in the work by Yi Sun-ji called *Calculation of the Motions of the Seven Celestial Determinants* (*Ch'ilchŏngsan*). Making use of both Chinese and Arabian calendar systems, in this work Yi Sun-ji developed new calculations suited to the specific geographical location of Korea. Finally, now in Sejo's reign, a triangulation device and surveyor's rod were created to measure land elevations and distances and these were put to use in making cadastral surveys.

In the medical field, in 1433 the *Compilation of Native Korean Prescriptions* (*Hyangyak chipsŏng pang*) appeared. This work continued a tradition that began in the Koryŏ period, and its systematic and comprehensive coverage brought to fruition the process of establishing an independent Korean medical science based on the Korean experience. It discusses diagnostic methods and prescribes remedies, classifying its material into major areas of medical specialty such as internal and external medicine and ophthalmology. In 1445 a medical encyclopedia entitled *Classified Collection of Medical Prescriptions* (*Ŭibang yuch'wi*) was completed; similar in format to the *Compilation of Native Korean Prescriptions*, it was based on the wide variety of both earlier and contemporary Chinese medical treatises that its compilers had assembled and consulted. In turn, the landmark *Exemplar of Korean Medicine* (*Tongŭi pogam*), completed in 1610, grew out of these early Yi efforts.

These state compilation activities inevitably led to the further development of printing technology. Metal movable type, in particular, was cast in great quantities and was widely used in book publication. A type casting foundry was established first in 1403 and the copper type made at that time was called *kyemi* type (after the cyclical year designation for 1403). Thus the way was opened for the Yi dynasty's development of new techniques for printing with metal movable type. At this stage, however, the type were fastened to a copper plate with beeswax, and their tendency to shift position made printing cumbersome. Sejong improved the system, fashioning the type so as to fit into squares on the copper plate, and this not only facilitated typesetting but made possible the consecutive printing of many copies. In 1434 Sejong ordered a new casting, the so-called *kabin* (1434) type famed for the exquisite style of its Chinese characters. As printing continued to undergo development still other font styles appeared.

In the realm of military technology, improvement in cannon manufacture was given impetus by their effectiveness in the campaigns against the Jurchen tribesmen that ensued from the settling of the northern regions, and the emphasis hitherto on defensive use of cannon shifted to their employment as offensive weapons. Techniques for casting and using cannon were described in detail, with diagrams accompanied by *han'gŭl* text, in a publication of 1448, the *Records on Gunpowder Weaponry (Ch'ong-t'ong tŭngnok)*. A projectile launching vehicle was invented soon thereafter, in 1451, an artillery piece that used gunpowder, ignited by fuse wicks, to fire one hundred arrow-like missiles and other rocket projectiles mounted on an undercarriage. For use in naval warfare a close-quarters attack galley was constructed by adding a protective covering to the standard Koryŏ warship used to ram and sink enemy vessels.

Fine Arts

The *yangban* of the Yi dynasty held the view that art was what artisans produced, not something that *yangban* should turn their hands to. And if *yangban* were to take an interest in such pursuits it would be merely as a pastime, or avocation. The result, in the realm of painting, was the popularity of ink and brush drawings known as "literati paintings." A master of this genre in the early Yi dynasty was Kang Hŭi-an (1419–1464), a well-born *yangban* official who served King Sejong. His genius has left marvelous creations for us to enjoy today, but, done as they were for his own pleasure, his paintings are too small in compass for the masterful brush strokes he employed. In contrast, the most highly praised early Yi painter, An Kyŏn of Sejong's time, as well as the renowned Ch'oe Kyŏng and Yi Sang-jwa, later fifteenth and early sixteenth century figures respectively, all were government artists. An Kyŏn synthesized the techniques of a number of great masters to produce famous landscapes like "Dream of Strolling in a Peach Garden" (*Mong yu towŏn to*), recognized then as now as a supreme achievement. It is said to have been an artistic representation of a dream of the Prince of Anp'yŏng, a son of King Sejong. Ch'oe Kyŏng was skilled in both landscape and portrait art, as was Yi Sang-jwa, born a slave but selected as a government artist when his outstanding talent was recognized.

The government artists, for the most part, painted landscapes on request from *yangban* in a style suited to their patrons' tastes. These landscape paintings portrayed idealized settings not found in the natural world, most often in the mode of the Northern Sung school of Kuo Hsi. But it should also be observed that, by such devices as focusing the composition of their canvases off-center, the Korean artists gave expression to styles of their own. The popularity of human likenesses, for its part, was owing to the need felt by the *yangban* for portraits to celebrate their rise to eminence in society. Portraits were valued not merely as lifelike representations but as animated portrayals of the inner spirit of their subjects.

In calligraphy the *sung-hsüeh* style of Chao Meng-fu continued to be popular, as it had been in late Koryŏ, and its acknowledged master was the Prince of Anp'yŏng. The third son of King Sejong, the prince took pleasure in artistic pursuits and, mastering the *sung-hsüeh* style, produced a supple and graceful calligraphy. Yang Sa-ŏn (1517-1584) for his cursive style and Han Ho (1543-1605) for his square or block style also were famed calligraphers of their day. Unlike painting, training in calligraphy was an essential adjunct of every *yangban*'s education, yet at this time there were not many calligraphic creations that ventured onto untried ground.

Ceramics occupies a special place in Yi dynasty art. In the early period pieces called *punch'ŏng* ("powder blue-green") were produced, like Koryŏ celadon only with a glaze that had devolved toward an ashy blue-green tone. This was a transition stage leading to the making of white porcelain (*paekcha*), a genre that departed from the smoothly curved shapes of Koryŏ celadon in favor of simple, warm lines. These creations also stood on broader bases, resulting in more practical vessels that give the viewer a sense of sturdy repose. This Yi dynasty ceramic ware, with its varying shadings of white ranging from pure white to milky to grayish hues, is said to constitute a fitting expression of the character of the *yangban* literati.

Literature and Music

In a Confucian state, music was a vital component of statecraft. Thus the arrangement of musical texts became a major task of the early Yi dynasty, and the man who contributed most to this endeavor was Pak Yŏn, in Sejong's reign. Subsequently, in 1493, the *Canon of Music* (*Akhak kwebŏm*) appeared, a work devoted to music to be played at court. Classifying its subject into the three categories of ceremonial music, Chinese music, and native songs, this illustrated treatise dealt thoroughly with matters ranging from scale and key to actual performance.

At the urging of Pak Yŏn, a book of lyrics to be sung to the various musical scores was compiled from the songs of Koryŏ and from the folk tradition. But this did not find great favor with the *yangban*, who composed many new texts (called *akchang*) to replace the traditional ones. Their texts were earnest and solemn celebrations of the founding of the new dynasty and the role of the literati in its achievements. Such creations were Chŏng To-jŏn's "Song of the New Capital" (*Sindo ka*) and the *Songs of Flying Dragons* (*Yongbi ŏch'ŏn ka*), a joint work by Chŏng In-ji and other literati. The "*kyŏnggi*-style poem" (*kyŏnggich'e ka*), popular among the literati from the late Koryŏ period, also belongs in this category, and a surviving example of an early Yi composition is Kwŏn Kŭn's "Song of the Censorate" (*Sangdae pyŏlgok*).

In 1478 Sŏ Kŏ-jŏng put together his *Anthology of Korean Literature* (*Tongmun sŏn*), a selection from past ages of poetry and prose written by Koreans in Chinese. At the same time, the literature of tales and anecdotes came to be in great vogue as a manifestation of the way the literati bureaucrats occupied their leisure hours. Works of this sort are Sŏ Kŏ-jŏng's *An Author's Trivia* (*P'irwŏn chapki*), Sŏng Hyŏn's *Assorted Writings of Yongjae* (*Yongjae ch'onghwa*), and Ŏ Suk-kwŏn's *Miscellany from a Storyteller* (*P'aegwan chapki*). This literature is considered also to be important as a rich source for the oral tradition of Korean history and culture. The *New Stories of the Golden Turtle* (*Kŭmo sinhwa*) by Kim Si-sŭp, a man of nonconformist spirit who turned away from the ordered world of Confucianist authority, also belongs to this period. *Kŭmo sinhwa* is valued as the precursor of the novel in Korea.

The Decline of Buddhism

Buddhism could not but wither in a society where Confucianism was paramount. T'aejo himself instituted a registration system to prevent the monk population from increasing, and he banned any new founding of temples. In short, while acquiescing in the power of Buddhism as it then existed, he prevented it from expanding any further. But while T'aejo was still alive his son T'aejong inaugurated a severe suppression of Buddhism, leaving only 242 temples throughout the whole country and disestablishing the rest, at the same time confiscating their lands and slaves (1406). This dealt Buddhism a blow of such magnitude that it never could recover.

Rendered thus impotent by T'aejong's oppression, Buddhism found hope in the personal faith of kings Sejong and Sejo. Defying the opposition of his Confucianist officials Sejong installed a Buddhist prayer hall within the palace, while Sejo built the Wŏn'gak-sa temple (today's Pagoda Park) and published *han'gŭl* explications of Buddhist sutras through the Superintendency for Sutra Publication that he established. Buddhism thus experienced a revival, and there appears to have been considerable rebuilding of temples and increase in the number of monks.

Under Sŏngjong, however, a strong policy of suppression again was adopted, leading to the complete abrogation of the monk registration system and a total ban on entering the priesthood. This was followed, in 1507, by abolition of the examination process by which monks hitherto had been selected for positions in the administrative hierarchy of the Buddhist establishment. This action signified that the formal relationship between Buddhism and the state had been severed. In the reign of Myŏngjong (1545–1567), under the regency of the Queen Dowager Munjŏng, the famous monk Pou was given important responsibilities in the encouragement of Buddhism, and for a time the Buddhist world again displayed some vitality.

It was at this juncture that Pongŭn-sa was made the main temple of the Sŏn (Contemplative) School and Pongsŏn-sa that of the Textual School, and the "monk examination" was reinstituted as well (in 1552). With the death of the queen dowager, however, Buddhism again suffered suppression, becoming a faith practiced principally by women.

Geometric design pottery, Neolithic Age; from excavations at Amsa-dong, Seoul.

Dolmen (table style), Bronze Age. Unyul county, Hwanghae province.

Tomb mural: hunting scene from the Tomb of the Dancers, Koguryŏ, 6th century.
T'ung-kou, Chi-lin province (Manchuria), China.

Gilt bronze meditating half-seated Maitreya.
Paekche, early 7th century. Seoul, National
Museum of Korea.

Gold crown, Tomb of the Heavenly Horse,
Kyŏngju. Silla, 6th century.
Kyŏngju National Museum.

Sakyamuni Buddha, Sŏkkuram, Kyŏngju. Unified Silla, mid-8th century.

Emille Bell, from the Pongdŏk-sa temple, Kyŏngju. Unified Silla, 771. Kyŏngju National Museum.

Pagoda of Many Treasures (Tabo-t'ap), Pulguk-sa, Kyŏngju. Unified Silla, mid-8th century.

Nine-tiered, octagonal pagoda, Wŏlchŏng-sa, Mt. Odae, Kangwŏn province. Koryŏ, 11-12th century.

Kundika (ritual water sprinkler), bronze with silver inlay and fittings.   Koryŏ, 11-12th century. Seoul, National Museum of Korea.

Woodblock for the *Koryŏ Tripitaka,* stored at the Haein-sa (near Taegu), S. Kyŏngsang province. Koryŏ, 1251.

Hall of Eternal Life (Muryangsu-jŏn), Pusŏk-sa, Yŏngju, N. Kyŏngsang province. Koryŏ, 13th century.

Mask (*yangban* protagonist), painted wood, used in Hahoe masked drama; from Hahoe village, Andong county, N. Kyŏngsang province. Koryŏ, 12th century (?). Seoul, National Museum of Korea.

"Portrait of the Willow Goddess of Mercy," by Hyehŏ (dates unknown). Koryŏ, 13-14th century. Tokyo, Sensōji temple.

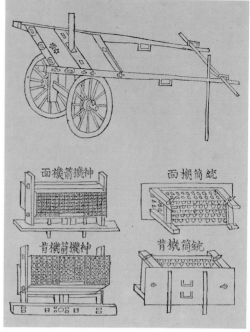

Portrait of Yi Sŏng-gye (1335-1408), founder of the Chosŏn dynasty. Artist unknown. Kyŏnggi-jŏn, Chŏnju, N. Chŏlla province.

Rocket artillery piece devised by King Munjong, Chosŏn dynasty, to fire arrow-like projectiles by means of wick-ignited gunpowder charges. 1451.

"Proper Sounds to Instruct the People" (*Hunmin chŏngŭm*), illustrating the pronunciation of the *han'gŭl* alphabetical letters. Promulgated in 1446.

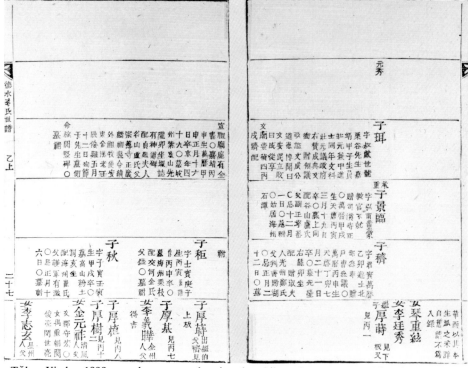

Tŏksu Yi clan 1898 genealogy, page showing the philosopher-statesman Yi I 李珥 (Yulgok), 1536-1584.

"Gourds and Mice" (*Hanult'ari wa chwi*), a typical painting of plant, insect, and animal life by Sin Saimdang (1512-1559), mother of Yulgok Yi I (李珥). Kangnŭng, Ojukhŏn Museum.

"Heroic Defense of Tongnae City" against Japanese invaders in 1592, by Pyŏn Pak (dates unknown), 1760. Seoul, Museum of the Korean Military Academy.

"Breach of the Peace" (*P'ajŏk*), genre painting by Kim Tŭk-sin (1754-1822). Seoul, Kansong Museum of Fine Arts.

"Boating Excursion" (*Chuyu to*), genre painting by Sin Yun-bok (1758-?). Seoul, National Museum of Korea.

Chunghwa-jŏn, the "Throne Hall" of the Tŏksu Palace, Seoul; 1906 reconstruction of an early Yi dynasty building.

Photograph of the first Korean diplomatic mission to the United States, 1883.
Yangban official members of the delegation are Hong Yŏng-sik, Min Yŏng-ik, and Sŏ Kwang-bŏm (seated, 2nd, 3rd and 4th from left), and Yu Kil-chun (standing, third from left); the Westerner is Percival Lowell, American escort and adviser to the delegation.

Soldiers of a "righteous army" (*ŭibyŏng*), anti-Japanese guerrilla fighters ca. 1907.

Portrait of the Yi royal family at dynasty's end, ca. 1910.
(from left to right) Crown Prince Yi Ŭn, Sunjong, Kojong, Sunjong's queen, and Kojong's youngest daughter, Princess Tŏkhye.

Throng gathered at Seoul Station on August 16, 1945, the day after Japan's surrender.
The large sign at upper left felicitates Korea's liberation from Japanese colonial rule.

Demonstration by professors
on April 25, during the Student Revolution of April 1960,
under a banner proclaiming
their determination that the
blood shed by protesting students a few days earlier must
not have been in vain.

A scene in central Seoul typifying the extreme destruction of the Korean War, 1950-1953.

A view of downtown Seoul today, with the area of rubble pictured above behind the high-rise buildings on the left.

Chapter 10

The Rise of the Neo-Confucian Literati

1. Changes in Society under Rule by the Meritorious Elite

Rule by the Meritorious Elite

It already has been noted that the class that dominated political, economic, and cultural life in the early Chosŏn period was the *yangban* literati. But within this class it was particularly the segment that usually is called the meritorious elite that in reality had stood at the helm of Yi society.

The meritorious elite were the likes of Chŏng To-jŏn and Cho Chun, men who had figured importantly in assisting Yi Sŏng-gye to found the dynasty and who had been amply rewarded for the support they had given him. They also were the ones who had stood at the side of succeeding kings and participated in ordering dynastic institutions; many of these, too, had been enrolled on "Merit Subject" rosters and given sizeable awards. Even the scholars of the Hall of Worthies in Sejong's time, in the larger view, belong to this group. But after Sŏng Sam-mun and his fellow *sa yuksin* (the "six martyred ministers") met their deaths at the hands of Sejo in 1456, along with many other scholars, the meritorious elite came to be composed most importantly of such figures as Chŏng In-ji, Ch'oe Hang, Yang Sŏng-ji, Sin Suk-chu, and Sŏ Kŏ-jŏng. They constituted the political force that held the reins of power, occupying high office and possessing an abundance of lands and slaves, wealth owed in substantial part to special merit awards bestowed for service under Sejo and Sŏngjong. They also were scholar-bureaucrats proficient in branches of learning having practical applications, and they had taken part in many of the government's compilation enterprises. Since for the most part they had their residences in the districts clustered around Seoul, this force also might appropriately be called the "capital faction."

There were many critical of these meritorious elite as well. First of all were those who had abandoned official careers, either remaining in seclusion behind their own gates or passing unsettled lives in havens outside the capital. Adjudging Sejo's usurpation to have been an immoral, unrighteous act, men of this persuasion invoked the Confucian principle that one should not serve two masters—that is, having pledged their loyalty to a previous monarch, they could not in good conscience serve a king who had seized the throne by force. The men known as the "six loyal subjects" (*saeng yuksin*), including Kim Si-sŭp, were such figures. Kim Si-sŭp's talent was recognized by his contemporaries, but he spent his life in wandering, in the guise of a monk, assuaging his feelings of unfulfillment through poetry and the writing of tales.

Another discontented group was made up of those who, scorning the society of that day, idled away their lives in "pure conversation," thus to preserve their moral integrity. Among these were Nam Hyo-on and his cohorts who modeled themselves after ancient China's "Seven Sages of the Bamboo Grove." In this group were included members of the royal house who by law were barred from government office, and there was also a man whose opportunities for government service were limited due to discrimination based on his social background, for he belonged to the *hyangni* class of petty local functionaries. It was such resentments that led these men to give vent to their feelings in poetry and song, and in lofty and witty discourse.

Thus the rule of the meritorious elite did not go unchallenged, but they enjoyed a solid political position, and they also had taken possession of large agricultural estates, thus securing their economic foundation.

Expanded Agricultural Estates and Increased Tribute Taxes

It has just been observed that the *yangban* bureaucrats who may be counted among the meritorious elite possessed large agricultural estates. They had first of all received "rank land" from the government, but then they had been given large amounts of "merit land" as well. When T'aejo founded the dynasty and subsequently whenever a succession crisis had arisen—T'aejong's struggle with his brothers, the deposing of Tanjong, Sejo making his throne secure—further awards of merit subject land had been awarded by successive kings. All of these lands, as has been noted, were to be held in perpetuity. There were other ways, too, by which the *yangban* bureaucrats expanded their holdings—by purchase, outright seizure, reclamation. Their eyes fastened in particular on the abundant state owned lands in the three provinces of the fertile southern third of the country, and they steadily encroached upon these. After the Office Land Law in turn was rescinded, the *yangban* bureaucrats' hunger for land grew still stronger, for now it was only by expanding their personal landholdings that they could secure their livelihood.

The expansion of agricultural estates brought about a reduction in government tax receipts, on the one hand, and at the same time it impoverished the life of the peasant farmers. But the hardship endured by the peasants was aggravated further by the tribute tax on special items of local provenance and craftsmanship, levied for the ultimate purpose of enriching the lives of the *yangban* bureaucrats. For not only was the amount of the tribute tax a heavy burden, but the process by which it was to be paid was itself troublesome in the extreme. In consequence, an "indirect payment" (*pangnap*) system developed, by which powerful individuals would deliver tribute goods to the state and then collect the cost of the goods from the peasants, the result being to add still more to the peasants' burdens. Unable to meet their tax obligations, more and more peasants abandoned their land, only to have collection enforced upon their kinsmen or upon their neighbors. Proposals eventually were aired to reform these abuses, such as Yi I's suggestion in the mid-sixteenth century to allow the tribute tax to be paid in rice. But the government of the *yangban* bureaucrats was painfully slow to take action on this problem.

Changes in the military service system added further to the woes of the peasantry. To begin with, the military service duty of the individual and the corvee labor obligation of a household had been kept distinct, but with the great enlargement of military rosters attendant upon adoption of the paired provisioner system (the peasant conscript system requiring alternate duty and direct provision of support for paired conscripts called in turn to active duty), it became impossible to fill the quotas for corvee labor duty. Inevitably, then, the soldiers themselves were mobilized for corvee duty, and to escape this double burden they in turn, with the support-in-kind they received from their *poin* "provisioners," hired laborers to stand corvee service in their place. But before long it was required that payment for corvee service be made directly to the office in charge of corvee labor mobilization in a particular locality. Once these officials got their hands on the payments for stand-in laborers, they employed government or private slaves, or landless wanderers, for the work to be done. Moreover, since the payment required for corvee labor substitution was excessively harsh, the number of provisioners and conscript soldiers who took to flight to escape this burden steadily increased, to the point where the ranks of the military were emptied and villages abandoned.

Finally, the grain loan system evolved into a form of usury at the expense of the peasants, causing them further distress. Designed to provide grain to the needy peasant farmer during the spring hunger season, before the winter barley crop came in, grain loans were to be repaid from the harvest in the fall. Management of the program originally was entrusted to government granaries (*ŭich'ang*, "righteous granaries") but they lacked adequate supplies for the task, and so the responsibility was transferred to the Ever-Normal Storehouses (*sangp'yŏngch'ang*), the government mechanism for controlling fluctuations in basic commodity prices. When grain was repaid an interest charge called "wastage grain" (*mogok*) was added; although set by regulation at ten percent, a number of ruses were used to increase the rate of interest, and this constituted another heavy burden on the peasantry.

The result of all this was to make the lives of the peasantry unsettled in the extreme. Many turned to a life of wandering, leaving their villages abandoned, and all over the country brigandage became rampant. The most famed brigand leader was Im Kkŏk-chŏng who was active for three years, between 1559–1562, in the region of Hwanghae province.

2. Emergence of the Neo-Confucian Literati

Rise of the Neo-Confucian Literati

Yi dynasty society, hitherto dominated by the meritorious elite, underwent a succession of upheavals with the appearance on the central government scene during the reign of Sŏngjong (1469–1494) of large numbers of rural Neo-Confucian literati (*sarim*). This term, "Neo-Confucian literati," is commonly used to designate a group of *yangban* scholars who had their base in the countryside. They were a force that had preferred to exert its influence, through the Local Agency, on administration at the county level rather than to seek to enter the capital bureaucracy.

Among the Neo-Confucian literati in Kyŏngsang province were many who carried on the teachings of Kil Chae, a man who had remained faithful to the royal house of Koryŏ by refusing to accept office under the Yi. The influence of this group became a force to contend with upon the emergence of Kim Chong-jik (1431–1492), son of the leading disciple of Kil Chae, and Kim Chong-jik's own disciples such as Kim Koeng-p'il, Chŏng Yŏ-ch'ang, and Kim Il-son. As students of Confucianism who esteemed above all deep learning in the Chinese classics, their scholarship had an idealistic and moral thrust that differed from that of the scholar-bureaucrats in the capital. Initially devoting themselves to the education of their youth in the countryside, they made their appearance in the central government when Sŏngjong appointed them in considerable number in an effort to prevent the further expansion of the preponderant power of the meritorious elite. In the main they held positions in the Censorate and in the Office of Special Advisers, where they had charge of remonstrance and the preparation of certain state documents. Presently, then, conflict developed between the two forces, the meritorious elite and the Neo-Confucian literati, and this in the end brought on a series of political convulsions known as the "literati purges" (*sahwa*).

The first literati purge, the Purge of 1498 (*muo sahwa*), broke out in 1498 under King Yŏnsan'gun. The reason this event also is called the "history purge" is that it owed its inception to a draft prepared for the official history, or annals, of Sŏngjong's reign. While serving as a state historian, Kim Il-son, a disciple of Kim Chong-jik, had incorporated into his draft history his teacher's "Lament for the Righteous Emperor." In this composition Kim Chong-jik had employed the metaphor of mourning the death of the young Chinese emperor I Ti at the hands of Hsiang Yü to criticize Sejo's usurpation of the throne and his subsequent execution of his nephew, the boy-king Tanjong. When the office for the compilation of the *Annals of King Sŏngjong* was established early in the reign of his son, Yŏnsan'gun (1494–1506), and Kim Il-son's draft was discovered, the meritorious elite incited Yŏnsan'gun to order Kim and those closely linked to him executed, while a number of other Neo-Confucian literati were sent into banishment. In consequence the power of the Neo-Confucian literati was sharply diminished.

In the years that followed, Yŏnsan'gun's addiction to a life of luxury and pleasure seeking led to massive squandering of the state's fiscal resources. Ultimately, in an effort to overcome his financial difficulties, Yŏnsan'gun would even attempt to confiscate the lands and slaves possessed by the meritorious elite, who naturally sought to frustrate the royal will. Yŏnsan'gun in turn looked for an opportunity to eliminate all sources of resistance to the exercise of his kingly authority. He already had launched a purge when a group of courtiers closely connected to the throne by marriage dredged up the incident in the previous reign of the ouster as Sŏngjong's consort and subsequent execution of Yŏnsan-gun's mother, the Lady Yun. Yŏnsan'gun thus was spurred on to decree death or banishment for many members of the meritorious elite as well as numerous Neo-Confucian literati who had survived the 1498 purge. This massive second purge, occurring in 1504, is therefore known as the *kapcha sahwa*.

After two years of terror, the king's cruelty and dissolute life having exceeded all bounds, Yŏnsan'gun was removed from the throne, by opportunists who had survived or even abetted his purges, and replaced by Chungjong (1506–1544). The new monarch, unlike his half-brother Yŏnsan-gun, was inclined to refrain from arbitrary exercise of royal authority and to respect the views of the Confucian literati. It was Chungjong who brought forward the young Neo-Confucian scholar Cho Kwang-jo (1482–1519) and rapidly appointed him to a succession of ever more influential positions. Cho Kwang-jo took as his political objective the establishment of a pattern of government by moral suasion, in accordance with the Confucian ideal. He rooted out superstitious beliefs that ran counter to Confucianist manners and mores, and he put into effect the so-called "village code" (*hyangyak*), a mode of local self-government infused with a spirit of basic justice for all and mutual assistance in time of need. He also encouraged the preparation of a number of vernacular translations of basic Confucianist writings, in an effort to inculcate Confucianist ideals among the populace at large. It was he, too, who proposed and secured the enactment of the so-called examination for the learned and virtuous (*hyŏl-lyangkwa*), whereby the responsible administrators in the capital and provinces were to recommend men of model integrity for recruitment into the bureaucracy by means of a much simplified examination held in the presence of the king. In consequence, still greater numbers of Neo-Confucian literati were enabled to secure appointment to prestigious government positions. As the power of Cho Kwang-jo and his faction grew, the animosity of the meritorious elite inevitably was aroused, and they presently found an opportunity to turn the king against the young zealots. Cho Kwang-jo had launched a campaign to rescind the awards bestowed on a large number of those rewarded for their merit in bringing Chungjong to the throne. Labeling their awards excessive, Cho succeeded in forcing the king to delete seventy-six names, nearly three-quarters of the total, from the merit roster that had been promulgated some thirteen years earlier. In the space of the next four days, however, the enraged Merit Subjects had so worked on Chungjong's fears that his own position might be in jeopardy, that he ousted the reform faction and even sanctioned death sentences for Cho Kwang-jo and his leading supporters. This event of 1519 is known as the *kimyo sahwa*, and the attendant purge once again broke the power of the Neo-Confucian literati.

Still another purge, the *ŭlsa sahwa* of 1545, occurred in consequence of events surrounding the successive enthronement, within the span of only eight months, of two sons of Chungjong by different queens. Even before Chungjong's death, factions of *yangban* officials had formed around brothers of the two queens, although both in fact were from the same leading aristocratic clan. The accession of Injong, Chungjong's eldest son, in significant measure represented a return to power of men identified with Cho Kwang-jo and the "men of 1519." A purge ensued, however, when Injong's untimely death brought the eleven year-old Myŏngjong to the throne and his strong-willed mother to power behind it. Once again, many leading Neo-Confucian voices were stilled, while those who set the purge in motion liberally rewarded themselves for their meritorious service to the state.

The circumstances surrounding the four literati purges differed in each case. But the principal theme from first to last was the struggle for power between the meritorious elite and the Neo-Confucian literati, a conflict that developed with the emergence of the latter as a political force in the arena of the central government. Over a period of half a century and more, the Neo-Confucian literati suffered blow after blow as victims in the recurrent purges. Despite these setbacks, however, they continued slowly but steadily to take dominant political power into their hands.

Private Academies and the Village Code

In the successive literati purges the Neo-Confucian literati were dealt repeated severe blows. Nevertheless, with their solid base in the society of the regions outside the capital, their power continued to develop through the private academies (*sŏwŏn*), the village code (*hyangyak*), and their agricultural landholdings. In the reign of Sŏnjo (1567–1608), then, they again were able to enter government service in the capital and, in the end, to dominate the political process.

Private academies called *sŏjae* that concerned themselves purely with education had existed from the end of Koryŏ, but schools that, like the *sŏwŏn*, also were shrines dedicated to worthies of an earlier period now appeared for the first time. The practice of honoring a personage from the past in this way arose out of the conviction that it would lend a spiritual aura to the authority of the school. Among the early *sŏwŏn* the most famous was the Paegundong Academy established by Chu Se-bung, then Magistrate of P'unggi county in Kyŏngsang province, in 1543. Wishing to honor An Yu, the famed Koryŏ proponent of Neo-Confucianism in Korea, Chu Se-bung adopted for his academy the rules Chu Hsi laid down for his Pai-lu-tung Academy in China. Subsequently, when Yi Hwang (the foremost Korean Confucianist philosopher of his age) became Magistrate of P'unggi, his memorial to the court persuaded the king to bestow a hanging board on this *sŏwŏn* inscribed in the king's own hand with the four characters "academy of received learning" (*sosu sŏwŏn*). Thenceforth known by this name, the Sosu Sŏwŏn was the first of the so-called royally chartered private academies.

Sŏwŏn now sprang up everywhere, and by the end of Sŏnjo's reign in 1608 they already numbered more than one hundred. The number of royally chartered *sŏwŏn* also increased at the same time, and it soon became a matter of course for the state to bestow on them grants of books, land, and slaves. Thus the *sŏwŏn* came to occupy a position in Yi society exactly like that enjoyed by the Buddhist temples in the Koryŏ period, and the moving force behind this development was none other than the Neo-Confucian literati. All but crushed by the literati purges, the Neo-Confucian literati found in the *sŏwŏn* the instrument with which they might lay the foundation for their revival and pave the way for their return to power.

The village code (*hyangyak*) was another mechanism by which the Neo-Confucian literati solidified their position in the countryside. The spirit of the village code was embodied in the four objectives that it emphasized: mutual encouragement of morality, mutual supervision of wrong conduct, mutual decorum in social relationships, and mutual succor in time of disaster or hardship. Cho Kwang-jo had sought to put the village code into wide effect in 1519, but his personal downfall brought failure to this effort as well. Thereafter the village code was put into practice on an ad hoc basis in a number of places, but it was only in Sŏnjo's time that it was instituted broadly throughout the whole country. It was normally powerful figures among the local Neo-Confucian literati who administered the village code, but the general farming population also automatically was included in it. In consequence the Neo-Confucian literati actually held a position of greater authority vis-a-vis the peasantry than did the magistrate and other local officials appointed by the central government, and this further solidified the ground on which the Neo-Confucian literati stood in local society.

The livelihood of the Neo-Confucian literati was dependent not merely on government service in Seoul but was sustained by their agricultural holdings in the countryside. Accordingly, though they might accept an appointment to serve in the central government, this did not at all mean that they were severing their ties with their lands and their locale. The locale they left behind was home as well to many of their kinsmen, and when their official careers were ended they would return to live out their days on the lands that had nurtured them. Moreover, it was these same lands that provided the means to establish the *sŏwŏn*, these same kinsmen who had joined in administering the village code. The victory of the Neo-Confucian literati was fashioned in the context of these socio-economic preconditions.

The Outbreak of Factional Strife

Along with the resurgence of the Neo-Confucian literati, a number of other factors—peace, population growth, and expanded examination quotas among them, combined to bring about a marked increase in the number of *yangban* eligible to serve as public officials. But the number of government positions in which a *yangban* might honorably serve was essentially fixed and did not much change over time. Thus if the many members of the *yangban* class all sought to occupy the limited number of official posts, confrontation and conflict inevitably would result. And so it did, in a form known in Korean history as "factional strife" (*tangjaeng*).

Factional strife began early in Sŏnjo's reign, the conventional date is 1575, with a confrontation between two segments of the officialdom centering respectively around Sim Ŭi-gyŏm and Kim Hyo-wŏn. The immediate cause of the conflict between the two men was a personal quarrel over appointments to the powerful and coveted positions in the Ministry of Personnel known collectively as *chŏllang*. Although these posts were only of middle rank and so well below ministerial level, the incumbents had major responsibilities in the process of recommending and selecting candidates for appointment to certain vital offices. Moreover, the importance attached to the *chŏllang* positions was such that it generally was necessary to serve therein if one hoped to progress steadily upward into the high ranking offices of minister or state councillor. Because of the power wielded by the *chŏllang*, not even the minister of personnel was permitted to involve himself in appointments thereto, and it became customary for an incumbent to recommend his own successor. To begin with, as a younger official of high repute, Kim Hyo-wŏn had been recommended for a *chŏllang* position, only to have Sim Ŭi-gyŏm, then third minister of personnel, accuse him of sycophancy and oppose his appointment. Nevertheless, in the end Kim Hyo-wŏn did secure the post, but when it came time for him to relinquish his duties the name of Sim Ŭi-gyŏm's younger brother was put forward as a potential successor, and this time it was Kim Hyo-wŏn who balked. Before long, then, the *yangban* bureaucrats of that day had begun to take sides with one or the other of the protagonists and to regard their opponents with hostility and contempt. The fact that the two factions known as Easterners (Tongin) and Westerners (Sŏin) came into being in consequence of such an affair, an incident centering on the government office having authority over personnel, says much about the nature of factional strife in the Yi dynasty.

The dominant characteristic of factional strife in Chosŏn is that it was a struggle among political cliques in which membership essentially was foreordained and forever. The descendants of those identified with a particular faction inherited their factional affiliation generation after generation, and their clansmen joined in factional politics with them. Their landholdings in the countryside, moreover, provided the economic sustenance that made it possible for their partisan feuds to continue. Factional strife of this nature was not likely to be brought to an end by a single incident, by one victory or defeat. Even if a faction was ousted from power for a time, from the stronghold of their lands in the countryside the descendants of the victims would await the time when they might again rise to office in the capital and vindictively exonerate their ancestors. In consequence, factional strife was a phenomenon that involved conflict not only among officials in the central government but also among Neo-Confucian literati everywhere throughout the country.

As factional strife intensified, the private academies (*sŏwŏn*) too became not merely halls of learning but seedbeds of partisan disputation. The hierarchical Confucian value system meant that the ties formed between student and teacher in the process of educating the youth of a clan became just as stifling a restraint on individual initiative and freedom of action as the blood relationship between a son and his father. The views of a teacher, however much in error they might be, could not be opposed by his young disciples. Furthermore, those who had studied in the same school formed fellowships that not only preserved the bond created by their shared experience, but also gave cohesion to their attitudes and actions on factional matters and on issues they faced as government officials, a solidarity that transcended all question of right or wrong.

3. The Struggle Against the Japanese and Manchus

The Japanese Invasion of 1592

When Korea began to suffer sporadic attacks on its coasts by the Japanese in the mid-16th century, the government created a Border Defense Council (*Pibyŏnsa*), jointly staffed by civil and military officials, and entrusted to it all matters in respect to the country's defense. But the *yangban* bureaucrats, accustomed to the ways of peace and not easily bestirred, were content to take only temporizing measures. At this very time a new situation was unfolding in Japan, as Toyotomi Hideyoshi brought an end to the internal disorders of the so-called age of Warring States. Having succeeded in unifying the country, Hideyoshi sought to direct the energies of his commanders outward, thereby to enhance the solidarity and tranquility of Japan itself. He had been stirred, too, by what he had learned of the wider world beyond Japan's shores, and there grew within him a reckless ambition to launch an invasion through Korea against the Ming empire itself.

The Japanese army made its landing at Pusan in the spring of 1592. Chŏng Pal, commander of the Pusan garrison, and Song Sang-hyŏn as the magistrate of Tongnae, defended the two beachhead areas to the death but in the end were overwhelmed, and the Japanese launched a three-pronged attack northward toward Seoul. The stunned government now pinned its hopes on Sin Ip, who had won repute in his successful campaign against the Yain (Jurchen) in the north. But when Sin Ip met defeat in a battle at Ch'ungju, King Sŏnjo took flight toward Ŭiju on the Yalu River, sending two of his sons to raise fresh troops in defense of the kingdom in Hamgyŏng and Kangwŏn provinces.

The populace at large was infuriated at the government's incompetence and irresponsibility. As Sŏnjo and his high officials abandoned Seoul in flight the people blocked their way, hurling insults at them. Once the king and his retinue had left Seoul, the city's slave population set fire to the registry where the slave rosters were kept and to the offices of the Ministry of Punishments. The two princes found none who would respond to their call to arms, and in the end they were captured by the Japanese. The blame for this wretched state of affairs lay with the government officials, who had failed to concern themselves with the welfare of the people and had caused the farming villages to fall to ruin. Nearly the whole of the country, now defenseless, was trampled over by the Japanese armies. They were a military force experienced in land warfare, blooded in the many campaigns of Japan's Warring States period, and moreover they possessed firearms. There was no reason to expect that Korea's meager, untrained battalions might hold out against them.

It was at this point that Yi Sun-sin, Naval Commander of Left Chŏlla province, began to make his presence felt in the struggle. Appointed to his post the year before, Admiral Yi had keenly felt the need to strengthen the country's naval forces, and he had energetically set about building warships and training their crews. In particular, on the model of vessels already in use in the mid-fifteenth century, he built his famed "turtle ships" (*kŏbuksŏn*) with a protective covering (thought to have been iron plated) to ward off enemy arrows and shells, and in addition with numerous spikes implanted to prevent the enemy from boarding. He also emplaced cannon around the entire circumference of the ships, so that attack could be made at will from any side. His preparations made, Yi Sun-sin set forth

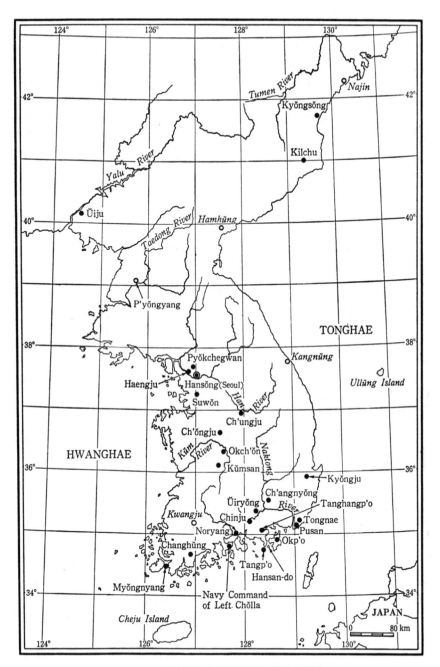

THE HIDEYOSHI INVASION (1592–1598)

with his warships to destroy the Japanese fleet whenever and in whatever waters it might appear. Victorious in his first encounter at Okp'o, he continued to carry the day in successive battles at Tangp'o, Tanghangp'o, Hansan Island, and Pusan [see map p. 211]. The battle in the seas off Hansan Island is especially famous as one of the three great victories of the war against the Japanese. Admiral Yi's successes gave complete control of the sea lanes to the Korean forces, with the result that the Japanese efforts to move north by sea and effect a link with their land armies were crushed. Moreover, the fact that the grain-rich region of Chŏlla province remained safely in Korea's hands also was owing to Admiral Yi's achievements. Not only this, but his operations imperiled Japanese supply routes, hampering their freedom to launch fresh attacks.

Meanwhile, within the borders of the country, guerrilla forces sprang into existence on all sides. The same populace that had reacted indifferently to the government's efforts to muster fresh troops now spontaneously took up arms in defense of their homes. Typically, *yangban*, peasant farmers, and slaves in a single district coalesced around a guerrilla leader and, as their strength grew, gradually expanded the area of their operations. The guerrilla leaders generally were Neo-Confucian literati of high repute in their locales, among them such outstanding figures as Cho Hŏn, Kwak Chae-u, Ko Kyŏng-myŏng, Kim Ch'ŏn-il, and Chŏng Mun-bu. Cho Hŏn rose in Okch'ŏn, in Ch'ungch'ŏng province, and routed the Japanese from Ch'ŏngju, only to be killed in an assault on Kŭmsan. Kwak Chae-u assembled a guerrilla force in Ŭiryŏng, Kyŏngsang province, and drove the Japanese out of the Ŭiryŏng-Ch'angnyŏng area; he went on to join with Kim Si-min in repulsing the enemy's first attempt to take Chinju. Ko Kyŏng-myŏng led a guerrilla force northward from his home in Changhŭng, but he too died in the attack on Kŭmsan. Kim Ch'ŏn-il repeatedly harassed the Japanese forces around Suwŏn and later took part in the second battle of Chinju, where he was killed. Chŏng Mun-bu, on the other hand, was active in Hamgyŏng province in the north, where he recaptured Kyŏngsŏng and Kilchu, and he also forced the Japanese to withdraw from Kangwŏn province. These constitute only a few of the hundreds of guerrilla units that sprang up large and small, among which even were bands of Buddhist monks led by such honored figures as the monks Hyujŏng (Sŏsan Taesa) and Yujŏng (Samyŏng Taesa). The hit and run thrusts of the Korean guerrilla forces often dealt severe blows to Japanese military operations.

Moreover, a Ming Chinese relief army had arrived, 50,000 strong. With Li Ju-sung at its head, the Ming army succeeded in recapturing P'yŏngyang and pursued the Japanese southward. But after being defeated in a battle at Pyŏkchegwan just north of Seoul, the Chinese pulled back to P'yŏngyang and for the time being remained there, inactive. Korean forces under Kwŏn Yul meanwhile had taken up positions in the mountain redoubt at Haengju on the north bank of the Han River, with the intent of attacking in concert with the Chinese forces to retake Seoul. But when the Ming army withdrew to P'yŏngyang the Korean defenders were left isolated, to face alone repeated large-scale assaults against their bastion launched by the Japanese. They succeeded in repulsing the Japanese in each of these bloody battles, and the victory they won there at Haengju is remembered too as one of the three great Korean triumphs in the 1592 struggle against the Japanese invaders.

Negotiations for peace now got underway and the Japanese forces withdrew to the southeastern littoral of Kyŏngsang province. About this time the Japanese, who had been beaten back by Kim Si-min in an earlier assault on Chinju, attacked the town once again, and despite a heroic defense led by Kim Ch'ŏn-il and Hwang Chin, in the end Chinju fell. The struggle to hold Chinju against these two separate Japanese sieges was no less fierce a conflict than the battle at Haengju, and the first, successful defense of Chinju occupies a special place among the three great Korean victories of the war.

Repulse of the Japanese and the Impact of the War

In the first flush of their invasion the Japanese land forces had swept over the whole country, but their navy had been defeated and control of the seas had been wrested from them. Moreover, harassed by Korean guerrilla attacks, the Japanese were beating a steady retreat southward. At the same time, the Ming army in P'yŏngyang finally was stirred to action by the Japanese withdrawal from Seoul. Instead of engaging the Japanese forces in battle, however, the Chinese advanced in screen formation in the wake of the retreating enemy, content thus simply to prevent the Japanese from regrouping and again attacking northward. It was this situation that led to the opening of truce talks between Ming and Hideyoshi. The negotiations, however, eventually were broken off. On the one hand, the Chinese sought to resolve the situation in their favor by accommodating Japan within the Chinese tributary system—enfeoffing Hideyoshi as the king of Japan and granting him the privilege of formal tribute trade relations with Ming. Hideyoshi, for his part, regarded himself as the victor, and so he responded with the absurdly unrealistic proposal that a daughter of the Chinese emperor be given to wed the emperor of Japan, that a portion of Korea be ceded to him, and that a prince of Korea and several of its high officials be sent to Japan as hostages. With such fundamental differences in bargaining positions, there was no prospect whatsoever for negotiations to succeed.

After the rupture of the long drawn out peace talks, the Japanese launched a second campaign to conquer Korea, in 1597. This time, however, things did not go as planned for the Japanese army, for the Koreans now were equipped and ready, and the Ming relief army too moved quickly into action. In consequence, the Japanese land forces could achieve no more than local success in engagements confined largely to Kyŏngsang province. At sea, on the other hand, the Japanese navy now was operating with unaccustomed audacity. This was because, as a result of intrigue against him in Seoul, Admiral Yi Sun-sin had been dismissed as Commander-in-Chief of the Naval Forces of the South and replaced by Wŏn Kyun, who then was overwhelmingly defeated in an encounter with the Japanese fleet. The dismayed government hastily reinstated Admiral Yi who, with the mere dozen warships remaining in his command, engaged a Japanese flotilla as it was sailing toward the Yellow Sea off Myŏngnyang, near Mokp'o, and won a resounding victory. Driven back into a shrinking perimeter along the south central and southeastern coastal regions, the Japanese army now found itself hemmed in both by land and sea. At this point in mid-1598 Hideyoshi died, and this led the Japanese to withdraw completely from the peninsula before the year was out. Attacking the retreating Japanese forces to the very end, Admiral Yi Sun-sin was felled by a chance enemy shot in the seas off Noryang point.

In the course of the seven-year struggle nearly the whole of Korea's eight provinces became an arena of Japanese pillage and slaughter, but Kyŏngsang province suffered most severely. The population markedly decreased, and whole villages were laid waste. Famine and disease ensued, and it was these conditions that gave impetus to the compilation after the war of great medical treatises such as the *Exemplar of Korean Medicine* (*Tongŭi pogam*). In order to overcome its financial difficulties resulting from the shortage of food grains, the government resorted to selling office titles and ranks in exchange for grain contributions (*napsok*) in fixed amounts. As a consequence of the terrible suffering the war had visited on the populace at large, uprisings also broke out on all sides, the most serious being that led by Yi Mong-hak in Ch'ungch'ŏng province in 1596. Moreover, with the destruction of land and census registers, the government was hard put to collect taxes and enforce corvee levies. The loss of cultural treasures in fires set by the Japanese troops also was substantial, including the wooden structures at Pulguk-sa in Kyŏngju and Kyŏngbok Palace, while the volumes stored in three of the four History Archives (*Sago*) were reduced to ashes. On the other hand the war with Japan brought advances in military tactics, for example the Chekiang order of battle used by Ming forces, and new weapons such as the "heaven-shaking explosive shell" and a kind of mobile rocket launcher were developed.

The impact of the war with Japan was felt not alone by Korea, for it was a conflict of a magnitude that shook the whole of East Asia. The Jurchen people who grew in power at this time in Manchuria, while Ming was busied in Korea, were soon to conquer Ming and make themselves masters of China. In Japan, too, the Tokugawa house established a new military regime. At Japan's request Korea entered into friendly relations with the Tokugawa Shogunate from 1606, but the animosity of the Korean people toward Japan remained alive long thereafter. Not only did the war bring about political changes in the countries of East Asia, but it had a marked cultural impact as well. Japan benefited in particular from the abduction of skilled Korean potters as prisoners of war, who then became the instruments of great advance in the ceramic art of that country. The numerous books seized by the Japanese in Korea also contributed to the development of learning in Japan, especially the study of Neo-Confucianism.

The Manchu Invasions

The beleaguered throne that Sŏnjo had occupied passed next to Kwanghaegun (1608-1623), a monarch who displayed uncommon capacities in directing both domestic and foreign affairs. He rebuilt the History Archives, printed many books, and reinstituted the *hop'ae* "identification tag" system, among other noteworthy domestic accomplishments. Beyond Korea's borders, Kwanghaegun's adroit foreign policy kept Korea from being drawn into the developing conflict on the continent, where the rise of the powerful Jurchen Manchus had created a perilous new situation for Chosŏn. When Ming sent an army to Manchuria to strike at the Manchu state of Later Chin, Kwanghaegun was unable to refuse the Ming request for help. But when he dispatched General Kang Hong-nip at the head of a force of some 10,000 troops, the king secretly enjoined the general to observe the situation carefully before determining his course of action. Thus when the tide of battle turned against Ming, General Kang found an opportunity to surrender to the Manchus. In consequence the Manchus took no punitive action against Korea at this time. Meanwhile, Kwanghaegun spared no effort to enhance his country's state of military preparedness, repairing defensive strongpoints, renovating weaponry, and instituting training programs. In the midst of this endeavor to shore up Korea's defenses Kwanghaegun was forced from the throne by the Westerners faction, to be succeeded by King Injo (1623-1649).

Under the influence of the Westerners who had put him on the throne, Injo abandoned Kwanghaegun's posture of watchful waiting in favor of a blatant pro-Ming anti-Manchu policy. This change was taken by the Manchus as a serious affront, and they were further alarmed when a Ming general, Mao Wen-lung, encamped on the Korean island of Kado near the mouth of the Yalu River as the first step in his plan to recapture the Liaotung Peninsula. The Manchus now came to feel it necessary to eliminate the threat to their rear posed by Korea and General Mao before proceeding with their campaign against Ming.

It was at this point, at the beginning of 1624, that the insurrection of Yi Kwal erupted. Yi Kwal was one of those cited for merit in bringing Injo to the throne but, rankled by receiving a lower level of reward than he thought he deserved, he rose in rebellion and for a time even occupied Seoul. When presently he was defeated by government forces some of his followers fled to Manchuria, where they appear to have urged the Manchus to invade Korea to redress the injustice of Kwanghaegun's removal from the throne. At any rate, it was under the pretext of righting this wrong that the Manchus launched their first invasion in 1627 (the so-called *chŏngmyo horan*). While some Manchu units struck at General Mao on Kado island, the main force penetrated quickly as far south as P'yŏngsan in Hwanghae province, whereupon Korea sued for peace. In exchange for a Korean pledge to do honor to Later Chin as would a younger to an older brother, the Manchus now withdrew their army from the peninsula.

Before long, Emperor T'ai Tsung of the Later Chin changed the name of his new state to Ch'ing and sent an embassy to Korea with the demand that Chosŏn acknowledge his suzerainty. The Korean response to this demand was one of total rejection, and King Injo refused either to receive the Ch'ing envoys or the documents they carried. Thus was visited upon Korea the second Manchu invasion, an assault led by the Ch'ing emperor himself in 1636 (the *pyŏngja horan*) at the head of a large force. Injo had sent his queen, his sons, and their wives to seek refuge on Kanghwa, but with the way to join them blocked, he instead betook himself to the Namhan-san fortress just south of Seoul. The fortress, unfortunately, was poorly supplied and the expected relief force did not arrive. To make matters worse, Kanghwa quickly fell to the Manchus and its royal refugees were taken prisoner. Heeding now the pleadings of Ch'oe Myŏng-gil and other officials who advocated peace, Injo decided to surrender, and at Samjŏndo (the Songp'a crossing, on the southern bank of the Han) he capitulated to the Manchu emperor in a ceremony staged in full view of the enemy encampment. By the terms of the surrender Chosŏn vowed to sever its ties with Ming, to deliver Injo's two eldest sons as hostages, to do homage to Ch'ing as the suzerain power, and to dispatch troops to assist the Manchus in their campaign against Ming. In consequence, Crown Prince Sohyŏn and his brother the Prince of Pongnim accompanied the Manchu army as hostages; Hong Ik-han, Yun Chip, and O Tal-che, the three scholar-officials who had argued most forcefully against making peace, were seized and executed; and Kim Sang-hŏn, a venerable scholar and high official already sixty-seven years of age, subsequently also was taken and held in harsh confinement in a Manchu prison for three long years.

In comparison with the war against the Japanese, the Ch'ing invasion was of short duration, only a small part of Korea became a battlefield, and the damage suffered was relatively slight. But the northwest region of Korea through which the Manchus had passed was ravaged by plunder and killing, and the smoldering enmity this aroused was fanned by Korea's feelings of cultural superiority to give rise to an intense hostility toward Ch'ing. The quixotic military official Im Kyŏng-ŏp's scheme to attack Ch'ing in concert with the waning Ming dynasty and the plan of Injo's successor, King Hyojong (the former Prince of Pongnim, who had been held as a Manchu hostage for eight years), to launch a northern expedition both were born of this festering hostility. At the same time, Hyojong was moved to strengthen Korea's defenses by repairing the mountain fortresses atop Pukhan-san and Namhan-san.

4. The Culture of the Neo-Confucian Literati

The Flourishing of Neo-Confucianism

The successive literati purges led many of the Neo-Confucian literati to abandon thought of careers in government and instead to devote their energies more than ever to pursuits centering on the private academies (*sŏwŏn*)—scholarly inquiry and the education of the younger generation. Having thus turned their backs on official life, it was natural for these men of learning to interest themselves in speculative and theoretical studies rather than in practical scholarship. It was for this reason that they had found Neo-Confucianism most appealing to their intellectual tastes. Neo-Confucianism is a doctrine that seeks to establish an ethical basis for an enlightened, Confucian political order through substantiation of the premise that the nature of man is fundamentally good, but it is also a metaphysical system of thought that endeavors to find the roots of this premise in the natural order of the cosmos. The exigencies of the time, then, called forth a number of great thinkers whose writings brought about the efflorescence of Neo-Confucian doctrine in Korea.

Neo-Confucians divide all existence into two inseparable components, *i* and *ki* (*li* and *ch'i* in Chinese). The one, *i*, is a patterning or formative element that accounts for what things are and how they behave, or normatively should behave, while the other, *ki*, is the concretizing and energizing element. The two are interdependent and inseparable, since *i* could not exist concretely without *ki* and *ki* would be but formless and directionless energy without *i*. Based on this dualism, two distinct schools of Neo-Confucian thought developed in Korea, one giving primary emphasis to *i*, the other arguing the primacy of the role of *ki*.

The pioneering thinker in the school that stressed the primacy of *i* was Yi Ŏn-jŏk (1491–1553), but it was Yi Hwang (T'oegye, 1501–1570) who proceeded to develop a full explication of this view. Yi Hwang is a giant figure in the history of philosophy in Korea, and he is known as Korea's Chu Hsi. In his elaboration of Chu Hsi's thought he further explicated the role of *i* in the function of the human psyche, and he established a position that gave emphasis to personal experience and moral self-cultivation as the essence of learning. He followed the dualistic position of Chu Hsi, which views *i* and *ki*, the forces that constitute the foundation of the universe, as inseparably related one with the other. But he stressed particularly the role of the formative or normative element, *i*, as the basis of the activity of *ki*; thus *i* comes to be seen as an existential force that masters or controls *ki*, a position that clearly attaches the greater importance to *i*. In this perspective, the understanding of the vital determinative pattern (*i*) that lies at the foundation of the universe is more important than cognizance of the principles governing individual substantive manifestations. Taken further, this reasoning acknowledges the importance of human moral volition, which is normatively and existentially based upon this vital determinative pattern of *i*. There follows from this a tendency toward introspection, in which personal, inner experience is highly valued. For it is in the individual's apperception of moral principle (*i*) and its realization in practice that personal integrity and one's spiritual essence are found. After Yi Hwang, this school of thought emphasizing the fundamental role of *i* was carried on by such figures as Yu Sŏng-nyong (1542–1607), Kim Sŏng-il (1538–1593), and Chŏng Ku (1543–1620), and it became known as the Yŏngnam (Kyŏngsang province) School. It exerted great influence on Confucian scholarship in Japan as well, eventually constituting one of the main streams in Japanese Confucian thought.

This emphasis on the role of *i* was countered by the school of thought that gave primary emphasis to *ki*, as the concretizing, energizing, more material element. Sŏ Kyŏng-dŏk (1489–1546), a man who spent his whole life in scholarly pursuits, was the pioneering proponent of this view. Ki Tae-sŭng (1527–1572) likewise emphasized the role of *ki* in his famed correspondence with Yi Hwang, but it was Yi I (Yulgok, 1536–1584) who completed its formulation. Fundamentally, the theory of the primacy of *ki* looked upon the material, energizing force of *ki* rather than the mysterious formative power of *i* as the fundamental factor in the existence of the universe. Ultimately this view leads to seeing *i* as nothing but the laws of motion or activity inherent in *ki*. Thus those who emphasize the primacy of *ki* are in a position to seek an objective grasp of the laws that govern things in the material world. Its advocates, as inheritors of Chu Hsi's philosophic system, also attached importance to the search for moral principles, but their approach emphasized looking outward rather than inward, intellectual rather than spiritual perception, and so they valued external experience and breadth of learning. Thus within Korean Neo-Confucianism two markedly different schools of thought developed. Yi I was famed not only as a philosopher but for the many reform proposals he put forward in regard to government, the economy, and national defense. The *ki* school of thought he championed was carried on by his contemporaries Sŏng Hon (1535–1598) and Song Ik-p'il (1534–1599), and by his disciples Kim Chang-saeng (1548–1631), Chŏng Yŏp (1563–1625), and others. These constituted what came to be known as the Kiho (Kyŏnggi and Ch'ungch'ŏng provinces) School.

Genealogy and the School of Rites

In Korea's *yangban* society of this age, now thoroughly Neo-Confucian in outlook and also strife-torn, the consanguineous clan unit comprised of descendants from a single patrilineal ancestor, and even identification with one of the branch or sub-lineages of which it was composed, had become major determinants of position in the society. An individual's relationship with powerful figures in his clan or sub-lineage was delineated in a written, and increasingly published, genealogy (*chokpo*). The genealogy clarified one's line of descent on the one hand and, on the other, it recorded one's position within the total clan structure. Thus the widespread compilation of clan genealogies from this time was due not only to the desire to demonstrate one's standing as a *yangban*, a status endowed with a variety of special privileges in that society, but also to the fact that it made explicit one's connections with other figures in the same clan. This need of the *yangban*, through the clan genealogy, to place themselves in relationship to famed members of their lineage led to the development of a field of study called by Koreans *pohak* ("lineage-ology"). For the ability to recite the lineage structures of the clan genealogy had become an essential skill that the *yangban* had to master.

Just as knowledge of intra-clan relationships was an important field of learning, so was knowledge of the funerary and memorial rituals that had to be observed in consequence of these relations. From the time Neo-Confucianism had been introduced into Korea, family rituals had been performed in accordance with the prescriptions of the *Family Rites of Chu Hsi* (*Chuja karye*), but Korea's *yangban* had observed these rites rather perfunctorily, with a certain sense of constraint. At this point, with the appearance of such works as *Exposition of Family Rites* (*Karye chimnam*) by Kim Chang-saeng, a theoretical foundation was given to the study of ritual (*yehak*) as a scholarly discipline, and Kim Chang-saeng became known as the "luminary" of this school in Korea. His view was that the true meaning of the doctrine of rites lies in conscious practice and deliberate involvement in ritual. His work was continued by his son Kim Chip, and in the ensuing centuries many treatises were written in this new field of study.

Kasa *and* Sijo *Poetry*

In the mid-Yi dynasty, in contrast to the heavily Chinese influenced *kyŏnggi*-style poems and the texts for court music *(akchang)* written in Chinese, the lyrical form known as *kasa* was widely composed. A kind of prose-poetry, the *kasa* normally was written in parallel lines each consisting of two four-syllable semantic units, its form thus exhibiting characteristics of typical Korean lyric verse. Through the *kasa*, then, the Neo-Confucian literati were able to vividly express their attachment to the beauties of nature that were a part of their life. Chŏng Ch'ŏl (1536-1593) is the poet who perfected the *kasa* form, creating such works as *Kwandong pyŏlgok* ("Song of Kangwŏn Scenes"), *Sa miin kok* ("Mindful of My Seemly

Lord"), and *Sok miin kok* ("Again Mindful of My Seemly Lord").

The *sijo* poetic form was born in the late Koryŏ period, but with its further development in the Yi dynasty it became a major genre of native literature, written in the Korean language. Although at times it was labeled the poetry of dilettantes, it became a necessary component of the education of every *yangban,* and statesmen, scholars, and military men alike have left to us their *sijo* compositions. Thus it may be said that the feelings of *yangban* toward life in their society were well expressed through the vehicle of the *sijo.*

Yi dynasty *sijo* literature, shaped by such as Pak Il-lo (1561–1643) and Sin Hŭm (1566–1628), reached the peak of its perfection in the hands of Yun Sŏn-do (1587–1671). There were numberless other composers of *sijo* too, of course, and the themes of which they sang were many and varied. There are *sijo* that express loyalty to the sovereign, and those that inculcate moral precepts. Along with those that sing of the valiant spirit of the warrior are *sijo* that depict the feelings of bitter rancor of those who suffered through the Japanese and Manchu invasions. Still others extol the beauties of nature, or give voice to a yearning to find haven in that natural world. Such a work is "New Songs from My Mountain Fastness" (*Sanjung sin'gok*) by that master of the *sijo* form, Yun Sŏn-do. In one of its verses, the "Song to Five Companions," he writes:

> How many friends have I, you ask?
>   The streams and rocks, the pines and bamboo;
> Moon rising over eastern mountain
>   You I welcome too.
> Enough. Beyond these five companions
>   What need is there for more?

In this way he expresses his desire to experience the tranquil pleasures of life in the company of five friends—the streams, the rocks, pine trees, bamboo, and the moon. He had left behind the world of political striving and sought to console himself in a life of upright but unrewarded endeavor. It cannot escape our attention that the greatest works of *sijo* literature were written on such themes as this.

Chapter 11

The Emergence of Landed Farmers
and Wholesale Merchants

1. Government by Powerful Lineages

Dominance of the Great Families

When the factional split between Easterners and Westerners first developed, the Easterners quickly achieved dominance and proceeded to suppress the Westerners. The Easterners faction consisted largely of the disciples of Yi Hwang and Cho Sik, whereas many of the followers of Yi I and Sŏng Hon were found among the Westerners, so that the factional lines of division bore a close relationship to the differences in the philosophical schools of thought. Within the Easterners, however, two sub-factions developed over the issue of Westerner Chŏng Ch'ŏl's proposal for designating an heir to the throne then occupied by King Sŏnjo, who had had no legitimate son. In the ensuing conflict between the two, the sub-faction known as the Northerners urged harsh condemnation and punishment of the Westerners, while the opposing Southerners took a more moderate stance. In terms of philosophic affinities this represented a rupture between the disciples of Cho Sik and those of Yi Hwang. Consolidating their power in the years following the war with Japan, the Northerners threw their weight behind the succession of Kwanghaegun, and accordingly they dominated the political scene during his reign (1608–1623). Meanwhile the political outs, the Westerners, were biding their time, and when Kwanghaegun was charged with misrule and deposed in 1623 they rallied behind the accession of King Injo. For a long time thereafter the Westerners had things essentially their own way, and during the reign of Hyojong (1649–1659) in particular, with the king's former tutor, Song Si-yŏl (1607–1689), occupying high position, they made their political base even more secure.

This is not to say that the Westerners met with no challenges to their exercise of power. In a dispute over the mourning rites to be observed by Hyojong's mother, the Queen Dowager Cho, the Westerners were driven from power and the Southerners took their place (1674). Again when King Sukchong (1674–1720), long without an heir, proposed to invest the newborn son of his favorite concubine, Lady Chang, as crown prince, the unyielding opposition of the Westerners once more brought about their downfall, while Song Si-yŏl paid with his life (1689). But on these occasions the Southerners were able to retain their hold on power only for a few short years, so that in effect the Westerners had enjoyed political supremacy for quite a long period of time. Meanwhile, the Westerners themselves had split into an Old Doctrine (Noron) faction led by Song Si-yŏl and a Young Doctrine (Soron) faction that coalesced around Yun Chŭng (1629-1711), after which it was principally the Noron who occupied the seats of power.

In the course of this prolonged political conflict along factional lines there emerged certain dominant lineages, especially in the Old Doctrine faction, that retained their grip on political power generation after generation. Taking advantage of their monopoly of high political office, these lineages were able to manipulate the examination and appointment processes to assure the preferment of their youth and thus perpetuate their hold on power. Two centuries earlier the Neo-Confucian literati had emerged onto the central government stage, there to contest for power with entrenched privilege as represented by the meritorious elite. By the end of the sixteenth century, Neo-Confucian doctrine in the realms of philosophy and social values had become accepted by all. The political legacy of this period, however, had been incessant factional strife and the concentration of power in the hands of a small number of great families belonging to the Old Doctrine faction.

Many Neo-Confucian literati, now excluded from participation in the political process, sought fulfillment in activities as members of a clan sub-lineage or as inheritors of a particular scholarly tradition. Near their homes in the countryside, then, these men laid a new foundation for their lives by establishing *sŏwŏn* (private academies), where they could both educate their youth and carry on the teachings of earlier generations of Neo-Confucian literati. The result was that nearly three hundred *sŏwŏn* were founded during Sukchong's reign (1674-1720). Content now to forego official careers, the scholars associated with the *sŏwŏn* concerned themselves with classical learning and moral conduct, to the exclusion of study undertaken to pass government examinations. In this way they came to represent the mainstream of Confucian scholarship and to win great respect as "rustic literati" (*sallim*). At the same time, as a matter of government policy aimed at preventing their further alienation, they sometimes were appointed to special sinecures such as votive officiant (*chwaeju*) in the National Confucian Academy, the officer who in theory presided over the national rites to Confucius. In this measure they were willing to compromise their principles and associate themselves with the great families, and to this extent they also allowed themselves to be used by the government.

A Lid on Factionalism

Reaction against the political dominance of the Westerners, the Old Doctrine faction in particular, and the consequent exercise of governmental power by a few great families, took other forms as well. Many who thus were barred from any meaningful political role lost faith in the justness of the Yi social order and harbored resentment against it. These men criticized the elevation of Neo-Confucianism to a position of unassailable dogma, and they discovered in themselves resources of spirit that made possible free and unorthodox thinking. It was in these critical minds that the ideas of the School of Practical Learning (*Sirhak*) took shape, a broad and varied approach to the reform of Yi dynasty institutions. It was in this milieu, too, that ideas rejecting the established order of that day took root—the geomantic and portentous formulations of the *Chŏnggam nok*, the subversive creed of Western Learning (Catholicism), and the individualist doctrines of the Wang Yang-ming school of Neo-Confucianism, anathema to the orthodox Chu Hsi philosophy. At the same time monarchic authority, which had been maintained up to this point in the equilibrium existing among the rival factions, had become threatened by the ongoing dominance of a single political coloration. The policy adopted as a measure addressed to the alienation of all these segments of the elite in Yi society was the *t'angp'yŏngch'aek* ("policy of impartiality").

First adopted by King Yŏngjo (1724–1776) and continued under Chŏngjo (1776–1800), the *t'angp'yŏngch'aek* aimed at according equal favor in official appointments to men of all the so-called four colors (*sasaek*)—to those of the Old Doctrine and of the Young Doctrine, to the Southerners and to the Northerners. As a result, factional strife became relatively quiescent and a new equilibrium was achieved among the *yangban* officials. Royal authority thus was greatly enhanced, with a consequent political stability during these two long reigns.

But the "policy of impartiality" could not eradicate the root cause of factional strife, which may indeed have been exacerbated by this approach. For a by-product of the policy was to increase still further the number of *yangban* seeking government appointments. Out of this situation arose the new conflict between the Party of Expediency (Sip'a) and the Party of Principle (Pyŏkp'a). These factions took shape within the officialdom over the issue of Yŏngjo ordering his son, Crown Prince Changhŏn, cruelly put to death, the Party of Expediency deploring his fate and the Party of Principle justifying the king's act. The conflict between the two groupings cut across factional lines, so that the phenomenon of political strife now took on the added complexity of factions within factions.

2. Changes in the System of Tax Collection

Enactment of the Taedongpŏp

During the period that political power was becoming concentrated in the hands of a few great lineages the most serious problem facing the nation was the desperate fiscal situation. Farmland had been laid waste in the wars and the area under cultivation had decreased. To make matters worse many land registers had been destroyed and the number of "hidden fields," those kept off the government registers, had increased. As a result, the 1,700,000 *kyŏl* of taxable land before the Japanese invasion was reduced to no more than 540,000 in the reign of Kwanghaegun (1608–1623), less than one-third of what it had been. Accordingly, the amount the nation collected in land taxes shrank in the same measure. How to make good this deficiency was an extremely serious problem.

In this context a radically different approach that would mandate payment of the tribute tax in rice, an idea already broached before the Japanese invasion, came under discussion once again. It has already been noted that a number of problems were associated with the tribute tax system, and that the growing practice of "indirect payment" (*pangnap*) made the burden on those who paid the tribute tax still more onerous. The continued flight of peasants from their land to escape this affliction had been the only protest they could make, however negative. The concept of a "rice payment law" had been put forward, then, as a means to alleviate the suffering of those who paid the tribute tax, insofar as it was caused by the abuse of "indirect payment."

In the end this proposal was not put into effect prior to the Japanese invasion. It was only afterwards, when faced with financial difficulties as tax collections fell off, that the government approved the measure as a means to replace its lost revenue. This was done in 1608, at the urging of Chief State Councillor Yi Wŏn-ik, and it was first carried out in Kyŏnggi province. In 1623 it was extended to Kangwŏn province, in Hyojong's reign (1649–1659) to Ch'ungch'ŏng and Chŏlla, and finally in 1708 it was enforced throughout the whole country.

By the terms of this new enactment, known as the Uniform Land Tax Law (*taedongpŏp*), twelve *tu* of rice (only about one percent of the harvest) was to be collected from each *kyŏl* of land, and the tax could be paid in cotton cloth (called *taedongp'o*) or in coin (called *taedongjŏn*) as well. The office created to administer the *taedongpŏp* was the *Sŏnhyech'ŏng* (literally "Agency to Bestow Blessings"). The government continued to collect tribute products from the peasants as necessity required, but in essence the tribute tax system had been abolished. This shift of the tribute tax to a land tax had a not inconsiderable impact on Yi society. In the first place, the economic burden on the peasant was lightened. Not only this, it fostered the accumulation of commercial capital by the government-designated merchants, known as "tribute men" (*kongin*), who served as purchasing agents for government requirements, and it concomitantly led to the emergence of independent artisans who produced goods on order for these "tribute men." These related phenomena combined to bring about a major transformation in the society of Yi Korea.

Changes in Corvee and Tax Laws

By the time of the Japanese invasion the Five Commands of the early Yi in fact existed in name only, and apart from the guerrilla bands that arose everywhere, the country possessed no military force worth mentioning. During the course of the war with Japan, however, a special agency was established to train fighting men, the Military Training Command (*Hullyŏn Togam*). There soldiers who formed a new garrison known as the three combat forces (*samsubyŏng*)—musketeers (*p'osu*), archers (*sasu*), and lancers and swordsmen (*salsu*)—were taught their skills. This training program was based on the book *New Text of Practical Tactics* (*Chi-hsiao hsin-shu*) by Ch'i Chi-kuang, an authority on the Chekiang order of battle that was developed in China to combat the attacks of Japanese marauders. From this beginning, by Sukchong's reign (1674–1720) a total of five new army garrisons had been created in the capital area—the other four were the Command of the Northern Approaches (*Ch'ongyungch'ŏng*), Command of the Southern Approaches (*Suŏch'ŏng*), Capital Garrison (*Kŭmwiyŏng*), and Royal Guards Command (*Ŏyŏngch'ŏng*)—and from this time on these Five Army Garrisons (*Ogunyŏng*) constituted the core elements of the Yi army.

This shift from the original Five Commands to the new Five Army Garrisons was not the result of any coherent plan or policy but rather was effected as occasion arose or circumstance required. In consequence it was not a model of consistency. One element of the new scheme had been the local levies of peasant-soldiers who were assigned on rotation to garrison duty in Seoul, but before long this arrangement broke down and in fact a system of paid recruits became the predominant means by which the army's ranks were filled. This did not mean, of course, that the able-bodied male population was simply exempted from the military service obligation. Instead of being called up for military duty themselves, the peasant-farmers now were asked to pay two bolts (*p'il*: about 2 by 40 feet) of cotton cloth per year, and this was used to defray the expenses of keeping the soldiery under arms. In other words, the required payment of cloth had become simply another tax.

This tax of two bolts of cloth per year was by no means an insubstantial burden. Some who should have paid it were able to gain exemption with the connivance of government officials, so that the tax was enforced mainly on the poor households who had no way to avoid it. On them the burden rested heavily indeed, for a number of unlawful practices added to their affliction, such as registering boys as adults and levying the tax on them as well (this was known as "fledgling legerdemain," *hwanggu ch'ŏmjŏng*), or keeping the names of dead men on the tax rosters (called "skeleton levies," *paekkol chingp'o*). As peasants fled their land to escape these onerous charges, their unpaid taxes were collected from their neighbors or from their kinsmen. This in turn resulted in still more peasants fleeing and the farm villages becoming ever more impoverished.

The Yi dynasty state was based on the agricultural economy, and it was clear that the dynasty could not stand on a foundation of ruined farm villages. The government was aware, then, that changes had to be made in the military cloth tax system. But it was too much to expect that the cloth tax itself might be abolished, for it was the principal source of government revenue and a source of private profit as well for the embezzling *yangban* officials. The government simply had no confidence that it could work out a plan to secure the revenue it needed through a fundamental economic reform. Finally, in 1750, Yŏngjo decreed that the cloth tax be reduced from two bolts to one, the loss in revenue to be made up by taxes on fish traps, salt production, and private fishing and trading vessels, and by a grain surtax. The latter tax, called *kyŏlchak*, was to be levied at the rate of two *tu* per *kyŏl* of land (about one-sixth of one percent) on harvests in every province except the two northernmost, P'yŏngan and Hamgyŏng. This represented an attempt to equalize the tax burden, and accordingly the new measure was called the Equalized Tax Law (*kyunyŏkpŏp*).

The Equalized Tax Law, however, belied its name in practice. As before, the *yangban* themselves were exempt from paying it. Moreover, since the peasants now had to pay a rice tax to compensate for the reduction in the cloth levy, for them it was a matter of exchanging one burden for another. Furthermore, all the abuses that had marked the collection of the cloth tax in the past remained unremedied, so that in fact the peasants paid more than the legal one bolt. Nevertheless, for all its negative aspects, as a desperately needed measure to counteract the flight of peasants from their land the Equalized Tax Law had some effect, since in some small degree it did alleviate the suffering of the peasants.

3. Economic Growth

Enlarged Scale Farming and the Polarization of the Rural Population

Agricultural technology underwent considerable advancement from early in the seventeenth century. First of all, the technique of transplanting rice seedlings was developed. That is, rice was first planted in a small seedbed and then, when it had reached a suitable stage of growth, it was transplanted to the paddy field, enabling the same plot of land to be used meanwhile for the ripening winter barley crop. The benefits of such a double-cropping system depended on the certain availability of water, both when the rice plants were in the seedbed and after they were transplanted, so that irrigation works became more than ever a pressing problem. Accordingly, many new ponds and dams were constructed to create reservoirs for irrigation. In 1662 an Office of Embankment Works was established, and in 1778 a comprehensive plan was promulgated to provide for the maintenance of irrigation works throughout the country. By the end of the eighteenth century, then, about 6000 reservoirs were in existence, and the result of the intensive use of the double-cropping system was a marked increase in agricultural production. A comparable advance took place in the technique of dry-field cultivation as well. That is, fields now were plowed so as to create alternate ridges and furrows, in which the seed was sown, a superior method that soon became widespread.

As opposed to the method of direct sowing, the techique of transplanting rice seedlings reduced dramatically the amount of labor required, so that the area of land one farmer could cultivate increased severalfold. The furrow-seeding method of cultivating dry-fields also greatly reduced the labor requirement. In consequence the practice called "enlarged scale farming" (*kwangjak*), the phenomenon of a peasant working a good-sized area of land by himself, soon became common. Generally it was the richer peasants who first succeeded in farming in this way, and they now became agricultural entrepreneurs, producing for the market as well as for their own consumption. This rich peasant class used not only the labor resources of their families but also hired farm laborers. The reduced requirements of the new agricultural technology had made large labor forces unnecessary, and so it was a simple matter to find hired hands among the rural unemployed. In short, the new technology produced a polarization in rural society between the rich peasant class and those who had been unable to hold on to their small plots of land. With their farming background most of the landless labor force in the villages became the hired hands of their wealthier neighbors, but others took up a life of vagrant begging or joined robber bands.

Enlarged scale farming was practised not only by absentee land owners and the independent landholding peasant, but by tenant farmers as well. By selling their labor to other landowners, these too in effect were engaged in enlarged scale farming, and their economic situation also gradually improved. This in turn gave rise to simple fee farming as the means by which the tenant farmer paid for his use of land owned by others. Up to this time share-cost farming had been the rule, whereby the tenant paid the landowner at the fixed rate of half the harvest. In this system the landowner shared equally with his tenant both the production costs and the risk of a bad harvest, but this inevitably meant that the landowner took part in making decisions as to how his land would be farmed. This often made it impossible for the tenant to manage the farming operation as he wished, since the social status of the landowner normally was higher than his. Now, however, with the advent of simple fee farming, the tenant paid a fixed amout for his use of the land, agreeing to bear the costs of production and the risks by himself. He thus was free of the landowner's supervision and, for the first time, could farm as he thought best. Moreover, in this land tenure relationship there was essentially no room for any social distinction between landowner and tenant to intrude. Finally, the gradual change from share-cost farming to a simple fee system laid the foundation for the development in the future of the practice of payment in cash instead of payment in kind.

At the same time, commercial production of specialized crops also developed, in particular ginseng, tobacco, and cotton. The ginseng grown in the Kaesŏng area was especially sought after and nearly all of it was grown for the market, some of the crop being exported even to China and Japan. Tobacco, first introduced in the early seventeenth century, also came to be widely cultivated. It too was grown not alone for domestic consumption but was exported to China, leading to a gradual expansion of the area devoted to tobacco production. The profit from tobacco was greater than from grain, and so some of the best and most fertile land was devoted to growing it. In the case of cotton, too, by this time its cultivation gradually had increased beyond the point of home consumption to production for the market.

In this way a new class of commoner landlords emerged, composed of peasant farmers who accumulated wealth through the increased production that resulted from advances in agricultural technology, through improvements in methods of farm management, and through the growth of farm production for the commercial market. In some cases, by contributing fixed amounts of grain, these wealthier farmers even purchased blank official appointment forms and, by inscribing their own names thereon, acquired the right to use a rank title normally reserved to *yangban*. At the same time there were *yangban* who, effectively excluded from office holding, sank to the status of tenant farmers. Thus the relationship between *yangban* and commoners, granted that the distinction itself did not disappear, was undergoing a significant change in character in the direction of a class structure based on economic wealth. To be sure, there were many peasants who fell into still more impoverished circumstances as tenant farmers, and there were others who became wage laborers or landless vagrants. But all these phenomena demonstrate plainly that changes were taking place in the status system of Yi dynasty society.

Development of Wholesale Commerce

In the realm of commerce during this period, the development that first commands attention is the active role of the *kongin*. With the elimination of local tribute payments following enactment of the Uniform Land Tax

Law (*taedongpŏp*), goods required by the government came to be procured through purchasing agents known as *kongin*. It naturally came about that these purchasing agents emerged from among the government licensed merchants, the *kyŏngjŏri* agents in Seoul of the county administrations, and the artisans—those who had been tied in to the old local tribute system. Under the new law they might receive the tax payments from the peasants first, then purchase the required goods and deliver them to the government. But at other times they would proceed to make purchases and delivery using their own resources and then later receive the tax payments from the peasants. In the process they gradually accumulated capital and so, despite the nature of their function as agents of the government, in terms of economic function they were quite different from the *pangnap* intermediaries of the past who merely had profited from illegal exaction of fees. They did business with the Six Licensed Stores in Seoul and with the inland market and coastal trade brokers (*kaekchu* and *yŏgak*), and they also dealt directly with the craftsmen who produced the goods. In time they developed into a specialized class of wholesale merchants, each handling large quantities of one particular type of goods.

At the same time, the activities of private merchants were becoming more evident in Seoul and throughout the country. Their activities were not limited to the area of their base of operations but extended along the major transportation routes to markets everywhere. For example, the river merchants of Seoul marketed their grain, salt, and fish all along the reaches of the Han River in Kyŏnggi and Ch'ungch'ŏng provinces. Since they transported their wares by boat they began to invest their capital in boatbuilding, thus coming to dominate that industry. Again, the merchants of Kaesŏng in Kyŏnggi province extended their activities over land routes to the Hwanghae and P'yŏngan regions in the north and into Ch'ungch'ŏng and Kyŏngsang provinces in the south, and in all of these areas they established branches known as "Kaesŏng Shops." The Kaesŏng merchants themselves managed the cultivation of ginseng, a major item in their trade, and they also undertook the processing of it into "red ginseng," the steamed and dried form in which it often is consumed. Like the private merchants, the government licensed merchants in Seoul also controlled the production of handcrafted articles and, by taking advantage of the privileged position accorded them by the government, gained monopolies in dealing in specified goods. Accordingly, whether private or licensed, the merchants of this period were wholesale dealers who controlled the production of the goods in which they traded, and this became the dominant form of commercial activity.

The merchants of this time were active not only within Korea but in foreign trade as well. In particular, the merchants of Ŭiju near the mouth of the Yalu carried on private trade with the Chinese at island sites in mid river and at the "palisade settlement" of Feng-huang well inside Manchuria. At Tongnae, too, near Pusan, merchants dealt privately with

Japan. Somewhat later a triangular trade developed, with the merchants of Kaesŏng, Ŭiju, and Tongnae serving as middlemen in transactions involving in the main Korean ginseng, Chinese silver, and Japanese copper. Through such international dealings many private merchants grew extremely wealthy, and among those who amassed capital in these international markets were official interpreters from Seoul's *chungin* (technical specialists) class.

As the activities of private merchants grew in scale, the appearance of Seoul's commercial streets also changed. With the exception of the original Six Licensed Stores themselves, the special privileges granted to the licensed merchants were entirely abolished in 1791, a measure known as the "commercial equalization" enactment. In this new situation three great markets operated by private merchants developed and flourished in Seoul—Ihyŏn inside East Gate, Chongnu in the modern Chongno area, and Ch'ilp'ae outside South Gate. These three markets traded not only in the products of every corner of Korea but in goods from China and Japan as well, and it was from these markets that the citizenry of Seoul bought their daily needs.

Markets in the countryside also underwent much development in this period. Markets existed at over a thousand locations in Korea in the eighteenth century, and the larger ones already had been established on a permanent basis. It was in these latter that wholesale merchants called *kaekchu* (inland market brokers) and *yŏgak* (coastal trade brokers) emerged to provide services to the itinerant pack and back peddlers. These were not simply wholesalers but engaged in warehousing, consignment selling, transportation, and innkeeping activities on the one hand, while also performing banking functions such as making loans, issuing checks or money drafts, and accepting deposits. They thus were the hub of commerce in the areas outside Seoul.

The development of commerce brought with it the formation of a variety of merchant organizations. The *kongin* purchasing agents first organized a *kongin kye*, or guild, to protect their rights and privileges, and the government licensed merchants with their base in the Six Licensed Stores also formed a guild called the "capital association" to preserve their monopolistic positions. In the countryside, too, the pack and back peddlers joined together in an association, the Peddlers Guild, to enhance their solidarity and mutual benefit.

Expanded commercial activity necessitated wider use of metal currency. Following the minting in 1678 of the copper coins known as "ever-constant treasure" (*sangp'yŏng t'ongbo*) large quantities of coins continued to be issued, and by around the end of the seventeenth century coins were in use throughout the whole country. At first, however, coins were employed not only as a medium of exchange but often were hoarded for their intrinsic value, becoming the means by which wealth was measured. Merchants amassed wealth in cash rather than putting their money into land, and they increased their wealth by loaning out their hoards at high interest. Shortages of coins, "coin famines" (*chŏnhwang*), developed as hoarding increased, but in spite of this their use penetrated into the far corners of the country and accelerated the commercialization of production. In this way marketing transactions, payment of wages, and payment of taxes in coin all gradually became more common, and eventually regulations came into effect requiring that land rents too be paid in money.

A New Phase in Handcraft Industry

As artisans and craftsmen broke away from government control during this period, production under state auspices gradually declined. The manufacture of weapons and of chinaware for palace use remained as government activities for still some time, but even in these areas the trend toward private industry went on unchecked. In large measure, therefore, the government's rosters of artisans became no more than lists of those on whom the "artisan tax" was to be assessed. Near the end of the eighteenth century, moreover, the keeping of these rosters was itself abolished. This signifies that craftsmen of all kinds had become private producers independent of government control.

This new development in handcraft production had a direct impact on the enactment of the Uniform Land Tax Law. This law stipulated that government needs be supplied through the *kongin* purchasing agents, and if the handcraft industry had not already developed to the point where it could produce an adequate supply of the required items, then the Uniform Land Tax Law hardly could have been enacted. On the other hand, after it was put into effect it served to stimulate handcraft industry into still greater growth, since craftsmen now produced goods on order from the purchasing agents and received their compensation in cash.

Nevertheless, craftsmen at this time had not yet become independent producers financing their operations with their own capital. Instead, they relied for the most part on capital provided by the merchants. At the same time that he accepted an order from a merchant a craftsman would receive the raw materials and advance payment for his labor, and so he could sell the finished goods only to the merchant who had financed him. Thus the merchant, as the financier, controlled production, and the craftsman found himself in the position of a wage laborer. For example, the merchants of the government licensed paper goods store controlled the output of the craftsmen of the Paper Manufactory and the merchants of the ironwares store that of the smiths they employed, while the artisans of the Kwangju Branch Pottery were dependent on the merchants who financed them. In the seventeenth and eighteenth centuries this was the most prevalent form of handcraft production.

At the same time, however, some craftsmen were beginning to produce and sell goods on their own, using their own capital. Fashioners of fur clothing and knife makers, for example, produced and sold fur neckpieces and decorative knives for women on their own, in competition with the licensed merchants. This was the case in particular with ironware and brassware manufacture. Pig iron artisans themselves enjoyed a monopoly on the manufacture and sale of cooking cauldrons. Similarly the makers of brassware, concentrations of whom were found in Ansŏng south of Seoul and in Chŏngju in northern P'yŏngan province, used their own capital to employ labor and sold their output to merchants on periodic market days. They employed their labor under contract and they paid wages in cash.

As for mining, in order to produce silver for the illicit trade with China, mines were opened in Tanch'ŏn in Hamgyŏng province and in P'aju and Kyoha just north of Seoul. The government permitted this private mining activity and taxed it, but the tax was so heavy that the private extractors came to be working essentially to provide revenue for the government, with the result that the number of officially sanctioned mines decreased. Subsequently, gold mining surpassed silver in importance and was carried on at Chasan and Sŏngch'ŏn northeast of P'yŏngyang and at Suan in Hwanghae province. Extraction of placer gold by panning, a method requiring simpler equipment than mining, attracted still more interest. The government authorized copper mining, too, at such locations as Suan and Yŏngwŏl (in Kangwŏn province), to supply the need for copper coins, but poor methods of refining the ore and excessive taxation made much development impossible. As a result copper mining came to be carried on without the government's knowledge, and these covert operations employed a wage labor force.

4. *Sirhak* and Other New Intellectual Concerns

The Birth of Practical Learning

As political power came to be monopolized in the seventeenth and eighteenth centuries by a small number of *yangban* houses, many *yangban* who did not belong to these select few lineages in effect fell from *yangban* status. In the countryside meanwhile, along with the emergence of peasants grown rich through the practice of enlarged scale farming, poor peasants were being forced to abandon their farms and the number of landless vagrants was increasing. In urban areas too a variety of changes were underway as wholesale merchants amassed wealth through their control of trade and handcraft production, while small merchants faced ruin and prices soared. As the numerous social ills attendant upon these phenomena became more grave, the problems Yi dynasty society now faced demanded serious reflection on the part of the members of its educated class. Their response is embodied in the scholarship and thought known today as "Practical Learning," or *Sirhak*.

The birth of *Sirhak*, therefore, connoted censure of those who held political power and an intent to bring about changes in the political and social order. There were, of course, government officials too who labored to effect reforms, but the chief critics were those who were not permitted to participate in the political process. Thus many *Sirhak* thinkers appeared from among the Southerners (Namin) faction that long had been excluded from important government positions.

The major concern of the *Sirhak* scholars was to illuminate the history and contemporary workings of political, economic, and social institutions. First preparing the ground by painstaking scholarly inquiries, they proceeded to elaborate their visions of how an ideal society might be achieved. By no means limiting their scholarship to fields of social science, such as politics and economics, they extended their inquiries to embrace many other areas—Chinese classical studies, historiography, geography, natural science, agriculture, and many more. Indeed it is not too much to say that the *Sirhak* scholars were concerned with virtually every branch of learning.

Although the objects of their study were many and diverse, there was a common ground on which all *Sirhak* scholars stood. Namely, the point of departure for their studies was the actual manifestation of things, their reality. Accordingly, while most *Sirhak* scholars were Chu Hsi Confucians, the emphasis of their inquiries was not on the theories of the primacy of formative principle (*i*) or of energizing force (*ki*), but on social science, natural science, and technology. Pragmatic scholarship naturally requires a pragmatic methodology, and so the *Sirhak* scholars sought always for explicit verification. No conclusion could be reached unless it was substantiated by certain fact. *Sirhak* scholars, therefore, were in no way inclined to blindly follow past tradition or to accept unchallenged the views of their predecessors. If they found another view to be at variance with the results of their own investigations they did not hesitate to criticize it, however hallowed it might be. Their scholarship, in short, was original, *de nouveau*. The realities with which they were concerned, of course, were precisely those confronting their society in their time, so that their thought inevitably had a Korea-centric thrust to it. Thus the *Sirhak* thinkers impelled Yi dynasty scholarship rapidly ahead in new directions.

Proposals for an Agriculture-Based Utopia

It has been said that *Sirhak* methodology took actual conditions as its starting point, and since the Yi dynasty order rested above all on the farming villages, it was to reform of the condition of agriculture that *Sirhak* scholars first addressed themselves. Their so-called institutional approach to government (*kyŏngse ch'iyong*) laid stress on reform in the vital areas of the land system, administrative structure, and military organization, with the aim of promoting the sound development of an agricultural economy based on the independent, self-employed farmer.

The scholar who systematized this institutional approach was Yu Hyŏng-wŏn (1622–1673). He passed his years in isolation in a farming village, engrossed in study based on his personal experience with the realities of the local society. The fruit of this lifetime of study was his treatise titled *Pan'gye surok*, completed in 1670. In it he examined and criticized in detail such features of the Yi dynasty order as the land system, education, appointments, government structure, official salaries, and the military service system.

Yi Ik (1681–1763) followed in Yu Hyŏng-wŏn's footsteps, extending his inquiries in both breadth and depth and establishing the institutional approach as a distinct school of thought. His basic work, *Sŏngho sasŏl*, displays the diversity of his scholarship. Almost encyclopedic in its coverage, it arranges its subject matter under the five broad headings of the physical environment, the world of living things, the human condition, Chinese classical scholarship, and belles-lettres. The section on the human condition, treating such subjects as government, the economy, and the family, is of particular interest for its detailed proposals, based on meticulous research and penetrating insight, for reordering each aspect of Yi society. But it was his work the *Kwagu-rok* (*Record of Concern for the Underprivileged*) that laid down the main principles of his reform ideas, setting forth his views on the full range of the dynasty's institutions. Yi Ik attracted many disciples, and thus *Sirhak* gradually emerged as the dynasty's dominant school of thought.

Chŏng Yag-yong (1762–1836) was the scholar who applied the institutional approach in the most comprehensive fashion. While living in banishment for eighteen years and forced retirement for seventeen more as a result of the Catholic Persecution of 1801, he wrote many works in which he analyzed and criticized conditions in Yi dynasty society on the basis of his personal experiences and investigations. His is judged to be the greatest name among *Sirhak* scholars. In his *Design for Good Government* (*Kyŏngse yup'yo*) he put forth his views on government structure, in his *Admonitions on Governing the People* (*Mongmin simsŏ*) he proposed reforms in local administration, and in his *Toward a New Jurisprudence* (*Hŭmhŭm simsŏ*) he offered his ideas on penal administration. In other works as well, such as "Outline of Ideal Government" (*T'angnon*) and *Treatise on Land* (*Chŏllon*), he further revealed his thinking on reforming the ills of his age.

Sirhak thinkers like Yu Hyŏng-wŏn, Yi Ik, and Chŏng Yag-yong, in their good-government approach to the solution of the problem of the farming villages, focused their attention not on the landlord class but on those who actually cultivated the soil. Accordingly, Yu Hyŏng-wŏn advocated a "public land system" under which the state would hold title to the land and allocate a fixed amount to each farmer; Yi Ik proposed an "equal field system" that would guarantee in perpetuity to each peasant household the amount of land minimally necessary to maintain its livelihood; and Chŏng Yag-yong urged adoption of a "village land system" whereby land would be owned and tilled in common by each village unit, the harvest then apportioned on the basis of the labor actually performed by each individual. Their common objective was to create a utopian state of independent, self-employed farmers who themselves held and tilled their lands. In short, they believed that the interests of the official class and of those who tilled the land were in fundamental harmony, and by abolishing social status distinctions, providing equal opportunities for education, and selecting officials on the basis of merit, they hoped to check the disintegration of rural life resulting from the development of commerce and the change to a money economy.

Proposals for Enriching the Nation and Securing the Livelihood of the People through Development of Commerce and Industry

A second school of thought developed within *Sirhak*, one that arose in the urban surroundings of Seoul and so took issue with the proponents of institutional reform aimed at the fostering of a healthy agriculture-based society. This alternative view owed much to the gradual expansion of commercial and manufacturing activities, and it sought to bring about prosperity in Yi society precisely through such activities. It thus added a new dimension to the development of *Sirhak* thought. Sometimes known as the "economic enrichment" school, this doctrine is more frequently called Northern Learning—i. e., a school of thought influenced by contemporary trends in scholarship in Ch'ing China.

The first important scholar of this persuasion was perhaps Yu Su-wŏn (1695–1755). His major work, modestly entitled *Usŏ* (*Idle Jottings*), was written in the early years of Yŏngjo's reign (1724–1776) and in it, framed in question and answer form, he presents a systematic plan for political, economic, social, and cultural reform. The author of *Jehol Diary* (*Yŏrha ilgi*), Pak Chi-wŏn (1737–1805), next deserves mention. Pak Chi-wŏn kept a diary of his journey to Peking in the entourage of a Korean embassy in 1780, and in it, in the course of describing aspects of contemporary Chinese life, he set forth his views on how poorly conditions in Korea compared with those in Ch'ing China. Hong Tae-yong (1731–1783) also wrote an account (titled *Yŏn'gi* or *Peking Memoir*) of his travel to China, but his work *Dialogue on Mount Iwulü* (*Ŭisan mundap*), cast in the form of a colloquy between an imaginary "Master Void" and "Old Man Substance," especially commands attention as a critique of conventional beliefs regarding the natural world, human society and institutions, and the thrust of history. Pak Che-ga (1750–?) and Yi Tŏng-mu (1741–1793), near contemporaries of the two scholars just noted, also wrote about their experiences in Peking in works entitled *Discourse on Northern Learning* (*Pukhak ŭi*) and *Peking Diary* (*Yŏn'gi*), respectively. The former work, that by Pak Che-ga, is not merely a journal of his travels but under separate headings addresses itself to reform of a variety of ills the Korea of his time confronted. It was this treatise that gave rise to the term "proponents of Northern Learning" as the designation of the school of thought they represented.

In the accounts they left of their journeys to Peking, these men recognized the superiority of the Chinese civilization they personally had seen and heard about, and they urged that it was necessary to understand what lay behind China's achievements before attempting to reform conditions in Korea. But the significance of the views expressed by the proponents of Northern Learning was not that they admired China but that they ardently wished to bring about change in Korea. Accordingly, their writings constitute a severe indictment of the *yangban* society of that age. They assailed the parasitic life of the *yangban* Confucianists who performed no productive labor themselves, and in contrast they attached great value to commercial and manufacturing activity and to agricultural work. They had particular interest in the growth of commerce and manufacturing, and they urged that production be expanded, through the introduction of new technology, and that means of transport by wagon and by ship be developed, so as to promote the flow of commerce both within and outside the country and thus enrich the nation. They went on to argue that the making and trading of goods were activities that ought to be pursued by people of whatever social status, of course including *yangban*, and that a new, model bureaucratic structure must be created around a core of professional public servants recruited through educational opportunities open to all. In sum, they took the position that the well-being of the people was to be achieved through abolishing the social status system and determining the division of labor in Yi society on the basis of ability alone.

New Interest in the Study of Korea

The actual conditions that the *Sirhak* thinkers wanted to reform were precisely those of the Yi dynasty society in which they lived, the legacy of their past that history had bequeathed to them. For this reason, although on the one hand they made an effort to discover a model for an ideal society in the ancient Chinese classics, they were equally concerned with their own history, geography, and culture.

Yi Su-gwang (1563–1628) must be accounted to be the first *Sirhak* scholar to display an interest in Korean history. He wrote his fundamental work, *Chibong yusŏl* (*Topical Discourses of Chibong*), in 1614. In these wide ranging volumes he discusses such subjects as astronomy, geography, Confucianism, and botany, and he offers, too, his own candid views on society and government in earlier Korean dynasties. Yi Ik's *Sŏnghŏ sasŏl*, discussed above, also is encyclopedic in range and includes treatment of many aspects of Korean history. A true encyclopedia, in which information on virtually every area of Korean history is brought together, is the *Tongguk munhŏn pigo* (*Reference Compilation of Documents on Korea*). Prepared in 1770 at King Yŏngjo's behest, the *Tongguk munhŏn pigo* is an encyclopedia of Korean studies that provides a chronological overview of the nation's geography, government, economy, and culture.

The major work of purely historical scholarship is An Chŏng-bok's superb *Tongsa kangmok* (*Annotated Account of Korean History*), written from an orthodox Confucian point of view. A disciple of Yi Ik, An Chŏng-bok (1712–1791) completed *Tongsa kangmok* in 1778, presenting a full chronological treatment of Korean history from Tan'gun through the end of Koryŏ, based on painstaking research. An Chŏng-bok also authored the *Yŏlcho t'onggi* (*Comprehensive Record of Successive Reigns*), which deals with the history of the Yi dynasty up to his time. An equally imposing figure as a historian is Han Ch'i-yun (1765–1814), who flourished in Chŏng-jo's reign. His *Haedong yŏksa* (*History of Korea*) is a remarkable account, in the annals-treatises-biographies format employed in the *Koryŏ sa*, incorporating an exhaustive selection of records on Korea found in Chinese and other non-Korean histories. The *Yŏllyŏsil kisul* (*Narratives of Yŏl-lyŏsil*), by Yi Kŭng-ik (1736–1806), is a description of major events in each Yi dynasty reign through Sukchong (1674–1720), drawn from a wide variety of individual accounts, often contemporary.

It must be noted, too, that there was great interest in the history of Manchuria at this time. An example is Yi Chong-hwi's (1731–1797) mono-graphic study *Tongsa* (*History of Korea*), a work that placed heavy empha-sis on the role of Koguryŏ in that area. But the most important work of this kind surely is the *Parhae ko* (*Study of the Parhae Kingdom*) written in 1784 by Yu Tŭk-kong (1748–1807). In it the author propounded the view that, since the so-called Silla Unification in fact did not put all of what had been Korea under one rule—for the Parhae kingdom existed simul-taneously in the north—the period instead should be known as that of the "Northern and Southern Kingdoms." Thus all of the *Sirhak* thinkers shared the view that the stage of the Korean historical experience extended beyond the peninsula into Manchuria, and this notion gave rise to a variety of new theories, such as that Old Chosŏn was located in the Liaotung Peninsula. In this context mention should be made of *Biographies of Famed Korean Generals* (*Haedong myŏngjang chŏn*); written in 1794 by Hong Yang-ho (1724–1802), with only one exception it treats the exploits of those who commanded Korean troops in battles against foreign invaders.

The flourishing of studies of historical geography also is a distinctive feature of this whole period. The pioneer work of this sort is *Tongguk chiri chi* (*Treatise on Korean Geography*) by Han Paek-kyŏm (1552–1615). Outstanding among later such works are *Kanggye ko* by Sin Kyŏng-jun (1712–1781), *Haedong yŏksa chiri ko* by Han Chin-sŏ (1777–?), and *Kangyŏk ko* by Chŏng Yag-yong (1762–1836), all of which are historical geographies of Korea.

An exceptionally fine cultural geography is the *T'aengni chi* (*Ecologi-cal Guide to Korea*; also known as the *P'aryŏk chi,* or *The Eight Provinces*), written by Yi Chung-hwan (1690–?). In this work Yi treats political and economic matters, as well as customs and community values, from the perspective of the advantages and disadvantages of establishing residence in a particular local area. Many other geographical treatises appeared in Yŏngjo's long reign (1724–1776), such as Sin Kyŏng-jun's *Toro ko* (*Routes and Roads*) and his *Sansu ko* (*Mountains and Rivers*). Chŏng Sang-gi (1678–1752) also completed his *Tongguk chido* (*Map of Korea*) at this time. Along with their concern as historians for factual depiction of the life of the nation, the *Sirhak* thinkers also approached geography from the standpoint of firsthand investigation of actual conditions, and as the network of commercial activity spread over the whole country their interest in such areas as transport and communications also steadily expanded.

At the same time there was marked interest in the study of the Korean language, and works on *han'gŭl* such as Sin Kyŏng-jun's *Hunmin chŏngŭm unhae* (*Explication of Korean Phonology*) and the *Ŏnmun chi* (*Treatise on Han'gŭl*) by Yu Hŭi (1773–1837) appeared.

The influence of these efforts by private scholars to achieve a new understanding of their own native land and its history was felt in government circles as well. This was particularly the case during the reigns of Yŏngjo and Chŏngjo, when *Sirhak* studies were at their height. Chŏngjo (1776–1800), in fact, established a research library and institute within the palace, called the *Kyujanggak*, and assigned scholars to it to prepare a large number of works of practical application in the administration of the country. Major works compiled under government auspices during Yŏngjo's reign (1724–1776) include the *Sok taejŏn* (*Supplement to the National Code*), a collection of decrees that had expanded or modified the original fifteenth century code (*Kyŏngguk taejŏn*); the *Sok oryeŭi* (*Supplement to the Five Rites of State*) that brought up to date the changes in these major ceremonial observances; the *Sok pyŏngjang tosŏl* (*Revised Illustrated Manual of Military Training and Tactics*) that updated a fifteenth century prototype; and the *Tongguk munhŏn pigo* (*Reference Compilation of Documents on Korea*) noted above. Under Chŏngjo many other important compilations were produced, including the *Taejŏn t'ongp'yŏn* (*Comprehensive National Code*) that brought together the previous statute books as well as the latest changes; the *Munwŏn pobul* (*Exemplar of Documents and Letters of State*), a selection of proclamations, royal admonitions, edicts, foreign relations documents and other state papers authored over the course of the dynasty by officials of the Office of Special Advisers and Office of Royal Decrees; the *Tongmun hwigo* (*Documents on Foreign Relations*), a compilation of Korea's diplomatic archives; the *Ch'ugwan chi* (*Records of the Ministry of Punishments*), documents on the history and practice of criminal law; the *T'akchi chi* (*Records of the Ministry of Taxation*), a detailed account of the structure and operations of that ministry; and the *Muye tobo t'ongji* (*Comprehensive Illustrated Manual of Martial Arts*), in which fighting techniques were detailed. A number of new castings of movable type were made in connection with this massive government compilation effort.

The Spread of Catholicism

Catholicism, known then as "Western learning" (*sŏhak*), came to Korea in the early stages of the transmission of Western culture, which first was introduced to Korea through European Jesuit missionaries residing in Ming China. It was the *Sirhak* thinkers who initially took an interest in the new religion. Already in the reign of Kwanghaegun (1608–1623), Yi Su-gwang made reference to Matteo Ricci's *True Principles of Catholicism* (*Ch'ŏnju sirŭi*) in his *Chibong yusŏl*. Later *Sirhak* scholars such as Yi Ik and An Chŏng-bok also were curious about Catholicism and discussed it in their writings. But theirs was purely an intellectual curiosity; they showed no disposition toward belief in Catholic doctrine as they understood it and, in fact, they leveled criticism at it.

During Chŏngjo's reign, however, the first stirrings of belief soon developed into a strong current, especially among Namin (the Southerners faction) scholars. A particularly significant event occurred in 1784 when Yi Sŭng-hun (1756–1801), who had accompanied his father in a diplomatic entourage, returned from Peking after being baptized by a Western Catholic priest. Namin figures among Catholic converts at that time included Yi Sŭng-hun, Yi Pyŏk, Yi Ka-hwan, the brothers Chŏng Yak-chŏn, Chŏng Yak-chong, and Chŏng Yag-yong, and the brothers Kwŏn Ch'ŏl-sin and Kwŏn Il-sin. Many of these were disciples of Yi Ik, but people from the *chungin* class, such as Kim Pŏm-u, also figured prominently. Thus Catholicism found many of its early converts among the Sip'a faction of the Namin, who long had had little access to political power, and among the *chungin* class of technical specialists.

It was not through the proselytizing of Western missionaries but rather on their own, through reading treatises brought back from China like *First Steps in Catholic Doctrine* (*Ch'ŏnhak ch'oham*), that these Korean Catholics developed a profound interest in the new religion. What they sought in Catholicism was the means to correct the distortions in the social and political order caused by concentration of political authority in the hands of a few powerful families. In an age beset by a host of social ills brought on by the oppression of the weak and the unbridled pursuit of personal gain by powerful families, wealthy farmers, and rich merchants, the Catholic doctrine of original sin, so unlike the dominant orthodoxy of Neo-Confucianism, evoked a warm response from many out-of-power scholars critical of the existing order. One can well imagine that those reform-minded *Sirhak* thinkers, desperately searching for ways to improve the dismal conditions surrounding them, took fresh hope for creating a heavenly kingdom on earth through belief in the new religion. Accordingly the acceptance of Catholicism constituted a kind of challenge to the oligarchic nature of *yangban* society and the intellectual rigidity of Neo-Confucianist orthodoxy. This psychology of the Catholic converts in the initial period is personified by Yi Pyŏk, a man of deep conviction and strong sense of mission.

The issue that brought to the surface Catholicism's challenge to the existing order, and that shook Yi society, was the so-called Rites Controversy. This arose in consequence of a papal ruling in 1742 that ancestor worship and belief in Christianity were incompatible. Chŏngjo had designated Catholicism a heresy and proscribed it in 1785, and in the next year the importation of books of any kind from Peking was banned. Then a few years later, in 1791, Yun Chi-ch'ung, from a *yangban* family in Chinsan, North Chŏlla, was sentenced to death for failing to prepare an ancestral tablet for his mother, a practice that was an essential adjunct of Confucian memorial ritual. Catholicism thus came to be suppressed on ritual grounds. But the activities of the Ch'ing Chinese priest Chou Wen-mo, who entered Korea secretly in 1795, revived the fortunes of the new religion, and before long the number of converts had reached about four thousand.

While Chŏngjo remained on the throne, with the Southerner Ch'ae Che-gong occupying a powerful position in the government, a course of tacit tolerance of Catholicism was followed and there was no severe persecution. But when Chŏngjo died and Queen Dowager Kim (Yŏngjo's queen) became regent for the new king, Sunjo (1800–1834), a cruel suppression immediately ensued. This is known as the Catholic Persecution of 1801, and during its course such prominent Korean Catholics as Yi Sŭng-hun, Yi Ka-hwan, and Chŏng Yak-chong, as well as the Chinese priest Chou Wen-mo, were put to death, while Chŏng Yak-chŏn and Chŏng Yag-yong were sent into banishment. There was a political motive for the persecution as well, in that the Pyŏkp'a clique of the Old Doctrine faction, which had ties with the regent Queen Dowager, saw therein an opportunity to bring down its rival Sip'a Southerners. The 1801 persecution also was the occasion when Hwang Sa-yŏng secretly attempted to send his famous "silk letter" to the Catholic bishop in Peking, a European, but Hwang was found out and was executed. His letter, written on silk, had asked Western nations to dispatch naval and land forces to compel the Korean government to grant religious freedom. But such traitorous actions on the part of Catholic converts led only to the intensification of the Catholic persecution policy.

Science and Technology

Interest in the development of agricultural technology was paramount in the seventeenth and eighteenth centuries, and the output of many works on agriculture is a hallmark of this period. Already in 1655 Sin Sok combined the early Yi treatises *Straight Talk on Farming* (*Nongsa chiksŏl*) and *Notes on Farming in Kŭmch'ŏn County* (*Kŭmyang chamnok*), added his own observations, and put out the *Compilation for Farmers* (*Nongga chipsŏng)*, the precursor of later Yi dynasty works. Not long thereafter the *Manual on Farming (Saekkyŏng)* by Pak Se-dang (1629–1703) appeared, in which he gave primary attention to the cultivation of fruit trees, raising of livestock, horticulture, irrigation, and weather. In his *Farm Management (Sallim kyŏngje)* Hong Man-sŏn (1643–1715) dealt item by item with the problems any farmer might face in the course of his daily activities, under such headings as agriculture, forestry, animal husbandry, sericulture, food processing, and storage. Later, in response to a royal command in Chŏngjo's reign, Sŏ Ho-su (1736–1799) compiled *Farming in Korea (Haedong nongsŏ)*, an attempt to systematize the whole range of Korea's agricultural science.

At the same time much attention was given to the sweet potato as a famine distress food, and a number of works on its cultivation appeared. In the reign of Yŏngjo, Kang P'il-li (1713–?) wrote *Observations on the Sweet Potato (Kamjŏ po)* and Kim Chang-sun wrote *New Observations on the Sweet Potato (Kamjŏ sinbo)*, while under Sunjo in 1833 Sŏ Yu-gu's *Growing Sweet Potatoes (Chongjŏ po)* appeared.

Although the works mentioned above discuss animals and plants in a variety of ways, the *Register of Hŭksan Fish (Chasan ŏbo)* by Chŏng Yak-chŏn, written in 1815 in banishment on Hŭksan Island off the southwest Chŏlla coast, is remarkable for its treatment of species of fish. Based on personal observation and analysis of specimens gathered from the seas around him, this work records the name, distribution, morphology, habits, and uses of 155 varieties of marine life. Also to be noted is a medical text written by Chŏng Yag-yong in 1798. Called the *Comprehensive Treatise on Smallpox (Makwa hoet'ong)*, this work refers to numerous Chinese writings on the subject in presenting a full discussion of the symptoms and treatment of this widespread disease.

Western science and technology came into Korea during this period and stimulated much new progress in this area. Initially knowledge about the West and its culture entered Korea through Ming China, and the very first firm information about the West was gained at the end of the reign of Sŏnjo (1567–1608) when a Korean envoy to China brought back a map of Europe. Subsequently, in 1631, Chŏng Tu-wŏn returned from his mission to Ming with a musket, telescope, alarm clock, world map, and books on astronomy and Western culture. Moreover, when Crown Prince Sohyŏn was a hostage in Ch'ing China, he became acquainted with the Jesuit missionary Adam Schall and in 1644 brought back to Korea a number of works on Western science. In 1628 a Dutchman, Jan Janse Weltevree, was shipwrecked on Korean shores; he took the name Pak Yŏn and lived out his life in Korea. Since he was experienced in casting cannon he was assigned to the Military Training Command and contributed to development in that area. He was followed in 1653 by Hendrik Hamel and his company of Dutch sailors who were cast ashore on Cheju Island. Brought to Seoul, a number of them later made good their escape to Nagasaki, and Hamel's account of his years of captivity gave the West its first direct knowledge of Korea.

In this way interest in Western science gradually increased from around the time of Injo (1623–1649). In this setting, through the efforts of Kim Yuk, new methods of calendrical computation were studied and a revised calendar was promulgated in 1653. Again, building on knowledge he gained from Jean Terrenz's *Descriptions of Ingenious Devices (Ch'i-ch'i t'u-shuo),* a manual contained in the Chinese *Collection of Books Old and New (Ku-chin t'u-shu chi-ch'eng)* that he acquired from Ch'ing at great cost, Chŏng Yag-yong devised pulley mechanisms that were put to use in constructing the fortifications at Hwasŏng (Suwŏn). Similarly, the insights they gained from Western science led such men as Kim Sŏng-mun, Yi Ik, and Hong Tae-yong to put forward their own views on terrestrial movement within a solar system. Thus a view of the world and a cosmology that had been based on the assumption that Asia constituted the center, if not the entirety, of man's habitation on earth underwent dramatic change.

Critiques of Neo-Confucian Philosophy

Some scholars within the Neo-Confucian school itself, dissatisfied with the orthodox interpretations, now offered their own dissenting views. Two such scholars were Yun Hyu (1617–1680) and Pak Se-dang (1629–1703), both of whom flourished in Sukchong's reign (1674–1720). In his *Exegesis of the Doctrine of the Mean (Chungyong chuhae)* Yun Hyu gave vent to his unhappiness with Chu Hsi's interpretations by expressing his own contrasting views, and this earned him the appellation of a "traitor to true Confucianism" who denigrated the master, Chu Hsi. When he lost out to Song Si-yŏl in the great mourning rites controversy of that day he was executed, and his *Exegesis of the Doctrine of the Mean* died with him. Pak Se-dang's major work in this area is his *Thoughtful Elucidations (Sabyŏn nok),* in which he presented an exegesis of the Four Books, the *Book of History,* and the *Classic of Songs.* Not only did he deviate from Chu Hsi's interpretations, but through his own analysis of the *Lao-tzu* and *Chuang-tzu* he offered a fresh view from the perspective of Taoist thought. For this reason he too was branded as a heretic. In short, these men approached the Confucian Classics from a fundamentalist point of view, attempting to discover the original intent of Confucius by penetrating through the Chu Hsi overlay. Chŏng Yag-yong was another creative interpreter of the Classics who sought to go back to Confucius' original concepts.

The acceptance meanwhile of Wang Yang-ming's ideas by some Korean scholars also is worthy of note. Such scholars are found principally among those in the Kyŏnggi area who belonged to the school stressing the primacy of the energizing force of *ki,* among those Neo-Confucian literati (especially of the Young Doctrine faction) excluded from the governing process. Members of the royal house and men of illegitimate descent, segments of society that alike suffered serious political disqualifications, also were much interested in Wang Yang-ming doctrine. Rather than seeing the ideas of Wang Yang-ming as antithetical to those of Chu Hsi, these scholars generally regarded the two schools of thought as mutually reinforcing and so sought to bring them into harmony.

But the leading Yi dynasty exponent of the Wang Yang-ming school, Chŏng Che-du (1649–1736), disassociated himself completely from orthodox Chu Hsi-ism. He could do this, it would seem, because he was able to move to Kanghwa Island and spend his life away from the political hazards of the capital. Chŏng Che-du's major work, *A Testament* (*Chonŏn*), presents his systematization of Wang Yang-ming doctrine, and at the same time it endeavors to go back beyond the Chu Hsi interpretations to find the original meaning of the Classics. To be sure, reluctant to be labeled heretical in an Yi society dominated by teachings of Chu Hsi Confucianism, these thinkers tended outwardly to profess loyalty to Chu Hsi doctrine. Yet their scholarship marked a new departure in its determination not to accept uncritically the orthodoxy of the Chu Hsi school.

5. New Modes of Expression in the Arts

The New Literature Written in Chinese

The spirit of *Sirhak* manifested itself not alone in scholarly writings but also appeared in new literary forms. Pak Chi-wŏn's fictional works perhaps best exemplify this. In his *Jehol Diary* (*Yŏrha ilgi*) are found the "Tale of Hŏ Saeng" (*Hŏ Saeng chŏn*) and "A Tiger's Rebuke" (*Hojil*), and in his *Random Jewels from Another Tradition* (*Panggyŏnggak oejŏn*) such pieces as "Tale of a *Yangban*" (*Yangban chŏn*) and "Tale of Elder Min" (*Min Ong chŏn*)—all bitingly satirical attacks against the parasitic *yangban* Confucian scholars. In telling these stories he used a natural, free-flowing style that avoided the overly mannered phrasings of earlier writing in Chinese.

At this time there also appeared many short stories that represented transcription in Chinese of tales that had passed down orally among the people. Since these stories treated themes from the oral tradition of the non-*yangban* classes, they were marked above all by an unaffected style. Among these works are those that vividly depict the ferment in traditional attitudes toward love and toward problems of social status arising out of the emergence of wealthy large-scale farmers and wholesale merchants. Two collections of such short stories are *Thrice-told Tales from Korea's Oral Tradition* (*Tongp'ae naksong*) and *Tales from the Green Hills* (*Ch'ŏnggu yadam*).

It is also important to take note of the fact that men from illegitimate *yangban* lineages (the descendants of secondary wives) and of *chungin* or petty clerk (*sŏri*) background, and even those of commoner status, produced anthologies of poetry. Already in the time of Sukchong (1674–1720), Hong Se-t'ae had compiled *Pearls from the Real Korean Poetry* (*Haedong yuju*), and in 1737 Ko Si-ŏn supplemented this with his *Poems of a Peaceful People* (*Sodae p'ungyo*). The term "poems of the people" (*p'ungyo*) was intended to indicate poetry of the lower social classes in contrast to the elegant creations of the *yangban* literati. Such anthologies were published thereafter at sixty-year intervals, the *Further Selection of Poems of the People* (*P'ungyo soksŏn*) appearing in 1797 and the *Third Selection of Poems of the People* (*P'ungyo samsŏn*) in 1857.

Traditional Novels and Sasŏl Sijo Poems

The greatest change in the literature field in the seventeenth and eighteenth centuries was the outpouring of works written in *han'gŭl*. It was not only that the words themselves were put into *han'gŭl* but there were changes in form as well, toward such genre as the novel and *sasŏl sijo* (a "long form" narrative *sijo*). Authorship changed too, away from the *yangban* class to those of lower social status such as petty clerks. These developments took place, in short, because this literary output was for a new, non-*yangban* clientele of readers. To be sure there were novels like *A Nine Cloud Dream* (*Kuun mong*), written about 1689 by Kim Man-jung, that in the tone it exudes of fascination for nobility and splendor bears the stamp of *yangban* literature—despite the author's professed high regard for his works written in *han'gŭl*. Yet most of the new fiction written in *han'gŭl*, drawn as it often was from the storyteller's repertoire, was new in style as well.

Novels in *han'gŭl* treated a variety of themes. Hŏ Kyun's *Hong Kiltong* (*Hong Kiltong chŏn*), written in the reign of Kwanghaegun (1608–1623) and considered to be the first vernacular novel, is a work of social criticism that scathingly attacked the inequities of Yi society with its discriminatory treatment of illegitimate offspring and its differences based on wealth. Such works as *Rose Flower and Pink Lotus* (*Changhwa Hongnyŏn chŏn*), *That Goodness Be Manifest and Righteousness Prized* (*Ch'angsŏn kamŭirok*), *Tale of Sim Ch'ŏng* (*Sim Ch'ŏng chŏn*), and *Tale of Hŭngbu* (*Hŭngbu chŏn*) may be seen as morality tales, wherein evil is punished and virtue rewarded. There also were novels like *The War With Japan* (*Imjin nok*) and *General Im Kyŏng-ŏp* (*Im Kyŏng-ŏp chŏn*) that related military exploits. The most widely read novels, however, *Dream of the Jade Chamber* (*Ongnu mong*), *The Story of Sukhyang* (*Sukhyang chŏn*), and *The Story of Ch'unhyang* (*Ch'unhyang chŏn*) all deal with themes of love. The contents of some of these do affirm the validity of Confucian morality. Yet many of these novels, the authors of which almost all are unknown, boldly express the candid feelings of the non-*yangban* classes and their discontent with the society in which they lived. Considered the greatest of the novels of this period, *Ch'unhyang chŏn* takes the stance that commoners and those of mean birth are no different in their human qualities than the *yangban*. Thus the heroine of its title is led to exclaim: "How can loyalty and filiality, or womanly virtue, differ between high born and low?"

The same tendency is apparent in *sijo* poetry as well. The early *sijo* were *yangban* literature, short poems that sang of Confucian virtue, or the joys of rusticity, or the heroic spirit of the warrior. Now, however, the *sijo* was taken over by those of status other than *yangban*, and their desire was not merely to convey a mood of emotional involvement but to let the *sijo* express their feelings in concrete form. Accordingly, the *sijo* became a long poem and its depictions took on a quality of realism. The themes too changed, to portray love between the sexes, the hardships of family life, and even unabashed lewdness. The authors of the new *sijo* most frequently were such government clerks of Yŏngjo's time as Kim Ch'ŏn-t'aek and Kim Su-jang, or were fallen *yangban*, or those of low social status such as female entertainers. In order to express their feelings more freely these writers frequently left their creations unsigned, for they did not wish to be bound by the conventions of the past.

> Pass where the winds pause before crossing over,
> Pass where the clouds too pause before crossing,
> High peaks of Changsŏng Pass where
> Wild hawks and trained hawks and
> Highest soaring falcons all,
> All must pause before crossing over.
> Were but my love waiting me across yonder pass,
> I should pause not once in my crossing over.   *Anonymous*

Many of the poems by known and unknown authors of other social origins were included in anthologies that contained the works of *yangban* writers of the past as well. The two major compilations were by the aforementioned government clerks Kim Ch'ŏn-t'aek and Kim Su-jang, whose *Enduring Poetry of Korea* (*Ch'ŏnggu yŏngŏn*) and *Songs of Korea* (*Haedong kayo*) appeared in 1728 and 1763 respectively. All in all, the appearance of the new *sijo* verse, like that of the new novel, gives ample evidence of the emergence of a fresh, new literature.

New Approaches in Art

In painting too the new trends are plain to see. First of all, this period marks the appearance of realism in landscape painting. Rather than attempt to portray idealized scenes on the model prescribed in manuals on Chinese landscape painting, Korean artists now came to depict Korea's natural surroundings as seen with their own eyes. Chŏng Sŏn (1676–1759) was the painter who developed this realistic landscape style. In fashioning his technique of realism he had to work out his own approach to composition, and he learned how to portray the craggy features of the Korean landscape with forceful splashes of black, to give a sense of looming mass. Paintings that perhaps best exhibit these characteristics are "Storm Lifting Over Inwang Mountain" (*Inwang chesaek to*) and "The Diamond Mountains" (*Kŭmgang chŏndo*). Although also a painter of the realism school, Kim Hong-do, who flourished in the latter half of the eighteenth century, depicted mountains, trees, and streams with swift brush strokes, conveying with the beauty of his lines a style that contrasts with that of Chŏng Sŏn. Typical of his landscape paintings is "The Steepled Rocks off Kŭmgang's Shore" (*Ch'ongsŏkchŏng to*).

Genre painting also flourished during this period. Kim Hong-do and Sin Yun-bok (1758-?) are the most famed masters of genre painting, the art that depicts scenes from the ordinary events of everyday life, and it is noteworthy that both were professional painters in government employ. Kim Hong-do was adept at delineating mountains and streams, Taoist immortals, flowers and grasses, and he is especially known for his way of depicting the branching of trees. In his masterful genre album (*P'ungsok hwach'ŏp*) his principal themes are the workaday lives of everyday people, as they till the fields, gather the harvest, or labor in a smithy, but his "Dancer with Musicians" (*Muak*) and "Wrestling" (*Ssirŭm*) are especially well-known works. Kim Tŭk-sin (1754-1822) is another genre painter of the same bent in style and subject matter as Kim Hong-do, while the paintings of Sin Yun-bok, on the other hand, depict mainly the mores of the townspeople of his time, with a focus on the activities of women. The best examples of his work are "A Beauty" (*Yŏin to*) and *An Album of Genre Scenes* (*P'ungsok hwach'ŏp*), in which are to be found girls on swings, housewives washing clothes in streams, women selling wine, and suggestive scenes of disporting libertines. The popularity of genre painting constituted an artistic protest against *yangban* Confucian society, an assertion of the worth of all humanity.

A noteworthy development in ceramics was the production of blue on white porcelains. In the early Yi dynasty the pigment known as "Mohammedan blue" was imported from China, making blue on white porcelain very precious, and its use among the common people was forbidden. During the time of Chŏngjo (1776-1800), however, when a pigment produced in Korea began to come into use, blue on white porcelain gained wide acceptance among the whole population and underwent considerable development. Quick brush strokes using only the blue pigment limned in mountains and streams, flowers and birds, grasses and trees. When fired, this blue on white porcelain ware was possessed of a beauty far different than that of the contemporary Chinese or Japanese ceramics of varied hues that employed blue, red, green, purple and other colors. From these Korean porcelains there emanated a simple poetry, an essential Korean flavor of unaffected naturalness.

Chapter 12

Instability in the *Yangban* Status System and the Outbreak of Popular Uprisings

1. Government by In-Law Families

Dominance of Royal In-Law Families

So long as Yŏngjo and Chŏngjo maintained their policy of appointment of officials without regard to factional affiliation, the policy known as *t'angp'yŏngch'aek*, the political scene generally remained stable. It is true that Hong Kug-yŏng held sway during the 1770's from his position as Chief Royal Secretary, having won favor by preserving the throne for Chŏngjo against those of the Pyŏkp'a faction who sought to keep him from it. He soon was driven out, however, and for the most part monarchic authority was secure enough during the seventy-five years that Yŏngjo and Chŏngjo occupied the throne.

But upon the death of Chŏngjo in 1800 and the accession of Sunjo, a boy of just ten years, the power of the royal in-law family completely dominated the authority of the throne, and the era of so-called in-law government (*sedo chŏngch'i*) began. As Sunjo's father-in-law, Kim Cho-sun of the Andong Kim clan was able to concentrate political power almost entirely in his own hands, and in consequence many of his close clansmen rose rapidly to occupy vital positions in the government. Subsequently the Andong Kim for a time had to yield their predominant position to another formidable in-law lineage, the P'ungyang Cho clan. This was because the mother of Hŏnjong (1834–1849), Sunjo's grandson and successor, was a daughter of Cho Man-yŏng, a leading P'ungyang Cho figure. The P'ungyang Cho thus held sway during much of Hŏnjong's reign, Cho In-yŏng (Cho Man-yŏng's younger brother) becoming chief state councillor and many of his clansmen securing appointments to important posts. But power once again reverted to the Andong Kim after the accession of Ch'ŏlchong (1849–1863), since his queen was the daughter of Andong Kim Mun-gŭn whose close kinsmen Kim Hŭng-gŭn and Kim Chwa-gŭn now came in turn to head the officialdom as chief state councillor.

In this situation the dynasty survived as that of the Yi royal house in name only, its authority overwhelmed by the power exercised by the

Andong Kim. The fact that there were those in the royal house who attacked the Andong Kim only to be sent into banishment, or charged with
treason and executed, bespeaks where real power lay. How insignificant,
then, was the power of the other *yangban* houses! A force that might
challenge the Andong Kim simply was not tolerated.

A time now had come when political power no longer was allocated
among all *yangban,* or even among those in the Old Doctrine faction, nor
was it seized by the winner of a factional struggle. At this point in the
latter half of the nineteenth century the political arena was dominated
by a single royal in-law sub-lineage.

Disarray in the "Three Administrations"

Concentration of power in the hands of a succession of royal in-law families brought with it disorder in the governing process, and the suffering
that ensued therefrom fell on the shoulders of the peasantry. This is because
the large sums offered in bribes to obtain appointments to office had to be
recovered through exactions levied on the peasantry. In consequence one
gets the feeling that the fiscal organs of the government had been converted
into embezzling instruments to fill the private purses of the officials.
The so-called three administrations, the agencies that administered the
three prime sources of government revenue—land tax, military service
tax, and the state granary system, consequently fell into extreme disarray.

The land tax actually was made up of a variety of charges levied on the
basis of the number of *kyŏl* under cultivation. First of all a tax of four
tu (about two bushels) was to be paid per *kyŏl,* in addition to which there
were levies of 1.2 *tu* earmarked for the support of the three combat forces
(*samsubyŏng*) attached to the Military Training Command, of another
12 *tu* of so-called *taedong* rice that the enactment of the Uniform Land
Tax Law (*taedongpŏp*) required in place of the former payment of tribute
goods, and finally of two more *tu* in consequence of the Equalized Tax
Law. Despite the multiplicity of these taxes the total amount came to less
than twenty *tu,* under one-tenth of the harvest, and so by no means a large
amount. Nevertheless the land tax indeed was a heavy burden, and the
reason for this was a variety of surcharges and handling fees. Although
practices differed from region to region, on the whole the addition of these
further charges and fees raised tax collections in some cases to as much
as one hundred *tu* per *kyŏl,* an amount equal to about half the harvest.
On top of all this officials might levy taxes on abandoned fields, a practice
known as the "bare field tax," and they frequently extorted payments above
the fixed amounts, the so-called added *kyŏl,* so that they might replace
the public funds they had spent for private purposes.

The military tax, for its part, levied payment of one "bolt" (*p'il*) of cloth
on each able-bodied male. To be sure, the rate had been cut in half by the
Equalized Tax Law, but one *p'il* was the equivalent of six *tu* of rice, and

so the miltary tax amounted to more than the basic land tax of four *tu*. Moreover, as has been noted earlier, the peasants were afflicted with an assortment of illegal exactions, such as demands for payment of cloth on behalf of family members who had died. In fact, then, since the military tax involved the production of cloth by the peasants themselves, it imposed a greater hardship, perhaps, than the land tax.

Finally, under the grain loan (*hwan'gok*) system, loans were made to poor peasants from government stores in the lean spring months and were to be repaid at harvest time with a "wastage" (*mogok*) charge of ten percent. A number of considerations lay behind the original concept of replacing losses by means of a wastage charge, but in reality it was only a pretext for charging interest. Accordingly, what was supposed to be a means of giving relief to hard-pressed peasants was converted into an instrument for making usurious loans, and the abuses of the grain loan system became the most severe among the three tax administrations. Officials forced peasants to borrow more than they needed, they fabricated false reports concerning their transactions, by a stroke of the brush they produced, on paper, rice in empty storehouses, they doubled the quantities of borrowed rice by mixing husks with the grain—in these and other ways the peasants were made to suffer still further.

Local officials thus grew fat on what they illegally extorted from the farm population in their charge. It was not the county magistrates alone, for the local functionaries (*hyangni*) at the bottom of the administrative ladder also profited. In order to obtain an appointment, the *hyangni* were required to pay a fee in advance to the local magistrate, and to recoup this amount they had to find suitable ways to collect taxes by force. In other words, taking advantage of their position as the actual operational and enforcement arm of local government, the *hyangni* were free to manipulate the situation and extort as they pleased. They were only *hyangni* but they wore the cloak of governmental authority, and the peasants had no way to refuse their demands. It was inevitable that the activities of the *hyangni* added heavily to the burdens of the peasantry.

The corruption of local administration not only brought grief to the peasantry but threatened the fiscal soundness of the central government as well. The government's response was to dispatch secret inspectors (*amhaeng ŏsa*) to bring charges against officials guilty of corrupt practices. Traveling incognito through the countryside, the *amhaeng ŏsa* investigated allegations of official misconduct and reported back to the throne. But this was not an effective way to get at the roots of the evil—though a comparatively honest official might be appointed a secret inspector, it was no longer possible to reverse the flood tide of dynastic decay.

2. Tremors in the *Yangban* Status System

Fallen Yangban *and the* Chungin *Class*

In broad conception, the *yangban* society of the Yi dynasty had been structured as a highly stratified society dominated by the *yangban* class. This *yangban* centered status system, however, gradually began to come apart from the seventeenth century on. By the nineteenth century, the occurrence of sharp upward and downward movements in social status had given an increasingly vague coloration to the term *yangban* as used to define a social class entity.

This phenomenon came about first of all because of the increase in the number of "fallen" *yangban*, those whose capacity to actually exercise their claim to *yangban* status had been eroded. It already has been noted that, during the period of rule by a few powerful families, political power was monopolized by the Noron (Old Doctrine) lineages alone, and that in the period of in-law government power resided almost exclusively in the hands of royal in-law families. In consequence, the many *yangban* thus excluded from government buried themselves in the countryside and fell to the status of a kind of local gentry. Furthermore, within *yangban* lineages unable to obtain a government appointment for any of their members for several generations, some had been forced by circumstance to become small-scale farmers. These were the so-called ruined *yangban* (*chanban*), who had sunk to the point where they no longer could maintain the dignity and authority that marked traditional *yangban* class status. Their numbers, moreover, were steadily increasing.

At the same time, the distinction between legitimate and illegitimate lines of descent was breaking down. Already in the latter part of the eighteenth century Chŏngjo had appointed men from illegitimate lineages to positions as editor-compilers in the *Kyujanggak* (the palace library), an indication that the discriminatory treatment to which they long had been subjected was becoming less severe. The *chungin* too, the hereditary class of technical specialists in the capital, were improving their social position. Not only were interpreters widening their horizons through coming into contact with a new culture on their travels to Ch'ing China, but they were amassing fortunes through private trading activities and thus were expanding their influence in the society. Accordingly, whether physicians, men versed in astronomical and meteorological science, government artists, or other professional men with their specialized knowledge and training on the one hand, or government clerks with their administrative talents and literary attainments on the other—all these *chungin* elements were pressing fresh claims to the position in Yi society to which their skills entitled them. At the same time, their situation readily induced feelings of affinity and common cause with the fallen *yangban*. Finally, it has been observed above that the wealthy farmers and great merchants too were in the process of raising their social status.

Another changing aspect of social class relationships was the growing strength of provincial society, which hitherto had suffered discriminatory treatment. For example, the number of successful higher civil service examination candidates from P'yŏngan province in northwest Korea increased sharply, to the point where the not very large county of Chŏngju came to produce more such degree holders than any other county north or south. To be sure, these men found it difficult to go on to have careers of importance in the central government, but the fact that such new elements appeared at all must be accounted a significant change. All of these developments, then, could not but constitute a threat to a ruling structure dominated by a few great families.

Changes in the Peasantry and the Liberation of Slaves

Currents affecting the *yangban* ruling structure also were rising at the base of Yi society. There were in fact instances of peasants becoming rich farmers and achieving the outward trappings of *yangban* status, but with the expansion of the landholdings of the royal house and in-law families many more peasants were reduced to precarious tenancy. At the same time, others lost their land entirely and became wage laborers, for it has been seen that the spread of the rice transplanting technique and ridge-furrow plowing methods resulted in a labor surplus in the farm villages. Some of the surplus was employed in the villages at the busy rice transplanting or harvest seasons, but other laborers left the villages to work as craftsmen or as miners. Among these was an element of temporary workers seeking to take advantage of the slack farming season to earn extra money, but others found it possible to leave for good and take up new lives as non-agricultural laborers. In the case of mine workers this sometimes resulted in the formation of new communities with periodic markets to service them.

Even if they lost their land, however, free peasants no longer fell into slavery, for slavery was gradually disappearing. The number of slaves on the government's rosters had fallen from 350,000 in the fifteenth century to less than 200,000 by the seventeenth century. This decrease was caused in part by the destruction of slave records and scattering of the slave population during the Hideyoshi invasion, but this was by no means the only reason. Slaves had come to be permitted to perform military service, the duty of the freeborn, and some were given their freedom on the basis of passing a test of their military skills, while others qualified for manumission on the ground of two successive generations of military service. Still others obtained free status by virtue of military valor or similar unusual service, and some simply bought their freedom. Even those government slaves still carried on the rosters no longer in fact performed labor for the government, nor did they pay a labor remission fee, so that they too were in effect free. This was true also of many of the privately owned slaves, whose hard-pressed *yangban* masters had difficulty keeping them.

Under these circumstances the government itself decided to free its re-maining slaves, and in 1801 the rosters of government slaves were ordered burned. Thus, with a few exceptions, government slaves cast off their low-born status and became free men. True, slaves attached to local govern-ment agencies remained unfreed, and the institution of private slavery had not been abolished. Nevertheless a social change of major dimensions had occurred, for the old status system that had so strictly upheld the distinction between master and slave now was crumbling.

3. Peasant Resistance

The Widespread Phenomenon of the Kye

Now grown more aware of the need to gain control over their own des-tinies in a society ground down by *yangban* misrule, the peasantry came to adopt a number of strategies for survival. First mention should be given to the development of the *kye*, a voluntary mutual assistance association. The *kye* was quite unlike the Confucianist "village code" (*hyangyak*) that operated under *yangban* leadership, attempting to enforce Confucianist moral prescriptions from above. The *kye*, in contrast, came into existence for the purpose of securing tangible benefit for its participants. Thus as the village code lost its meaning with the disintegration of *yangban* soci-ety, the *kye* in contrast flourished all the more.

Most *kye* associations to begin with were formed for mutual assistance or simply as social gatherings. Examples of this are lineage *kye*, *kye* or-ganized by those born in the same year, wedding and funeral *kye*, and neigh-borhood *kye*. It is clear, too, that many *yangban* and wealthy households participated in *kye* of these sorts. But later the dominant form of *kye* became those organized to overcome economic hardship through the pool-ing of resources. Naturally many poor village people participated in these. Such *kye* were formed to repair a reservoir indispensable to all, for the common purpose of paying the military cloth tax, or to purchase an ox or farm tools for shared use. It may be said, then, that the widespread use of the *kye* voluntary association was a reflection of the changing face of village life.

The great interest aroused in the potato and sweet potato as famine foods also is a phenomenon closely related to village life around this time. Sweet potato seeds were brought to Korea from Tsushima in 1763 by Cho Ŏm, an official returning from a diplomatic mission to Japan. Its cultivation spread, then, through the efforts and encouragement of a number of dedicat-ed people, until it became a meaningful adjunct to the Korean diet. But the sweet potato is not well suited to Korea's climate nor is it easy to cultivate, and so the white potato spread more widely from the moment of its introduction from China around 1840. Because of the way it came into Korea the white potato was called the "northern potato," while the sweet potato was known as the "southern potato."

Landless Wanderers and Brigandage

Despite all their efforts at self-help, the life of peasants reduced to tenantry on small plots of land was one of grinding poverty. In poor harvest years there were multitudes of famine stricken people everywhere, and thousands died of hunger. Inevitably forced to abandon their villages, large numbers of peasants took up lives of vagrant wandering. So deserted were the villages in some areas that a whole township (*myŏn*) might be left with scarcely ten households. Some peasants sought to survive in the upland areas as "fire-field people" (*hwajŏnmin*). They moved from place to place, with no fixed abode, burning off the vegetation cover and farming the hilly land as best they could. The harvests of course were small and their lives were poor, but at least they could hope to take some pleasure in having escaped the exactions of the government. Yet the grasping hands of the officials reached out to extract taxes even from the fire-field people. In consequence the number of peasants who migrated across Korea's borders into the Chien-tao (Korean: Kando) region of Manchuria or the Russian Maritime Territory was rising.

The discontent and grievances of the peasantry now began to be made manifest in covert ways. One expression of this was the repeated appearance all over the country of inflammatory streamers (usually hung from trees) and wall placards. In 1804, for example, a "Secret Account of Conditions in P'yŏngan Province" was affixed to the four main gates of Seoul, and in the same year a slanderous denunciation of the court appeared in Anak county, Hwanghae province, in the form of a cryptically written *kasa* poem. Again, in 1826 a streamer was hung in Ch'ŏngju cursing the government for its corruption and abuses; its contents were considered so seditious that Ch'ŏngju was downgraded in the hierarchy of local administrative jurisdictions and its name changed. These and many other similar incidents offer clear insight into the state of mind of the common people at this time.

Given such grounds for discontent, it is understandable that peasant protest did not long remain so passive. First of all many peasants turned to brigandage, shattering the public peace on all sides. Such bands roamed the countryside and ranged up and down the coastlines. There were men on horseback armed with muskets, known as "fire brigands" (*hwajŏk*), and there were those called "water brigands" (*sujŏk*) who pillaged by boat along the rivers and seashores. Gradually this lawlessness became better organized, as smaller bands that had arisen separately merged into more powerful forces. Their names often were taken from the areas in which they operated, like the West River Band and the Northwest Frontier Band, or from the background of those who formed them, like the Vagabond Band made up of landless wanderers.

Outbreak of Popular Uprisings

A rash of popular uprisings now broke out, centered naturally on the peasantry. Leadership generally was provided, however, by discontented *yangban* elements, the "fallen" *yangban,* and in a number of instances originally localized disturbances grew into large-scale rebellions. This was the case with the Hong Kyŏng-nae Rebellion in 1811. A fallen *yangban* from P'yŏngan province, Hong Kyŏng-nae was frustrated by his inability to pass the civil examinations and enter on an official career, and he conspired with others in his area, like U Kun-ch'ik and Kim Sa-yong, who shared his discontent. Declaring that discrimination against the populace of P'yŏngan province must end, they plotted a rebellion with prosperous *yangban*-turned-farmers of local civil and military service background, as well as with a number of Kaesŏng merchants and other private tradesmen. Just at this time the people of P'yŏngan were in a volatile mood, due to severe famine conditions and the unusually large numbers of landless wanderers. Under the pretext, then, of assembling laborers for mining operations, Hong Kyŏng-nae and his fellow conspirators gathered and drilled their motley force and rose in open rebellion. Nearly the whole region north of the Ch'ŏngch'ŏn River immediately came under their control, but presently they were defeated by government forces at Songnim-ni in Pakch'ŏn county. After falling back to the fortified town of Chŏngju they continued to hold out for some months, but Hong himself was killed in the final battle for the town and his rebellion was suppressed.

The Hong Kyŏng-nae Rebellion was put down, but its result was only to fuel the deepening popular discontent. Rumors that Hong Kyŏng-nae was still alive were widespread, and there also were local risings by bands claiming earlier to have been under his command. Thus over the years small-scale outbreaks continued almost uninterruptedly throughout the whole country. The Chinju Uprising of 1862 was the most serious of these. Unable to endure the rapacious exploitation of the Provincial Army Commander Paek Nak-sin, the populace armed themselves with bamboo spears and rose under the leadership of Yu Kye-ch'un, a peasant of fallen *yangban* background. The rebels killed local government functionaries, set fire to government buildings, and wrought considerable destruction. The Chinju Uprising too was suppressed, but it ignited a succession of similar outbreaks. Some forty days later, for example, a peasant uprising occurred at Iksan in Chŏlla province and simultaneously almost every region of the three southern provinces was beset by popular disturbances. The tide of uprisings spread elsewhere too, up and down the land, with even the fishermen on Cheju Island rebelling against the local authorities.

These popular uprisings mostly were spontaneous in character, having the objective of getting rid of vicious local officials. But at the same time they represented an attack against *yangban* society itself, plagued by the abuses of power of a few powerful or royal in-law lineages.

4. Development of a Popular Culture

Scholarship and Thought

Out of the *Sirhak* (Practical Learning) tradition of the seventeenth and eighteenth centuries came new scholarly achievements in the nineteenth century. The basic thrust of nineteenth century scholarship remained the same, an attempt to find solutions to the pressing problems of the day by searching for their roots in the Korean historical process. But the perspective of Korean scholars now changed, as they sought to apply the results of their work in new directions. There thus emerged a body of scholarship known as "enlightenment thought" (*kaehwa sasang*).

The most noteworthy aspect of the scholarship of this period was the effort to give it an overall structure. It was in the early nineteenth century that the thought of Chŏng Yag-yong, the great synthesizer of the full range of *Sirhak* scholarship, ripened into maturity. There had been further works of an encyclopedic nature on the model of Yi Su-gwang's *Chibong yusŏl* and Yi Ik's *Sŏngho sasŏl*, but now in Sunjo's reign (1800–1834) appeared two remarkable compilations: *Sixteen Treatises Written in Retirement* (*Imwŏn simnyuk chi*; also known as *Imwŏn kyŏngje chi*) by Sŏ Yu-gu (1764–1845), and *Random Expatiations* (*Oju yŏnmun changjŏn san'go*) by Yi Kyu-gyŏng (1788–1856). The former treated agriculture most comprehensively but also dealt with the full spectrum of life in Yi dynasty society, from daily activities to economic output to *yangban* intellectual and recreational pursuits. Yi Kyu-gyŏng's work is a vast assemblage and meticulous examination of data in the whole range of scholarly endeavor— astronomy, geography, government, economics, society, history, and other disciplines. Then at the very end of the dynasty, in 1908, a group of scholars led by Pak Yong-dae (1849–?) completed an expanded version (titled *Chŭngbo munhŏn pigo*) of the late eighteenth century *Reference Compilation of Documents on Korea* (*Tongguk munhŏn pigo*), a work that truly may be called an encyclopedic collectanea of materials for the study of traditional Korea. Again, in 1865, Cho Tu-sun (1796–1870) headed a compilation team that prepared the *Taejŏn hoet'ong*, a comprehensive update of the dynasty's administrative code. Such revised editions and new compilations of materials are a hallmark of the scholarly work of this period.

Another characteristic of nineteenth century scholarship lies in its research methodology. Yi Kyu-gyŏng's striking concern for substantiating the data he used, his efforts at empirical verification, already have been remarked, but Kim Chŏng-hŭi (1786–1856) was the leading practitioner of this methodology. He adopted the approach of the Ch'ing empirical school and is known in particular for his deeply learned studies of historical inscriptions. A work typical of his meticulous scholarship is the *Observations on Examining Two Stone Inscriptions* (*Kŭmsŏk kwaan nok*), a study of two of the monument stones erected by Silla King Chinhŭng in the mid-sixth century as he toured the frontiers of his kingdom. In the field of cartography Kim Chŏng-ho (?–1864) completed his "Detail Map of Korea" (*Taedong yŏjido*) in 1861 on the basis of a lifetime spent in direct observation of the geographical features of the whole of the Korean Peninsula.

It is important to note next that numbers of scholars now emerged from among the fallen *yangban* and from the *chungin* ("middle people"), and that their work contained points of view that reflected the interests of the social class of their origin. Foremost among this group was Ch'oe Han-gi (1803–1875), a scholar of fallen *yangban* background. In a typical work completed in 1860, *Personnel Administration* (*Injŏng*), he argued that the way to restore good government was through proper recruitment of officials, and he proposed that men of talent be educated and employed from *yangban*, peasant, craftsman, or merchant backgrounds, without discrimination. He had a progressive view of history, one that made him confident the future held a better life for mankind in an enlightened world. Accordingly he urged that Korea abandon its policy of isolation, open its doors, and live in concert with the other nations of the world. Ch'oe Sŏng-hwan was a *chungin* who advocated reform and rationalization of government administration in a work called *Brief Words of Counsel* (*Komun piryak*). Among the positions he took were that the traditional practice of forced mobilization of commoners to labor on state construction projects should be replaced by a wage labor system, and that taxes should be paid in cash, not kind. Such writings as these displayed a common viewpoint, a concern for issues affecting urban economic interests or the problems of those in direct charge of the day to day operations of the government.

A history of the problem of illegitimate offspring of *yangban* and their concubines also appeared. Called *Sunflowers* (*Kyusa*), it was compiled in 1859 by men who suffered this stigma and it urged an end to all discriminatory treatment directed against them. A little earlier, about 1848, a *History of the Clerkly Class* (*Yŏnjo kwigam*) was published. Put together in the course of the previous century principally by Yi Chin-hŭng, a man of *hyangni* (local functionary) origin, this work argued that since the bloodlines of *hyangni* and *yangban* originally were the same, the two classes ought to be accorded the same treatment. Moreover, in such works as *Chronicles of Forgotten Men* (*Hosan oegi*) by Cho Hŭi-ryong (1789–1866; a noted painter, calligrapher, and writer perhaps of *chungin* lineage), *Village Observations* (*Ihyang kyŏnmun nok*) by a government clerk named Yu Chae-gŏn, and *Those This Age Has Overlooked* (*Hŭijo ilsa*) by Yi Kyŏng-min (1814–1883), a *yangban* from an impoverished family, are found biographies of men of outstanding accomplishments or virtuous enterprises whose low social origins prevented their recognition by inclusion in the conventional compilations. Representing a new phenomenon in Korean historiography, all these works reflect the changes that were taking place in the society of that time.

The Spread of Catholicism

Once the Andong Kim lineage led by the young king's father-in-law, Kim Cho-sun, had secured power early in the reign of Sunjo (1800–1834), Catholicism no longer was severely suppressed. From the beginning, policy with respect to the alien religion had been inextricably bound up with factional politics, the Pyŏkp'a taking a harsh anti-Catholic stance and the Sip'a, to which Kim Cho-sun belonged, a moderate position. During this long interlude the Vatican had appointed a vicar apostolic for Korea and French priests began to enter the country, Maubant in 1836 and Chastan and Imbert the following year. The Catholic faith thus had begun to win wider acceptance. But presently a policy of suppression was initiated by the Pyŏkp'a P'ungyang Cho, who had come to dominate the court as the current in-law family, and in the ensuing Catholic Persecution of 1839 the three foreign priests and many Korean converts were executed. A few years later the first Korean priest, Kim Tae-gŏn, who had been trained at a seminary in Macao, secretly returned to Korea and began to proselytize. He tried to maintain contact with missionaries in China by sea rather than via the long and dangerous land route, but he soon was apprehended and suffered martyrdom, in 1846. With Ch'ŏlchong (1849–1863) on the throne the Andong Kim again held power and again the anti-Catholic policy was relaxed. As a result a number of Western priests entered Korea, the number of converts reached 20,000, and a variety of Catholic books and tracts were published.

At the outset Catholicism had attracted many *yangban* converts from among the Namin (Southerner) Sip'a scholars who were excluded from access to political power. Persecution brought a gradual decline in their numbers, however, and from the turn of the nineteenth century most converts came from among people of lower social status. While there were some from the *chungin* class, such as medical practitioners, a decided majority were peasants, craftsmen, or those in commercial occupations. Moreover, there were even substantial numbers of converts from among wage laborers, while women adherents also increased remarkably. In short, it was people from the lower social classes rather than the higher, the uneducated rather than the educated, and the poor rather than the better off who now were attracted to Catholicism. Still, Catholic believers were concentrated mainly in Seoul and nearby areas, and rather than a religion of the villages Catholicism remained a faith for urban dwellers.

It is clear that what attracted Koreans to Catholicism was above all its creed of equality, its tenet that the whole of humankind are alike the children of God. It must have been a moving experience for *chungin* and commoners to be able to number themselves among God's children and worship Him on a basis of equality with the *yangban*. For women as well Catholicism surely had a corresponding appeal. Moreover, those who found themselves in circumstances of despair doubtless responded with joyous belief to sermons about the kingdom of God. Indeed this vision of an afterlife likely constituted a powerful inducement to embrace Catholicism. It is clear, then, that belief in Catholicism was in itself a grave and growing indictment of *yangban* society.

Appearance of the Tonghak ("Eastern Learning") Doctrine

If it was Catholicism that propagated its faith in the region of the capital, then it was Tonghak that was nurtured among the people of the farming villages. For the grievances of the peasants against the society in which they lived found expression in a religious movement called Tonghak, or "Eastern Learning." Tonghak began to be propounded by its founder, Ch'oe Che-u (1824–1864), during the reign of Ch'ŏlchong. Although he asserted he had taken the best precepts of Confucianism, Buddhism, and Taoism so as to oppose "Western Learning" (Catholicism) with "Eastern Learning," his doctrine included elements from Catholicism and also embraced features of popular shamanistic beliefs. His ideas, thus eclectically shaped, are expressed in his writings such as *Bible of Tonghak Doctrine* (*Tonggyŏng taejŏn*) and *Hymns from Dragon Pool* (*Yongdam yusa*).

Ch'oe Che-u believed in the unity of man with God, that mankind and the Supreme Being are one and the same. He preached that the mind or spirit of man was a replica of that of God and that, accordingly, serving man constituted service to God. His ideas thus proclaimed an equality for all human beings that transcended social status or class, and this is the primary reason why his doctrine was welcomed by the oppressed peasantry. Another factor in the acceptance of Tonghak by the peasant population was that it incorporated such practices as the chanting of magical formulas and worship of mountain deities, aspects of traditional shamanistic beliefs that were readily understood by village people.

Tonghak was not simply a religious movement but a social movement as well, one concerned primarily with the peasantry and the betterment of the conditions in which the villagers lived. Tonghak urged that the nation be strengthened and the livelihood of the people be ensured, and it called for reform of the corruption ridden government. Moreover, Tonghak went on to assert that the turning wheel of time had brought near the day when these goals might be achieved. It was this millenarian aspect that led the government to view with alarm the spreading popularity of the Tonghak faith. Accordingly, in 1863 Ch'oe Che-u was arrested on charges of misleading the people and sowing discord in the society, and he was executed the following year. Ch'oe Che-u had predicted that the year 1864 would bring "welcome tidings," and this is why the government, fearing a popular uprising might ensue, brought him under arrest in the year preceding. His trial and execution sent many of his followers into hiding in the mountains, and for a time the popularity of Tonghak waned. But the discontent of the peasantry, the hotbed that had nurtured Tonghak, had not been assuaged. Before long the Tonghak faith would revive, infused with new vigor.

The Flourishing of a Popular Literature

As an example of native Korean literature, the *Anthology of Korean Poetry* (*Kagok wŏllyu*), an imposing collection primarily of *sijo* poetry, appeared in 1876, compiled by Pak Hyo-gwan and An Min-yŏng. But the "one-man opera" or *p'ansori* form is the most noteworthy achievement in Korean literature of this period. *P'ansori* were tales sung by professional artists to an outdoor audience in a performance extending over several hours. The origins of the *p'ansori* form can be traced rather far back in time, but it only flourished in the nineteenth century when masterly singers like Song Hŭng-nok and Mo Hŭng-gap emerged to bring *p'ansori* to the peak of its popularity. The lyrics sung by the *p'ansori* performers were adapted from earlier Korean vernacular novels, and eventually a repertoire of twelve tales was created. The man who contributed most to the development of this corpus of *p'ansori* texts was Sin Chae-hyo (1812–1884), who put his own creative stamp on his story material by transforming mere words into emotion-charged phrasings. *P'ansori* texts contained satirical passages that lampooned the *yangban* class, thus providing a vehicle for the artists who performed them, as well as the populace who heard them, to give vent to their grievances against the inequities of late Yi society.

Literature written in Chinese by members of lower social classes, by illegitimate descendants of *yangban*, by *chungin*, and by petty clerks, already had begun to appear and now it truly flourished. In 1857 Yu Chae-gŏn (1793–1880), primarily, completed the compilation of the *Third Selection of Poems of the People* (*P'ungyo samsŏn*), in which works by monks and by women also were included, thus giving fuller expression to the wide authorship and readership of the selected poems. The fact that this anthology contained works by some three hundred five different authors is itself a measure of the plethora of writers now to be found among the members of the non-*yangban* social classes. These literary artists formed "fellowships of poets" (*sisa*), and one well-known such company was the group of seven poets that included Chang Chi-wan (1806–?), a *chungin*. The creations of satirical poets like Chŏng Chi-yun (1808–1858; also known as Chŏng Su-dong) and Kim Sakkat (original name Kim Pyŏng-yŏn; 1807–1863) also provide insight into the nature of literature in Chinese produced during this period.

Masked dance, a drama form aimed at an audience of the common people, also flourished at this time. Interspersing dance and song and narrative, masked drama contained shamanistic elements, and this made it still more appealing to the mass audience. Furthermore, satirical passages contained in the narrative usually mocked the *yangban* class, as in this passage from the drama *Festival at Naval Headquarters* (*Suyŏng yayu*) spoken by a snake-like creature called Yŏngno:

> I'll eat them raw at low tide, cram my maw at high tide,
> Devour my *yangban* masters nine and ninety.
> Then I'll eat one more and lo!
> A dragon now become, mount the throne of Heaven.

Such frank expression of feelings of hostility against the *yangban* explains the popularity that masked drama enjoyed among the common people.

Changes in the World of the Arts

Painting by men of letters in an abstract style derived from the art of calligraphy was the dominant genre of this period. Kim Chŏng-hŭi (1786–1856) is the most renowned such artist, and in his outstanding work "Winter Scene" (*Sehan to*) one sees not the real landscape of Korea but a portrayal of an other-dimensional idealized world. The orchids of the Taewŏn'gun and Min Yŏng-ik also exemplify such expressionism. This predilection for subjective representation was not limited to the *yangban* literati but spread as well to the professional painters in government employ, to the point where it became the predominant trend of this age. It may well be that hostility among the literati to the corrupted values of Korean society of that time, when the royal in-law families held sway, gave birth to this propensity toward idealization of the painter's subject matter. It appears, moreover, that the earlier trend toward naturalism in landscape painting, and in portrayal of scenes from everyday life, was arrested by the development of this new expressionist school. At the end of the nineteenth century the most renowned figure is Chang Sŭng-ŏp (1843–1897), a painter frequently accounted one of the three great masters of the Yi dynasty, along with An Kyŏn and Kim Hong-do. Chang Sŭng-ŏp was an orphan who learned to paint by looking over the shoulders of his foster brothers, but his talent soon was recognized and he was given employment as a government artist. A genius who would not take up his brush for anyone he did not like, no matter in how high a station, Chang Sŭng-ŏp is best known for such paintings as "Plum Blossoms Red on White" (*Hongbaengmae pyŏng*), a depiction that quickens into life the ethereal beauty of its subject.

In calligraphic art the hidebound style of the past, one that had degenerated into mere formalism, was swept away and new modes of brushwork appeared. Kim Chŏng-hŭi, the great painter and scholar of epigraphy, was a foremost master of the new calligraphy. He studied the work of famed calligraphers of the past and fused their different characteristics into a style bursting with boldness of spirit, a form generally called the Ch'usa style after his penname. No lesser talents were the likes of Sin Wi (1769–1847) and Cho Kwang-jin (1772–1840), who also contributed greatly to the innovations in calligraphic style.

The art of woodworking also underwent considerable development. Wardrobes, chests, mirror stands, cabinets for storing writing materials, stands for displaying ceramic art, bookcases, dining tray-tables, and other items of furniture are famed for their simple, unadorned elegance that preserves the natural beauty of the wood grain. At the same time, many superbly crafted articles were fashioned from bamboo, and bone, and lacquered wood with mother-of-pearl inlay.

5. The Reforms and Isolation Policy of the Taewŏn'gun

Reforms of the Taewŏn'gun

Kojong succeeded Ch'ŏlchong in 1864 at the tender age of twelve. The new king's father, the Hŭngsŏn Taewŏn'gun, himself assumed direction of the government and set in motion a resolute program of reform aimed at creating a strong monarchy. To this end he determined to appoint higher officials in equal proportion from each of the "four colors" (*sasaek*), the four major factions, nor would he be overly concerned with the question of a man's regional or social class background. By this resolute policy of basing official appointments on merit, then, the Taewŏn'gun sought to destroy the pattern of rule by a few powerful lineages or royal in-law families.

The Taewŏn'gun's basic approach to the political problem was reflected as well in his economic policy. He converted the military cloth tax, hitherto levied on the commoner population alone, into a household tax assessed alike against *yangban* and commoners. Furthermore, he reorganized the grain loan system by establishing a network of locally administered village granaries (*sach'ang*), and he made efforts to purify official mores by investigating the stores of grain actually held in the granaries and sentencing to death or banishment those officials who had enriched themselves at public expense.

In order to enhance the dignity of the royal house the Taewŏn'gun set about to reconstruct the Kyŏngbok Palace, which had been destroyed by fire during the Hideyoshi invasion and never rebuilt, since the resources to do so could not be found. Heedless of the precarious state of the government's finances, however, the Taewŏn'gun now proceeded to order the reconstruction begun, in 1865, and completed it only two years later. To meet the huge costs of the project a special "land surtax" (*kyŏltujŏn*) of one hundred "coins" per *kyŏl* was levied on all landholders regardless of social class, and a "gate tax" was even charged on goods transported in and out of the gates of Seoul. The Taewŏn'gun also extracted contributions to the undertaking by force, euphemistically calling them "voluntary offerings." Moreover, since a large force of laborers had to be mobilized for the construction work, the Taewŏn'gun could not but earn their resentment as well. It was also at this time that the "arbitrary hundred cash coin" (*tangbaekchŏn*) was minted, with a value set far above its intrinsic worth, and this gave rise to considerable economic disorder. Nevertheless, the restoration of the Kyŏngbok Palace was completed on a grand scale, graced by such structures as the Hall of Diligent Rule (Kŭnjŏng-jŏn), the Pavilion of Felicitous Gatherings (Kyŏnghoe-ru), and the Gate of Radiant Transformation (Kwanghwamun).

The Taewŏn'gun also moved decisively to close down the private academies (*sŏwŏn*). By this time the hundreds of *sŏwŏn* possessed large agricultural estates and slaves to work them, and they enjoyed the special privilege of exemption from taxation and corvee labor. Thus the *sŏwŏn* were ravaging the economic foundation of the state, and this was not all—they were a political problem as well, a force free of government control that wielded authority on its own in the countryside. The extreme case was that of the Hwayangdong Academy honoring the seventeenth century Noron patriarch Song Si-yŏl, for the views it expressed on public affairs were greeted with more deference than were even government decrees. Accordingly, so long as the *sŏwŏn* were permitted to exist, it would not be possible to create a strengthened administrative hierarchy under the paramount authority of the throne. Already in 1864, then, the Taewŏn'gun banned the rebuilding or unauthorized construction of *sŏwŏn* and shrines to local worthies, and in the next year he abolished the Mandongmyo, the shrine erected to honor the last two emperors of Ming China in accordance with the dying wish of Song Si-yŏl. In 1868 he ordered that taxes be levied on *sŏwŏn*, and finally, in 1871, he carried out a drastic reduction in their number, closing all but a scattered forty-seven. His suppression of the *sŏwŏn* provoked bitter opposition from the Confucian scholars of that day, and in the end his campaign against the *sŏwŏn* was one factor in the set of circumstances that forced the Taewŏn'gun to relinquish power.

Isolation Policy

From early in the nineteenth century, Western nations displayed ever greater interest in establishing contact with Korea for trade and other purposes. Britain and France eastward through the Indian Ocean and then north, America westward across the Pacific, and Russia southward after crossing Siberia—one after another the Western powers came knocking on Chosŏn's doors. In 1832 an English merchant ship appeared off the coast of Ch'ungch'ŏng province seeking to trade, and in 1845 an English warship spent more than a month in Korean waters, surveying the island studded sea between Cheju and the southern coast. In 1846 three French warships dropped anchor off the Ch'ungch'ŏng coast, left a letter for forwarding to the court and departed, while in 1854 two armed Russian vessels sailed along the Hamgyŏng coast, causing some deaths and injuries among the Koreans they encountered. In 1866, the German adventurer Oppert twice asked permission to trade, and after his request was denied it was he who came ashore two years later to attempt to rifle the tomb of the Prince of Namyŏn, the Taewŏn'gun's father, in Tŏksan county of Ch'ungch'ŏng province. In the same year of 1866 the American trading ship *General Sherman* sailed all too brashly up the Taedong River to P'yŏngyang, only to be burned to the water line by a mob of the local populace and soldiery, with all who were on board perishing.

The repeated appearances of these strange vessels could only be regarded as still another menace by a dynasty already troubled by a variety of internal ills. Korea also was aware of the fate that had befallen China in consequence of continuing clashes with Western nations—the Opium War of 1839–1842, the Arrow Incident in 1856, and others. The Korean government, then, looked upon rejection of Western demands for trade as a means of preventing such disasters from overtaking Korea as well.

There was another reason for Korea's rejection of Western demands for trade relations—fear of the spread of Catholicism. It has been seen that Catholicism, whose original appeal primarily had been to disaffected Namin scholars, subsequently had won more and more converts from among *chungin*, commoners, women, and other lower or oppressed segments of the population. This development led to the proscription of Catholicism as a heterodox doctrine opposed to traditional Confucian teachings, and there had been several major persecutions. But Catholicism had been reinvigorated by the proselytizing activities of twelve French priests, including Berneux and Ridel, who entered Korea during the reign of Ch'ŏlchong (1849–1863), and by the early years of Kojong's reign more than 20,000 converts already had been won.

At the outset the Taewŏn'gun was relatively tolerant of Catholicism. Concerned about Russia's southward advance he even adopted the proposal of a Catholic, Nam Chong-sam, to attempt to block Russian expansion by enlisting the aid of France. Negotiations did not go well, however, and reports also were being received of suppression of Catholicism by the Ch'ing government of China. Persuaded at this point to follow the exclusion policy advocated by Chief State Councillor Cho Tu-sun and other high officials, the Taewŏn'gun launched a full-scale persecution early in 1866. Before it was over, nine French missionaries had been executed and large numbers of Korean converts, including Nam Chong-sam, had met their deaths. Clearly, the underlying purpose of Chosŏn's isolation policy was less to exclude Western trade than to avoid contamination by Western ideas.

Clashes with the Western Nations

Korea's doors now were tightly closed. All contact with Westerners was regarded as fraught with peril. Even contact with Japan, which had established relations with the Western powers, was looked upon as dangerous. Relations with Ch'ing China alone were permitted. To establish commercial relations through peaceful negotiations with a Korea ruled by the Taewŏn'gun, the architect of this policy of strict seclusion, was completely out of the question. The Western nations, thereupon, attempted to compel Korea to treat with them by the threat of military force. This resulted in the eruption of two major "foreign disturbances" (*yangyo*), military clashes with Western nations.

The first was the "Foreign Disturbance of 1866," which was ignited by Korea's suppression of Catholicism. Nine of the twelve French missionaries who were active in Korea at that time had been apprehended and martyred, while three remained in hiding in the provinces. One of these, Father Ridel, made good his escape to China, contacted the commander of the French Asiatic Squadron, Admiral Roze, and secured his pledge to take punitive action against Korea. Deciding first to make a show of force, Admiral Roze crossed the Yellow Sea with three of his ships and steamed up the Han River, reconnoitering within sight of Seoul itself before returning for the moment to his station at Chefoo, China. Shortly, however, Admiral Roze again entered Korean waters, this time with a flotilla of seven warships, and after effecting a preliminary landing for reconnaissance purposes, he sent a detachment to seize the administrative center for Kanghwa Island, pillaging it and carrying away the weapons and documents stored there. But another French force attempting to make its way toward Seoul was beaten back by Korean troops led by Han Sŏng-gŭn at Munsusan Fortress, on the mainland just opposite the town of Kanghwa. Moreover, the French troops sent to attack the Chŏngjok-san fortifications at the southern end of Kanghwa were repulsed by units under the command of Yang Hŏn-su [see map p. 265]. In the end, therefore, the French squadron was forced to withdraw without having accomplished its mission.

Five years later, the "Foreign Disturbance of 1871" occurred. The destruction in 1866 of an American merchant ship, the *General Sherman*, on the Taedong River below P'yŏngyang already has been recounted. Now, belatedly, the U. S. government decided to use the incident as a pretext to force Korea to open its ports to trade. Accordingly, the U. S. Minister to Peking, Frederick F. Low, and the Commander of the U. S. Asiatic Squadron, Rear Admiral John Rodgers, were ordered to proceed into Korean waters with a detachment of five warships. By this time, however, in the aftermath of the French reprisal expedition, the Taewŏn'gun had repaired the fortifications, built new gun emplacements, cast more cannon, and had energetically strengthened Korea's defenses in other ways as well. When the American warships steamed boldly up through the Kanghwa

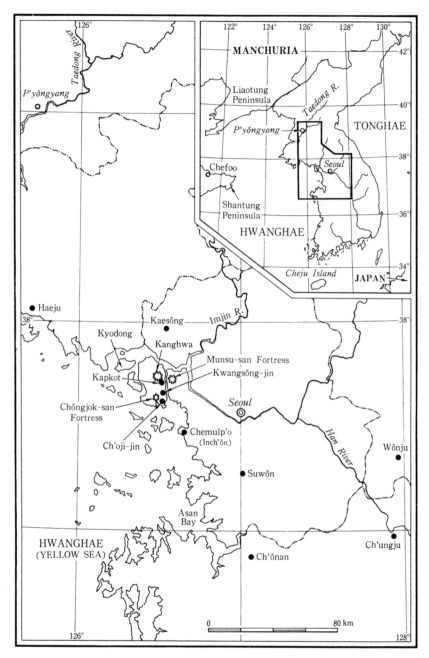

THE "FOREIGN DISTURBANCES" OF 1866 AND 1871

Strait, then, Korean shore batteries opened fire. U.S. marine detachments succeeded in capturing the Ch'oji-jin and Kwangsŏng-jin forts on southern Kanghwa, but the stubborn defense of Kwangsŏng-jin by Ŏ Chae-yŏn inflicted a heavy toll of casualties on the American attackers. Moreover, a marine force attempting a landing at Kapkot point just below Kanghwa's administative center [see map p. 265] was driven back by Korean counterattacks. At this point, then, the U.S. force withdrew and returned to its station in Chinese waters.

Exultant at his victories over the attacking French and American warships, the Taewŏn'gun now further hardened his exclusion policy. To demonstrate his resolve to reject all contact with the Western nations, he had monument stones set up on the Chongno main thoroughfare in Seoul and at points throughout the country, incised with this admonition: "Western barbarians invade our land. If we do not fight we must then appease them. To urge appeasement is to betray the nation." Determination so demonstrably unyielding as this could not easily be shaken. Despite the two reprisal expeditions, the Taewŏn'gun's policy of national isolation remained strictly in force.

The failure of the two Western attacks on Kanghwa was due in part to the stubborn Korean resistance, but it was also true that the French and Americans had lacked a resolutely aggressive purpose. Neither nation had any thought of sending an army of occupation to Korea, or of annexing its territory; both believed instead that intimidation alone might achieve the opening of Korea to commerce with the West. The Taewŏn'gun, however, was both determined enough and strong enough to stand firm against such limited, merely punitive attacks. This was a period when France was busied with the problems of governing Annam (Vietnam), while American energies, in the aftermath of the Civil War, were consumed in the settling of the West. When they encountered the unexpectedly tenacious Korean resistance, they simply were not prepared to bring to bear sufficient force to overcome it. Similarly, England then was engaged in putting down revolt in India, and Russia was occupied with the colonization of the Maritime Territory of Siberia. They too, therefore, had no strong desire at this time to force Korea to open its doors.

To the contrary, however, Japan now was ready to pursue an active and forceful Korea policy. After signing a treaty of friendship with the United States in 1854, Japan had concluded commercial treaties one by one with the major Western powers. The Meiji government, having overturned the Tokugawa Shogunate and effected an imperial restoration, had adopted a policy of fostering economic and military strength by conscious emulation of the material aspects of Western civilization. Before long, then, Japan's ambition to invade Korea lay revealed, the only question being that of suitable opportunity. The Taewŏn'gun, therefore, was no less apprehensive about a modernizing Japan than he was about the Western powers, and his anti-Western policy was equally anti-Japanese.

Chapter 13

Growth of the Forces of Enlightenment

1. Enlightenment Policy and Reaction Against It

Proponents of Foreign Trade and "Enlightenment"

As early as the late eighteenth century Pak Che-ga, a scholar of Ch'ing or Northern Learning, had argued that only by developing trade relations with Japan and the Western nations could Chosŏn become a rich and powerful nation. Yi Kyu-gyŏng, too, when English merchant ships asked to be allowed to trade with Korea in 1832, urged that permission be granted. Ch'oe Han-gi as well, in his book *Descriptions of the Nations of the World* (*Chigu chŏnyo*), which he wrote on the basis of information acquired through reading such Chinese works as *Illustrated Treatise on Nations Across the Sea* (*Hai-kuo t'u-chih*) and *A World Cultural Geography* (*Ying-huan chih-lüeh*), not only introduced his readers to knowledge about foreign lands but took the position that it was necessary for Korea to open itself to foreign intercourse. Moreover, these writers were not merely concerned with acquiring wealth through foreign trade but also were anxious to introduce Western technology.

The argument for foreign trade was put still more forcefully by such men as Pak Kyu-su, O Kyŏng-sŏk, and Yu Hong-gi. Pak Kyu-su (1807–1876), a grandson of the *Sirhak* titan Pak Chi-wŏn, carried on in the tradition of his grandfather—he too was widely read on the material culture of the Western nations and argued that Korea should open its doors to Western ideas and ways. O Kyŏng-sŏk (1831–1879) was a translator-interpreter of the *chungin* class; he had acquired books like the *Illustrated Treatise on Nations Across the Sea* in the course of his journeys to Ch'ing China and he continuously urged his countrymen to read them. Yu Hong-gi (1831–1885?; often called by his penname Yu Taech'i) also was a *chungin*, one who practiced the medical profession. He was a close friend of O Kyŏng-sŏk, from whom he obtained books concerning Western civilization, and his reading led him to advocate that Korea engage in foreign trade and initiate a process of enlightened reform. Thus the voices clamoring for this sort of change grew ever more powerful, while at the same time conditions within Korea conducive to opening the country to foreign trade were becoming more favorable.

One such factor was that in 1873, the tenth year of his long regency, the staunchly isolationist Taewŏn'gun at last relinquished his grip on power. Actually, the Taewŏn'gun was driven out at this juncture, by a combination of the Confucian officials whom he had so antagonized and the power of the newly emerged Min family. Aware of the abuses that had developed under the Andong Kim in-law government, the Taewŏn'gun had arranged for his son to take a queen from a branch of the Yŏhŭng Min clan that lacked powerful political connections. The young King Kojong, however, fell under Queen Min's control, and when Ch'oe Ik-hyŏn submitted a memorial denouncing the Taewŏn'gun, she seized the opportunity to effect his retirement as regent, thus ending his active political role. The departure of its staunchest advocate inevitably hastened the abandonment of Korea's policy of isolation.

The Opening of Ports

Aware of these changing conditions, the Japanese government seized the opportunity to force a commercial treaty on Korea that would further Japan's aggressive designs. To this end, Japan deliberately brought about a confrontation with Korea, the so-called *Unyō* Incident. This occurred in 1875 when the Japanese navy vessel *Unyō* appeared in the waters off Kanghwa and promptly was fired upon by Korean defenders at the Ch'oji-jin fortifications on the southeast tip of the island [see map p. 265]. The Japanese government protested that Korea was guilty of an unprovoked attack on a Japanese ship engaged on a peaceful mission, but in fact before departing from Japan the ship's commander had been given orders to create some sort of incident. The *Unyō*, then, had deliberately violated Korean territorial waters with the intent of drawing fire from the Korean defenders at Ch'oji-jin. In short, the *Unyō* Incident was a drama played out in exact conformance with a scenario scripted by Japan.

Using the incident as a pretext, Japan appointed Kuroda Kiyotaka as minister plenipotentiary and dispatched him to Korea the next year at the head of a force consisting of two warships and three troop transports carrying about four hundred soldiers. Landing at Kapkot promontory on the east coast of Kanghwa, Kuroda demanded that Korea enter into treaty negotiations. Although a majority of Korea's high officials insisted that there should be no dealings with Japan, the translator-interpreter O Kyŏng-sŏk persuaded Third State Councillor Pak Kyu-su to adopt a policy of trade and amicable relations. The government then dispatched Sin Hŏn to receive Minister Kuroda and negotiate with him, with the result that a treaty eventually was concluded. This agreement usually is referred to as the 1876 Treaty of Friendship or simply as the Treaty of Kanghwa. Most important among its twelve articles were one proclaiming that, as an autonomous nation, Korea possessed equal sovereign rights with Japan and another stipulating that Korea would open Pusan and two other ports within the ensuing twenty months. Moreover, the treaty permitted Japan to survey Korean coastal waters at will and it also contained an extra-territoriality clause authorizing the establishment of Japanese settlements on land to be leased in the opened ports, with their Japanese residents subject to Japanese law as applied by Japanese courts.

Japan asserted that the acknowledgment of Korea's status as an autonomous nation contained in the treaty constituted proof that Japan harbored no aggressive designs. But the real objective of this article was the opposite: to open the way for Japanese aggression without interference from China, whose claims to suzerainty over Korea the treaty thus had rejected. Furthermore, the Treaty of Kanghwa was an unequal treaty. Japan had obtained extraterritorial rights, thus forcing on a Korea ignorant of international law the same unequal provisions the Western nations earlier had demanded from Japan itself. The mere fact that Japan came to negotiate a commercial agreement with an intimidating force of warships and combat soldiers amply suggests the one-sided nature of the treaty.

The provision for opening Korean ports, however, constituted the most important feature of the Treaty of Kanghwa. Pusan was a port where Japan had traditionally enjoyed the right to trade through the Sō lords of Tsushima, and two other ports also were to be opened. The designation of these was left to the discretion of Japan. Accordingly Japan dispatched naval vessels to make a thorough survey of potential port sites along Korea's coast. Japan wanted to select a site suitable not merely for commercial trading activity but one that could serve as well to block Russia's southward advance. After much debate, therefore, the Bay of Wŏnsan on the north-central east coast was designated. On the west coast, on the other hand, it was thought that the opening of Inch'ŏn, the gateway to Seoul, would be useful for political purposes. However, the export of rice from Inch'ŏn was banned, which meant that shipments to Japan from the rice granary region of Chŏlla province could be made only after costly overland transport to other ports. Japanese extraterritorial settlements were established in the newly opened ports, and the Japanese residing there, on Korean sovereign territory, enjoyed the special privilege of being governed by their own laws.

After the conclusion of the Treaty of Kanghwa, Japan approached every aspect of its relations with Korea from the perspective of advancing its aims of political, military, and economic aggression. Nevertheless, despite Japan's singleminded aggressive intent, the Treaty of Kanghwa holds great historical significance for Korea. This is because it brought Korea for the first time out onto the international stage. It was the impetus that led the Western powers as well gradually to begin trading with Korea, thus opening Korea's doors to the outside world. The introduction of Western civilization to Korea was an inevitable consequence. At the same time, however, and just as inevitably, the new cultural influences were accompanied by the aggressive actions of Japan, in particular, and of the Western powers as well. In effect, therefore, the opening of Korean ports imposed a great historical ordeal on the Korean people, for how might they achieve at once the twin objectives of enlightenment, or modernization, and the preservation of their independence as a nation?

Pursuit of an Enlightenment Policy

The same year the Treaty of Kanghwa was concluded, in 1876, the Korean government appointed Kim Ki-su as a special envoy and dispatched him to Japan. Upon his return Kim presented to the king his *Record of a Journey to Japan* (*Iltong kiyu*), the journal of his observations on his mission. The content of this record, however, was filled with a reasoned but negative assessment of the course Japan was following in adopting the new Western ways. In the meantime Japan had sent Hanabusa Yoshitada as its minister of legation in Korea, and after protracted negotiations he was permitted to occupy a government building outside West Gate as temporary quarters for his mission.

Korea learned in rather more detail about the world beyond its shores upon the return of Kim Koeng-jip (1842–1896; later known by the name Kim Hong-jip) from a mission to Japan in 1880. Having observed the startling evidence of Japan's progress and been made aware of the thrust of developments elsewhere in the world, Kim Koeng-jip conceived a profound desire to bring such enlightenment to his own country. When he left Japan Kim had obtained from Huang Tsun-hsien, counselor of the Chinese legation in Tokyo, copies of two treatises that were to have a considerable impact back in Korea. One of them, "A Policy for Korea" (*Ch'ao-hsien t'se-lüeh*), was written by Huang himself, who argued that to create a strong nation Korea must adopt Western institutions and technology, and that to secure itself against Russian aggression Korea should seek to achieve self-strengthening under the umbrella of a foreign policy of close friendship with China, treaty ties with Japan, and diplomatic relations with America. The other work, *Presumptuous Views* (*I-yen*) by the Ch'ing thinker Cheng Kuan-ying, asserted that to strengthen a nation like his own, it was not enough to merely import Western technology; the political and other institutions that underlay Western technological development also must be adopted. Moved by such influences as these, government authorities in Korea gradually turned to a policy of enlightenment.

In 1881, the year following Kim Koeng-jip's return, Cho Chun-yŏng, Pak Chŏng-yang, Ŏ Yun-jung, Hong Yŏng-sik and a number of others were sent to Japan as members of a mission of inspection, the so-called gentlemen's sightseeing group (*sinsa yuramdan*). This was in essence a technical mission whose aim was to survey a wide spectrum of Japan's modernized facilities. For more than seventy days the delegation traveled about Japan inspecting administrative agencies first of all, but military, educational, industrial, and other facilities as well. At the same time, at the urging of the Ch'ing government, Kim Yun-sik led a large group of students from *yangban* families and artisans on a mission to Tientsin. There they were taken to the Chinese government arsenal, where they studied the methods of modern weapons manufacture and the military applications of basic science. Korea thus was making a conscious, visible effort to bring itself abreast of advances in the outside world.

On the basis of the new knowledge it had gained, Korea now carried out governmental reforms along enlightenment lines. King Kojong himself was particularly interested in reform of the military. Already in 1881 he reorganized the five garrisons of the traditional army structure into two, the *Muwiyŏng* (Palace Guards Garrison) and *Changŏyŏng* (Capital Guards Garrison), and to head these he appointed generals who would serve also as his close confidants. Meanwhile the king had invited Horimoto Reizō, a lieutenant in the engineering corps of the Japanese army, to instruct a newly organized unit in the methods of modern warfare, and on this unit (the *Pyŏlgigun*, or Special Skills Force) the king lavished his especial favor. Further, he formed a select group of so-called cadet officers from among young and talented *yangban* sons and had them instructed in the new military arts. His plan thus was to do away entirely with the traditional military structure in the near future. It would appear, however, that the need Kojong felt so keenly to strengthen his army derived above all from a desire to enhance the power of the throne.

Meanwhile a reform of administrative mechanisms also was underway. In general conformity to the Ch'ing administrative structure, an overarching Office for Extraordinary State Affairs (*T'ongni Kimu Amun*) was established. Under it were ranged twelve departments, to deal with relations with China, diplomatic matters involving other foreign nations, military affairs, border administration, coastal surveillance, foreign trade, machinery production, military ordnance, shipbuilding, personnel recruitment, foreign language schooling, and special procurement. As can be seen in the duties assigned to these new agencies—such as foreign trade, machinery production, military ordnance, and shipbuilding—the new administrative structure reflected a desire to come to grips with the new situation in which Korea found itself.

The Movement to "Reject Heterodoxy" and the Military Mutiny of 1882

The Confucian literati had opposed the Treaty of Kanghwa itself from the beginning. While the treaty negotiations were still going on, for example, Ch'oe Ik-hyŏn had expressed his opposition in a memorial to the throne he titled "Five Reasons Against." In it he pointed out that Japan was no different from the Western "barbarians," and that if a treaty were concluded the Catholic religion would enter Korea. At the same time he expressed his concern that Japan would attack Korea when the time was ripe.

It was related above that Kim Koeng-jip brought back with him from Japan a treatise called "A Policy for Korea." King Kojong had his high officials examine it and they had it copied and distributed, with the idea of opening the eyes of the Confucian literati who opposed the enlightenment policy. But these worthies, to the contrary, reacted strongly against the arguments "A Policy for Korea" set forth. A deluge of opposing memorials soon flooded the government, among them the famous "Memorial of Ten Thousand Men of Kyŏngsang Province" (*Yŏngnam manin so*) initiated by Yi Man-son. In this and similar outpourings, the Confucian literati propounded the doctrine of "defending orthodoxy and rejecting heterodoxy" (*wijŏng ch'ŏksa*), violently assailing the enlightenment policy. So outraged were these guardians of Chosŏn's traditional ways that they even came to look upon the Taewŏn'gun, the former enemy whom they had ousted from political power, as a figure worthy of their esteem.

Taking advantage of this situation, the Taewŏn'gun now made plans to bring himself back into power. His first scheme, in 1881, was to put his eldest son Yi Chae-sŏn, born of a secondary wife, on the throne in Kojong's stead, at the same time getting rid of the advocates of enlightenment, those who were establishing ties with the Western Powers and Japan. The plot was revealed by an informer, however, and Yi Chae-sŏn and more than thirty of his fellow conspirators were put to death. It was widely known that the Taewŏn'gun was behind the whole affair, but as the father of the reigning monarch he alone was not brought under investigation. Thus the conflict between the enlightenment and conservative forces intertwined with the struggle between the Taewŏn'gun and Queen Min to bring the government into new disarray. Moreover, the hostility of the people toward the expansion of Japanese influence in Korea acted to make the situation still more volatile. The eruption that ensued in consequence was the Military Mutiny of 1882 (*imo kullan*).

The elite corps (*Pyŏlgigun*) established in the reform of the military structure carried out earlier had been regarded with special favor by Kojong, and it was anticipated that before long the traditional military units would be scrapped entirely. As a result, the treatment of the old line units had worsened, and moreover it had been some thirteen months since these troops had been given their pay and rations. At this point several transports arrived carrying grain taxes from the Chŏlla region, and it was determined to use these funds to first pay out the arrears to the soldiers. But the depot clerks of the *Sŏnhyech'ŏng* (the office created to administer the Uniform Land Tax Law), with an eye to their personal profit, adulterated the rice rations with chaff. When the infuriated soldiers fought with the ration clerks, the high official who superintended the operations of the *Sŏnhyech'ŏng*, Min Kyŏm-ho, had the ringleaders among the soldiers arrested and sentenced them to death. At this fresh outrage the soldiery stormed Min

Kyŏm-ho's house, forcing him to flee to the protection of the palace (for his brother was the adopted heir of Queen Min's father). The soldiers then hastened to the Taewŏn'gun to see whether he would give them his support. Although outwardly he offered only soothing words, the Taewŏn'gun proceeded to meet secretly with the leaders of the mutiny and had his own trusted subordinates direct their actions. The soldiers now seized weapons, attacked the prison where their comrades were held, and freed them. They then killed the Japanese training officer, Horimoto Reizō, and descended in force on the Japanese legation. Hanabusa, the Japanese minister, barely extricated himself and his staff and found his way back to Japan by way of Inch'ŏn, but the legation building was burned to the ground. The next day the mutinous soldiers invaded the palace precincts, killed Min Kyŏm-ho, and tried to find Queen Min for the same vengeful purpose. But she managed to hide and escape unharmed in the confusion.

To cope with this perilous situation, Kojong had no choice but to bring the Taewŏn'gun back into the palace, and so now he was restored to power. An edict was issued requiring that henceforth all governmental matters be submitted to the Taewŏn'gun for decision, thus once again putting full authority in his hands and enabling him, for the moment, to do as he wished. At the same time the military mutiny subsided. In deference to the demands of the soldiery, the Taewŏn'gun dismantled the two new commands and the Special Skills Force (*Pyŏlgigun*) and revived the former Five Army Garrisons structure. He also abolished the recently created Office for Extraordinary State Affairs. The initial efforts to institute a policy of enlightenment thus had come to naught.

Chinese and Japanese Aggression and Commercial Treaties with the Powers

The Taewŏn'gun's resurgence was a victory for reaction and for an exclusionist policy. His triumph was short-lived, however, for both Japan and China now intervened in Korea's affairs. Hanabusa returned with fresh instructions from Tokyo and, backed by powerful army and navy forces, initiated negotiations with the Korean government. Indicating that ultimate resort to hostilities by no means had been ruled out, Japan readied a mixed combat brigade at Fukuoka in Kyushu and had transports stand by, thus demonstrating its ability to mount war operations at any moment. Japan also was prepared to demand the outright cession of the Korean islands of Kŏje and Ullŭng, should the opportunity present itself. When the negotiations Hanabusa pressed forward so urgently reached a deadlock, he issued an ultimatum and withdrew to Inch'ŏn. But the military show of strength he had planned was now impossible, for by this time a superior Chinese force already had arrived on the scene (August 20, 1882).

Ch'ing China had been deeply disturbed by Japan's dispatch of armed forces to Korea. China agreed with the Korean envoy Kim Yun-sik, then still in Tientsin, on the necessity of sending troops to confront the Japanese, and so a force of 4,500 men immediately was dispatched under the command of Wu Ch'ang-ch'ing. China's position was that, as the suzerain power, it must assist its client state in time of internal disorder. This was a direct contradiction of assertions China had made in the past: that its suzerainty conveyed no right to intervene in Korea's domestic affairs. What China sought to do, of course, was to utilize this opportunity to restore the Chinese position of supremacy in Korea that had been usurped by Japan. Entering Seoul at the head of his columns of troops, General Wu first stationed Chinese soldiers at strategic points in the capital. He then seized the man responsible for the mutiny, the Taewŏn'gun, as he paid a courtesy call on the Chinese headquarters and sent him under protective custody to Tientsin. Thus once again the Taewŏn'gun was driven from power.

China's abduction of the Taewŏn'gun brought a swift change in Japan's highhanded attitude. Japan not only had no stomach for confronting the quickly mobilized Chinese troops, but the Taewŏn'gun, the leader of the anti-Japan forces in Korea and the man responsible for the mutiny, now had been removed from the scene. Negotiations between Korea and Japan immediately resumed and the Treaty of Chemulp'o (Inch'ŏn) was concluded. By its terms the leaders of the mutiny were punished, the families of the Japanese victims were indemnified, 500,000 yen in reparations was paid to the Japanese government, and Japan was permitted to station a company of guards at the Japanese legation in Seoul.

The provisions of the Treaty of Chemulp'o notwithstanding, Japan had failed to achieve its aim of strengthening its position in Korea. To the contrary, Ch'ing China had reasserted its rights as the suzerain power and had greatly expanded the authority it wielded in Korea. The Min family, the dominant force in the Korean court, became a pro-China faction, looking to China for support. Unable to deal effectively with its many vexing foreign relations problems, the Korean government now sought China's help. In response China recommended the appointment of two special advisers on foreign affairs, the German P. G. von Möllendorff, who had served for many years in China, and the Chinese diplomat Ma Chien-ch'ang. As these two men took up their posts another administrative reorganization was effected, since the Taewŏn'gun had done away with the new structure created the year before. This time two organs were established at the highest level, one for handling foreign affairs (*Oeamun* or Foreign Office) and one for internal affairs (*Naeamun* or Home Office); the former dealt with all aspects of foreign relations and trade, while the latter undertook responsibility for military matters and the full range of domestic administration. With regard to military structure, a Capital Guards Command (*Ch'in'gunyŏng*) was created with Four Barracks Commands under it, those of the Right, Left, Front, and Rear, and the new force was trained along Chinese lines by Ch'ing General Yüan Shih-k'ai.

The Korean government at this time thus was under the strong influence of Ch'ing China. This was particularly the case with regard to economic matters and foreign relations. A set of Regulations for Maritime and Overland Trade was agreed upon with Ch'ing whereby Chinese merchants, as citizens of the suzerain power, obtained the right to reside, conduct business, and travel freely within Korea. In consequence the number of Chinese traders increased dramatically, dealing a severe blow to the interests of Korean merchants. This of course gave rise to anti-Chinese feelings among the Korean populace.

Again at the urging of China, which saw it as one way to block Japanese inroads, Korea now concluded treaties of commerce with the U.S., France, and other Western nations. The treaty with the United States was the first to be signed, in 1882, and it was ratified that year. A treaty with England was negotiated at the same time, but when England balked at ratification it was revised and ratifications were not exchanged until spring 1884. Similarly, a treaty with Germany was concluded in 1882, revised the next year, and the ratifications were exchanged later. Treaties with Italy and Russia were signed also in 1884 and one with France in 1886. Subsequently, treaties of commerce were concluded with Austria, Belgium, Denmark, and other nations.

2. The Reform Movement of the Progressive Party

Birth of the Progressive Party

As knowledge of the outside world spread, in spite of the intense reaction against it, what Koreans call "enlightenment thought" began to exert a powerful influence on the *yangban* officialdom. Not only prominent political figures of the time, like Kim Hong-jip (Kim Koeng-jip), Kim Yun-sik, and Ŏ Yun-jung, but also such men from the royal in-law family as Min Yŏng-ik supported enlightenment policies. These officials, however, favored a gradualist approach, and moreover they thought in terms of carrying out their plans with the aid of Ch'ing China.

In contrast, another persuasion had taken form around younger men like Kim Ok-kyun, Pak Yŏng-hyo, Sŏ Kwang-bŏm, and Hong Yŏng-sik—*yangban* officials whose advance was blocked by the royal in-law Min clan's control over appointments to high position, a group that pushed for a policy of rapid change. These all were disciples of Yu Hong-gi (Yu Taech'i) in whom was epitomized the enlightenment thought of that day, a man not only a practitioner of medicine from the *chungin* class but one who believed in the Buddhist faith. Such Buddhist monks as Yi Tong-in belonged to this new progressive movement, as did Pyŏn Su, another *chungin*, military men like Yu Sang-o and his son, and even merchants such as Yi Ch'ang-gyu. Thus membership in the progressive camp transcended social class status, as like-minded men banded together under the banner of enlightenment thought and searched for ways to bring about reform.

Firm believers in the doctrine of equality, the aim of the progressives was to do away with class distinctions, renovate the political process on the model of Japan's Meiji Restoration, and at the same time make the Korean nation independent in reality, as well as in name, by bringing an end to China's interference in Korean affairs. They believed that their goals could be achieved only through taking extraordinary steps, and they hoped to obtain Japanese support for their plans. They necessarily constituted rather a clandestine force, and in consequence their numbers were limited. Nevertheless, they were a conspicuous element in the political world of that time and were referred to as the Progressive Party (Kaehwadang) or the Independence Party.

The activities of this group first became noticeable after the Military Mutiny of 1882, when Pak Yŏng-hyo was sent as a special envoy to Japan and was accompanied by Kim Ok-kyun and Sŏ Kwang-bŏm. Because of their knowledge of the wider world outside Korea, these men won the confidence of King Kojong and, as their influence grew, they succeeded in winning approval of a number of reform measures. Acting on their proposals, an Office of Culture and Information (*Pangmun'guk*) was created and a thrice-monthly gazette, the *Hansŏng Sunbo*, was published; students were sent to Japan to study military and technical subjects; a Postal Administration was established to provide modern postal service; and a modern army unit was formed at Kwangju near Seoul, albeit opposition from the Min family clique quickly led to its disbanding. Moreover, aware of the importance of diplomatic activity for the preservation of their country's independence, the progressives took every opportunity to develop contacts with foreign representatives.

For all their desire to bring about rapid change, the progressives could do little more than effect these few measures. They had earned the enmity of the Min clan faction, for one thing, and could not secure appointments to pivotal positions. The attitude of Japan, too, had become decidedly cool, and when the progressives asked for a loan to meet the costs of the new army unit and of other reforms they wanted to implement, Japan refused. Accordingly, it had become impossible for the progressives to push ahead with their plans as they wished.

The Coup d'Etat of 1884 (Kapsin Chŏngbyŏn)

The progressives now were prepared to consider taking whatever extreme steps might be necessary to put their policies into effect. It would appear that they began to lay their plans in 1883, around the time Kim Ok-kyun went to Japan in an attempt to secure a loan of 3,000,000 yen, for when he returned he brought gunpowder back with him. But his efforts to obtain this loan so central to his plans came to naught, and for the moment he was forced to bide his time.

In 1884, however, hostilities between France and China broke out over Annam, and this was viewed as an opportune time to drive the Ch'ing presence out of Korea. The progressives now rushed ahead with a detailed blueprint for a coup, and they succeeded in enlisting Sŏ Chae-p'il, freshly returned from study at a Japanese military academy, into the core group of conspirators. Meanwhile Japan's attitude had undergone a change, the Japanese minister, Takezoe Shinichirō, promising that in the event of a coup the Japanese legation guards stationed in Seoul would be called out to render positive assistance. The plans of the progressives were now complete. It must be said, however, that it was a fundamental miscalculation, despite Takezoe's assurances, to allow the fate of the enterprise to hinge on the support of no more than 140 Japanese troops, when even with the withdrawal of some contingents there still were at least 1,500 Chinese soldiers stationed in Seoul.

The coup took place on the 17th day of the 10th month, 1884 (December 4 by the Western calendar). The conspirators made opportune use of a banquet hosted by Hong Yŏng-sik, the director of the Postal Administration, to celebrate the opening of that new agency. The guests of honor were the various foreign diplomats, but the commanding officers of the Four Barracks Commands also had been invited, and the plan was to set fire to the nearby detached palace in An'guk-tong, dispose of the four commanders, and then proceed to secure custody of the king. Although matters at the banquet hall did not go according to plan, Kim Ok-kyun and his cohorts went to the palace, falsely reported to the king that the Chinese troops had created a disturbance, and asked the Japanese legation guards to provide protection. Having escorted the king to Kyŏngu Palace, a site better suited to defense against attack, they summoned the Barracks commanders—for it was they who had authority to call out the troops—and the other senior officials of the conservative faction and killed them one by one as they appeared. Returning at length to Ch'angdŏk Palace, they formulated a program of political reform and, as Kim Ok-kyun tells us in his *Journal of 1884 (Kapsin illok)* which he later wrote in exile, decided to take the following actions:

1. Seek the immediate return of the Taewŏn'gun and an end to the empty formalities of the tributary relationship with China.
2. Abolish ruling class privilege and establish equal rights for all; stop making appointments on the basis of finding suitable office for privileged seekers of position and instead seek out men whose talents suit them for official appointment.
3. Revise the land tax laws for every region of the country and root out the extortionate practices of the petty officials who administer them, thus alleviating the distress of the people and at the same time ensuring receipt

  of sufficient revenue to meet government expenditures.
4. Abolish the Office of Eunuch Attendants (*Naesibu*), but employ those eunuchs who are men of superior talent.
5. Punish the crimes of those most notorious officials whose evil and venal acts past and present have brought the nation to its present state of infirmity.
6. Cancel all outstanding grain loan debts owed the government.
7. Abolish the *Kyujanggak* (the palace library).
8. Quickly establish police patrols in order to prevent thievery.
9. Abolish the Office for the Benefit of Trade (i.e., the "Peddlers Bureau").
10. Review the cases of those who have been banished or barred from office and, as warranted, revoke their sentences.
11. Merge the Four Barracks Commands into a single unit, then select the most able soldiers among them and immediately form a Royal Guards Division under the command of the Crown Prince.
12. Put all internal fiscal administration under the jurisdiction of the Ministry of Taxation, abolishing all other fiscal agencies.
13. Have the ministers and councillors convene on a regular schedule at the State Council chamber within the palace to discuss policy, submit proposals to the king, make his decisions known, and then transmit them for implementation.
14. Abolish all superfluous government agencies, with the ministers and councillors to study the matter and submit proposals to the throne.

The very first measure, to press for the immediate return of the Taewŏn-gun from China, appears to reflect not only the hostility of the progressives toward China but also an awareness of the need to make use of the Taewŏn-gun for the moment—they could not work with him in the long run—in overcoming the entrenched Min faction. The pronouncement of equal rights for all of course was aimed at eliminating social status differences. Punishment of those whose venal conduct had done injury to the nation would strike a blow at the royal in-law power of the Min. The reform of fiscal administration as well as that of the land tax law were designed to bring about an increase in state revenues. The renovations in the office system and the stipulation that important policy matters be decided at State Council discussions were efforts to bring an end to the arbitrary exercise of the power of the throne and so to expand the authority of ministerial deliberations. The progressives assumed, of course, that they would dominate these deliberations and thus be able to carry out their reform program.

Before their reform measures even were made public, however, the Chinese troops had moved into action and the fate of the progressives was sealed. Kim Ok-kyun, Pak Yŏng-hyo, and a few of their colleagues accompanied the retreating Japanese guards and made good their escape to Japan. Minister Takezoe set fire to his legation building and joined in the exodus. But some Japanese guards were killed when their headquarters was attacked and a few Japanese civilians also died in the fighting.

Great Power Inroads

The coup itself was finished, but Korea's complex foreign affairs problems had become still more complicated. The government of course assailed Minister Takezoe's wrongful interference in internal Korean politics and insisted that he be held accountable. Japan was aware that Takezoe's conduct was improper but nevertheless took a negotiating position that sought to sidestep this issue. Thus Japan's envoy to the talks, Foreign Minister Inoue Kaoru, worked toward a solution that emphasized appropriate redress for Japanese losses rather than the question of responsibility for the violence. In the end the Treaty of Hansŏng (Seoul) contained provisions for indemnities to the Japanese victims and compensation for the cost of rebuilding the Japanese legation.

Japan was anxious not to lose this opportunity to weaken China's dominant position in the peninsula. To this end Japan hoped to achieve a mutual withdrawal of Chinese and Japanese troops from Korea. Japan's prime minister, Itō Hirobumi, paid a visit to China to discuss the matter with his powerful Chinese counterpart, Li Hung-chang, and the resulting Convention of Tientsin, signed on April 18, 1885, effected a solution of this issue. The agreement called for troops of both nations to be withdrawn within four months of its signing, stipulated that neither signatory send military instructors to Korea, and provided for prior notification to the other party if troops were to be dispatched to Korea in the future.

Although the Convention of Tientsin removed foreign troops from Korean soil, this did not mean that Korea had been fully restored to a position of independence. China's Yüan Shih-k'ai remained in Seoul, now bearing the imposing title of "Director-General Resident in Korea of Diplomatic and Commercial Relations," and his influence was pervasive. Under his protection Chinese merchants inundated both Seoul and the countryside, taking their profits at the expense not only of Japanese merchants but Korean as well. (Incidentally, as Korean ill-feeling toward the Chinese mounted, Yüan Shih-k'ai brought those in the capital together into a single settlement, thus bringing into being Seoul's "Chinatown.") In point of fact China had lost no ground in Korea at all. In contrast, Japan's position remained weak, and what is more Japan had become an object of anathema to those who dominated Korean government councils.

But now a new power appeared in Korea, hostile to Ch'ing designs. In consequence of the treaty concluded between Korea and Russia in 1884, a Russian minister, Karl Waeber, now was stationed in Seoul. He was an extraordinarily able diplomat, and as he paid his frequent visits to the court he endeavored to foster a pro-Russian force in the government. In revulsion against China's excesses a pro-Russian inclination in fact gradually began to appear in the officialdom, a development given further impetus by Möllendorff, the special adviser on foreign affairs China had recommended to the Korean government. Möllendorff believed that Chinese and Japanese influence in Korea needed to be counterbalanced by that of a third power, and to that end he worked to create a Russian presence. The king and queen, then, began to lean toward an anti-Ch'ing pro-Russian policy, and it even was believed that they had reached a secret agreement with Russia.

Alerted to the danger to their position posed by the tilt toward Russia, the Chinese countered first by returning the Taewŏn'gun to his homeland. As a means to maintain China's position Yüan Shih-k'ai even thought to depose Kojong, by employing the pretext that he had come to a secret understanding with the Russians. China also had Möllendorff replaced as foreign affairs adviser by the American Owen N. Denny, at the same time subordinating the administration of the Korean Maritime Customs Service, which owed its inception to Möllendorff, to that of China. But unexpectedly Denny too advocated ties with Russia as the best way to bring Chinese interference to an end and eliminate the pernicious influence of Yüan Shih-k'ai.

So far as is certain, no treaty granting Russia special privileges in Korea was signed before 1888, when an Overland Trade Agreement opened Kyŏnghŭng (a Tumen River town near the border with Russia) to Russian trade, permitted Russians to live there in an extraterritorial settlement, and even granted Russia full navigation rights on the Tumen River. Early in 1885, however, it was widely rumored that, by the terms of an agreement then being negotiated, Russia would secure major concessions from Korea and achieve a position of unrivaled strength in the peninsula. Substance seemingly was lent to these reports, moreover, by the behavior of the Russian minister in Seoul, Karl Waeber.

Not only China but England too was aroused by the inroads of Russian power. In confrontation with Russia along the length of its southern perimeter, England could not look lightly upon Russia's southward advance in Korea. Accordingly, with the full knowledge of China, England dispatched a naval force in 1885 to occupy Kŏmun-do, off the southern coast of Chŏlla, so as to be prepared to counter any further Russian movement. By constructing troop encampments and gun emplacements, England gave every indication that its occupation of Kŏmun-do was intended to be permanent.

Kŏmun-do is located at the gateway to the Korea Strait, and it lay athwart the sea lanes along which the Russian naval forces in East Asian waters had to steam. England's intent to frustrate Russian designs thus was clear, and the alarmed Russian authorities took immediate countermeasures. On the one hand Russia made it ominously clear to the Korean government that the English action would not be tolerated, while at the same time pressuring China with the threat that it too would occupy Korean territory. At this point China interceded, and after nearly two years of negotiations the English forces were removed from Kŏmun-do, in 1887.

England's condition for withdrawal, however, was a Russian pledge that no nation would be permitted to seize Korean territory. England's actions, then, served as a major restraint on the advance of Russian power. Be that as it may, the Kŏmun-do incident made it clear that Korea was not the arbiter of its own destiny but that its fate would be decided by outside powers motivated by their particular selfish interests.

Beset thus by the conflicting ambitions of the great powers, Korea found itself in great peril from the world beyond its borders. The sending of Pak Chŏng-yang to America in 1887 as a specially empowered envoy, charged with fostering closer relations between Korea and the United States, was conceived of as one means to overcome this crisis. The proposal in 1885 by the German vice-consul, Hermann Budler, that Korea attempt to secure international guarantees as a neutral and unaligned nation sprang from the same motivation. This advice was ignored, but it constitutes another measure of the gravity of Korea's international position at that time.

3. The Revolutionary Uprising of the Tonghak Peasant Army

Unrest Among the Peasantry

Despite the critical international situation Chosŏn now faced, the government lacked any coherent policy. This government of King Kojong and the Min family oligarchs could only think to maintain itself in power by seeking the backing of foreign states, not by winning the support of the Korean people. Meanwhile the nation's chronic financial crisis had further worsened. On the one hand special exemptions, abandoned fields, and tax evasion had diminished the government's receipts, while at the same time developments subsequent to the opening of Korean ports—the exchange of diplomatic missions, the payment of indemnities to Japan, and the introduction of modern facilities—required new and heavy expenditures. These needs in part were met from customs receipts and from foreign loans, but government activities still had to be financed preponderantly by the farming villages. The burdens on the peasantry thus doubled or even tripled, as every pretext was used to impose fresh levies and the petty functionaries who collected them resorted to ever more harsh methods of extortion. Under these circumstances the grievances harbored by the peasants toward their *yangban* rulers gave every indication of erupting into violence. Indeed, popular uprisings were breaking out in many areas, while armed bandits were raiding periodic markets and other centers of goods distribution with alarming frequency.

At the same time, Japanese economic penetration was further eroding Korea's village economy. Although Japan had been the first to take aggressive advantage of Korea, Japan's position in the peninsula inevitably deteriorated because of its involvement in the failed 1884 coup. Nevertheless, by the early 1890's Japanese economic activity had reached astonishing proportions that no other nation could rival. The establishments of Japanese merchants were to be found on a large scale in each of the open ports, Inch'ŏn, Pusan, and Wŏnsan, and statistics for 1896 show that 210 of 258 such businesses were Japanese. Japan also enjoyed a heavy preponderance with respect to numbers of merchant vessels entering Korean ports. Among 1,322 merchant ships with a gross tonnage of 387,507 entering Korea's ports in 1893, 956 weighing 304,224 tons were Japanese; in percentage terms 72% of the vessels and over 78% of the gross tonnage came in under the Japanese flag. Accordingly, Japan's proportion of the total volume of Korea's foreign trade loomed correspondingly large: over 90% of exports went to Japan and more than 50% of imports came from Japan. A full breakdown is shown in the following table.

KOREA'S FOREIGN TRADE BY COUNTRY IN 1893   Unit: yen

COUNTRY	EXPORTS (%)	IMPORTS (%)
China	134,085 (7.9)	1,905,698 (49.1)
Japan	1,543,114 (90.9)	1,949,043 (50.2)
Russia	20,917 (1.2)	25,414 (0.7)
TOTAL:	1,698,116 (100.0)	3,880,155 (100.0)

The principal import item, cotton cloth, came in both from China and Japan, but whereas Chinese merchants simply were reexporting English cotton goods, Japanese traders increasingly brought in cloth manufactured in their own country. Korean exports, chief among which were rice, soybeans, gold, and cowhides, went almost entirely to Japan. It must be noted, too, that Japanese traders mostly were from the lawless or depressed elements of Japan's society, and they showed no scruples in their eagerness to make their fortunes at the expense of the Korean peasant. Shrewdly taking advantage of the fact that the village people could only buy Japanese cotton goods, kettles, pots and pans, farming tools, kerosene, dyestuffs, salt, and other things by selling their rice, Japanese traders would loan their victims the money with which to make purchases and then at harvest time claim a part or even all of the peasant's crop. Living as they were in such straitened circumstances, the Korean peasants could not resist the glitter of the Japanese goods, only to find themselves made destitute by the exorbitant interest extorted by the profit-hungry Japanese.

One way the government found to resist Japan's economic penetration was to prohibit the export of rice from certain provinces. Such bans were put into effect for Hamgyŏng province in 1889 and for Hwanghae in 1890, but Japanese protests rendered them ineffective. Due to a combination of factors, then, the villages continued to sink into destitution, while the peasantry harbored a mounting hostility toward its exploiters, Korean and foreign alike.

Uprising of the Tonghak Peasant Army

After the execution in 1864 of its founder Ch'oe Che-u, the Tonghak ("Eastern Learning") movement for a time could not operate in the open. But under its second Patriarch, Ch'oe Si-hyŏng (1829-1898), despite great difficulties the *Bible of Tonghak Doctrine* (*Tonggyŏng taejŏn*) and *Hymns from Dragon Pool* (*Yongdam yusa*) were compiled, thus systematizing the tenets of the new religion. At the same time a network of churches was successfully established, organizing members into "parishes" (*p'o*) and creating a hierarchy of church leadership. This movement to bring new converts under Tonghak discipline owed its success to the peasantry's deep hostility toward the *yangban* class and its resistance to the inroads of foreign powers.

As the Tonghak grew to become a force in Korean society, its energies were channeled into a movement to clear the name of the founder of the false charges under which he had been sentenced to death. This effort took overt form first in 1892, when several thousand Tonghak members gathered at Samnye in Chŏlla province [see map p. 286] and made demands on the governors of Chŏlla and Ch'ungch'ŏng that Ch'oe Che-u be posthumously exonerated and that suppression of the Tonghak be ended. The former demand was rejected on the ground that the governors lacked authority to take such action, but a pledge was given that local functionaries would be ordered to stop their persecution of Tonghak believers. Not satisfied with this, the assembled Tonghak followers resolved to carry their struggle to Seoul, to try to achieve their objective by petitioning the throne directly from in front of the palace gates. They carried out this resolve the following year, and when this form of protest also met with rejection, the petitioners in fact being dispersed by force, the order was given for Tonghak members to assemble again, this time at Poŭn in Ch'ungch'ŏng province. More than 20,000 heeded the summons to Poŭn, where they proceeded to erect defensive barricades, hoist banners, and call for a "crusade to expel the Japanese and Westerners." The disconcerted authorities barely succeeded in dispersing the Tonghak throngs by threatening the use of force, while at the same time soothing them with further promises to punish the functionaries who had persecuted the Tonghak most harshly. Thus the growing strength of the Tonghak made continued prohibition of the faith futile, and this in turn led to still further expansion of the movement's appeal.

In 1894 the now expanded, well organized Tonghak movement erupted into a revolutionary peasant struggle employing military operations on a large scale. The magistrate of Kobu county, Cho Pyŏng-gap, was known for his tyrannical cruelty, and since assuming his post he had taken every opportunity to inflict torment on the hard-pressed people he governed.

He illegally extorted large amounts from the peasantry, for example collecting over 1000 *yang* (equivalent perhaps to 1500 contemporary U.S. silver dollars) to erect a covering structure over his father's tombstone. But what most evoked their bitter protests was the tax he enforced on irrigation water from the Mansŏkpo reservoir. He had mobilized the peasants to labor on a new reservoir constructed on a site just below the old one, and yet he now extorted more than 700 *sŏk* of rice in water use charges from the very peasants whose sweat and toil had built the reservoir. The enraged people of Kobu had repeatedly petitioned for redress of their grievances, but to no effect. At this point, under the leadership of the head of Kobu county's Tonghak parish, Chŏn Pong-jun, the peasants occupied the county office, seized weapons, distributed the illegally collected tax rice to the poor, and then destroyed the Mansŏkpo reservoir. When a report of the incident reached the government, a specially empowered inspector was dispatched to investigate. This official, however, charged the Tonghak with responsibility for the uprising and, drawing up a roster of Tonghak members, arrested some and summarily executed others, meanwhile committing the further outrage of burning Tonghak homes. Further inflamed by this cruel denial of simple justice, the peasants rallied around Chŏn Pong-jun, Kim Kae-nam, Son Hwa-jung, and other Tonghak members and rose again. A call to arms now went out to the peasants, appealing to them to rise in defense of the nation and to secure the livelihood of its people. The peroration of this proclamation read as follows:

> The people are the root of the nation. If the root withers, the nation will be enfeebled. Heedless of their responsibility for sustaining the state and providing for its people, the officials build lavish residences in the countryside, scheming to ensure their own well-being at the expense of the resources of the nation. How can this be viewed as proper? We are wretched village people far from the capital, yet we feed and clothe ourselves with the bounty from the sovereign's land. We cannot sit by and watch our nation perish. The whole nation is as one, its multitudes united in their determination to raise the righteous standard of revolt, and to pledge their lives to sustain the state and provide for the livelihood of the people. However startling the action we take today may seem, you must not be troubled by it. For as we felicitously live out the tranquil years ahead, each man secure in his occupation — when all the people can enjoy the blessings of benevolent kingly rule, how immeasurably joyful will we be!

Now peasants from all the surrounding areas came to join forces with the Tonghak army, swelling its ranks to some several thousands. They wrapped multicolored cloth around their heads and waists, and for weapons they had a few rifles or swords or lances they had seized, but otherwise they mostly had only bamboo spears and cudgels. Nevertheless, holding aloft their distinctive yellow flags and protected from bullets, they believed, by the amulets they wore, the Tonghak peasant soldiers were fairly spoiling for a fight. After occupying Kobu they moved their base a little northward to Paeksan, where they paused to group their formations into battle array. It was there that Chŏn Pong-jun assumed overall command and on his banner in large letters inscribed the exhortation to "sustain the nation and provide for the people" (*poguk anmin*).

Creation of Local Directorates and the Struggle against Japan

Massed now in battle formation, the Tonghak peasant army first crushed the government troops sent from Chŏnju at Hwangt'ohyŏn hill in Kobu county, then in turn seized Chŏngŭp, Koch'ang, and Mujang, and still further southward took control of Yŏnggwang and Hamp'yŏng [see map p. 286]. Their ranks meanwhile had increased to over 10,000 men. The government in Seoul already had dispatched Hong Kye-hun to suppress the revolt, in command of an elite battalion of about 800 men from the capital garrison. By the time he reached Chŏnju, however, his force had been cut in half by desertions, and so despite its superiority in weapons and the timely arrival of reinforcements, there was no way it could defeat the confident, spirited Tonghak soldiery. Routing Hong Kye-hun's troops in a clash at Changsŏng, the Tonghak army pushed north against virtually no resistance and occupied Chŏnju.

In a state of panic, the government hastily appealed to China for military support. China's response was immediate, and within a month a sizeable Chinese force had landed at Asan Bay. Japan, however, also sent in troops, so that the two powers faced each other in an increasingly tense confrontation. Convinced now that the Tonghak must be appeased by whatever means and its army of peasants dispersed, the government proposed that a truce be negotiated. Informed of the government's willingness to listen to Tonghak demands, Chŏn Pong-jun regarded this as an opportunity to achieve his objectives without further recourse to warfare. In consequence hostilities came to an end, on condition that an end also be put to government misrule. The Tonghak demands in this regard were the same as when they took up their arms: first that the *yangban* be prevented from draining the life-blood of the peasants by their illegal extortions; and secondly, that the government block the inroads of foreign merchants.

At this point the Tonghak peasant soldiers withdrew from Chŏnju and returned to their homes, while a separate Tonghak force that had arisen in Ch'ungch'ŏng province also dispersed. But with the announced aim of establishing congregations in every village, the Tonghak extended their organized network into area after area. In the fifty-three counties of Chŏlla province in particular, so-called Local Directorates (*Chipkangso*) were established and set about reforming local government abuses. These popular organs, headed by a director and staffed by clerks, existed in parallel with the formal county administration, and in the provincial capital at Chŏnju a Headquarters Directorate (*Taedoso*) was established with Chŏn Pong-jun at its helm. On the whole the positions in the Local Directorates went to

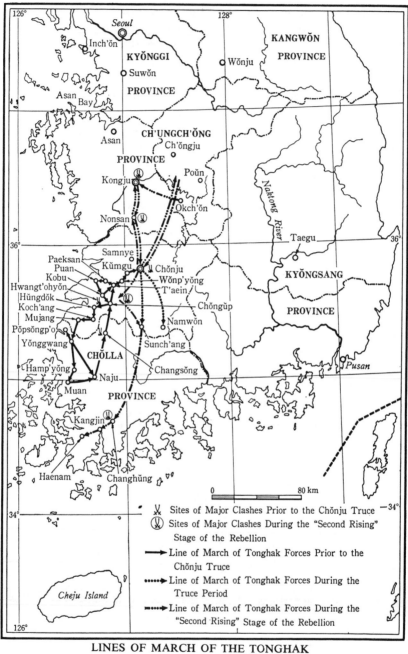

LINES OF MARCH OF THE TONGHAK
PEASANT ARMY

those with knowledge of administrative matters, the "fallen" *yangban* and the county level petty functionaries (*hyangni*), and the essentials of the reform program it was proposed to carry out were as follows:

1. Eliminate the chronic mistrust between Tonghak believers and the government and cooperate in dealing with problems of administration.
2. Investigate the crimes of venal and corrupt officials and punish the guilty severely.
3. Sternly punish men of wealth who owe their fortunes to high-handed extortionate practices.
4. Discipline those *yangban* in or out of office whose conduct is improper.
5. Burn all documents pertaining to slaves.
6. Rectify the treatment of those engaged in the "seven despised occupations" (lackeys attached to government offices and laborers assigned to perform certain arduous services for the state) and free the *paekchŏng* outcasts once and for all from the wearing of their distinctive "P'yŏngyang hat."
7. Permit the remarriage of young widows.
8. Ban collection of all arbitrary and irregular taxes.
9. In employing officials, break the pattern of regional and class discrimination and appoint men of talent.
10. Severely punish those who collaborate with the Japanese.
11. Cancel all outstanding debts, whether owed to government agencies or to private individuals.
12. Distribute land equally for cultivation by owner-farmers.

The principal concerns expressed here are, in sum, that the oppressive treatment of the Tonghak by the government and the *yangban* be stopped, that an end be put to excessive economic exploitation of the peasantry, that discriminatory treatment based on social class status be abolished, and that those guilty of collusion with the Japanese in their aggressive designs be punished. This revolutionary program to be implemented through the Local Directorates was welcomed with the greatest enthusiasm by the peasantry. Thus the powerful appeal of the Tonghak movement was felt not only in Chŏlla but spread into the other southern provinces as well, and even far northward into P'yŏngan and Hamgyŏng.

The pause in the fighting, however, had worked to the disadvantage of the Tonghak peasant army, for the explosive situation created by the presence of both Chinese and Japanese troops in Korea soon led to the outbreak of the Sino-Japanese War (in late July, 1894) and Japan's exercise of virtual control over all internal security matters in Korea. Later in the year, in October, the Tonghak again took up their arms and began to move northward, with the avowed intent of expelling the Japanese. But they were defeated in fighting at Kongju against government troops reinforced by a Japanese army contingent, and they met defeat again at T'aein. Many of the leaders of the peasant army, including Chŏn Pong-jun, were captured or killed and before long the Tonghak army had been scattered.

The Tonghak rebellion was a widespread revolutionary movement of the peasantry against Chosŏn's oppressive *yangban* society. Cohesion and direction were given the movement by the Tonghak religion, through its institutional structure. In spite of the opposition of the Northern Assembly of Tonghak led by Ch'oe Si-hyŏng, who denounced an armed uprising as an act of treason against the nation and a betrayal of the teachings of the founder, it was not possible to shake the determination of the peasants of the Southern Assembly to fight to achieve their aims. At the same time, the rebellion of the Tonghak peasant army also was a struggle against the economic aggression of the Japanese. The outcry to "expel the Japanese" at first had been a demand upon the government for action on this problem, but once Japan intervened in the rebellion militarily, the Tonghak fought the Japanese face to face. The second rising of the Tonghak peasant army following the short-lived truce with government forces was the direct consequence of Japan's intervention. This time the Northern Assembly also joined in the anti-Japanese struggle, fighting hand in hand in the common cause. But the Tonghak peasant army lacked the strength to successfully confront the modern weapons and training of the Japanese troops. In the end, then, struggle as they might against the *yangban* power structure within and the aggressive forces of foreign imperialism from abroad, the Tonghak peasant soldiers were caught in a vise between the two and were crushed.

China and Japan Compete for Ascendancy

Unable to suppress the struggle of the Tonghak peasant army with its own forces, the Korean government had requested assistance from Ch'ing China. Perceiving this to be an opportune occasion to solidify its deteriorating position in Korea, China dispatched a force of 3000 men under Yeh Chih-ch'ao to land at Asan Bay. This action was reported to the Japanese government, in accordance with the terms of the Convention of Tientsin.

No less than China, Japan too now saw an opportunity to expand its influence in Korea. Japan not only hoped to restore its position of political primacy but also was keenly aware of the need to ensure a Korean market

COMPARISON OF KOREA'S IMPORTS FROM CHINA AND JAPAN
Unit: Mexican Dollars

YEAR	CHINA (%)	JAPAN (%)
1885	313,342 (19)	1,377,392 (81)
1886	455,015 (18)	2,064,353 (82)
1887	742,661 (26)	2,080,787 (74)
1888	860,328 (28)	2,196,115 (72)
1889	1,101,585 (32)	2,299,118 (68)
1890	1,660,075 (35)	3,086,897 (65)
1891	2,148,294 (40)	3,226,468 (60)
1892	2,055,555 (45)	2,555,675 (55)

for its products. Japan's generally unrivaled economic position in Korea in the early and mid-1890's has been discussed above. Japan's exports to Korea, however, now were steadily declining relative to those of China and had begun to decrease in absolute terms as well. The extent to which Japan's export activity was being undercut by Chinese competition is revealed in the above statistics.

In 1885, the year following the 1884 coup, Japan had provided 81% of Korea's imports from the two countries, but just seven years later Japan's advantage had been cut to 55%. This statistic vividly depicts the rapid penetration of Korean markets by goods from China in the wake of Japan's political setback in 1884. As has been seen, moreover, the two countries shared the Korean market almost equally in 1893, the year before the outbreak of the Sino-Japanese War. Furthermore, imports from China largely were of goods produced elsewhere whereas Japan was exporting its own manufactures, so that the impact on Japan in fact was more severe than the statistics indicate. In addition, the Japanese merchants were loath to give up the exorbitant profits that extortionate practices had secured for them. It was this set of circumstances that made it necessary for Japan to exert political and military pressure on Korea, and it was for this reason that Japan viewed China's action of dispatching troops as a welcome opportunity.

Accordingly, under pretext of protecting its citizens resident in Korea, Japan landed a large force of 7000 troops at Inch'ŏn, backed by seven warships. By this time, however, the Tonghak peasant army already had withdrawn from Chŏnju, so that the ostensible reason for stationing Chinese and Japanese troops in Korea no longer existed. Recognizing this, China proposed a joint withdrawal to Japan, and this proposal was supported both by the Korean government and by the foreign powers. However, determined to take advantage of the situation to completely eliminate Chinese power in Korea, Japan rejected the Chinese plan. In turn, then, Japan suggested that the two powers jointly undertake to reform Korea's internal administration. For the record, Japan argued that reform was absolutely essential if internal unrest were not again to flare into open rebellion, and that peace in East Asia depended on preventing such an occurrence. This was merely a pretext, however, and in fact Japan's purpose was to raise an issue unacceptable to China and then seize upon it as an excuse to open hostilities. China of course rejected the proposal as constituting interference in the internal affairs of another nation, whereupon the talks became deadlocked and a clash between China and Japan became inevitable.

The Sino-Japanese War began with a preemptive attack by Japanese warships at Asan Bay in July, 1894, and it ended in a Japanese victory early in 1895. In the ensuing Treaty of Shimonoseki concluded between the two powers, China's acknowledgment of the full independence of Korea was detailed in the very first article. But to reiterate a point made several times before, the purpose of this clause was not in fact to guarantee Korea's independence but rather to repudiate China's claim to suzerainty over Korea. The treaty also called for China to cede the Liaotung Peninsula and Taiwan to Japan, thus revealing that Japan's territorial ambitions extended even to Manchuria. Naturally Japan believed that Korea now had been brought firmly within its grasp.

4. The Reform of 1894

The Reform Enactments

With its preparations for launching an attack on China now well under-way, Japan demanded still more insistently that the Korean government carry out the internal reforms Japan earlier had proposed. But the Korean government refused to yield to the Japanese pressure, demanding in turn that Japan withdraw its forces as a precondition to any reform enactments. At the same time, the Korean side rejected the Japanese plan for reform itself on two grounds: that most of its provisions were to be found in Chosŏn's existing canon of law and that, in regard to the few new measures Japan had proposed, a Board of Review and Rectification now had been created and was proceeding with a program of reform. From the outset Japan had intended to use the issue of reform as a pretext to start a war with China, and moreover Japan was more interested in wringing economic concessions from Korea than in reform itself. To this end it was necessary to gain control over the Korean government, and so at this point Japan used the troops it had sent to Korea to occupy the Kyŏngbok Palace by force and restore the Taewŏn'gun to power. A new government then was formed from pro-Japanese elements and others not identified with the China orientation of past years, and it was this "cabinet," headed by Kim Hong-jip, that pushed ahead with the Reform of 1894 (*kabo kyŏngjang*) almost entirely on its own.

The Reform of 1894 was carried out by an organ that may be called the Deliberative Council (*Kun'guk Kimuch'ŏ*), created by the new government for this purpose. Under the direction of Kim Hong-jip, the eleven officials who served actively on this council carefully reviewed each reform proposal and rendered a decision on it. Men identified with the Progressive Party that had initiated the abortive 1884 coup, like Yu Kil-chun, constituted the core group in the council. It may be said, therefore, that the Reform of 1894 was the reform movement of the old Progressive Party in a new manifestation. The Deliberative Council itself not only operated outside the purview of the king and Queen Min but also constituted a threat to the position of the Taewŏn'gun, to whom the king had delegated authority over governmental affairs. It would appear, in fact, that the express purpose of establishing the Deliberative Council as a supra-governmental body was to ensure its autonomy and so prevent interference with its work.

But once the throne and the Taewŏn'gun found themselves in actuality to be excluded from decision making in the political sphere, the Deliberative Council was abolished, although to be sure its reform proposals were carried out. The major reforms put into effect largely through the efforts of this extraordinary council were as follows.

To look first at reforms of a political nature, by adopting an official calendar based on the year the dynasty was founded, Korea demonstrated that the traditional suzerain-tributary relationship with Ch'ing China had been severed. A fundamental internal structural change was the separation of the palace apparatus from the government proper. A Department of the Royal Household (*Kungnaebu*) was created to subsume, in streamlined form, the various agencies that had dealt with matters related to the palace and the royal family. The State Council (*Ŭijŏngbu*) was reorganized under a prime minister, with ministries for foreign affairs and agriculture and commerce added to the original six. The eight ministries were subdivided into bureaus, the responsibilities of each and its place in the administrative hierarchy being carefully delineated. Subsequently this structure was further refined, resulting in a Cabinet (*Naegak*) composed of seven ministries—those for foreign affairs, home affairs, finance, justice, education, defense, and agriculture, commerce and industry, with bureaus and sections under each. In conjunction with this change, modifications also were made in the office rank system, and a monthly salary to be paid in cash rather than in kind was stipulated for each rank level. The traditional examination system then was abolished and the procedures for selecting officials that replaced it eliminated the former distinctions between *yangban* and commoners. Former social and ritual distinctions that had marked relations between officials in the civil and military branches of service were formally denounced.

Local government also was restructured. Initially the former eight provinces were replaced by twenty-three prefectures, in an effort to better adapt local administration to local conditions. The prefectures were subdivided into uniform county (*kun*) units, thus simplifying the somewhat more complex earlier structure. The county unit of local government was left intact when subsequently the twenty-three prefectures were reorganized into thirteen provinces. The judicial and military powers hitherto exercised by the local government offices were taken away, weakening their authority over the local populace and thus reflecting more modern concepts of local administration.

Next, the administration of justice was separated from the executive power. A law establishing a system of courts was promulgated and all judicial matters were placed under their jurisdiction. District courts, including those specially established at the open ports, were created at the lower level, with appellate jurisdiction assigned to so-called high and circuit courts. A similar hierarchic restructuring of the police power also was effected. A Metropolitan Police Board in Seoul was given responsibility for public safety in the capital, while police offices under the jurisdiction of the provincial governors were charged with maintaining public safety in the local areas; these latter were made independent of the county-level administration.

A thorough rationalization of fiscal administration also was undertaken. On the model of the reform projected by the progressives in 1884, all fiscal matters—accounting, receipts and expenditures, taxation, government bonds, currency, banking, and the like—were placed under the jurisdiction of the new Ministry of Finance (*T'akchibu*). In accordance with this policy two hundred twenty tax collection agencies were established throughout the country, under the supervision of nine regional offices, to enforce tax laws and deal with other local revenue matters. The currency system too was changed. The new regulations put the country on the silver standard, with nickel, copper, bronze, and brass coins made subsidiary units of exchange; the old coins still could be used for the time being but gradually were to be replaced by the new. Accompanying the currency change was a stipulation that taxes be paid in cash rather than in kind. At the same time the system of weights and measures, hitherto a chaotic array of differing standards, was revised and made uniform.

Social reform was a vital component of the sweeping changes enacted in 1894. First of all the social class status system was, in point of law, totally abrogated. Class distinctions between *yangban* and commoners were eliminated, making it possible to open the ranks of officialdom to men of talent irrespective of social background. The statutes that had perpetuated the owning of public and private slaves were abolished, and the buying and selling of human beings was prohibited. Moreover, post station attendants, actor-entertainers, the outcast *paekchŏng,* and others similarly stigmatized were freed from their traditional lowborn status. These were momentous social reforms, signifying the demise of the *yangban* dominated status structure.

In addition, legislation was enacted against a wide variety of malignant social practices and conventions. Torture of criminal suspects and extension of punishment to family members of those convicted of heinous crimes were banned. Early marriage was prohibited and minimum age requirements of twenty for men and sixteen for women were set. Widows of whatever social class were allowed to remarry. The pursuit of careers in business or commerce by government officials no longer in office, even by those who had occupied the highest positions, was formally sanctioned. The regulations governing adoption to continue family lines were revised to give illegitimate sons the right to succeed their fathers. Sumptuary laws were changed, to simplify the regulations on modes of dress that had distinguished higher and lower official ranks and differentiated *yangban* from commoners, and also to encourage the wearing of more practical clothing.

Aftermath of the Reforms

It is evident from the above that the measures enacted in 1894 constituted a sweeping reform that affected many vital aspects of the administration, the economy, and the social fabric of Korea, and as such it holds great significance for Korea's modernization process. At the same time, the Reform of 1894 had the incidental effect of facilitating the further penetration into Korea of Japan's developing capitalist economy. For example, the currency reform contributed to the stabilization of the monetary system, a precondition for Korea continuing to serve as a major market for Japanese products. The standardization of weights and measures, too, was a welcome convenience to Japanese traders. On the other hand, the absence of concern for remedying defects in so vital an area as the military system constitutes a serious flaw in the reform program. The reforms, then, did nothing to ensure adequate military manpower resources or the provision of new weaponry, both of which are essential to the security of a modern state. The only change worthy of note was to place existing military units, which had a combined strength of only about three thousand troops, under the authority of the new defense ministry.

Another shortcoming of the reform was the requirement that taxes be paid in cash. This visited great hardship on the peasants, since coinage was not in widespread circulation in the villages at that time. It was necessary, therefore, for the peasants first to exchange their grain for cash and then to pay their taxes, a two-stage process made still more burdensome by the fact that banks had not yet been established in Korea. To overcome this difficulty the government encouraged experienced grain merchants to establish rice brokerages that would serve as banking facilities for converting grain tax payments into cash revenue, but the government lacked the means to finance such a scheme and it was not effective.

The reform program, moreover, encountered the bitter opposition of the Taewŏn'gun, who went so far as to plot a military coup that would depose Kojong and replace him on the throne with the Taewŏn'gun's grandson, Yi Chun-yong. For his scheme to succeed, it would first be necessary to force Japan to withdraw its troops from Korea. To this end the Taewŏn'gun made contact with both the commander of the large Chinese force that had just taken up positions in P'yŏngyang and with the Tonghak peasant army then still engaged in fighting the Japanese. The plot was uncovered and came to naught, but it caused the Japanese considerable anxiety. Fearing that its representative in Seoul, Ōtori Keisuke, might lose control of the situation, Japan recalled him and appointed the prestigious senior statesman Inoue Kaoru as minister in his place. Making use of the secret communication from the Taewŏn'gun to the Chinese, a document that had come into Japanese possession when their forces captured P'yŏngyang, Inoue succeeded in forcing the Taewŏn'gun to retire from the political scene. Inoue then persuaded the king to appoint Pak Yŏng-hyo, and others now returned from long exile in Japan, to the Kim Hong-jip cabinet, thus in effect creating a coalition government headed jointly by Kim and Pak. It was at this point early in January, 1895, that Kojong, at the head of the officialdom and flanked by the Taewŏn'gun, the Crown Prince, and members of the royal family, visited the Royal Ancestral Shrine and there before the tablets of his ancestors vowed to push forward with the task of reform. The proclamation of fourteen articles he read on this occasion, entitled "Guiding Principles for the Nation" (*Hongbŏm*), has been called Korea's first constitution, but it is memorable rather for its embodiment of the basic thrust of the 1894 reform program.

Inoue's appointment as minister had increased Japan's pressure on the Korean government. But when the tripartite intervention of Russia, France, and Germany forced Japan to retrocede the Liaotung Peninsula, a prize Japan had won in the Sino-Japanese War, the situation underwent a dramatic change. Japan's weakness had been exposed, and now a consensus arose in the Korean government for freeing the country from Japanese domination, an undertaking that would require Russian assistance. Queen Min and her kinsmen were behind the new policy of reliance on Russia to counter Japan, for their power had been weakened as Japan's pressure had grown stronger. When reports reached Queen Min that Pak Yŏng-hyo was plotting to force her to abdicate, she was able instead to drive him and his pro-Japanese cohorts from the government. Pak once again had to flee to Japan and men of the pro-Russian faction, led by Yi Pŏm-jin and Yi Wan-yong, now obtained cabinet appointments, giving the government a dominant pro-Russia orientation.

Japan naturally was loath to see the appearance of Russian influence in Korea. Japanese policy, therefore, was aimed at eliminating the pro-Russian faction and the influence on the court wielded by Queen Min, and in its desperation to restore pro-Japanese forces to power Japan was prepared to resort to any means. In the end, then, Inoue's successor as Japanese minister, Miura Gorō, authorized an attempt on Queen Min's life which was carried out on October 8, 1895. The nation's queen thus met a cruel death at the hands of foreign assassins. Fearing an outcry of condemnation from abroad Japan recalled Miura to stand trial in Japan, but in the end he was declared not guilty on grounds of insufficient evidence.

After the murder of Queen Min a new cabinet was formed with Kim Hong-jip again at its head. The new government pushed ahead with still more radical reform measures, as both a continuation and expansion of those already enacted. The Western calendar was adopted, smallpox vaccinations for children were prescribed, elementary schools were established in Seoul, postal service was inaugurated in Ch'ungju, Andong, Taegu, and Tongnae, a new era name system was inaugurated (a single era name was to be used during the entirety of each king's reign, that of Kojong thenceforth to be known as *Kŏnyang*, the "Lustrous Inauguration"), the military structure was reorganized to provide for a capital guards unit in Seoul and defense garrisons in provincial areas, and an order to cut the Korean male's traditional topknot was issued and was enforced.

These later reforms, carried out while the nation was in a state of shock following the assassination of the queen, and filled with outrage at Japanese aggression, aroused intense popular opposition. The order for the cutting of topknots was particular anathema, and resistance to it even took the form of cries to "Cut off my head, but my hair—never!" The atmosphere of hostility toward Japan was such that guerrilla bands, so-called righteous armies (*ŭibyŏng*), rose up throughout the country to wage an armed struggle against the Japanese troops still encamped on Korean soil. The leaders of these bands were such men as Yu In-sŏk, Yi So-ŭng, and Kim Pok-han, and to suppress the guerrillas the government was forced into the painful decision to dispatch most of the newly formed capital guards unit to fight against their countrymen in the rural areas.

5. Commerce, Industry, and Currents of Thought in the Enlightenment Period

Changes in Commerce and Industry Subsequent to Opening the Ports

The activities of foreign traders who took up residence in Korea's newly opened ports brought a rapid increase in the country's foreign trade. The Koreans who responded most receptively to the changed situation were the wholesale commodity brokers, the *kaekchu* and *yŏgak*. These wholesale merchants, strategically situated on the Han River at Seoul and river and sea ports in the provinces, had amassed capital by dominating trade in a variety of commodities. Unlike the conservative merchants who operated the Six Licensed Stores in the shelter of their government-bestowed privileges, the wholesale merchants were an aggressive and enterprising lot, and it was they who now undertook new commercial activities in collaboration with the foreign traders. When the ports were first opened, the activities of foreign traders were restricted to an area not far beyond the confines of the ports themselves, and for this reason the foreign traders had no choice but to conduct their activities through Korean wholesale merchants. Thus by selling imported goods through the network of pack and back peddlers and by buying up items for export by the foreign traders, the Korean *kaekchu* and *yŏgak* further added to their capital.

But the Korean wholesale merchants and the peddlers too suffered a serious blow when foreign traders came to be able to operate in the interior as well as in the port areas. In consequence, the more enterprising *kaekchu* and *yŏgak* organized trading companies to cope with the foreign competition. The forerunner of a large number of such commercial ventures— more than forty have been identified in records from the time of the 1894 reforms—was the Taedong Company organized by merchants in P'yŏngan province. Among these were some enterprises that involved the pooling of private capital, such as the Kwangin-sa, a publisher of books, and the Changch'un-sa, which was in the business of brewing and selling alcoholic beverages. At the same time, government companies also came into existence and in fact were more numerous than the private companies. But these, like the Six Licensed Stores in the past, were granted certain special privileges by the government, and this tended to restrict their freedom of operation.

Merchant associations also were organized. In 1883 the government had established an agency called the Office for the Benefit of Trade (*Hye-sang Kongguk*) to protect the interests of the pack and back peddlers, whose monopolistic position was threatened by the removal of restrictions on trade after the opening of the ports. This office sought to preserve the privileges and profits of its charges by preventing foreign merchants from engaging in illegal or unethical practices. Thus protected by the government, the Peddlers Guild (Pobu Sangdan), the peddlers' own association, could not free itself from a psychology of dependence on its traditional privileges, and this prevented its development as a modern merchants organization. In contrast, the wholesale merchants at the ports organized bodies that gradually developed the form and functions of modern mercantile associations. Organizations of this type were established at Wŏnsan in 1883, at Inch'ŏn in 1885, and at Pusan somewhat later. These mercantile associations exposed the activities of the Japanese merchants who violated the conditions governing trade at the ports and filed complaints against them, and in other ways too they sought to combat the economic penetration of the foreign traders. At the same time they gradually adapted themselves to the new Western business practices.

In the area of industry the government took the lead in establishing a variety of manufacturing enterprises. An arsenal to produce modern weapons, the government mint, and a publishing organ all were established in 1883; a textile factory was founded in 1885; and in 1887 both a paper manufactory and a bureau to develop mines employing new methods of extraction were created. In the first years following the opening of the ports, therefore, the characteristic of modern industry in Korea was that factories were owned and operated by the government rather than by private entrepreneurs.

In shipping, too, as Japanese merchant vessels strengthened their dominant position, the Korean government at first attempted to compete in a cooperative venture with a Western shipping company. This initial effort failed, however, when the government found itself unable to pay in its share of the investment capital. Then in 1886 the government established a bureau with responsibility for maritime shipping, bought four modern steam powered vessels, and undertook to provide shipping services. A few years later, in 1892, operation of the steamships was entrusted to a newly created company jointly owned by the government and private interests. It was intended that this shipping firm undertake primarily the transport of tax grain, but the volume of business decreased as the reform measure requiring payment of the grain tax in cash took effect. Shortly thereafter, when the steamships were commandeered by the Japanese army during the Sino-Japanese War, the government's efforts to provide state-controlled shipping services essentially came to an end.

The Development of Enlightenment Thought

What we call "enlightenment thought" was a continuation of the traditions of the school of Northern Learning within the *Sirhak* movement. Accordingly, it had the same aim of achieving national prosperity and military strength through introducing new technology and developing commerce and industry. The new technology discussed in enlightenment thought, however, was that of the West rather than that of China, and in consequence the enlightenment thinkers urged that their objectives could be more swiftly attained by opening Korean ports and so entering into commercial relations with the West.

Western weapons technology was the first item of concern to Korea at this time. In the five years between the two "foreign disturbances" (the French reprisals of 1866 and the American expedition in 1871), Korea had built a new style warship as well as cannon on the basis of descriptions in the Chinese work *Illustrated Treatise on Nations Across the Sea* (*Hai-kuo t'u-chih*). The steamship had failed to operate satisfactorily but the cannon had been deployed in the defense of Kanghwa against the American attackers. Following the opening of the ports, of course, Korea still more actively imported new weapons and also instituted modern military training. Koreans also were much interested in acquiring new agricultural technology that would enrich the nation. A pioneer in this effort was Ch'oe Kyŏng-sŏk, who raised livestock and cultivated seeds imported from America on his experimental farm. A newly created public sericulture enterprise invited a German technical expert to experiment with new methods of raising silkworms. At the same time, An Chong-su's 1881 work *New Approaches to Farm Management* (*Nongjŏng sinp'yŏn*) and Chŏng Pyŏng-ha's *Essentials of Farm Management* (*Nongjŏng ch'waryo*), appearing in 1886, were written to introduce modern farming methods from the West.

This initial concern with the introduction of new technology gradually gave way to a more radical stream of enlightenment thought that assigned a higher priority to political and other institutional change. Yu Kil-chun's *Observations on a Journey to the West* (*Sŏyu kyŏnmun*) represents an exemplary reflection of this thinking. There is also Kim Ok-kyun's *Contemporary Korea and Japan* (*Kihwa kŭnsa*), in which he compared the stages of development in those two nations with that of the West, but no other work compares with Yu Kil-chun's in breadth of coverage or in terms of idea content. Yu had studied in Japan and the United States in the early 1880's, had visited Europe, and was well acquainted in the foreign community in Seoul. Written in 1889, *Observations on a Journey to the West* describes the geography, history, politics, economy, society, and learning of various Western nations, measuring Korean conditions against these and advocating that Korea strive for modernization on the model of Western civilization.

In the view of Yu Kil-chun the process of enlightenment might take two courses, the one sterile and the other fruitful. The former process, a merely wasteful approach, would slavishly imitate the ways of others without first gaining an understanding of the context in which they had developed. The enlightenment process would bear fruit, on the other hand, if the operative principles at the root of the material civilization of the West were first perceived and these were then adapted to the realities of one's own country. From this perspective Yu proceeded to formulate a program for political and economic reform in his contemporary Korea. His ultimate objectives were to establish a constitutional democracy and create a free enterprise capitalist economy, but for the Korea of his day he believed that a political structure in which governance was exercised jointly by the sovereign and his subjects, in other words a constitutional monarchy, was best suited.

Earlier, in 1883, a now unknown author had published an article titled "Explanation of a Corporation" (*Hoesa sŏl*) in the newly founded government gazette *Hansŏng Sunbo.* In it he spoke of the necessity of creating Western style business organizations, joint stock companies, explaining how capital was obtained from a number of individual investors, discussing the issuance of shares, and setting forth the principles that govern the election of the president of such a corporation. In short, he argued the need for Korea to move toward the adoption of modern business institutions.

The "Reject Heterodoxy" Persuasion

The conceptual basis for "rejecting heterodoxy" was that Chu Hsi Neo-Confucianism was the sole valid system of belief and that, therefore, civilizations based on any other ideology must be kept from Korean shores. This belief was strongest among those Confucian literati who did not participate in the political process, and it was inevitable that these men should react with hostility toward introduction of the values represented by the civilizations of the West and Japan. Accordingly they took a stance in strong opposition to the ideas of the enlightenment thinkers.

Because the foreign attacks on Kanghwa in 1866 and 1871, and the 1876 Treaty of Kanghwa, were consequences of French, American, and Japanese aggression against Korea, the "reject heterodoxy" thinking first of all took the form of protest against coming to terms with these enemies. Yi Hang-no (1792-1868) was a foremost proponent of this position, and in a memorial submitted to the throne in 1866 upon resigning as a Royal

Secretary, he set forth the extreme Confucianist ideological argument for continued armed resistance against foreign inroads, asserting that to advocate peaceful relations would be to abandon the values on which all moral civilization must rest, thereby causing man to sink to the level of animal behavior. In *Reflections of the Master Hwasŏ* (*Hwasŏ aŏn*), the record of his lifetime of thought and activity compiled by his disciples in 1867, Yi Hang-no discussed the recent foreign attacks on Kanghwa, again arguing that Western values lead men to adopt the ways of the brute beast that honors neither father nor sovereign. Yi Hang-no was not merely attempting to rouse his countrymen to do battle against foreign aggression, for he insisted that to achieve this external objective internal transformation too was essential. When government paid heed to its policy critics, when the state of military readiness was improved, when men of moral uprightness were appointed to office—only after such changes in governmental policies and practices had been effected, he thought, would a strong stance against foreign aggression be possible. He went even further, to argue that men of standing in the local areas be encouraged to form guerrilla bands to fight in concert with government forces against the foreign enemy. The later phenomenon of "righteous armies," guerrilla bands springing up throughout the country to fight the Japanese, owes much to this ringing call to arms.

Concerned not only with military aggression, Yi Hang-no also warned against the consequences of economic aggression by the capitalist powers. Since the Western nations were in a different stage of economic development than Korea, trading with them, he believed, would only exhaust the basic resources Korea needed for its own consumption. Accordingly, his position was that Koreans simply should not use Western goods, in which event trade naturally would become unnecessary.

From the time that trade with Japan began to develop as a result of the Treaty of Kanghwa, the thinking of those of the "reject heterodoxy" persuasion had come to be directed not only against the Western nations but against Japan as well. This view that Japan and the West were one and the same in the threat they posed to Korea was well expressed in the 1876 memorial of Ch'oe Ik-hyŏn, cited earlier, in which he detailed "Five Reasons Against" concluding the Treaty of Kanghwa with Japan. At the same time, however, there were those who, while supporting the concept of "rejecting heterodoxy," went on to argue that Korea should selectively accept one thing from the West, its technology, as the only realistic way to strengthen the nation. This way of thinking, that Korea must preserve its cultural values while mastering Western technology, is sometimes termed the concept of "Eastern ways, Western machines."

Chapter 14

Nationalist Stirrings and Imperialist Aggression

1. Activities of the Independence Club

Inauguration of the "Great Han Empire"

The assassination of Queen Min roused the hostility of the Korean people toward Japan to a fever pitch, and guerrilla bands had risen throughout the country to harass the Japanese troops still encamped on Korean territory. Taking advantage of this turmoil, the Russian minister, Waeber, brought one hundred marines to Seoul under pretext of guarding his legation. Then Yi Pŏm-jin and others of the pro-Russian faction made secret arrangements with Waeber to bring King Kojong under Russian protection. Now in fear for his own life, Kojong was desperate to escape from Japanese intimidation. Accordingly, in February 1896, he allowed himself to be smuggled out of the palace to the security of the Russian legation. The king's flight of course turned the political situation completely around. Pro-Japan cabinet members like Kim Hong-jip and Ŏ Yun-jung were killed, while Yu Kil-chun and others fled to Japan. A new pro-Russian cabinet was formed to include such figures as Yi Pŏm-jin and Yi Wan-yong.

During the year the king remained in the Russian legation the government came under strong Russian influence. Japanese advisers in whatever Korean ministry and Japanese military instructors all were dismissed, Russian advisers and instructors being appointed in their stead. Russian arms, too, were procured, and a Russian language school was established. The actions of the Russian adviser to the Ministry of Finance gave the distinct impression that it was he, in fact, who headed the ministry, and now a variety of economic concessions were handed over to the Russians. But when Russia gained concessions the other powers too were encouraged to demand equal favor, and so in the aftermath of the king's removal to the Russian legation a large number of such concessions fell into the hands of foreign governments and businesses.

The Korean people were united in their condemnation of their king's flight to a foreign legation and the continuous granting of economic concessions to foreigners. Their outrage coalesced in particular around a campaign launched by the recently inaugurated Independence Club. In response to this, in February 1897, Kojong moved out of the Russian legation to the Kyŏngun Palace (today's Tŏksu Palace), in August he changed his reign name to *Kwangmu* ("Martial Brilliance"), and in October he proclaimed to the nation and the world the establishment of the independent "Great Han Empire." In formal structure Korea now had become an empire, and this may be said to have been a victory for the pressure of Korean public opinion. Korean realities, however, had not changed. The reason the king had gone to Tŏksu Palace rather than return to his Kyŏngbok Palace residence was that he thought thus to avail himself of the protection of the Russian, American, English, and other nearby legations. Although in the capital of his own country, out of fear of Japan the king had lost his freedom of action and was no longer his own master. In consequence economic concessions continued to be wrung from Korea,

THE SCRAMBLE AMONG THE POWERS FOR CONCESSIONS

YEAR	COUNTRY	CONCESSION
1883	Japan	Laying of Pusan - Nagasaki undersea cable
1885	China	Construction of Inch'ŏn - Ŭiju telegraph line
	Japan	Construction of Pusan - Inch'ŏn telegraph line
1886	Japan	Permission to establish coaling station on Yŏngdo, off Pusan
1888	Japan	Coastal fishing rights
1891	Japan	Permission to establish coaling station on Wŏlmi Island, off Inch'ŏn
		Territorial fishing rights off Kyŏngsang province
1894	Japan	Building of Seoul - Pusan railway line
1895	U.S.	Gold mining rights at Unsan, P'yŏngan province
1896	U.S.	Building of Seoul - Inch'ŏn railway line
	Russia	Mining rights in Kyŏngwŏn and Chongsŏng counties, Hamgyŏng province
		Permission to establish coaling station on Wŏlmi Island, off Inch'ŏn
		Timber rights in the Yalu river basin and Ullŭng Island areas
	France	Building of Seoul - Ŭiju railway line
1897	Germany	Gold mining rights at Kŭmsŏng, Kangwŏn province
1898	Russia	Permission to establish coaling station on Yŏngdo, off Pusan
	U.S.	Laying of electricity and water mains in Seoul
	Russia	Authorization to establish Russo-Korean Bank
	England	Gold mining rights at Ŭnsan, P'yŏngan province
	Japan	Exclusive purchase rights to coal produced at P'yŏngyang
		Building of Seoul - Inch'ŏn railway (concession bought from U. S.)

bringing fresh degradation to the nation and humiliation to its people.

Founding of the Independence Club

Seeing that the king and his high officials were prepared to rely on the support of foreign powers to preserve Korea's territorial integrity, the public at large attacked the government's ineffective policy and fought dauntlessly to maintain the nation's independence and freedom. This was particularly true of a new intellectual class that had been exposed to the ideas of Western liberalism. These men formed a variety of political organizations and battled to secure the nation's independence and the rights of the people. The Independence Club (Tongnip Hyŏphoe) was the first of these organizations and it also was the most energetically active.

The Independence Club was founded in 1896 by Sŏ Chae-p'il (Philip Jaisohn), who had exiled himself to America in the wake of the abortive 1884 coup and now had returned to Korea. Membership in the Club at first was drawn from the Kŏnyang Club (a name symbolizing the end of the traditional Chinese suzerain relationship), a group organized by Yu Kil-chun and other leading figures in the 1894 reforms, from the Chŏngdong Club formed by Yun Ch'i-ho and Yi Sang-jae, men active in the nation's diplomatic affairs, and from men like Namgung Ŏk in the middle levels of the government. Initially, therefore, the Independence Club largely was comprised of men who were incumbent or former government officials.

Before long, however, membership in the Independence Club was thrown completely open, so that anyone might freely join without need of recommendation or sponsor. Moreover, selection of the Club's officers and the conduct of its business were handled democratically, with matters decided by a simple majority of the members present. Consequently the character of the Club gradually changed, as more and more of the citizenry of Seoul in general joined its ranks. The Club, moreover, expanded its network of members into the countryside. The first branch was that formed in Kongju in 1898, to be followed by branch clubs in P'yŏngyang, Taegu, and other places. After branches had been established in a sufficient number of provincial towns, one in each province was designated to represent that provincial area and these in turn maintained regular contact with Independence Club headquarters in Seoul. Even after the headquarters club in Seoul had been dissolved, these branches remained and continued their activites.

As the Independence Club's criticism of the government and denunciation of its policies mounted, higher level officials deemed it politic to resign their membership. Leadership of the Club thereupon fell to representatives of the new intelligentsia like Sŏ Chae-p'il, Yun Ch'i-ho, and Yi Sang-jae, men influenced by Western bourgeois thought. Next in importance was a group including Namgung Ŏk and Chŏng Kyo that might be characterized as a Confucianist reform party, a persuasion that evolved out of the "Eastern ways, Western machines" school of thought. In addition to these two principal elements, other Club participants included Han Kyu-sŏl, a military official who had much in common with the progressives, various townsmen who directed the affairs of the trading associations or the new joint stock companies, and in some few cases even *paekchŏng* outcasts or those of similar background who recently had been freed from base social status. There were still others: the Independence Club was joined and supported by peasants who had become politically aware through the activities of the Tonghak peasant army, by new elements in Korean society such as mine laborers and dock workers at the open ports, by pioneering women, and by students. The leadership of the Independence Club, in short, came from the new intelligentsia, while it grew and prospered with the support of a wide spectrum of newly awakened townspeople.

Activities of the Independence Club

The Independence Club originally was established for the purpose of carrying out two symbolic projects: first, to erect an Independence Gate on the recently razed site of the Yŏngŭn ("Welcoming Imperial Grace") Gate, through which envoys from China had been escorted, and second, to renovate the Mohwa-gwan ("Hall of Cherishing China"), where Chinese embassies had been entertained, and create there an Independence Hall and Independence Park. In the context of the international crisis Korea then was facing, these announced objectives evoked a warm response from the populace, and support and sizeable contributions came, as expected, from the citizenry as a whole and from the royal family and highest officials as well. Success thus was assured, and the cornerstone laying ceremony for Independence Gate was carried out in November 1896, the year the Independence Club was founded, while in May of the next year the completion of Independence Hall was marked by the formal hanging of its signboard.

As the Independence Club transformed itself into a citizens assembly, it went beyond such symbolic activities and began to initiate direct social and political programs. The first priority of the Club was to launch a campaign of public education. One device employed was the sponsorship of a debating forum, and another was a newspaper. Several hundred Club members and spectators attended the debating forums, held each Sunday at Independence Hall, and through their participation in the fervent discussions a public consensus took form. The official organ of the Independence Club was the fortnightly *Bulletin of the Independence Club of Great Chosŏn* but an unofficial organ was published daily and was called *The Independent*, in Korean *Tongnip Sinmun*. With the backing of the government obtained through some of the men of the Progressive Party who had taken leading roles in the 1894 reforms, Sŏ Chae-p'il published the first issue of *The Independent* even before the Independence Club was formed. To attract a wide readership among the populace in general it was put out in *han'gŭl*, without the use of any Chinese characters. Then, once the Independence Club came into existence, *The Independent* served as a vehicle for its views and in particular for the views of the new intelligentsia and their Western liberal ideas, and in this way it played a major role in advancing public awareness and understanding. At the same time another daily paper, the *Hwangsŏng Sinmun*, served as a spokesman for the Confucianist reform element within the Independence Club.

The activities of the Independence Club were aimed on the whole at three principal goals. Its energies first of all were directed toward safeguarding the nation's independence in the face of external aggression. Needless to say, it condemned foreign interference in Korea's governmental processes, but it also opposed the granting of economic concessions and demanded that those already extorted be recovered. The Club also urged that Korea adopt an independent and neutral foreign policy, favoring none of the rival powers seeking to advance parochial interests in the peninsula. Secondly, the Club initiated a popular rights movement as a means of bringing about wider participation in the political process. Setting forth such ideological grounds as the right of the individual to the security of his person and property, the rights of free speech and assembly, the full equality of all people, and the doctrine of the sovereignty of the people, the Club argued the right of the governed to participate in their governing. For the first time in Korea, then, the Independence Club in effect had launched a movement for political democracy. The specific measure proposed by the Club to further this end was to convert the Privy Council (*Chungch'uwŏn*) into a parliamentary assembly, and at one point Kojong even accepted this proposal. Thirdly, the Club sought to promote a self-strengthening movement. The principal points in this program were to establish schools in each village to provide a new-style education; to build textile and paper mills and ironworks, thus furthering the country's commercialization and industrialization; and to ensure the nation's security by developing a modern national defense capacity.

It was due to the activities of the Independence Club that the Russian military instructors and finance adviser were recalled, that the Russo-Korean Bank was forced to close, and that the king left the Russian legation to take up residence in Tŏksu Palace. But the agitation of the Independence Club reached its peak with the convening of a mass meeting of officials and the citizenry at the Chongno intersection in October 1898. Constantly at odds with those in power, who hated him and the ends toward which he worked, Sŏ Chae-p'il by this time had decided to return to the United States, but the ardor of the Independence Club had not been dampened. With high government officials also in attendance and with the fervent support of the people of Seoul who had thronged to the meeting, the assemblage resolved to submit the following six proposals to the king (herebelow as reported on the English page of *The Independent,* issue of November 1, 1898):

I.   That both officials and People shall determine not to rely on any foreign aid but to do their best to strengthen and uphold the Imperial prerogatives.

II.   That all documents pertaining to foreign loans, the hiring of foreign soldiers, the grant of concessions, etc., in short every document drawn up between the Korean government and foreigners, shall be signed and stamped by all the Ministers of State and the President of the Privy Council.

III.   That no important offender shall be punished until after he has been given a public trial and an ample opportunity to defend himself either by himself or by a counsel.

IV.   That to His Majesty shall belong the power of appointing his ministers, but that in case the majority of the Cabinet disapproves a man, he shall not be appointed.

V.   That all sources of revenue and methods of raising taxes shall be placed under the control of the Finance Department, no other department or office, or private corporation being allowed to interfere therewith, and that annual estimates and balances shall be made public.

VI.   That existing laws and regulations shall be faithfully enforced.

The words "existing laws and regulations" referred to the fourteen articles of the "Guiding Principles for the Nation" (*Hongbŏm*) promulgated in 1895 and to the administrative regulations of the various government agencies. Thus what the mass meeting in fact called for was constitutional government and the rule of law. When the six proposals were conveyed to Kojong he actually promised to put them into effect, and in fact the Privy Council was restructured to enable half its councillors to be elected by "public associations," by which was meant, "for the time being," the Independence Club alone. But this was no more than a delaying tactic to calm public agitation while suppressive countermeasures were being readied. Presently, charging that the real aim of the Independence Club was to abolish the monarchy and in its stead establish a republic headed by an elected president, the government ordered that the Club be dissolved and at the same time arrested Yi Sang-jae and sixteen others of its leaders. Club members immediately mounted a campaign to force the release of those imprisoned, holding a continuous mass protest meeting day after day. As the crisis worsened the government countered by ordering the Imperial Association, a body newly created as a tool of the government, to employ violence against the demonstrators by bringing in thugs from the Peddlers Guild. The government then called in troops to clear the streets and banned any further protest meetings. With this, the efforts of the Independence Club to effect fundamental reform of the ailing dynasty came abruptly to an end.

2. Japanese Aggression and the Struggle of the "Righteous Armies"

Russo-Japanese Rivalry for Domination over Korea

It was of course between Russia and Japan that the most intense rivalry over Korea developed. This was the time when Russian power was penetrating so remarkably into Northeast Asia. After forcing Japan to retrocede the Liaotung Peninsula to China in 1895, Russia had concluded a secret military agreement with Ch'ing and had acquired the right to build the eastern end of the Trans-Siberian Railway down through Manchuria. Next Russia obtained twenty-five year leases on Port Arthur and Talien (Dairen) and the right to link these two Manchurian ports by rail to the Trans-Siberian. Having thus solidified its control over Manchuria, Russia had launched a powerful drive to penetrate into Korea as well.

Needless to say, Japan more than any other nation watched this thrust of Russian power into the Far East with apprehension. At the same time, Japan was not yet ready to oppose the Russian push by force. The policy that Japan pursued in Korea, therefore, was a compromise: to proceed with economic penetration while looking ahead to an opportunity to commit overt aggression in the future. Russia too, busied with its Manchurian ventures, for the time being was willing to reach an accommodation with Japan. After prolonged negotiations, therefore, the two rivals reached an understanding in April, 1898. Neither country would interfere in Korea's internal administration, neither would send military instructors or financial advisers without prior mutual agreement, and on Russia's part a pledge was given not to obstruct Japanese economic activity in Korea. The signing of this agreement with Japan did not mean, of course, that Russia had abandoned its designs on Korea, and in fact Russian machinations continued as before. One instance of this was the Russian effort in 1900 to lease land in Masan on which to construct a naval base, a site that would serve as a midway point in a sea link between Vladivostok and Port Arthur. This plan was frustrated due to Japanese obstruction, but at the same time it caused Japan much concern.

It was at this time, in 1900, that the Boxer Rebellion broke out in China. A nationalistic resistance movement against foreign aggression, the Boxer Rebellion finally was put down only by combined contingents of troops dispatched from the major Western powers and Japan. Russia had taken advantage of this opportunity to send a large force into Manchuria, and even after the rebellion had been subdued the Russian troops were not withdrawn, giving the distinct impression that Russia's intent was to remain in permanent occupation. This would constitute a grave menace not merely to Japan but to England as well, already in confrontation with

Russia at points all over the Eurasian land mass. The result was the signing of the Anglo-Japanese Alliance in January 1902, an agreement aimed at containing the Russian threat. By its terms England's rights and interests in China were recognized by Japan and in exchange England acknowledged Japan's special interests in Korea. And the two countries pledged assistance to each other in the event either became involved in a war against a third power.

The Anglo-Japanese Alliance strengthened Japan's position and now, in concert with England and the United States, Japan demanded that the Russian army withdraw from Manchuria. Russia's response in April 1902 was a promise to effect the withdrawal in three stages, but only the first stage was carried out on schedule. Thus the Russian military occupation of Manchuria continued as before, and not only this—in July 1903 a Russian force crossed the mouth of the Yalu into Yongamp'o, bought land, and constructed housing, and before long formally requested to lease a port area there. Once again Japanese opposition compelled the Russians to back down, but Russia at least did achieve the opening of Yongamp'o as a trading port.

By now the aggressive ambitions of Japan and Russia with regard to Korea and Manchuria were bared for all to see. That a war would ensue if neither imperialist power yielded to the other was a foregone conclusion. Nor did either of the two show any signs of yielding. When the Russians reneged on their pledge to evacuate their troops from Manchuria, Japan immediately proposed that the two powers enter into negotiations. At these negotiations the Japanese side demanded that Russia recognize Japan's "preponderant" interests in Korea. For its part, Japan would acknowledge Russia's special position with regard to the operation of its railway in Manchuria, but at the same time the development of Japanese commercial activities was to be permitted. Russia, on the other hand, offered to recognize the paramountcy of Japan's political and economic interests in Korea, providing Japan would guarantee not to use the peninsula as a staging base for military operations, but all of Manchuria was to remain outside the sphere of Japanese interests. Russia went on to propose that the territory of Korea north of the thirty-ninth parallel be declared a neutral zone into which neither country would be permitted to introduce troops. The tortuous negotiations went on through several sessions but no ground for compromise could be found. Having failed to achieve its purpose through diplomatic means Japan determined to seek a military solution, and in February 1904 Japan carried out a surprise attack on the Russian installations at Port Arthur. The rivalry between the two powers now was to be resolved by war.

International Recognition of Japanese Aggression

As the outbreak of war between Russia and Japan became imminent, Korea formally proclaimed its neutrality, in January 1904. In spite of this,

Japan displayed its military might by sending troops into Seoul and occupying a number of buildings. Then, by threat of force, Japan compelled Korea to sign a protocol agreement. This document contained the ritualistic provision that Japan undertook to respect the independence of Korea and the integrity of Korean territory. But the agreement also called for Korea to accept Japanese counsel with regard to improvements in governmental administration, it authorized Japan to take necessary measures in the event the personal safety of the Korean monarch were threatened by a third country or by internal disorder, and to this end it permitted Japan to occupy strategic points throughout the country. The agreement, in short, provided legal justification for whatever political or military actions Japan might wish to take in Korea. Concurrently with the signing of this protocol, Korea declared all its agreements with Russia to be void. Japan now started construction on the Seoul-Ŭiju and Seoul-Pusan railroads, so necessary to the prosecution of the war against Russia, commandeered the Korean telegraph network, and took for itself navigation rights on Korean rivers and in Korean coastal waters. This was not all: as the first step in its planned land grab in Korea, Japan demanded the right to open up all uncultivated state owned lands to development by Japanese colonists. This last demand was withdrawn, however, in the face of strong opposition from the Korean government and the general public.

In exchange for abandoning its designs on uncultivated land, Japan insisted that Korea install Japanese advisers in strategic Korean ministries. By this means Japan would be able to interfere even in the inner workings of the Korean government. This latest Japanese demand was incorporated into a new agreement signed in August 1904. By its terms Korea agreed to employ a Japanese financial adviser named by Japan and to conduct all matters related to fiscal administration entirely in accordance with his advice. A foreign affairs adviser also was to be engaged, a foreigner selected by Japan, and this man would be responsible for concluding treaties with foreign governments and for handling other important diplomatic matters— always after advance consultation with Japanese authorities. The first Japanese financial adviser was Megata Tanetarō, a high official of the Japanese Ministry of Finance, while an American, Durham W. Stevens, was named as foreign affairs adviser. (When Stevens returned to America in 1908 to praise the record of the Japanese Residency-General in Korea, he was assassinated in San Francisco by two Korean expatriates, Chŏn Myŏng-un and Chang In-hwan.) Subsequently, although this was not stipulated in the agreement, Japan installed an adviser in the Korean Ministry of Defense, a police adviser, an adviser on royal household affairs, and an adviser on educational matters. Japan thus had created what was known at the time as a "government by advisers" in Korea. The situation was exactly as if actual administrative authority had passed into Japanese hands. This was particularly evident with regard to diplomatic affairs, as the Korean ministers who had been accredited to Germany, France,

Japan, China, and other nations were recalled.

Contrary to expectations around the world, the Russo-Japanese War saw a succession of Japanese victories from beginning to end. With Russia ready to sue for peace, the American president, Theodore Roosevelt, stepped in to mediate the terms. Horace N. Allen, the U. S. minister of legation in Seoul, urged his government to intervene in the Korean situation in order to block Japanese aggression, but Roosevelt would not listen. He took the view, rather, that Japanese control over Korea was an appropriate means to prevent the further expansion of Russian power. Roosevelt felt, moreover, that it was necessary to acquiesce in Japanese domination of Korea as a *quid pro quo* for Japan's recognition of U. S. hegemony over the Philippines. This deal between the U. S. and Japan is revealed in the secret Taft-Katsura Agreement of July 1905. England too, in renegotiating the terms of the Anglo-Japanese Alliance in August 1905, acknowledged Japan's right to take appropriate measures for the "guidance, control, and protection" of Korea. The Treaty of Portsmouth ending the Russo-Japanese War was concluded in September 1905, in this setting of international recognition of Japan's paramountcy in Korea.

The most important provisions of the Treaty of Portsmouth were Russia's acknowledgment that Japan possessed paramount political, military, and economic interests in Korea, and Russia's pledge not to hinder Japan from taking whatever actions it deemed necessary for the "guidance, protection, and control" of the Korean government. By the terms of the treaty, further, Japan succeeded to all rights in Port Arthur and Dairen formerly held by Russia, and Japan secured the right to develop its commercial interests in Manchuria on a basis of equality with Russia. In sum, Japan now had won all of the concessions it had sought in the earlier abortive negotiations with Russia, and considerably more as well. Most significantly for Korea, the Treaty of Portsmouth meant that Japan had succeeded in removing the last threat to its dominant power position in Korea. Japan now was free to proceed to make Korea its colony, without any let or hindrance.

The 1905 Protectorate Treaty

Having won recognition from Russia, England, and America of its paramount interests in the peninsula, Japan moved immediately to establish a protectorate over Korea. As an initial step toward this objective, Japan propagandized the necessity for a protectorate treaty through a front organization, the Ilchinhoe, headed by Song Pyŏng-jun and Yi Yong-gu. The purpose of this charade was to create the impression that a protectorate treaty was not a demand on the part of Japan but rather a response to the wishes of the Korean people. But the Ilchinhoe had been formed by an interpreter for the Japanese army headquarters in Seoul, Song Pyŏng-jun, and by a Tonghak apostate, Yi Yong-gu, with financial support from the

Japanese and under the direction of Japanese advisers. How could it be other than an instrument of Japanese designs in Korea? Not surprisingly, then, despite the presence of the Japanese occupation forces, another group emerged to take a stand against the Ilchinhoe and to speak for the Korean people in condemning its betrayal of the nation. This was the Society for the Study of Constitutional Government (Hŏnjŏng Yŏn'guhoe), led by Yi Chun and Yang Han-muk.

But it no longer mattered what Koreans wanted, for Japan's policy already was set. Japan sent its elder statesman, Itō Hirobumi, to conclude the protectorate treaty. Itō and the Japanese minister, Hayashi Gonsuke, entered the palace with an escort of Japanese troops, threatened the emperor and his ministers, and demanded that they accept the treaty draft Japan had drawn up. When the Korean officials refused to accede to this demand, the one who had expressed the most violent opposition, Han Kyu-sŏl, the prime minister and a former Independence Club member, was dragged from the chamber by Japanese gendarmes. Japanese soldiers then went to the Foreign Ministry to bring the seal of the Minister of Foreign Affairs, which was affixed to the treaty by Japanese hands (November 17, 1905). Thus the treaty was validated despite the illegal nature of the whole proceeding. Often referred to in English as the "Protectorate Treaty," Koreans know it simply as the Treaty of 1905. Itō Hirobumi, who thus served as the principal instrument of this Japanese act of aggression against Korea, met his end in 1909, the victim of an assassin's bullet fired by An Chung-gŭn.

The Treaty of 1905 first of all gave full authority over all aspects of Korea's relations with foreign countries to the Japanese Foreign Office. Secondly, it forbade the Korean government from entering into any further treaties or agreements of an international character "except through the medium" of the Japanese government. Thirdly, it provided for the appointment of a Japanese resident-general to a position directly under the Korean emperor, to take charge of Korea's foreign relations. In sum, Japan had completely divested Korea of the sovereign power to maintain relations with foreign governments.

Thus Korea's standing in the international community as an independent nation was all but destroyed. Japan's relinquishing of Korea's claim to the Chien-tao (Korean: Kando) region of southeast Manchuria in 1909, in exchange for China's permission to reconstruct the rail line between An-tung and Mukden (now Tan-tung and Shenyang) in Manchuria, is illustrative of the complete control over Korea's foreign affairs that Japan had gained. Another example of the sort of arbitrary actions Japan took in respect to Korean territory was its seizure by force of the island of Tokto, an administrative dependency of Ullŭng-do, during the Russo-Japanese War in 1905. But control over Korea's foreign relations was not the end of it. Although the wording of the treaty limited the authority of the Japanese resident-general "primarily" to matters relating to diplomatic affairs, in fact the whole of Korea's internal administration had come under his control as well. In consequence the very substance of Korean sovereignty in effect had been stripped away.

The Treaty of 1905 evoked bitter anger and opposition from the whole of the Korean people. Despite strict Japanese censorship of both news and editorial content, the Korean press took the lead in rousing public opinion against the treaty. Once aroused, public outrage quickly reached the boiling point. Endless memorials streamed in and countless oral protests were voiced, demonstrations were held and places of business closed their doors. In an excess of indignation and anger, Min Yŏng-hwan, the military aide-de-camp to the king, left an impassioned testamentary letter to the nation and took his own life. Many other outraged officials—Cho Pyŏng-se, Hong Man-sik, Song Pyŏng-sŏn, and Yi Sang-ch'ŏl among them, one by one followed Min Yŏng-hwan's example, while earlier self-martyred patriots included Yi Han-ŭng. At the same time, guerrilla forces, "righteous armies," rose throughout the country to resist Japan by force of arms. Min Chong-sik seized Hongsŏng in Ch'ungch'ŏng province and controlled the surrounding countryside, Ch'oe Ik-hyŏn and Im Pyŏng-ch'an rose in Sunch'ang, Chŏlla province, and Sin Tol-sŏk went into action in Kyŏngsang province. But none of these acts of defiance brought any change in Japanese policy. Japan awaited only an opportunity to put a proper face before the international community on the extinction of Korean independence in name as well as in fact.

The Secret Mission to The Hague and a New Korea-Japan Agreement

The Treaty of 1905 of course was not something Kojong had desired. This was made clear in a royal letter published on February 1, 1906, in the *Taehan Maeil Sinbo* newspaper, in which he stated that he had not consented to the treaty and appealed for the joint protection of the powers. The next year, when the Second Hague Peace Conference was about to open in June 1907, Kojong gave credentials to Yi Sang-sŏl, Yi Chun, and Yi Wi-jong and dispatched them to the Netherlands to appeal the injustice done Korea. But the president of the Conference ruled that Korea was not entitled to participate, having lost authority over its own diplomatic affairs when it became a protectorate of Japan. The Korean envoys protested that without the seal of the king the treaty was invalid, but in the end their request to be seated was denied. A sympathetic newsman, however, arranged for Yi Wi-jong to appear before an international meeting of journalists being held at that same time at The Hague. There he assailed the Japanese aggression and sought to enlist support for the restoration of Korean sovereignty by revealing his country's true state of affairs. But this effort too failed and one of the three envoys, Yi Chun, became overwrought with grief and died there at The Hague.

Although the secret mission to The Hague did not succeed, the worldwide publicity it received did create a considerable international furor.

Ignoring this, Japan instead used the incident as a pretext to further strengthen its grip on Korea, demanding that Kojong accept responsibility for the incident by yielding his throne to the crown prince. When Kojong balked at this, the Japanese indicated a willingness to allow his son to rule as prince regent. Thinking it was this that was being arranged, Kojong unexpectedly found he had been tricked into relinquishing the throne itself. Thus Sunjong became emperor in July 1907, with the reign title of *Yunghŭi* ("Abundant Prosperity"). When the edict announcing the abdication was made public, the extreme agitation of the stricken people drove them into a rash of massive protest demonstrations, while the building housing the newspaper organ of the Ilchinhoe was destroyed by the mob and Japanese everywhere were attacked.

But Japan quelled this violence with military force and, not content with Kojong's abdication alone, moved to put Korea under a still harsher yoke. A new agreement was signed giving the Japanese Resident-General formal authority to intercede in all matters of internal administration. Specifically, it was now required that the Korean government act "under the guidance" of the Resident-General in regard to reforms in administration, that legislative enactments and major administrative measures receive his prior consent, that appointment and dismissal of high officials be done only with his concurrence, and that his consent be obtained too in the employment of any foreign advisers. The agreement went even further, to make mandatory the appointment to office of Japanese subjects as recommended by the Resident-General. Thus Japan abandoned its previous method of governing through advisers in favor of a so-called system of government by vice-ministers, as numbers of Japanese bureaucrats were appointed in each ministry at the second in command level or to other strategic posts.

Immediately following the signing of this new agreement Japan dissolved the entire remaining Korean army units, already reduced in strength to a relative handful of men (August 1, 1907). In Seoul at that time there were about 3600 troops in two infantry guards regiments and scarcely 400 men in mounted guards, artillery, and transport units, while outside of Seoul there were approximately 4800 infantry soldiers in eight local garrison regiments—a combined strength of barely 8800. Even this pitiful force stood in the way of Japan's determination to work its will in Korea. Accordingly, Japan proceeded to dissolve the Korean army, pleading fiscal stringency and asserting that it was a temporary measure until a conscription system could be introduced. At this point, lacking any capacity at all for self-defense, Korea became a mere puppet, an empty shell of a nation. On the day the army was dissolved the commander of the First Infantry Guards regiment, Pak Sŏng-hwan, killed himself in mortification, while his officers and men took up their weapons and, supported by the troops of the Second Infantry Guards regiment, engaged the Japanese army of occupation in battle in the streets of Seoul. After their ammunition was exhausted they retreated from the city to join forces with the guerrilla bands in the countryside. The garrison troops in the provinces also joined up with these "righteous armies" to continue armed resistance against the Japanese.

Korea Becomes a Japanese Colony

The scheme of imperial Japan to annex Korea, planned from long before and awaiting only a decision on its timing, now at last was to be carried out. In May 1910, Japan appointed General Terauchi Masatake as the new Resident-General, and explicitly entrusted to him the mission of effecting the annexation. While still in Tokyo, before taking up his new post, he had secured an agreement yielding police power in Korea to Japan, and he had beefed up the Japanese gendarmerie forces by 2000 men and given them charge of police functions. Immediately upon arriving in Seoul he ordered publication of the *Hwangsŏng Sinmun, Taehan Minbo, Taehan Maeil Sinbo,* and other Korean newpapers suspended, so as to prevent the public from learning what was transpiring. Then, together with Prime Minister Yi Wan-yong, he formulated the terms of the annexation treaty and finally, on August 22, 1910, secured the prime minister's signature to it. In the aftermath of Kojong's forced abdication in 1907 Yi Wan-yong's house had been burned to the ground by an enraged populace, and in December, 1909, he had suffered stab wounds in an assassination attempt by the young independence activist Yi Chae-myŏng. But not even these acts of violence against him awakened Yi Wan-yong to the enormity of his betrayal, and he proceeded to assure his place in history as an arch traitor to his country. His only concern at the time the annexation agreement was being drafted was how to preserve the position of the royal household and that of his fellow traitors. The treaty now had been concluded but, fearing the intensity of the popular reaction against it, the Japanese were hesitant to make it public immediately. First, to prepare the ground for the announcement, the authorities dissolved Korean patriotic organizations and carried out summary arrests of leading dissidents. Finally, then, on August 29, 1910, Sunjong was forced to issue a proclamation yielding up both his throne and his country. Thus the Korean nation, against the will of its entire people, was handed over to the harsh colonial rule of Japan by a coterie of traitors.

In its preamble, the treaty declared that Japan's annexation of Korea was intended "to promote the common weal of the two nations and to assure permanent peace" in Asia. Japan, however, was not a friend of Korea but its enemy. Japan had annexed Korea to enhance the prosperity of the Japanese people at the expense of the people of Korea. Moreover, in the years ahead Korea would provide Japan a springboard for its invasion of China, which would in fact shatter still further the peace of Asia. Japan, it is clear, merely had cloaked its aggression in high-sounding but empty phrases.

Having made Korea its colony, Japan exercised its rule through a Government-General, which took the place of the former Residency-General. The governor-general was to be appointed from the ranks of Japanese generals or admirals on active duty, and all legislative, executive, and judicial powers resided in his hands alone. The rule of the first governor-general, Terauchi Masatake, was characterized by unmitigated repression. He declared the maintenance of law and order to be the highest priority of his administration, and to achieve this end he employed a gendarmerie police system. In 1911, some 7749 military police, or gendarmes, and 6222 regular police were deployed throughout the country, over half of them Korean auxiliaries recruited from the dregs of Korean society. The commanding officer of the Japanese gendarmerie in Korea served as the director of the national police headquarters in Seoul, while gendarmerie battalion commanders were in charge of police headquarters in each province.

Under such a police system, the slightest word or act by a Korean was potentially subject to punishment. In consequence, in 1912 over 50,000 and in 1918 the incredible number of more than 140,000 Koreans were brought under arrest. In the aftermath of the unsuccessful attempt on Governor-General Terauchi's life by An Myŏng-gŭn in December 1910, over six hundred prominent Koreans were arrested arbitrarily, including Yun Ch'i-ho, Yang Ki-t'ak, Yi Sŭng-hun, and other members of the New People's Association (Sinminhoe), the strongest Korean nationalist organization at that time. Among those arrested one hundred and five subsequently were indicted, so that the incident is known as the "Case of the One Hundred Five" (or the Korean Conspiracy Trial); the case became widely known both in Korea and abroad for the blatant fabrication of the criminal charges against the accused and for the vicious torture to which they were subjected.

In short, Japan made all those who did not cooperate with the rule of its Government-General in Korea subject to arrest. In innumerable cases summary judgments of floggings or fines were meted out without recourse to due judicial proceedings. All newspapers that aired nationalist sentiments were closed down to forestall expression of adverse public opinion. To further intimidate the Korean populace, all Japanese officials and even school teachers were made to wear uniforms and carry swords. Needless to say, all political activity by Koreans also had to be banned. Using the provisions of the 1907 Peace Preservation Law, the Japanese now prohibited meetings for political purposes or public assembly for any purpose, and many additional regulations aimed at inhibiting Korean freedom of expression also were issued.

As an adjunct to the Government-General Japan created a Central Council. Its membership composed of Koreans, it was a consultative body established to discuss and make recommendations on matters referred to it by the governor-general. The president of the Central Council, however, was the Japanese administrative superintendent, the second highest official in the Government-General, and the councillors all were appointed by Japan. The Central Council's initial vice-president, understandably, was Yi Wan-yong, and the others who had collaborated in selling out their country filled nearly all of the councillor positions. Judged by its membership alone, the Central Council clearly could not represent the will of the Korean people. But its character as the creature of its Japanese masters is even more apparent from a look at the range of matters the governor-general referred to it. Instead of being asked to consider important political or economic questions, for example, the Central Council was set the task of studying traditional Korean customs and practices. What the Japanese wanted from the Central Council, in other words, was only information needed by them in ruling Korea. Accordingly, it was simply false for Japan to assert that the Central Council was an instrument through which Koreans could express their will by participating in the political process. In fact, Japan wanted Koreans to make no political utterances whatsoever and, indeed, Japan regarded all Koreans who had any concern for political matters as subversive elements or, worse, openly seditious.

Intensification of the Resistance of the Righteous Armies

Resistance to the Japanese aggression in Korea took many forms. First there was the struggle of the royal house to restore its disintegrating sovereign power. The secret mission to The Hague was such an effort. Some among the *yangban* officialdom had acted in concert with this endeavor. Almost from the beginning, however, the king and his ministers had chosen to place their reliance primarily on outside forces, to avail themselves of the support of one foreign power or another in order to block the Japanese aggression. In the end this policy only forced Korea to satisfy other aggressive appetites; it did nothing to guarantee that support would be forthcoming in Korea's hour of need. Thus, when Russia was defeated in the Russo-Japanese War, there was no way to cope with Japan's unrelenting pressure. Those few officials who did resist the Japanese only made gestures as lone individuals—they did not think to resist by joining forces with the people. The fact is that Kojong and his government feared the censure of the people they governed more than they feared the threat from Japan. This was why they suppressed the Independence Club and why the deliberations on the Protectorate Treaty and the Treaty of Annexation were conducted in secret, without the knowledge of the people. Consequently, under circumstances in which the traitorous pro-Japan elements already were in the cabinet, prepared to do the bidding of the Residency-General, it was impossible for the resistance of the king or a few individuals to thwart Japan's aggression.

Among the Confucian literati there were those who resisted Japan in a way hallowed by tradition—by attempting to bring about the adoption of a national policy of resistance through offering memorials to the throne. At times several hundreds of literati assembled at the palace gates to petition the king for such a policy. But neither the king nor the government, already under the watchful eyes of the Japanese, were able to act on these pleas. In their despair, then, a number of men chose suicide as the only way out. On the other hand, there also were those who engaged in an active, armed struggle against Japan by forming "righteous armies."

The main component of the righteous armies that were organized under the leadership of the literati was the peasantry. But the combat effectiveness of these guerrilla bands was much enhanced when soldiers from the disbanded Korean army joined with the peasant fighters. It already has been related that when the Korean army was disbanded in 1907, the guards units in Seoul battled with the Japanese troops in the streets of the capital, and that when their ammunition ran out they retreated into the countryside and joined forces with the righteous armies. Among the provincial garrisons there was the one in Wŏnju that took up arms in a body under the leadership of Min Kŭng-ho, and then proceeded to inflict a series of defeats on the Japanese—at Wŏnju, Ch'ungju, Yŏju, Ch'unch'ŏn, and elsewhere in central Korea. The Kanghwa garrison under Yu Myŏng-gyu overcame the Japanese forces there and then moved on to Hwanghae province to join up with the righteous armies. In another instance Hŏ Wi, who had resigned his high post and gone into retirement after submitting an anti-Japanese memorial in 1905 attacking the Protectorate Treaty, took command of a force of like-minded literati and disbanded soldiers and was active in Chŏksŏng and other counties in the Imjin river region. Yi In-yŏng, too, was active in Kangwŏn province; Yi Kang-nyŏn operated in the Kangwŏn-North Kyŏngsang area, his guerrilla band augmented by troops from the Andong garrison; and Sin Tol-sŏk fought in Kyŏngsang province. Sin Tol-sŏk is particularly noteworthy as a non-*yangban*, a man of commoner origin who nevertheless commanded a righteous army.

The activities of the righteous armies, as was observed above, began from the time of the assassination of Queen Min in 1895. But these forces had arisen only out of a fierce spirit of resistance against Japan, and they possessed neither military discipline nor weapons of any account. When their ranks were joined by the soldiers disbanded in 1907, however, they acquired both the military organization and the weapons with which they could mount effective resistance. Min Kŭng-ho had several thousand men under his command and both Hŏ Wi and Yi Kang-nyŏn's forces numbered over a thousand. To be sure, none of the many other righteous armies had a strength of more than several hundreds, while there were some bands of only a few score men. Most of these guerrilla bands based themselves in the mountainous areas, attacking Japanese garrisons and destroying the railways and telegraph facilities. Supported by the populace and familiar with the local terrain, these guerrilla fighters were able to compensate for their deficiencies in manpower and in arms.

The righteous armies were particularly active in Kyŏngsang, Kangwŏn, Kyŏnggi, and Hwanghae provinces, but their operations extended over virtually the whole country. There was hardly one county in all of Korea where the guerrilla fighters did not make forays at one time or another. Korean guerrilla units in Kando in southeast Manchuria even crossed the Tumen River to harass Japanese garrisons inside north Korea. In 1907 Yi In-yŏng and Hŏ Wi brought together about 10,000 guerrilla troops from all over the country to attack the Residency-General headquarters, and the advance units were able to penetrate to positions within eight miles of Seoul's East Gate. This incident alone demonstrates how vigorously the righteous armies carried on their struggle against the Japanese. Guerrilla activity reached a peak in 1908 but rapidly declined thereafter, and following the annexation the scene of operations shifted to Manchuria and the Russian Maritime Territory. There the guerrilla soldiers became independence fighters and dauntlessly continued their warfare against Japan. By 1910 more than 17,600 guerrilla fighters had given their lives in the struggle, including Min Kŭng-ho, Hŏ Wi, Yi Kang-nyŏn, and other commanders. Although the following are official Japanese statistics, they provide an indication of the dimensions of the operations of the righteous armies. In fact, however, the scale of operations must have been much larger than shown here.

SCALE OF OPERATIONS OF KOREA'S RIGHTEOUS ARMIES

YEAR	GUERRILLAS UNDER ARMS	NUMBER OF CLASHES WITH JAPANESE FORCES
1907	44,116	323
1908	69,832	1,451
1909	25,763	898
1910	1,891	147
Total		2,819

3. Japanese Economic Aggression and Korean Capital

The Japanese Land Grab

After the opening of the ports, Japanese traders had penetrated into the Korean villages and through a variety of methods seized more and more of the peasants' land. Subsequently, when major Japanese financiers began actively to invest in Korean farmland, the land grab greatly accelerated. It has been observed that in mid-1904 Japan even went so far as to attempt to take over large tracts of Korean land by force, under the pretext of bringing uncultivated areas into production. But this outrageous demand foundered against the intense opposition of Korean public opinion. The recently formed Agriculture and Mining Company, set up by Yi To-jae and other Korean businessmen in collaboration with a number of power- ful officials, asserted that the opening of new lands to cultivation was a task to be performed by Koreans themselves, not one to be put into Jap- anese hands, and the company received permission from the government for the undertaking. At that time, too, the Korea Preservation Society (Poanhoe) initiated a public campaign against the Japanese demand through public lectures and other pronouncements. In consequence Japan withdrew its proposal to take over uncultivated Korean lands. Nevertheless, after the establishment of the Residency-General, Japan enacted a "Law for the Development of Uncultivated State Lands" and in this way finally attained its objective.

At this point Japanese entrepreneurs vied with one another to establish companies that seized possession not only of uncultivated state land but even of the paddy lands that the Korean government formerly had set aside for the support of the military, government agencies, and such state services as the network of post stations. Beginning with the Korea Agriculture Company, Ltd. in 1904, a number of Japanese companies with such names as Korea Enterprises and Sanin Agricultural Products were formed and quickly acquired large tracts of land, initially in the granary region of the three southern provinces but before long throughout the whole country, and their acquisitions of Korean farmland kept growing. The Oriental Development Company was particularly notorious; established in 1908, in its first eighteen months of operation it acquired possession of about 30,000 *chŏngbo* (73,500 acres) of land. Along with this accelerat- ing land grab went a dramatic increase in the numbers of immigrant Jap- anese farmers. At first some of the Japanese farmers came as owner-cul- tivators, but on the whole they were landlords bent on increasing their landholdings.

The Japanese land grab was furthered as well by expropriation, under the pretext of needing land for railroad rights of way or for military in- stallations. In these instances state-owned land was taken without com- pensation, while private land had to be purchased by the Korean govern- ment and then presented to the Japanese—although the government was able to pay for the land only after first obtaining loans from Japan. In the most flagrant cases Japanese speculators would swell their profits by ferreting out information as to where a railroad would be built, buying up the right of way from the Korean owners for a song, and then demanding exorbitant prices from the Korean government.

After the annexation, with Korea reduced to the status of a colony, the Japanese seizure of Korean land was still further accelerated through the mechanism of a comprehensive cadastral survey, which was conducted with the full weight of the colonial regime behind it. It began to be carried out in earnest with the establishment of the Land Survey Bureau in 1910. The land survey law was promulgated in 1912 and required that a landholder, in order to have his ownership rights recognized, report his name, address, and the name under which his land was registered—as well as the type of land use, the dimensions, and other pertinent data. This report was to be made to the director of the Land Survey Bureau within a comparatively short stipulated time period.

Koreans, however, felt very uneasy about reporting their landholdings to the Japanese Government-General. Moreover, the registration procedures were not adequately made known to the general farming population and many peasants were negligent about making their reports. Nevertheless, all those who failed to register their land had it confiscated by the Government-General. In addition, all land that formerly had been allocated to state instrumentalities, such as the Department of the Royal Household or the various government offices or even the post stations, automatically became the property of the Government-General. This is because the Japanese regarded the ownership rights to privately held land to be vested in the landlord (incidentally according no recognition to the rights of the tenant farmer) and to state land in the government agency that had control over it. The Government-General thus became Korea's largest landowner. What is more, by the provisions of a newly enacted forest lands law, all former state owned lands of this type also became the property of the Government-General. In consequence, according to statistics for 1930, the combined total of agricultural and forest land held by the Government-General was 8,880,000 *chŏngbo*, 40% of the total land area of Korea.

A portion of the land thus taken over by the Government-General was sold at a fraction of its worth to companies under Japanese management, in particular the Oriental Development Company, or to Japanese immigrants. The area of Korean land held by the mammoth Oriental Development Company alone, in fact, amounted to nearly 110,000 *chŏngbo*, 269,000 acres, by 1930. The tenant rents received in one year from these holdings reached the huge amount of 500,000 *sŏk* (about 2.5 million bushels, or some 3% of the country's total harvest) of rice and in addition probably twice that amount of other grains. Accordingly, the so-called cadastral survey belied its name, for its effect was to enable the Japanese Government-General and Japanese companies and individuals as well to become great landowners.

Japan's Monopolization of Korea's Natural Resources

Japan was interested not only in land but in all of Korea's natural resources. For the further development of its capitalist economy Japan had to convert to the gold standard, and it relied on Korea for an assured supply of that precious metal. Accordingly, Japan took gold from Korea by whatever predatory methods, and the availability of Korean gold played a decisive role in Japan's adoption of the gold standard. Following the annexation the Government-General surveyed Korea's mineral deposits and turned them over to the Japanese *zaibatsu* conglomerates for exploitation. The result was a dramatic increase in mining output. Such minerals as gold, silver, iron, lead, tungsten, and coal registered increases that were five- or six-fold in some cases or even several thousand times in others. The expansion of mining production was particularly marked during World War I, since Japan was an important supplier of raw materials to the Allies. The following table graphically depicts the phenomenal growth in the output of minerals from Korea's mines, especially toward the end of the war from those owned by Japanese concerns.

MINING OUTPUT BY NATIONALITY OF MINE OWNERS

unit: Japanese yen

YEAR	KOREAN	JAPANESE	OTHERS	TOTAL
1909	325,979	1,297,074	2,964,562	4,587,615
1910	331,248	1,968,034	3,768,670	6,067,952
1911	296,019	1,401,569	4,488,370	6,185,958
1912	181,769	1,683,931	4,949,418	6,815,118
1913	276,359	1,934,072	5,987,095	8,197,526
1914	313,335	1,783,577	6,425,506	8,522,418
1915	384,010	2,820,682	7,311,274	10,515,966
1916	1,042,284	3,622,695	9,413,209	14,078,188
1917	857,839	7,615,982	8,584,281	17,058,102
1918	299,110	24,673,745	5,865,219	30,838,074

Japan also encouraged reforestation, asserting that its purpose was to safeguard Korea's forestry resources, but in fact Japan took far more timber than was replaced by new plantings. Reforestation of the hills around the cities was promoted, but on the other hand the stands of large trees on the more remote mountain slopes were felled. This trend grew only more pronounced after 1920.

Japan had begun quite early to take steps to protect Japanese fishermen. The illegal incorporation of Tokto island into Japan proper was prompted by this consideration. After the annexation Japanese fishermen were encouraged to emigrate to Korea, with the result that their numbers among Japanese residents in Korea increased rapidly. Their fishing boats and

THE FISHING INDUSTRY BY NATIONALITY OF OPERATOR

YEAR	KOREAN OPERATORS			JAPANESE OPERATORS		
	VESSELS	NO. OF CREW	VALUE OF CATCH(in yen)	VESSELS	NO. OF CREW	VALUE OF CATCH(in yen)
1912	10,502	160,809	5,989,375	5,653	22,488	6,629,981
1913	18,570	114,160	5,055,051	12,059	49,646	6,001,232
1914	22,158	177,791	5,615,459	11,135	48,451	6,449,226
1915	30,187	261,213	6,365,669	11,995	54,772	6,869,272
1916	34,627	216,295	7,960,982	10,621	63,186	7,994,940
1917	45,892	247,139	9,760,592	11,897	70,184	11,152,700
1918	39,000	272,077	14,670,068	14,118	74,349	18,193,334

equipment were superior to those of their Korean competitors, and so the Japanese share of the fishing catch swelled disproportionately. This may be seen in the above table.

Thus the exploitation of Korea's natural resources was predominantly carried on by Japanese companies, with the benevolent backing of the Government-General. In fact the Government-General was itself simply another, and by far the largest, Japanese entrepreneurial complex in Korea. The Government-General operated all such facilities as railways, harbors, communications, and airports, as well as establishing monopolies on products like ginseng, salt, tobacco, and opium, and the profits from all these enterprises were enormous. In short, Japanese businesses, with the Government-General itself in the forefront, came close to monopolizing Korea's natural resources and, operating under such favorable conditions, reaped ever fatter profits.

Japanese Control of Public Service Enterprises

With regard as well to public service enterprises like transportation and communications, it is abundantly clear that Japan's aim from the beginning was to have exclusive control in Japanese hands. Initially Japan had argued that its restrictive policies in this area were necessary to block the inroads of foreign capital. But in making this assertion Japan conveniently ignored the fact that it too was a foreign country looking for opportunities to invest its predatory capital in Korea. In any case, the Japanese Residency-General had devoted considerable effort to developing the transport and communications links Japan needed to further its objectives in Korea, and these activities were carried on in turn by the Government-General.

Korea's first telegraph facilities were installed in 1885, linking Seoul and Inch'ŏn with Ŭiju at the mouth of the Yalu. This line soon was extended to Feng-huang (now Feng-ch'eng) inside Manchuria in response to the need that was perceived by both Korea and Ch'ing China for a means of rapid communication between the two countries. But this Seoul-Ŭiju line in its entirety was under the control of China, and its construction was actually a corollary to China's aggressive Korea policy. The Seoul-Pusan telegraph line was built in 1888 and was linked to Japan by undersea cable. The Seoul-Pusan facility initially was operated by the Korean government but during the Russo-Japanese War it passed completely into Japanese hands. It then was placed under the administration of the Residency-General and in 1910 its operation automatically devolved upon the Government-General.

The postal service that had been established in 1884 collapsed with the failure of the 1884 coup. A postal bureau was created anew in 1895 and in 1900 it undertook for the first time to exchange mail with foreign countries. But this service too fell under Japanese control at the time of the Russo-Japanese War and subsequently passed from the hands of the Residency-

General into those of the Government-General.

The laying of railroads was undertaken from the beginning in the furtherance of Japan's aggressive aims. Japan looked upon Inch'ŏn as the gateway through which its military would move into the capital region, and so it exacted the consent of the Korean government to build the needed Inch'ŏn to Seoul rail line. But before Japan's plans for constructing this link could materialize, the Seoul-Inch'ŏn railway concession was turned over, in 1896, to an American enterprise. Work on the roadbed began in the next year but was stymied by Japanese opposition, whereupon the project reverted to Japan and was completed in 1900. Korea's main rail artery, the Seoul-Pusan and Seoul-Ŭiju lines, was a military necessity for Japan's prosecution of the Russo-Japanese War, and for that reason Japan pushed through its construction with great urgency. Thus built for military objectives, the line presently came under the railroad bureau of the Residency-General and then passed to the Government-General. Electric power services, on the other hand, were inaugurated in 1898 by a company capitalized jointly by Korean and U. S. interests, and therefore its streetcar and electric lighting facilities were not taken over by the Residency-General. But these too were brought under the control of the Government-General after the annexation.

Thus modern transportation and communications facilities were built and operated almost exclusively by Japan, not for the benefit of Korea but in the interests of the colonial power itself. The railroads well illustrate this point: built with Korean labor mobilized by force, and on Korean land bought at paltry prices, Korean railroads were scarcely utilized by Koreans but mainly served the Japanese. In consequence these modern facilities were more cursed than welcomed by the Korean people.

Japanese Control of Finance

The Japanese fiscal adviser who was appointed in 1904 under the Korea-Japan agreement of August of that year, Megata Tanetarō, possessed broad powers, in fact virtual control, over Korean fiscal administration. The task he first addressed himself to, in 1905, was the reform of Korean currency, which at that time consisted mainly of the so-called *yŏpchŏn* brass coin and a nickel coin. On the ground that many of the coins in circulation were of substandard fineness, Megata had the existing currency replaced by coins newly minted by a Japanese bank, Daiichi Ginkō. In accordance with the exchange procedures laid down by Megata, the old nickel coins were classified into three grades, depending on their intrinsic worth, and A-grade coins were assigned a value of 2.5 "cents" (*sen*) in the new coinage and B-grade one cent, but C-grade coins were declared to be valueless and therefore non-exchangeable. However, the C-grade coins represented two-thirds of the nickel coins then in circulation, and the consequence was that Korean businessmen sustained fearsome losses. Worse, many Korean merchants had no faith in the new currency and so before the exchange went into effect they instead invested their old coins in land or houses, thus ending up in the serious predicament of having no capital with which to finance their businesses. In fact, however, the new currency appreciated in value, bringing windfall profits·to the Japanese. In short, the result of the currency reform was to open the way still more widely to the economic advance of Japanese commercial interests. Not only this, but it became the decisive factor in enabling Japanese banks to dominate the financial sector in Korea.

Japanese financial institutions appeared in Korea just after the opening of the ports. By around 1900 a number of Japanese banks—the Daiichi Ginkō most importantly but many others as well—had established branch or agency offices in Korea and had come to play the leading role in the country's financial activities. Early in 1905, when the Korea branch of the Daiichi Ginkō was given authority to issue currency, it assumed the role of a central bank for Korea, buying gold and silver bullion, making loans to the Government, collecting customs duties at the open ports, and otherwise undertaking a wide range of central banking functions. With the establishment of the Bank of Korea in 1909 these functions became its responsibility, but the manager of the Daiichi Ginkō's general offices in Seoul was concurrently appointed to the governorship of the new bank. Then after the annexation, in 1911, the Bank of Korea was transformed into the Bank of Chōsen (the Japanese pronunciation of Chosŏn and the name by which Japan called Korea) and it was given the duties of a central bank. A major Japanese bank of another kind was the Industrial Bank (Shokusan Ginkō), originally established in 1906 under another name to assist in the development of agriculture and industry in Korea. After Korea became a colony, the Shokusan Ginkō became an instrument for supporting mostly Japanese businessmen and farmers.

During the Protectorate period the Korean government was forced to borrow substantial amounts from Japan. The borrowed funds were needed to finance the activities of the Japanese Residency-General in Korea, such as supporting the newly established banking institutions, improving roads, and employing Japanese officials. Loans were obtained both from the Japanese government and from Japanese banks, through the intermediacy of the Residency-General. For example, the Daiichi Ginkō provided a loan of 3,000,000 yen to underwrite the currency reform, then handled the changeover itself and made a huge profit. The Japanese policy of paying for its programs in Korea by Korean government borrowings was carried out particularly aggressively just prior to the annexation, and by 1910 Korea's debt had reached the immense sum of 45,000,000 yen.

The burden of this debt only made the Korean government all the more dependent on Japan. Because of this there was a nationwide movement to redeem the debt, by collecting suitably scaled contributions from the entire Korean populace. In a certain sense this is what happened in the end, for after the annexation the Japanese Government-General repaid the debt from taxes collected from the Korean people.

The Difficulties Faced by Native Korean Enterprises

It was in the wake of the Independence Club's ambitious efforts to create a public spirited concern for Korea's ongoing development as a nation, and thus in the closing years of the nineteenth century, that modern entrepreneurial activities financed with Korean capital began to flourish. During this period such activities were undertaken in a variety of commercial and industrial fields, not through government initiative but by private Korean companies.

About this same time the modern mercantile associations that had been organized by the wholesale merchants at the ports began to change into something like chambers of commerce. This followed the government's promulgation of "Regulations Governing Chambers of Commerce" in 1895, and by 1905 such a businessmen's association, the Hansŏng (Seoul) Chamber of Commerce, had been established in the capital as well. The Russo-Japanese War had erupted by then, Japan had tightened its political hold on Korea, and the Korean business community was struggling in the grip of the severe financial panic brought on by Megata's currency reform. The Hansŏng Chamber of Commerce, then, was established by the businessmen of Seoul to devise a means of saving themselves from financial disaster. Their immediate objective was to find a way to overcome their critical shortage of working capital, and when their proposals to the government went unheeded due to Japanese obstruction, they decided in 1906 to found their own bank, which they called the First Bank of Korea (Hanil Ŭnhaeng). In addition to the main banking facility they built a merchandise display hall, and they also published a monthly commerce and industry bulletin in which they provided a wide variety of information concerning domestic and international economic trends to their fellow businessmen. But the Hansŏng Chamber of Commerce was dissolved after Korea became a Japanese colony, and Korean businessmen then were absorbed into the Japanese dominated Keijō (Seoul) Chamber of Commerce.

Korean entrepreneurs also began to take an interest in modern industry at this same time, from about 1897. They built modern manufacturing facilities out of an awareness that they could compete successfully against Japanese business only by producing quality goods not inferior to those made in Japan. The field of enterprise in which there was most interest was textiles, and a number of well-known textile concerns were founded during these years—An Kyŏng-su's Korea Textile Works in 1897, the Chongno Textile Company established in 1900 by the old government licensed cotton cloth shop on Chongno, the Kim Tŏk-ch'ang Textile Company in 1902, a modernized rebuilding of his antiquated factory, and others. In addition to textiles, factories for ceramics, rice cleaning, tobacco products, and milling gradually increased in number.

As the foreign powers fought with each other to obtain concessions to construct railroads in Korea, the conviction arose that rail lines had to be built with Korean capital as well. This was the purpose behind the establishment in 1898 of the Pusan and Southwest Perimeter Railway Company headed by Pak Ki-jong, which planned to link Pusan with the region at the mouth of the Naktong River. Other railway companies followed, in particular the Korea Railway Company formed in 1899 to construct trunk lines between Seoul and Ŭiju, Seoul and Wŏnsan, and from Wŏnsan northward in Hamgyŏng province. But capital was inadequate to start construction, and when the government established a railway bureau in 1900 it decided to proceed with the construction of these lines as a direct government undertaking. A new government agency, then, was created to be responsible for the Seoul-Ŭiju line, and in 1902 its director, Yi Yong-ik, held a ceremony marking the beginning of construction. Delays ensued, however, and when the Russo-Japanese War broke out in 1904 Japan took over the right to build this vital rail link.

As for shipping, after the joint government-private venture of the early 1890's ceased to operate, it was not until 1897 or so that a purely private shipping industry began to emerge. In 1900 several cargo carrying lines were founded (Korea Joint Mail and Shipping, Inch'ŏn Mail and Shipping, Inhan Steamship Company) and subsequently full service freight forwarding and shipping companies came into existence.

Nevertheless, these commercial and industrial activities carried on with native Korean capital were rather insignificant in comparison with those of the Japanese. Opportunities for the development of enterprises by Korean capital were still further restricted after the annexation in 1910. The Residency-General already had enacted a law to regulate all business companies, and in 1911 this law was toughened to give the Japanese Government-General absolute discretionary power over the formation and dissolution of business concerns. Accordingly, if even Japanese companies were restricted in their freedom to develop by Japanese controls, then clearly the problems experienced by companies operating with Korean capital would be far more serious. This situation is graphically evident in the following table giving statistics on industrial output in 1917 by nationality of factory owner. The number of factories owned by Koreans was not so much less than those owned by Japanese, but the Korean companies were capitalized in only one-eighteenth the amount of the Japanese and their output was scarcely one-tenth as great. This reflects the fact, of course, that industrial concerns in Korean hands mostly were small-scale, almost trifling operations.

The fundamental reason why Korean owned industry remained undeveloped was that, in the context of a Japanese colonial regime backed by military force, it was inevitable that access to capital in Korea would be controlled by Japanese banks. Beyond that, the critical shortage of financing

FACTORIES BY INDUSTRY AND NATIONALITY OF OWNER IN 1917

INDUSTRY	OWNER	NUMBER OF FACTORIES	CAPITAL (in yen)	PRODUCTION (in yen)
Cotton Cloth, Dyeing and Weaving	Korean	70	236,390	612,073
	Japanese	36	6,894,989	6,230,739
Paper, Pulp	Korean	51	15,886	58,022
	Japanese	4	15,000	144,116
Hides and Tanning	Korean	37	52,900	229,139
	Japanese	8	1,991,036	3,531,663
Ceramic Products	Korean	115	137,720	169,350
	Japanese	67	506,500	631,944
Soap, Fertilizer	Japanese	20	474,200	763,627
Metalworking	Korean	106	202,250	378,695
	Japanese	57	279,270	1,590,729
Lumber, Wood-working	Korean	22	33,917	80,529
	Japanese	43	544,010	1,344,906
Milling, Rice Cleaning	Korean	154	546,420	5,855,153
	Japanese	152	3,682,906	41,685,923
	Other	1	500	4,500
Noodles, Con-fectioneries	Japanese	36	170,250	350,974
Tobacco Products	Korean	5	211,880	539,627
	Japanese	21	2,214,413	6,016,332
Brewing	Korean	6	101,000	97,216
	Japanese	108	1,968,485	1,835,318
	Other	3	23,000	53,363
Ice, Salt, Soft Drinks	Japanese	47	786,281	1,321,951
Printing	Korean	11	103,110	65,546
	Japanese	59	617,965	1,400,014
Smelting and Refining	Korean	2	15,000	10,330
	Japanese	26	8,832,555	14,801,381
	Other	7	2,207,582	5,975,230
Electricity, Gas	Korean-Japanese	3	384,733	134,769
	Japanese	17	4,402,548	2,176,297
	Other	1	850,000	14,442
Other Industries	Korean	26	226,320	268,073
	Korean-Japanese	1	25,000	22,000
	Japanese	35	279,950	575,671
	Other	1	5,000	2,545
Total	Korean	605	1,882,793	8,363,753
	Korean-Japanese	4	409,733	156,769
	Japanese	736	33,660,358	84,401,585
	Other	13	3,086,082	6,050,080

Note: Factories with less than five employees and government owned enterprises are not included.

engendered by the currency reform forced Korean entrepreneurs into a desperate struggle for enough capital just to survive. The first banking facility established by Koreans was Kim Chong-han's Bank of Chosŏn in 1896, and a number of other Korean banks—including the First Bank of Korea noted above—subsequently came into existence. These banks were founded by rich Seoul merchants with the support of former government officials, and in 1903 the government even promulgated an ordinance for the creation of a central bank. But these were all small scale efforts that could not compare with the banks the Japanese had launched, and even the Korean government's plans for its own central bank failed to materialize.

4. The Patriotic Enlightenment Movement

Activities of Political and Social Organizations

After the demise of the Independence Club many other political and social organizations were formed, contributing greatly to raising the political and social consciousness of the educated class, especially in the cities. Believing that the solution to the political and social problems Korea then faced was to be sought in the strength of the Korean people themselves, these organizations were active in promoting programs for the edification of the Korean people as a whole.

The first such organization was the Korea Preservation Society (Poanhoe) inaugurated in 1904. It was organized by Song Su-man and others in response to the Japanese effort to seize possession of Korea's uncultivated land, and by arousing public opposition through a campaign of public lectures and pronouncements, in the end it succeeded in forcing Japan to withdraw its demand. Under the leadership of Yi Sang-sŏl the Poanhoe continued to grow, developing into an ongoing organization with broader objectives, but before long it was dissolved under Japanese pressure.

This political and social movement not only fought against Japanese aggression but also waged a struggle for internal political reform. This was the objective, for example, of the Kongjinhoe organized in 1904 by former members of the Independence Club. A year later the Kongjinhoe evolved into the Society for the Study of Constitutional Government (Hŏnjŏng Yŏn'guhoe), the position of which was that both the monarch and the government must observe the nation's laws and that the people must be free to enjoy the rights guaranteed to them under law. A number of other political and social organizations, including one called the Society of Spokesmen for the People (Inmin Taeŭihoe), came into existence around this time.

The activities of such political organizations as these were anathema alike to both the Korean government and to Japan, and ultimately a ban was placed on public political assembly in Seoul. When it thus became impossible to carry on political activities lawfully, social and cultural movements arose that sought to establish a foundation for the recovery of Korean sovereignty through promoting the development of native industry and making educational opportunities more widely available to the Korean populace. The major organization with a program of this sort was the Korea Self-Strengthening Society (Taehan Chaganghoe), formed in 1906 as the successor to the Society for the Study of Constitutional Government. It was this organization that led the opposition to Japan's demand for Kojong's abdication in the wake of the secret mission he sent to The Hague, and in consequence it was forced to dissolve by the Residency-General. It soon reappeared under the name of the Korea Association (Taehan Hyŏphoe) and continued its social and cultural programs.

In 1907 the Association for Redemption of the National Debt was organized to launch a campaign to repay the immense amounts the government had borrowed from abroad, nearly all from Japan. This was a plan to liquidate the huge obligation artfully forced upon the government by Japan, a plan born out of the belief that the existence of the debt threatened the nation's independence. Men from Taegu like Sŏ Sang-don and Kim Kwang-je were the first to develop the concept that the nation's borrowings might be repaid through the united efforts of the Korean populace, but the idea quickly spread to Seoul and then throughout the whole country. The various organs of public opinion, the *Korea Daily News* (*Taehan Maeil Sinbo*), the *Imperial Post* (*Cheguk Sinmun*), the *Capital Gazette* (*Hwangsŏng Sinmun*), the *Independence News* (*Mansebo*), and others were particularly active in collecting "pledges for the nation" (*ŭigŭm*). Toward the common end men joined in a no-smoking movement while women and girls responded by selling their ornamental hairpins and rings. The Residency-General looked upon this as an anti-Japanese movement and used every means to suppress it. False charges of embezzlement of contributions entrusted to the *Taehan Maeil Sinbo* were brought against its editor, Yang Ki-t'ak, and he was placed under arrest. In the end the charges were dropped and he was released, but the movement to redeem the nation's foreign debt had lost its momentum and was thwarted.

As both political and social movements came under the many restrictions imposed by the vigilant Residency-General, Koreans finally resorted to forming clandestine organizations. The New People's Association (Sinminhoe), formed in 1907 around members of the press, military men, and businessmen—men such as An Ch'ang-ho, Yi Tong-hwi, Yi Kap, Yang Ki-t'ak, and Yi Sŭng-hun, was in one vital dimension such a secret organization. While it openly promoted Korean industry by establishing a ceramics factory, promoted Korean education by establishing schools, and promoted Korean public awareness by operating bookstores, the Sinminhoe also was making preparations for armed operations—to promote Korean independence. But the organization's directors all were arrested in connection with the so-called Case of the One Hundred Five in 1911, with the result that the activities of the Sinminhoe were brought to a standstill.

Development of a Korean Press

In consequence of the greatly heightened political and social consciousness of the Korean general public, especially the businessmen and intellectuals, it became essential to publish newspapers—modern organs of opinion through which this aroused public might speak. Korea's first newspaper can be said to have been the thrice-monthly *Hansŏng Sunbo*, published by the government's newly created Office of Culture and Information in 1883 through the efforts of Kim Ok-kyun and other members of the Progressive Party. True, this was a government publication with first priority given to government news, but it also played a significant role in informing its readers on current developments within Korea and abroad, and also in introducing the new Western civilization. But it stopped publication after only one year due to the failure of Kim Ok-kyun's 1884 coup.

It was then in 1896 with Sŏ Chae-p'il's founding of *The Independent* that a genuinely modern newspaper first appeared. At first published three times a week, *The Independent* subsequently became a daily and, writing only in the Korean *han'gŭl* alphabet, it provided impartial news reports to the general public while at the same time fighting to preserve the nation's independence and expand the rights accorded its citizens. *The Independent* also served as a vehicle for expressing the views of those of the new intellectual class within the Independence Club who had been exposed to Western culture.

Another newspaper, the *Capital Gazette* (*Hwangsŏng Sinmun*) founded by Namgung Ŏk in 1898, also served as an organ of the Independence Club, but it spoke rather for what may be called the Confucianist reform element. Appealing on the whole to readers from the middle and upper classes who were proficient in classical Chinese, the *Capital Gazette* published in a mixed Chinese-*han'gŭl* script. Hence its pages did not convey a sense of modernized values in quite the same way the vernacular *The Independent* did. But the *Capital Gazette* was in the very forefront of the resistance to Japanese aggression. The response of its editor, Chang Chi-yŏn, to the signing of the Protectorate Treaty in 1905 is justly famed: together with reporting the full particulars of how the treaty came into being, he inflamed public opinion with an editorial titled "Today We Cry Out in Lamentation," and to avoid Japanese censorship (still exercised on the basis of military security regulations put into effect during the Russo-Japanese War), he had the paper delivered free house to house. After denouncing Japan's perfidious aggression and bemoaning the incompetence of the Korean government, Chang Chi-yŏn closed his editorial with these words of raging indignation:

> Alas! What sorrow! O now enslaved twenty million countrymen of mine!
> Are we to live or are we to die? Our Korean nationhood, nurtured over four
> thousand years since Tan'gun and Kija—is it thus in a single night to be so
> abruptly extinguished, forever? What sorrow, oh my countrymen!

In the same year, 1898, that the *Capital Gazette* appeared, Yi Chong-myŏn and his associates began publication of the *Imperial Post* (*Cheguk Sinmun*). This was a purely vernacular newspaper that aimed at a readership from the middle and lower classes and among women. Accordingly, its political overtones were muted and it concentrated instead on social issues.

When Japanese censorship tightened and newspapers lost the freedom to criticize openly Japan's policies of aggression, the English journalist Ernest T. Bethell joined with Yang Ki-t'ak to found the bilingual *Korea Daily News* (*Taehan Maeil Sinbo*), in 1905. Since it was controlled by an Englishman, and Japan and England were allies, the *Korea Daily News* was able to remain free of Japanese censorship. Over the door to the newspaper offices a sign was hung proclaiming "No Entry to Japanese," and the paper proceeded to attack Japanese acts of aggression with impunity. The *Korea Daily News* used the mixed Chinese-Korean script, but later it published a purely *han'gŭl* edition designed to reach a broader public, and there was also the English language edition for foreign readers. To counteract its influence the Japanese authorities had a variety of newspapers published under individual Japanese ownership, but none of these was a match for the *Korea Daily News*. It was this paper, too, that stunned the Japanese with the publication of Kojong's personal letter denying that he had approved the Protectorate Treaty and appealing for the protection of the Western powers. The Japanese subjected Bethell to all sorts of harassment and also pressed charges against him in the British consular court. Before long, then, he felt compelled to sever his connection with the paper, but the *Korea Daily News* continued to publish as before.

The next year, in 1906, Son Pyŏng-hŭi, O Se-ch'ang, and other Ch'ŏndogyo (the new name for the Tonghak religion) leaders founded the *Independence News* (*Mansebo*), and the particular target of its criticism was the pro-Japanese Ilchinhoe. In 1909, again, the Korea Association began publication of the *Korea People's Press* (*Taehan Minbo*), and it too set itself squarely against the Ilchinhoe.

Thus the organs of the Korean press made a major contribution to raising the level of political consciousness of the Korean people. The Korean newspapers of that day already boldly proclaimed that the armed struggle against Japan was being waged by "righteous armies," not by rebels as the Japanese would have it. This explains why the first Japanese resident-general, Itō Hirobumi, once said that a single word in a Korean newspaper had greater power to move the Korean people than a hundred words of his. And this is why, by 1907, the Residency-General had enacted a law governing newspaper publication, by which the native Korean press was brought under strict control. The difficulties thus faced by the Korean press were compounded after the annexation in 1910 when, with the *Korea Daily News* essentially the only remaining organ that spoke for the people, it too was converted into a mouthpiece for the Government-General, under the abridged name of the *Daily News* (*Maeil Sinbo*). During the period of the protectorate Koreans overseas also published newspapers—the *New Korea People's Press* (*Sinhan Minbo*) in the United States and the *Mainstream* (*Haejo Sinmun*) in Vladivostok, and these had some circulation in Korea as well. But in 1908 these too were banned, and Koreans thus became a people without a press to speak for them.

The Growing Passion for Education

In 1886 the Korean government established a special institute (called the Yugyŏng Kongwŏn) to provide education in the new knowledge from the West, and after the 1894 reforms a new educational system was created, with a new curriculum offered in government schools of several types—from primary and middle schools to normal schools and schools for foreign languages. In 1895 King Kojong handed down an edict on education for the nation's future, in which he stressed the importance of education in these words:

> When one looks at the state of affairs in the world, one finds that in all those nations that maintain their independence through wealth and power and thus have gained ascendancy, the citizens are enlightened in their knowledge. Enlightened knowledge is attained through excellence of education, and so education truly is of fundamental importance in preserving our nation.

But the government schools on the whole were established to train future officials and they were attended mainly by the sons of high-ranking *yangban*. Accordingly these schools could not meet the demands of the time.

The passion for education during this period burned still more brightly in the public at large. Numerous private schools were established, serving the growing interest in the education of the younger generation. That "knowledge is power" was a conviction shared by the whole of the intellectual class. In consequence, many Korean patriots who had been active in political movements directly committed themselves to educational endeavors, with the intention thus of laying the foundation for an independent Korea. This phenomenon became still more pronounced after Korea became a Japanese protectorate in 1905, since at that point open political activity became almost impossible.

The first modern private school was the Wŏnsan Academy (Wŏnsan Haksa) founded at Wŏnsan in 1883. It was established by Chŏng Hyŏn-sŏk, the magistrate of Tŏgwŏn county (in which Wŏnsan is located) and a man of progressive views, in response to the request of the Wŏnsan Traders Association and other local residents. It is significant that Korea's very first modern school was established at the initiative of the residents of a newly opened port city, with their own resources, in response to the challenge the nation confronted from abroad. Three years later, in 1886, the Paejae school and several other private institutions were founded by American missionary organizations. Following the Protectorate Treaty of 1905, however, private schools were established by the Koreans themselves in almost unending succession. Meanwhile, with the founding of Ewha Women's School by U. S. missionaries in 1886, Korea's first educational institution for women came into being, and subsequently several other girls schools were established under Korean auspices. These schools performed a vital role in freeing Korean women from their subservient position in traditional *yangban* society. In the scant few years before Korea fell completely under Japanese colonial domination, the number of private schools that were founded reached some 3000, being particularly numerous in the northern half of the country. The listing herebelow of a number of the more important private schools reveals several aspects of this phenomenon.

Those most eager to establish private schools were not from the *yangban* class but from the public at large. Many of those educated in the new schools also were of non-*yangban* origin. The subject matter taught at these schools in the main was the new Western learning and thought. There was instruction in history, geography, politics, and law, and also in such subjects as arithmetic and algebra. The private schools of that day served not only to disseminate the new learning but also are renowned as hotbeds of the nationalist movement. Debates, oratorical contests, and campaigns of various sorts were held under the sponsorship of these schools, fanning the patriotic ardor of the students. Some of those who entered the new schools already were advanced in years, while one also could find students at higher level schools who were active as teachers at lower level schools. Conservative elements in Korean society remained convinced of the impropriety of the new education, but the private schools nevertheless continued to flourish, wrapped in the mantle of the growing nationalist fervor.

Japan was not at all pleased with the existence of these private schools. Accordingly, a law was enacted during the Residency-General period requiring that private schools be operated only with government sanction, and that only authorized textbooks be used. As a result many of the private schools were forced to close. After the annexation Japan's educational policy changed, as the Government-General put emphasis on a vocational education that would instruct Koreans in simple manual skills. One reason for this was Japan's fear that, if given a higher level of education, Koreans would be critical of the colonial administration and would actively embrace the cause of Korean independence. But beyond this, seeing no need to produce future leaders of a Korean nation, Japan's only concern was to educate Koreans to perform menial tasks for Japanese bureaucrats and

PRIVATE SCHOOLS OF THE LATE YI PERIOD

YEAR FOUNDED	NAME OF SCHOOL	FOUNDER	LOCATION
1883	Wŏnsan Academy	Chŏng Hyŏn-sŏk	Wŏnsan, Hamgyŏng
1886	Paejae Academy	U.S. Methodists (North)	Seoul
	Ewha Girls School	//	Seoul
	Kyŏngsin School	U.S. Presbyterians (Northern)	Seoul
1890	Chŏngsin Girls School	//	Seoul
1897	Sungsil School	//	P'yŏngyang, P'yŏngan
1898	Paehwa Girls School	U.S.Methodists (South)	Seoul
1903	Sungŭi Girls School	U.S.Presbyterians (Northern)	P'yŏngyang, P'yŏngan
1904	Hosudon Girls School	U.S.Methodists (South)	Kaesŏng, Kyŏnggi
	Young Men's Academy	Chŏn Tŏk-ki	Seoul
1905	Posŏng School	Yi Yong-ik	Seoul
	Yangjŏng School	Ŏm Chu-ik	Seoul
	Hwimun School	Min Yŏng-hwi	Seoul
1906	Sinsŏng (Boys) and Posŏng Girls School	U.S. Presbyterians (Northern)	Sŏnch'ŏn, P'yŏngan
	Chinmyŏng Girls School	Lady Ŏm	Seoul
	Sungmyŏng Girls School	Lady Ŏm	Seoul
	Poin School	Poin School Association	Seoul
	Yanggyu (Girls) School	Chin Hak-sin	Seoul
	Chungdong School	Sin Kyu-sik	Seoul
	Sŏjŏn Lyceum	Yi Sang-sŏl	Kando, Manchuria
1907	Sinhŭng (Boys) and Kijŏn Girls School	U.S. Presbyterians (Southern)	Chŏnju, Chŏlla
	Taesŏng School	An Ch'ang-ho	P'yŏngyang, P'yŏngan

Osan School	Yi Sŭng-hun	Chŏngju, P'yŏngan
Osŏng School	North and West Educational Ass'n.	Seoul
Pongmyŏng School	Yi Pong-nae	Seoul
1908 Kiho School	Kiho Educational Association	Seoul
Tongdŏk Girls School	Yi Chae-gŭk	Seoul
Taedong Technical School	Taedong School Association	Seoul
1909 Soŭi School	Chang Chi-yŏng	Seoul

Note: Schools listed without indication of sex of students educated boys only.

technicians. Accordingly, Japan directed its efforts toward an elementary level, vocational education. At the heart of this concept of a basic education for Koreans was the Japanese language, which was the foundation on which Japanese rule would rest, and the essence of the doctrine of a vocational education was to teach only the more vapid forms of handwork. Nevertheless, even under the oppression of Japanese colonial rule, the surviving private schools were the key instruments of a Korean national education and served as a locus of the Korean nationalist movement.

Religious Movements

Christianity, and Protestantism in particular, exerted a tremendous influence on the political and educational activities carried on by the intellectual class. In 1884 Horace N. Allen, an American Presbyterian (Northern) missionary, arrived in Korea, while Horace G. Underwood of the same denomination and the Methodist Episcopal (North) missionary, Henry G. Appenzeller, came from the U. S. the next year. They were quickly followed by representatives of a number of other Protestant sects who joined them in actively carrying on a variety of missionary works. As one means of propagating their faith the missionaries undertook medical work, contributing much in this way to Korean society, and they also played an important role, through instilling the ideas of Western liberal thought, in arousing a national consciousness among the Korean people. Korean Protestants like Sŏ Chae-p'il, Yi Sang-jae, and Yun Ch'i-ho, all of them central figures in the Independence Club, threw themselves into political activities. The Protestant private schools, not only those in Korean hands but those run by the missionary societies as well, gave every appearance of being organs for the propagation of nationalist thought. Such Christian organizations as the Seoul Young Men's Christian Association, founded in 1903, carried on active political and social programs, and this provided the stimulus for the formation of similar Korean youth organizations. These groups of young people were interested not alone in politics and education but aroused new social awareness with their campaigns against drinking, smoking, and superstitious practices, and for equality of the sexes, strict monogamy, and the simplification of popular ceremonial observances.

Protestantism was most warmly received by the new intellectual class and by the business community, and this was particularly the case in regions of developing economic activity, such as P'yŏngan province. The growing vitality of the Protestant church in Korea was demonstrated in 1905 with the inauguration of large-scale Bible study conferences at which participants read passages from the Bible to stir the listeners to self-reflection, thus deepening the ardor of their faith. In 1909 "A Million Souls for Christ" campaign was launched in an effort to make massive new conversions to the Protestant faith. Protestantism was warmly welcomed not only as a religious creed but also for its political, social, educational, and cultural ideals and activities. The strength of its appeal was due in part to a psychological factor— the acute feeling of the Korean people that belief in Christianity would atone for the failings of their society that led to the loss of Korea's nationhood.

On a lesser scale there were other religious movements that also served to instill a deeper sense of nationalist consciousness into the Korean people. One segment of the Tonghak was absorbed into the pro-Japanese Ilchinhoe, whereupon its Third Patriarch, Son Pyŏng-hŭi, led the Tonghak mainstream into active participation in the nationalist movement under the newly created name of Ch'ŏndogyo, or Religion of the Heavenly Way. Ch'ŏndogyo too carried on an extensive cultural program that included publication of the nationalist newspaper *Independence News* (*Mansebo*).

The Confucianists, on the whole, adhered to their tradition by taking a conservative stance, and accordingly they often opposed the trends toward modernization. But they too believed strongly that the Japanese must be expelled from Korea, and to this end they memorialized the throne and they raised "righteous armies" to fight against Japan. At the same time efforts were made to reform Confucianism, to adapt it to the changing conditions of the times. This Confucian reform element, as has been observed, joined forces with the Christian members of the new intellectual class and participated in the activities of the Independence Club. Within Buddhism, too, a reform movement arose, one fruit of which was the appearance in 1913 of Han Yong-un's work *On the Revitalization of Korean Buddhism* (*Chosŏn Pulgyo yusin non*).

Finally, seeking to revive ancient belief in Tan'gun as the divine progenitor of the Korean race, Na Ch'ŏl and O Hyŏk founded a religion called Taejonggyo. Although this too was a conservative force, it was a religious movement with strong nationalist overtones.

Enlightenment Scholarship

In this period of deepening national crisis, it was not possible for scholarly inquiry as such to flourish. Nevertheless, the efforts of scholars to inform and educate the people were greater at this time than ever before. Theirs was a nationalistic perspective and it led them to strive to foster awareness of the meaning of independence and to disseminate the new Western learning broadly throughout the society.

A number of scholarly organizations now came into existence to further these ends. Some were formed around scholars in particular provincial areas, such as Yi Kap's North and West Educational Association (Sŏbuk Hakhoe), Yi Kwang-jong's Kyŏnggi-Ch'ungch'ŏng Educational Association (Kiho Hŭnghakhoe), Chang Chi-yŏn's Kyŏngsang Educational Association (Yŏngnam Hakhoe), Yi Ch'ae's Chŏlla Educational Association (Honam Hakhoe), and Namgung Ŏk's Kangwŏn Educational Association (Kwandong Hakhoe). There were other, more broadly based bodies of this kind, such as Yu Kil-chun's Hŭngsadan (Society for the Fostering of Activists), Kim Yun-sik's Korea Educational Association (Taedong Hakhoe), and Chin Hak-sin's Association for Women's Education (Yŏja Kyoyukhoe). Most of these organizations of scholars put out journals that whetted the public's appetite for knowledge, and among these the monthly publications of the North and West Educational Association, the Kyŏnggi-Ch'ungch'ŏng Educational Association, and the Chŏlla Educational Association were perhaps the most influential. Many other educational magazines also were published, such as the monthly organ of the Independence Club, the *Korea Self-Strengthening Society Monthly*, and *Children* (*Sonyŏn*). A number of commercial publishing companies were founded, like the Kwanghak Sŏp'o and Hoedong Sŏgwan, and put out numerous books whose contents reflected the new learning.

Study of the Korean language broke new ground toward the end of the nineteenth century with Yu Kil-chun's *Grammar of Korean* (*Chosŏn munjŏn*), the first such modern work. Subsequently Chu Si-gyŏng founded the Society for the Standardization of Korean Writing (Kungmun Tongsikhoe) and Chi Sŏg-yŏng the Society for the Study of the Korean Script (Kungmun Yŏn'guhoe), both organizations that devoted themselves to studying the problems of spelling and writing in *han'gŭl*. In 1907, with the establishment of a Korean Language Institute by the Ministry of Education, acting upon the proposal of Chi Sŏg-yŏng, work was begun in earnest on the fundamental task of standardizing Korean language spelling and usage. Among the scholars who joined in this effort the one with the most outstanding record of accomplishment was Chu Si-gyŏng himself, who authored such works as *A Korean Grammar* (*Kugŏ munpŏp*) and *A Phonology of Korean* (*Mal ŭi sori*). Chu Si-gyŏng had many disciples, and these were the scholars who later formed the Korean Language Society (Chosŏnŏ Hakhoe).

Key figures in the study of Korean history who flourished during this period were Chang Chi-yŏn, Pak Ŭn-sik, and Sin Ch'ae-ho. Through their research and writing these men strove above all to foster a sense of national pride and self-respect. This is evident from the prominence among their publications of such works as the *Biography of Ŭlchi Mundŏk, Biography of Kang Kam-ch'an, Biography of Ch'oe Yŏng,* and *Biography of Yi Sun-sin,* all of them accounts of the lives of heroes who fought against foreign invaders. There also was much interest in historical geography, and it is noteworthy that works in this field too laid stress on the love a people must have for the land of their forebears. Efforts to rediscover old texts and to gain a new understanding of their value were made. The outstanding example of work of this kind was done by Ch'oe Nam-sŏn, who founded the Chosŏn Kwangmunhoe and published a series of reprints of old Korean texts under its auspices.

There was great interest in world history as well. Koreans were drawn in particular to histories of nation building that might serve as a model in their own situation, and to accounts of the fall of nations that could offer salutary lessons upon which to reflect. Thus there appeared such works as *The Creation of the Swiss Nation, History of American Independence, History of Italian Independence, Poland's Final Struggle,* and the *Fall of Vietnam.* For the same reasons biographies of heroic world figures— *Three Heroes of Italian Nationhood, Biography of George Washington, Emperor Peter the Great, Biography of Joan of Arc*—were read eagerly by the Korean public.

The New Novel and Song

It was during this period, too, that the "new novel" was born, a literary mode that served as a bridge between the old novel and a modern Korean literature. The new novel was written entirely in *han'gŭl* and so could be read for pleasure by everyone, but as a transitional form it could not escape the influence of many features of its predecessor. For example, the new novel continued to develop the theme of encouraging good and punishing evil, and the characters ran true to old familiar types, as if cast from the same mold. The characters in the new novels nevertheless were contemporary people placed in a contemporary setting, and the words they spoke were conveyed to the reader in the phraseology of the vernacular language—these all were clear signs that the new novel was evolving toward the modern form that presently would emerge. Furthermore the new novels had their characters, by both actions and words, cry out for the independence of the Korean nation, they forcefully argued the necessity of the new education, they called for a new family morality based on equality between the sexes, and they asserted the necessity for eradicating superstitious beliefs and constructing a rational, enlightened society.

In short, the new novels that so ardently championed the new modes

of thought reflected the values of the contemporary enlightenment movement, and they represent an important stage of development in Korean
literature. Yi In-jik was the pioneer figure among the new novelists, with
such representative works as *Tears of Blood* (*Hyŏl ŭi nu*), *Pheasant Mountain* (*Ch'iaksan*) and *Voice of a Demon* (*Kwi ŭi sŏng*). Yi Hae-jo's *Liberty
Bell* (*Chayu chong*) and *The Peony Screen* (*Moran pyŏng*), Ch'oe Ch'an-
sik's *Color of the Autumn Moon* (*Ch'uwŏl saek*), and An Kuk-sŏn's *Proceedings of the Council of Birds and Beasts* (*Kŭmsu hoeŭi-rok*) appeared at
about the same time. The "new novel" constituted the mainstream of
fiction writing in Korea until about the time of the March First Movement
in 1919, reaching the height of its achievement with the publication of Yi
Kwang-su's *The Heartless* (*Mujŏng*) in 1917.

So-called *ch'angga*, songs of a new type sung to Western melodies,
were immensely popular at this time. Their appeal started with the introduction of Protestant hymns, and they became songs of the whole
people that were sung everywhere throughout Korea. Many *ch'angga*
were inspiring glorifications of love of country, independence, and the new
education and culture, and in this respect they clearly mirrored the age in
which they were created. Such *ch'angga* were sung joyously by students,
or by independence fighters, to uplift their spirits, and many of these were
permeated with intense national feeling.

The introduction of Western literature into Korea also expanded around
this period. The Bible of course was the first work of Christian literature
to be translated into Korean, and *Pilgrim's Progress* was another. There
were also numerous translations of literature that appealed to younger
readers, such as *Aesop's Fables*, *Robinson Crusoe*, and *Gulliver's Travels*.

5. The March First Movement

Exile and Clandestine Organizations

After Korea became a Japanese colony and an overt independence movement became an impossibility, many Korean nationalist activists fled to the
safety of overseas havens. The independence movements they launched
outside Korea's borders in general reflected two distinct approaches. One
of these advocated establishing bases for the movement in neighboring territories, from which operations might be expanded until Korean independence could be restored by military force. Those independence fighters who
fled just across the Yalu or Tumen rivers into West or North Kando
(Chien-tao) in Manchuria or into the Russian Maritime Territory mainly
engaged in activities of this kind. One famous base for armed independence
operations was established under the leadership of Yi Si-yŏng, Yi Tongnyŏng, and Yi Sang-nyong at San-yüan-p'u in West Kando. Here, in 1911,
the Military School of the New Rising (Sinhŭng Mugwan Hakkyo) was

opened to train freedom fighters. In the Russian Maritime Territory, in 1914, Yi Sang-sŏl and Yi Tong-hwi established the Government of the Korean Restoration Army (Taehan Kwangbokkun Chŏngbu), organized a military force, and laid plans for an armed struggle against Japan. The determination to wage a military struggle by training freedom fighters was in the tradition of the struggle of the "righteous armies," and in fact many of the men who had fought in those guerrilla bands joined the new forces in exile.

On the other hand, there were those who advocated that Korea should attempt to recover its independence by diplomatic means. To this end Korean exiles active in the Shanghai area maintained a covert relationship with China. One such major figure was Sin Kyu-sik, who organized the Mutual Assistance Society (Tongjesa) in 1912 and formed ties with Chinese revolutionaries. On the other hand, Yi Sŭng-man (Syngman Rhee) founded the Korean National Association (Kungminhoe) in Hawaii in 1909 and proceeded to conduct his international activities from a base in America. In the same year Pak Yong-man established a military school for Korean youth in the U. S., thus demonstrating his conviction that the diplomatic approach had to be backed by a readiness to resort to force of arms. After the annexation, every possible opportunity was taken to lay Korea's case before international gatherings. When an International Socialist Congress was convened in Stockholm in 1917, Korean independence activists in exile in China were dispatched as representatives to present a demand for the independence of Korea. Again, Korean representatives attended the World Conference of Small Nations held in New York in the same year and appealed to world opinion to restore Korea's nationhood.

Despite the numerous difficult conditions they faced, nationalist activists within Korea maintained contact with patriots abroad and carried on the struggle for independence. This could be done, of course, only through clandestine organizations. One such was the New People's Association (Sinminhoe) organized in 1907 by An Ch'ang-ho around a core of Korean Christians who carried on the tradition of the Independence Club. An Ch'ang-ho himself had taken refuge in America, but he argued that there were two prerequisites to Korea recovering its independence— raising the level of knowledge and moral standards of the Korean people through fostering education, and achieving economic strength by developing industry. Accordingly, he put his primary emphasis on broadly educational activities within Korea, while working at the same time to create a base for the independence movement overseas. However, so many of its leaders were among those arrested and imprisoned in the Case of the One Hundred Five in 1911 that the Sinminhoe itself soon dissolved. Nevertheless, its ideals survived and were widely disseminated through the educational and other outreach activities conducted by its former members. There also was the Association of the Korean People (Chosŏn Kungminhoe) organized in 1917 under the leadership of Chang Il-hwan; again a

Christian group, it carried on the work of the patriotic enlightenment movement. Other organizations, meanwhile, carried on the tradition of the "righteous army" movement—the Righteous Army for Korean Independence (Tongnip Ŭigunbu) organized principally by Im Pyŏng-ch'an in 1912, the Society for the Restoration of Korean National Sovereignty (Chosŏn Kukkwŏn Hoeboktan) established by Sŏ Sang-il in 1915, and the Restoration Association (Kwangbokhoe) formed by Ch'ae Ki-jung in 1913 and later strengthened by Pak Sang-jin and others are noteworthy examples. The ultimate objective of all such organizations was to restore their country's freedom by force of arms.

Whether the armed struggle of independence forces outside Korea, or the diplomatic maneuvers of patriots who had taken refuge in foreign lands, or the energetic work within Korea of the clandestine organizations and educational bodies—all these activities sustained the will of the Korean people to oppose Japan and strengthened their spirit of resistance. All over Korea, then, popular disturbances broke out one after the other. Under the harsh colonial rule of imperial Japan the nationalistic spirit of resistance had grown and spread to all segments of Korean society and had almost reached the point of explosion. The Korean people were only awaiting an opportune moment to arise, when the turn of international events brought on the inevitable eruption.

The Outbreak of the March First Movement

It was the doctrine of the self-determination of nations that provided the impetus to transform the Korean nationalist movement—a movement that hitherto had trusted in the activities of exiles and of clandestine organizations, or had placed its faith in educational activities or religious movements—into a full-scale, nationwide effort to regain Korea's lost independence. This doctrine was put forward by the American President, Woodrow Wilson, as an integral part of the post-World War I peace settlement, in response to the burgeoning independence movements that had arisen among the national minorities of Europe. The spirit of revenge that dominated the deliberations leading to the Treaty of Versailles made it impossible to give full realization to the principle of the self-determination of nations. Nevertheless, to some extent the principle was applied, and from within the former Austro-Hungarian Empire such nations as Czechoslovakia, Yugoslavia, and Rumania emerged as independent entities, while Poland, Finland, Estonia, Lithuania, and Latvia, formerly under Russian domination, all became independent.

The principle of the self-determination of nations naturally was greeted with the greatest enthusiasm by the Korean people, suffering as they were under the harsh colonial rule of imperial Japan. Koreans were persuaded that at last the world was ready to bring an end to the "age of force" and usher in an "age of justice." It was the belief that the principle of self-determination also could bring independence to Korea that thrust the Korean nationalist movement forward as a single great crying out for freedom.

Korean patriots in exile meeting in Shanghai in January, 1919, organized the New Korea Youth Association (Sinhan Ch'ŏngnyŏndang) and sent Kim Kyu-sik as its representative to the peace conference in Paris to make an appeal for Korean independence. The new organization also sent representatives to Korea, Japan, Manchuria, Siberia, and other areas to explore ways to develop specific independence activities. At the same time, Ch'oe P'ar-yong and other Korean students in Tokyo formed the Korean Youth Independence Corps (Chosŏn Ch'ŏngnyŏn Tongniptan) and laid out a course of action. In consequence, some six hundred students met at the Y.M.C.A. Hall in Kanda, Tokyo, on February 8, 1919, where they adopted a series of resolutions and issued a declaration demanding independence for their country. This event gave immense encouragement to those in Korea who had been seeking means to bring the independence movement into the open, and within a month nationwide demonstrations had erupted.

Within Korea this new phase of the movement was coordinated through the various religious organizations, Ch'ŏndogyo (Religion of the Heavenly Way), Christian, Buddhist, and others, and the central figures were those who signed the Korean Declaration of Independence as representatives of the whole Korean people—those thirty-three men led by Son Pyŏng-hŭi for Ch'ŏndogyo, Yi Sŭng-hun for the Christian groups, and Han Yong-un for the Buddhists. Taking advantage of the fact that funeral rites for the former king, Kojong, were scheduled for March 3, observances that would bring throngs of people to Seoul from all over the country, they determined to act two days before this event. On March 1, 1919, then, the thirty-three representatives of the Korean people met at the T'aehwagwan restaurant (often called the Myŏngwŏlgwan) near the Chongno Intersection, formally promulgated a Declaration of Independence, and proclaimed that Korea now had become an independent nation. At the same time, students gathered in Seoul's Pagoda Park to hear the Declaration read aloud, after which they marched through the streets in peaceful procession, shouting "Long live Korean independence!" (*Tongnip manse!*). The March First Movement, the greatest mass movement of the Korean people in all their history, had begun.

Unfolding of the March First Movement

The March First Movement began with the promulgation of the Declaration of Independence framed by the thirty-three representatives of the Korean people. The fact that a formal Declaration of Independence was drafted and proclaimed, despite the urging of some that a simple petition for independence be read instead, provided the main impetus for the development of the March First Movement into a struggle for freedom carried on by the whole of the Korean nation. The opening lines of the declaration read as follows, in a translation made shortly after the event:

> We herewith proclaim the independence of Korea and the liberty of the Korean people. We tell it to the world in witness of the equality of all nations and we pass it on to our posterity as their inherent right. We make this proclamation, having back of us five thousand years of history and twenty millions of a united loyal people. We take this step to insure to our children, for all time to come, personal liberty in accord with the awakening consciousness of this new era. This is the clear leading of God, the moving principle of the present age, the whole human race's just claim. It is something that cannot be stamped out, or stifled, or gagged, or suppressed by any means.

The Korean Declaration of Independence proclaimed the overarching principles of the just right of a people to its own national existence and of the equality of all mankind, and it did not incite acts of vengeance against Japan's harsh colonial rule. Accordingly, as the covenant appended to the declaration pledged, the Korean people, in their insistence on self-determination, would not give way to expressions of hostility toward others, every individual from first to last would willingly abide by this common consensus, and orderly procedures would be respected for the sake of national honor and rectitude. The March First Movement, in other words, was intended to be entirely peaceful.

As soon as they finished proclaiming the Declaration of Independence at the T'aehwagwan, the thirty-three signers themselves informed the Japanese authorities of their action and so were immediately arrested. It was their plan that the independence movement they had launched be carried forward first of all by the students and then be spread by the entire people. Accordingly, the students gathered as planned at Pagoda Park and, after a formal reading of the Declaration of Independence, began their demonstration in the streets, holding aloft the Korean flag and shouting in unison "Long live Korean independence!" With the street demonstration of the students the March First Movement took on added fervor. Not only students but shopkeepers, farmers, laborers, and other citizens joined in, while Koreans employed by the Government-General also found ways of showing their sympathy. The demonstrations for independence gradually spread into the countryside, until the cries of *"Tongnip manse!"* could be heard all across the length and breadth of the nation. From men and women, from old and young, from people in every walk of life, the single outcry of the whole population was for independence. Indeed, the solitary weapon of the March First Movement was this cry itself—"Long live Korean independence!" These independence demonstrations by the Korean people on so vast a scale caught the Japanese authorities by surprise. Japan was stunned by the enormity of the movement,

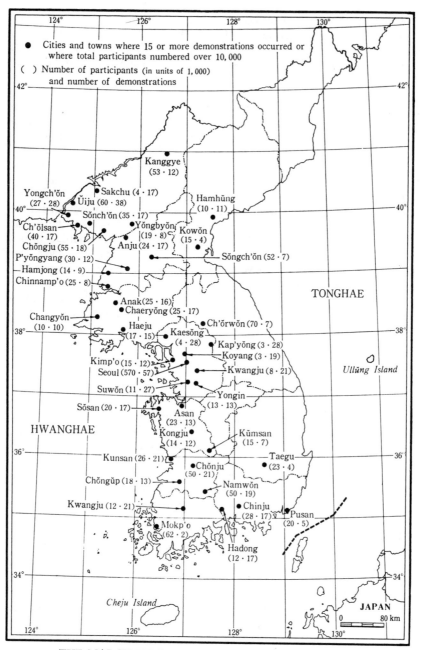

THE MARCH FIRST 1919 INDEPENDENCE MOVEMENT
MAJOR SITES OF POPULAR DEMONSTRATIONS

in which more than two million Koreans directly participated, in more than 1500 separate gatherings, in all but seven of the country's 218 county administrations [see map p.343]. The demonstrations quickly spread as well to Manchuria, to the Russian Maritime Territory, and to other overseas areas.

These peaceful demonstrations were crushed by military force. Japan not only mobilized its constabulary and police forces in Korea but contingents of its army and navy as well. The unarmed and peaceful demonstrators were met with a hail of bullets, while with equal wantonness the Japanese set fire to schools, and churches, and private dwellings as well. The reports issued by the Japanese authorities themselves record 46,948 demonstrators arrested, 7,509 killed, and 15,961 injured, while as many as 715 houses were destroyed or burned, along with 47 churches and two schools. But in reality the numbers in all these categories far exceeded those officially reported. In the most cruel acts of suppression, like that at the village of Cheam-ni near Suwŏn, twenty-nine people were herded into a church which was then set afire to burn them alive. Japan, however, was one of the victorious allies in World War I, and its international position was strong. For this reason, despite the fact that the Korean people had only their bare fists with which to oppose so inhumane a policy of repression, the March First Movement failed to win the support of the Western powers and so in the end could not achieve its purpose.

Formation of the Korean Provisional Government

The March First Movement was carried out by religious organizations and educational bodies, but these did not constitute a strong and closely knit structure. The independence movement overseas, too, had been carried on independently by a variety of Korean activist exiles. Moreover, several different provisional governments were established both inside and outside Korea in the immediate wake of the March First Movement. It was felt necessary, therefore, to have a headquarters organization able to give overall direction to the further activities of the independence movement, and efforts were put underway to create just such a unified provisional government in exile.

The Provisional Government of the Republic of Korea (Taehan Minguk Imsi Chŏngbu) was established in Shanghai in April, 1919, and it included both those already active overseas and others who had gone into exile in the aftermath of the March First Movement. Structurally, the Provisional Government consisted of a deliberative organ and an administrative organ, and although it was a government in exile, nevertheless it is significant that, for the first time in Korean history, a government was formed in accordance with the principles of democracy. The fact that the Provisional Government was created not as a restoration of the old monarchy but as a republic reflected the power the Korean people had manifested in the March First Movement. It further demonstrated that the political consciousness of the Korean people already had reached a new stage of awareness.

Contact between the Provisional Government and the Korean people was maintained through a liaison mechanism designed especially for that purpose. Responsibility for liaison was assigned to individuals in every province, county, and township, a system that opened the way to participation in the independence movement by anyone in any part of the country. For one thing, funds needed for continued independence activities abroad were collected from the Korean public and transmitted through this mechanism.

The Provisional Government immediately initiated a series of diplomatic moves, dispatching Kim Kyu-sik as envoy plenipotentiary to the Paris Peace Conference in May of 1919 to plead the cause of independence, and sending a representative to the International Socialist Party Congress, held in Switzerland in August of the same year, which then adopted a resolution calling for Korean independence. At the same time, the forces of independence fighters in Manchuria and the Russian Maritime Territory were regrouped under a single banner with the creation of the General Headquarters of the Restoration Army (Kwangbokkun Ch'ongyŏng) in An-tung prefecture in Manchuria, thus preparing the way for continuing the struggle for independence by military means. Finally, as its principal publication, the Provisional Government put out the *Independence News* (*Tongnip Sinmun*), a newspaper that accomplished much in making known the circumstances of the independence movement both within Korea and to the outside world and in keeping alive, indeed invigorating, the idea of freedom in the minds of the Korean people.

Chapter 15

Development of the Nationalist Movement

1. Changes in Japan's Colonial Policy

The Proclaimed "Enlightened Administration"

The March First Movement made it inevitable that Japan change its colonial policy in Korea, if only cosmetically. Japan's propaganda claims, that the Korean people had willingly submitted to Japanese colonial rule, now were exposed as the sheerest fabrications, and accordingly world opinion had become extremely critical of Japan's actions in Korea. At this point, then, Japan announced that it was abandoning reliance on its gendarmerie police forces to maintain control in Korea in favor of a so-called enlightened administration (*munhwa chŏngch'i*). This would require modification of certain aspects of Japanese colonial policy, and with the appointment of Admiral Saitō Makoto as the new governor-general, the major changes contemplated under the proclaimed "enlightened administration" were made known.

First, the previous requirement that the governor-general of Korea be selected from among generals or admirals on active duty was to be changed to permit appointment of civil officials as well. Next, the gendarmerie police system would be abandoned, thus demilitarizing police operations in Korea. Finally, the educational system for Koreans was to be expanded and its standards raised to the same level as that available to Japanese, while control of the press would be relaxed to permit the publication of Korean owned newspapers in *han'gŭl*.

But all this simply represented a different approach to the pursuit of the very same objectives as before. The new policy, therefore, was largely fraudulent and deceptive. First of all, up to the time Japan was ejected from Korea by force in 1945, not one single civil official was appointed to the post of governor-general. Moreover, although the announced change was made in the police system, on the other hand police organs in fact were expanded and the number of police personnel increased. Including the gendarmerie, police strength had grown to about 15,000 in the immediate aftermath of the March First Movement in 1919, and by 1938 it reached

21,782. At the same time more prisons were built and the number of arrests for "ideological crimes" swelled. Furthermore, the widely advertised expansion of educational opportunities for Koreans, as will be explained in detail later, was more propaganda than reality, while the former discriminatory practices continued as before. Again, Korean owned newspapers published in *han'gŭl* were founded, true enough, like the *Tonga Ilbo, Chosŏn Ilbo,* and the *Sidae Ilbo.* But for Japan this simply provided a means by which to exercise control over the voicing of Korean opinion. Accordingly, the Japanese censorship remained strict and instances of deletion of text, confiscation, levying of fines, and suspension of publication occurred continuously, averaging as many as five or six times a month. No wonder, then, that behind the mask of benevolence Koreans tended to see the real face of Japan in the inhumane treatment of their countrymen in Japan on the occasion of the great earthquake in Tokyo in 1923, when many Koreans were slaughtered senselessly by the frenzied Japanese populace.

In sum, Japan's professed "enlightened administration" was no more than a superficial and deceptive moderation of its earlier policy of forceful repression, carried out under pressure of world opinion. There was no basic change, therefore, in Japan's colonial policy. The only policy shifts that did occur were made in consequence of changes in Japan's demands upon Korea, and these in turn were dictated by adverse developments within the fabric of Japanese society itself or by the consequences of Japan's imperialist expansion abroad.

The Plundering of Korea's Rice Production

In the 1920's new developments within Japan itself forced certain changes in Japan's colonial policy in Korea. The first of these was a decision to ship huge quantities of Korean rice to Japan, to overcome a severe crisis in Japan's own food supply brought on by maladjustments in its rapidly industrializing economy. In particular, in 1918 the price of rice in Japan had skyrocketed, resulting in so-called rice riots erupting all over the country. In consequence, Japanese demand for Korean rice increased sharply.

From the time of the Kanghwa treaty in 1876 there had been a continuous outflow of Korean rice to Japan, and after Korea became a Japanese colony this process was further accelerated. Now faced with a serious crisis in its domestic food supply, Japan had a greater need than ever for Korean rice and so adopted special measures to boost rice production in its colony. The first such plan envisaged the expenditure of 168,000,000 yen over a fifteen year period starting in 1920, with rice production to increase by more than 9,200,000 *sŏk* as a result of irrigating 427,500 *chŏngbo* of land and improving methods of cultivation. More than half of the projected increase, 5,000,000 *sŏk*, would be earmarked for annual export to Japan.

But even so this would mean an increase of 4,200,000 *sŏk* of rice for Korea, so that Korea too would benefit from the plan.

In fact, however, the plan to increase rice production did not achieve the results anticipated. Revised downward in 1926, it still fell far short of its goals. Rice production between 1912-1916 had averaged 12.3 million *sŏk* annually, and in the 1922-1926 period had increased to no more than 14.5 million. Even another ten years later, during 1932-1936, the rice harvest averaged only 17.0 million *sŏk*. The total increase in production, then, was less than a third of the amount originally projected. On the other hand, the amount of rice exported (essentially all of it to Japan) rose from an annual average of only 1.06 million *sŏk* in 1912-1916 to more than four times that in 1922-1926, and during the next decade it soared again, to 8.76 million *sŏk* in the 1932-1936 period. At this point the amount of Korean rice exported to Japan had reached a figure that was over half of Korea's total rice production. Thus in the course of the twenty-five year period covered in the accompanying table, Korean rice production had increased by less than 40%; in contrast, exports of rice during these same years expanded by more than eight times.

PRODUCTION AND EXPORT OF RICE

unit: million *sŏk*

PERIOD	1912-1916	1917-1921	1922-1926	1927-1931	1932-1936
Average Production	12.3	14.1	14.5	15.8	17.0
Production Index	(100)	(115)	(118)	(128)	(138)
Average Exported	1.06	2.20	4.34	6.61	8.76
Export Index	(100)	(208)	(409)	(624)	(826)
Consumed In Korea	11.24	11.90	10.16	9.19	8.24
Consumption per capita (in *sŏk*)	(0.72)	(0.69)	(0.59)	(0.50)	(0.40)

Since rice exports to Japan exceeded the targeted amount while increase in production was well under the goal set by the Japanese planners, the Korean consumer had to suffer, for despite the larger rice harvests the amount available to the Korean population (which grew by 3.7 million between 1919-1934) had decreased significantly. As a result, in contrast to a Japanese annual per capita rice consumption of over 1.0 *sŏk*, the figure for Koreans had steadily declined to less than half that. With what, then, could Koreans fill their half-empty stomachs? With a variety of less palatable grains brought in from Manchuria—millet, kaoliang, soybeans, and others. Imports of Manchurian millet, barely 15,000 *sŏk* in 1912, soared more than a hundred-fold to 1,720,000 *sŏk* in 1930, to help replace the Korean rice that had been taken to feed the Japanese.

The further implementation of Japan's plan to increase Korean rice production was suspended in 1934. This was because Japan had been caught up in the worldwide depression and feared that imports of still more

Korean rice would aggravate the deteriorating price conditions faced by Japanese farmers. On the other hand, although the plan had been suspended, while it had been in effect improvements had been made to increase acreage output. These principally involved irrigation works, which were undertaken through local irrigation associations. By 1931 some one hundred thirty-eight such projects had been completed throughout Korea and twenty-three more were underway, with total expenditures amounting to more than 100,000,000 yen. But, due to the immense cost of these irrigation works, the irrigation associations fell into serious financial difficulties, and the water charges that had to be levied on land within the irrigation districts, therefore, were substantially increased. It was for this reason that the price of newly irrigated land, which should have risen, in many cases instead began to fall off. In the end, then, the new irrigation facilities that ought to have benefited the farmers in actuality drove large numbers of them into poverty. In consequence, opposition movements against the irrigation associations now arose throughout Korea.

Korea as a Market for Japanese Goods

Japan not only looked to Korea as a supplier of food grains but also as a market for the output of Japanese industry. With the elimination of all duties on exports from Korea in 1920 and free entry granted to most imports from Japan by 1923, Japan's monopolistic market position vis-a-vis Korea became still further strengthened. As a result, by 1931 95% of total Korean exports were going to Japan and in that year 80% of all Korea's imports came from Japan. The importance of the Korea market for Japanese industry is underscored by the proportion of Japan's total exports that Korea absorbed, the figure for which reached 34% in 1939.

Furthermore, a preponderance of Korea's imports from Japan was in the form of manufactured products; in 1919, for example, this percentage was 79.1, and it remained at essentially that level. These imports consisted mostly of such items as clothing, yarn and thread, alcoholic beverages,

COMPOSITION OF KOREA'S TRADE WITH JAPAN
(in percentages of current value)

Year	EXPORTS				IMPORTS			
	1919	1929	1935	1939	1919	1929	1935	1939
Raw Materials	(85.2)	(83.0)	(73.7)	(49.5)	(6.8)	(13.3)	(16.3)	(14.5)
Food	72.0	68.9	57.2	27.9	1.6	9.8	6.0	5.7
Industrial	13.2	14.1	16.5	21.6	5.2	3.5	10.3	8.8
Manufactures	(10.4)	(13.3)	(22.9)	(45.8)	(79.1)	(79.5)	(79.6)	(80.9)
Food	0.4	2.5	1.6	2.5	5.1	8.1	6.6	5.1
Semi-finished	9.7	8.8	17.2	32.4	9.3	10.4	14.2	14.4
Finished	0.3	2.0	4.1	10.9	64.7	61.0	58.8	61.4
Miscellaneous	(4.4)	(3.7)	(3.4)	(4.7)	(14.1)	(7.2)	(4.1)	(4.6)
Total	100.0	100.0	100.0	100.0	100.0	100.0	100.0	100.0

sugar, tobacco products, and paper goods—in other words, a high proportion of imports from Japan were items of everyday use. To the contrary, the majority of Korean exports to Japan consisted of foodstuffs, most notably rice, while at least until 1930 exports of raw materials and semifinished goods were next in importance. Korea's role as a colony of Japan is amply evident from this perspective alone.

In the 1930's, however, a change took place in the nature of Korea's trade with Japan. Of course Japan's position as Korea's almost exclusive trading partner was further solidified, and the continuing growth of exports to Japan of industrial raw materials was typical of a colonial relationship. At the same time, however, the proportion of manufactured products among Korea's exports to Japan also began rapidly to rise. It was only 10.4% in 1929, had increased substantially by 1935, and in 1939 was approaching half of total exports. On the other hand, the proportion of food, mostly rice, exported to Japan, and even the absolute amount, was falling off. In percentage terms, food exports dropped from 72% to 57.2% between 1919 and 1935, and fell sharply to only 27.9% in 1939. But it would be a hasty conclusion to assume from these facts that the character of Korea's relationship with Japan as a colonial dependency was undergoing transformation. This is because the increase in Korea's exports of manufactured goods to Japan was a reflection of the fact that Japanese capital investment in Korea was increasing. This in turn tells us that a shift in the thrust of Japan's colonial policy once again had taken place.

Japan Invests in Heavy Industry

In 1920 the Government-General rescinded the law regulating business concerns in Korea. In consequence, the establishment of a company no longer required permission but simply had to be registered, so that those who wished to launch new business enterprises were freed from the tedious procedures hitherto required for obtaining a permit. But it would be a mistake to think that Japan took this step in order to encourage capital investment by Koreans. In fact it was done to develop a profitable market in Korea for the investment of Japanese capital, now swollen by the World War I prosperity Japan enjoyed as a supplier to the Allied nations. Japan's purpose was to convert Korea from a market in which to sell only Japanese finished products into a market for Japanese capital as well. The cost of the cheap Korean labor was no more than half that of Japanese workers. Moreover, it was possible to demand more than ten hours work per day from a Korean labor force. These favorable labor conditions, taken together with the potential for an abundant supply of cheap hydroelectric power, had attracted the attention of Japanese investors. Thus in 1926 the Chōsen Hydroelectric Power Company was formed to develop a site on the Pujŏn River in Hamgyŏng province. In the next year the Chōsen Nitrogenous Fertilizer Company was founded in Hŭngnam where it could utilize the new power supply. The fertilizer factory that was built there was on a scale unknown not only in Korea but not yet found even in Japan.

Thus begun, the large scale investment of Japanese capital in Korea was greatly accelerated with the outbreak of the Manchurian Incident in 1931, the creation of the Japanese puppet state of Manchukuo, and the exercise of full Japanese control over Manchuria. Now transforming itself into a so-called national defense state, Japan felt a heightened need to develop resources in Korea for the Japanese munitions industry. Accordingly, Japan's great *zaibatsu* competed with each other to build factories in Korea, so that the proportion of manufacturing industries within Korea's industrial structure grew at a rapid rate.

Specifically, in 1925 the proportion contributed by manufacturing industries to Korea's gross commodity product was 17.7%; in 1931 it had increased to 22.7%, in 1936 to 31.3%, and in 1939 to 39%. In contrast, agricultural production, which stood at 72.7% of total commodity output in 1925, declined to 63.1% in 1931, 51.8% in 1936, and 42% in 1939. Consequently, if the 6% represented by mining output is added to the 39% figure for manufacturing industries in 1939, in that year mining and manufacturing combined constituted the most significant component of total Korean output, surpassing even agriculture. Eventually, then, certain regions of Korea became the sites of major concentrations of new industrial plant, and among these Hamgyŏng province was particularly significant. Hamgyŏng province took on importance strategically as well, as a new avenue of Japanese access to Manchuria.

But it is the character of the manufacturing industry sector in Korea that commands the greater attention. The following table indicates percentages of output of manufacturing industries contributed by each component.

MANUFACTURING OUTPUT BY INDUSTRY (in percentages)

INDUSTRY	1930	1936	1939
Textile	12.8	12.7	13.0
Metal	5.8	4.0	9.0
Machine and Tool	1.3	1.0	4.0
Ceramic	3.2	2.7	3.0
Chemical	9.4	22.9	34.0
Lumber and Wood Products	2.7	2.7	1.0
Printing	3.1	1.8	1.0
Food	57.8	45.2	22.0
Gas and Electric	2.4	5.6	2.0
Others	1.5	1.4	11.0
TOTAL	100.0	100.0	100.0

The first observation to be made from these statistics is that the amount contributed by the food processing industry, originally far and away the most significant, steadily and markedly decreased, and in its place the chemical industry quickly rose to the position of primacy. In 1939 the chemical industry contributed 34% to the total output of manufacturing industries, and if the 9% of the metal industry and the 4% of the machine and tool industry are added to that figure, then the contribution of the heavy industry sector reached 47% in that year. This signifies, of course, the one-sided emphasis in Japan's development plans on creating a munitions industry in Korea. In other words, Korea was being transformed into a supply base for Japan's aggression against China.

Despoliation of Korea's Mineral Resources

That mineral production too increased at no less a pace than the manufacturing industries can be seen in the following statistics. In 1930, just before the Manchurian Incident, the output of Korea's mines was valued at 24,650,000 yen, while in 1936, on the eve of Japan's attack on China, it had expanded more than four and one-half times, to 110,430,000 yen. Moreover, by 1942 it had undergone another precipitous rise, reaching 445,420,000 yen. At first glance, so phenomenal an increase in the short span of twelve years seems truly astonishing.

Japan's primary emphasis in developing Korea's mining industry in this way was on gold. Gold production in 1936 was 17,490 kilograms worth 59,350,000 yen, equal to over one-half the value of total mining output. The reason why gold mining was so encouraged by the Japanese government was that gold was essential to financing Japan's purchases, from the U.S. and elsewhere abroad, of oil, scrap iron, machine tools, and other resources needed for the war against China.

But with the outbreak of war between Japan and the U.S. in 1941, the emphasis in the mining industry shifted from gold to those minerals directly required by Japan's war industry—iron, tungsten, graphite, magnesite, and molybdenum. In consequence, production of iron ore rose over six times between 1930 and 1944, coal 8 times, tungsten about 700 times, graphite 5 times, molybdenum 29 times, and output of magnesite, which had not been mined at all in 1930, more than doubled between 1940 and 1944. Here again is evidence of the role of Korea as a supplier to Japan's war machine.

PRODUCTION OF MAJOR MINERALS

unit: metric tons

YEAR	GOLD	IRON ORE	COAL	TUNG-STEN	GRAPH-ITE	MOLYB-DENUM	MAGNE-SITE
1930	5.876	532,497	884,138	12	20,073	26	—
1940	22.060	1,185,426	5,740,941	4,218	94,581	195	73,540
1944	0.598	3,331,814	7,048,776	8,333	103,306	760	157,745

Japan's Assimilation Policy

In 1937 Japan launched a full-scale assault on China and in 1941 boldly attacked even the United States. In prosecuting this hopeless war, Japan carried out a so-called total national mobilization policy and even in Japan itself put into effect a variety of extraordinary measures. Needless to say, this policy was implemented with still greater severity in its Korean colony, as Japan launched a sweeping campaign to eradicate Korean national identity under the slogan "Japan and Korea are One Entity" (*Nai-Sen ittai*).

As a first step in carrying out its assimilation policy Japan banned all forms of cultural expression that might be considered nationalistic. The *Tonga Ilbo, Chosŏn Ilbo,* and other newspapers published in *han'gŭl*, as well as *han'gŭl* magazines like *Literature* (*Munjang*) all were ordered to cease publication. The leading figures in the Korean Language Society were arrested in October 1942, on charges of fomenting a nationalist movement, and as a result of the severe torture to which they were subjected by the Japanese police, Yi Yun-jae and some others among the Korean linguists died in prison. Novelists, poets and other creative writers were forced to produce their works in Japanese, and in the end it was even required that Japanese be exclusively used in the schools and in Korean homes. Not only the study of the Korean language but also of Korean history was regarded as dangerous, and accordingly even the activities of the Chindan Hakhoe, Korea's leading historical society, came to a halt. Worship by Koreans at Japanese Shinto shrines was required, and there were some Christians, like Chu Ki-ch'ŏl, who refused and so lost their lives. Kim Kyo-sin and a score or more of his colleagues who had been publishing the *Korea Bible News* (*Sŏngsŏ Chosŏn*) were subjected to the rigors of imprisonment. Finally, a policy of "identity creation" (*ch'angssi*) was enforced, under which Koreans were compelled even to adopt Japanese style family and personal names. In short, Japan's aim was to eradicate consciousness of Korean national identity, roots and all, and thus to obliterate the very existence of the Korean people from the face of the earth.

Japan also enforced measures for the requisition of Korean grain production and certain items made of metal, and for the mobilization of the Korean labor force. Korean farmers were compelled to deliver their rice harvests directly to the government, and metal articles of many kinds were required to be donated to the Japanese war effort. Moreover, as the fighting grew in scale and intensity and Japan's own manpower resources became strained, an all-out mobilization of Korean manpower was put into effect. Many Koreans were pressed into forced labor, conscripted for work in coal mines, in munitions factories, and at Japanese bases in forward areas. The number of Koreans transported to Japan alone for these purposes was more than 700,000. Even young, unmarried women were mobilized in so-called volunteer brigades and forced to serve as "comfort girls" for Japanese front-line soldiers. Koreans also were conscripted for Japanese military service. At first a volunteer system was in effect, with Koreans simply being urged to present themselves for military duty, but then college students were forced into service, and from 1943 Koreans too were subject to conscription. Many Koreans, of course, died as soldiers in Japan's armies, but there also were many who refused to join the student battalions or to serve as conscripts and so were sent into forced labor in the coal mines or elsewhere. There were still others who, even though they had been dragged off to fight for Japan, found opportunities once at the front to escape and go over to the side of the Allies.

2. Native Capital and the Condition of Korean Farmers and Workers

Korean Entrepreneurial Capital

Under the political protection of Japanese imperialism, Japanese capital investment in a wide range of industries in Korea was growing apace. War related industry in particular was established in Korea by the great *zaibatsu* of Mitsui, Mitsubishi, and Noguchi, hand in hand with Japan's war ministry. Accordingly, the development of these industries did not signify a growth of Korean capital investment. In fact, as the following table for capital investment in manufacturing plant in Korea as of 1938 vividly shows, the domination of Japanese capital was overwhelming—87.7% in contrast to 12.3% for Korean capital. Moreover, if the monopolistic position of the Japanese in the electric power industry, representing an investment of 213,065,000 yen, is included in the calculation, then the proportion of Korean capital becomes still smaller. When these statistics

CAPITAL INVESTMENT IN MANUFACTURING INDUSTRIES BY NATIONALITY, 1938   unit: 1,000 yen

INDUSTRY	PAID-UP CAPITAL (and percentage)		AVERAGE CAPITAL PER COMPANY	
	Korean Companies	Japanese Companies	Korean Companies	Japanese Companies
Textile	6,075 (20.8)	23,103 (79.2)	164	593
Metal and Machinery	1,852 (7.3)	23,654 (92.7)	32	249
Brewing	12,054 (46.7)	13,772 (53.3)	38	107
Pharmaceutical	1,676 (64.2)	934 (35.8)	51	37
Ceramic	432 (2.7)	15,791 (97.3)	36	395
Flour and Rice Cleaning	2,526 (20.4)	9,860 (79.6)	27	141
Processed Food	217 (2.2)	9,621 (97.8)	13	128
Lumber and Woodworking	594 (5.3)	10,553 (94.7)	31	129
Printing	625 (30.0)	1,461 (70.0)	14	35
Chemical	2,954 (2.8)	100,736 (97.2)	80	1,340
Others	1,193 (18.6)	5,220 (81.4)	18	39
Total	30,198 (12.3)	214,705 (87.7)	41	267

are further analyzed on the basis of capital investment per company, then it becomes evident that the Korean concerns were small-scale enterprises in comparison with the large size of the Japanese companies. Under these circumstances, there also were occasions when businesses launched with Korean capital came to be controlled by the Japanese investors from whom they had to borrow in order to survive.

The same situation is found in the mining industry, since most mining operations were in the hands of the Japanese. Japanese capital represented 94.8% of the total investment in coal mining in 1945, while the Japanese share of investment and facilities in other mining industries was even higher, 96%. Accordingly, as in the case of the manufacturing industries, development took place not with Korean capital but with Japanese.

Pointing to this growth of Korea's manufacturing industries, Japan painted a propaganda picture of a "rapidly developing Chōsen." But this rapid advance was not achieved by Koreans but by Japanese. Accordingly, it was not economic development undertaken for the benefit of Koreans but instead to serve the interests of the Japanese. In point of fact, Korea's industrial economy was built in pursuit of Japanese goals, on a foundation of Korean suffering and sacrifice.

But even under these circumstances there was a persistent growth of native Korean capital investment. A good example is Kim Sŏng-su's Seoul Textile Company (Kyŏngsŏng Pangjik Hoesa). Established in 1919, it was a purely Korean enterprise launched with Korean capital provided mainly by large landowners in Chŏlla province. As such it produced durable, heavy cloth suited to Korean preferences, and it found its market principally among the rural population. Its products were received with particular favor by the people of the northwest, the P'yŏngan province region, where nationalist sentiment was strong. Furthermore, the Seoul Textile Company announced a policy of hiring only Koreans and it maintained this special characteristic of a native Korean enterprise throughout its history. At the same time, Kim Sŏng-su undertook to offer Koreans an education with Korean content through a middle school he operated and at Posŏng College (Posŏng Chŏnmun Hakkyo; now Korea University). Also one of the founders of the *Tonga Ilbo* newspaper in 1920, he remained the principal support of this staunchly nationalist voice for the expression of Korean public opinion. In addition to the Seoul Textile Company, An Hŭi-je's Paeksan Trading Company, established in Pusan with capital invested by landowners in Kyŏngsang province, is well known as a general trading company. The Paeksan company contributed significant sums to the Korean independence movement, while also engaging actively in the work of Korean education and promoting the Korean cooperative movement.

The knitwear and rubber goods factories of P'yŏngyang also are notable as examples of native capital investment. The knitted goods industry, which began to flourish in the years after 1920, produced mainly Western style socks and stockings. The owners of these factories, like Yi Chin-sun of Kongsin Hosiery and Son Ch'ang-yun of Samgong Hosiery, in many cases had been struggling small merchants. Accumulating capital by hard work and frugality, eventually they were able to build their own factories. As for the rubber goods factories, they won popular acceptance of their chief product, rubber shoes, and began to flourish after developing a styling modeled on the traditional Korean footwear. Yi Pyŏng-du, the man who created this design, became the plant superintendent of the Chŏngch'ang Rubber Goods Company operated by Ch'oe Kyu-bong. It was typical of the owners of these P'yŏngyang knitwear and rubber goods factories that their business practices were marked by industry and frugality, honest dealing, and an enterprising spirit, while in private life they were practicing Christians. These industries that began their development in P'yŏngyang grew into a major area of native Korean entrepreneurial activity in which the Japanese could not well compete.

The Impoverishment of the Korean Farmer

Japan asserted that the cadastral survey it carried out between 1910-1918 was an undertaking for the modernization of land tenure relationships in Korea. But it has been seen above that in fact this survey paved the way for Japanese seizure of vast amounts of Korean land. The result was that the number of large-scale Japanese landowners increased, while some among the former Korean *yangban* class also became great landholders and continued to maintain the specially privileged position they had enjoyed in the past. In the process, however, many of those who tilled the land inevitably fell to the level of marginal tenant farmers. Since they now labored under a contractual relationship with the landowner, they were placed in the further disadvantageous position of losing the rights of tenancy that in the past had enabled many tenant farmers to acquire eventual ownership of the land they worked. Moreover, the vast majority of those who managed to survive as independent farmers toiled at subsistence level, unable to acquire more than a miniscule plot of land. Many of these farmers, therefore, were forced to work as tenants on others' land as well.

The landlord class, of course, was small in number, but in consequence of the developments traced above, the proportion of owner-farmers (those who owned all the land they cultivated but had no surplus to rent out) also was unusually low. According to statistics for 1916 [see accompanying table], among 2,641,000 total farm households only 2.5% were absentee or other landlords (rich farmers who rented their surplus land to tenants), while scarcely more than 20% were owner-farmers. In contrast, 40.6% of farm households were owner-tenants renting a part of the land they tilled and 36.8% were pure tenants, with the total of these two tenancy categories reaching 2,045,000 households, or 77.4%. A majority of these, nearly 60% of all farm households, worked small holdings of less than one *chŏngbo* (2.45 acres).

FARM HOUSEHOLDS BY LAND TENURE RELATIONSHIP (1916)

TYPE OF LAND TENURE	NUMBER OF HOUSEHOLDS	PERCENTAGE
Absentee and Other Landlords	66,391	2.5
Owner-Farmers	530,195	20.1
Owner-Tenants	1,073,360	40.6
Pure Tenants	971,208	36.8
Total	2,641,154	100.0

The lives of these marginal farmers, fallen to subsistence level, could not but be miserable. Even by the count of the Japanese Government-General, among 2,728,921 total farm households in 1924 fully 44.6%, 1,273,326 households, were unable to earn enough to sustain their lives. In other words, close to half of Korean farm households had to burden themselves with debt each year in order to survive. But it is clear that this number in fact was greater than the official statistics indicate. Poverty stricken farmers, once their food supplies were exhausted, were forced to eat roots or the bark of trees. Even the pronouncements of the Government-General itself admit that, at times, the number of these starving farmers exceeded half of all farm households.

Given Japanese colonial policy, these trends in rural Korea could only become more pronounced as time went on. The numbers of owner-farmers and owner-tenants who fell into pure tenancy rose rapidly, while a simultaneous increase occurred in the number of absentee Japanese landlords. This is revealed in the following statistics: the percentage of absentee and other landlords, which had been 3.4% of total farm households in 1919, was 3.6% in 1930, with the increase attributable to growth in the number of Japanese absentee landlords. In the same period, the proportion of owner-farmers declined from 19.7% to 17.6%, while that of owner-tenants went down from 39.3% to 31%. In contrast the percentage of pure tenant farmers climbed from 37.6% in 1919 to 46.5% in 1930.

The proportion of the harvest paid to landlords by their tenant farmers averaged about one-half. But in addition the tenant was responsible for the cost of fertilizer, irrigation charges, the cost of transporting his harvest, and for the land tax; moreover, the tenant had to provide labor services to the landlord on demand. No wonder, then, that the life of the Korean farmer was one of intensifying hardship, and often the only recourse was flight from the land. The number of "fire-field people" (those who slashed and burned off the cover of vegetation in uninhabited upland areas and then cultivated small patches of the bared ground before moving on to repeat the process) nearly tripled from 245,626 in 1916 to 697,088 in 1927, and in 1936 this lowest stratum of the Korean farming population was officially recorded at over 1.5 million. Meanwhile, the numbers of Koreans who migrated to Manchuria and Japan rose with every passing year. Korean immigrants in Manchuria numbered 560,000 in 1927, 800,000 in 1931, and 1,450,000 by 1940. There had been less than 250 Korean residents in Japan in 1910, but the figure for 1930 was 419,000 and by 1941 it had swollen to 1,469,000. Yet whether as a farmer in Manchuria or a laborer in Japan, the life of the Korean emigrant was seldom less harsh than that he had left behind. Moreover, friction with the indigenous population led to unfortunate interracial outbursts of violence such as the Wan-pao-shan incident in Manchuria (a clash between Chinese and Korean farmers over use of water resources), events that Japan twisted to its own purposes to justify its aggression against China.

As a resistance movement among Korean farmers gathered momentum under these desperate circumstances, Japan launched a so-called Rural Revival Movement. Initiated in 1933 as a self-help program, the plan sought to revitalize the rural economy by eliminating the chronic "spring famine" problem and wiping out the farmer's burden of debt. To this end farmers were encouraged to lead a "rational life" and to develop secondary sources of farm income. But given the circumstance that a preponderance of the rural population barely eked out a living as tenants on small plots of land, it was too much to expect that the anticipated results could be achieved. The policy, after all, was a mere expedient contrived by the Japanese in an attempt to defuse the growing resistance movement among the Korean farmers.

The Life of Korean Workers

With the development of the mining and manufacturing industries the number of Korean wage laborers rose sharply with each passing year. In 1931, the year of the Manchurian Incident, there had been but 106,781 factory workers and 35,895 mine laborers. Already in 1937, when hostilities between Japan and China broke out, the numbers had risen to 207,000 and 162,000 respectively, and by 1942, the first year of the Pacific War, had grown dramatically again, to 520,000 and 224,000. With the war at its peak in 1944, then, there were close to 600,000 Koreans laboring in factories in Korea and 350,000 in mines. When workers in construction, transport, and other sectors of the economy are added in, then the total number of

COMPOSITION OF KOREAN WAGE-LABOR FORCE BY INDUSTRY

INDUSTRY	NUMBER OF LABORERS	PERCENTAGE	DATE OF REPORT
Manufacturing	591,494	27.9	1945. 1
Mining	346,424	16.3	1944. 9
Construction	437,752	20.6	1944
Forestry	205,911	9.7	1944.10
Marine Products	211,520	10.0	1944
Transportation	198,896	9.4	1944
Agriculture	130,377	6.1	1943
Total	2,122,374	100.0	

Korean wage laborers in 1944 reaches well over the two million mark. Taken together with their family members, this wage-labor force constituted a substantial portion of the total Korean population.

These laborers were required to work long hours: 47% of factory workers and 34% of mine workers put in work days of twelve hours or more. Nor was such arduous labor rewarded with generous wages. As the accompanying table indicates, in 1929 Japanese adult male factory workers in Korea were paid 2 yen 32 sen per day, while in contrast Koreans received less than half that, only one yen; Japanese juvenile male labor received 71 sen as against 44 sen for Koreans; Japanese adult female laborers got 1 yen 1 sen but Korean women only 59 sen; and Japanese juvenile female workers were paid 61 sen, while Korean girls got just 32 sen per day. On such wages it was difficult for a family to maintain even a minimal standard of living, and there was nothing left to spend for cultural or leisure activities or for the education of one's children.

DAILY WAGES OF FACTORY WORKERS BY NATIONALITY IN 1929

KOREANS				JAPANESE			
MALE		FEMALE		MALE		FEMALE	
Adults	Juveniles	Adults	Juveniles	Adults	Juveniles	Adults	Juveniles
1.00 yen	0.44 yen	0.59 yen	0.32 yen	2.32 yen	0.71 yen	1.01 yen	0.61 yen

It was natural under these conditions that the health of the workers could not be satisfactorily maintained. As a result many workers became the victims of industrial accidents or disease. But so few precautions were taken against this as to be almost meaningless. The life of these workers, therefore, can only be described as one of misery. Yet the number of Koreans who could not even find such employment as this was substantial. Statistics for 1931 show a level of unemployment of 15% among Koreans in the sample investigated, a figure more than double the 6.7% rate in Japan in the same year. Matters related to labor conditions clearly were pressing problems for Korean society at that time.

3. The Korean National Movement Enters a New Phase

The "Movement to Buy Korean" and Labor Disputes among Korean Tenant Farmers and Workers

With many Korean merchants and landowners emerging as entrepreneurs in the 1920's, a number of Korean owned enterprises came into being. Nevertheless, capital resources were too meager to enable Korean businesses to compete in scale with those of the Japanese; therefore, without the support of the Korean public there would be no way for them to grow. This led to the launching of a "movement to buy Korean," aimed at giving a positive stimulus to investment in modern industry by Koreans. In 1923 the Society for the Encouragement of Native Products (Mulsan Changnyŏhoe) was formed and began a campaign to persuade Koreans to refrain from buying Japanese goods and instead favor their own Korean manufactures, employing the slogan "Our livelihood with our products." The campaign began in the large cities like Seoul and P'yŏngyang and then spread throughout the country, and with the enthusiastic response of youth groups, women's organizations, and the Boy Scouts, in a remarkably short span of time it developed into a nationwide movement.

Meanwhile, the problems faced by the growing number of tenant farmers gave rise to increasing conflict, and this was further intensified with the formation of a variety of tenant farmer organizations. As has been seen above, the farming population was not only poverty stricken but faced the threat of being deprived of their rights of tenancy by the owners for whom they toiled. Their resistance against these conditions now took the form of concerted confrontations with their landlords. In 1922 there were 124 such incidents involving 2,539 farmers, a number that grew to 204 with 4,002 participants in 1925 and to 726 incidents involving 13,012 farmers in 1930. Some 60% of all these incidents were caused by tenant farmer resistance against transfer of their tenancy rights to other farmers, while another 18% were characterized by demands for reduction in the amount of rent charged by the landlord. Still another issue in these disputes was the demand of the farmers that the landowner bear the burden of such imposts as the land tax and irrigation charges. It already has been noted that harm done to Korean farmers by Japan's agricultural policies also was a contributing factor to the rise of unrest among tenant farmers. Moreover, many of the disputes arose on the lands of the giant Japanese landholding corporations, such as the Oriental Development Company and the Fuji company. Particularly serious instances of disputes with Japanese landlords broke out on Oriental Development Company land at Kowŏn in South Hamgyŏng province and on Fuji land at Yongch'ŏn in North P'yŏngan. It is understandable, then, that unrest among Korean tenant farmers was not simply a struggle for economic justice but also took the form of a resistance movement against Japan.

As the great Japanese business enterprises took advantage of cheap Korean labor to invest ever more heavily in mining and industry in Korea, labor unrest also grew apace. From 6 disputes involving 1,573 workers in 1912 the number rose rapidly to 36 cases and 3,403 workers in 1921, to 81 cases and 5,984 workers in 1926, and to 205 cases and 21,180 workers in 1931. These labor disputes acquired added impetus with the organization of the Workers Beneficial Association (Nodong Kongjehoe) in 1920 and its successor the Korean Workers Alliance (Chosŏn Nodong Yŏnmaeng-hoe) in 1922. The result was such work stoppages as the strikes called by

Pusan dockworkers in 1921 and by female rubber goods workers in Seoul in 1923, but the most dramatic instance was the general strike by the workers of Wŏnsan in 1929. This was occasioned by an assault on a Korean worker by a Japanese foreman in an English-owned oil company, and the strike began when the workers walked out demanding that the Japanese foreman be fired. At this point the Wŏnsan Federation of Labor involved itself in the issue and the strike spread, until nearly all of the workers in Wŏnsan had joined in. A flood of contributions soon came in from all over the country to support the livelihood of the striking workers. The Japanese authorities then tried to settle the dispute through a hastily organized group of workers willing to cooperate with the government, but this effort failed. The strike ultimately was resolved by compromise, but it had clearly demonstrated the interrelationship between labor unrest and the nationalist movement. Most labor disputes arose over demands for higher wages, but as time went on there were more and more demands for granting the right of collective bargaining and implementing the eight hour work day. This struggle of the Korean workers gradually spread throughout the country, as one facet of the resistance movement against Japan.

Taken overall, the buy Korean movement of the 1920's and the labor unrest among Korean tenant farmers and factory workers posed a considerable threat to Japan's colonialism in Korea. To counter this, Japan consistently enforced a policy of suppression. And with the Japanese war of aggression against China in the 1930's, Japan's acts of repression became ever more harsh.

Activities of the Sin'ganhoe

After the March First Movement, the Korean struggle for independence sought to find its direction in a variety of alternative stratagems, and one of these was to effect ties with international socialism. The Bolshevik Revolution in Russia had just triumphed, and Lenin was urging support for independence movements among the oppressed peoples of the world. This development gave rise to the organization of the Koryŏ (Korean) Communist Party in Shanghai in 1920, under the leadership of Yi Tong-hwi, and its securing of substantial financial support from the Soviets.

At the same time an anarchist movement arose among Korean students in Tokyo. This movement championed absolute freedom for the individual, denying the legitimacy of any political authority whatsoever, and it adopted the extreme tactics of terrorism. One concrete manifestation of this approach was the assassination attempt on the Japanese emperor by Pak Yŏl in 1923. There was also a group of Marxist theoreticians who argued that Korean independence could be won only through the overthrow of Japanese capitalism, and to this end they formed the Chosŏn Communist Party in 1925 and launched an organized anti-Japanese struggle based on the fostering of labor unrest. The left-wing movement in Korea, however, was weakened by the formation of numerous splinter groups.

In response to this challenge from the radical left, democratic nationalists in Korea sought to form their own political organization, but they could not overcome the stumbling block of the intense opposition of all Koreans to any legal organization that perforce would have to compromise with Japanese colonial rule. In 1927, however, the year after the "June 10 Independence Demonstration" (described below), the nationalist and Communist forces joined in a common front to form the Sin'ganhoe as a single, united nationalist organization. At this time the Japanese authorities still were pursuing their heralded policy of "enlightenment," and they also were motivated by the underlying consideration of thus gaining insight on the inner workings of the Korean nationalist movement, and these factors led to the Sin'ganhoe being accorded recognition as a legal organization.

The guiding principles of the Sin'ganhoe were set forth in the following threefold pledge:

1. To promote political and economic awakening
2. To strengthen national solidarity
3. To disavow any form of opportunism

Accordingly, despite its status as an officially approved organization, it is clear from this manifesto that the aim of the Sin'ganhoe was to participate actively in the struggle for Korean independence. Among the policy proposals it put forward were the dismantling of those Japanese instrumentalities (such as the Oriental Development Company) that exploited Koreans, an end to Japanese policies that encouraged Korean migration to Manchuria and Japan, establishment of an educational system that would serve Korean needs, teaching of the Korean language as part of the school curriculum, freedom to study the "scientific thought" of Marxism-Leninism, and abolition of special laws and regulations imposing restraints and controls on the Korean populace. In short, the Sin'ganhoe took a nationalist position on the full range of issues confronting the Korean people at that time.

Although the overt activities of the Sin'ganhoe were subject to the pressure of constant Japanese surveillance, it succeeded in establishing well over a hundred branches outside of Seoul and its membership reached some 30,000. A parallel women's organization, the Kŭnuhoe, acted in concert with the Sin'ganhoe in pursuing its aims, thus providing a further indication of the fervent support of the Korean people for the nationalist movement. On the occasion of the Kwangju student demonstrations in 1929, the Sin'ganhoe dispatched an investigation team and demonstrated its sympathy for the student activists by such other means as holding mass protest meetings. This resulted in the arrest of many of the Sin'ganhoe's leading members, making its continued operation as an organized body almost impossible. Then in May, 1931, it was dissolved at the insistence of its Communist wing, and from this point on the struggle against Japan was forced to go underground.

The June 10, 1926, Independence Demonstration and the Kwangju Student Movement

A salient feature of the Korean nationalist movement during the period of Japanese colonial rule was the outbreak of student-led demonstrations focusing specifically on demands for independence. The initial beacon fire heralding the March First Movement had been lit by Korean students in Tokyo, and the demonstrations in the streets of Seoul that transformed the movement into a nationwide struggle also had been carried on by the students. This was the case as well with the June 10, 1926, Independence Demonstration and the Kwangju Student Movement in 1929.

The last ruler of the Yi dynasty, Sunjong, died in April 1926, and the deep sorrow of the Korean people combined with their hostility toward Japan to produce an outpouring of grief for his passing. With left-wing activists in the forefront, a plan was set in motion to seize this opportunity to hold a massive anti-Japanese demonstration on the day of the late monarch's state funeral, June 10. But mindful of their earlier experience, when Koreans had taken advantage of the death of King Kojong to launch the March First Movement, the Japanese police maintained the strictest vigilance and discovered what was underway before the funeral. Accordingly, the leaflets that had been printed were seized and throughout the country important figures of standing in Korean society were placed under precautionary arrest. The Japanese authorities even went so far as to prohibit travel to Seoul to join in the funeral observances, and the security net was tightened to enforce this ban. Nevertheless, two other plans developed independently by the students remained undetected, and so street demonstrations did break out after all on June 10. As the funeral cortege passed each new location along the route to the burial ground, groups of students shouted "Long live Korean independence!" and scattered handbills on which was written: "Twenty million countrymen! Drive out the enemy. The price of liberty is blood. Long live Korean independence!" As a consequence, more than two hundred students were arrested, and the incident came to be referred to widely as "The June 10 Independence Demonstration."

Student nationalist activities took not only the form of street demonstrations but also were carried out through organized school strikes. Among the demands presented on these occasions were an educational curriculum suited to Korean interests and needs, an end to the discriminatory features of Japanese colonial education, full implementation of Korean language teaching in the schools, the teaching of Korean history by Korean instructors, and separate schools for Koreans and Japanese. These student strikes in opposition to Japanese colonial policies spread throughout

Korea, culminating in the Kwangju student uprising of 1929.

The Kwangju Student Movement was sparked by the insulting language used by three Japanese male students to three Korean girl students waiting for a train to take them home after school. A clash ensued between Korean and Japanese students and by November 3, 1929, the conflict had escalated into open fighting in the streets of Kwangju. The Japanese police, of course, put the blame for the incident entirely on the Korean students and arrested some four hundred of those involved. At this, students throughout the city rose as one, setting off demonstrations that echoed with cries for release of their jailed comrades, abolition of racial discrimination, liberation of oppressed peoples, and the overthrow of imperialism. These demonstrations did not remain confined to Kwangju alone but by early the next year had spread across the country, involving 194 schools and some 54,000 students. Meanwhile, public sympathy had been thoroughly aroused and, as has been related, the Sin'ganhoe was moved to conduct an on the spot investigation and hold mass protest rallies. In the end, 582 students were expelled from their schools and 2,330 placed under indefinite suspension, while the number of those arrested reached 1,642. The disturbances arising out of the Kwangju Student Movement, then, constituted the largest nationalist demonstration to occur in Korea since the March First Movement of 1919.

The Overseas Independence Movement

Among the overseas independence movements, the activities of the independence fighters in Manchuria deserve first mention. Due to its geographical propinquity, Manchuria had been a center for efforts to regain Korean independence by force of arms ever since the "righteous army" leader Hong Pŏm-do had conducted operations there at the end of the Yi dynasty. The Manchurian villages where fully one million emigrant Koreans lived provided a natural base for such resistance activities. Units of independence fighters were organized in particular numbers in the wake of the March First Movement, to transform the longing for independence that event had aroused into a lasting, tenacious struggle against Japan. These units possessed weapons much inferior to those of the Japanese army, but they nevertheless constituted a powerful force thoroughly schooled in the aims and ideals of Korean nationalism.

On numerous occasions these Korean guerrilla forces attacked Japanese army units and police both in Manchuria and across the border on Korean territory as well. Two of their most spectacular victories occurred in 1920 in battles at Feng-wu-tung and Ch'ing-shan-li, just across the Korean border in southeast Manchuria. In the former instance the Korean Independence Army led by Hong Pŏm-do joined forces with the soldiers of Ch'oe Tong-jin's Military Directorate to surround a Japanese army contingent, inflicting casualties of over 160 killed and more than 300 wounded.

In the Ch'ing-shan-li battle the resistance fighters of the Northern Route Military Command, led by Kim Chwa-jin, crushed a Japanese force vastly superior in numbers and arms, killing over 1,000 Japanese soldiers. The Japanese Army retaliated by attacking Korean villages in Manchuria in what is known as the "1920 massacre," in which many houses were burned and many Korean young men slaughtered.

The effect of the "1920 massacre" was to scatter Korean resistance units into more inaccessible areas, including Russian territory. But before long they began to regroup, despite the adverse conditions confronting them, at the same time combining smaller units under a single command in order to mount more effective operations. As a result, a General Staff Headquarters was established under direct command of the Korean Provisional Government in the region of the mid-Yalu, centering on Chi-an prefecture. At the same time, a Righteous Government was formed in Chi-lin and Feng-t'ien provinces, serving in effect as a governing authority for the Korean population of southern Manchuria. In northern Manchuria the New People's Government was created through coalescence of a number of independence army units around a core of those forces that had returned from Soviet territory in the aftermath of the Free City Incident of 1921, in which Soviet Korean and Bolshevik forces attacked Korean nationalist fighters who refused to allow themselves to be disarmed. Thus Korean independence forces in Manchuria came to be organized under three distinct jurisdictions. These all were democratic organs of civil government through which the Koreans living in Manchuria practiced self-rule, and at the same time they were organs of military administration exercising jurisdiction over the training of resistance forces and their deployment in the armed struggle against Japan. Although the ultimate unity of these three bodies was not achieved, they never slackened their resistance against the common enemy.

As the operations of the independence forces in Manchuria continued with new resolve on the firmer foundation now established, Japan hastened to devise countermeasures. Thus in 1925 Japan sent Mitsuya Miyamatsu, the chief of the Government-General's Police Bureau, to conclude an agreement with the Manchurian warlord Chang Tso-lin to cooperate in stamping out Korean resistance activities. As a result many Korean independence fighters, who had continued to look upon the Chinese regime in Manchuria as sympathetic to their cause, were seized and turned over to the Japanese. This dealt a serious blow to the operations of the independence forces. But after the Manchurian Incident of 1931, with Manchuria under increasingly effective Japanese control, Korean units joined with Chinese forces that were fighting against the new puppet regime in Manchuria and continued their struggle. In the end, however, they were forced to disperse into China proper or the Soviet Maritime Territory.

Whereas the independence movement in Manchuria was carried on mainly through armed resistance, there were those Korean exiles in China who adopted terrorist tactics in their fight against Japan. The best known organizations of this sort were Kim Wŏn-bong's Ŭiyŏltan (Righteous Brotherhood) and Kim Ku's Aeguktan (Patriots Corps). The bombing and assassination plots carried out by these groups were almost too numerous to count, but the best known are the terrorist attacks on the offices of the Oriental Development Company and other targets in Seoul in 1926 by Na Sŏk-chu (1892-1926) of the Ŭiyŏltan, the attempt to assassinate the Japanese emperor by hand grenade in 1932 by Yi Pong-ch'ang (1900-1932) of the Aeguktan, and the bomb set off by Yun Pong-gil (1908-1932), also a member of the Aeguktan, in Shanghai's Hung-k'ou Park in 1932, killing or wounding a number of high-ranking Japanese military and civil officials.

As for the Korean Provisional Government, dissension developed over such issues as the assumption of the presidency by Yi Sŭng-man (Syngman Rhee), who advocated that Korea be made a League of Nations mandated territory, and the use of funds obtained by Yi Tong-hwi from Lenin. In an attempt to restore unity a National Representatives Conference of independence activists from both within and outside Korea was convened in Shanghai in 1923, but to no avail. A chronic shortage of funds added to these woes, and the Provisional Government could do no more than barely keep itself alive. But with the outbreak of the Sino-Japanese War in 1937 a movement to effect a united front gradually got underway, and at length the fresh impetus provided by the U. S. entry into the war against Japan in 1941 brought the disparate elements together again under the banner of the Korean Provisional Government. By this time the Provisional Government had followed the Chinese government in its move to the wartime capital of Chungking, and on the day after Japan's attack on Pearl Harbor the Korean Provisional Government proclaimed a declaration of war against Japan and proceeded to mount an active diplomatic campaign to enlist support abroad.

Along with the diplomatic offensive, military operations also became more vigorous. The new-found political unity brought unity as well to the armed independence fighters, who combined to form the Restoration Army (Kwangbokkun) under the overall command of the Korean Provisional Government, and this force conducted military operations against Japan in cooperation with the Allied armies. From 1942 in particular, in accordance with an agreement reached with the Chinese government, the Restoration Army carried out its operations in close concert with the Chinese forces. At the same time, units of the Restoration Army sent to the Burma-India theatre fought alongside the British armies there. In addition to the Restoration Army, Koreans attached directly to Chinese army units constituted a substantial manpower resource, and many Koreans in America contributed to the common war effort by volunteering their services. Thus the struggle of the Korean people to free their nation from the bondage of Japanese imperialism overcame all obstacles and went forward with renewed vitality.

4. The Preservation of Korean Culture

Resistance Through Nationalist Educational Activities

With the implementation of the so-called enlightened administration strategy following the March First Movement, Japanese educational policy in Korea also underwent the appearance of change, for Japan had professed the intention of providing a level of education for Koreans equal to that available to Japanese. There was, in fact, a remarkable increase in the number of schools, while a university as well was established in Seoul. Nevertheless, what Japan professed in regard to education for Koreans was as hollow as before. This becomes clear from the statistics in the table below. Even on the elementary level the proportion of Korean children attending school was no more than one-sixth that of Japanese. This disparity became progressively greater at the higher levels of education. In the colleges the ratio was 1:26, and at the university level well over 1:100. In short, the expansion of educational facilities in Korea was undertaken more for the benefit of the Japanese colonists than for the native Korean population. This fact alone provides solid evidence of the farcical nature of Japan's touted "enlightened administration."

SCHOOL ENROLLMENT IN KOREA BY NATIONALITY IN 1925

SCHOOL LEVEL	NATION-ALITY	ENROLL-MENTS	PER TEN THOUSAND POPULATION	RATIO
Elementary	Koreans	386,256	208.20	1:6
	Japanese	54,042	1,272.35	
Boys Higher Schools	Koreans	9,292	5.01	1:21
	Japanese	4,532	106.70	
Girls Higher Schools	Koreans	2,208	1.19	1:108
	Japanese	5,458	128.50	
Vocational Schools	Koreans	5,491	2.96	1:21
	Japanese	2,663	62.70	
Normal Schools	Koreans	1,703	0.92	1:16
	Japanese	611	14.39	
Colleges	Koreans	1,020	0.55	1:26
	Japanese	605	14.24	
University	Koreans	89	0.05	1:109
	Japanese	232	5.46	

From the decade of the 1930's Japan's educational policy in Korea took a new direction. Invoking the doctrine of "education for everyday life," Japan now laid stress on teaching the Japanese language and on vocational education. This was because, with the development of war industries in Korea, Japan required a labor force that understood Japanese and possessed some degree of skill. Then, toward the end of the war, in accordance with the policy of eradicating Korean cultural identity, the teaching of Korean was discontinued and exclusive use of Japanese in the schools was enforced. In sum, from beginning to end Japan's educational policy in Korea was the handmaiden of its overall designs for its Korean colony.

Under these circumstances Koreans again had to look to Korean schools for the education to which they aspired. More than half of the Korean students enrolled in colleges studied in private Korean institutions. At the same time, Korean students journeyed abroad—to Japan, where discrimination against them was less severe than in Korea, or to the United States—to obtain a higher education. In 1931, 3,639 Korean students were enrolled in schools in Japan, while as many as 493 were studying in America. When one considers that the majority of these were college students the numbers become all the more impressive. It is evident, then, that the dissemination of modern currents of thought and scholarship among Koreans owed much to the education many of them received in Korean private schools and by study abroad. The movement to establish a Korean university as an alternative to Japan's Keijō (Seoul) Imperial University also may be said to have been a conscious response to this demand for a higher education that would prepare Koreans for their future as a free people.

However, to say nothing of the educational institutions at the college and university level, even the number of middle and elementary level schools were too few to enable them to meet the needs of the Korean people. For this reason a demand arose for additional educational facilities, and to fulfill this demand the traditional *sŏdang* (village study halls) were reorganized into so-called improved *sŏdang*, and these performed an important role in providing an elementary education to village children. Some of these private rural schools eventually were given accreditation as primary schools within the framework of the Government-General's educational system.

Another type of supplementary educational institution was the night school for laborers. The first of these was established in Masan by Ok Ki-hwan as early as 1907, but their large-scale expansion took place after the 1919 March First Movement. It already has been noted that organized movements among farmers and workers developed vigorously in this same period, and the establishing of night schools for laborers was simply the way in which this phenomenon found expression in the area of education. Such schools were opened in cities and towns and villages throughout the whole country, but they were particularly numerous in the southern provinces where private schools hitherto had been relatively few. In the main the night schools for laborers provided an opportunity for a rudimentary education to poor tenant farmers and laborers or to their children, and a considerable number of night schools attended only by women and girls also came into being. On the whole the night schools offered only one year's instruction, mainly in *han'gŭl* and arithmetic, but they demonstrated concern as well for the social and national issues that Korea faced. Since no education fees were assessed, the expenses of these schools had to be met by contributions from the interested public, and often it was a struggle just to keep a school in operation. With the intensification of repressive Japanese control measures following the Manchurian Incident in 1931, the number of night schools gradually decreased. Meanwhile, however, a rural enlightenment movement had developed among Korean students, who utilized their summer vacations to go into the countryside to help the farmers overcome their illiteracy and improve their daily lives. Korean newspapers such as the *Chosŏn Ilbo* and *Tonga Ilbo* gave important support to this movement.

Scholarly Work on Korea

In the field of Korean language study, the Korean Language Society (Chosŏnŏ Hakhoe, a name change that dates from 1931), formed by disciples of Chu Si-gyŏng, played the pivotal role. Inaugurated in 1921 as the Society for the Study of the Korean Language (Chosŏnŏ Yŏnguhoe) and known today as the Han'gŭl Hakhoe, this association of Korean linguists made its greatest contribution in the standardization of *han'gŭl* orthography and usage. Through its monthly journal, *Han'gŭl*, the Society worked to broaden and popularize the use of the native Korean alphabet, *han'gŭl*, in a nation whose educated elite still preferred to write in literary Chinese. At the same time, the Society began the compilation of a dictionary of the Korean language and, to lay a proper foundation for this undertaking, carried out such preparatory tasks as devising rules for *han'gŭl* spelling, differentiating between standard and variant forms of native words, and creating a uniform system for transcribing foreign words in *han'gŭl*. Thus the substantial accomplishments of the Korean Language Society constituted a practical response to the contemporary needs of the Korean people. The Society also did much to enhance appreciation of Korean culture among the public at large by commemorating as "Han'gŭl Day" the date in 1446 when the newly devised Korean alphabet first was promulgated.

The writing of nationalist histories of Korea, in the tradition of those published during the time of the patriotic enlightenment movement at the end of the Yi dynasty, was a phenomenon of the decade of the 1920's. In his works *The Tragic History of Korea* (*Han'guk t'ongsa*) and *The Bloody History of the Korean Independence Movement* (*Han'guk tongnip undong chi hyŏlsa*), Pak Ŭn-sik not only attacked Japan's policies of aggression but at the same time sought to provide spiritual support for the independence movement, asserting that the soul of the Korean race must be preserved. Sin Ch'ae-ho was a historian whose energies were mainly directed to the study of early Korean history, also from the perspective of arousing a spirit of patriotism in his readers, and he laid particular stress on the distinctive Korean *hwarang* ideal, that of dedicating one's life to the service of the nation. His representative works are *Exploratory Studies in Korean History* (*Chosŏnsa yŏn'gu ch'o*) and *Early History of Korea* (*Chosŏn sanggosa*). Chŏng In-bo, too, emphasized the preservation of Korea's unique "soul" or cultural identity in his *Studies in the History of Korea* (*Chosŏnsa yŏn'gu*), which also appeared under the title of *The Spiritual Essence of Korea's Five Thousand Years of History* (*Och'ŏnnyŏn'gan Chosŏn ŭi ŏl*). Ch'oe Nam-sŏn, for his part, interpreted the Tan'gun myth as a manifestation of the shared cultural identity of the Korean people, and in his *The Dawning of Korean History* (*Asi Chosŏn*) he put forward a view of Korean history as constituting the mainstream of northeast Asian culture. Mun Il-p'yŏng as well sought an understanding of Korean history as the expression of the distinct Korean cultural identity; his best known work, however, is *The Fifty Year History of Korean-American Relations* (*Han-Mi osimnyŏnsa*). Most of these studies bore a close relationship to the struggle to regain Korea's independence, in the sense that they all were concerned with defining the vital spirit or essence that uniquely infused the history of the Korean people. These nationalistic Korean histories were suppressed by the Japanese authorities, and Pak Ŭn-sik, Sin Ch'ae-ho, and other like-minded historians were forced to suffer the hardship of continuing their work in exile from their homeland.

From the 1930's, in contrast, emphasis in the study of Korean history was put mainly on the processes through which Korean society evolved, and a school arose that sought to explain these successive stages of development in economic terms. Some scholars of this bent attempted to impose a Marxist historical materialism construct on the historical development of Korea. But there also emerged a methodological school of historiography that believed a more penetrating understanding of Korean history could be gained through objective study of individual historical problems than by setting the Korean historical experience within a rigid theoretical framework. The research activities of the scholars who founded the Chindan Hakhoe (The Chin-Tan Society) in 1934 were among those of this persuasion. The Society's journal, *Chindan Hakpo*, provided a counterweight to the studies of Japanese scholars, and in it there appeared many excellent monographs in a wide range of disciplines, including political history, folklore, fine arts, and intellectual history.

The Development of a Modern Literature

A major turning point in the history of Korean literature came in the wake of the March First Movement. Literature in Korea now broke away from the constraints of the didacticism that characterized the prose of the novels of enlightenment, which had reached the pinnacle of their development with Yi Kwang-su, and came to be recognized as a mode of artistic expression constituting an end in itself. A new wave of literary artists launched the publication of a number of writers' magazines—such as *Creation* (*Ch'angjo*) in 1919, *Ruins* (*P'yehŏ*) in 1920, and *White Tide* (*Paekcho*) in 1922. In the vanguard of the new literary movement that found its outlet in these magazines was Kim Tong-in (1900-1951). In works like his "Potatoes" (*Kamja*) his aim was to create a literature of naturalism that portrayed hunger, and greed, and instinctual sexual behavior with studied candor. At the same time the works of Yŏm Sang-sŏp (1897-1963), such as "Three Generations" (*Samdae*), gave expression to a literature of realism, depicting with careful fidelity the mundane features of the society in which he lived. A literature imbued with sentimentalism, or romanticism, also developed as one stream of Korean literature in the early 1920's.

In the mid-1920's two new trends developed in reaction against what was deemed the effete sentimentality of much literary expression. One of these sought to infuse an awareness of cultural identity, a literary endeavor typified by Han Yong-un (1879-1944). In his poem "The Silence of Love" (*Nim ŭi ch'immuk*) he gave expression to his profound love for his fellow countrymen. The efforts of Yi Pyŏng-gi (1892-1968) and others to adapt the *sijo* to contemporary sensibilities may also be considered to have been similarly inspired. The other trend was toward a literature designed to instill a social consciousness, and works of this kind in the main were produced by writers of the so-called new trend school. This literature was influenced by the Socialist and Communist movements that arose in this period, and on the whole it portrayed the lives of people afflicted with poverty. The work of these writers soon developed into proletarian literature, a politicized literature that looked upon literary activity as serving purely political ends.

As Japanese militarism intensified in the decade of the 1930's a mood of deepening crisis swept over the Korean people. In this milieu writers in Korea shifted course once again, toward a "pure" literature that deliberately avoided confronting the threatening realities of that time. With the publication of the magazine *Literature* (*Munjang*) in 1939 the tendency to seek to safeguard literature from political involvement—to insist that literature remain, as it were, immaculate—grew still more pronounced. This newest movement was essentially escapist, but by discovering the unpretentious beauty of native Korean language expressions, eschewing reliance on hallowed usages borrowed from Chinese, this literature too contributed to enhancing Korean cultural identity.

With the enforcement of the cultural assimilation policy at the end of the Japanese colonial period, the writings of the school of pure literature too were suppressed, for the publication of any work in the Korean language no longer was permitted. At this juncture Korean literature faced its darkest hour, its very survival in peril. Many Korean writers succumbed to Japanese pressures, publishing their work in Japanese or even allowing their art to serve Japan's purposes. In this context the words of the young poet Yun Tong-ju (1917-1945), who died in prison in Japan just before Korea's liberation, are especially poignant. In the poem that, as a statement of the poet's faith, introduces his posthumous work "Sky, Wind, Stars, and Poetry," he writes:

> The constancy of Heaven is my lodestone
>   Till the day I die,
> So that the slightest ground for shame
>   Shall not exist for me.
> The alluring rustle of the wind among the leaves
>   But bestirs me to renewed steadfastness.

In these words Yun Tong-ju gave voice to the agonizing struggle of one solitary Korean soul to follow the dictates of his conscience as a human being.

Chapter 16

The Beginnings of Democracy

1. The Liberation of Korea, August 15, 1945

Liberation

With Italy's surrender in June 1943, the prospects of victory for the Allied cause in the Second World War gradually became more certain. This meant that the day of Korea's liberation from Japanese oppression also was drawing near. In fact, at a summit conference held this same year in Cairo among the leaders of the United States, Great Britain, and China, the so-called Cairo Declaration was adopted, on December 1, 1943, in which it was proclaimed that:

> "The aforesaid three great powers, mindful of the enslavement of the people of Korea, are determined that in due course Korea shall become free and independent."

The inclusion of this statement, there can be no doubt, was owing to the untiring struggle of the Korean national movement for independence. A year and a half later, in May of 1945, Germany too surrendered, and when the leaders of the same three Allied nations met again in the Berlin suburb of Potsdam in July 1945, they reaffirmed the principles agreed upon earlier at Cairo. A month later, the Soviet Union also subscribed to the Potsdam Declaration. As a result of this international commitment on the part of the major Allied Powers, the Korean people were convinced that their independence would be achieved at the moment of Japan's final defeat.

On August 15, 1945, Japan at last surrendered unconditionally to the Allies. Korea had been liberated from thirty-six years under the tyrannical rule of Japanese imperialism. Amidst an outpouring of popular rejoicing the streets of Korea's towns and villages no longer flew the blood-red sun symbol of the flag of Japan but were bedecked instead with the *yin-yang* and trigram patterned banner of Korea. The people of Korea harbored no slightest doubt that their liberation meant their immediate independence.

But liberation from Japan's harshly oppressive rule had come with unexpected suddenness, and the difficulty in obtaining accurate information from abroad while Japan still controlled all channels of communication engendered confusion among Korean leaders as to what preparatory measures they might appropriately take. Song Chin-u and his followers anticipated that the Allied forces would occupy Korea forthwith and that the returning Korean Provisional Government would take over governmental authority. Acting on a sharply different premise, those who shared the views of Yŏ Un-hyŏng (Lyuh Woon-hyung) saw a need to create popular representative organs in advance of the arrival of the Allied forces. While the former remained inactive, awaiting the return to Korea of the officials of the Provisional Government, the latter organized a Committee for the Preparation of Korean Independence. Although some democratic nationalist figures participated in the activities of this committee, it was the Communist members who exerted the greater influence. Before long, therefore, non-Communist leaders such as An Chae-hong, who at first had accepted membership on the committee, disassociated themselves from it. At this point the committee's left-wing forces hastily put together a kind of administrative mechanism called the Korean People's Republic (Chosŏn Inmin Konghwaguk), thus in effect setting themselves in opposition to the Korean Provisional Government in Chungking. Whereupon their opponents countered by holding a preparatory meeting to plan for the convening of an "Assembly of the People," the purpose of which would be to support the Provisional Government and consolidate a broad national consensus behind it.

The Division at the Thirty-Eighth Parallel and Military Government

Just as the confrontation between the democratic nationalist and Communist forces within Korea thus was growing sharper, the U.S. and Soviet armies of occupation appeared on the scene. The Soviets, due to their common border with Korea, were the first to arrive. Having declared war only on August 9, when it was all but certain that Japan would capitulate, the Soviet Union crossed the frontier into Korea and, following the Japanese surrender, proceeded to occupy P'yŏngyang, Hamhŭng, and other major cities in the north. U.S. forces landed at Inch'ŏn a month later, on September 8, entered Seoul, then gradually stationed troops throughout the southern half of the peninsula. The line that divided the U.S. and Soviet zones of occupation was drawn at the 38th parallel of north latitude. This artificial line of demarcation became the principal external factor that brought division and tragedy to the Korean people in the years ahead.

The U.S. and Soviet forces administered their respective zones of occupation in south and north Korea through radically different instrumentalities. In the north, the Soviet authorities made use of the so-called Provisional People's Committee for the Five Provinces [of northern Korea], which had been organized around those active in the independence movement and included even democratic nationalists like Cho Man-sik, entrusting to it actual governmental administration under the policy direction of the Soviet military command. But before long the Soviets formed the so-called Provisional People's Committee for North Korea under the chairmanship of Kim Il-sŏng (Kim Il Sung) and, after Cho Man-sik and many other nationalist figures had been ousted from the committee, a policy of Communization was enforced. The number of Koreans who could not endure life under this Communist authoritarianism and so crossed over the 38th parallel into south Korea rose sharply, totaling more than 800,000 by the end of 1947.

On the other hand, the U.S. forces that somewhat later took up their stations in south Korea established a military government and opted to conduct the administration of the south themselves. Accordingly, the U.S. Military Government refused to recognize either the so-called People's Republic or the Provisional Government in Chungking as sovereign governmental organs. The U.S. armed forces that were entrusted with governmental authority, however, had practically no advance knowledge of conditions within Korea, and they were unable to meet the expectations of the people they governed. To make matters worse, in contrast to the situation in north Korea, freedom of political activity was permitted in the south and this led to a chaotic profusion of political parties. More than fifty were formed in all, the chief among them being Song Chin-u's Korean Democratic Party (Han'guk Minjudang), An Chae-hong's Nationalist Party (Kungmindang), Yŏ Un-hyŏng's Chosŏn People's Party (Chosŏn Inmindang), and Pak Hŏn-yŏng's Korean Communist Party (Chosŏn Kongsandang). Under this circumstance political unity hardly could be expected, and the return of Yi Sŭng-man (Syngman Rhee) from the United States and Kim Ku and other key figures in the Provisional Government from China did nothing to calm the political turbulence.

The south Korean people now suffered not only from the political disarray but from grave economic dislocations as well. The contours of Korea's economy had taken shape abnormally, with emphasis on war-related industry and a high degree of reliance on Japan. Accordingly, the severance of all ties with Japan following liberation inevitably dealt a severe blow to the economy. Moreover, the partition of the country at the 38th parallel separated the predominantly light industry and agricultural zone of the south from the heavy industry of the north [see following table], while production at those facilities in the south that remained operable often suffered from a shortage of qualified Korean technicians. Furthermore, the huge amount of currency, 3.6 billion yen (compared to the approximately five billion yen total of banknotes outstanding at the time of liberation), put into circulation in the first weeks following Japan's surrender—most of it by Japanese authorities prior to the landing of U. S. forces—brought on severe inflation. Finally, more than two million Koreans crossed into the southern zone from the north or returned home from China, Japan, and former Japanese occupied areas elsewhere in the two years or so following liberation. The combined effect of all these adverse factors was to produce economic chaos.

COMPARISON OF PRODUCTION IN SOUTH AND NORTH KOREA
(in percentages as of 1945)

CATEGORY	SOUTH KOREA	NORTH KOREA
Steel	5	95
Hydroelectric Power	10	90
Chemicals	15	85
Coal	20	80
Food	65	35
Machinery	65	35
Consumer goods	80	20

2. The Establishment of the Republic of Korea

The Anti-Trusteeship Movement and the U.S.-Soviet Joint Commission

At a conference in Moscow in December 1945, the foreign ministers of the U.S., Great Britain, and the Soviet Union adopted a trusteeship plan as a means of solving the Korean problem. This plan, which would have placed Korea under four power trusteeship (U.S., Britain, China, Soviet Union) for a period of up to five years, met with the violent opposition of the Korean people. To give expression to this public outrage, an anti-trusteeship movement was launched under the aegis of a Committee for Total National Mobilization Against Trusteeship, organized around Provisional Government leaders. In Seoul stores and businesses were closed and demonstrations held in the streets, while the employees of the U.S. Military Government went out on strike. Demonstrations then spread throughout the whole country. At first the Communists too joined in the anti-trusteeship movement but then suddenly shifted position to support trusteeship, and this created a serious obstacle to a campaign of national unity based on cooperation between leftist and rightist forces. At this point the Provisional Government leadership summoned an "extraordinary people's assembly" for the purpose of establishing a sovereign governmental authority, thus to block the implementation of the trusteeship plan.

Such was the political atmosphere when preparatory talks for convening the U.S.-Soviet Joint Commission, the body that was to implement the Moscow Agreement, were held in January 1946, and in March the meetings of the Joint Commission itself got underway. There the Soviet side contended that political parties and social organizations opposed to trusteeship should be excluded from those Korean bodies to be consulted with respect to the creation of the provisional government structure that the trusteeship plan envisaged. This position was designed to exclude the democratic nationalists from the interim government, leaving it to be organized by the Communists alone. In response, the U.S. delegates asserted the principle of freedom of political expression and argued that even those Koreans who were opposed to trusteeship ought to take part in the consultative process. Deadlocked over this issue, the first round of talks at the Joint Commission soon was broken off, in May 1946.

The deadlock at the Joint Commission brought further disarray to the Korean political scene, and in consequence there were a number of different approaches attempted to break through the political impasse. The reaction of the Korean Democratic Party, which now was headed by Syngman Rhee, was to organize a National Headquarters for Unification and seek to establish an autonomous Korean goverment. Rhee's demand was that the agreement at Yalta and the Moscow decisions be nullified, thus doing away with both the 38th parallel and the trusteeship concept, and that an independent transitional government be established immediately. Rhee personally traveled to the United States in an effort to achieve this end. On the other hand the Korean Independence Party, led by Kim Ku and others from the Korean Provisional Government, formed a "national assembly" (the successor to the earlier "extraordinary people's assembly") whose main activity was to oppose trusteeship but which, at the same time, sought to bring about accord between left and right, thus to achieve unification of the peninsula. There was also a moderate right under the leadership of Kim Kyu-sik that worked with the moderate left of Yŏ Un-hyŏng to promote unity of action between leftists and rightists. These moderate forces came to receive the backing of the U.S. Military Government and comprised the membership of the South Korean Interim Legislative Assembly established by the U.S. in 1947.

Meanwhile the left-wing political parties formed the so-called Democratic National Front and carried on a unified pro-trusteeship campaign, urging support of the Moscow Agreement and the reconvening of the Joint Commission. By giving positive support to the work of the Joint Commission, the left-wing hoped to enhance its position within the governmental authority that was to be created under the trusteeship concept. At the same time the leftists employed a variety of means to disrupt the political, economic, and social processes in south Korea. But when the police found evidence of large-scale currency counterfeiting at a press used by the Korean Communist Party (May 1946), the U.S. authorities put out an order for the arrest of its leaders, whereupon the Communists went underground. Even then the Communists continued to foment sedition, the most serious such instance being the Taegu uprising that developed on the occasion of the railroad strike in early October 1946.

In the meantime the U.S. Military Government had created a legislative organ with completely Korean membership, the South Korean Interim Legislative Assembly, and had appointed a Korean chief justice and a Korean chief civil administrator. Formal administrative authority thus was turned over to Koreans, in a structure that was called the South Korean Interim Government.

The Establishment of the Republic of Korea

The U.S.-Soviet Joint Commission reconvened in May 1947, one year after the initial talks had been broken off. For a time, in response to the request of the Commission, suggestions as to the form and political orientation of the prospective provisional government were submitted by Korean political parties and social organizations. But the Soviets reiterated the position they had taken before, that those bodies which had opposed the trusteeship plan should be excluded from the consultative process. This Soviet intransigence brought the Commission's deliberations to a standstill.

At this juncture the U.S. proposed that the Korean issue be referred to a conference of the foreign ministers of the U.S., Soviet Union, Britain, and China for further discussion. When the Soviet Union also rejected this proposal, the United States submitted the question of Korea's independence to the United Nations. The U.S. recommendation was that general elections be held in Korea under U.N. supervision, that U.S. and Soviet troops be withdrawn from Korea upon the establishment of a government based upon the outcome of the elections, and that a U.N. Temporary Commission on Korea be created to oversee and facilitate the carrying out of these provisions. With minor modifications the U.S. resolution was adopted, despite Soviet opposition, by an overwhelming majority of the U.N. General Assembly. The United Nations Temporary Commission on Korea created by the terms of this resolution began its operations in January 1948, but Soviet opposition frustrated the Commission's efforts to gain entry to north Korea. On the basis of the Commission's report, in February 1948, the Interim Committee of the U.N. General Assembly authorized elections to be held in those areas of Korea open to the supervision of the Commission and the creation of an independent government based on the outcome of the elections. Thus the way was cleared for Korean independence, although an independent government under U.N. auspices would be established only in the southern half of the country.

The first general election in the history of Korea was carried out on May 10, 1948. Those who favored direct talks between political leaders of the north and south boycotted the elections, and one hundred seats allocated to the northern provinces were left unfilled, but 198 representatives of the Korean people nevertheless were chosen by the voters. The first National Assembly was convened on May 31 and it immediately set about its priority task, framing a constitution. By July 12 a constitution had been adopted by the National Assembly and on July 17 it was formally promulgated. In accordance with its provisions a presidential election was held on July 20 (at that time the Korean constitution prescribed that the president be elected indirectly, by the National Assembly) and Syngman Rhee emerged the winner. An administrative structure then was created and on August 15, 1948, the establishment of the government of the Republic of Korea (Taehan Min'guk) was announced to the Korean people and to the world. In December of the same year the Republic of Korea was acknowledged by the U.N. General Assembly to be, in effect, the only lawfully constituted government in Korea. Soon thereafter the Republic of Korea was accorded recognition by the United States and some fifty other nations.

3. The Korean War

Solidification of Communist Control in North Korea

The Provisional People's Committee for North Korea had been formed in P'yŏngyang in February 1946, and was designed to function as an interim government under the policy control of the Soviet military authorities. Through a variety of enactments, foremost among then a thoroughgoing land reform, this People's Committee laid a firm foundation for a Communist political system. Then, in February 1947, the People's Committee of North Korea (no longer labeled "provisional") was created and this was tantamount to establishing an autonomous governmental authority in north Korea.

Refusing to permit the United Nations Temporary Commission on Korea to carry out its mission in north Korea, the Communist authorities proposed instead that direct negotiations be pursued between political leaders of the north and south. Their objectives were to obstruct the Commission's activities, to effect a simultaneous withdrawal of U.S. and Soviet occupation forces, and then to seek an opportunity to extend Communist dominion over all of Korea by force of arms. Accordingly a powerful military force was organized and trained in north Korea from an early date, and after the formal establishment of an independent government, called the Democratic People's Republic of Korea (Chosŏn Minjujuŭi Inmin Konghwaguk), in 1948, military preparations were further strengthened. Immediately prior to the outbreak of the Korean War on June 25, 1950, North Korean military power consisted of as many as ten infantry divisions, 242 tanks, and 211 planes. In contrast, despite President Syngman Rhee's insistent clamor for unification of Korea by military force, South Korea's army consisted of no more than eight divisions. More seriously than that, South Korea's military was poorly equipped, lacking even a single tank and with an air force consisting of some twenty training aircraft but not one fighter plane.

The Korean War

South Korea's second general elections were held in May, 1950. The result of the election gave 56 seats in the National Assembly to the government party, 26 to members of the Democratic Nationalist Party and other opposition parties, and 128 to independents. This clearly was an expression of the people's lack of confidence in the government and in the existing political parties as well. At about this same time the view was being expressed in Washington that Korea lay outside the U.S. defense perimeter in East Asia. The North Korean Communists, who had been trying to subvert the Republic of Korea by fomenting armed rebellion (such as that at Yŏsu and Sunch'ŏn in 1948), now were led to believe that the time was ripe for an all-out invasion of South Korea.

On June 25, 1950, then, North Korea launched a surprise attack across the 38th parallel. The under strength and poorly equipped Republic of Korea army was quickly forced to retreat to a line along the Naktong River in the southeast corner of the country. The United Nations, however, quickly resolved to give military support to the Republic of Korea, at whose birth as an independent nation the U.N. had acted as midwife. A United Nations Command was established and troops from sixteen countries—including the United States, Britain, France, Canada, Australia, the Philippines, and Turkey—arrived in Korea to fight side by side with the South Korean army under the flag of the United Nations.

Seoul was recaptured on September 28, 1950, following the successful amphibious landing at Inch'ŏn. On September 30 the U. N. forces poured across the 38th parallel and continued to push northward, before long reaching Ch'ŏngjin on the northeast coast, the Yalu River in the areas of Hyesanjin and Ch'osan in north-central Korea, and Sŏnch'ŏn in the northwest. But the fighting took a sharp turnabout with the intervention of Communist Chinese armies. In this new war the U.N. forces for a time retreated to positions south of the Han River, but then the Communists were driven back above the 38th parallel, suffering huge losses in the process. The fighting gradually fell into a stalemate, and eventually (on July 27, 1953) an armistice agreement was reached between the U.N. and Communist forces. The bitter warfare thus came to an end.

The Korean War was one of the most tragic such episodes in the nation's history. The suffering that it caused was cruel beyond expression. South Korean casualties in the fighting alone are estimated at 150,000 dead, 200,000 missing, and 250,000 injured, while more than 100,000 civilians were abducted to North Korea and the number of war refugees reached several million. North Korean casualties were several times these figures.

It is difficult to give an accurate account of the material losses resulting from the Korean War, but the damage to property has been estimated at something over 3 billion (1953 U.S.) dollars. About 43% of manufacturing facilities, 41% of electrical generating capacity, and 50% of the coal mines in South Korea were destroyed or damaged. One-third of the nation's housing was destroyed, and substantial proportions of the country's public buildings, roads, bridges, ports, and the like also were reduced to ruins.

PRODUCTION INDICES FOR SOUTH KOREA IN THE FIRST TWO YEARS OF THE KOREAN WAR

PRODUCT	1949	1950	1951
Grains	100	96	73
Marine Products	100	73	92
Anthracite Coal	100	53	10
Tungsten Ore	100	60	86
Cotton Cloth	100	85	47
Rubber Shoes	100	16	57
Common Bricks	100	74	58
Cement	100	48	30

But the damage wrought by the Korean War cannot be measured in material terms alone. This is because the war forced the Korean people, long conscious of their ethnic unity, painfully to face the tragic reality that their nation had been partitioned and that hope for eventual reunification had become still more remote. It is not that no attempt at reunification was made after the signing of the armistice. The Geneva Conference called for in the armistice accord indeed was convened in April 1954. At Geneva the representatives of the Republic of Korea proposed first that the authority of the United Nations over the Korean problem be acknowledged and, secondly, that free elections be held under U.N. supervision for the purpose of creating a united and independent democratic Korea. But the North Korean Communists rejected this approach, bringing about the rupture of the Geneva talks. In subsequent years, this "Geneva formula" for the reunification of Korea was reaffirmed annually by the U.N. General Assembly.

4. The April 1960 Revolution

The Growth of Authoritarian Government

In the midst of the national peril occasioned by the Korean War, a political crisis took shape within the country as well. This was because of a gradually deepening drift toward authoritarian rule. Syngman Rhee's dictatorial inclinations were apparent from the beginning, when he stubbornly insisted on a constitution giving disproportionate powers to the office of the president. Moreover, it was due to his opposition that the intent of extraordinary legislation enacted to punish those who had flagrantly collaborated with Japanese colonial rule was frustrated and remained unenforced.

Then with the Korean War still raging in 1952, when Syngman Rhee realized how dim were his prospects for reelection by the National Assembly to a second term as president, he brazenly resorted to dictatorial tactics to keep himself in power. When his plan to amend the constitution to provide for direct popular election of the president was rejected by the National Assembly, he openly took steps to coerce the Assembly into doing his bidding. First declaring a state of martial law, he then, on May 26, imprisoned a large number of Assemblymen who opposed him, an event known as the Political Turmoil of May 26. This state of political siege continued until the National Assembly passed the so-called Selective Constitutional Revision Bill, which included provision for direct election of the president. In the end Rhee had forced the vote to be taken by show of hands, and many Assembly members were afraid to stand openly against him.

Subsequently Syngman Rhee's Liberal Party (Chayudang), which had triumphed in the general elections of May 1954 by means of coercive tactics, proposed a constitutional amendment that would exempt the "present incumbent only" from the prohibition against more than two terms as president, a measure transparently aimed at securing President Rhee's indefinite continuance in office. Lacking the statutory two-thirds majority by a fraction of one vote, the amendment was declared to have been defeated, but the next day it was announced that in fact it had passed, on the ground that the number of affirmative votes required for passage, 135.3, might reasonably be rounded down to the next whole number. The opposition Democratic Nationalist Party and independent Assemblymen now formed an Association for the Preservation of the Constitution, and this body eventually fathered the Democratic Party (Minjudang), an amalgam of political opposition forces. This resulted in the victory of the vice-presidential candidate of the Democratic Party in the 1956 elections, and in the 1958 elections for the National Assembly the Democratic Party was able to prevent the Liberal Party from obtaining the two-thirds majority needed for further amendment of the constitution. On this occasion the Liberal Party suffered a crushing defeat in the cities, winning only in the countryside where it was easily able to obtain votes by employing a variety of highhanded tactics. Facing almost certain defeat in the next presidential elections, in December 1958 the Liberal Party sought to strengthen its hand by amending the National Security Law (to tighten government controls) and the Local Self-Government Law (to enable the government to appoint the heads of major units of local administration). Encountering strong resistance from opposition Assemblymen, the Liberal Party members called in police specially trained in the martial arts to arrest their opponents. Then, at a session of the National Assembly attended only by the Liberal Party members, the controversial revision bill was passed, an incident known as the Political Turmoil of December 24 (1958).

The Emergence of New Business Tycoons

Accompanying the growth of authoritarian government a new phenomenon appeared in the economic sphere as well, with the emergence of monopolistic business concerns. The severe destruction of the Korean War had brought industrial production to a virtual standstill, and the Korean government's printing of money to pay the costs of the war and to meet the huge requirements of the U.N. forces for Korean currency had fueled a raging inflation. In consequence, in the course of the war, commodity prices came to double every six months, an inflationary spiral that posed a severe threat to the livelihood of the whole of the general populace. Nevertheless, the government gave special treatment in the distribution of imported raw materials and commodities to a favored few industrialists and business houses, enabling them to reap windfall profits at public expense. Similarly, special bank loans, allocations of U.S. dollars at favorable rates of exchange, and capital sums imported in connection with foreign aid programs were made available by the government to those entrepreneurs who supported it. Accordingly, although industrial output and Korea's infrastructure in general actually had expanded beyond the pre-war levels within a few years after hostilities ended, due in large part to U.S. foreign aid, this redounded to the benefit of a few privileged businessmen rather than to that of the people as a whole. Moreover, as the designated recipients of shareholdings in banks formerly vested in the government, these new tycoons were given control of the major organs of finance as well, thus enabling them to strengthen their grip still further on the Korean economy. As the following table shows, the result of all this was that large enterprises employing two hundred or more workers accounted for a highly disproportionate percentage of total shipments of finished products.

**CONCENTRATION OF PRODUCTION IN MAJOR
INDUSTRIES IN 1962**

(unit: million wŏn)

INDUSTRY	TOTAL ENTERPRISES	LARGE ENTERPRISES*		TOTAL SHIPMENTS	LARGE ENTERPRISES	
Milling	58	2	3.4%	2,337	233	10.0%
Sugar	44	2	4.5	3,480	3,173	91.2
Textiles	174	33	19.0	11,089	9,834	88.7
Tires and Tubes	10	2	20.0	1,105	1,023	92.6
Soap	98	1	1.0	518	255	49.2
Rubber Shoes	48	9	18.8	1,845	1,437	77.9

* 200 or more employees

Thus within the space of a few short years a group of new business concerns emerged in close collusion with the government and achieved a dominant position in the production and distribution of many basic commodities. The result was that economic inequities grew ever more severe. For one thing, small and medium size enterprises, unable to obtain adequate financing, had no way to halt their slide toward bankruptcy. But the inequity between urban and rural sectors of the economy was particularly glaring. The farmers had received land in accordance with the land reform carried out in 1949, but the bare subsistence pattern of farmholding prevailed as before. With the price of rice arbitrarily set by the government even below the cost of production, the poor rural population became even more impoverished. In such ways as this the dominant economic position of a few new business tycoons, operating hand in glove with an authoritarian government, fostered serious unrest in Korean society.

The April Revolution

The social unrest spawned by Syngman Rhee's authoritarian rule reached a climax in the presidential elections of March 1960. Syngman Rhee and his Liberal Party mobilized government employees and the police in particular to carry out the most blatant acts of election rigging. A system experimented with earlier requiring open marking of ballots by voters in groups of three, stuffing of ballot boxes, ballot switching, obstruction of opposition party election campaigning, use of terrorist tactics—the government resorted to all these devices and more. At the same time huge election campaign funds were squeezed out of the business houses that had grown fat from their parasitic relationship with the Liberal Party government.

Opposition to these flagrant illegalities manifested itself even before the election with the student demonstration in Taegu on February 28. This demonstration, however, had the professed objective of protesting political interference on the campuses. But the student demonstration held in Masan on March 15, the day of the election, was aimed squarely at the election irregularities themselves. The demonstrators were dispersed when the police fired live ammunition, killing or wounding some one hundred participants. But on April 11, when the brutality of the police toward the demonstrators became known with the discovery of the body of a high school boy in Masan harbor, the aroused students and citizenry of Masan again took to the streets.

The Masan demonstration was the spark that ignited Seoul. On their way back to their campus after holding a rally in the center of Seoul on April 18, the students of Koryŏ (Korea) University were set upon by government-hired thugs, many of them suffering injuries. The next day, on the 19th, students from nearly all of Seoul's colleges and universities, and from many high schools as well, poured into the city's downtown streets, shouting such slogans as "We demand new elections!," "Defend democracy to the death!," and "The Syngman Rhee government must resign!" After holding a demonstration in front of the National Assembly building the students headed for the Kyŏngmudae, the presidential mansion, only to be met by a hail of police bullets when they reached its vicinity. Roused to a frenzy by the sight of comrades dying before their eyes, the students set fire to a number of government structures and committed other violent acts of destruction. Alarmed by the gravity of the situation the government declared martial law and called in the army, thus for the moment restoring order in the streets.

But in the wake of a demonstration by university professors on April 25, culminating in the reading of a far-reaching set of demands to an enthusiastic crowd in front of the National Assembly building, students and citizenry joined in an all night demonstration that swelled in numbers and stridency as the next day wore on. The martial law troops refused to fire on the demonstrators, giving President Rhee no further hope of maintaining himself in power. His formal resignation on April 26 brought an immediate end to the demonstrations, and the students themselves took the lead in bringing about a restoration of public order.

The April Revolution was the first in the history of Korea wherein a people armed with nothing but their bare fists succeeded in overthrowing an oppressive government. The leading role in this revolution was performed by the students. Their loss of faith in the established generation and its political order led them to take their position in the vanguard of the April 1960 revolutionary struggle. At the same time, the revolution could not have been won without the wholehearted support of the people. The power of the people, united in their opposition to a dictatorial government and the exploitative economic interests allied with it, had been given expression through the vigor and elan of the youthful student demonstrators. The April Revolution, therefore, held out bright prospects for the development of democracy in Korea.

DYNASTIC LINEAGES*

Old Chosŏn
古朝鮮

Tan'gun Wanggŏm ·· Pu Wang ——————— Chun Wang
檀君王儉 (2333 B.C.-?)   否王   準王 (?-194 B.C.)

Wiman Chosŏn
衞滿朝鮮

Wiman Wang ————————————— ◯ ————————— Ugŏ Wang
衞滿王 (194 B.C.-?)   右渠王 (?-108 B.C.)

Puyŏ (Hae)
夫餘 (解)

·············Si Wang ——————— Wigut'ae ······························ Put'ae Wang ······
         始王   尉仇台 (fl. 121)   夫台王

···· Wigut'ae Wang ——————— Kanwigŏ Wang ——————— Mayŏ Wang ——————— Ŭiryŏ Wang ······
尉仇台王 (?-ca.200)   簡位居王   麻余王   依慮王 (?-285)

                                ···· Ŭira Wang ·············· Hyŏn Wang
                                   依羅王 (286-?)   玄王 (?-346)

Pon Kaya (Kim)
本加耶 (金)
(42-532)

1. Suro Wang ——————— 2. Kŏdŭng Wang ——————— 3. Map'um Wang ——————— 4. Kŏjilmi Wang ——
首露王 (42-199)   居登王 (199-259)   麻品王 (259-291)   居叱彌王 (291-346)

└── 5. I(si)p'um Wang ——————— 6. Chwaji Wang ——————— 7. Ch'wihŭi Wang ——
     伊(尸)品王 (346-407)   坐知王 (407-421)   吹希王 (421-451)

└── 8. Chilchi Wang ——————— 9. Kamji Wang ——————— 10. Kuhyŏng Wang
     銍知王 (451-492)   鉗知王 (492-521)   仇衡王 (521-532)

Tae Kaya
大加耶

1. Ijinasi Wang ·············· 9. Inoe Wang ——————— Wŏlgwang T'aeja ·········· 16. Tosŏlchi Wang
伊珍阿鼓王 (ca. 42-?)   異腦王 (fl. 522)   月光太子   道設智王 (?-562)

   * For the ancient period, including the Three Kingdoms and Parhae, records giving the surname of a royal house (in parentheses following the name of the kingdom), the names and titles of kings, and the dates of their reigns (in parentheses under the king's name) in many cases are at variance or are problematical. Foundation dates and the reign dates of the founding kings of these early dynasties are regarded as mostly unreliable but are provided here as in Korean historiographic tradition.

Koguryŏ (Ko)
高句麗 (高)
(37 B.C.-668)

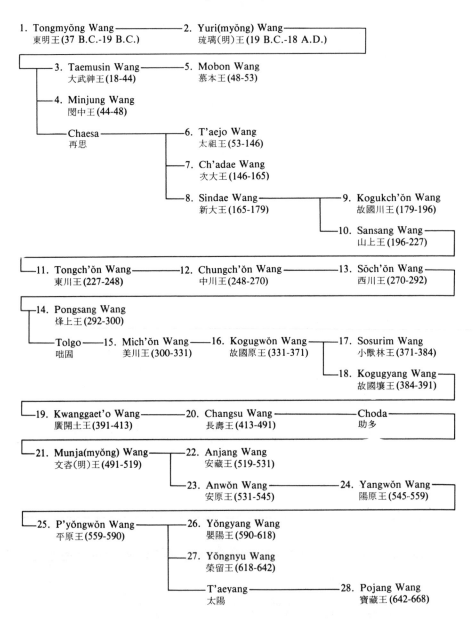

Paekche (Puyŏ)
百濟 (扶餘)
(18 B.C.-660)

1. Onjo Wang ——————————— 2. Taru Wang ——————————— 3. Kiru Wang
   溫祚王(18 B.C.-28 A.D.)   多婁王 (28-77)   己婁王 (77-128)

4. Kaeru Wang ———— 5. Ch'ogo Wang ———— 6. Kusu Wang ———— 7. Saban Wang
   蓋婁王 (128-166)   肖古王 (166-214)   仇首王 (214-234)   沙伴王 (234)

                                                              11. Piryu Wang
                                                                  比流王 (304-344)

                     8. Koi Wang ———— 9. Ch'aekkye Wang ——10. Punsŏ Wang
                        古尒王 (234-286)   責稽王 (286-298)   汾西王 (298-304)

                                                              12. Kye Wang
                                                                  契王 (344-346)

13. Kŭn Ch'ogo Wang ———————— 14. Kŭn Kusu Wang ——————— 15. Ch'imnyu Wang
    近肖古王 (346-375)   近仇首王 (375-384)   枕流王 (384-385)

                                                              16. Chinsa Wang
                                                                  辰斯王 (385-392)

17. Asin (Ahwa) Wang ——————— 18. Chŏnji Wang ——————————— 19. Kuisin Wang
    阿莘(華)王 (392-405)   腆支王 (405-420)   久爾辛王 (420-427)

20. Piyu Wang ———— 21. Kaero Wang ———— 22. Munju Wang ———23. Samgŭn Wang
    毗有王 (427-455)   蓋鹵王 (455-475)   文周王 (475-477)   三斤王 (477-479)

                                          Konji ————————24. Tongsŏng Wang
                                          昆支   東城王 (479-501)

25. Muryŏng Wang ——————————— 26. Sŏng Wang ——————————— 27. Widŏk Wang
    武寧王 (501-523)   聖王 (523-554)   威德王 (554-598)

                                                              28. Hye Wang
                                                                  惠王 (598-599)

29. Pŏp Wang ——————————————— 30. Mu Wang ——————————————— 31. Ŭija Wang
    法王 (599-600)   武王 (600-641)   義慈王 (641-660)

Silla (Pak, Sŏk, Kim)
新羅 (朴,昔,金)
(57 B.C.-935)

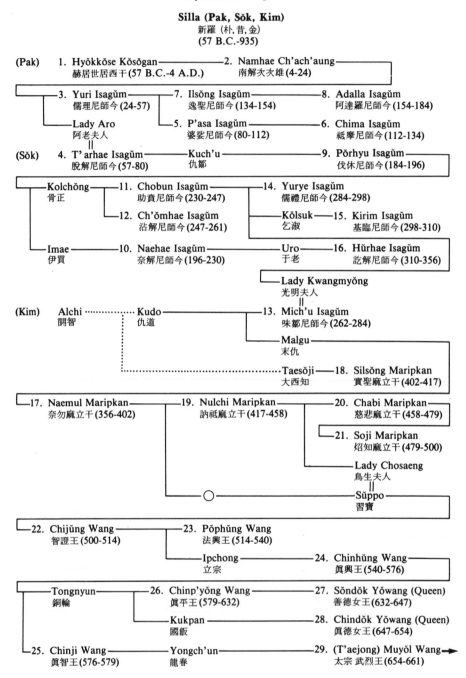

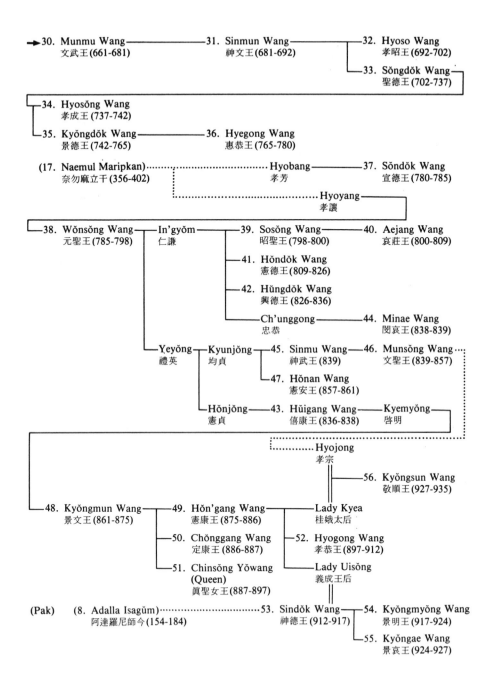

→ 30. Munmu Wang ———————— 31. Sinmun Wang ———————— 32. Hyoso Wang
文武王 (661-681)   神文王 (681-692)   孝昭王 (692-702)

33. Sŏngdŏk Wang
聖德王 (702-737)

34. Hyosŏng Wang
孝成王 (737-742)

35. Kyŏngdŏk Wang ———————— 36. Hyegong Wang
景德王 (742-765)   惠恭王 (765-780)

(17. Naemul Maripkan) ············· Hyobang ———————— 37. Sŏndŏk Wang
奈勿麻立干 (356-402)   孝芳   宣德王 (780-785)

Hyoyang
孝讓

38. Wŏnsŏng Wang ——— In'gyŏm ——— 39. Sosŏng Wang ——— 40. Aejang Wang
元聖王 (785-798)   仁謙   昭聖王 (798-800)   哀莊王 (800-809)

41. Hŏndŏk Wang
憲德王 (809-826)

42. Hŭngdŏk Wang
興德王 (826-836)

Ch'unggong ———————— 44. Minae Wang
忠恭   閔哀王 (838-839)

Yeyŏng ——— Kyunjŏng ——— 45. Sinmu Wang ——— 46. Munsŏng Wang
禮英   均貞   神武王 (839)   文聖王 (839-857)

47. Hŏnan Wang
憲安王 (857-861)

Hŏnjŏng ——— 43. Hŭigang Wang ———————— Kyemyŏng
憲貞   僖康王 (836-838)   啓明

Hyojong
孝宗

56. Kyŏngsun Wang
敬順王 (927-935)

48. Kyŏngmun Wang ——— 49. Hŏn'gang Wang ———————— Lady Kyea
景文王 (861-875)   憲康王 (875-886)   桂娥太后

50. Chŏnggang Wang ——— 52. Hyogong Wang
定康王 (886-887)   孝恭王 (897-912)

51. Chinsŏng Yŏwang ———————— Lady Uisŏng
(Queen)   義成王后
眞聖女王 (887-897)

(Pak)   (8. Adalla Isagŭm) ············· 53. Sindŏk Wang ——— 54. Kyŏngmyŏng Wang
阿達羅尼師今 (154-184)   神德王 (912-917)   景明王 (917-924)

55. Kyŏngae Wang
景哀王 (924-927)

Parhae (Tae)
渤海 (大)
(698-926)

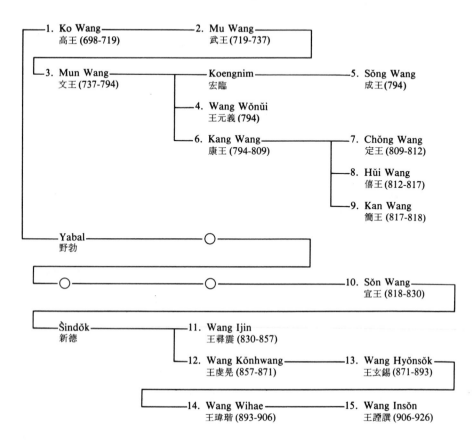

1. Ko Wang
   高王 (698-719)

2. Mu Wang
   武王 (719-737)

3. Mun Wang
   文王 (737-794)

Koengnim
宏臨

5. Sŏng Wang
   成王 (794)

4. Wang Wŏnŭi
   王元義 (794)

6. Kang Wang
   康王 (794-809)

7. Chŏng Wang
   定王 (809-812)

8. Hŭi Wang
   僖王 (812-817)

9. Kan Wang
   簡王 (817-818)

Yabal
野勃

10. Sŏn Wang
    宣王 (818-830)

Sindŏk
新德

11. Wang Ijin
    王彝震 (830-857)

12. Wang Kŏnhwang
    王虔晃 (857-871)

13. Wang Hyŏnsŏk
    王玄錫 (871-893)

14. Wang Wihae
    王瑋瑎 (893-906)

15. Wang Insŏn
    王諲譔 (906-926)

Koryŏ (Wang)
高麗〔王〕
(918-1392)

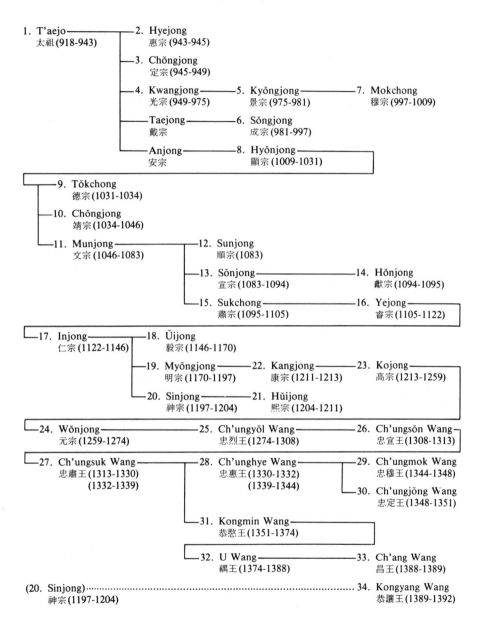

1. T'aejo
太祖 (918-943)

2. Hyejong
惠宗 (943-945)

3. Chŏngjong
定宗 (945-949)

4. Kwangjong
光宗 (949-975)

5. Kyŏngjong
景宗 (975-981)

7. Mokchong
穆宗 (997-1009)

Taejong
戴宗

6. Sŏngjong
成宗 (981-997)

Anjong
安宗

8. Hyŏnjong
顯宗 (1009-1031)

9. Tŏkchong
德宗 (1031-1034)

10. Chŏngjong
靖宗 (1034-1046)

11. Munjong
文宗 (1046-1083)

12. Sunjong
順宗 (1083)

13. Sŏnjong
宣宗 (1083-1094)

14. Hŏnjong
獻宗 (1094-1095)

15. Sukchong
肅宗 (1095-1105)

16. Yejong
睿宗 (1105-1122)

17. Injong
仁宗 (1122-1146)

18. Ŭijong
毅宗 (1146-1170)

19. Myŏngjong
明宗 (1170-1197)

22. Kangjong
康宗 (1211-1213)

23. Kojong
高宗 (1213-1259)

20. Sinjong
神宗 (1197-1204)

21. Hŭijong
熙宗 (1204-1211)

24. Wŏnjong
元宗 (1259-1274)

25. Ch'ungyŏl Wang
忠烈王 (1274-1308)

26. Ch'ungsŏn Wang
忠宣王 (1308-1313)

27. Ch'ungsuk Wang
忠肅王 (1313-1330)
(1332-1339)

28. Ch'unghye Wang
忠惠王 (1330-1332)
(1339-1344)

29. Ch'ungmok Wang
忠穆王 (1344-1348)

30. Ch'ungjŏng Wang
忠定王 (1348-1351)

31. Kongmin Wang
恭愍王 (1351-1374)

32. U Wang
禑王 (1374-1388)

33. Ch'ang Wang
昌王 (1388-1389)

(20. Sinjong)
神宗 (1197-1204)

34. Kongyang Wang
恭讓王 (1389-1392)

Chosŏn (Yi)
朝鮮 (李)
(1392-1910)

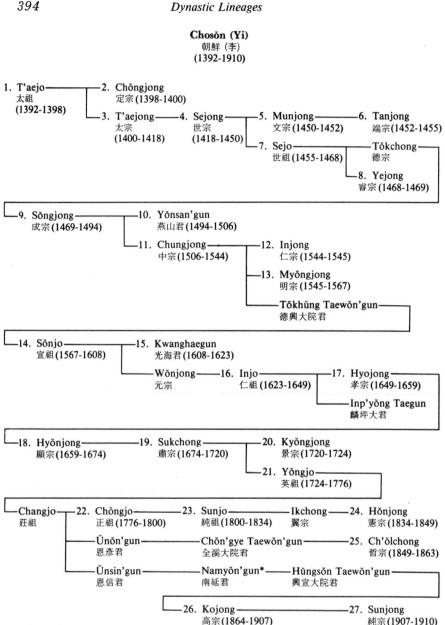

* A sixth generation descendant of the Inp'yŏng Taegun, third son of Injo; adopted to continue the lineage of the already deceased Ŭnsin'gun in 1815.

SELECT BIBLIOGRAPHY

One attractive and useful feature of *Han'guksa Sillon* is its comprehensive bibliography. At the end of each subsection of his original Korean-language text, Professor Lee has appended a listing of relevant published work, principally journal articles by Korean and Japanese scholars. These listings range in length from only two or three items to thirty or more, comprising a select bibliography of scholarly work relating to the contents of the particular section. In addition, Professor Lee has provided a bibliographical essay in a fifty-eight page appendix, listing and evaluating, under twenty subject headings, an extensive selection of book-length publications in Korean, Japanese, and English, primarily, but also a number in other Western languages and in modern Chinese. These publications, of course, belong preponderantly to the more recent years of the twentieth century, but many traditional works written in classical Chinese are included as well.

Korean readers, especially students of Korean history on the college or university level, have found these bibliographies to be convenient and helpful. The contents of the works listed, however, are accessible only to those who command the languages in which they are written. Accordingly, a translation of either the subsection listings or of the bibliographical essay has not been attempted, since it would serve a rather narrow purpose.

The Select Bibliography prepared to accompany this translation contains only book-length publications and is essentially limited to works in English. Periodical, dissertation, archival, and other literature in the Korean studies field can be approached through the bibliographies cited herein and, in turn, through their bibliographies. Since the more recent of these works already are some years out of date, an effort has been made to be more inclusive here in listing books published after 1975. Finally, it should be noted that the brief annotations given for most selections are intended, on the whole, to describe rather than to evaluate.

BIBLIOGRAPHIES

Courant, Maurice, *Bibliographie Coréene*. Paris: E. Leroux, 1894–1896. *Supplement*, 1901. Reprint, New York: B. Franklin, 1968. Annotates about 3,200 traditional Korean works.

Kim, Han-Kyo, *Studies on Korea: A Scholar's Guide*. Honolulu: University Press of Hawaii, 1980. Comprehensive annotated bibliography of books, articles, and Ph. D. dissertations mostly in English but also in other Western languages, with a separate chapter on works in Russian. Coverage generally ends with 1976. Valuable essays preface the bibliographical entries in each topical chapter.

Kim, Tai-Jin, transl. and ed., *A Bibliographical Guide to Traditional Korean Sources*. Seoul: Asiatic Research Center, Korea University, 1976. Annotated bibliography with detailed descriptions of 148 major traditional Korean works.

Marcus, Richard, ed., *Korean Studies Guide*. Berkeley: University of California Press, 1954. Carefully annotated bibliographies of works in Korean, Japanese, literary Chinese, English, and other Western languages, classified under seventeen fields of study.

Shulman, Frank Joseph, *Japan and Korea: An Annotated Bibliography of Doctoral Dissertations in Western Languages, 1877–1974*. Chicago: American Library Association, 1970. An invaluable tool for work in the Korean field, since so many Ph.D. dissertations remain unpublished or, when they do appear, suffer considerable abridgement. This exhaustive bibliography first was updated by the compiler under the title *Doctoral Dissertations on Japan and Korea, 1969–1974*. Ann Arbor: University Microfilms International, 1976. Dissertations on Korea now are included in the semi-annual *Doctoral Dissertations on Asia* also compiled by Frank Joseph Shulman and published for the Association for Asian Studies by Xerox University Microfilms, Ann Arbor.

Song, Minako I., and Masato Matsui, *Japanese Sources on Korea in Hawaii*. Honolulu: Center for Korean Studies, 1980.

GENERAL

Hoefer, Hans J., *Insight Guides: Korea*. Hong Kong: APA Productions, 1981. An unusual and unusually beautiful guidebook, with a wealth of superb photographic illustrations and first-rate essays introducing Korean history, society, and culture.

McCann, David R., John Middleton, and Edward J. Shultz, ed., *Studies on Korea in Transition*. Honolulu: Center for Korean Studies, Univ. of Hawaii, 1979. Conference papers on history, literature, language, and society by ten Peace Corps Volunteers who went on to pursue Korean studies in U.S. graduate schools.

Pihl, Marshall R., ed., *Listening to Korea: A Korean Anthology*. New York: Praeger, 1973. Translations of essays and short stories by contemporary writers on both contemporary themes and events of Korea's recent past.

HISTORY, General

Han, Woo-keun. *The History of Korea*. Translated by Kyong-shik Lee, edited by Grafton K. Mintz. Honolulu: University Press of Hawaii, 1971. A detailed survey history by a leading Korean historian; coverage ends at 1960.

Hatada, Takashi, *A History of Korea*. Translated and edited by Warren W. Smith, Jr. and Benjamin H. Hazard. Santa Barbara: ABC Clio, 1969. A translation of perhaps Japan's most widely read Korean history text. Coverage originally stopped with the Japanese annexation in 1910 but later was supplemented, to 1950, by the author.

Henthorn, William E. *A History of Korea*. New York: Free Press, 1971. A concise history from antiquity to the nineteenth century.

Hulbert, Homer B., *The History of Korea*. 2 vols. Edited by Clarence N. Weems. New York: Hilary House, 1962. Based uncritically on traditional Korean sources. Originally published in 1905, this work now has only historiographical value.

Joe, Wanne J. *Traditional Korea: A Cultural History*. Seoul: Chungang University Press, 1972. Comprehensive survey of Korean history from antiquity to the mid-nineteenth century, with emphasis on Korea's cultural development.

Rutt, Richard, *James Scarth Gale's History of the Korean People*. Seoul: Royal Asiatic Society, Korea Branch, 1975. Not so much a history as a structured sequence of vignettes, the book both entertains and informs as it narrates highlights from the Korean historical and cultural experience. Bishop Rutt's biography of Gale, as well as his annotations and commentary, are useful features of this recent edition of the 1927 original.

Sohn, Pow-key, Chol-choon Kim, and Yi-sup Hong. *The History of Korea*. Seoul: Korean National Commission for UNESCO, 1970. Translation of a collaborative effort by three contemporary Korean historians.

HISTORY, Traditional

Dallet, Charles, *Histoire de l'Église de Corée*. Paris: V. Palme, 1874. 2 vols. Reprint, Seoul: Royal Asiatic Society, Korea Branch, 1975. An account of the Catholic church and socio-political conditions in late Yi Korea. An English translation of the latter material is included.

Gardiner, K.H.J., *The Early History of Korea: The Historical Development of the Peninsula up to the Introduction of Buddhism in the Fourth Century A.D.* Honolulu: University of Hawaii Press, 1969. A short work based heavily on Japanese archeological and historical studies.

Henthorn, William E., *Korea: The Mongol Invasions*. Leiden: Brill, 1963. A detailed account of the warfare itself and the exactions imposed by the conquerors on Korea. A brief discussion of Koryŏ military institutions is appended.

Iryŏn, *Samguk Yusa: Legends and History of the Three Kingdoms of Ancient Korea*. Translated by Tae-Hung Ha and Grafton K. Mintz. Seoul: Yonsei University Press, 1972. Not always a reliable translation, this work nevertheless provides access to the distinctive flavor and invaluable contents of the original 13th century work on the Koguryŏ, Paekche, and Silla kingdoms.

Kang, Hugh H.W., ed., *The Traditional Culture and Society of Korea: Thought and Institutions*. Honolulu: Center for Korean Studies, Univ. of Hawaii, 1975. Three interpretive studies—on the traditional military and land systems, and on *Sirhak* thought; an epilogue offers a critical commentary.

Kim, Jeong-hak, *The Prehistory of Korea*. Translated by Richard J. Pearson and Kazue Pearson. Honolulu: University Press of Hawaii, 1979. Authoritative rendering of a work by a leading Korean archeologist; originally written in Japanese.

Ledyard, Gari, *The Dutch Come to Korea*. Seoul: Royal Asiatic Society, Korea Branch, 1971. An account of the experiences of Dutch sailors shipwrecked on the Korean island of Cheju in the mid-17th century; based on Hendrik Hamel's *Narrative* as well as contemporary Korean, Japanese, and Dutch sources.

Meskill, John, *Ch'oe Pu's Diary: A Record of Drifting Across the Sea*. Tucson: University of Arizona Press, 1965. A translation of the late 15th century *P'yohae-rok*, an account of a Korean official's shipwreck on the coast of China and subsequent sojourn there. Much valuable information on Korean society and institutions is contained in Ch'oe Pu's conversations with Chinese officials.

Park, Yune-hee, *Admiral Yi Sun-shin and his Turtleboat Armada*. Revised edition. Seoul: Hanjin Publishing Company, 1978. Recounts the glorious career of Korea's most honored military figure, the naval hero of the 1592–98 struggle against Japanese invading armies.

Wagner, Edward W. *The Literati Purges: Political Conflict in Early Yi Korea*. Cambridge, Mass.: East Asian Research Center, Harvard University, 1974. A monograph on institutional power conflicts as manifested in three major political purges, 1498 to 1519.

HISTORY, Modern (to 1945)

Choe, Ching Young, *The Rule of the Taewŏn'gun, 1864–1873: Restoration in Yi Korea*. Cambridge, Mass.: East Asian Research Center, Harvard University, 1972. A detailed examination of the regency of King Kojong's father, the Taewŏn'gun, and his reform program to reinvigorate the Yi dynasty.

Chung, Henry, *The Case of Korea*. New York: Revell, 1921. A documentary account of the Japanese seizure of Korea and the subsequent March First Movement of 1919.

Conroy, Hilary, *The Japanese Seizure of Korea, 1868–1910: A Study of Realism and Idealism in International Relations.* Philadelphia: University of Pennsylvania Press, 1960. An in-depth study of events leading up to the Japanese annexation of Korea, the author's interpretations evoke heated dissent from Korean historians.

Cook, Harold F., *Korea's 1884 Incident: Its Background and Kim Ok-Kyun's Elusive Dream.* Seoul: Taewon Publishing Co., 1972.

Dennett, Tyler, *Americans in Eastern Asia: A Critical Study of the Policy of the United States with Reference to China, Japan and Korea in the Nineteenth Century.* New York: Macmillan, 1922. Reprint, New York: Barnes and Noble, 1963.

Deuchler, Martina, *Confucian Gentlemen and Barbarian Envoys: The Opening of Korea, 1875–1885.* Seattle: University of Washington Press, 1977. A meticulously researched, richly documented, lucidly written account of the complex events of these years.

Grajdanzev, Andrew J., *Modern Korea.* New York: Institute of Pacific Relations, 1944. Reprint, Seoul: Royal Asiatic Society, Korea Branch, 1975. A well documented examination of the exploitation of Korea and its economy under Japanese rule, with treatment of social and political issues as well.

Harrington, Fred Harvey, *God, Mammon, and the Japanese: Dr. Horace N. Allen and Korean-American Relations, 1884–1905.* Madison: University of Wisconsin Press, 1944. An enduring study centering on the major role played by Dr. Allen in the history of the period, first as a medical missionary and then as the senior U.S. diplomat in Seoul.

Hulbert, Homer B., *The Passing of Korea.* New York: Doubleday Page, 1906. Reprint, Seoul: Yonsei University Press, 1969. Valuable account of Korean society and politics at the end of the 19th and beginning of the 20th century by an American missionary who witnessed much of what he relates.

Kim, C.I. Eugene, and Han-Kyo Kim, *Korea and the Politics of Imperialism, 1876–1910.* Berkeley and Los Angeles: University of California Press, 1967. A study of Korea as the focal point of international rivalries in the age of imperialism.

Kim, C.I. Eugene, and Doretha E. Mortimore, ed., *Korea's Response to Japan: The Colonial Period.* Kalamazoo: Center for Korean Studies, Western Michigan University, 1975. A volume of conference papers.

Kim Key-Hiuk, *The Last Phase of the East Asian World Order: Korea, Japan, and the Chinese Empire, 1860–1882.* Berkeley: University of California Press, 1980.

Lee, Chong-sik, *The Politics of Korean Nationalism.* Berkeley: University of California Press, 1965. Describes and analyzes the Korean nationalist movement from the Tonghak uprising in 1894 to 1945.

McCune, George, and John A Harrison, ed., *Korean-American Relations: Documents Pertaining to the Far Eastern Diplomacy of the United States. Vol. I.: The Initial Period, 1883–1886.* Berkeley: University of California Press, 1951.

McKenzie, Frederick A., *Korea's Fight for Freedom.* New York: Revell, 1920. Reprint, Seoul: Yonsei University Press, 1969. A thoroughly sympathetic account of Korea's struggle against the Japanese from the late 19th century through the March First Movement of 1919.

———, *The Tragedy of Korea.* London: Hodder and Strongton, 1908. Reprint, Seoul: Yonsei University Press, 1969. The history of Japanese penetration into Korea from 1876 to the time of writing, by a Canadian journalist who witnessed "Righteous Army" resistance activities in Korea in 1907.

Nahm, Andrew C., ed., *American-Korean Relations 1866–1976. The United States and Korea*: Kalamazoo: Western Michigan University, 1979. Conference papers focusing primarily on American figures and their role in the development of Korean-American relations.

———, ed., *Korea under Japanese Colonial Rule: Studies of the Policy and Techniques of Japanese Colonialism.* Kalamazoo: Center for Korean Studies, Western Michigan University, 1973. A conference volume.

Nelson, M. Frederick, *Korea and the Old Orders in Eastern Asia.* Baton Rouge: Louisiana State University Press, 1945. Reprint, New York: Russel and Russel, 1967. Historical study of Korean foreign relations under the traditional Confucian system and, from 1876 to 1910, in a Western international legal framework.

Palais, James B., *Politics and Policy in Traditional Korea.* Cambridge, Mass.: Harvard University Press, 1975. A careful study of the period 1864–1876, with an analytical overview of the political, social, and economic order of premodern Korea.

Palmer, Spencer J., ed., *Korean-American Relations: Documents Pertaining to the Far Eastern Diplomacy of the United States.* Vol. II: *The Period of Growing Influence, 1887–1895.* Berkeley: University of California Press, 1963.

Suh, Dae-sook, and Chae-jin Lee, ed., *Political Leadership in Korea.* Seattle: University of Washington Press, 1975. A collection of papers dealing with both institutional and human factors determining patterns of political leadership in 20th century Korea.

Swartout, Robert R., Jr., *Mandarins, Gunboats and Power Politics: Owen Nickerson Denny and the International Rivalries in Korea.* Honolulu: University Press of Hawaii, 1980. A study focusing on the career of a U.S. foreign affairs adviser to the Korean government at the end of the 19th century.

Weems, Benjamin B., *Reform, Rebellion and the Heavenly Way.* Tucson: University of Arizona Press, 1964. A monograph on the Tonghak movement and the development of Ch'ŏndogyo.

Wilkinson, William H., *The Corean Government: Constitutional Changes, July 1894 to October 1895, with an Appendix on Subsequent Enactments to 30th June 1896.* Shanghai: Statistical Department of the Inspectorate General of Customs, 1897. Detailed description of the Kabo Reforms (1894–1895), providing unique material on late Yi dynasty institutions.

HISTORY, Contemporary (post-1945)

Allen, Richard C., *Korea's Syngman Rhee: An Unauthorized Portrait.* Rutland, Vt.: Tuttle, 1960. A critical account of Syngman Rhee and Korea's First Republic.

Baldwin, Frank P. Jr., ed., *Without Parallel: The American-Korean Relationship since 1945.* New York: Pantheon Books, 1974. A collection of eight provocative essays on the U.S. role in post-liberation Korea.

Boettcher, Robert, and Gordon L. Freedman, *Gifts of Deceit: Sun Myung Moon, Tongsun Park and the Korean Scandal.* New York: Holt, Rinehart and Winston, 1980. The first book-length treatment of these major irritants in the U.S.-Korean relationship.

Buss, Claude, A., *The United States and the Republic of Korea: Background for Policy.* Stanford: Hoover Institution Press, 1982. An American diplomatic historian's analysis of South Korea's special relationship with the U.S., particularly in the last fifteen years.

Cho, Soon Sung. *Korea in World Politics, 1940–1950: An Evaluation of American Responsibility.* Berkeley: University of California Press, 1967.

Cumings, Bruce, *The Origins of the Korean War: Liberation and the Emergence of Separate Regimes, 1945–47.* Princeton: Princeton University Press, 1981. Likely to remain the definitive work.

Han, Sungjoo, *The Failure of Democracy in South Korea.* Berkeley: University of California Press, 1974. Examination of Korea's unsuccessful attempt to introduce representative democratic institutions during the Second Republic, 1960–61.

Henderson, Gregory, *Korea: The Politics of the Vortex.* Cambridge, Mass.: Harvard University Press, 1968. A wide-ranging study concerned particularly with internal Korean political developments and history since World War II; by a former U.S. Foreign Service officer and scholar of Korea who served in Seoul during much of the period he treats.

Kim, Chong Lim, ed., *Political Participation in Korea: Democracy, Mobilization, and Stability.* Santa Barbara: ABC Clio Press, 1980. Conference papers dealing with political developments in the post-Korean War period.

Kim, Joungwon Alexander, *Divided Korea: The Politics of Development*

1945-1972. Cambridge, Mass: East Asian Research Center, Harvard University, 1975. An analysis of the two Korea's and their varying political styles.

Kim, Kwan Bong, *The Korea-Japan Treaty Crisis and the Instability of the Korean Political System*. New York: Praeger, 1971. A study of the early years of the Third Republic under Pak Chŏng-hŭi, with full treatment of the critical issue of establishing formal relations with Japan.

Kim, Quee Young, *The Fall of Syngman Rhee*. Berkeley: Institute of East Asian Studies, Univ. of California, 1983. A trenchant analysis of the "Student Revolution" of April, 1960, with extensive discussion of background factors and a day-by-day description of the climactic events that forced President Rhee's resignation.

Kim Se-jin, *The Politics of Military Revolution in Korea*. Chapel Hill: University of North Carolina Press, 1971. A detailed account of the 1961 military coup and the subsequent military government.

Kwak, Tae-Hwan, ed., *U.S.-Korean Relations: 1882–1982*. Seoul: Kyungnam University Press, 1982. Papers read at a 1982 conference commemorating the centennial of U.S.-Korean diplomatic relations.

Lee, Hahn-Been, *Korea: Time, Change and Administration*. Honolulu: East-West Center Press, 1968. An assessment of South Korea's administrative development and governmental performance.

McCune, George M., *Korea Today*. Cambridge, Mass.: Harvard University Press, 1950. A political and economic study of Korea under the American and Soviet military occupations immediately after World War II.

Meade, E. Grant, *American Military Government in Korea*. New York: King's Crown Press, 1951. A critique of the United States Military Government in Korea, especially at the provincial and local levels, by a former military government officer.

Morse, Ronald, ed., *A Century of United States-Korean Relations: Proceedings of a Conference at the Wilson Center, June 17–19, 1982*. Washington, D.C.: University Press of America, Inc., 1983.

Oh, John Kie-chiang, *Korea: Democracy on Trial*. Ithaca: Cornell University Press, 1968. A study of Korean politics in the 1950s and early 60s.

Oliver, Robert T., *Syngman Rhee: The Man Behind the Myth*. New York: Dodd Mead, 1954. A favorable biography of the Republic of Korea's first president, based on Rhee's private papers.

_____, *Syngman Rhee and American Involvement in Korea, 1942–1960: A Personal Narrative*. Seoul: Panmun Book Company, 1978. A friend and adviser to Rhee, relying on his own recollections and Rhee's correspondence, recounts this period of American-Korean relations.

Reeve, W.D., *The Republic of Korea: A Political and Economic Study*. London: Oxford University Press, 1963. An examination of South

Korea's First Republic under Syngman Rhee, in whose government the author served as an adviser.

Wright, Edward R., ed., *Korean Politics in Transition*. Seattle: Univ. of Washington Press, 1975. A collection of essays on both historical and contemporary topics.

Yi, Pangja, *The World is One: Princess Yi Pangja's Autobiography*. Translated by Sukkyu Kim. Seoul: Taewon Publishing Company, 1973. The life story of the Japanese princess married to the last Crown Prince of the Yi royal family of Chosŏn.

HISTORY, Communism and North Korea

Burge, Frederick, ed., *North Korea: A Country Study*. Washington, D.C.: Government Printing Office, 1982.

Hyun, Peter, *Darkness at Dawn: A North Korean Diary*. Seoul: Hanjin Publishing Company, 1981. The account of his recent travels in northeast China and North Korea by a well-known Korean-American writer.

Kim, C.I. Eugene, and B.C. Koh, ed., *Journey to North Korea: Personal Perceptions*. Berkeley: Institute of East Asian Studies, 1983. The account of the summer, 1981, visit to North Korea by seven Korean-born professors at U.S. universities.

Kim, Youn-Soo, ed., *The Economy of the Korean Democratic People's Republic, 1945–1977* (Mon. der Deutschen Korea-Studien Gruppe, 2). Leiden: E.J. Brill, 1979.

Koh, Byung Chul. *The Foreign Policy of North Korea*. New York: Praeger, 1969.

Lee, Chong-sik, transl. and ed., *Materials on Korean Communism, 1945–1947*. Honolulu: Center for Korean Studies, Univ. of Hawaii, 1977.

Scalapino, Robert A. ed., *North Korea Today*. New York: Praeger, 1963. A collection of articles covering the period of the 1950s and early 1960s.

Scalapino, Robert A., and Jun-yop Kim, ed., *North Korea Today: Strategic Issues*. Berkeley: Institute of East Asian Studies, Univ. of California, 1983. Papers delivered at a 1981 conference by seventeen Korean and U.S. specialists.

Scalapino, Robert A., and Chong-sik Lee. *Communism in Korea*. 2 vols. Berkeley: University of California Press, 1972. An exhaustive treatment of the Communist movement in Korea from its earliest beginnings.

Suh, Dae-sook, *Documents of Korean Communism, 1918–1948*. Princeton: Princeton University Press, 1970. Sixty-six documents translated from Korean, Japanese, Chinese, and Russian.

_____, *The Korean Communist Movement, 1918–1948*. Princeton: Princeton University Press, 1967.

_____, *Korean Communism, 1945–1980: A Reference Guide to the Pol-*

itical System. Honolulu: University of Hawaii Press, 1981.

HISTORY, The Korean War

Appleman, Roy E., *United States Army in the Korean War: South to Naktong, North to Yalu (June-November, 1950)*. Washington: Department of the Army, Office of the Chief of Military History, 1961.

Berger, Carl, *The Korea Knot: A Military-Political History*. Philadelphia: University of Pennsylvania Press, 1957. Emphasis is on U.S.-Korean relations and the Korean War.

Goodrich, Leland M., *Korea: A Study of U.S. Policy in the United Nations*. New York: Council on Foreign Relations, 1956.

Goulden, Joseph C., *Korea: The Untold Story of the War*. New York: Times Books, 1982. Relying on previously unused sources, this work presents a critical assessment of the Truman Administration and its prosecution of the Korean War.

Noble, Harold Joyce, *Embassy at War*. Edited with an introduction by Frank P. Baldwin, Jr. Seattle: University of Washington Press, 1975. Contemporary account of the early stages of the Korean War by a U.S. Embassy official in Seoul.

Paige, Glenn D., *The Korean Decision, June 24–30, 1950*. New York: Free Press, 1968. Detailed analysis of the making of the U.S. decision to enter the Korean War.

Rees, David, *Korea: The Limited War*. New York: St. Martin's Press, 1964. Includes an extensive bibliography, major documents, and statistical material.

Riley, John W., and Wilbur Schramm, *The Reds Take a City: The Communist Occupation of Seoul, with Eyewitness Accounts*. New Brunswick, N.J.: Rutgers University Press, 1951. A scholarly analysis of the North Korean occupation of Seoul in 1950, together with narratives of their personal experiences by a number of leading Korean figures.

Simmons, Robert, *The Strained Alliance: Peking, Pyongyang, Moscow, and the Politics of the Korean Civil War*. New York: Free Press, 1975. An examination of developments in the relationships among North Korea, China and the Soviet Union brought about by the Korean War.

Spanier, John W., *The Truman-McArthur Controversy and the Korean War*. Cambridge, Mass.: Belknap Press, 1959.

Stone, I. F., *The Hidden History of the Korean War*. New York: Monthly Review Press, 1952. A well documented account charging U.S. and South Korean culpability in triggering the North Korean invasion.

Stueck, William Whitney, Jr., *The Road to Confrontation: American Policy Toward China and Korea, 1947–1950*. Chapel Hill: University of North Carolina Press, 1981.

ART

Choi, Sunu, *5000 Years of Korean Art*. Seoul: Hyonam Publishing Company, 1979. Nearly 400 plates, over half in full color, illustrating the full spectrum of traditional Korean artistic achievement.

Choi, Sunu, and Young-kyu Park, *Korean Furniture*. Seoul: Kyoungmi Publishing Company, 1982. Treats the full range of traditional furniture; the 145 color plates both portray individual pieces and present close-ups of their brass and iron fittings.

Gompertz, G. St.G. M., *Korean Celadon and Other Wares of the Koryŏ Period*. London: Faber and Faber, 1963.

_____, *Korean Pottery and Porcelain of the Yi Period*. London: Faber and Faber, 1968.

Honey, William B., *Corean Pottery*. London: Faber and Faber, 1947. Introduction to Korean ceramics with important artistic observations.

Kim, Chewon, and Won-yong Kim. *Treasures of Korean Art: 2000 Years of Ceramics, Sculpture and Jeweled Arts*. New York: Abrams, 1966.

Kim, Chewon, and Lena Kim Lee, *Arts of Korea*. Tokyo: Kodansha International, 1974. The most recent, comprehensive treatment in English of traditional Korean art forms, with superb plates.

Kim, Won-yong, et al., ed., *The Arts of Korea*. Seoul: Dong Hwa Publishing Company, 1979. A six-volume set, discussing and illustrating ancient art objects, paintings, Buddhist art, ceramics, handicrafts, and architecture.

Kyemongsa, comp., *The Folkcrafts of Korea*. Seoul: Kyemongsa, 1980. Copiously illustrated, comprehensive treatment of its subject. Text is in both Korean and English.

Kyoungmi, comp., *Korean Folk Painting*. Seoul: Kyoungmi Publishing Company, 1980. Discusses, and amply illustrates, the development of this folk art in Korea, its characteristics, and the cultural patterns it reflects.

McCune, Evelyn, *The Arts of Korea: An Illustrated History*. Rutland, Vt.: Tuttle, 1962. Coverage includes archaeology, architecture, sculpture, painting, and ceramics, as well as minor art forms.

ECONOMY

Ban, Sung Hwan, Pal Yong Moon, and Dwight H. Perkins, *Rural Development*. Cambridge, Mass.: Council on East Asian Studies, Harvard University, 1980. A comprehensive study of the period 1945–75, with emphasis on the more recent years.

Hasan, Parvez, et al., *Korea: Policy Issues for Long-Term Development*. Baltimore, Johns Hopkins, 1979.

Jones, Leroy, P., and Il Sakong, *Government, Business, and Enterpreneurship in Economic Development: The Korean Case*. Cambridge, Mass.:

Council on East Asian Studies, Harvard University, 1980.

Kim, Kwang Suk, and Michael Roemer, *Growth and Structural Trans-formation.* Cambridge, Mass.: Council on East Asian Studies, Harvard University, 1979. An analysis of the different economic factors that have contributed to Korea's rapid economic growth.

Krueger, Anne O., *The Developmental Role of the Foreign Sector and Aid.* Cambridge, Mass.: Council on East Asian Studies, Harvard University, 1979. An examination of the contribution of foreign aid and international loans to Korea's economic growth.

Kuznets, Paul W., *Economic Growth and Structure in the Republic of Korea.* New Haven: Yale University Press, 1977. Detailed analysis of economic development since 1953, identifying the factors responsible for accelerated growth.

Lee, Hoon Koo, *Land Utilization and Rural Economy in Korea.* Chicago: University of Chicago Press, 1936. Reprint, New York: Greenwood Press, 1969. A study of the Korean agricultural economy in the 1920s and early 1930s.

Mason, Edward S., Mahn Je Kim, Dwight H. Perkins, Kwang Suk Kim, David C. Cole, et al. *The Economic and Social Modernization of the Republic of Korea.* Cambridge, Mass.: Council on East Asian Studies, Harvard University, 1980. Summarizes the research results and conclusions of the *Studies in the Modernization of the Republic of Korea: 1945–1975* series, with additional interpretive and historical essays.

McGinn, Noel E., Donald R. Snodgrass, Yung Bong Kim, Shin-Bok Kim, and Quee-Young Kim, *Education and Development in Korea.* Cambridge, Mass.: Council on East Asian Studies, Harvard University, 1980. Detailed analysis of the Korean education system and its contribution to economic development.

Mills, Edwin S. and Byung-Nak Song, *Urbanization and Urban Problems.* Cambridge, Mass.: Council on East Asian Studies, Harvard University, 1979. Examines the urbanization process, applying theories regarding population concentration to the case of contemporary Korea.

Repetto, Robert, and Tai Hwan Kwon, Son-Ung Kim, Dae Young Kim, John E. Sloboda, and Peter Donaldson, *Economic Development, Population Policy, and Demographic Transition in the Republic of Korea.* Cambridge, Mass.: Council on East Asian Studies, Harvard University, 1981.

Suh, Sang Chul. *Growth and Structural Change in the Korean Economy, 1910–1940.* Cambridge, Mass.: Council on East Asian Studies, Harvard University, 1978.

GEOGRAPHY

Bartz, Particia M., *South Korea.* Oxford: Clarendon Press, 1972. Well-illustrated technical and descriptive geography of South Korea.

McCune, Shannon, *Korea's Heritage: A Regional and Social Geography.* Rutland, Vt.: Tuttle, 1956. Additionally valuable for its bibliographic notes, photographic illustrations, and statistical appendices.

LANGUAGE

Cho, S.B., *A Phonological Study of Korean.* Uppsala: Almqvist & Wiksells, 1967. Comprehensive treatment of its subject, including historical aspects.

Lee, Ki-moon, "A Historical Study of the Korean Writing Systems." English synopsis of the author's *Kugŏ p'yogipŏp ŭi yŏksajŏk yŏn'gu.* Seoul: Han'guk Yŏn'guwŏn, 1963.

_____, *Geschichte der Koreanischen Sprache.* Translated by Bruno Lewin. Wiesbaden: Dr. Ludwig Reichert Verlag, 1977. Authoritative history of the Korean language by a foremost Korean linguist.

Martin, Samuel E., *Korean Morphophonemics.* Baltimore: Linguistic Society of America, 1954. A classic treatise, considered the best work in the structural tradition on phonological alternations in Modern Korean.

Ramstedt, G.J., *A Korean Grammar.* Facsimile reprint, Oosterhout, Netherlands: Anthropological Publications, 1968. Helsinki: Suomalais-ugrilainen Seura, 1939. The classic work in its field.

_____, *Studies in Korean Etymology.* 2 vols. Helsinki: Suomalais-ugrilainen Seura, 1949–1953.

Sohn, Ho-min, ed., *The Korean Language: Its Structure and Social Projection.* Honolulu: Center for Korean Studies, Univ. of Hawaii, 1975. Conference papers by established Korean linguists in the United States.

LAW

Choi, Dai-kwon, Bong Duck Chun, and William Shaw, *Traditional Korean Legal Attitudes.* Berkeley: Institute of East Asian Studies, 1980. Each of the three authors is concerned with aspects of the ideological and legal institutional setting in which modern Korean society developed.

Hahm, Pyong-Choon, *The Korean Political Tradition and Law: Essays in Korean Law and Legal History.* Seoul: Royal Asiatic Society, Korea Branch, 1967. Nine essays by an eminent legal scholar, three of which deal with historical issues.

Kim, Chan-jin, ed., *Business Laws in Korea: Investment, Taxation, and Industrial Property.* Seoul: Panmun Book Company, 1982. An 800-page handbook covering nearly all the business laws in force at the time of compilation.

Park, Byoung-ho, Choo-soo Kim, Kwun-sup Chung, Hyung-bae Kim, and Tai-joon Kwan, *Modernization and Its Impact upon Korean Law*. Berkeley: Institute of East Asian Studies, 1981. Five Korean legal scholars discuss issues involving conflict between traditional customs and values and modern egalitarian legal principles.

Park, Choon-ho, Jae Schick Pae, and Nam-Yearl Chai, *Korean International Law*. Berkeley: Institute of East Asian Studies, Univ. of California, 1982. Treats major aspects of Korea's adoption and application of Western concepts of international law.

Shaw, William. *Legal Norms in a Confucian State*. Berkeley: Institute of East Asian Studies, University of California, 1981. A scholarly exposition of the Yi dynasty legal system derived in large part from an analysis of 18th century court cases. Includes abridged translations of the records of one hundred such cases.

Song, Sang Hyun, ed., *Introduction to the Legal System of Korea*. Seoul: Kyung Mun Sa Publishing Company, 1983. The editor's primary purpose is "to present the historical, sociological and conceptual background of Korea's present legal system." For the most part this voluminous and comprehensive work brings together the writings of Korean and Western legal scholars during the past fifteen years, but new material also is included.

LITERATURE

Carpenter, Frances, *Tales of a Korean Grandmother*. Rutland, Vt.: Tuttle, 1973. A collection of thirty-two folk stories presented in sprightly English versions.

Grant, Bruce K., and Chin-man Kim, transl., *Han Joong Nok: Reminiscences in Retirement*. Larchmont, N.Y.: Larchwood Publications, 1980. The personal account by Hyegyŏng-gung Hong-ssi, princess consort of Crown Prince Changhŏn (Sado), of her husband's tragic relationship with his father, King Yŏngjo, culminating in the prince's cruel death in 1762.

Hoyt, James, transl., *Songs of the Dragons Flying to Heaven: A Korean Epic*. Seoul: Korean National Commission for UNESCO, 1979. 2nd ed. A translation with commentary of the 15th century eulogy of the Yi Chosŏn dynastic founder and his forebears.

Hwang, Sun-won, *The Stars and Other Korean Short Stories*. Translated by Edward W. Poitras. Hong Kong: Heinemann Educational Books (Asia), 1980. A selection from the work of one of Korea's most widely acclaimed contemporary writers.

Hwang [Whang] Sun-won, *Trees on the Cliff: A Novel of Korea and Two Stories*. Translated by Wang-rok Chang. Larchmont, N.Y.: Larchwood Publications, 1980.

Kang, Younghill. *The Grass Roof*. New York: Scribner's, 1931. Reprint, Chicago: Follett, 1966. Autobiographical novel of a Korean boy growing up in the changing world of early 20th century Korea.

Kim, Donguk, *History of Korean Literature*. Translated by Leon Hurvitz. Tokyo: Center for the Study of East Asian Culture, Tōyō Bunko, 1980. Translated from the Japanese original written by a leading contemporary Korean scholar.

Kim, Jaihiun, transl., *The Contemporary Korean Poets: Korean Poetry Since 1920*. Larchmont, N.Y.: Larchwood Publications, 1980.

_____, transl., *The Immortal Voice: An Anthology of Modern Korean Poetry*. Seoul: Inmun Publishing Co., 1974.

Kim, Richard E., *The Innocent*. New York: Ballantine, 1969. A novel of contemporary Korea using the May 16, 1961 military coup as a background.

_____, *Lost Names: Scenes from a Korean Boyhood*. New York: Praeger, 1970. An autobiographical novel of a boy living under Japanese colonial rule in Korea.

_____, *The Martyred*. New York: G. Braziller, 1964. A novel exploring the spiritual and moral dilemmas arising from the execution of twelve Christian ministers by the retreating North Korean army during the Korean War.

Kim, Sowol, *A Lamp Burns Low*. Translated by Jaihiun Kim. Seoul: Seongji-Sa Publishing Company, 1977. A selection of the poems of perhaps Korea's best loved modern poet. A lyric genius and ardent nationalist, Kim was only thirty-one when he died in 1934.

Kim, Tongni, *Ulhwa the Shaman: A Novel of Korea and Three Stories*. Transl. by Junghyo Ahn. Larchmont, N.Y.: Larchwood Publications, 1979. The novel, depicting conflict between Western Christian beliefs and traditional Korean religious practices, is based on the author's acclaimed short story, "The Portrait of a Shaman," published in 1936.

Korean National Commission for UNESCO, ed., *Modern Korean Short Stories*. Seoul: Si-sa-yong-o-sa Publishers, 1983. One hundred nine selections, from the 1920s to the present, published in ten volumes.

Lee, Peter H., comp. and ed., *Anthology of Korean Literature from Early Times to the Nineteenth Century*. Honolulu: Univ. of Hawaii Press, 1981. A selection including myths and fables, tales of adventure, satirical stories, fictionalized biographies, and poems of all ages and genres. Informative introductory remarks preface each chapter.

_____, comp. and transl., *Anthology of Korean Poetry from the Earliest Era to the Present*. New York: John Day, 1964. Translation with commentary by the foremost scholar of Korean literature in the West. A revised edition is *Poems from Korea: A Historical Anthology* (Honolulu: University Press of Hawaii, 1974).

_____, ed., *Flowers of Fire: Twentieth Century Korean Stories*. Honolulu: University Press of Hawaii, 1974.

_____, *Korean Literature: Topics and Themes*. Tucson: University of Arizona Press, 1965. Treats both traditional and modern literature.

_____, *Songs of Flying Dragons: A Critical Reading.* Cambridge, Mass.: Harvard University Press, 1975. A translation and broadly learned literary analysis of the 15th century eulogy cycle composed to celebrate the founding of Yi Chosŏn.

_____, ed., *The Silence of Love: Twentieth-Century Korean Poetry.* Honolulu: University Press of Hawaii, 1980. Presents the work of sixteen modern poets each represented by a substantial selection.

Li, Mirok, *The Yalu Flows: A Korean Childhood.* East Lansing: Michigan State University Press, 1956. Autobiographical novel of a boy growing up in an early 20th century Korea about to succumb to Japanese aggression. English translation of the original German-language work (*Der Yalu Fliesst.* Munich: 1946).

McCann, David. R., *Black Crane: An Anthology of Korean Literature I & II.* Ithaca: East Asian Papers nos. 14 & 24, Cornell University Press, 1977 & 1980. Translations of Korean vernacular literature, traditional and contemporary.

_____, transl., *The Middle Hour: Selected Poems of Kim Chi Ha.* Stanfordville, N.Y.: Human Rights Publishing Group, 1980. A collection of the works of contemporary Korea's most vocal poet of protest.

Moh, Yoon Sook, *Wren's Elegy.* Translated by Peter Hyun and Chang-soo Ko. Larchmont, N.Y.: Larchwood Publications, 1980. Also contains the author's "*The Pagoda, an Epic,*" and a broad selection of her poems.

O'Rourke, Kevin, transl., *A Washed-Out Dream.* Larchmont, N.Y.: Larchwood Publications, 1980. Revised and expanded version of the translator's *Ten Korean Short Stories* (Seoul: Yonsei University Press, 1973), a selection of works written during the past fifty-some years.

Rutt, Richard, *The Bamboo Grove: An Introduction to Sijo.* Berkeley: University of California Press, 1971. Translations, bibliographical notes, and textual comments on 260 *sijo* poems.

Rutt, Richard, and Chong-un Kim, transl., *Virtuous Women: Three Masterpieces of Traditional Korean Fiction.* Seoul: Korean National Commission for UNESCO, 1974. Translation of three classical works: *Kuun mong, Inhyŏn wanghu chŏn,* and *Ch'unhyang ka.*

Skillend, W.E., *Kodae Sosŏl: A Survey of Traditional Korean Style Popular Novels.* London: School of Oriental and African Studies, University of London, 1968. A cataloguing, with descriptive data and other information, of 531 titles in this popular traditional genre.

Zong, In-sob, *Folk Tales from Korea.* London: Routledge & Kegan Paul, 1952. Revised edition, Elizabeth, N.J.: Hollym International, 1970.

MUSIC

Lee, Hye-Ku, *Essays on Korean Traditional Music.* Translated by Robert C.

Provine. Seoul: Royal Asiatic Society, Korea Branch, 1981. A selection of articles by Korea's leading scholar of its classical music.

Song, Bang-song, *Source Readings in Korean Music*. Seoul: Korean National Commission for UNESCO, 1980. Translations of selections on music from Korean traditional texts, with ample introductory and explanatory notes.

RELIGION and THOUGHT

Buswell, Robert E., Jr., *The Korean Approach to Zen: the Collected Works of Chinul*. Honolulu: University of Hawaii Press, 1983. The first major work on Korean Buddhist doctrine to appear in a Western language, this book contains nearly all the extant treatises written by Chinul (1158–1210)—the founder of the indigenous Chogye sect of Sŏn (Zen) Buddhism.

Choi, Min-hong, *A Modern History of Korean Philiosophy*. Seoul: Seong Moon Sa, 1980. The third part of the author's Korean-language *History of Korean Philosophy*, this volume treats the development of Korean philosophy from the beginning of the Yi dynasty (1392) to the present.

Clark, Charles Allen, *Religions of Old Korea*. New York: Revell, 1932. Reprint, Seoul: Christian Literature Society of Korea, 1961. Lectures delivered at Princeton by an American Protestant missionary who taught theology in a seminary in Seoul. Outdated but still useful descriptions of Buddhism, Confucianism, Ch'ŏndogyo, shamanism, and the early phase of Christianity in Korea.

Kim, Yong Choon, *The Chondogyo Concept of Man: An Essence of Korean Thought*. Seoul: Pan Korea Book Company, 1978. Introduction to the history and doctrine of this native Korean religion that originally developed in the mid-19th century under the name of Tonghak, in response to dynastic decline, the authoritarianism of Neo-Confucian orthodoxy, and the spread of Catholicism.

Lancaster, Lewis R., with Sung-bae Park, *The Korean Buddhist Canon: A Descriptive Catalogue*. Berkeley: University of California Press, 1979. A reference guide to the 13th century *Koryŏ Tripitaka*, with title indices for Sanskrit, Pali, Chinese, Korean, and Tibetan renderings, for authors and translators, and for place names, as well as other useful research aids.

Lee, Jung Young, *Korean Shamanistic Rituals*. Hawthorne, N.Y.: Mouton Publications, 1981. Portions of this book are unacknowledged translations from Japanese studies of the 1930s.

Lee, Peter H., *Lives of Eminent Korean Monks: The Haedong Kosŭng Chŏn*. Cambridge, Mass.: Harvard University Press, 1969. Meticulously rendered translation of extant chapters of this 13th century Buddhist hagiographical text.

Paik, Lak-Geoon George, *The History of Protestant Missions in Korea,*

1832–1910. P'yŏngyang: Union Christian College Press, 1927. Reprint, Seoul: Yonsei University Press, 1970.

Palmer, Spencer J., *Korea and Christianity: The Problem of Identification with Tradition*. Seoul: Royal Asiatic Society, Korea Branch, 1967. Assesses the factors in traditional Korean society that may account for the remarkable success Protestant Christianity has achieved in Korea.

Yoon, Hong-key, *Geomantic Relationships between Culture and Nature in Korea*. Taipei: Orient Cultural Service, 1976. A photographic reproduction of the author's University of California (Berkeley) Ph. D. dissertation.

SCIENCE and TECHNOLOGY

Jeon, Sang-woon, *Science and Technology of Korea: Traditional Instruments and Techniques*. Cambridge, Mass.: M.I.T. Press, 1974. A pioneering work of exceptionally high standard.

Underwood, Horace H., *Korean Boats and Ships*. Seoul: Yonsei University Press, 1979. Reprint of the original 1934 study of traditional Korean sea-going vessels.

SOCIETY

Brandt, Vincent S.R., *A Korean Village: Between Farm and Sea*. Cambridge, Mass.: Harvard University Press, 1971. A social-anthropological study of a Korean village on the Yellow Sea.

Crane, Paul, *Korean Patterns*. 4th ed. rev. Seoul: Royal Asiatic Society, Korea Branch, 1978. A delineation of traditional values, attitudes, customs, and personality by a long-time U.S. medical missionary in Korea.

Eikemeier, Dieter, *Documents from Changjwa-ri: A Further Approach to the Analysis of Korean Villages*. Wiesbaden: Otto Harrassowitz, 1980. Exposition based on a cache of documents found on the southwestern coastal island of Wando. Document texts and translations are appended.

Harvey, Youngsook Kim, *Six Korean Women: The Socialization of Shamans*. St. Paul. Minn.: West Publishing Co., 1979. Observations of an anthropologist on the nature of Korean shamanism and its role in Korean society.

Janelli, Roger L., and Dawnhee Janelli, *Ancestor Worship and Korean Society*. Palo Alto: Stanford University Press, 1982. Describes Korean rites for the dead in the context of kinship structure, Confucian doctrine, and property inheritance patterns. Includes a systematic comparison of ancestor worship in Korea, China, and Japan.

Kendall, Laurel, and Mark Peterson, ed., *Korean Women: View from the*

Inner Room. New Haven: East Rock Press, 1983. A collection of essays, mostly historical, on the role and position of women in Korean society.

Kim, Yung-Chung, ed. and transl., *Women of Korea: A History from Ancient Times to 1945*. Seoul: Ewha University Press, 1979. A translated and revised version of a 1972 Korean-language study of the status, role, and activities of Korean women throughout their nation's history.

Koh, Hesung Chun, *Korean and Japanese Women: An Analytic Bibliographical Guide*. Greenwood Press: Westport, Conn., 1982.

Lee, Changsoo and George A. Devos, *Koreans in Japan, Ethnic Conflict and Accommodation*. Berkeley: University of California Press, 1981. Collection of essays on the contemporary Korean minority community in Japan.

Lee, Man Gap, and Herbert Barringer, ed., *A City in Transition: Urbanization in Taegu, Korea*. Seoul: Hollym, 1971. A team study of the Republic of Korea's third largest city, with chapters on history, government, the economy, social structure, migration, education, and religion.

Mattielli, Sandra, ed., *Vitues in Conflict: Tradition and the Korean Woman Today*. Seoul: Samhwa, 1977. Collection of articles on traditional behavioral influences on the lives and roles of contemporary Korean women.

Mitchell, Richard H., *The Korean Minority in Japan*. Berkeley, University of California Press, 1967. A historical treatment culminating in a discussion of issues and problems arising after 1945.

Osgood, Cornelius, *The Koreans and Their Culture*. New York: Ronald Press, 1951. Early village study, with an interpretation of Korean social culture.

Pak, Ki-hyuk, with Sidney D. Gamble, *The Changing Korean Village*. Seoul: Royal Asiatic Society, Korea Branch, 1975. Describes economic and social life in three "clan villages," using data from investigations of Ich'ŏn in Kyŏnggi province, Miryang in Kyŏngsang, and Chŏngŭp in Chŏlla.

Rutt, Richard, *Korean Works and Days: Notes from the Diary of a Country Priest*. 2nd ed. Seoul: Royal Asiatic Society, Korea Branch, 1964 (Reprint, 1978). Reflections and impressions of country life, adroitly conveying the atmosphere and character of the people in a rural community "poised between the old dispensation and the new."

Explanatory Note
to the
Index-Glossary

The primary purpose of this INDEX-GLOSSARY is to provide reference to the people, places, and events of Korean history, to the terms by which Koreans have designated their political, social, and economic institutions, to the monuments of Korean cultural achievement, to the creations of Korean science and technology—in short, to the numerous and varied specific manifestations of the long and rich Korean historical experience. On the other hand, the INDEX-GLOSSARY is less concerned with analytical classification under general subject headings of the exceptional wealth of data presented in this history text. The detailed table of contents separately lists all of the seventy-three sections and two hundred forty-three subsections into which the book's sixteen chapters are divided. In most cases, then, the CONTENTS should serve as a satisfactory means of locating material relating to a particular subject of broader interest.

Wherever appropriate, the INDEX-GLOSSARY provides the Chinese characters or Korean *han'gŭl* letters with which an indexed item is written. If the Korean (or other East Asian) name or term appears in the text in romanized form, then the applicable characters or *han'gŭl* syllables are given in the INDEX-GLOSSARY under the romanization entry and are not repeated under the entry for an English translation or other brief English designation. When only the English version appears in the text, then the characters or *han'gŭl* appear under that entry.

The location of indexed items that are found on the maps and charts is indicated by italicized page numbers.

Alphabetization follows the common "all-through" method of index preparation—that is, alphabetical sequence is determined by the spelling of the full entry, disregarding spaces or hyphens that divide the words or syllables within the entry. For example, CHO TU-SUN (a nineteenth century senior official) is alphabetized *after* the CHOSŎNŎ HAKHOE (KOREAN LANGUAGE SOCIETY) and also after CHŎNG TU-WŎN (a seventeenth century envoy to China) or CH'OE YŎNG (the end-of-Koryŏ military commander). The apostrophe (as in the CH'OE surname) and the breve (as over the vowel in the CHŎNG surname) also are ignored in determining alphabetical sequence, except when the spelling of two entries, in full, is otherwise identical. Thus the entry for the ancient Chinese state of CH'IN is listed *after* seven entries spelled simply CHIN.

Index - Glossary

A

Abiji 阿非知, 63

"able-bodied land" (*chŏngjŏn*), 80

Abridged Chronological History (*P'yŏnnyŏn t'ongnok*), 167

absentee landlords 不在地主, 159, 160, 227

Academy of Letters 翰林院, 168

"academy of received learning" (*sosu sŏwŏn*), 207

Accounting College (*Sanhak*), 119, 120

Account of a Pilgrimage to T'ang in Search of the Law (*Nyū Tō kyūhō junrei kōki*), 95

"Account of the Eastern Barbarians" (*Tung-i chuan*), 29

ach'an 阿飡, 50, *51, 52*

"added *kyŏl*" 都結, 248

Administrative Code of Chosŏn (*Chosŏn kyŏngguk chŏn*), 172

administrative superintendent 政務總監, 315

Admonitions on Governing the People (*Mongmin simsŏ*), 234

Ado 阿道, 59

Aeguktan 愛國團 (Patriots Corps), 366

Aesop's Fables 이솝이야기, 338

"Again Mindful of My Seemly Lord" (*Sok miin kok*), 220

"Agency to Bestow Blessings" (*Sŏnhye-ch'ŏng*), 224, 272

"agricultural estates" (*nongjang*), 157, 158–159, 160, 164, 183, 184, 202, 208, 262

agricultural technology, 184, 195, 226, 227 228, 240, 297

Agriculture and Mining Company 農鑛 會社, 318

ajŏn 衙前 (local civil functionaries), 175, 178; *see also hyangni*

Ajwa, Prince 阿佐太子, 64

akchang 樂章 (musical texts), 198, 219

Akhak kwebŏm 樂學軌範 (*Canon of Music*), 198

Ak pon 樂本 (*Book of Music*), 84

A-ku-ta 阿骨打, 128

Album of Genre Scenes, An (*P'ungsok hwach'ŏp*), 246

Alchi 閼智, 6

Alch'ŏn 閼川, 74

Allen, Horace N., 309, 334

alsŏngsi 謁聖試 (Royal Visitation Examination), 181

amhaeng ŏsa 暗行御史 (secret inspector), 249

Amitabha Buddha, 阿彌陀佛, 82, 87, 136

Amitabha sutra 阿彌陀經, 82

Amsa-dong 岩寺洞, 3, *4*, 8

Amur River 黑龍江, 3, 73

Anak 安岳, 253, *343*

Analects 論語, 83, 120

Anapchi 雁鴨池, 78

Anbuk 安北, *115*, 116, *127*

Anbyŏn 安邊, *115*, 116

ancestor worship, 34

An Chae-hong 安在鴻, 374, 375

anch'alsa 按察使 (superintendent), 116

An Ch'ang-ho 安昌浩, 328, *333*, 339

An Chŏng-bok 安鼎福, 237, 239

An Chong-su 安宗洙, 297

An Ch'uk 安軸, 168

An Chung-gŭn 安重根, 310

Andong 安東, 101, *102*, *115*, 116, 162, 168, 294, 316

Andong Kim clan 安東 金氏, 247, 248, 257, 268

Anglo-Japanese Alliance, 307, 309

An Hŭi-je 安熙濟, 355

Anju 安州, *177*, *343*

An Kuk-sŏn 安國善, 338

C

Cabinet (*Naegak*), 291, 294, 305

cadastral surveys, 164, 196; of 1910—1918, 土地調査事業, 318, 319, 356

Cairo Declaration, 373

Calculation of the Motions of the Seven Celestial Determinants (*Ch'ilchŏngsan*), 196

calligraphy, 88, 109, 136, 170, 198, 260, 261

Calligraphy College (*Sŏhak*), 119, 120

Canada, 380

Canon of Music (*Akhak kwebŏm*), 198

"capital association" 都中, 230

capital district (*pu*), 44

"capital faction" 近畿派, 201

Capital Garrison (*Kŭmwiyŏng*), 225

Capital Gazette (*Hwangsŏng Sinmun*), 304, 313, 328, 329, 330

Capital Guards Command(*Ch'in'gunyŏng*), 274

Capital Guards Division (*Kammunwi*), 117

Capital Guards Garrison (*Changŏyŏng*), 271

capital guards unit 親衛隊, 294

Capital Liaison Office (*Kyŏngjaeso*), 178

Case of the One Hundred Five 百五人事件, 314, 329, 339

"castle lord" (*sŏngju*), 54, 55, 97, 98, 103

Catholicism ("Western Learning" or *sŏhak*), 223, 239-240, 257-258, 263, 264, 271

Catholic Persecution of 1801, *see* Persecution of 1801

Catholic Persecution of 1839, *see* Persecution of 1839

Catholic Persecution of 1866, *see* Persecution of 1866

cavalry corps (*Sin'gigun*), 127, 128

celadon, 134, 135, 198

Censorate, in Chosŏn, 199, 204; in Koryŏ, *see Ŏsadae*

"census household" 計烟, 80

census register of 755, 80

census registers 戶籍, 111, 214

"Central Capital" (Chunggyŏng), 70, 90

Central Council (*Chungch'uwŏn*), 314, 315

centralized aristocratic states 中央集權的 貴族國家, 31, 37, 38, 43, 48, 54, 55, 58, 60

ceramics 198, 246; *see also* celadon

Chabi 慈悲麻立干 (Silla king), 41

Chabiryŏng Pass 慈悲嶺, 17, 18, 19, 152, 157

ch'ach'aung 次次雄, 29

ch'a-ch'onju 次村主 ("secondary village headman"), 57; *see also* village headmen

Chaebu 宰府 (Directorate of Chancellors), 113, 114

Ch'ae Che-gong 蔡濟恭, 240

chaein 才人 (entertainers), 124

ch'aekhwa 責禍 ("responsibility for damages"), 6

Ch'ae Ki-jung 蔡祺中, 340

Chaeryŏng 載寧, 343

Chajang 慈藏, 60, 61, 81

Chakchegŏn 作帝建, 95

"chambers" (*pang*), 178

ch'an 湌, 53

chanban 殘班 ("ruined *yangban*"), 250

Chancellery for State Affairs (*Chungsŏmunhasŏng*), 113

Chancellery Office (*Chipsabu*), 75, 76, 89, 93

Ch'ang 昌王 (Koryŏ king), 163, 164

Changan 長安國, 93

Chang Chi-wan 張之琬, 259

Chang Chi-yŏn 張志淵, 329, 336, 337

Chang Chi-yŏng 張志暎, 334

Changch'un-sa 長春社, 296

changdŏk 將德, 52

Ch'angdŏk Palace 昌德宮, 277

changga 長歌 ("long poem"), 168

ch'angga 唱歌, 338

changgun 將軍 ("generals"), 97

Changgunbang 將軍房 (Council of Commanders), 117

Changgun Ch'ong 將軍塚 (Tomb of the General), 63

Changhŏn, Crown Prince 莊獻世子, 223

Changhŭng 長興, 108, 211, 212, 286

Changhwa Hongnyŏn chŏn 薔花紅蓮傳 (*Rose Flower and Pink Lotus*), 244

Chang Il-hwan 張日煥, 339

Chang In-hwan 張仁煥, 308

Ch'angjo 創造 (*Creation*), 371

changmun 場門 ("market gate"), 187

Ch'angnim-sa temple 昌林寺, 108

Ch'angnyŏng 昌寧, 42, 44, 211, 212

Changŏyŏng 壯禦營 (Capital Guards

N